THE CAMBRIDGE COMPANION T

HUME'S *TREATISE*

Revered for his contributions to empiricism, skepticism, and ethics, David Hume remains one of the most important figures in the history of Western philosophy. His first and broadest work, *A Treatise of Human Nature* (1739–40), comprises three volumes, concerning the understanding, the passions, and morals. He develops a naturalist and empiricist program, illustrating that the mind operates through the association of impressions and ideas. This companion features essays by leading scholars, who evaluate the philosophical content of the arguments in Hume's *Treatise*, while considering their historical context. The authors examine Hume's distinctive views on causation, motivation, free will, moral evaluation, and the origins of justice, which continue to influence present-day philosophical debate. This collection will prove a valuable resource for students and scholars exploring Hume, British empiricism, and modern philosophy.

Donald C. Ainslie is the Principal of University College and Associate Professor of Philosophy at the University of Toronto. He has published articles in numerous journals, including *Philosophy and Phenomenological Research*, *Journal of the History of Philosophy*, the *Canadian Journal of Philosophy*, *Hume Studies*, and *Theoretical Medicine and Bioethics*.

Annemarie Butler is Associate Professor of Philosophy and Religious Studies at Iowa State University and book review editor for *Hume Studies*. Her articles have appeared in the *British Journal for the History of Philosophy*, *History of Philosophy Quarterly*, *Journal of Scottish Philosophy*, *Hume Studies*, and *Dialogue*.

CAMBRIDGE COMPANIONS TO PHILOSOPHY

OTHER RECENT VOLUMES IN THIS SERIES OF CAMBRIDGE
COMPANIONS:

The Cambridge Companion to

HUME'S
TREATISE

Edited by

Donald C. Ainslie
University of Toronto

Annemarie Butler
Iowa State University

CAMBRIDGE
UNIVERSITY PRESS

CAMBRIDGE
UNIVERSITY PRESS

32 Avenue of the Americas, New York, NY 10013–2473, USA

Cambridge University Press is part of the University of Cambridge.

It furthers the University's mission by disseminating knowledge in the pursuit of education, learning, and research at the highest international levels of excellence.

www.cambridge.org
Information on this title: www.cambridge.org/9780521529143

First published 2015

Printed in the United States of America

A catalog record for this publication is available from the British Library.

Library of Congress Cataloging in Publication Data
The Cambridge companion to Hume's Treatise / [edited by] Donald C. Ainslie, University of Toronto; Annemarie Butler, Iowa State University.
    pages cm. (Cambridge companions to philosophy)
1. Hume, David, 1711–1776. Treatise of human nature.
2. Knowledge, Theory of.   I. Ainslie, Donald C., editor.   II. Butler, Annemarie, editor.
B1489.C36 2015
128–dc23   2014034327

ISBN 978-0-521-82167-4 Hardback
ISBN 978-0-521-52914-3 Paperback

Contents

Contributors

KATE ABRAMSON is an Associate Professor in the Department of Philosophy at Indiana University. Her work focuses principally on eighteenth-century philosophy (especially Hume and Smith) and contemporary ethics. Her work has been supported by a fellowship from the Rockefeller Center for Human Values at Princeton and a grant from the ACLS.

DONALD C. AINSLIE is an Associate Professor in the Department of Philosophy and the Principal of University College at the University of Toronto. His primary research focus is early modern philosophy, and he has published extensively on the works of David Hume. He has a secondary research project in bioethics.

ANNEMARIE BUTLER is an Associate Professor in the Department of Philosophy and Religious Studies at Iowa State University. She is book review editor of *Hume Studies*. Her publications focus on Part 4 of Book 1 of Hume's *Treatise* and Hume's first *Enquiry*.

LORNE FALKENSTEIN holds the rank of Professor in the Department of Philosophy at Western University in London, Canada. His work is principally focused on spatial perception and mental representation in eighteenth-century philosophy.

DON GARRETT is Professor and Chair of the Department of Philosophy at New York University. He has taught previously at Harvard University, the University of Utah, and the University of North Carolina at Chapel Hill, where he was Kenan Distinguished Professor for Teaching Excellence. He is the author of *Cognition and Commitment in Hume's Philosophy* (1997) and the forthcoming *Hume*. In addition, he is the editor of *The Cambridge Companion to Spinoza* and has served as editor of *Hume Studies* and as North American editor of the *Archiv für Geschichte der Philosophie*.

TITO MAGRI is Professor of Philosophy at Sapienza University, Rome. He has done historical and theoretical research in political philosophy, in the philosophy of emotions, and in ethics and rational choice. He is currently working on Hume's theory of imagination and on action theory.

DAVID OWEN teaches in the Department of Philosophy at the University of Arizona. He has edited several volumes on the history of early modern philosophy and is the author of *Hume's Reason* (1999) as well as several articles on Locke and Hume.

TERENCE PENELHUM is Professor Emeritus of Religious Studies at the University of Calgary, Canada, where he was formerly Head of the Department of Philosophy, Dean of Arts and Science, and Director of the Calgary Institute for the Humanities. In 1988 he was awarded the Canada Council Molson Prize in the Humanities. His books include *Themes in Hume* (2000) and *God and Skepticism* (1983).

AMÉLIE OKSENBERG RORTY is a Visiting Professor at Tufts University and a Lecturer at the Harvard Medical School. Author of *Mind in Action* (1991) and numerous articles on the history of moral psychology, she has edited *Explaining Emotions* (1976) and *Philosophers on Education* (1988) as well as volumes on Descartes's *Meditations* and on Aristotle's *Ethics*, his *Rhetoric*, and his *Poetics*. She is currently working on a book, *On the Other Hand: The Ethics of Ambivalence*.

PAUL RUSSELL is Professor in Philosophy at the University of British Columbia. His publications include *Freedom and Moral Sentiment: Hume's Way of Naturalizing Responsibility* (1995) and *The Riddle of Hume's* Treatise: *Skepticism, Naturalism, and Irreligion* (2008). He is also the editor of *The Oxford Handbook of David Hume* (forthcoming).

NICHOLAS L. STURGEON is Susan Linn Sage Professor of Philosophy, emeritus, at Cornell University. He has joined in contemporary debates about metaethics, while also writing about Hume and other British moral philosophers of the eighteenth and nineteenth centuries.

JACQUELINE TAYLOR is Professor of Philosophy at the University of San Francisco. She has published numerous articles on David Hume as well as articles on moral psychology and metaethics.

KENNETH P. WINKLER is Professor of Philosophy at Yale University. His books include *Berkeley: An Interpretation* (1989) and an abridgment, with introduction and notes, of Locke's *Essay Concerning Human Understanding* (1996). A collection of his essays, *Matters of Reason: Essays in Early Modern British Philosophy*, is forthcoming. From 2011 to 2012 he was the Sir Isaiah Berlin Visiting Professor in the History of Ideas at Oxford University, where he delivered a series of lectures on philosophical idealism in America. From 2000 to 2005 he was editor, with Elizabeth Radcliffe, of the journal *Hume Studies*.

Preface

The idea for this project was conceived in the late 1990s, and most of the contributors joined it with the expectation that it would appear in the early 2000s. The volume's delayed appearance was the result, in part, of the normal problems associated with edited volumes: a few recalcitrant contributors, last-minute withdrawals, and the like. But my personal shortcomings, as I tried to balance a demanding administrative role with my research responsibilities, also contributed significantly. I owe many thanks to Annemarie Butler for joining the project as a coeditor; she did the heavy lifting required to bring the project to completion. I also would like to thank the other contributors for their patience and apologize to them for the long gestation of the volume.

Donald C. Ainslie

Method of Citation

References to Hume's texts are normally given parenthetically, but on some occasions these references may be placed in a note. Parenthetical references follow the form of these examples:

A Treatise of Human Nature: T, followed by Book, Part, Section, and paragraph numbers of the Clarendon Edition (see T in the list of abbreviations); after this, SBN is followed by page number(s) from the Selby-Bigge and Nidditch edition. References to this work will produce, for example, the form (T 1.4.7.14, SBN 272–73).

Dialogues Concerning Natural Religion: DNR, followed by the Part and page numbers of the Norman Kemp Smith edition. References to this work will produce, for example, the form (DNR 1, 137).

An Enquiry Concerning Human Understanding: EHU, followed by the Section and paragraph numbers of the Clarendon Edition (see EHU in the list of abbreviations); after this, SBN, is followed by page number(s) from the Selby-Bigge and Nidditch edition. References to this work will produce, for example, the form (EHU 1.5, SBN 8).

An Enquiry Concerning the Principles of Morals: EPM, followed by the Section and paragraph numbers in the Clarendon Edition (see EPM in the list of abbreviations); after this, SBN, is followed by page number(s) from the Selby-Bigge and Nidditch edition. References to this work will produce, for example, the form (EPM 7.16, SBN 256).

Essays: E-, followed first by an abbreviation of the title of the particular essay cited (for these abbreviations see E in the list of abbreviations) and then by the relevant page number(s) of the edition of Hume's *Essays Moral, Political, and Literary* described at E, to produce, for example, the form (E-Sc 172).

Abbreviations

Abs.　An *Abstract of a Book Lately Published; Entituled* A Treatise of Human Nature, &c. *Wherein the Chief Argument of that Book is farther Illustrated and Explained* (first published 1740). Cited from the Clarendon Edition of *A Treatise of Human Nature*, edited by David Fate Norton and Mary J. Norton (Oxford: Clarendon Press, 2007), and the 2nd edition of *A Treatise of Human Nature*, edited by L. A. Selby-Bigge, revised by P. H. Nidditch (Oxford: Clarendon Press, 1978).

D　*A Dialogue* (first published 1751), cited from the Clarendon Edition of *An Enquiry Concerning the Principles of Morals*, edited by Tom L. Beauchamp (Oxford: Clarendon Press, 1998), and the 3rd edition of *Enquiries Concerning Human Understanding and Concerning the Principles of Morals*, edited by L. A. Selby-Bigge with notes by P. H. Nidditch (Oxford: Clarendon Press, 1975).

DNR　*Dialogues Concerning Natural Religion* (first published 1779), edited by Norman Kemp Smith (Oxford: Clarendon Press, 1935). Subsequent editions are uniformly paginated.

DP　*Dissertation on the Passions* (first published 1757), cited from *A Dissertation on the Passions and the Natural History of Religion*, edited by Tom L. Beauchamp (Oxford: Clarendon Press, 2007).

E　*Essays Moral, Political, and Literary*, edited by Eugene F. Miller (Indianapolis: Liberty Classics, rev. ed., 1987). Abbreviations of the individual essays cited in this volume, with date of the first publication, follow this entry.

E-DM　Of the Dignity or Meanness of Human Nature (1741; "or Meanness" added in 1770)

E-DT　Of the Delicacy of Taste and Passion (1741)

E-MSL　Of the Middle Station of Life (1742)

E-OC　Of the Original Contract (1748)

E-PO　Of Passive Obedience (1748)

E-RA   Of Refinement in the Arts (1752; title changed from "Of
        Luxury" in 1760)
E-Sc   The Sceptic (1742)
E-SE   Of Superstition and Enthusiasm (1741)
E-SR   Of Simplicity and Refinement in Writing (1742)
E-St   The Stoic (1742)
E-ST   Of the Standard of Taste (1757)
EHU   *An Enquiry Concerning Human Understanding* (first
        published 1748 as *Philosophical Essays Concerning Human
        Understanding*). All quotations and references are to the
        Clarendon Edition, edited by Tom L. Beauchamp (Oxford:
        Clarendon Press, 2000), and the 3rd edition of *Enquiries
        Concerning Human Understanding and Concerning the
        Principles of Morals*, edited by L. A. Selby-Bigge with notes by
        P. H. Nidditch (Oxford: Clarendon Press, 1975).
EPM   *An Enquiry Concerning the Principles of Morals* (first
        published 1751). All quotations and references are to the
        Clarendon Edition, edited by Tom L. Beauchamp (Oxford:
        Clarendon Press, 1998), and the 3rd edition of *Enquiries
        Concerning Human Understanding and Concerning the
        Principles of Morals*, edited by L. A. Selby-Bigge with notes by
        P. H. Nidditch (Oxford: Clarendon Press, 1975).
HL   *The Letters of David Hume*, edited by J. Y. T. Greig, 2 vols.
        (Oxford: Clarendon Press, 1932).
NHL   *New Letters of David Hume*, edited by Raymond Klibanksy and
        Ernest C. Mossner (Oxford: Oxford University Press, 1954).
T   *A Treatise of Human Nature* (first published 1739–40). All
        quotations and references are to the Clarendon Edition, edited
        by David Fate Norton and Mary J. Norton (Oxford: Clarendon
        Press, 2007), and the 2nd edition of *A Treatise of Human
        Nature*, edited by L. A. Selby-Bigge, revised by P. H. Nidditch
        (Oxford: Clarendon Press, 1978).

1 Hume's Early Biography and *A Treatise of Human Nature*

David Hume was born David Home[1] in Edinburgh on April 26, 1711 (o.s.) to Joseph Home (1681–1713) and Katherine Home (née Falconer) (1683–1745). He had an older brother, John, and a sister, Katherine. In "My Own Life," Hume describes his family as "not rich" (HL 1:1). However, it is clear that they were not poor either. Joseph Home was an admitted advocate in Edinburgh,[2] and he was a laird at Ninewells,[3] along the southern border of Scotland. He employed shearers who, along with farmers and a weaver, rented houses from him (Mossner 1980: 23–24). This provided stable income for the family. Joseph Home died suddenly in 1713 from unknown causes, leaving a widow with three young children.

The details of Home's early education are scant. J. Y. T. Greig (1931: 33–35) speculates that John and David attended school in neighboring Chirnside. E. C. Mossner speculates that the boys had tutors, who would likely have been young clergymen recently out of school (1980: 31; see also Stewart 2005: 17–18). Either way, boys were expected to develop reading and writing skill in Latin, typically reading Aesop, Ovid, Corderius, and Horace (Emerson 2009: 59–60).[4] The boys were raised Presbyterian, and the Homes were Whigs. James Boswell reports that later in life Hume admitted that he took religion seriously when he was young, having read carefully *The Whole Duty of Man*[5] (a very popular book of English Protestant devotional exercises) and examined his character against the vices cataloged therein (Mossner 1980: 34; see also 34n2).

Both John and David Home were sufficiently prepared for Edinburgh University, whose goal was "to train students for virtuous living in a society regulated by religious observance" (Stewart 2005: 12). It was typical for boys to enter university in their early teenage years. David Home, aged 11, signed the matriculation book in February 1723 on a page for William Scot, the professor of Greek (Mossner 1980: 39). The numeral 2 next to David's name is taken to indicate that this was his second year, meaning that he had followed the usual course of a year of Humanity first (Stewart 2005: 17–19).[6] Prior to 1708, the university operated with

rotating regents. A student would study under the same regent throughout his time at the university, and the regent would be compensated with
fees from each graduate. Regents were incentivized to retain and graduate
as large a student class as possible. In 1708, the university adopted a
professorial system in which professors taught subjects in their own
fields (Mossner 1980: 38–39; Sher 1990: 89–90). The typical coursework
was four years: Humanity (Latin language and culture), Greek language
and culture, Metaphysics and Logic, and Natural Philosophy.[7] Since only
the professor of natural philosophy received graduation fees, professors
no longer had an incentive to see students through to graduation.
Accordingly, graduation rates dropped (Mossner 1980: 38–39). In this
light, it is not remarkable that neither David nor John graduated from
Edinburgh University.

Upon leaving Edinburgh University, it was clear that John would
become laird at Ninewells. David's patrimony was approximately £50
(sterling), forcing him to pursue a career. David's father and maternal
grandfather had been advocates, and this may have influenced David's
decision to study law (Mossner 1980: 53). There is no evidence that he
attended Edinburgh University for the study of law, although Roger
Emerson claims that this is likely (2009: 82).[8] In "My Own Life," Hume
reports, "I found an unsurmountable Aversion to every thing but the
pursuits of Philosophy and general Learning; and while they [sc. family]
fancyed I was poring over Voet and Vinnius, Cicero and Virgil were the
Authors which I was secretly devouring" (HL 1:1).

Home was splitting time between Edinburgh and Ninewells. In 1727,
David wrote to his friend, Michael Ramsay, claiming to be "entirely
confind to my self & Library for Diversion," reading "sometimes a
Philosopher, sometimes a Poet" (HL 1:9–10). In a 1734 letter to a
physician,[9] he wrote,

I found a certain Boldness of Temper, growing in me, which was not enclin'd to
submit to any Authority in these Subjects, but led me to seek out some new
Medium, by which Truth might be establisht. After much Study, & Reflection on
this, at last, when I was about 18 Years of Age, there seem'd to be open'd up to me a
new Scene of Thought, which transported me beyond Measure, & made me, with
an Ardor natural to young men, throw up every other Pleasure or Business to apply
entirely to it. (HL 1:13)

By the end of the law session of 1728–29, he had quit studying law
(Stewart 2005: 29). He intensely pursued reading and studying, which
made him "infinitely happy" until September 1729, when he began to
have difficulty concentrating. Compounding his difficulty, he was
reading "Books of Morality, such as Cicero, Seneca & Plutarch, & being
smit with their beautiful Representations of Virtue & Philosophy, I

undertook the Improvement of my Temper & Will, along with my Reason & Understanding. I was continually fortifying myself with Reflections against Death, & Poverty, & Shame, & Pain, & all the other Calamities of Life" (HL 1:14). The effect was "to waste the Spirits" (ibid.). He discovered symptoms of scurvy, and in April 1730 he was diagnosed with the "Disease of the Learned" (ibid.), the remedy for which was bitters, anti-hysteric pills, daily exercise, and wine.

Around this time, David had a religious crisis. In 1751, Hume described to Gilbert Elliot:

tis not long ago that I burn'd an old Manuscript Book, wrote before I was twenty; which contain'd, Page after Page, the gradual Progress of my Thoughts on that head. It begun with an anxious Search after Arguments, to confirm the common Opinion: Doubts stole in, dissipated, return'd, were again dissipated, return'd again; and it was a perpetual Struggle of a restless Imagination against Inclination, perhaps against Reason. (HL 1:154)

It is likely that this religious crisis contributed to David's "Disease of the Learned" (Stewart 2005: 30–31; Baier 2011: 11–13).

From 1731 to 1734, David managed to read and write, despite continued difficulty concentrating:

Having now Time & Leizure to cool my inflam'd Imaginations, I began to consider seriously, how I shou'd proceed in my Philosophical Enquiries. I found that the moral Philosophy transmitted to us by Antiquity, labor'd under the same Inconvenience that has been found in their natural Philosophy, of being entirely Hypothetical, & depending more upon Invention than Experience. Every one consulted his Fancy in erecting Schemes of Virtue & of Happiness, without regarding human Nature, upon which every moral Conclusion must depend. This therefore I resolved to make my principal Study, & the Source from which I wou'd derive every Truth in Criticism as well as Morality. (HL 1:16)

He was now disenchanted with the ancient moral philosophy and was working to develop a new theory of morality and criticism,[10] based on human nature.[11] "[W]ithin these three Years," he had "scribled many a Quire of Paper, in which there is nothing contain'd but my own Inventions" (ibid.). Home still struggled to think clearly and worried that this would frustrate clear exposition of his new views (HL 1:16–17). Despairing that he would never recover, Home wrote to a physician, seeking advice about whether and how his concentration could be restored (HL 1:18). Home then resolved to take up a different occupation.

Around this time, the intellectual climate in Scotland was hostile to atheism and freethinking. In Duns, a town near Chirnside, lived Andrew Baxter, a strident defender of Samuel Clarke's philosophy: matter is inert, God's existence can be demonstrated a priori, and God creates and sustains the material world (Russell 2008: 40). In 1732, William

Dudgeon (also from southern Scotland) published *The State of the Moral World Considered*, in which he argued that the natural and moral world are governed by necessity and denied the existence of moral or natural evil (Russell 2008: 43). Baxter sharply criticized Dudgeon's work in *Reflections on a Late Pamphlet*. Soon afterwards, Dudgeon was charged with "lybel," a charge that occupied the local presbytery (which included David's uncle, George Home) and synod for several years (Russell 2008: 43–44). Paul Russell speculates that this climate contributed to David's decision to leave Scotland (2008: 45).

In March 1734, David left Ninewells for Bristol, "having got Recommendation to a considerable Trader" (HL 1:18). The trader was Michael Miller, a sugar merchant. David served as a clerk – Mossner speculates because sailing caused seasickness (1980: 89). While in Bristol, Home changed the spelling of his name to "Hume," to reflect the correct pronunciation (Mossner 1980: 90). Greig speculates that it may have been to signal independence from his disappointed family (1931: 26), but Annette Baier doubts that David would have been so affectionate toward his family later in life had this been the case (2011: 14). Hume did not last long as a clerk. He repeatedly made critical remarks about Miller's writing, to which Miller was not receptive.

Hume left England for France, arriving in Paris in midsummer 1734. Why he left England is not known. Mossner thinks that it is because of the quarrels with Miller (1980: 90). John P. Wright speculates that Hume delivered his "letter to a physician" to Dr. George Cheyne in Bath, who then recommended a sojourn in France (2003: 131–33). David Fate Norton suggests that Hume was motivated to distance himself from his family, "who may have wondered about his lack of visible progress or success" (2007: 441). In Paris, he stayed with Chevalier Ramsay, cousin of Michael Ramsay. This proved expensive, and Chevalier Ramsay and Hume did not get along well. The former provided Hume with introductions to "two of the best Families" in Rheims (HL 1:22). While in Rheims, Hume enjoyed access to the library of Abbé Noel-Antoine Pluche. There he read and re-read various classics and contemporary works in French and English, including Locke's *Essay* and Berkeley's *Principles* (Mossner 1980: 626). Although he enjoyed the parties and libraries in Rheims, it too was expensive.

In 1735, Hume moved to La Flèche, where René Descartes had been a student at the Jesuit College. Hume was able to live cheaply, enjoy access to the library, and engage in philosophical conversations with Jesuit priests. One such conversation Hume later related to George Campbell:

[I] engaged in a conversation with a Jesuit of some parts and learning, who was relating to me, and urging some nonsensical miracle performed in their convent, when I was tempted to dispute against him; and as my head was full of the topics of my *Treatise of Human Nature*, which I was at that time composing, this argument immediately occurred to me, and I thought it very much gravelled my companion; but at last he observed to me, that it was impossible for that argument to have any solidity, because it operated equally against the Gospel as the Catholic miracles;—which observation I thought proper to admit as a sufficient answer. (HL 1:361)

Hume's argument likely was included in an essay he composed, then entitled "Reasonings concerning Miracles."

In September 1737, Hume returned to London, seriously looking for publishers. In advance of his arrival, Hume wrote to Michael Ramsay that he would supply him with a draft of the book to read. Hume recommended that, in preparation, Ramsay read Malebranche's *Recherche de la Verité*, Berkeley's *Principles*, Bayle's *Dictionary* (particularly the articles on Zeno and Spinoza), and Descartes's *Meditations*. "These Books will make you easily comprehend the metaphysical Parts of my Reasoning and as to the rest, they have so little Dependence on all former systems of Philosophy, that your natural Good Sense will afford you Light enough to judge of their Force & Solidity" (Mossner 1980: 626–27).

In a letter to his cousin, Henry Home (later Lord Kames), in December 1737, Hume expressed excitement about his new opinions, which he had been negotiating unsuccessfully to have printed.[12] He said that he would likely not include the section on miracles, "afraid [that it] will give too much offence, even as the world is disposed at present" (HL 1:24). He asked his cousin to read it, perhaps show it to William Hamilton, and then burn it. (Home advised suppressing the section [Mossner 1980: 112].) Hume also asked for an introduction to Dr. Joseph Butler, reporting, "I am at present castrating my work, that is, cutting off its nobler parts; that is, endeavouring it shall give as little offence as possible, before which, I could not pretend to put it into the Doctor's hands" (HL 1:24).[13] In the meantime, Hume was anxiously editing his *Treatise*, beginning "to feel some Passages weaker for the Style & Diction than I cou'd have wisht. The Nearness & Greatness of the Event [sc. publishing] rouz'd up my Attention, & made me more difficult to please than when I was alone in perfect Tranquillity in France" (NHL 1–2).

Part of the difficulty in finding a publisher was that Hume had three terms that he insisted on. First, he would not solicit subscriptions or dedicate the work to a patron. Second, he insisted on anonymity.[14] Third, Hume would sell rights to the first edition only, and he refused to sign a contract for any future volumes (Mossner 1980: 113–14). In September 1738, John Noon agreed to publish Books 1 and 2 of *A Treatise of Human Nature* under these terms, adding further stipulations. Hume would receive £50 and twelve bound copies in six months, and one thousand copies would be printed. Second, Hume agreed not to publish a second edition of the *Treatise* without first buying all the unsold copies of the first edition at the standard rate (Norton 2007: 452–53), which would have been approximately 10 *s.* per volume (Norton 2007: 584).

In early 1739, Books 1 and 2 of *A Treatise of Human Nature* were published (HL 1:26). Hume expressed worries to his cousin about its reception: "Those who are accustomed to reflect on such abstract subjects, are commonly full of prejudices; and those who are unprejudiced are unacquainted with metaphysical reasonings. My principles are also so remote from all the vulgar sentiments on the subject, that were they to take place, they would produce almost a total alteration in philosophy: and you know, revolutions of this kind are not easily brought about" (HL 1:26). Back in Ninewells, Hume anxiously awaited reviews of his work. He sent a copy to Bishop Butler (HL 1:27), and he also wrote to Pierre Desmaizeaux, needling him to read the work (HL 1:29). Later, in "My Own Life," Hume wrote, "Never literary Attempt was more unfortunate than my Treatise of human Nature. It fell *dead-born from the Press*; without reaching such distinction as even to excite a Murmur among the Zealots" (HL 1:2). Although the sales were poor, some copies were sold and read. Nor was it ignored: Mossner cites a comment in the *Weekly Magazine, or Edinburgh Amusement*, in 1771 that stated, "I was in Edinburgh soon after the original publication, and well remember how much and how frequently it was mentioned, in every literary conversation" (Mossner 1980: 133; Norton 2007: 520). It seems, then, that Hume was expressing disappointment with how widely it was misunderstood.

A short announcement of its publication appeared in the "Literary News from London" section of *Bibliothèque raisonnée des ouvrages des savans de l'Europe*: "A Gentleman, named Mr. *Hume*, has published *A Treatise of Human Nature*" (Mossner 1980: 120). Hume's goal of anonymity had been frustrated. Mossner speculates that Desmaizeaux wrote the "puff piece" (ibid.).

The earliest brief critical comments on Books 1 and 2 were not favorable. In May 1739, *Neuen Zeitungen von gelehrten Sachen* published a brief description, including: "The author's evil intentions are sufficiently betrayed in the sub-title of the work, taken from Tacitus" (Mossner 1980: 120). A more neutral comment was published in October in The Hague, noting the similarity between the views of Hume and Hutcheson. Another: "This is a system of logic, or rather of metaphysics, as original as can be, in which the author claims to rectify the most ingenious philosophers, particularly the famous Mr. *Locke*, and in which he advances the most unheard-of paradoxes, even to maintaining that the operations of the mind are not free" (Mossner 1980: 121).

Meanwhile, Hume worked on Book 3, "Of Morals." He corresponded with Francis Hutcheson, Professor of Moral Philosophy at Glasgow University, to whom he provided a draft of Book 3. Hutcheson complained that "there wants a certain Warmth in the Cause of Virtue" (HL 1:32). Hume defended his presentation, using an analogy in which he likened his approach to the human mind and body to an anatomist's and Hutcheson's approach to a painter's (ibid.). Furthermore, he defended his claim that justice is an "artificial" virtue and contested whether benevolence is the only virtue (HL 1:33–34). Hutcheson clearly advised Hume to be careful about tone and some of the more controversial claims. Hume replied, "I must own, I think you a little too delicate. Except a Man be in Orders, or be immediately concern'd in the Instruction of Youth, I do not think his Character depends upon his philosophical Speculations, as the World is now model'd; & a little Liberty seems requisite to bring into the public Notice a Book that is calculated for so few Readers" (HL 1:34).

Toward the end of 1739, Hume continued to be frustrated that no full review of his work had appeared. Hoping to pave the way for a more favorable reception, he composed a summary of the core argument.[15] But before Hume could have it published as an anonymous letter to the editor of the *History of the Works of the Learned*, a review appeared in the November issue. Indeed, the review was so long that its second half was printed in the December issue (Mossner 1980: 121). The review, a collection of quotations from the text interspersed with commentary, was not kind. The reviewer complained about excessive use of the first person and Hume's lack of modesty. The reviewer misrepresented Hume as holding that in fact anything may cause anything. The reviewer scoffed: "A most charming System indeed! one can hardly conceive the Uses it may be put to, and the different Purposes it will serve: It is to be hoped, the inimitable Inventor will one Day give us a large and ample Account of them" (Mossner 1980: 123). The author of the review was likely William Warburton, close friend of Andrew Baxter, who – surprisingly – was unaware of the authorship of the *Treatise* (Mossner 1980: 124). Other reviews followed in other publications, similarly panning the work; objecting to his accounts of the will, necessity, and belief; and accusing him of paradoxes, Pyrrhonism, and posing a danger to religion (Norton 2007: 494–519).

Following Warburton's "abusive review," Hume wrote again to Hutcheson, noting "that the Alterations I have made [to Book 3] have improv'd it very much both in point of Prudence & Philosophy" (HL 1:36). He also enclosed "the *Conclusion*, as I have alter'd it, that you may see I desire to keep on good Terms even with the strictest & most rigid" (HL 1:37). The alteration Hume made was to strike out "both our Selfishness and Pride" in the first sentence of T 3.3.6.6 (SBN 620). R. W. Connon speculates that Hume was selective in what he allowed Hutcheson to see: "several passages seem calculated to give Hutcheson the impression that Hume was also revising his work in a more generally *Hutchesonian* direction" (1977: 195). On this hypothesis, Connon explains Hume's single mention of a "moral sense" in the title of T 3.1.2 and "its extraordinary concession to revealed religion ... as well as its rather uncharacteristic panegyric on the beauty of noble and generous actions" (1977: 197–98).

Hume abandoned the plan of having his abstract published in *History of the Works of the Learned*; instead, he had it published anonymously[16] as a pamphlet in March 1740, initially to be entitled *An Abstract of a late Philosophical Performance, entitled A Treatise of Human Nature, &c. Wherein the chief Argument and Design of that Book, which has met with such Opposition, and been represented in so terrifying a Light, is further illustrated and explain'd*. The published title was *An Abstract of a Book lately Published; Entituled, A Treatise of Human Nature, &c. Wherein the Chief Argument of that Book is farther Illustrated and Explained* (Mossner 1980: 124–25). With this pamphlet, Hume aimed to correct the misreading of the *Treatise*.

Hume informed Hutcheson that he would travel to London to have Book 3 published, asking Hutcheson to send a letter of recommendation for a publisher so that Hume could negotiate with multiple publishers. Hutcheson recommended Thomas Longman (HL 1:38). Hume had been revising Books 1 and 2 of the *Treatise*, but because of poor sales and the terms of his contract with John Noon, he was unable to publish a second edition; indeed, no second edition was published in his lifetime.[17] Thus, Hume included with Book 3 an Appendix "Wherein some Passages of the foregoing Volumes are illustrated and explain'd." These were published in November 1740 at a cost of 4 s. (Mossner 1980: 138).

In 1741, *Bibliothèque raisonnée* published a review that complained of paradoxes and "passages calculated to excite the curiosity of people who do not like the beaten path" (Mossner 1980: 138–39). The reviewer characterized Hume's view as a mixture of the sentiment theory of Hutcheson and the egoism of Hobbes.

Hume continued to pursue his ambition of literary fame. In 1741 and 1742, he published two volumes of moral and political *Essays*. In a letter to Henry Home in June 1742, he reported, "The *Essays* are all sold in London, as I am informed by two letters from English gentlemen of my acquaintance. There is a demand for them ..." He added, "I am also told that Dr Butler has every where recommended them; so that I hope they will have some success. They may prove like dung with marl, and bring forward the rest of my Philosophy, which is of a more durable, though of a harder and more stubborn nature" (HL 1:42–43).

Meanwhile at Edinburgh University, the professor of pneumatics, Dr. John Pringle, was frequently absent, because he was personal physician to the commander of the British forces in Flanders (HL 1:55–56n7). Pringle retained his chair, paying substitutes (including William Cleghorn) to hold his place (Sher 1990: 102). In 1744, the town council sought to replace Pringle, and Hume expressed interest in filling the vacancy (HL 1:56). By all indications, Hume had reason to expect a groundswell of support for his nomination. Pringle managed to finagle another year of leave, and Cleghorn served as substitute once more (Mossner 1980: 155).

At this point, things took a turn for the worse.[18] Hutcheson failed to include Hume's name among candidates he recommended for the position. The principal of the university, William Wishart, collected quotations from the *Treatise* and charged Hume with scepticism, atheism, undermining morality, and other grave errors (Wright 2006: 10–11).[19] In May 1745, in advance of the town council's vote, the ministers of Edinburgh voted 12 to 3 against recommending Hume. In response, Hume hastily composed a letter to a friend on the town council defending himself against Wishart's charges. Henry Home received a copy and had it printed as *A Letter from a Gentleman to his Friend in Edinburgh: Containing some Observations on a Specimen of the Principles concerning Religion and Morality, said to be maintain'd in a Book lately publish'd, intituled, A Treatise of Human Nature, &c*. It was anonymous and advertised in the *Caledonian Mercury* and *Edinburgh Evening Courant* on May 21, 1745 (Mossner 1980: 160).

Sensing that his campaign would not be successful, Hume wrote a letter on June 1 to the town council to withdraw his candidacy (Mossner 1980: 161). The letter did not arrive in time, but it did not matter (ibid.). On June 5, the town council met and named Cleghorn to the professorship of pneumatics.

Hume's *Essays* were extremely popular, and he published several more. With *Philosophical Essays on Human Understanding* in 1748, he tried again to publish for a more philosophical audience, this time including controversial parts on natural and revealed religion. In 1751, he published *An Enquiry concerning the Principles of Morals*. He had another unsuccessful bid to become a professor, this time of logic at Glasgow University in 1752. He became librarian of the Advocates Library in Edinburgh. In 1757, he recast Book 2 and published it as one of the *Four Dissertations*. Over his lifetime, he held a variety of positions, including secretary to Lord Hertford and undersecretary in Edinburgh. He researched and published six volumes of *The History of*

England (first published between 1754 and 1762), which were extremely popular after an initially bumpy reception. He died in August 1776. In accordance with his wishes, his nephew had *Dialogues concerning Natural Religion* published posthumously.

Throughout his life, Hume criticized the *Treatise* for its manner and inelegant wording. Some scholars have maintained that Hume disavowed the *Treatise*. In support of this view, they point to an Advertisement Hume composed in 1775 to serve as "a compleat Answer to Dr Reid and to that bigotted silly Fellow, Beattie" (HL 2:301), who profitably published works in which they criticized Hume's views in the *Treatise* instead of those of his later publications. In January 1776, the Advertisement was affixed to the *Essays and Treatises on Several Subjects* (a four-volume set that contained his moral and political essays, *Philosophical Essays, An Enquiry concerning the Principles of Morals*, and *Political Discourses*):

MOST of the principles, and reasonings, contained in this volume, were published in a work in three volumes, called *A Treatise of Human Nature*: A work which the Author had projected before he left College, and which he wrote and published not long after. But not finding it successful, he was sensible of his error in going to the press too early, and he cast the whole anew in the following pieces, where some negligences in his former reasoning and more in the expression, are, he hopes, corrected. Yet several writers, who have honoured the Author's Philosophy with answers, have taken care to direct all their batteries against that juvenile work, which the Author never acknowledged, and have affected to triumph in any advantages, which, they imagined, they had obtained over it: A practice very contrary to all rules of candour and fair-dealing, and a strong instance of those polemical artifices, which a bigotted Zeal thinks itself authorized to employ. Henceforth, the Author desires, that the following Pieces may alone be regarded as containing his philosophical sentiments and principles. (EHU Adv. 1; SBN 2)

Nevertheless, it is not clear that this should be understood as complete repudiation of the *Treatise*. In publishing it, Hume had exerted effort to protect his anonymity. David Fate Norton observes that Hume's 1776 essay, "My Own Life," and the Advertisement "constitute printed, public acknowledgement that the *Treatise* is his work" (2007: 588). To this day, scholars dispute whether we should accept Hume's assessments of the *Treatise* at face value.[20]

NOTES

I am deeply grateful to Donald Ainslie, Travis Butler, and Paul Russell for comments on earlier drafts of this essay.

1.   David Hume's change of surname is discussed in this chapter.
2.   There is dispute about how much he practiced law. Compare Greig 1931: 27 to Mossner 1980: 19.

3. Ninewells was named for its nine wells (or springs), but Greig notes that the estate actually had thirteen (1931: 30n1).

4. See Emerson 2009, ch. 4, for a discussion of the variety of books that eighteenth-century Scottish youth encountered from childhood to university.

5. The authorship of this anonymous work usually is thought to be that of Richard Allestree. See Elmen 1951.

6. In contrast, Graham (2004: 8) concludes that John and David "went immediately into the second year."

7. There is scholarly disagreement about what topics were covered in the required courses and which electives Home took. Stewart observes that readings from Locke's *Essay* were not common until after Home left the university (2005: 16). Stewart adds that the logic course distinguished between natural and supernatural gifts from God, according to which philosophy's aim is to use the natural gifts to better understand man's relationship with God (2005: 11). See Echelbarger 1997: 140 for further description of logic coursework at this time. Barfoot (1990) describes the typical natural philosophy course as studying Boyle's hydrostatics. Stewart comments that although it would have been possible to do so, there is no evidence that the professor of natural philosophy lectured on ethics (2005: 22). Mossner (1980: 41) speculates that Home took electives in French and mathematics; Emerson (2009: 82) disputes this but thinks that Home took three years of mathematics to prepare for natural philosophy. Stewart (2005: 23) fails to find Home's name on the attendance logs for history, but Emerson (2009) finds evidence that Hume studied a fair amount of history and geography, supporting his interpretation that Hume was interested in history for his entire life.

8. Emerson (2009) points out that the study of law would have additionally involved the study of history and languages. In the 1990s, a discovery was made: a transcription in Home's handwriting of lectures notes from George Campbell's 1726 course on fluxions. It is unknown whether they are Home's own notes or copied from someone else's notes (Stewart 1990: 8 and 2005: 21n37).

9. There is a scholarly dispute about whether the letter was to Dr. John Arbuthnot, Dr. George Cheyne, or no one. Mossner (1980: 83–87) argues that it was composed for Arbuthnot but acknowledges that there is no evidence that Home sent it. Against this conclusion, see Wright 2003. Graham (2004: 36) argues that it is to no one but was kept as a reminder to David of his overcoming adversity.

10. Around this time, in 1727, Hume wrote Michael Ramsay to tell him that he admired Longius, who is "an Author that may be be [sic] cited for an Example to his own Rules by any who shall be so adventurous as to write upon his Subject" (HL 1:11). Brandt speculates that Hume attempted literary criticism in the style of Longius to rival Addison and Pope (1977: 119). In 1739, in the Advertisement to the *Treatise*, Hume announced that after Books 1 and 2 he would "*proceed to the examination of* Morals, Politics, *and* Criticism; *which will compleat this* Treatise of Human Nature" (T Adv.; SBN xii). No such fourth volume ever appeared. Brandt (ibid.) speculates that Hume intended to include his "An Historical Essay on Chivalry and Modern Honour" and the

paragraph on poetry that he excised from Section 3 of *An Enquiry concerning Human Understanding* (Beauchamp 2000: 237). There is a dispute about the date of the essay on chivalry. See Wright 2012, in which it is argued that it should be dated 1732 or 1733.

11. Stewart (2005: 32–35) cautions us not to conflate the "new Scene of Thought" (HL 1:13) with this new moral philosophy founded on human nature (HL 1:16). (Compare Mossner 1980: 72–74.) The former occurred before the onset of Home's scurvy and broken concentration, when he was studying and applying ancient "schemes of Virtue & Happiness." After medical treatment, in 1730–31, Home became critical of the ancient philosophy and pursued his own philosophical view. This leads Stewart to date the "plan" of the *Treatise* to 1731, when the author was 20. This accords nicely with Hume's 1751 letter to Gilbert Elliot, in which he claims that the *Treatise* was "plan'd before I was one and twenty, & compos'd before twenty five" (HL 1:158). See also Brandt 1977: 118–19.

12. Graham (2004: 91) interprets Hume as expressing embarrassment at failing to find a publisher, thus explaining why he did not return to Edinburgh.

13. A manuscript fragment on evil was discovered in 1993. Stewart offers the educated guess that it is from the late 1730s. He speculates further that it may have been intended for *Treatise* Book 1, Part 4, along with suppressed essay on miracles and immortality (1995: 164). To this list of excised topics, Wright adds belief in the afterlife and the existence of God (2006: 5–6). For a discussion of the irreligious elements that remain in the published *Treatise*, see Russell 2008.

14. Mossner (1980: 113) notes that this was a common practice; for example, Locke, Baxter, Hutcheson, Mandeville, and Wollaston had all published some work anonymously.

15. In a letter to Hutcheson, Hume mentions an Abstract of the *Treatise* possessed by "Mr Smith." Greig notes that Adam Smith was then a senior student of Hutcheson's (HL 1:37n3), and it was common for students to compose abstracts of new philosophical works (HL 1:37n4). (Against this second claim, see Norton 2007: 461n85.) Nelson uses this fact to defend the claim that Adam Smith authored the Abstract (Nelson 1976 and 1991); Raynor (1993) and Norton (1993b) convincingly refute this claim, holding that the "Mr Smith" is William Smith, a publisher of *Bibliothèque raisonnée*. See also Norton 2007: 459–71.

16. Spencer (2003) observes that the 1827 edition of *The Universal Biographical Dictionary* (but not earlier editions) identifies the author of the Abstract as Hume.

17. Norton (2007: 583–84) notes that in February 1763, the late John Noon's stock still included 290 sets of Volumes 1 and 2. It would have cost over £500 for Hume to purchase those unsold copies; and it is safe to assume that there would have been even more unsold copies in 1740, and thus prohibitively expensive.

18. Mossner contends that Hume's failure is to be explained mainly by political disputes between Hume's backers and opponents (1980: 158). Sher persuasively points out that this viewpoint does not explain Whig and Presbyterian opposition to Hume's candidacy (1990: 105–6). Instead, Sher holds, "For these clergymen and academics, Hume's philosophical acumen

and factional attachments were a good deal less important than his lack of moral fervor and his political and religious scepticism" (1990: 106).

19. For challenges to the claim that Wishart was Hume's accuser, see Russell 1997.

20. On the topic of whether Hume "disowned" the *Treatise* for its philosophical errors, compare, for example, Cummins 1973 and Baier 2008: ch. 13; see also Wright 2006. Stuchbury (1989: 250–53) speculates that Hume was motivated by sluggish sales. On whether Hume's claims in "My Own Life" show that *An Enquiry concerning Human Understanding* constitutes abandonment of philosophy for literary fame, see Buckle 1999.

2   From Impressions to Justice and the Virtues: The Structure of Hume's *Treatise*

I

Hume's *A Treatise of Human Nature* is an extended eighteenth-century essay, a reflective exploration that twists and turns through a vast terrain. Of course it contains definitions, arguments, and conclusions; but they are embedded within the labyrinth of a constantly shifting reflective investigation, an assay that sifts and measures our beliefs and practices. We should read the work as if we were reading Montaigne's *Essais*, being careful not to detach arguments and conclusions from the contexts in which they occur. Both Montaigne and Hume are engaged in a meditative examination of their own turns of mind. Both nevertheless intend to address Everyman, inviting him to recognize that his experience is like theirs. Both are suspicious of illicit abstraction and decontextualization, yet both believe that the human mind is nevertheless everywhere alike, subject to the same general laws. Both are naturalists, sceptical of appeals to supernatural explanations, trusting in human nature to provide remedies for its own shortcomings and defects. Both are dialectical: no sooner do they articulate a view than they turn to its antithesis. Although both adopt an ironic and even sometimes a sceptical attitude, each (in his own distinctive way) reaffirms common sensibility. Hume uses scepticism as an antiseptic against the inflated pretensions of religious dogmatism and its secular replacement, the dogmatic and equally vacuous claims of metaphysical rationalism.[1] But in his deft hands, dogmatic scepticism fares no better than any other overextended claim. Indeed – to shift the metaphor – Hume sees that scepticism bears all the marks of disappointed romantic love: it takes its direction and its energy – and in the end, its rage – from its hopelessly idealized conceptions of the power of reason.

For all that, both Montaigne and Hume exhibit a strong Stoic influence on their lives and their thought: their disdain of religious superstition, their contempt for the fears of death, their dual allegiance to the civic virtues and to private reflection. Hume's attempt to combine Montaigne's Stoicism with his naturalism and dialectical irony is announced in his choice of epigraphs for the *Treatise*. Books 1 and 2 carry a quotation from Tacitus's politically charged *History*, in which Tacitus – a republican who nevertheless managed to receive the patronage of Vespasian, Titus, and Domitian – praises the new age. It is, he says, in phrases that ring more with hope than with experience, freed from the need for flattery and servility: "Rara temporum felicitas, ubi sentire, quæ velis; & quæ sentias, dicere licet." ("Rare is the good fortune of an age in which we can feel what we wish, and say what we feel.") The epigraph for Book 3 is even more veiled. It comes from Lucan's *Pharsalia*, Book IX, 561–63. Labienus is speaking to Cato, urging him to consult an oracle to determine whether the civil wars are finally over, and whether the people will at last be allowed to enjoy their laws and liberties. "Duræ semper virtutis amator, Quære quid est virtus, et posce exemplar honesti." ("As a lover of austere virtue, ask what virtue is and demand [to see her] worthy presence.") Lucan continues by praising Cato's answer as "worthy of the oracle itself," even though it was "inspired by the god he bore in his own heart." But Cato replies to the suggestion that he consult an oracle with a set of questions: Is it better to die in battle as a free man or to live in tyranny? Is it better to have a short or a long life? Can the virtuous be hurt by violence? Does "Fortune threaten in vain when Virtue is her antagonist?" Is noble purpose sufficient for virtue, or must virtue be capped by success? Although these questions first appear to be merely rhetorical, they clearly have a bite, particularly since Cato, standing by an altar in the temple of Ammon, adds, "The gods have no need to speak; for the Creator told us – once and for all – everything that we are permitted to know." Cato's questions are, of course, only superficially rhetorical: he is posing serious and difficult problems that even Stoic moral theory must address. If Hume intended the *Treatise* as a work in normative epistemology, with application to selected problems in psychology, ethics, and political theory, these epigraphs would be singularly ill-chosen and ill-placed. But if the *Treatise* is intended to be an investigation of "moral subjects" – that is, of psychology largely and broadly considered as encompassing all the operations of the human mind – these epigraphs reveal his sensitivity to the moral and political dimensions of his task.

To be sure, one of Hume's many voices is not to be found among any of Montaigne's own ventriloquist arts, and it is this voice that misleads many readers. This is the sober, dry voice that opens the pages of the *Treatise*, the voice introduced in the subtitle of the work: "an attempt to introduce the experimental method into moral subjects." Despite the wildness of his images and examples, Montaigne's *assays* are juridical; he brings the ancient voices that have constituted his mind to trial, to charge and answer one another. And despite the wildness of his images and examples, Hume's *assays* are those of a chemist who initially isolates, measures, and purifies the elements that are normally inseparable in experience and practice, and then analyzes the forces of attraction that compound them. Like the analytic scientist, the analytic philosopher separates independent varia- bles that form an "uncompounded and inseparable" motion (T 3.2.2.14, SBN 493). Hume provides an elegant statement of the principle that under- lies his general method: "Human nature [is] compos'd of two principal parts, which are requisite in all its actions, the affections and understand- ing; 'tis certain, that the blind motions of the former, without the direction of the latter, incapacitate men for society.... The same liberty may be permitted to moral, which is allow'd to natural philosophers; and 'tis very usual with the latter to consider any motion as compounded and consist- ing of two parts separate from each other, tho' at the same time they acknowledge it to be in itself uncompounded and inseparable" (ibid.).

Hume begins parsimoniously, by postulating only a series of simple impressions and ideas, the presumptively bare and basic constituents of all meaningful thought. In the opening Sections of the *Treatise*, the motto that "whatever objects are separable are also distinguishable, and that whatever objects are distinguishable are also different" (T 1.1.7.3, SBN 18) appears to govern the work of analysis. Because it quickly becomes evident that ordinary beliefs – about causation, about the continued existence of the external world, about the nature of personal identity – are metaphysically inflated, Hume sets himself the task of discovering the processes and rules by which these impressions and ideas are com- bined to form the proper significance of ordinary belief, freed of its metaphysical pretensions. This requires locating the points at which the austere beginnings are to be expanded. Having established that the operations of the imagination, the understanding, and the passions are analytically distinct, and that the imagination is capable of moving beyond the scope of present impressions (T 1.1.1.10, SBN 6), Hume moves to show that they are psychologically conjoined – and that it is to our benefit that they continue to be conjoined.

If Hume begins in Montaigne, he ends in Hegel. Indeed, the plot of the *Treatise* is an elegant, British proto-version of *The Phenomenology of Spirit*. The structures of the works are parallel. The argument starts from perceptual sensations and moves to an account of how we construct ideas of physical objects. From there, it moves to the idea of a system of objects forming the world of experience, and then to the experience and con- structor of that system, the self apparently composed of nothing more than the very items that compose the world. It becomes evident that the interpretive self exists in a social world, its mentality partially formed by its interactions with others. The argument ends with the moral and political world – its beliefs, convictions, and practices evaluated by the experience of history.

Like Hegel, Hume came to see the study of history – the study of political history as well as the natural genealogy of our ideas and sentiments – as the best route to understanding the long-standing, and perhaps even honorably functional, habits of the human mind. But instead of constructing a new, historicized metaphysics, Hume uses history to support an alliance between common sense and philosophy. He sets for himself the program of saving the phenomena, to analyze sensible meaning that lies behind common sense and common practice. A reconstruction of this kind – particularly one that is historically sensitive – sometimes uses the shards and stones, the ruins of previous metaphysical edifices. Sage and equitable statesman that he is, Hume thinks that an understanding of the sources of philosophic folly reveals the habits and the proper limitations of the human mind.

Unwary readers are easily misled by Hume's dialectical modes. Those who select and abstract their favorite passages – say, those on causation, on personal identity, or on the conventionality of justice – will invent their favorite Hume. Not surprisingly, the technique of raiding rather than reading does not provide the portrait of a well-integrated philosopher; rather, it introduces us to a large and disparate family. Some find Hume a proto-positivist and even an emotivist; others see him as an early, somewhat timid Romantic; some find him expressing the last pretensions of the Enlightenment; still others see him primarily as a pragmatic, political Tory. But the utilitarians also claim him, and there are even those who discern the lineaments of a proto-Kantian. Like greedy offspring who each abscond with a small part of the inheritance, Hume's grandchildren are left with bits and pieces pathetically displaced from the grand mansion in which they were deftly placed and ironically counterbalanced.

Hume is notorious for his treatment of the philosophic clichés of the time: the distinctions between matters of fact and the relations between ideas, between belief and the imagination, between reason and sentiment, between the natural and artificial virtues, between 'is' and 'ought,' between the virtues of self-interested prudence and the social virtues. He presents the current, accepted analysis of each term of the opposition and proceeds to trace its role in thought and experience. Having set forth the claims of the fashionably favored partner, he then stuns the reader by arguing the case in the other direction. It then seems – for a time – as if we are to reverse accepted truths: the idea of strict personal identity is wholly vacuous; morality rests solely on the passions and the sentiments; matters of fact are entirely irrelevant to the determination of moral obligations; justice is an artificial virtue, its principles conventional. Having apparently subverted accepted philosophic opinion, Hume's investigation takes yet another turn, and it emerges that there is more of a subterranean connection between the terms of the naïvely paired opposition than it first seemed. Although they may be separable in thought, we would be unwise to attempt to separate or oppose them.

2

I propose to trace six of Hume's arbitrations between fashionable but false oppositions. The first opposition – that between belief as a purely cognitive state, identified by its content and belief as a "certain feeling or sentiment" (T App. 2, SBN 624) that renders a conception "more present and intense" (T App. 4, SBN 625) – is resolved by treating belief as emerging from the natural and custom-bound operation of the imagination in the association of ideas. The second opposition – that between the operations of reason and those of the passions – is resolved by introducing sentiment as a third mediating faculty, a faculty that combines some of the functions of the passions with those of reason and the understanding. The third opposition – that between the idea of the self as a continuing identical substance and radical scepticism about strict personal identity – is resolved by Hume's reconstruction of the idea of self as arising from the passion of pride and self-interest reflecting the judgment of others. The fourth opposition – that between 'is' and 'ought' – is resolved by tracing the operations of sympathy on the sentiments. The fifth opposition – between the motives of self-interest and those of the social virtues – is overcome by showing how the motives of narrow self-interest naturally expand to include those of the social virtues of justice. Finally, the sixth opposition – between natural talents and artificial virtues – is shown to be overstated, and to depend on social practices rather than on the postulate of a free will.

Causality: Two Senses of Belief

The first sense of belief designates the content of an idea; for instance, that whatever exists must have a cause for its existence (T 1.3.3.1, SBN 78–79). But it seems that Hume's analytic maxim that ideas correspond to the impressions from which they derive casts a sceptical shadow on beliefs about causality. Like the ideas of the continued existence of physical objects and of personal identity, the idea of causation cannot be traced to a set of originating impressions of sensation.[2] It is nevertheless evident that these ideas or beliefs naturally and "invariably" guide our inferences and practices. The opposition between an unsubstantiated dogmatic claim in causality and an equally dogmatic nihilistic scepticism is resolved by introducing causality as a "philosophical" as well as a "natural" relation derived from an idea of reflection (T 1.3.14.31, SBN 170). Hume announces a shift in the focus of his heuristic strategy. Having established (by means of his "experiment" with the missing shade of blue) that the imagination is capable of supplying ideas beyond the scope of its present impressions, Hume is free to extend his search for the origins of complex ideas (T 1.1.1.10, SBN 6). Instead of looking for the sensory origin of the idea of causation as a relation among physical objects, he looks for its origin in the natural and invariable activity of the imagination in the principled association of ideas. This shift allows Hume to find the origin of the idea of causation – and the tendency to believe specific causal claims – in the natural and customary "determination" of the mind by the principles of the association of ideas. Under certain conditions – the temporal priority, contiguity, and constant conjunction of impressions and ideas – the imagination renders the ideas of cause and effect with a certain degree of lively vivacity or force (T 1.3.6–8). Hume's statesmanly arbitration reconciles the two apparently opposed senses of belief: it is a "wonderful and unintelligible instinct in our souls, which ... arises from past observation and experience" (T 1.3.16.9, SBN 179), "a certain feeling or sentiment" (T App. 2, SBN 624) that under specific conditions renders a conception "more present and intense" (T App. 4, SBN 625). "[P]robable reasoning is nothing but a species of sensation" (T 1.3.8.12, SBN 103). The feeling, the sentiment of belief, is itself a species of sensory experience, a vivid and forceful impression of reflection associated with a patterned set of impressions and ideas. The apparent tension between the two senses of belief – belief as identified by its content and belief as identified by its vivacity – is reconciled. The liveliness, the force and vivacity, of a specific idea-content derives from the imagination operating according to specific rules governing the relations among their content; that is, their resemblance, contiguity, and constant conjunction. Scepticism is rebutted, but its impulse has been acknowledged (T 1.2.5.26n12.2, SBN 639n).

Two Sources of the Ideas of Good and Evil

Hume opens his discussion of the sources of morality with a vigorous attack against the friends of reason who claim that reason alone distinguishes moral good and evil. Since Hume has already provisionally defined reason as a purely speculative (i.e., observational) faculty, he can, by remaining strictly within the boundaries of the argument he has so far developed, claim a cheap and easy victory. Reason, which is limited to judgments about matters of fact or about relations among ideas, is incapable of giving rise to any new idea (T 1.3.14.18, SBN 164). It cannot prove the continued existence of external objects (T 1.4.2.14, SBN 193).

And though it cooperates with the imagination in making particular causal inferences, it is not the source of our idea of causation (T 1.3.3.3, SBN 79). And most significantly, it alone "can never produce any action, or give rise to volition" (T 2.3.3.4, SBN 414). Even if morality were only a matter of forming evaluative judgments, even if it were strictly limited to assigning grades to actions and character – this one is excellent, that one is unworthy – reason could not be the source of our moral ideas. It could not provide general criteria for what is morally obligatory, or for virtue and vice. The terms 'good' and 'vicious' do not refer to properties that are intrinsic to objects, qualities, or events as such, independently of their complex relations to us. They express what, on the basis of experience, we tend to judge to be generally useful, pleasurable, harmful, or painful. But Hume's argument against the friends of reason is even stronger. Because the point of morality is to influence actions and affections, "to go beyond the calm and indolent judgments of the understanding" (T 3.1.1.5, SBN 457), it falls in the practical rather than the speculative domain. Even if moral distinctions – the criteria for moral judgment and evaluation – were in the province of reason, they could not provide a motive for following the judgments of morality.

Having dispatched the claims of reason as the guide to morality, Hume turns to those of sentiment. First, however, we have to address difficult terminological questions: What is the relation between the motivating impulses of the passions analyzed in Book 2 of the *Treatise* and the sentiments that are, in Book 3, argued to be the sources of moral distinctions? How are we to understand the notorious passage that so misleads even readers sympathetic to Hume – the passage in which he says, "Reason is, and ought only to be the slave of the passions, and can never pretend to any other office than to serve and obey them" (T 2.3.3.4, SBN 415)? Although reason is not the sole source of the sentiment, or even the general idea, of justice, judicious deliberation enters into the way in which issues of justice are determined and settled; it can, and properly should, play some role in affecting the passions and sentiments.

Hume's rhetorical antirationalist outburst occurs within the course of an argument that considerably diminishes its force. It appears within the context of his expounding a view that he shares with Descartes and Spinoza, that there is no direct combat between reason and the passions. "Nothing," he says, "can oppose or retard the impulse of passion, but a contrary impulse" (ibid.). But we have already seen that reason is not an active force of any kind. It is the passions and the passions alone, as they are conjoined with pleasure and pain, that motivate us. The passions nevertheless bear extremely complex relations to representational ideas and to beliefs. For the passions are not in and of themselves representational: taken simply as psychological facts, they are only contingently connected with representational ideas.

Hume distinguishes three categories of passions. According to their *origins*, passions are *direct* when they arise immediately from pleasure or pain, *indirect* when they are mediated through a "double relation" between impressions and ideas. Although some simple passions, like pleasure and pain, are in principle capable of being directly motivating, the specific motivational direction of an indirect passion like pride – to pursue *this* or avoid *that* – depends on the beliefs and ideas with which it is conjoined. Although indirect passions may not have immediate motivational force, they are given direction by the ideas with which they are contingently but regularly conjoined (T 2.2.6.3, 2.3.9.3–4, SBN 367, 438–39). It is this basic, mutually reinforcing associative conjunction between passions and specific correlated ideas that effectively (though not strictly logically) makes the passions cognitive. For as Hume puts it, "'tis not the present sensation or momentary pain or pleasure, which determines the character of any passion, but the general bent or tendency of it from the beginning to the end," described by enumeration of the circumstances that attend the passions (T 2.2.9.11, SBN 384–85). So they are in part identified and individuated by the ideas with which they are typically conjoined, and in part by the behavior they, together with their associated ideas, typically generate.

But passions are also classified by their felt emotional intensity or turbulence as *calm* or *violent* (T 2.3.3.9, SBN 417) and, according to the extent of their influence on our thoughts and actions, as *strong* or *weak*. The three categories of passions intersect: a direct passion can be calm and weak; an indirect passion can be violent and strong. It is central to Hume's whole enterprise that some calm, indirect passions – the sentiment of justice, for instance – can be strong.

Sentiments are calm, indirect dispositional passions. It is for this reason that their operations are often confused with those of reason. Like other passions, they are not in themselves representational: the complex, general ideas that identify them do not directly refer to properties of objects. Yet since sentiments are attitudes toward objects that are conceived as good or evil, they can be straightaway motivating. Like the Cartesian *habitudes* of *generosité* and *éstime de soi meme* – dispositions that also combine ideas and passions – Hume's *sentiments* are descendants of Stoic *eupatheiai*: they are strongly cognitive, dispositional passions that are in principle powerful enough to outweigh narrow, immediate passions. The seventeenth- and eighteenth-century descendants of Stoic *eupatheiai* have, as it were, double-entry bookkeeping: they are motivating passions, yet they are also sound, well-formed general cognitive attitudes.

Two Conceptions of the Self

Hume notoriously attacks the standard received conception of the continued, uninterrupted, and invariable self as a simple, unified entity (T
1.4.6.1, SBN 251). Because impressions are distinct, because they are as
various as their contents, they cannot – individually or collectively – give
rise to the idea of such a self. "[T]here is no impression [that is] constant
and invariable.... I never can catch *myself* at any time without a perception, and never can observe any thing but the perception ... of heat or
cold, light or shade, love or hatred, pain or pleasure.... [W]ere all my
perceptions remov'd,... I shou'd be ... a perfect non-entity" (T 1.4.6.2–
3, SBN 251–52). Shifting from the idea of the identity of the person to the
identity of the mind, Hume finds that the mind, properly conceived,
consists of nothing but a sequence of distinct impressions. Yet the idea
of the continued existence of the self as mind seems as persistent – as
embedded in speech and practice – as the ideas of causation and the
continued, uninterrupted existence of objects. What, then, is the source
of this apparently fictional idea? It is, not surprisingly, the imagination
that ascribes "invariableness and uninterruptedness" to a sequence of
variable, interrupted impressions or perceptions. The imagination does
so, following the same laws of association that prompt it to ascribe
continued existence to physical objects, by projecting from the relations
of resemblance and causation, which are, along with contiguity, "the
cement of the universe" (Abs. 35, SBN 662). The idea of the identity of
the mind is at best a fiction of the imagination (T 1.4.6.21–23, SBN 262–
63). Hume himself is evidently not altogether convinced that his account
of the idea of personal identity "as it regards our thought or imagination"
(T 1.4.6.5, SBN 253) is as successful as his reconstruction of the ideas of
causation and the existence of physical objects. Nowhere is the necessity
of the expansion of the austere reductionist beginning of the *Treatise*
more evident than in the devastation of the idea of the continued, invariable existence of a unified, substantial mind (T 1.4.6.21, SBN 262). The
Appendix is severe: "*we have no notion of it* [the mind], *distinct from the
particular perceptions*" (T App. 19, SBN 635). At this point, the idea of the
self is not even accorded the status of a fictional idea.

But Book 1 and its appended notes are not the end of the *Treatise*, nor
the end of the story of the construction of the idea of the self as an agent.
Although "it is by means of thought only that any thing operates upon
our passions, and [the principles of association] are the only ties of our
thoughts" (Abs. 35, SBN 662), "we must distinguish betwixt personal
identity, as it regards our thought or imagination, and as it regards our
passions or the concern we take in ourselves" (T 1.4.6.5, SBN 253).
Attempting to trace the origins of the idea of the self as an agent, Hume

turns to the passions – as impressions of reflection – to legitimize the fictional idea of agency. Nature provides a remedy: "nature has given to the organs of the human mind, a certain disposition fitted to produce a peculiar impression or emotion, which we call *pride*: To this emotion she has assign'd a certain idea, *viz.* that of *self*, which it never fails to produce" (T 2.1.5.6, SBN 287). Moreover, we are also naturally disposed to be affected by the sentiments of our fellows, and indeed to acquire them, as it were by sympathetic contagion. Moved by the desire for approval and by the concerns of others, the passions and sentiments can acquire a moral force (cf. Rorty 1990).

Two Sources of Moral Obligation

If the passions have introduced the idea of the self as an agent, they have not delivered the idea of the self as a fully formed moral agent subject to moral obligations and capable of acquiring moral virtues. The notorious – and much misunderstood – passage on the abrupt transition from *is* to *ought* announces the theme: "In every system of morality,... the author proceeds... in the ordinary way of reasoning [about what he supposes are matters of fact]... when of a sudden,... instead of the usual copulations of propositions, *is*, and *is not*, [we] meet ... *ought* or an *ought not*" (T 3.1.1.27, SBN 469). Hume's complaint is that the shift in verbs marks the introduction of a wholly new and unargued thesis. If claims about moral obligations – say, that it is morally obligatory to fulfill promises – cannot be demonstrated by empirical or a priori reasoning, does it follow that such claims are nonsensical?

Of course they are not. If they were, common sense and common practice would be endangered as well as unintelligible. Having attacked the friends of reason, Hume announces the claims of the friends of the sentiments. "[S]ince vice and virtue are not discoverable merely by reason, or the comparison of ideas, it must be by means of some impression or sentiment they occasion, that we are able to mark the difference betwixt them.... Morality, therefore, is more properly felt than judg'd of" (T 3.1.2.1, SBN 470).

Typically, Hume does not leave the matter as it stands, with the sentiments in full charge. He straightaway looks for the psychological laws that govern our sentiments concerning morality. After all, even if morality is more properly felt than judged, moral sentiments are distinguishable from other kinds of feelings – for instance, those that arise from an attack of the gout, from spite, or from hearing a good musical performance. Even if moral distinctions and obligations are not demonstrated or refuted by the same methods that are used to establish mathematical or empirical claims, there are still considerations beyond mere personal or idiosyncratic sentiment that substantiate one obligation over another. It may not be *irrational* to prefer the destruction of a nation to splitting an infinitive or a fingernail, but it is preposterous, contemptible, and even vile to have such preferences (T 2.3.3.6, SBN 416).

The natural operations of sympathy, in conjunction with the imagination, enlarge the scope of the passions so that they become morally motivating sentiments, sensitive to the well-being of others. Sympathy is not a particular feeling akin to pity or compassion; it is, rather, a disposition to acquire the interests and opinions of those we judge to resemble ourselves. Hume's metaphors derive from music and from medicine: we are so attuned with someone that his condition strikes a sympathetic chord; or we are susceptible to infectious contagion. We are, by nature, so constructed that we infer the psychological state of others by observing them. Seeing a person's posture and her countenance, hearing her voice and intonation, we conclude that she is sad; other expressions indicate disapproval or indignation. When we think that the person bears a significant resemblance to ourselves, the *idea* of her condition becomes imaginatively enlivened so that it acquires the force and vivacity of a passion, an impression of reflection. The psychological resonance of sympathy is not limited to passions and sentiments; it can also produce a harmony of beliefs and attitudes. If my friend is indignant about his government's educational policy, I can acquire his attitudes through the mechanism of sympathy rather than through any experience or reflection of my own. It is, indeed, through the active working of the sympathetic imagination that a population can give meaning and motivation to a set of cultural and political convictions beyond their individual experiences. The introduction of sentiments has moved at least some passions closer to the understanding, and reason and belief have also made their compromises and accommodations.

The friends of reason might still hope to find a sounder psychological basis for moral motivation than the passions, enlarged though they might be by sympathy and the imagination. As the account stands so far, a person's motives are largely contingently formed: they consist of a heterogeneous collection of passions acquired through the accidents of sympathetic contagion. We would be in serious trouble if this were the end of the story. After all, a person might sympathetically acquire murderous as well as generous passions. Although its operations are natural and lawlike, sympathy is likely to leave us with a set of contingently (and even randomly) acquired, tensed, and perhaps even conflicted motives. We do not yet have the kinds of sentiments that can reliably serve as the basis of morality.

There is, however, a good deal more that can be said about why irrational attitudes are vicious. It turns out that there are steady, general principles implicit in the patterns of moral sentiments: "An action, or sentiment, or character is virtuous or vicious," Hume says, "because its view causes a pleasure or uneasiness of a particular kind" (T 3.1.2.3, SBN 471). "'Tis only when a character is consider'd *in general*, without reference to our particular interest, that it causes such a feeling or sentiment, as denominates it morally good or evil" (T 3.1.2.4, SBN 472; emphasis added). Moral sentiments presuppose the operations of sympathy, but they also involve surveying what is (regarded as) *useful* and *pleasing* to our fellows, generally considered. These sentiments arise only after we have taken a general point of view – one in which we consider an action or character as it might be generally found useful or pleasant. Only those sentiments that arise from an adequate, sympathetic understanding can be denominated as moral. Although morality is more aptly felt than judged, it cannot be felt without having been reasonably judged. Indeed, on closer examination, it turns out that the constraints on moral sentiments are as stringent as those on the most rigorous causal laws. Moral sentiments involve the approval or disapproval of a sympathetically sensitive judicious spectator, as he judges the general utility or pleasure of a character, quality, or action.

Hume has bridged the gap between *is* and *ought* by arguing that moral judgments are formed through the mechanism of sympathy; they involve a projected judgment about what would please or be useful to the general run of mankind. Even though a moral judgment is an emotional response of approval or disapproval that cannot be empirically or analytically demonstrated, it is an emotional response arising "from the constitution of your nature" (T 3.1.1.26, SBN 469) to something seen or conceived *as* useful or pleasing. "We do not infer a character to be virtuous, because it pleases: But in feeling that it pleases *after such a particular manner* [that is, a pleasure in the general utility and agreeableness of a character, action, or quality], we in effect feel that it is virtuous" (T 3.1.2.3, SBN 471; emphasis added).

Hume's account of moral sentiments is doubly intellectualized: the sentiments involve the sympathies we would have if we were to assume the position of a judicious spectator, and they involve the sympathies that a judicious spectator would have when he judges the effects an action or character would have under normal circumstances.

Two Sources of the Idea of Justice

So far, Hume has established the sources of moral distinctions and moral approbation. He has yet to show why attitudes succeed in motivating. He first establishes what seems a naïve egoism and then shows how the natural course of events will, in the best of circumstances, lead an individual toward being moved by the sentiment of justice. The movement from narrow self-interest to the institution of just practices and institutions occurs, he says, like a law of nature, "common ... [and] inseparable from the species" (T 3.2.1.19, SBN 484). The story of the origins of the rules of justice and of their ready acceptance is a simple but subtle story. We have no innate idea of justice; its rules are not part of the original constitution of the human mind. Apart from its relation to our natural sentiments, we have no fixed motives to serve the general public welfare as such. Our initial, basic motives are and remain those of self-love and self-interest, as they are naturally extended by our affections and by the mechanism of sympathy (T 3.2.2.5–6, SBN 487). To be sure, we are also inclined to the virtues of benevolence, charity, and kindness to children. Because the exercise of these virtues arises from our affections, they are always pleasant to us, regardless of what might come of them. But in their original, untutored forms, these sentiments are relatively weak, unable to outweigh the strong force of self-interest. Indeed, we suffer one passion that outweighs any natural general benevolence we might have. The desire for possessions – our avidity and greed – is, as Hume puts it, "insatiable, perpetual, universal, and directly destructive of society" (T 3.2.2.12, SBN 492). So powerful is this motive that nothing but its own force, as it might be reasonably redirected to its own interests, can restrain it. In its most rhetorical form, Hume's dialectical irony has its full play: "'tis only from the selfishness and confin'd generosity of man, along with the scanty provision nature has made for his wants, that justice derives its origin" (T 3.2.2.18, SBN 495).

Having had his ironic turn in tracing the idea of justice from self-interest, Hume still must show that the sentiment of justice can become an active habit, a virtue with a reliable motivational force. Although self-interest is argued to be self-limiting and self-checking, it becomes evident that the movement from the passion of greed to the sentiment of justice also requires the active collaboration of the imagination and the understanding. Justice is an artificial idea: its rules are thoughtful and deliberate contrivances to regulate and coordinate our behavior (T 3.2.1.19, SBN 484). Intelligent reflection on experience – deliberation and the experimental method of reasoning – is required to recognize that the desire for possession is best served by being constrained by the socially formed conventions of justice. The details of the story mitigate the irony of the reversal: greed recognizes that it must check itself to serve itself only when it receives the cooperation of the understanding, of acute judgment and reasoning.

Although initially the conventions, and eventually the rules of justice, are artificial, they are not arbitrary. The interests they serve are as steadfast, immutable, and commanding as if they had been instinctual

(T 3.3.6.5, SBN 620). Like the shelters we contrive for our safety and protection, the structure and content of the conventional rules of justice are carefully and astutely designed. Far from being arbitrary, they conform to our needs and our situations, taking the conditions of scarcity and our natural dispositions into account. The practices of justice gradually arise out of a recognition of the convenience and benefits of following a convention – literally, a coming together in agreement – of acknowledging one another's "established rights" and respecting one another's possessions. To be sure, individual instances of justice may sometimes conflict with our passions, sentiments, and interests. But here, as elsewhere, Hume argues that we are guided by a consideration of what happens *as a general rule*, following projectable expectations of the benefits of the institutions of justice.

The genealogy of justice explains why we try to institute it, to promote and to educate it. But it does not yet establish its moral worth; nor does it explain why we esteem justice as a virtue and why we are moved by issues of justice that have no conceivable practical effect on our own welfare. As Hume puts it, *"self-interest* is the original motive to the *establishment* of justice: But a *sympathy* with *public* interest is the source of the *moral* approbation, which attends that virtue" (T 3.2.2.24, SBN 499–500). Reflection on the experience of history shows that a refined sense of justice and a devotion to the public good have been beneficial and agreeable at all times and in all places. Since we approve of a character trait as virtuous when we judge that it typically serves our fellows, it should be no surprise that justice is a highly prized virtue, the primary defense against the major threat to the harmony of social life. Because we are sympathetically affected by the evaluations of those we esteem, the strong social approbation of justice as a central virtue further strengthens our resolve to conform to its rules.

The Two Sources of the Virtues

Having introduced the familiar distinction between the artificial virtues (justice, promise-keeping, and chastity) and the natural abilities (such as wit, intelligence, equanimity of temper, and good humor), Hume again moves to show their interconnections. Both indicate mental qualities, both are socially useful, and a judicious spectator finds both pleasurable and estimable. Moreover, the natural abilities enhance and indeed support the exercise of the artificial virtues: intelligent justice is far more admirable, even as a virtue, than dense, unimaginative justice. And though our attitudes toward natural abilities and virtues are typically different from those toward the artificial virtues – for instance, we love the natural abilities of wit and humor but esteem courage and benevolence – still each of the virtues elicits a distinctive and particular response (T 3.3.4.2, SBN 607–8).

The strongest argument for distinguishing artificial virtues from natural abilities is that the former are thought to depend on liberty and free will, whereas the latter are believed to be entirely involuntary (T 3.3.4.3–4, SBN 608–9). Hume's reply is, by now, predictable: the phenomena elude simplistic dichotomies. Many of the traits that enter into the moral virtues – constancy, fortitude, and magnanimity – are as constitutionally based as natural abilities; moreover, many involuntary responses enter into the determination of whether a particular virtue is exercised. Someone suffering overwhelming pain is – however virtuous she may be – not held by a small promise. In any case, since Hume has already cast doubt on the metaphysical existence of a free will, it is an unlikely source for a working distinction between the natural and artificial virtues. Still, many practices appear to rest on the distinction; the phenomena need to be explained, and diplomatic courtesy to moral philosophers requires that we understand why they were drawn to it. In practice, we attempt to motivate the exercise of some virtues by praise and reward. As Hume puts it, "to punish a man for folly,... wou'd have but little effect; tho' the same punishments and exhortations, with regard to justice and injustice, might have a considerable influence" (T 3.3.4.4, SBN 609). We call those qualities that are responsive to rewards and sanctions "moral virtues," and classify those that seem invariable as "natural abilities." The significance of the distinction between the natural and the artificial virtues lies wholly and solely in successful social practices.

3

Hume has brought the passions into their own, no longer marks of invasive forces but our own motivating attitudes. From being merely reactive responses, the passions became the primary sources of action. Although passions are analytically distinct from ideas, they are so constantly conjoined with specific ideas in mutually reinforcing patterns of association that their individuation and identification is cognitively charged. And though reason can neither create nor oppose the passions, the two – forming a partnership in the articulation of the calm, indirect sentiments – are the conjoint sources of our moral ideas and our moral motives. To counterbalance the claims of dogmatic rationalism, Hume emphasizes the role of the sentiments in morality; but it quickly becomes apparent that although reason is never sufficient either to produce the idea of virtue or to motivate it, its cooperation in the activities of the sentiments is absolutely necessary. Perhaps not fully recognizing the import of his constructive originality, Hume also marks the social and political contributions to the formation and directions of the passions, as affected by sympathy, by the social patterns of admiration and contempt, and by the political structures that define property. He so enlarges the conception of the passions that he can classify justice as a cognitively formed motivating sentiment, derived from the recognition of the benefits of cooperative activity. Justice receives approval as a virtue because it generally conduces to the public good. More significantly, sympathy and the imagination so enliven ideas of justice's distant advantages that, feeling them as our own, we are prepared to act on its behalf.

We can now understand why the major objections to the *Treatise* come from the very (opposed) positions that he attempted to reconcile. Neo-Kantians argue that the moral sentiments are unreliable grounds for morality, even when they are supported by deliberation and reasoning. From that point of view, a developmentally oriented, naturalistic moral psychology is inadequate to account for the normative force of moral obligations. Indeed, as such neo-Kantians see it, the introduction of the experimental method of reasoning into the moral sciences is nothing more than a suspiciously empiricized analytic psychology, incapable of explaining the phenomena of morality, let alone providing its foundations. On the other side, Nietzsche and his successors see Hume as duped by – and ready to perpetuate – custom and convention, gulled by what he mistakenly takes to be the lessons of history. Ironically, both sides charge him with attempting to derive *ought* from *is*.

Hume's persona as an eighteenth-century essayist would not incline him to engage neo-Kantians in counter-transcendental arguments. His response would predictably be practical, psychological, and naturalistic. On the one hand, reason cannot, even in its most powerful forms, provide the kinds of directions that neo-Kantians believe morality requires. Unless it is supported by sentiment, habit, and custom, reason can provide only a criterion to determine the propriety of the intentions of a (fictional) will: it is too general to command specific actions – indeed, too general to provide specific intentions. If morality depends on the power as well as the authority of reason, morality is in deep trouble. Moreover, the authority of reason over moral obligations extends only as far as successful experience can warrant. On the other hand, the operations of the passions and the sentiments are as regular and invariable as any other natural phenomena: they conform to similar sorts of laws. Checked by the judgments of a judicious spectator, they are as reliable sources of morality as anything can be.

Hume's response to Nietzsche would be equally debonair: neither power nor energetic exuberance carries any more claim to intrinsic worth than does the vast range of goods that we normally prize and attempt to realize. As Nietzsche himself is the first to insist, the general experience of mankind does not accept the forms of excellence that he thinks represent its highest values. And if Nietzsche's "moralizing" is directed solely to those who are ready to set aside the values tested by experience, and if it is addressed to an audience that is not moved by ordinary passions and sentiments, then he has no claim on those of us who recognize ourselves in Hume's mirror.[3]

NOTES

1. Hume's "modest" or "moderate" scepticism marks him as a cautious fallibilist (T 1.4.7.15, SBN 273–74).
2. Hume is notoriously evasive about the relation between impressions and ideas. In what sense do ideas "correspond" to impressions? In what sense are they "*derived*" from them? In what sense do they "represent" and "resemble" them (T 1.1.1.3–4, SBN 3)? In what sense are they "images" of impressions (T 1.1.1.11, SBN 6)? Although I believe that Hume's main focus – his schematic account of the origins of complex ideas of reflection – is neutral between different emphases on his initial analytic maxim, developing this interpretation would deflect us from the main concerns of our investigation.
3. Some sections of this paper appeared in Rorty 1993. Those sections are reprinted here with the permission of *History of Philosophy Quarterly*. I am greatly indebted to Donald Ainslie for his detailed comments and suggestions and to Annemarie Butler for her careful editing.

3 The Ideas of Space and Time and Spatial and Temporal Ideas in *Treatise* 1.2

Part 2 of Book 1 of Hume's *Treatise*, "Of the ideas of space and time," is peppered with a number of apparently inconsistent claims:

(1A) [T]he capacity of the mind is limited, and can never attain a full and adequate conception of infinity. (T 1.2.1.2, SBN 26)

(1B) [W]ere I to carry on the addition *in infinitum*, I clearly perceive, that the idea of extension must also become infinite. (T 1.2.2.2, SBN 30)

(2A) [T]he idea of a grain of sand is not distinguishable, nor separable into twenty, much less into a thousand, ten thousand, or an infinite number of different ideas. (T 1.2.1.3, SBN 27)

(2B) [W]e can form ideas, which shall be no greater than the smallest atom of the animal spirits of an insect a thousand times less than a mite. (T 1.2.1.5, SBN 28)

(3A) [T]he minute parts of distant bodies convey not any sensible impression. (T 1.2.1.4, SBN 27)

[S]ound reason convinces us that there are bodies *vastly* more minute than those, which appear to the senses. (T 1.2.4.24, SBN 48)

(3B) Nothing can be more minute, than some ... images, which appear to the senses. (T 1.2.1.5, SBN 28)

(4A) Nothing can be more minute, than some ... images, which appear to the senses; since these are ... images perfectly simple and indivisible. (T 1.2.1.5, SBN 28)

(4B) A microscope or telescope ... gives parts to impressions, which to the naked eye appear simple and uncompounded. (T 1.2.1.4, SBN 28)

(5A) 'Tis universally allow'd, that the capacity of the mind is limited, and can never attain a full and adequate conception of infinity: And tho' it were not allow'd, 'twou'd be sufficiently evident from the plainest observation and experience. (T 1.2.1.2, SBN 26)

(5B) We may hence discover the error of the common opinion, that the capacity of the mind is limited on both sides, and that 'tis impossible for the imagination

31

to form an adequate idea, of what goes beyond a certain degree of minuteness as well as of greatness. (T 1.2.1.5, SBN 28)

(6A) [T]he images, which I form in my mind to represent [the thousandth and ten thousandth part of a grain of sand], are nothing different from each other, nor inferior to that image, by which I represent the grain of sand itself. (T 1.2.1.3, SBN 27)

(6B) [O]ur ideas are adequate representations of the most minute parts of extension. (T 1.2.2.1, SBN 29)

(7A) [E]very idea, with which the imagination is furnish'd, first makes its appearance in a correspondent impression. (T 1.2.3.1, SBN 33)

(7B) The idea of time is not deriv'd from a particular impression mix'd up with others, and plainly distinguishable from them; but arises altogether from the manner, in which impressions appear to the mind, without making one of the number. (T 1.2.3.10, SBN 36)

In what follows, I argue that these claims are not in fact incoherent. Their coherence can be established by accepting two tenets: that visual and tactile impressions and the ideas that copy them are extended, and that impressions and ideas represent objects by more or less closely resembling them, so that what it means to have an idea or impression of an object is not so much "to think, about it, that it is a certain way," as for there to be a more or less accurate and complete replica of it in the bundle of impressions and ideas that constitutes a mind.[1]

I am not sure that invoking these tenets is the only way to establish the coherence of Hume's claims. I confine myself to arguing that the tenets do make Hume's claims coherent, that Hume thought that they did, and that he made the claims with so little concern to address their apparent inconsistency because he was so thoroughly wedded to the tenets. If I am right on these points, then it is incumbent on those who have denied that Hume seriously meant to describe perceptions as extended or representation as replication to come up with an alternative, equally coherent account of the claims of *Treatise* 1.2, on pain of having to admit that their views fail to reflect the course of Hume's thought in all the parts of the *Treatise*.[2]

I argue for these conclusions by presenting a close commentary on the text of the opening Sections of *Treatise* 1.2.

I. THE ARGUMENT OF TREATISE 1.2.1.2

Treatise 1.2 is nominally about the ideas of space and time. Hume proposed to "begin this subject" with an examination of "the doctrine of infinite divisibility" (T 1.2.1.1, SBN 26). We need to be careful not to be misled by this remark. It is natural to assume that by "the doctrine of infinite divisibility" Hume meant either the geometrical doctrine that space and time are infinitely divisible or the metaphysical doctrine that the infinite divisibility of space entails the correspondingly infinite divisibility of material objects. These were the topics of concern for other early modern philosophers who considered the "doctrine," such as Bayle, Leibniz, and Kant. But Hume seems to have understood the doctrine more broadly, or at least to have approached the doctrine from an odd angle. He did not begin by asking whether space, time, or the objects in space are infinitely divisible. Instead, he began by asking whether we can form ideas that consist of infinitely many parts. Witness the title of *Treatise* 1.2.1, "Of the infinite divisibility of our ideas of space and time," as contrasted with the title of *Treatise* 1.2.2, "Of the infinite divisibility of space and time." Witness further the conclusion of *Treatise* 1.2.1.2 (SBN 27; emphasis added), which contains Hume's opening and foundational argument: "the *idea*, which we form of any finite quality, is not infinitely divisible, but ... by proper distinctions and separations we may run up *this idea* to inferior ones, which will be perfectly simple and indivisible."

Appreciating this point takes some of the oddness out of the way Hume began *Treatise* 1.2. If we think that his project was to examine the ideas of space and time, then it seems odd that he would not have started by inquiring into what impressions these ideas are derived from. But if we think that his initial project was rather to inquire into those of our ideas that are spatially extended and temporally ordered, then the beginning is less suspect. We can see the study of the origin and the kinds of ideas undertaken in *Treatise* 1.1 being complemented in *Treatise* 1.2 with a further inquiry into their mereological structure, centered on the claim that compound ideas can be composed of only finitely many simple ideas.

Hume's argument for this conclusion was a simple one: the capacity of the mind is limited, and therefore none of its products – in particular no idea – can be infinitely complex. Most notably, the ideas we form of any finite ""quality" (Hume's term)" (including, crucially, a finite extension) cannot be infinitely complex. Since no idea can be infinitely complex, it must be possible to "run up" any idea into a finite number of "inferior ideas" by "proper distinctions and separations" (T 1.2.1.2, SBN 27).

There are two things worth noting about this argument. The first is that, as Hume stated it (though not as I restate it in the previous paragraph), it contains a red herring. After observing that the mind is able to conceive of only finitely complex ideas, Hume tossed in a contrasting comment that whatever is infinitely divisible must consist of infinitely many parts. Commentators have charged that he was wrong about this,[3] but it does not matter, because the remark has no bearing on the conclusion that ideas are only finitely divisible. That conclusion follows from Hume's appeal to the finite capacity of the mind, regardless of what one might think it means for something to be infinitely divisible.

The second thing worth noting about this argument is the precise nature of its conclusion. Hume did not say that, because the mind is limited, the idea it forms of any finite quality can only be an idea *of* a quality with a finite number of parts; he said, rather, that it can only be an idea *with* a finite number of parts. It is not some "finite quality" represented by the idea that is said to have only finitely many parts – at least not at this stage in Hume's argument. It is the idea itself. Note Hume's very words: "the *idea*, which we form of any finite quality, is not infinitely divisible"; and again, "by proper distinctions and separations we may run up *this idea* to inferior ones, which will be perfectly simple and indivisible" (emphasis added); and again, "In rejecting the infinite capacity of the mind, we suppose it may arrive at an end in the division *of its ideas*" (emphasis added); and still again, a little further on toward the end of the following paragraph, "whatever we may imagine of the thing, the idea of a grain of sand is not distinguishable,... into ... different ideas"; and yet again, toward the end of *Treatise* 1.2.2, "this idea, as conceiv'd by the imagination, tho' divisible into parts or inferior ideas, is not infinitely divisible, nor consists of an infinite number of parts" (T 1.2.2.9, SBN 32); and finally, "*our ideas of* [spaces and times] *are compounded of parts, which are indivisible*" (T 1.2.3.12, SBN 38), "let us take one of those simple indivisible ideas, of which the compound one of *extension* is form'd" (T 1.2.3.13, SBN 38), "the idea of extension consists of parts" (T 1.2.3.14, SBN 38), "the compound idea of extension, which is real, is compos'd of such [perfectly simple and indivisible] ideas" (ibid.), "the idea of extension ... is compos'd of the ideas of these points" (T 1.2.3.16, SBN 39), "no idea of extension or duration consists of an infinite number of parts or inferior ideas, but of a finite number, and these simple and indivisible" (T 1.2.4.1, SBN 39), "[t]he" parts, into which the ideas of space and time resolve themselves, become at last indivisible" (T 1.2.4.2, SBN 39). Hume was saying this: "Reflect on your idea of any finite quality. Make this idea itself, as opposed to the quality it is 'of,' into the object of your thought and you will find that it is only finitely divisible. You can even know this to be true in advance if you consider that all ideas are products of your own mind, which has only finite capacities."

2. THE CONSISTENCY OF TREATISE 1.2.1.2
AND TREATISE 1.2.2.2 (CLAIMS 1A AND 1B)

Hume could not consistently have intended to establish that objects could not have infinitely many parts, particularly if those objects are infinitely, as opposed to finitely, extended. For he said the opposite.

I first take the least idea I can form of a part of extension, and being certain that there is nothing more minute than this idea, I conclude, that whatever I discover by its means must be a real quality of extension. I then repeat this idea once, twice, thrice, *&c.* and find the compound idea of extension, arising from its repetition, always to augment, and become double, triple, quadruple, *&c.* till at last it swells up to a considerable bulk, greater or smaller, in proportion as I repeat more or less the same idea. When I stop in the addition of parts, the idea of extension ceases to augment; and were I to carry on the addition *in infinitum*, I clearly perceive, that the idea of extension must also become infinite. (T 1.2.2.2, SBN 29–30)

Here, Hume not only allowed (a) that there can be infinitely extended things, but also (b) that we can "clearly perceive" that they are infinitely extended, and even (c) that we can "clearly perceive" that an "idea of extension" would, under certain conditions, "become infinite." None of these claims is inconsistent with the argument of *Treatise* 1.2.1.2, however:

a. The argument of *Treatise* 1.2.1.2 establishes only that *ideas* cannot have infinitely many parts; it does not rule out the possibility that there might be other things that have infinitely many parts.

b. We might "clearly perceive" that some things have infinitely many parts, as long as what it means to have a "clear perception" is properly qualified. Early modern philosophers often drew careful distinctions between the clarity, the distinctness, and the adequacy of conceptions.[4] Although the manner of drawing these distinctions was by no means uniform, it would not be far off the mark to say that a conception was taken to be clear when it could be distinguished from other conceptions; distinct when its features could be distinguished from one another; and adequate when all of its features, the features of those features, and so on down to fundamental features could be exhaustively identified. The visual metaphor is obvious, and this makes the point readily transferrable to visual perception and to perception in general. A perception of an infinite object can be said to be "clear" as long as it involves something that permits us to infer that the object must have more parts than any finite object (and so is different from any finite object), even if it does not contain an exhaustive representation of all of those parts, and so is not "adequate." Stipulating that the object is constructed by a process of adding parts to parts that goes on without end would suffice for such a purpose, and that appears to have been Hume's point in *Treatise* 1.2.2.2. The infinitely extended object is not clearly perceived to be infinite because we perceive each of its infinitely many parts, but because we infer that it would have that many parts.

c.   However, adding parts to parts forever is not a condition that we can satisfy. Consequently, even though Hume claimed that we can "clearly perceive" that the idea of an extension would "become infinite" were this condition to be satisfied, any idea that we are successfully able to generate would have to be one built up from only finitely many parts. It is just that some finite ideas might serve as inadequate representations of infinite objects.

3. EXTENDED IDEAS AND MINIMAL PARTS

In addition to being consistent with *Treatise* 1.2.1.2, *Treatise* 1.2.2.2 tells us something important about how Hume conceived of at least some ideas. The passage makes clear that he did not just take extension and location to be features of space and the objects in space. He also maintained that some ideas are themselves extended. These ideas are compounds that consist of a number of "inferior" ideas that have been set alongside one another. The compound ideas are divisible into the component ideas, and the compound ideas have a size that is a function of the number of component ideas they contain. The simple component ideas, for their part, are indivisible, but they nonetheless have location relative to one another. Witness the following claims: "I first take the least [i.e., the smallest in size] idea I can form ..."; "and being certain that there is nothing more minute than this idea ..."; "I then repeat this idea once, twice, thrice, &c. and find the compound idea of extension, arising from its repetition, always to augment, and become double, triple, quadruple, &c. till at last it swells up to a considerable bulk, greater or smaller, in proportion as I repeat more or less the same idea" (T 1.2.2.2, SBN 29). Note that it is the compound idea of extension that is said to augment – become double, triple, quadruple, etc., and swell up to a considerable bulk – not just the extension this compound idea is of. Further indication of Hume's commitment to the extension of ideas can be gleaned from passages such as the following: "This idea of *Rome* I place in a certain situation on the idea of an object, which I call the globe" (T 1.3.9.4, SBN 108). "That table, which just now appears to me, is only a perception, and all its qualities are qualities of a perception. Now the most obvious of all its qualities is extension. The perception consists of parts. These parts are so situated, as to afford us the notion of distance and contiguity; of length, breadth, and thickness" (T 1.4.5.15, SBN 239).[5] "[T]he very idea of extension is copy'd from nothing but an impression, and consequently must perfectly agree to it. To say the idea of extension agrees to any thing, is to say it is extended" (T 1.4.5.15, SBN 239–40).

Some might object that it is simply absurd to suppose that ideas could have spatial features such as location or size. However, this objection gains its strength from the tacit supposition that ideas are states of being of an immaterial mind, and that is not a supposition that we can accuse Hume of having shared.

There is another objection that poses a more serious problem for Hume. How, it might be asked, could any aggregation of indivisible and ipso facto unextended components give rise to something extended?

There are (at least) two answers to this question – a modern answer and Hume's answer. The modern answer is that there is no contradiction in the mathematics of a discrete space.[6] A discrete space is a set of locations governed by an immediate successor relation. On any line in such a space, and for any location B on that line, there is a location A that is immediately before B and a location C that is immediately after B. ("Immediately before" and "immediately after" mean that there is no further location that comes between A and B on the one side or B and C on the other.) A computer monitor is an example of such a space. Objects (colored dots) exist only at a discrete set of locations on the monitor and cannot exist between these locations. Admittedly, we think of the monitor as existing in a larger, continuous space that contains it, and we think of the dots on the monitor as being separated by intervals of this containing space, and indeed as being themselves extended. But there is no contradiction in supposing a space where the dots are unextended points and where there simply are no intervening locations. Such a discrete space has some surprising features: most importantly, not every two points can be joined by a straight line,[7] there are no perfectly smooth curves, and lines can intersect only at certain angles.[8] But the space contains step-shaped lines that are close approximations of perfectly straight lines, perfectly smooth curves, and arbitrarily acute angles. Moreover, up to certain tolerances, geometrical operations performed upon these figures (bisection, erection of perpendiculars, etc.) yield comparable results to those that result when those same operations are performed upon corresponding figures in a continuous space. Indeed, for all we can tell just by looking, our space might be a discrete space. This is in fact how things are on a computer screen, even though the objects on the screen can appear smoothly curved, triangular, or continuously moving. The objects in the space around us might be similarly discrete and discontinuous, though at a level of detail that has up to now not had any observable consequences.

Granting the consistency of the notion of a discrete space, we can explain how an extended object can be supposed to be produced by the aggregation of a number of unextended parts, supposing that it is produced in such a space. The parts need merely be set one immediately beside the other. In a discrete space, this is possible without creating either an overlap (which for simple parts would mean that one would have to be on top of the other and no extension would be created by their aggregation) or a gap between parts (since in a discrete space there are no further locations between immediately adjacent locations – that is, there is such a thing as immediate adjacency).

Hume's own answer to the question of how an extended object could be composed of a number of unextended parts is given in *Treatise* 1.2.4.4–6 (SBN 40–41). It comes very close to this modern answer, insofar as it appeals to our intuition that two unextended but differently colored dots might touch one another without either overlapping (and so being coincident at a point) or leaving a gap.

A blue and a red point may surely lie contiguous without any penetration or annihilation. (T 1.2.4.6, SBN 41)

Hume here utilized the resources at his disposal to forge his own approximation of the modern notion of a manifold governed by an immediate successor relation. In doing so, he overcame a significant intellectual hurdle. Like his contemporaries, he thought that two mathematical points cannot touch without overlapping (T 1.2.4.3, SBN 40), not realizing that this is due to the presumed continuity or density of the space in which the points are contained rather than to the extensionlessness of the points themselves. This view prevented his contemporaries from accepting that a space could consist of a discrete set of locations – that is, of points set immediately adjacent to one another. Hume did not transcend this view so far as to invoke the notion of a different kind of space, in which locations are governed by an immediate successor relation. On the contrary, he shared the then common antipathy to the notion that space might be a thing in its own right that imposes constraints on the possible locations of objects. But he did give a new direction to the common view that the features of space are determined by the features of the objects in space. He did so by arguing that there is a domain of objects that are governed by an immediate successor relation and that objects in this domain can therefore compose a discrete extension. This domain is the domain of points of color. The objects in this domain are impressions and ideas. They are not mathematical objects (such as points) or physical objects (such as atomic bodies). Hume took it to be introspectively evident that there is an immediate successor relation governing the locations of the minimally visible points of color that occur on the visual field, and governing the locations of the smallest color points we are able to imagine while still keeping track of all of their imagined surroundings. And, as has already been pointed out, granting that there are immediate successors, it is possible to have extended composites that arise from an aggregation of unextended components.

This is perhaps the best place to address a pervasive misconception of Hume's position. The misconception was alluded to (though, to his credit, not explicitly endorsed) by Antony Flew, who observed that "Anyone familiar with the theories and the paintings of Seurat might also mischievously characterize the Hume of this Section [Flew means *Treatise* 1.2.3, but *Treatise* 1.2.1–2 could apply just as well] as 'the Father of Pointillisme' " (Flew 1976: 265), and it has led commentators such as C. D. Broad to think that they can refute Hume by simply looking at a sheet of white paper to convince themselves that what they see is a continuous white surface and not an aggregate of discontinuous, punctiform elements (Broad 1961: 166). The fallacy in this objection is that it represents Hume as holding that there are gaps or fissures between immediately adjacent points, as there are in a pointillist painting. This is actually a sophisticated way of begging the question. It tacitly presupposes that the space (or canvas) that contains colored points is itself dense or continuous. If the space is dense or continuous, then any two colored points must either overlap or, if they do not overlap, there must be some space between them, however close they may be to one another, and any aggregate of nonoverlapping points will have a granular or gappy structure. But if we deny that space is dense or continuous, then this pointillist caricature of the appearance of Humean ideas and impressions cannot be sustained. In a space governed by an immediate successor relation, points can be immediately adjacent to one another. But if points are *immediately* adjacent, there are no gaps between them. For there to be a gap between two points, there would have to be a location between them that is not occupied by either of them. And if there is an unoccupied location between them, they are not immediately adjacent, or the space in which they are located is not a discrete space. The moral is that one cannot distinguish between a continuous and a discrete manifold by such facile means as simply looking at them. (One needs to reason from experiments such as Hume's with the inkblot or appeal to evidence for the finite discriminative powers of the sense organs or the imagination.) The difference between a continuous and a discontinuous manifold is that there is an immediate successor relation governing locations in the latter but not in the former – not that the latter looks granular or gappy.

A different sort of objection to Hume's position has been resurrected by Robert Fogelin, citing Bayle. Fogelin charged that color points must always be extended and divisible.

Returning to Bayle's criticism, would such a point have both a right side and a left side? I suppose that the answer to this must be yes, for something could be on the right side of such a point and something else could be on the left side of that point. For example, the right side of the point might be contiguous with something green, the left side contiguous with something red. From this Bayle would argue that the point must now divide into parts, for something is true of one feature that is not true of the other. (Fogelin 1985: 32)

The fallacy in this argument lies in the way it equivocates on the term *side* (which can refer either to a direction, as in the expression "what lies to the left side of me," or to a part, as in the expression "there is a pain in my left side") to surreptitiously transform a spatial relation that something else can bear to a point (being on the right "side" or the left "side" of that one, single, undivided point – i.e., being to the left or the right) with a property of that point (having a right "side" or a left "side" – i.e., consisting of distinct right-hand and left-hand parts). Just because A lies to the left of B, and C is to the right of B, it does not follow that B has to have distinct right and left parts. All that follows is that there have to be locations to the left and to the right of B.

4. THE ILLUSTRATIONS OF TREATISE I.2.1.3 (CLAIMS 2A AND 2B)

Throughout *Treatise* 1.2.1.3 (SBN 27) Hume attempted to illustrate the position he had reached by making a number of claims about a grain of sand. It is important to appreciate that these claims involve a distinction between what can be thought of a grain of sand considered (rightly or wrongly) as an object existing independently of being perceived and what can be thought of the *idea* of a grain of sand. Witness the closing sentence of the paragraph: "whatever we may imagine of the thing, the idea of a grain of sand is not distinguishable,... into ... different ideas."

If we accept that at least some ideas have extension and size, and that those that do are divisible into finitely many, simple parts that cannot be further divided without being destroyed, then it should be possible for there to be ideas that consist of just one of these simple parts. Hume seems to have supposed that the idea of a grain of sand would paradigmatically be like this. It would be a point of color that is so small that it could not be diminished without being destroyed. Were it any larger, it would not be the idea of a grain of sand, but of a flint, flake, or pebble.

It would seem to follow that the *idea* of a grain of sand ought to be a smallest possible thing. After all, if it cannot be considered to be divisible into parts, it cannot take up any space. So nothing could possibly be smaller than it is. Yet, Hume worried, is it not possible for there to be an idea of a thousandth or a ten thousandth part of a grain of sand? If it is, as certainly seems to be the case, would the ideas of these smaller parts not be smaller than the idea of a grain of sand? To answer these questions, Hume invoked a distinction between an idea and the object the idea is of. His claim was that although a thousandth or ten thousandth *part* is, *ex hypothesi*, smaller than the whole of which it is a part, the *idea* of a thousandth or ten thousandth part might be no smaller than the *idea* of the whole. (Keep in mind that ideas are themselves things that take up space and so can have size.)

To further clarify, Hume remarked that an idea of a thousandth or ten thousandth part involves an idea of the numbers 1 and 1,000 or 1 and 10,000 and of their relative proportions to one another. But the ideas of numbers and proportions are abstract ideas. They refer, respectively, to any collection of one or one thousand or ten thousand things. And according to Hume's account, abstract ideas never occur apart from some particular idea. So the thought of a thousand pennies must be accompanied by some particular idea (say, the idea of the space taken up on my desk by 20 rolls of pennies), and the thought of ten thousand soldiers must be accompanied by another particular idea (say, of the space that many soldiers would take up on a battlefield). The thought of a ten thousandth part of a grain of sand must be accompanied by yet another particular idea. But in the case of the ten thousandth part of a grain of sand, Hume claimed, the particular idea is no different from the particular idea that is involved in the idea of a thousandth part of a grain of sand, or from the idea of the grain of sand itself. In all of these cases, the idea is a single point of color. And although one of these ideas may be of one of ten thousand objects that are all supposed to be contained in a grain of sand, the idea is not itself a ten thousandth part of the idea of a grain of sand. It is, rather, exactly the same size as the idea of a grain of sand. This simply means that the idea of a grain of sand is that much more inadequate a representation of its object, because the object purportedly contains (at least) ten thousand parts, whereas the idea has only one, indivisible part.

It follows that although it is possible to form an idea of a thousandth or ten thousandth part of an object such as a grain of sand, it is not possible to form the idea of a thousandth or ten thousandth part of *the idea* of an object such as a grain of sand. Granting that such an idea is the idea of an indivisible point of color, it cannot without contradiction be conceived to have any parts. The grain of sand, in contrast, can be conceived to have further parts, as long as we stipulate that any idea that consists of just one part is an inadequate representation of it.

This account resolves the apparent tension between claims 2A and 2B. Even though the hypothetical "least atom of the animal spirits of an insect a thousand times less than a mite" is a much smaller object than a grain of sand, the *idea* of such an atom could be no smaller than the *idea* of a grain of sand. If both of these ideas are indivisible points of color, then they are objects that cannot be made any smaller than they are. The objects they represent, in contrast, can still be conceived to have parts. Accordingly, the smallest atom of the animal spirits of an insect a thousand times less than a mite could turn out to be larger than the idea of a grain of sand, as the combination of 2A and 2B implies. This is not a contradiction, because even though the grain of sand may be much larger than the atom, it is only the *idea* of the grain of sand that is smaller.

5. THE SIZE OF IDEAS, IMPRESSIONS, AND OBJECTS (CLAIMS 2B, 3A, AND 3B)

Even granting that some ideas have size, it sounds odd to make a claim about the size of any idea relative to the size of an object such a grain of sand or a part of a mite, as Hume does in 2B. The oddness arises because it seems natural to think that ideas occupy an internal or imagined space that is distinct from external or physical space. If we take measurements to be made by coincidence with a measuring standard such as a ruler, then, because there is no object that exists in both the imagined and the physical space, there is no way to measure the size of ideas relative to the size of objects.

However, there are other ways to make measurements than by relation to a standard object. In a discrete space, we can count up the number of points or immediately adjacent locations there are along the sides of an object. This yields an absolute value that depends on the intrinsic features of the object (the number of immediately adjacent points it occupies) rather than a relative value that depends on comparison to some standard object. Because Hume treated ideas as things existing in a discrete space, he naturally adopted this method of measurement and treated the size of compound ideas as a function of the number of inferior, pointal ideas they contain. Witness the following claim: "I ... repeat this idea once, twice, thrice, &c. and find the compound idea of extension, arising from its repetition, always to augment, and become double, triple, quadruple, &c. ... in proportion as I repeat more or less the same idea" (T 1.2.2, SBN 29).[9]

In a discrete space there is a minimal size, the size of an object that takes up just a single point. Nothing can be smaller than this without ceasing to exist in the space. In a dense or continuous space, in contrast, there is no minimal size. Any object, however small, can always be divided into further parts, and so it can be seen as composed of more than one part. Otherwise put, any object in a dense or continuous space, however small that object may be, must have an intrinsic size greater than one point. This seems to be what motivated Hume's odd claim that we can form ideas that are at least as small as certain very small objects, such as the atom of animal spirits. If objects such as the atom of animal spirits occupy a discrete space, then they cannot have an intrinsic measure of less than one point, and so no pointal idea can be greater than they are, in terms of intrinsic measures. If the objects occupy a continuous or dense space, then they must have an intrinsic measure greater than one point, and so every pointal idea must be less than they are, in terms of intrinsic measures.

This result is nonetheless still troubling when carried over to the parallel case of impressions, for reasons indicated by the 3A-3B pair of claims. As Broad once put it, we appear compelled to accept that "even those material things which are too small for us to perceive by sight must be larger than some of our actual visual sense-data" (1961: 164). This perplexing result can be explained if we accept that impressions are almost always vastly more minute than the objects they represent, and hence are usually "disproportion'd" and inadequate representations of all the parts that objects contain. Exceptions would arise only if objects were only finitely divisible and only if they were viewed under such extreme magnification that only a few of their smallest parts appear. Otherwise, objects that are quite "large" in terms of the number of parts they contain might still be too small to produce even pointal impressions.

6. IMPRESSIONS (CLAIMS 4A AND 4B)

Hume proceeded to argue that what he had said about ideas could also be said about impressions (T 1.2.1.4, SBN 27-28).[10] Some of them – those of vision and touch – are extended and divisible into a finite number of simple and indivisible parts. Again, it is the *impressions* that Hume was concerned with, not any objects that might be supposed to cause the impressions or any objects that the impressions might be supposed to be of or to represent. Hume's conclusion was not that impressions are caused by finitely divisible objects or are of objects that are only finitely divisible; it was that impressions themselves are only finitely divisible.[11]

Put a spot of ink upon paper, fix your eye upon that spot, and retire to such a distance, that at last you lose sight of it; 'tis plain, that the moment before it vanish'd *the image or impression was perfectly indivisible.* (T 1.2.1.4, SBN 27; emphasis added)

The finite divisibility of impressions is proven, for the case of visual impressions, by the experiment of putting an inkblot on paper and retreating from it until it becomes just barely visible. Presumably, while retreating from the inkspot, a series of impressions occurs, and each later impression in the series is smaller in relation to the previous member. Thus, the experiment provides evidence both that impressions have size (presumably it is not the inkblot that gets any smaller as we retreat from it, but the impressions of it) and that there is an inverse relation between the size of the impression and the distance to the inkblot. However, the experiment also shows that a distance is reached at which, rather than there being a smaller impression, there is no impression. Putting these two facts together – that increased distances are correlated with decreased sizes of impressions and that there is a distance beyond which no impression occurs – we can infer that the last impression to occur prior to disappearance cannot be diminished without being destroyed, and so must be an indivisible or smallest possible impression.

As just mentioned, though the impressions that occur at increasing distances from the inkblot are ever smaller, Hume granted that the ink-blot itself continues to be composed of the same number of parts it had at first. Witness the distinction between parts of bodies and "their impressions" in the sentence following the one just cited: "[the parts of bodies] are remov'd beyond that distance, at which their impressions were reduc'd to a *minimum*." Presumably, the parts continue to exist even though removed beyond the point at which "their impressions" are reduced to a minimum and so disappear. This suggests that although there may (optimistically) be one pointal part of the impression corresponding to one small region of the inkblot when the blot is set up close, at increasingly great distances there is one pointal part of the impression for each increasingly large neighborhood of adjacent small regions of the inkblot, until, at the crucial distance, there is only one, pointal impression for the entire inkblot. In other words, the impressions produced at increasingly remote distances are increasingly confused and inadequate replicas of the part-whole structure of the object. One part of those impressions corresponds to many adjacent parts of the object.

Reciprocally, impressions of increasingly proximate objects are increasingly distinct and adequate. The closer one gets to the object, the closer one gets to a situation in which there is a one-to-one relation between distinct parts of the object and distinct parts of the impression. At an extreme, a very distinct and adequate (and also a very large) impression ought to be produced when looking at the object through a microscope or telescope – an impression so large that (so to speak) it cannot all be seen at once.

Reflecting on this result, Hume remarked that "[a] microscope or telescope ... gives parts to impressions, which to the naked eye appear simple and uncompounded, and advances to a *minimum*, what was formerly imperceptible" (T 1.2.1.4, SBN 28). This is a startling comment. Read one way it suggests that a distinction ought to be drawn between impressions and the appearances of those impressions to the naked eye, and that a microscope or telescope ought to be understood to reveal that apparently simple impressions are not simple after all, but further divisible. But, though Hume thought that ideas can often appear to be otherwise than they really are (this is why we need to trace them back to original impressions to clarify them), there is no suggestion that he would have accepted a distinction between impressions and appearances of impressions. On the contrary, at *Treatise* 1.4.2.7 (SBN 190) he wrote that impressions "must necessarily appear in every particular what they are, and be what they appear." Moreover, to concede that apparently simple impressions might be further divisible would be disastrous. It would mean that the inkblot experiment proves nothing.

However, there is another way of reading Hume's odd remark. Perhaps he meant only to say that the view through a microscope or telescope produces impressions with parts in the same circumstances in which a naked eye view would produce a simple and uncompounded impression. On this reading, there are two different impressions that occur when viewing the same object by different means. One is a simple and indivisible impression, hence a smallest possible impression, and an inadequate or indistinct representation of an actually compound object. The other is a comparatively large, compound impression, consisting of a number of smallest possible parts, and is a more adequate and distinct representation of the object. The compound impression is not a more correct or complete appearance of the simple impression, but instead a more distinct and adequate representation of the object. It does not reveal parts contained in the simple impression; it contains more parts for each distinct part contained in the object. Rather than contain parts that are smaller than the simple impression, its smallest parts are no smaller than the simple impression. They just correspond to distinct parts of the object, whereas the one part of the simple impression corresponds to the whole of the object.

This second way of understanding Hume's remark is admittedly not as natural a reading of the text as the first, but the first is so much at variance with Hume's intentions and his other views that it would be charitable to allow that he expressed himself ineptly and really meant to write "gives parts to objects, which to the naked eye appear simple and uncompounded" rather than "gives parts to impressions, which to the naked eye appear simple and uncompounded."

Accepting this second reading resolves the paradox that would otherwise be presented by claims 4A and 4B. The view through a microscope or telescope is only misleadingly described as a better view of the naked-eye impression. It is a view of the object, a view that gives us a different impression than the naked-eye impression. That impression is a much larger impression than the naked-eye impression, despite being of much smaller parts of the object. Accordingly, Hume can hold that a simple and indivisible impression is the most minute thing possible. The impressions that occur when looking through a microscope or a telescope are not smaller, just of smaller objects.

7. THE ADEQUACY ARGUMENT (AND CLAIMS 5A AND 5B)

We are now in a position to understand the very perplexing *Treatise* 1.2.1.5. Hume opened the paragraph by questioning appeals to the limited capacity of the mind (claim 5B). This may seem odd given that he had earlier rested his case on just such an appeal (claim 5A). But the circumstances are not precisely the same. In 5A Hume claimed that the finite capacity of the mind entails that it cannot form a "full and adequate conception of infinity." In 5B he claimed that its finite capacity does not prevent it from forming "an adequate idea, of what goes beyond a certain degree of minuteness," though its finite capacity does prevent the mind from forming an adequate idea of what goes beyond a certain degree of greatness.[12] These claims are not inconsistent. To see why, consider what would be the case if objects were only finitely divisible but the world were infinite in extension. Then the mind's incapacity to form a full and adequate conception of infinity would require that it could not form an adequate idea of what goes beyond a certain degree of greatness. But if there is a bound to how small the parts of objects can be, the mind's incapacity to form a full and adequate conception of infinity would not necessarily entail that it could not form an adequate idea of smallest possible objects.

Of course, by *Treatise* 1.2.1.5 Hume had said nothing that would prove that anything other than impressions and ideas must be only finitely divisible. But he proceeded to offer an argument, which I will call the "adequacy argument," that evaded the necessity of proving this point:

Nothing can be more minute, than some ideas, which we form in the fancy; and images, which appear to the senses; since these are ideas and images perfectly simple and indivisible. (T 1.2.1.5, SBN 28)

Stated somewhat more completely: Nothing can be smaller than a thing with no parts into which it can be further divided. Since we have impressions and ideas that have no parts, nothing can be smaller than they are. Therefore, it is wrong to suppose that there is any object so small that the imagination could not form an adequate idea of it. The problem is, rather, forming adequate ideas of objects that are complex or compound to any significant extent, because as the number of parts increases, it becomes difficult to form an idea that represents them all.

8. COMPARISONS BETWEEN PERCEPTIONS AND OBJECTS (CLAIMS 6A AND 6B)

This understanding of the sense in which impressions and ideas are adequate allows us to see how Hume could claim that ideas are adequate representations of the smallest parts of extension (claim 6B) despite maintaining that the ideas of a thousandth and ten thousandth part of a grain of sand are no different from the idea of the grain of sand (claim 6A). The solution to the paradox rests with appreciating that although ideas can be adequate representations of the smallest parts of extension, they are inadequate representations of the larger parts of extension. Supposing that a grain of sand consists of ten thousand parts, an idea of its ten thousandth part would be adequate, and an idea of its thousandth part might be adequate (insofar as it contains ten distinct "ten thousandth" parts), but an idea of the grain would necessarily fail to include so many parts or would confuse them with one another.

At this point, it remains unclear just how many parts a grain of sand might have – and so just what fraction of a grain of sand might be the one that is adequately represented by an indivisible idea – if indeed there are any. Were the grain of sand infinitely divisible, all ideas of it and its parts, however small, would necessarily be inadequate (not because the ideas are too large, but rather because they are too small to copy the infinite complexity of any part of an infinitely divisible object). This is a possibility that cannot be definitely ruled out at this stage.[13] *Treatise* 1.2.1 argues only for the finite divisibility of ideas and impressions, not of any other objects. Hume admitted that we can form distinct ideas of arbitrarily large numbers, and hence of arbitrarily small fractions, and it remains a question whether any of these ideas are fictions or whether arbitrarily small fractions might always refer to some actually existing object.

All we can say for sure at this point is that, however many parts a grain of sand might have, the *impression* of a grain of sand has only one part (supposing it is a naked-eye impression), and the *idea* of a grain of sand can have as little as one part (supposing it is a copy of the impression) or as many parts as it is possible for a finite mind to distinctly conceive of at once (though in this case the idea would better be described as an idea of a stone). The idea of a grain of sand containing any large number of parts, such as one thousand or ten thousand, is an abstract idea of a number, involving a particular image that contains far fewer parts than the number names.

Hume appealed to the uncertain correspondence between parts of ideas or impressions and parts of objects in order to explain how we fall into the absurd belief that objects might have parts that are vastly smaller than any impressions or ideas.

[T]aking the impressions of those minute objects, which appear to the senses, to be equal or nearly equal to the objects, and finding by reason, that there are other objects vastly more minute, we too hastily conclude, that these are inferior to any idea of our imagination or impression of our senses. (T 1.2.1.5, SBN 28)

The impressions we receive from the senses can be inadequate, not in the sense that they might fail to represent as simple what is simple, but in the sense that they can fail to represent as compound what is compound. We do not always appreciate this, but rather assume that the object has no more parts than the impression. When we afterwards have experiences that tell us that the object has more parts than the impression revealed, we do not think that the object is larger than we had at first supposed. Instead, we retain the belief that it is the same size as the impression and think that, since it has parts, those parts must be vastly smaller than the impression. However, this is impossible, as the adequacy argument has shown. Given that nothing can be smaller than a thing that has no parts, we ought rather to conclude that the original impression is a "disproportion'd" representation of a much larger object, with more parts than first appeared.

9. THE NATURE OF REPRESENTATION

Throughout *Treatise* 1.2.1 Hume drew a distinction between impressions and ideas on the one hand and objects on the other. He treated impressions and ideas as representations of objects and suggested that one and the same object (one and the same inkblot, mite, or grain of sand) can be represented by different impressions or different ideas. He also suggested that these different impressions and ideas can be more or less adequate representations of their objects. Some of them can be "disproportion'd" in the sense that they have fewer parts than, and so are smaller than, the objects they represent. Others, such as the smallest atom of the animal spirits of an insect a thousand times less than a mite, might be fictions – imaginative compilations of abstract ideas of numbers and simple ideas of colored points that do not correspond to any actually existing object. To be an adequate representation of an object, in contrast, an impression or idea would have to copy the features of some actually existing object as faithfully as possible.

Wherever ideas are adequate representations of objects, the relations, contradictions and agreements of the ideas are all applicable to the objects. (T 1.2.2.1, SBN 29)

This is a significant remark. Hume did not write that where ideas are adequate, the relations, contradictions, and agreements *that they attribute to objects* are all in fact true of those objects. Rather, he wrote that the relations, contradictions, and agreements *of the ideas* are all applicable to the objects those ideas are taken to represent. This suggests that the comparison is not between the object as it is conceived through having the idea and the object as it is in itself; it is rather between *the idea*, considered as itself a kind of object, and another object that the idea is understood to sculpt or depict. The context in which this passage occurs lends further support to this reading.[14] The "relations, contradictions and agreements" that Hume went on to mention are ones that he had, up to this point, proven to be true only of our ideas and not of the objects those ideas represent (namely, their consisting of smallest possible parts that, when set alongside one another, cause the compound idea they form to increase in size).

It would seem, therefore, that Hume was not working with the notion that ideas are acts of thinking something about an object, where the action of thinking is one thing and the object that is thought about is something else. He was, rather, working with the notion that ideas are objects and that they can more or less adequately represent other objects by more or less closely resembling them. This may be why he wrote, at *Treatise* 1.1.7.6 (SBN 20), that "to form the idea of an object, and to form an idea simply is the same thing; the reference of the idea to an object being an extraneous denomination, of which in itself it bears no mark or character." If an idea resembles some other object that is known to exist, then the idea can be considered a representation of that object. But knowledge of the existence of a resembling object is a merely "extraneous denomination." Were there no resembling object, or were there no knowledge of a resembling object, the idea could still exist. Its function as a representation is therefore accidental.

By now, none of this should be surprising. The account of ideas and impressions as extended, finitely divisible objects that have parts that more or less adequately correspond to the parts of other objects has been shown to run throughout *Treatise* 1.2.1 and explains all the otherwise paradoxical claims of that Section.

Further support for this understanding of Hume's account of the nature of representation can be gleaned from the following passage:

As every idea is deriv'd from a precedent impression, had we any idea of the substance of our minds, we must also have an impression of it; which is very difficult, if not impossible, to be conceiv'd. For how can an impression represent a substance, otherwise than by resembling it? And how can an impression resemble a substance, since, according to this philosophy, it is not a substance, and has none of the peculiar qualities or characteristics of a substance? (T 1.4.5.3, SBN 232–33)

Hume here suggested that the only way an impression could represent a substance is by quite literally taking on its features – that is, by itself being a substance. Because there is no reason to think there is something special about the case of substance, we can infer that he would have generalized the suggestion and maintained that the only way any impression can represent any object is by resembling it. Accordingly, we find that Hume made remarks such as the following: "'tis impossible our idea of a perception, and that of an object or external existence can ever represent what are specifically different from each other" (T 1.4.5.19, SBN 241); "We have no idea of any quality in an object, which does not agree to, and may not represent a quality in an impression" (T 1.4.5.21, SBN 243).

On this understanding, the "adequacy" of an impression is a function of how good a copy it is of its object. An adequate impression of an object has the very features of the object. If the object is extended, the impression is extended. If the object is red, the impression is red. If the object consists of spatially disposed parts, the impression consists of an identical number of parts, disposed in identical relations to one another. This is what it means for the relations, contradictions, and agreements of the impressions to be applicable to the objects. Since ideas are in turn "copies" of impressions, the same can be said of them.

10. MANNERS OF DISPOSITION (CLAIMS 7A AND 7B)

Treatise 1.2.1 and significant parts of 1.2.2 are not about the ideas of space and time. Rather, they are about the spatiality of ideas and impressions. The main point of *Treatise* 1.2.1 and 1.2.2 – that at least some ideas and impressions are extended composites of finitely many "inferior" ideas or impressions set immediately adjacent to one another in a discretely ordered manifold – sets the stage for *Treatise* 1.2.3, which does deal with the ideas of space and time. The main point of that later Section is that these ideas are not ideas of some distinct kind of thing. Instead, they are ideas of the manners in which other things – "inferior" impressions and ideas – are disposed in compound impressions and ideas.

To justify this conclusion, Hume argued that if the ideas of space and time were ideas of some distinct thing, there would be distinct impressions of that thing. After all, "every idea, with which the imagination is furnish'd, first makes its appearance in a correspondent impression" (T 1.2.3.1, SBN 33). But there are no distinct impressions of space or time arising either through sensation or reflection. The idea of space is not copied from any "internal impression" or impression of reflection.

Our internal impressions are our passions, emotions, desires and aversions; none of which, I believe, will ever be asserted to be the model, from which the idea of space is deriv'd. There remains therefore nothing but the senses, which can convey to us this original impression. (T 1.2.3.3, SBN 33)

However, the senses do not give rise to any distinct impression of space either. Ideas of space are copied from only two of the senses, sight and touch, and neither of these senses produces distinct impressions of space. Instead, they produce impressions of other things (colors and tactile qualities). The impressions of colors and tactile qualities do, however, occur at different locations in space. As Hume put it, they are "dispos'd in a certain manner."

[M]y senses convey to me only the impressions of colour'd points, dispos'd in a certain manner.[15] If the eye is sensible of any thing farther, I desire it may be pointed out to me. (T 1.2.3.4, SBN 34)

This observation led Hume to his position. There are no distinct impressions of space in the way there are distinct impressions of color or solidity. But there are compound, spatially extended impressions, which consist of "inferior" impressions of colors or tactile qualities disposed alongside one another to form a spatially extended aggregate. Consequently, while impressions of particular colors or tactile qualities can be separated from the other impressions of particular colors and tactile qualities that surround them and can be made into the object of distinct simple ideas, there is no impression of space that can be separated from the surrounding impressions and made into the object of a distinct simple idea. Because there can be no manner of disposition of impressions of color or tactile quality if there are no colors or tactile qualities to be disposed, there are impressions of space only insofar as there are a number of impressions of color or tactile quality· that are disposed.

Admittedly, there may be abstract ideas of space. One composite of colored or tactile points may resemble another in having its points disposed in a certain fashion, though the points themselves differ in color or tactile quality, and this makes it possible for there to be ideas that focus on this common manner of disposition. But such abstract ideas "are really nothing but particular ones, consider'd in a certain light" (T 1.2.3.5, SBN 34) – namely, as standing in for all the ideas in a particular resemblance class. Thus, even abstract ideas of space and geometrical figures do not occur apart from ideas of some particular collection of spatially arranged colored or tangible points.

The same may be said of time. The idea of time is not copied from an impression of reflection. It is not that we must first have a number of ideas and then get the impression of time only after reflecting on those ideas. The ideas occur sequentially over time to begin with, and if they do not, but are simultaneous, no amount of reflection on them will produce an impression of time.

[T]he mind [cannot], by revolving over a thousand times all its ideas of sensation, ever extract from them any new original idea, unless nature has so fram'd its faculties, that it feels some new original impression arise from such a contemplation. But here it only takes notice of the *manner*, in which [different things] make their appearance. (T 1.2.3.10, SBN 37)

But granting that ideas do occur sequentially, their sequence is not to be accounted for by appealing to distinct impressions of time that accompany them, the way distinct impressions of red or green may accompany impressions of heat and solidity.

The idea of time is not deriv'd from a particular impression mix'd up with others, and plainly distinguishable from them; but arises altogether from the manner, in which impressions appear to the mind, without making one of the number. Five notes play'd on a flute give us the impression and idea of time; tho' time be not a sixth impression, which presents itself to the hearing or any other of the senses. Nor is it a sixth impression, which the mind by reflection finds in itself. (T 1.2.3.10, SBN 36)

It takes time for five notes to be played in succession upon a flute, and Hume made it clear that the impression of the time that it takes is nothing other than the compound impression that consists of the successive occurrence of these five component impressions. As with the idea of space, the idea of time is copied from a compound impression that consists of a number of "inferior" impressions that are disposed in a certain manner. Only in this case the impressions are disposed one after the other along one dimension rather than one alongside the other over three dimensions. The compound impression that the idea of time is copied from is thus an impression that itself takes time to occur, just as the compound impression that the idea of space is copied from is an impression that is itself extended.

Of course, as with space, there can be abstract ideas of time in general or of longer or shorter intervals of time. But as with abstract ideas of space, abstract ideas of time are really ideas of some particular number of other, particular ideas or impressions or objects occurring in a particular sequence. These particular ideas are merely closely associated with a number of other resembling sequences.

[The mind] may afterwards consider [the manner in which the different sounds make their appearance] without considering these particular sounds, but may conjoin it with any other objects. The ideas of some objects it certainly must have, nor is it possible for it without these ideas ever to arrive at any conception of time. (T 1.2.3.10, SBN 37)

Many commentators have charged that when Hume declared that the ideas of space and time are not copied from any antecedent simple impression, but rather are ideas of two different manners in which component impressions and ideas may be disposed in compound impressions, he violated the fundamental tenet "that every idea, with which the imagination is furnish'd, first makes its appearance in a correspondent impression" (T 1.2.3.1, SBN 33).[16] But the ideas of space and time do first make their appearance in a correspondent impression. It is just that the impression is not a distinct, simple *impression of space* or of time but a compound, *spatially extended impression* or temporally altering impression. Admittedly, no simple impression is extended, as *Treatise* 1.2.1 argues, and no single impression or idea can properly be said to be enduring, as *Treatise* 1.2.3.7–8 goes on to argue. But because single impressions of vision and touch occur at different locations and can be situated immediately alongside one another and all impressions occur before or after others, collections of simple impressions constitute compound impressions that are more than just the collection of their parts and that have properties of extension and duration that the parts lack.[17] Particular ideas of space and time are copies of these compound impressions, and abstract ideas of space and time necessarily involve particular ideas. Consequently, the rule that all ideas copy impressions has not been violated.

This explains how to reconcile claims 7A and 7B. Although every idea first makes its appearance in a correspondent impression, that impression need not be a *simple* impression. It may instead be a compound impression that consists of a number of simple impressions that are distinguishable one from another, but an impression that also exhibits these particular impressions as disposed in a certain manner.

II. PERCEPTIONS OF RELATIONS AND RELATED PERCEPTIONS

If there are no simple impressions of space, but only compound impressions that consist of a number of particular impressions disposed alongside one another over space, and if what it means for an idea to represent an impression is just that it copies or replicates that impression, then it follows that an idea of space is a spatially extended idea. Hume occasionally said as much. Witness *Treatise* 1.4.5.15 (SBN 239–40): "the very idea of extension is copy'd from nothing but an impression, and consequently must perfectly agree to it. To say the idea of extension agrees to any thing, is to say it is extended."

The same holds true of time. An idea of an interval of time is not the sort of thing that can occur at a moment. It is a compound that consists of a number of component ideas, more or less adequately corresponding to the parts of the time it represents,[18] that occur after one another in a sequence similar to the sequence of the corresponding parts of the time. An idea of a time is an idea that itself takes time to occur. For example, a memory of the first four notes of Beethoven's Fifth Symphony is not something that now, in the present moment, somehow manages to represent all four notes and the order of their occurrence at once; it is rather a thought that takes time to occur and that consists of ideas of four notes thought one after the other. The sequence of these thoughts may be much more rapid than the corresponding impressions, in the sense that a large number of notes may succeed one another in the time marked by an impression of just two or three, but were there no limits in this regard, it would be possible to have infinitely many ideas in a finite time.[19]

This account of the idea of time (and by implication of space) has been found wanting. As M. R. Annand (1930: 589) classically objected,

A succession of perceptions is one thing, a perception of succession is quite another, and from the former to the latter there is "no road." How could a sequence of impressions of which no two are present together, undetermined by relation to anything other than the impressions themselves, yield a consciousness of the relation between the moments in which the impressions are given, or of the sum of such moments?

Annand's argument that there is "no road" from a succession of perceptions to the perception of succession invokes the notion of consciousness. Presumably, according to Annand's account, to have a perception is to be conscious of something. To have a succession of perceptions is to be conscious of one thing, then to be conscious of something else, then to be conscious of something else, and so on. To be conscious of a succession of perceptions is not simply to be conscious of one thing and then another and another, but instead to be conscious of the relation between the moments when these different acts of consciousness occur and of the entire interval they compose. The latter, Annand claimed, is something more than the former and so cannot be reduced to it. To see why, consider the case in which a sentient being is born, hears the first note of Beethoven's Fifth Symphony, and then dies. At the moment of its death, a second sentient being is born, hears the second note of Beethoven's Fifth, and dies. At the moment of its death, a third sentient being is born, hears the third note, and dies. And so on. Here there is a sequence of perceptions. But there is no consciousness of the relation between the moments in which the perceptions are given or of the sum of the moments. The challenge for Hume is to explain how there could ever be anything more than this – how there could ever be any such thing as a compound impression as opposed to a collection of successively existing simple impressions.

The challenge is one that Hume can meet. He can meet it rather more easily in the case of time than in the case of space, but the fact that he can meet it in the easier case supports the viability of dealing with the harder case in a similar way. The case of time is easier to deal with because the phenomenology of time consciousness lends some support to the Humean view that to be conscious of an interval of time is for there to be a thought that takes time to occur and that consists of a successive series of consciousnesses. When I hear the first four notes of Beethoven's Fifth Symphony, I hear those notes in succession. There is no time at which I simultaneously perceive all four. Nor do I find that I am able to subsequently remember them all in an instant. I might give that interval of time a name or a tag and be conscious of that symbol for the interval in a moment. But I cannot think of the meaning of that name or tag in a moment. The best I can manage to do is replay the notes to myself and thereby come to be conscious of a subsequent perception (or memory) of each note in succession as I do so. It takes time to do this, however, and during the time it takes, I remember only one note at a time. If someone asks me to conceive of the temporal relation between any two notes, I find that I can do it only by first conceiving the one and then conceiving the other. Again, if someone asks me to report which of two notes ought to come first, I find I can do so only by first reconceiving the one and naming it as I do so and then reconceiving the other and naming it, so that the composition of my report itself takes time and occurs in tandem with a replay of the sequence of perceptions. The verbal report of the relation between the notes, the memory of the sequence of the notes, and the original consciousness of the sequence between notes all seem to be indistinguishable from the occurrence of a succession of perceptions.

Supposing that this is the case, it poses Annand's question: If I am never conscious of more than one moment of an interval of time at a time, then how is my consciousness of an interval of time distinct from the separate consciousnesses of a number of distinct, successively existing minds, each of whom lives for only a moment? Posed in this context, the answer seems easy: I am conscious of the temporal interval consisting of the first four notes of Beethoven's Fifth Symphony to the extent that I can reproduce a successive series of those four notes in the right order whenever the occasion arises. This is not something that any one of the four different minds, each of whom hears just one note, is in a position to do. It is therefore what entitles me to claim to be conscious of an interval of time.

The same approach could be taken to deal with a parallel problem with space. Just as Annand objected that a succession of perceptions is not the same thing as the perception of a succession, so he might have objected that a collection of simple impressions disposed in the configuration of a square is not the same thing as the compound impression of a square. Imagine four distinct subjects, each of whom is capable of perceiving only a single colored point and each of whom is ignorant of what is happening to the others but all of whom happen to be standing in the configuration of a square where each is experiencing an identically colored, minimally visible point. Then there are four simple impressions disposed in the configuration of a square. But there is no such thing as the compound impression of a square. The challenge for Hume is, again, to explain what more there could possibly be to the compound impression of a square than there is to the occurrence of four simple impressions disposed in the configuration of a square. And here the challenge is rather more daunting, because the phenomenology is not as obviously in his favor. It does seem, introspectively, that I see all the parts of a figure at once. I cannot as plausibly claim to be merely conscious of one point but capable of imagining each of the others in some appropriate order upon request.

However, the same sort of answer that Hume could have given to the temporal case could still be given in this case. What makes a picture a composite object, as opposed to an aggregate of accidentally and temporarily adjacent parts, is that the parts persist in the same relation to one another over time. If, for example, I pick up the picture by a corner, the other parts get carried along with it. So, similarly, one thing that makes the case of the four different subjects perceiving four different minimally visible points different from the case of a single subject perceiving a square is that the four different subjects can walk away from one another, and when they do so each contains a memory only of the point that particular subject previously saw. The single subject, in contrast, carries away a memory that consists of four colored points disposed in a certain configuration relative to one another, and the simple ideas of those four points persist in that order in the bundle of impressions and ideas constitutive of that subject.

Admittedly, to account for the difference between the multiple-subject and single-subject cases in this way is not to account for the phenomenological experience that we take to be uniquely characteristic of the single-subject case: that of a simultaneous awareness of four distinct points and of their manner of disposition relative to one another. But to assume that this sort of consciousness must occur at a point or could not possibly be distributed over a series of points and divisible into parts is to beg the question. The question is whether to be conscious of a perception is not simply for there to be a perception, and whether for there to be a perception of a relation between parts is not simply for there to be operations performed on a perception that consists of parts disposed in that relation, such as navigating correctly from one location to another. Annand's objection that the perception of a relation is not the same thing as a collection of related perceptions is compelling insofar as it raises a question about Hume's ability to account for the fact that there can sometimes be cases where there is a collection of related perceptions even though there is no perception of the relation. But if there are criteria that Hume could have invoked to account for the difference, then the objection loses its force.

APPENDIX. HUME'S CONCLUSIONS

In addition to articulating a position on the nature of representation in general and on the representation of space and time in particular, *Treatise* 1.2 attempted to defend two further tenets: that there are no infinitely divisible objects of any sort (not just no infinitely divisible ideas or impressions) and that we have no impression, and consequently no "real" idea, of a vacuum. Hume attempted to derive the first of these tenets from his position on the finite divisibility of impressions and ideas and the second from his position on the nature of the idea of space. Both attempts are failures. This is fortunate, because it means that appeals to the possibility of infinitely divisible objects or impressions of vacua cannot be invoked in a *modus tollens* refutation of Hume's position on representation.[20]

In what follows, I pinpoint where Hume arguments against the infinite divisibility of objects and impressions of vacua go wrong.

The Finite Divisibility of Objects

Hume offered four arguments against the infinite divisibility of objects. They occur in *Treatise* 1.2.2.1–2, 1.2.2.3, 1.2.2.4, and 1.2.2.5, respectively. However, only the first of these arguments was based on his account of representation. The others appealed to other considerations. Since my purpose is just to show that Hume's rejection of the infinite divisibility of other objects could not have been supported by his position on the finite divisibility of ideas and impressions, I pass over the latter arguments here.[21]

It is commonly supposed that Hume's initial argument against the infinite divisibility of objects was offered in the second paragraph of *Treatise* 1.2.2, whereas the first paragraph merely serves to introduce some preliminary points. We ought, however, to understand the opposite to have been the case. Aside from its first three sentences, which contain a red herring, the second paragraph talks about ideas only. The argument that what the second paragraph says about ideas should also be considered to hold for objects is actually given in the first paragraph. In reviewing Hume's case, I begin with the observations of the second paragraph and then turn to the argument of the first.

a. *Treatise* 1.2.2.2. As has already been noted, Hume took it to be empirically evident that impressions and ideas are governed by an immediate successor relation. A pointal blue impression or idea can occur next to a pointal red impression or idea in such a way that there is neither any gap nor any overlap between the two. Otherwise put, there is a limit to how closely two pointal impressions or ideas can be set next to one another. The same holds of any three, four, or five pointal impressions or ideas occurring on a line. Imagine five pointal impressions occurring at some noticeable distance from one another along a line. Then imagine the impressions at the end points of the line being squeezed toward one another, so that the distances between the five impressions are reduced while still preserving their linear order. If no impressions are destroyed, a point of maximal compression is reached at which each impression is immediately adjacent to its neighbors on either side. This maximally dense line of impressions has a length that is in direct proportion to the number of impressions set immediately adjacent to one another. Had there been only four impressions to begin with, the line would have been 20 percent shorter. Had there been only three, it would have been 40 percent shorter, and so on. As Hume put it,

> I first take the least idea I can form of a part of extension.... I then repeat this idea once, twice, thrice, &c. ... till at last it swells up to a considerable bulk, greater or smaller, in proportion as I repeat more or less the same idea. (T 1.2.2.2, SBN 29)

Although Hume did not make this point as forthrightly as he might have, it follows that the line we have been considering cannot be composed of arbitrarily many proportional parts. (Proportional parts are the parts that arise at successive stages when one divides a finite extension into parts, then divides those parts into parts, and so on. At each stage, the parts generated are proportionally smaller in relation to those generated at the previous stage, and proportionally more numerous. But though more numerous, because they are smaller, they still sum to the same finite extension that was present to begin with. Even if the division were carried on without end, this would be the case at any arbitrarily chosen stage in its progress, however far on.) Because there is a limit to how closely two pointal impressions can be set next to one another, an infinite number of pointal impressions cannot be compressed into a finite length. Any finite line of pointal impressions can consist only of a finite number of those impressions and can be divided into halves, thirds, quarters, etc., only to the extent that the division produces parts that are larger than or equal to these points. An attempt to divide further would destroy the points and the line.

Hume claimed that the distinction between proportional (i.e., progressively smaller) and aliquot (i.e., equally sized) parts is "frivolous" (T 1.2.2.2n6, SBN 30n1). The distinction is not frivolous, particularly when the question concerns the constitution of external objects. But when the question concerns the constitution of impressions and ideas, appealing to the distinction between proportional and aliquot parts is beside the point. Hume gave reasons for concluding that impressions and ideas are only finitely divisible, and hence that there are limits to how many proportional parts any impression or idea can have. Someone wishing to challenge Hume's position would need to attack those reasons and show that there is no limit to the number of proportional parts an impression or idea can be divided into, not simply appeal to the bare notion of a proportional part.

b. *Treatise* 1.2.2.1. In *Treatise* 1.2.2.1, Hume allowed that impressions and ideas might be inadequate representations of objects that consist of a large number of parts. However, the adequacy argument of *Treatise* 1.2.1.5 establishes that impressions and ideas are adequate representations of things that have just a few parts, and that they are certainly adequate representations of the smallest possible parts, if there are any. As has just been noted, for Hume, to be an adequate representation is just to be a good replica, and since nothing can be smaller than a thing with no parts, a pointal impression or idea is an adequate representation of a smallest possible part.

Given these preliminary reminders, we can proceed to Hume's argument:

Premise 1: Where ideas are adequate representations of objects, the relations, contradictions, and agreements of the ideas must all be applicable to the objects; otherwise, the ideas would not be good copies of the objects and hence not adequate.

Premise 2: But, as is explained in more detail in *Treatise* 1.2.2.2, pointal ideas are governed by an immediate successor relation. There is a closest distance at which one idea can be set next to another without annihilating the other and occupying its location or leaving a gap. Setting a series of ideas at the closest possible distances to one another produces an extension that increases in proportion to the number of ideas added to the compound. In fact, it takes only a comparatively small number of pointal ideas to produce a compound that is considerably vast – perhaps just a few score or a few hundred, though in this context thousands or tens of thousands would still be a comparatively small number.

Conclusion: Consequently, the parts of objects are governed by an immediate successor relation. Therefore, no finite object could be infinitely divisible. For if the opposite were true, there would be no limit to the number of parts that could be contained in a finite volume. But if the parts are governed by an immediate successor relation, then there is such a limit, however far we may have to go to reach it.

In his own statement of this argument, Hume once again presented his point by making the contrasting claim that an infinitely divisible object would have to consist of infinitely many parts. But the argument does not depend on that claim. It turns, rather, on the claim that since there is an immediate successor relation governing pointal ideas, there must be an immediate successor relation governing the parts of objects, and so only a finite number of parts in any finite space.

Hume's argument is nonetheless a failure. The conclusion follows only if we accept the antecedent of the first premise – that pointal ideas are adequate representations of at least some of the parts of objects. But were objects infinitely divisible, pointal ideas would never be adequate. Any part of an object, however small, would always contain many more parts than are replicated by the idea. Consequently, even though it might be true that the pointal parts constituting ideas are governed by an immediate successor relation, it does not follow that the very different, infinitely divisible parts of objects, which are only ever inadequately represented by ideas or their parts, must also be governed by such a relation.

Despite its failure, the argument can seem very compelling. It gains its plausibility from the natural assumption that if nothing can be smaller than a thing with no parts, then, however many parts an infinitely divisible object may be divided into, those parts must always be larger than a thing with no parts ("thro' whatever divisions and sub-divisions we may suppose these parts to be arriv'd at, they can never become inferior to some ideas, which we form" [T 1.2.2.1, SBN 29]). But if the aggregation of a comparatively small number of things with no parts produces a considerably large volume, then it would seem to follow that the vast number of parts into which an infinitely divisible object can be divided would have to produce an immense volume. After all, each of the parts into which an infinitely divisible thing is divided would always have to be vastly greater than a thing with no parts. So it might seem that their aggregation would have to produce a vastly greater extension.

Seeing the error in this reasoning is not easy. It rests in recognizing that the aggregation of a comparatively small number of pointal ideas produces only a comparatively large extension because the pointal ideas are governed by an immediate successor relation, and that this is not something we can simply assume to be true of the parts of objects. The parts of objects might be located in a different kind of space from the parts of ideas – a space constituted by a dense or continuous, as opposed to a discrete, set of locations. In a space where locations are densely or continuously packed, infinitely many parts can be located in a finite volume.

The Idea of a Vacuum

Hume's position on the idea of a vacuum provides occasion to address another potential conflict in his account.

(8A) '[T]is certain we have an idea of extension; for otherwise why do we talk and reason concerning it? (T 1.2.2.9, SBN 32)

(8B) The frequent disputes concerning a vacuum, or extension without matter, prove not the reality of the idea, upon which the dispute turns; there being nothing more common, than to see men deceive themselves in this particular. (T 1.2.5.22, SBN 62)

Claims 8A and 8B are not strictly contradictory. Claim 8A makes an assertion concerning the existence of ideas, whereas claim 8B concerns their "reality." The claims can be reconciled by allowing that there is indeed an idea of a vacuum, understood as the idea of "extension without matter" (as is proven by our talking and disputing concerning it), but that this idea has no "reality."

An idea might be said to have no "reality" if it has not been copied from any impression (like the idea of the New Jerusalem). In Hume's account, this is the case with our idea of a vacuum. There are impressions of space or extension *with* matter, understood as compound impressions consisting of visible or tactile points disposed in a certain manner. However, impressions of different visual or tactile points are customarily accompanied by certain further sensations specific to the particular parts of the eye that are affected by light (or so Hume supposed) and to the muscles of the eyes or limbs as they move from one location to the other. These further sensations are not the sort of impressions that are disposed in space (they are like sensations of smell or taste in this regard), and so, considered purely on their own, they are incapable of conveying any idea of extension. However, because these further sensations are constantly associated with impressions of visible and tangible extensions, they come to be confused with our ideas of visible and tangible extensions. The idea of a vacuum is the product of this confusion. It arises because the same muscle sensations and specific nerve impulses that occur when viewing objects separated by a visible or tangible extension can occur when viewing objects in the absence of any intervening visual or tactile impressions. In this circumstance, the specific nerve impulses and muscle sensations evoke the associated idea of extension, whereas the absence of any intervening visual or tactile impressions produces the idea that this extension contains no matter. In fact, according to Hume, there is no impression of an empty extension corresponding to this idea; there are only specific nerve impulses and muscle sensations that are not in space at all but that are confused with extension because they have been so constantly associated with visible and tangible extensions. Thus, the idea of vacuum has no "reality."

Problems with Hume's Position

Hume's account of the origin of the "confused" idea of a vacuum is premised on the claim that we do not have any impression of a vacuum, and so could not obtain a "real" idea of a vacuum by copying such an impression. His case flounders at this point.

According to *Treatise* 1.2.3, the impression of space is not a "separate" and "distinct" impression. Rather, it arises from the manners in which "separate" and "distinct" impressions of color or tactile qualities are disposed in compound impressions. From this point it follows that there can be no impressions of space without *some* other impressions. Accordingly, there can be no impression of a *completely* empty space. But it does not follow that there can be no impression of a *partially* empty space – that is, of an empty space between objects.

Hume nonetheless tried to argue that there could be no such impression. According to *Treatise* 1.2.5.11 (SBN 57),

We may observe, that when two bodies present themselves, where there was formerly an entire darkness, the only change, that is discoverable, is in the appearance of these two objects, and that all the rest continues to be as before, a perfect negation of light, and of every colour'd or visible object. This is not only true of what may be said to be remote from these bodies, but also of the very distance, which is interpos'd betwixt them; *that* being nothing but darkness, or the negation of light; without parts, without composition, invariable and indivisible. Now since this distance causes no perception different from what a blind man receives from his eyes, or what is convey'd to us in the darkest night, it must partake of the same properties: And as blindness and darkness afford us no ideas of extension, 'tis impossible that the dark and undistinguishable distance betwixt two bodies can ever produce that idea.

The problem with this argument is that it accepts the very thing it proposes to deny. According to Hume's theory of representation, impressions represent objects by resembling them. Therefore, just as an impression of extension represents extension by being an extended aggregate of component impressions set next to one another, an impression of a vacuum between bodies, or an unoccupied extension, would be an extended aggregate of component impressions set at a distance from one another, so as to create a hole or a gap. To deny that such an impression can be obtained from vision, one would need to have some special reason for holding that simple impressions of color must occur at every point in a compound visual impression. Hume did not do this in the argument cited above. On the contrary, he allowed the very opposite.[22] He did not attempt to prove that if two bodies present themselves where there was formerly an entire darkness the impressions of these bodies can occur only immediately alongside one another. Instead, he allowed that there might be a "distance, which is interpos'd betwixt them" yet not occupied by any other color. When he made this allowance, he gave up his case. A compound impression that consists of two visible points disposed in such a way that there is an unoccupied distance between them is an impression that contains a gap between its parts. And according to Hume's account of representation, an impression with a gap between its parts is an impression of a gap – that is, of an empty space.

It makes no difference that the unoccupied distance is dark, "without parts, without composition, invariable and indivisible," and "no ... different from what a blind man receives from his eyes, or what is convey'd to us in the darkest night." We can grant that these features entail that the unoccupied distance can "afford us no ideas of extension." No idea of a minimally visible point of color affords us an idea of extension either. Imagine two cases: that the two visible points Hume described are separated from one another by a single, intervening red point, and that they are separated from one another by a single unoccupied point. The unoccupied point, we can grant, does not afford us an idea of the distance between the other two points. But neither does the red point. Hume's main idea in *Treatise* 1.2.1–3 was that the compound idea of extension is not a product of the extension of its component parts, but rather of the manner in which these component parts are disposed alongside one another. The red point does not take up an extension between the two other visible points any more than the unoccupied point does. If it did, it would be divisible into parts and not a point. But even though it is unextended, because it is set immediately to the right of the one and immediately to the left of the other without overlapping with either, this manner of disposition of unextended parts produces something extended. By parity of argument, an unoccupied point, similarly disposed, ought to do the same.

It will not do to object that insofar as darkness is "without parts, without composition, invariable and indivisible," or "undistinguishable," we could never judge there to be any more than a single unoccupied point between any two visible points. For one thing, the same could be said of any uniformly colored expanse set between two visible points. It is just as "undistinguishable" and so could with just as much right be said to be without parts, composition, or variability. For another, if the question at issue is just whether we can form a "real" idea of a vacuum, all we need is a single unoccupied point, be it truly single or be it actually an "undistinguishable" plurality – a plurality that appears as a single point. Measurements of the size of "undistinguishable" extensions, whether colored or colorless, are in any case not difficult to make. All one needs is a third visible point off the line of the other two. The third point forms the vertex of an angle that is visibly greater or lesser depending on the distance between the other two points. (Hume made things artificially easy for himself by considering a case where only two points appear. Had he considered as few as three – let alone an illuminated square with a dark center – he would not have found it so easy to mount even a shadow of an argument to prove that the unoccupied extension between any two of them cannot be perceived because of the darkness between them.)

The argument that Hume offered to attempt to prove that touch cannot supply an impression of vacuum is even worse.

> I suppose two cases, *viz.* that of a man supported in the air, and moving his limbs to and fro, without meeting any thing tangible; and that of a man, who feeling something tangible, leaves it, and after a motion, of which he is sensible, perceives another tangible object; and I then ask, wherein consists the difference betwixt these two cases? No one will make any scruple to affirm, that it consists merely in the perceiving those objects, and that the sensation, which arises from the motion, is in both cases the same: And as that sensation is not capable of conveying to us an idea of extension, when unaccompany'd with some other perception, it can no more give us that idea, when mix'd with the impressions of tangible objects; since that mixture produces no alteration upon it. (T 1.2.5.13, SBN 58)

In this passage, Hume spoke as if the only way for an impression or idea of space to arise from the sense of touch is as a consequence of motion. But according to *Treatise* 1.2.3, simple tactile impressions and ideas are disposed alongside one another to compose extended compounds, as is the case with simple visual impressions. And according to Hume's account of representation, an extended impression is the same thing as an impression of extension. Consequently, motion should not be required for there to be an impression of a space composed of tactile impressions. It should suffice that a number of tactile impressions occur alongside one another. Indeed, insofar as motion produces a temporal sequence of impressions as opposed to a compound impression of simultaneously existing, spatially disposed component impressions, Hume ought to have been bewildered how motion could give rise to an idea of extension, even when the distance traversed is filled with tangible objects.

When considering whether the idea of a vacuum can be copied from compound impressions of touch, the question Hume ought to have asked is whether simultaneous tactile sensations must occur alongside one another without leaving any gaps or holes. If a mosquito bites me on the shoulder as I stand with a foot pressed against the ground and I have no other tactile sensations at the time, must the sensation of the bite in my shoulder be experienced as immediately adjacent to the sensation of solidity in my foot, or would I experience these simultaneously occurring tactile sensations as disposed at some distance from one another? If the latter, then the compound impression that consists of these two simple impressions disposed in this manner contains a gap. And an impression that contains a gap is an impression of a gap and hence an impression of an empty space. Since Hume failed to offer any reason for supposing that simultaneously occurring tactile sensations must be disposed immediately alongside one another, he failed to make a case against the possibility of a "real" idea of an empty space between tangible bodies.

NOTES

1. Or, more accurately, "thinking, about it, that it is a certain way" is simply making a replica, and this is all that it means to have a thought of an object. (I borrow the "about it, that" locution from Nicholas Wolterstorff [2001], who has employed it to attempt to describe how Reid's account of representation differs from that invoked by proponents of what Reid called the "ideal theory," among whom Hume is traditionally taken to have pride of place.)

2. For a paradigm statement of the view that Hume did not seriously mean to describe perceptions as extended or representation as replication see Yolton 1980, 1984. For alternative attempts to offer a coherent account of Hume's views in *Treatise* 1.2, see Frasca-Spada 1998 and Jacquette 2001. While I have profited from all of these works, readers familiar with them will note a number of points of disagreement.

3. See Flew 1976: 259–60, endorsed by Fogelin 1985: 27–28 and 175.

4. See, e.g., Locke 2.29, 31 [1690] 1975: 362–72, 375–84; Leibniz [1684] 1956: 448–50; and Descartes *Principles* I.45 ([1644] 1985 1:207–8).

5. It might be objected that Hume was not speaking in his own voice in this passage but merely reporting on a teaching of "the most vulgar philosophy." But the text does not support this charge. All that it attributes to "the most vulgar philosophy" is the teaching that external objects are known only through the interposition of images or perceptions.

6. See Franklin 1994: 87–89. I have benefited from Franklin's broad and illuminating paper in reaching the conclusions of this work. For further treatment, see the discussion of "discrete series" in Huntington 1917.

7. Imagine a corner A, B, C, D on a discrete plane formed by a line A, B, C three points in length and perpendicular to a line C, D two points in length. There can be no straight line from A to D. For the midpoint X of such a line would have to be closer to B than D is to C. But D and C are supposed to be immediately adjacent and so as close as possible. The point X would either have to be orthogonal to D, in which case the line A, X, D is not straight, or coincident with C, in which case A, X, D is again not straight.

8. Were it possible for lines to intersect at any angle, the space would be infinitely divisible.

9. At T 1.2.4.19 (SBN 45), Hume complained that it is "useless" to attempt to measure objects by counting up the number of points they contain because the parts are too small and "confounded" with one another. However, he also declared the standard to be "*just*, as well as obvious." The problems with it concern its application; it is right in theory. In cases such as the present one, in which we are stipulating how many points an idea or an object contains rather than trying to discover how many there are, it is appropriate to invoke this means of measurement.

10. The questions of the infinite divisibility of ideas and the infinite divisibility of impressions are entirely distinct. We might grant that the mind's finite capacities prevent it from forming ideas that have infinitely many parts, while maintaining that there is no limit to the acuity of the senses and hence to the number of parts exhibited in impressions. Alternatively, we might grant that the senses are only finitely acute, while maintaining that the mind has infinite capacities to imagine further divisions within its ideas. Trying to derive the finite divisibility of ideas from the finite divisibility of impressions by invoking the claim that ideas are copied from impressions would beg an important question. Hume recognized that even though many ideas are copied from impressions, many others are formed by compounding previously formed ideas in ways not exhibited by any impression. It is at least a question, therefore, whether original ideas may not equally well be formed by dividing previously formed ideas into parts not exhibited in isolation in any impression. Indeed, the idea of the smallest parts of the animal spirits of an insect a thousand times less than a mite may be an example of just such an idea. This is why a separate argument for the finite divisibility of ideas is necessary and why it is a mistake to represent Hume's argument for finite divisibility as resting on an appeal to the inkblot experiment (which establishes only the finite divisibility of visual impressions), backed up by appeal to the claim that ideas must copy impressions. Hume can be read as having attempted to forestall precisely this misinterpretation by first offering an independent argument for the finite divisibility of ideas at T 1.2.1.2–3 (SBN 26–27) and only subsequently turning to consider impressions at T 1.2.1.4 (SBN 27–28).

11. Fogelin (1985: 29) found this bewildering. Referring to Hume's claim that it is the impression or image itself that vanishes and is indivisible just before vanishing, not the object, he wrote, "It is very difficult to find your footing in this argument. We might make sense out of this claim that the impression vanished by translating it into: the spot seemed to vanish. But this produces no candidate for indivisibility. We can also make sense out of the claim that the impression is indivisible by translating it into: just before the spot seems to vanish it seems to be indivisible. This, however, is just false." What Fogelin failed to explain is why we may not make sense of these claims by taking them to be claims about impressions themselves considered as a special kind of object (one that might loosely be called a mental representation or a mental image) rather than about the spot or the judgments we are inclined to make about the spot. Since Fogelin was aware that Hume intended the claims to be made about the impressions themselves, but did

not mention this as a way of "making sense" of the claims, he must have thought that the claims make no sense when understood in this way. But he never explained why this makes no sense, and the reason why is far from obvious.

12. The words "as well as of greatness" in claim 5B need to be taken as drawing a contrast rather than making an addition. The point is that it is wrong to think that the imagination has the same problems forming adequate ideas of smallest possible objects that it does (i.e., "as it does") forming ideas of arbitrarily great ones.

13. In this case, Hume would still have been entitled to claim that our ideas are adequate representations of the smallest parts of extension. It would just be that there are some forms of extension (or some extended objects) that have no smallest parts, and so we cannot form any adequate ideas of them. Further to this point, see Appendix above.

14. For a fuller development of this point, see Appendix above.

15. This sentence can be parsed in two different ways: as "my senses convey to me only (the impressions of coloured points), (disposed in a certain manner)" or as "my senses convey to me only the impressions of (coloured points disposed in a certain manner)." According to the latter reading, the impressions are not themselves said to be disposed, but only the points that they are "of." However, both Hume's use of the plural (impressions of colored points, as opposed to a single impression of many disposed colored points) and the placement of the comma suggest that he wanted the sentence to be parsed in the former way, as stating that the senses convey impressions of colored points, which impressions are disposed in a certain manner – i.e., in space. T 1.2.3.5 (SBN 34) bears this out: "the impressions of touch are found to be similar to those of sight in the disposition of their parts." Of course, if we accept that what it means, for Hume, for an impression to be of an object is that the impression has the features of that object, then even the latter reading carries the same implication: the only way for an impression to be of colored points that are disposed in space is for it to consist of colored, pointal impressions that are disposed in space.

16. See, classically, Kemp Smith 1941: 209.

17. I suspect that those who have criticized Hume's appeal to manners of disposition have done so because they supposed that, for Hume, compound impressions must be analyzed *without remainder* into distinct and separable simple impressions. Accordingly, when they saw that Hume identified the "manner of disposition" as a component part of compound impressions, they expected to find him affirming the existence of some particular simple impression, like a Lockean simple idea of space, from which ideas of the "manner" might subsequently be copied. See Hendel 1963; Kemp Smith 1941: 274; Weinberg 1965: 115–16; and Rosenberg 1993: 83. There is no warrant for this expectation. Nothing Hume said implies that compound impressions could not consist of something more than their component parts. Granting that this is the case, we should expect that there would be some (compound) ideas that can originally be copied only from compound impressions and not from simple ones.

18. For Hume, just as a spatially pointal impression or idea may "inadequately" correspond to an object that consists of a vast number of parts, so a single

impression or idea in the temporal sequence of perceptions may correspond to a temporal interval over which a number of events occur in succession. See T 1.2.3.7, SBN 35.

19. For a fuller explanation of this point, see Baxter 2001a.

20. Hume himself appears to have come to view his position on finitism in geometry as flawed. Although a degree of commitment to that position continued to be evident in his notes to Section 12 of *An Enquiry concerning Human Understanding*, sometime over the years immediately subsequent to the publication of that work (in 1748), Hume wrote a paper on "some Considerations previous to Geometry & Natural Philosophy" (HL 1:223) and planned to have it included in the collection eventually published in 1757 under the title *Four Dissertations*. (This was reported to Andrew Millar in letter 111 on 12 June 1755.) However, a chance disclosure of the work to Philip Stanhope led him to withdraw the essay just prior to printing and, so far as now appears, destroy it. Twenty years later, Hume wrote (in letter 465 to William Strahan on 25 January 1772) that Stanhope had convinced him "that either there was some Defect in the Argument or in its perspicuity; I forget which" (HL 2:253).

21. The best and most recent reviews of these arguments are Holden 2001 and Baxter 2001b.

22. He could not easily have done otherwise, for reasons that are rather deeply rooted. As he himself observed, "as every idea, that is distinguishable, is separable by the imagination; and as every idea, that is separable by the imagination, may be conceiv'd to be separately existent; 'tis evident, that the existence of one particle of matter, no more implies the existence of another, than a square figure in one body implies a square figure in every one" (T 1.2.5.3, SBN 54). In this passage, Hume was engaged in laying out an argument he proposed to go on to refute, but this particular part of his exposition is one that is uncontroversially Humean. The consequence of this passage is one that he went on to endorse independently at T 1.2.5.24 (SBN 63): "a body interpos'd betwixt two others may be suppos'd to be annihilated, without producing any change upon such as lie on each hand of it" (notably, without causing them to approach one another). Note also T 1.2.5.15 (SBN 58–59): "two visible objects appearing in the midst of utter darkness, affect the senses in the same manner, and form the same angle by the rays, which flow from them, and meet in the eye [i.e., have the same angular separation on the visual field], as if the distance betwixt them were fill'd with visible objects."

4 Hume's Theory of Causation: Inference, Judgment, and the Causal Sense

Book 1 Part 3 of *A Treatise of Human Nature*, entitled "Of Knowledge and Probability," is the longest of the ten Parts that constitute the *Treatise*, and Hume devotes nearly all of it to a sustained and multi-faceted endeavor to "explain fully" the relation of *causation* (T 1.3.2.3, SBN 74). The discussion of the causal relation he provides there – together with the corresponding "recasting" of it in Sections 4 to 7 of his later *An Enquiry concerning Human Understanding* – constitutes one of his best-known and most important contributions to philosophy. Yet the wealth of arguments and claims it contains have led to competing interpretations of his theory of the nature of causation itself – particularly in recent years.[1] Hume holds that a "necessary connexion" is required as an "essential ... part" of the relation of cause and effect (T 1.3.6.3, SBN 87). He goes on to argue that what we take to be such a "necessity and power [lying] in the objects" is in fact merely an internal feeling of "the determination of the mind, to pass from the idea of an object to that of its usual attendant," a feeling that the mind erroneously treats as a quality of the objects observed (T 1.3.14.25, SBN 167), even though the ideas derived from this feeling of determination "represent not any thing, that does or can belong to the objects" (T 1.3.14.19, SBN 164). Thus, it seems that he *denies* that there are any such things as real causal relations in nature, admitting instead only fictitious projections of internal sentiments onto objects that cannot genuinely be qualified by them. At the same time, however, he also offers what he calls a "precise definition" of *cause* as "[a]n object precedent and contiguous to another, and where all objects resembling the former are plac'd in like relations of precedency and contiguity to those objects, that resemble the latter" (T 1.3.14.30–31, SBN 169–70). He then cites and employs this definition in the remainder of the *Treatise*. Thus, it seems that by a method of semantic analysis he *reduces* the relation of cause and effect to nothing more than what he calls "constant conjunction" between pairs of event types. Yet he goes on to allow that this same definition may "be esteem'd defective, because drawn from objects foreign to the cause" (T 1.3.14.31, SBN 170). In addition, he alludes variously to "the power, by which one object produces another" (T 1.3.1.1, SBN 69), the "internal structure or operating principle of objects" (T 1.3.14.29, SBN 169), and "the ultimate connexion of ... objects," concluding that "we can never penetrate so far into the essence and construction of bodies, as to perceive the principle, on which their mutual influence depends" (T 2.3.1.4, SBN 400) and that "[w]e cannot penetrate into the reason of the conjunction" (T 1.3.6.15, SBN 93). Thus, it seems that he *affirms* that there are real (even if epistemically inaccessible) causal powers and relations that go beyond both the projection of internal sentiments and mere constant conjunction. Each of these seemingly incompatible elements of the *Treatise* is repeated in *An Enquiry concerning Human Understanding* – often with only minor variation, but sometimes (as in the case of references to "powers" and "ultimate principles") with even greater force or frequency. Accordingly, Hume has seemed to some readers to hold a *projectivist* theory of causation, to some a *reductionist* theory, and to some a *realist* theory; and many have concluded that he either equivocates among them or simply holds an inconsistent mixture of all three.[2]

Although the outcome of his discussion may seem equivocal, Hume makes it clear why he devotes such a preponderance of Book 1 Part 3 to an explanation of the causal relation. All reasoning, Hume claims, is a "discovery of ... relations" (T 1.3.2.2, SBN 73). "Demonstrative" reasoning, as he characterizes it, is based on unchanging intrinsic "relations of ideas" and so can provide certain knowledge; but its employment, at least beyond obvious truths, is largely limited to mathematics. All other reasoning, according to his Lockean scheme of classification, qualifies as "probable" reasoning, the kind that predominates both in ordinary life and in philosophical enquiry; but all probable reasoning, he argues, "discovers" and depends on the relation of cause and effect, proceeding in one way or another from some immediately perceived or remembered "objects" (in a sense of the term broad enough to include states and events) to other "objects" treated as their causes or effects.

Having explained its importance, Hume proceeds to investigate this crucial relation by "examination of the idea" of it. In order to do so as "perfectly" as possible, he invokes his prime methodological principle – grounded in the doctrine that ideas (or their simpler component ideas) are always copied from resembling impressions – that one should seek to clarify the content of an idea by examining the impression or impressions from which it is derived (T 1.3.2.4, SBN 74–75). He quickly determines that causes precede and are, at least typically, contiguous with their effects. However, he then finds himself stymied by the nature of a third element or aspect that is of "much greater importance": the "necessary connexion" of cause and effect (T 1.3.2.11, SBN 77). Because the impression from which *this* idea is copied is not obvious in the observation of either the cause or the effect, he proposes to approach his quarry obliquely, by examining two questions – which he calls "neighbouring fields" – about the necessity of causes (T 1.3.2.13, SBN 78):

First, For what reason we pronounce it *necessary*, that every thing whose existence has a beginning, shou'd also have a cause?

Secondly, Why we conclude, that such particular causes must *necessarily* have such particular effects; and what is the nature of that *inference* we draw from the one to the other, and of the *belief* we repose in it? (T 1.3.2.14–15, SBN 78)

The investigation of the first question initially yields only a negative answer: the belief is not the result of either demonstration or immediate intuition (T 1.3.3). Hume then moves on to the second question, hoping that its investigation will also yield the positive answer to the first. Most of Book 1 Part 3 is thus an investigation of the nature of causal inferences – that is, probable reasonings, which are based on the relation of cause and effect – that is intended to lead to the discovery of the impression of necessary connection and, with that discovery, to an understanding of the causal relation itself.

In what follows, I try to explain Hume's own explanation of causation and of our "discovery" of it, in such a way as to resolve the appearance of equivocation among incompatible projectivist, reductionist, and realist theories of causation. I begin by explaining his theory of the nature of *causal reasoning* – that is, of what occurs when one reaches a conclusion about a matter of fact through probable reasoning, the kind of reasoning that "discovers" and depends on the relation of cause and effect. Next, I draw on that explanation, together with other aspects of his cognitive psychology (including his theories of relations, abstract ideas, and the correction and location of sensed qualities) to explain his theory of *causal judgment* – that is, of what occurs when one judges explicitly that two things stand in the relation of cause and effect. In doing so, I argue that Hume in effect recognizes a "causal sense," analogous in some ways to the visual sense of color (along with other external senses), the moral sense, and the sense of beauty. Finally, I draw on that theory of causal judgment to argue that Hume has a coherent theory of causation that can concede something of importance to projectivism, to reductionism, and to realism, without collapsing into a simple version of any of them.

I. HUME'S THEORY OF CAUSAL REASONING

Hume identifies (in T 1.3.4) three elements or "component parts" of causal reasoning: first, a present "impression" (i.e., a sensation or internal feeling) or memory (explained in T 1.3.5); second, an inference from the present impression or memory to a believed idea (explained in T 1.3.6); and third, the believed idea itself (explained in T 1.3.7). The reasoning is "causal" because it effectively treats the object of the impression or memory and the object of the believed idea either as cause and effect or as effect and cause.

Three Elements of Causal Inference

The starting point for belief-generating causal reasoning, Hume argues, must have two characteristics. First, it must have the high degree of "vivacity" or "liveliness" that he identifies as characteristic of an impression or memory – otherwise, there may still occur an associative transition and even "hypothetical reasoning," but no genuine belief will result. Second, objects *like* that represented by the impression or memory, on the one hand, and objects *like* that represented by the resulting believed idea, on the other, must have been constantly conjoined, in a consistent order of temporal priority, in the reasoner's experience. For the representation of a cause and the representation of its effect are always entirely distinct "perceptions" – "perception" being Hume's most general term for the contents of the mind, including impressions, memories, and other ideas – and nothing can be discovered in either perception that would indicate what (if anything) must follow or be followed by its object. This is confirmed by the mind's evident inability to make any causal inferences about objects that are entirely unlike any that the mind has perceived before. Because a causal inference cannot occur *prior* to the experience of a constant conjunction between two types of objects or events, the question then naturally arises of how this inference is made even *after* the experience of constant conjunction. The negative first stage of Hume's answer to this question is the famous, if often misunderstood, conclusion that the inference is *not* "determin'd by reason" (T 1.3.6.4, SBN 88) – a conclusion often described as Hume's "inductive scepticism."

It is important to understand clearly the question that Hume is asking, to which "not reason" constitutes a negative part of his answer. Reason, for Hume, is the faculty of reasoning or inference, the exercises of which are demonstrative and probable reasonings or inferences. Thus, Hume is *not* asking whether probable or causal inferences are themselves examples or instances of reasoning, exercises of the faculty of reason; they obviously are, and he continues to characterize them as reasonings throughout his writings, including his argument denying their "determination" by reason. Nor is he asking, at this point, either whether one is justified in making such inferences or whether their conclusions will be true. Rather, he is asking whether, within an episode of causal reasoning, the transition that occurs *from* the impression or memory *to* the believed idea following exposure to a constant conjunction of objects of the two kinds in question is *itself mediated* by a component inference or piece of reasoning. The outline of his argument is well known. In order for the mind to move, after some prior observation of a constant conjunction of two kinds of objects, from an impression or memory of one to a believed idea of the other, the mind must, in some way, make a "presumption" to the effect that "*instances, of which we have had no experience, must resemble those, of which we have had experience, and that the course of nature continues always uniformly the same*" (T 1.3.6.4, SBN 89), at least with respect to the conjunction in question, in application to the present case. If that presumption of uniformity were itself produced by a piece of reasoning, the presumption would take the form of a conclusion that affirmed such uniformity and was produced by either demonstrative or probable reasoning. Such an affirmed conclusion could not be caused by genuine demonstrative reasoning, however, for there is nothing in the intrinsic relations among the ideas that requires nature to remain uniform in an as-yet-unobserved case – as we can see simply from the *conceivability* of a change in the course of nature in the relevant respect. Yet the presumption of the uniformity of nature could not be the product of probable reasoning either; for *all* probable reasoning, Hume has already argued, depends without exception on the relation of cause and effect precisely *by* effectively presuming that nature will be uniform in respect of the relevant constant conjunction. In other words, the presumption of uniformity in question cannot be *caused* by probable reasoning because the presumption must *already have occurred* in order to make possible *any* probable reasoning about the subject. Hence, Hume concludes, the presumption of the uniformity of nature that facilitates the crucial step within causal reasoning is not itself caused by any reasoning at all.[3] Instead, it must be the result of some associative mechanism.

Having reached this largely negative conclusion about the cause of the inference, Hume examines the third element of causal reasoning: the idea believed. He concludes that the belief consists in the liveliness or vivacity that the idea acquires from the mind's enlivenment by the initiating impression or memory with which the idea is now associated (as a result of the experienced constant conjunction). In turn, this conclusion allows him to offer a more specific positive answer to the question of how the inference occurs by identifying the mechanism behind the implicit presumption of the uniformity of nature: it is not reasoning but "custom" or "habit,": the mechanism by means of which something that has been often repeated in the mind is renewed again "without any new reasoning or conclusion" (T 1.3.8.10, SBN 102).

Further Influences on Belief

Hume next offers evidence to confirm his theory that belief resulting from causal inference consists of an idea that has been enlivened by its association with a present impression or memory. He does so by noting that the three relations already identified in *Treatise* 1.1 as associative relations – resemblance, contiguity, and causation itself (whatever exactly it may turn out to be) – all have some enlivening influence on ideas when the objects of those ideas are taken to be related to the objects of current impressions or memories in those ways, even when the circumstances required for inference are absent (T 1.3.8), and by noting that the associative relations of resemblance and contiguity can further strengthen beliefs resulting from causal inference when the circumstances for inference are present (T 1.3.9). After a consideration of the influence of beliefs on action (T 1.3.10), he goes on to analyze – in Sections devoted to species of "philosophical" and "unphilosophical" probability – various influences on the strength or weakness of belief in cases in which the transition to a particular believed idea does not convey the fullest degree of liveliness (T 1.3.11–13).

The Impression of Necessary Connection

On the basis of this account of the components of causal inference and the variety of influences on belief, and now armed with an understanding of the association-generating role played in causal inference by the experience of constant conjunction, Hume returns to the question of the origin of the idea of the necessary connection that he has declared to be such an important aspect of causation. Because experienced constant conjunction of some kind is required before one can make a causal inference, one never perceives a necessary connection after a first experience of one kind of object being followed by another; instead, the impression of necessary connection arises only after the experience of their constant conjunction. Yet the mere repeated perception of the same types of objects cannot reveal anything new in the objects themselves. Hence, the impression of necessary connection cannot be the sensory perception of something external to the mind and located in the cause and effect; rather, it must be something new that arises in the mind itself as the result of the repeated conjunction. Hume concludes that the impression of necessary connection is an "internal impression" of the mind caused by other perceptions – an "impression of reflection" rather than an "impression of sensation," in his terminology – and is identical with the felt "determination of the thought to pass from causes to effects and from effects to causes, according to their experienc'd union" (T 1.3.14.22, SBN 166; cf. T 1.3.14.1, SBN 155).

Of course, in calling the impression of necessary connection a felt "determination" of the mind, Hume cannot mean that the mere occurrence of this impression in the mind constitutes immediate awareness, independent of prior experience, of a causal relation of mental determination holding between the impression or memory and the believed idea that results from the customary transition of thought that he has described. Since *all* discovery of causal relations depends on the experience of constant conjunction, according to Hume, the discovery of the causal relations among one's own perceptions does as well. The impression of necessary connection is nevertheless properly characterized as an impression "of" the mind's "determination," for one in fact feels this impression whenever the mind makes, or is about to make, a custom- or habit-based inference. Indeed, given its *own* constant conjunction with the occurrence of such inferences, the impression of necessary connection may well be a state of mind that itself constitutes an essential contributing cause to the completion of the inference from the impression or memory to the believed idea; and it may therefore even be characterized as "the determination of the mind" itself, and not merely as an impression "of" the presence of such a determination.

Hume concludes that the "necessity" of causes is constituted by this determination, or "propensity," of the mind (T 1.3.14.22, SBN 165). In doing so, he strongly implies that the impression of determination that he has identified as that of "necessary connexion" is indeed properly characterized as an impression *of necessity*. This implication is legitimate, because he holds that, in general, the application of the term *necessity* reflects the mind's determination to conceive things in a certain way – that is, its inability to conceive and affirm otherwise – whether the necessity in question is that of "relations of ideas" (which are always either self-evident or demonstrable) or that of causes. Thus, he writes:

[A]s the necessity, which makes two times two equal to four, or three angles of a triangle equal to two right ones, lies only in the act of the understanding, by which we consider and compare these ideas; in like manner the necessity or power, which unites causes and effects, lies in the determination of the mind to pass from the one to the other. (T 1.3.14.23, SBN 166)

In the latter case, "[t]he objects seem so inseparable, that we interpose not a moment's delay in passing from the one to the other" (T 1.3.8.13, SBN 104).

Yet although necessary "relations of ideas" and necessary causal relations both involve an inability to think otherwise, there remains a crucial difference between the two cases. In the case of relations of ideas, the inability to conceive otherwise is grounded in the intrinsic character of the ideas themselves, which (at least when they are "adequate representations" [cf. T 1.2.2.1, SBN 29]) represent the intrinsic characters of their objects; whereas in the case of causal necessity, the inability is more properly a psychological *difficulty* in separating two perceptions (and a psychological inability to believe their objects to be separated), a difficulty resulting not from the intrinsic characters of the objects as we conceive them but from the habitual association between them established by constant conjunction. Thus, Hume writes:

'Tis natural for men, in their common and careless way of thinking, to imagine they perceive a connexion betwixt such objects as they have constantly found united together; and because custom has render'd it difficult to separate the ideas, they are apt to fancy such a separation to be in itself impossible and absurd. (T 1.4.3.9, SBN 223)

Nevertheless, we may say that much as one "discovers" the necessity of twice 2 making 4 by being *determined* by intrinsic content to conceive of 4 in the act of conceiving twice 2 and by being *unable to conceive* twice 2 making any other quantity, so one "discovers" the necessity of causes by being psychologically determined (by the observation of genuine constant conjunction) to infer the existence of one object from that of another and by finding it difficult even to think of the one object without thinking of the other. It is precisely in making such inferences that one "discovers" the necessity of causes and, in effect, represents the two objects involved as being related by cause and effect.

2. HUME'S THEORY OF CAUSAL JUDGMENT

On Hume's account, causal reasoning consists of an inference from an impression or memory to a lively idea – an inference that occurs after a previously experienced constant conjunction of objects like the former with objects like the latter and is accompanied by an impression of necessary connection that is a felt determination of the mind to make the inference. Such reasoning, as he describes it, presupposes no uniquely human capacities. Indeed, he argues in the final Section of *Treatise* Book I Part 3 (T 1.3.16, "Of the reason of animals") that this fact constitutes a very important point in favor of his account, because animals as well as humans show by their behavior that they perform causal reasoning. But although animals, like humans, effectively presume the uniformity of nature in the course of their causal reasoning, they do not formulate the principle of the uniformity of nature as an explicit doctrine to which they give assent, as at least some reflective humans ultimately come to do. Similarly, although animal reasoning implicitly discovers and depends on causal relations in order to infer one thing from another, animals do not make explicit judgments of the form "Object A and Object B stand in the relation of cause and effect." Human beings, however, do make explicit causal judgments of this form; and in order to understand Hume's theory of *what* they are judging when they do so, we must understand his theory of how such causal judgments occur. In order to do this, in turn, we must understand something of his general theory of judgments of relations, of which his theory of causal judgment is an application.

Relations and Abstract Ideas

For Hume, perceptions may have, and may represent their objects as having, many different qualities; for example, they may represent their objects as being round and a particular shade of red. Similarly, perceptions may stand in, and may represent their objects as standing in, many different relations, either "natural" or "philosophical."[4] For example, a pair of perceptions may represent one object as similar in shape but double in size to another, while also representing the objects as existing simultaneously but at a distance equal to the height of the smaller. In order for perceptions to represent objects as having particular qualities and relations – and also in order for the perceptions themselves to have qualities and relations that determine the nature of further cognitive operations – it is not always necessary for the mind to have what Hume calls "general or abstract ideas" (what we would call "concepts") *of* the qualities or relations in question. In order to think with generality *about* qualities and relations, however, or about the classes of things that have them, it *is* necessary to form abstract ideas of them.

No idea, Hume argues, is general or indeterminate in its own nature. Therefore, in order to have thoughts with generality, the mind must employ what he calls the "imperfect" device of abstract ideas (T 1.1.7.2, SBN 17). Such ideas arise in the mind, on his view, in the following way. When perceptions resemble one another in some respect, it is natural to apply the same sound or mark to each, notwithstanding their difference. Later uses of the sound or mark come to elicit a particular and determinate idea (which we may call the "exemplar") together with a disposition to revive and "survey," as needed for reasoning or other purposes, the other ideas (which we may call the "revival set") whose objects resemble one another in the operative respect (T 1.1.7.7–8, SBN 20–21). Thus, the abstract idea of the quality *red* is a determinate idea of a particular thing having a particular shade of red but associated with the word *red* in such a way that the mind is disposed by them to revive and survey any of a set of other ideas of red things for use as needed. If, for example, one's abstract idea exemplar of red is an idea of a dark red circle and the claim is made that all red things are dark red circles, the ideas of red things of other shades or other shapes will immediately come to mind, allowing one to reject the claim proposed. Similarly, we may infer, the abstract idea of a relation consists, for Hume, of a determinate idea of a pair (or triple, etc.) of particular things taken to stand in that relation and associated with a word in such a way that the mind is disposed to revive and survey for use as needed any of a set of ideas of other pairs (triples, etc.) whose objects are taken to be similarly related. His application of this theory to the relation of causation is confirmed by his remark that "[w]e must not here be content with saying, that the idea of cause and effect arises from objects constantly united; but must affirm, that 'tis *the very same with the idea of these objects*" (T 2.3.1.16, SBN 405; emphasis added).

Judgment and Correction

To judge that a particular object has a specified quality, then, is to include a lively idea of that object – an idea constituting belief in its existence – within the revival set of the abstract idea of that quality; and to judge explicitly that two particular objects stand in a specified relation is to include a lively idea of that pair of objects in the revival set of the abstract idea of that relation. To judge that two objects, A and B, stand in the relation of cause and effect, therefore, is to include a lively idea of the pair A and B in the revival set of the abstract idea of the causal relation – a revival set that has resulted from the effect on the mind of the resemblance that holds among the various object pairs that, following the experience of constant conjunction of like pairs, sustain causal inference with its characteristic impression of determination or necessary connection. Hume aims to capture this revival set with "two definitions" of *cause* that – because "the nature of the relation depends so much on that of the inference" (T 1.3.14.30, SBN 169) – he offers only after his account of the impression of necessary connection:

(1)   We may define a CAUSE to be "An object precedent and contiguous to another, and where all the objects resembling the former are plac'd in like relations of precedency and contiguity to those objects, that resemble the latter."

(2)   "A CAUSE is an object precedent and contiguous to another, and so united with it, that the idea of the one determines the mind to form the idea of the other, and the impression of the one to form a more lively idea of the other."

(T 1.3.14.31, SBN 170)

These two definitions express what we might call "productive" and "responsive" conditions – constant conjunction and association-plus-inference, respectively – that lead to the impression of necessary connection and the inclusion of an object pair in the revival set of the abstract idea of cause and effect.

In Book 3 of the *Treatise*, Hume discusses distinctive sentiments of moral approbation and disapprobation. These sentiments are, like the impression of necessary connection, impressions of reflection; and he characterizes our ability to feel them as a "moral sense" that enables us to discriminate vice and virtue (T 3.1.2). In the *Treatise* and even more clearly in *An Enquiry concerning the Principles of Morals*, Hume goes on to offer two definitions of "virtue," one appealing to productive features *external* to the moral spectator ("the possession of mental qualities, *useful* or *agreeable* to the *person himself* or to *others*" [EPM 9.1, SBN 268]) and the other appealing to responsive features *internal* to the moral spectator ("*whatever mental action or quality gives to a spectator the pleasing sentiment of approbation*" [EPM App. 1.10, SBN 289]). This analogy suggests that the mental operations by which constant conjunction leads to association, inference, and the impression of necessary connection may also be viewed as a kind of "causal sense," one that allows the mind to distinguish those pairs of objects that are *causally related* from those that are not.

Of course, senses need not be, and generally are not, infallible; not all things that appear to resemble each other in a given respect truly do resemble each other in that respect. Hence, not every object that we might initially include in the revival set of an abstract idea is properly so classified. The sizes, shapes, and relative positions of bodies as they are initially sensed will often be corrected, Hume allows, by consideration of the position of the observer (T 3.3.3.2, SBN 602-3); and the apparent colors, sounds, tastes, and smells of objects will also sometimes be corrected, he notes, for features of the circumstances of observation, including the health of the sense organs. He emphasizes how the immediate deliverances of the moral sense are likewise "correct[ed]" by taking into account differences of perspective on the individuals judged, so as to reduce the "contradictions" in felt response that the same character would otherwise produce among different observers and even within the same observer at different times (ibid.). The initial deliverances of the sense of beauty will often be corrected as well, both by a consideration of the physical circumstances of observation (T 3.3.1.15, SBN 582) and by reflectively developed rules of criticism (T 2.2.8.18, SBN 379).

In parallel fashion, Hume offers in the penultimate Section of *Treatise* Book 1 Part 3 a set of eight "rules by which to judge of causes and effects" (T 1.3.15), rules that serve to guide the refinement of the revival set of one's abstract idea of the relation of cause and effect. These rules "are form'd on the nature of our understanding, and on our experience of its operations in the judgments we form concerning objects" – that is, by reflection on the mechanism of causal reasoning in light of the past predictive successes and failures of causal inferences of various kinds – and by means of them "we learn to distinguish the accidental circumstances from the efficacious causes" (T 1.3.13.11, SBN 149).[5] Of course, the greatest problem of perspective or situation in discerning causal relations lies in the limitation of our experience to only a small part of what actually occurs in the world, with the resulting danger of insufficient or unrepresentative samples. Enquiry into causes involves the development and use of both experiments and rules for judging causes that mitigate this insufficiency as much as possible. Just as the *correct* or *true* revival set for the abstract idea of a sensible, moral, or aesthetic quality is that which would arise in an *idealized* human observer judging in accordance with associated rules of correction, so the correct or true revival set for the abstract idea of cause and effect is the set that would arise in an ideal observer having the human causal sense, possessing enough observations to constitute a sufficient and representative sample for any causal judgment, and employing the associated rules for judging of causes and effects.

Judgment and Mislocation

Hume's distinction between "impressions of sensation" (such as those of color, sound, heat, and hunger) and "impressions of reflection" (such as passions, moral and aesthetic sentiments, and the impression of necessary connection) is itself a purely causal one: impressions of sensation are caused directly and externally, without the mediation of other perceptions, whereas impressions of reflection arise in the mind through the causal operations of other perceptions. Given Hume's theory about the prerequisites for causal inference, it follows that this distinction between impressions of sensation and impressions of reflection can itself be drawn only after repeated experience. Within the class of impressions of sensation, our drawing of the further distinction between those impressions that resemble continuing qualities of the objects that cause them (such as shape and motion) and those that do not (such as the pain produced by a sharp knife) arises as the result of a complex cognitive process depending on aspects of "constancy" and "coherence" in the occurrence of impressions of sensation (T 1.4.2.2–19, SBN 187–95). Accordingly, it is possible to make mistakes both about whether an impression is one of sensation or of reflection and about whether an impression of sensation does or does not bear a resemblance to any quality in its cause. Furthermore, once an impression is taken either to *be* or to *represent through resemblance* a quality of an external cause,[6] the association of ideas also leads the mind, erroneously, to attribute literal spatial location in the objects to such nonspatial sensory qualities as sounds and smells (T 1.4.5.12–13, SBN 237–38; cf. T 1.4.3.5, SBN 221).

In *An Enquiry concerning the Principles of Morals*, Hume appears to suggest that the mind has a tendency to locate both moral and aesthetic sentiments – all of which are in fact impressions of reflection that do not resemble qualities in objects – in the objects of evaluation themselves, thereby "gilding or staining... natural objects with the colours, borrowed from internal sentiment" (EPM App. 1.25, SBN 294). In *Treatise* 1.4.4, he argues that (what he calls) "the modern philosophy," while subject to many objections, has a "satisfactory" argument for the conclusion that there is nothing resembling the impressions of so-called "secondary" sensible qualities (such as color, sound, taste, smell, and heat and cold) in external bodies themselves – contrary to our usual way of conceiving bodies (T 1.4.4.3–4, SBN 226–27). Hume claims that a similar process of attribution and location occurs erroneously in the case of necessary connection:

[T]he mind has a great propensity to spread itself on external objects, and to conjoin with them any internal impressions, which they occasion, and which always make their appearance at the same time that these objects discover themselves to the senses. Thus as certain sounds and smells are always found to attend certain visible objects, we naturally imagine a conjunction, even in place, betwixt the objects and qualities, tho' the qualities be of such a nature as to admit of no such conjunction, and really exist no where.... Mean while 'tis sufficient to observe, that the same propensity is the reason, why we suppose necessity and power to lie in the objects we consider, not in our mind, that considers them; notwithstanding it is not possible for us to form the most distant idea of that quality, when it is not taken for the determination of the mind, to pass from the idea of an object to that of its usual attendant. (T 1.3.14.25, SBN 167)

As a result of this misattribution and mislocation, our ideas of cause-and-effect pairs themselves may include as a part an idea of necessary connection, copied from the impression of reflection. Because we thereby treat the necessity of causes as if it were grounded in the intrinsic character of the idea of particular cause-and-effect pairs, rather than in the custom-based psychological difficulty of their separation that is the true basis of causal necessity, we erroneously suppose, Hume thinks, that we can observe causal necessity or power as a quality or relation in the objects themselves. Moreover, he continues, we fail to distinguish the necessity of causes from the kind of necessity that pertains to demonstrations of "relations of ideas," a necessity that *is* grounded in the intrinsic character of ideas.

3. CAUSAL PROJECTIVISM

Does Hume's explanation of the causal relation, expressed in his theories of causal inference and causal judgment, entail that causality is merely projected and not ultimately real? Four reasons might be given for thinking that Hume must deny the reality of causal relations. These concern the topics of truth, determinacy, mind-independence, and explanatory role, respectively.

Projection and Truth

Hume acknowledges and emphasizes the importance of "necessary connexion" to the causal relation. Yet he identifies the impression of necessary connection with a mere feeling of determination that we typically project, through misattribution and mislocation, onto the pairs of objects taken to be causes and effect – despite the fact that this feeling cannot really represent "any thing, that does or can belong to the objects" (T 1.3.14.19, SBN 164). It seems to follow that Hume cannot regard ascriptions of causality as literally true and must instead regard them either (1) as false or (2) as neither true nor false, but merely as ways of expressing one's feeling of determination or perhaps of the accompanying readiness to make inferences or of both. The first option is an "error theory" of causation; the second is an expressivist theory. Both may be understood as projectivist interpretations.

Yet Hume constantly implies that many causal judgments are straightforwardly true. He writes, for example, of "prov[ing]" and "know[ing]" the causal "dependence" of ideas on preceding impressions (T 1.1.1.8, SBN 4–5), of "the true and real cause of [an] idea, and of the belief which attends it" (T 1.3.8.8, SBN 102); of the sufficiency of constant conjunction to render something a "real cause" (T 1.3.14.32, SBN 171); of having established "the truth of my hypothesis" about the causes of causal inference itself (T 1.4.1.8, SBN 183–84); and of having "prov'd" the causes of pride and humility (T 2.1.12.1, SBN 324–25). Indeed, Hume declares himself in the Introduction to the *Treatise* to be pursuing nothing less than the "truth" (T Intro. 3, SBN xiv) about the "principles of human nature" (T Intro. 6, SBN xvi), a project that requires forming a "notion of [the] powers and qualities" of the mind and "explaining all effects from the simplest and fewest causes" (T Intro. 8, SBN xvii).

The "quasi-realist" version of causal expressivism first developed by Simon Blackburn (2000) cleverly proposes that Hume can characterize some causal judgments as "true" in a way compatible with a fundamentally expressivist orientation in virtue simply of their meeting *accepted norms* governing attitudes of willingness to make causal inferences and their expression. Whatever the philosophical merits of this sophisticated deflationary conception of truth, however, it is not one that Hume himself would sanction. On the contrary, Hume treats truth as straightforward correspondence between an idea and what it represents, defining "truth or falshood" as "an agreement or disagreement either to the *real* relations of ideas, or to *real* existence and matter of fact" (T 3.1.1.9, SBN 458; cf. T 2.3.3.5, SBN 415). He clearly aims at least to contribute to the development of a true account of the causal relations governing the human mind in his own literal and non-expressivist sense of "truth."

Hume can retain this aim, despite the acknowledged projective misapplication and mislocation of the impression of necessary connection, for two reasons. First, a Humean idea need not always precisely resemble its object in every respect in order to "agree with" it and so represent it truly. For example, a true idea of New York and Boston as being 190 miles apart need not include ideas that are themselves 190 miles apart; some conventional way of representing large distances (which may include proportions among ideas, ideas of standard units, and ideas of numbers or numerals[7]) is sufficient. Nor, obviously, need the ideas of New York and Boston resemble the actual cities in every particular. Hume's definition of truth and falsity in terms of "agreement or disagreement" echoes the terms of Locke's definition of "truth"; and in the Lockean tradition, the ideas provided by a *sense* can provide a true representation without perfect resemblance. Thus, Locke holds, for example, that nothing in external bodies resembles our sensory ideas of colors or other secondary qualities; but he insists that the representation of a body using these ideas can nevertheless constitute "real Knowledge" of color or other secondary qualities, for the sensory ideas are reliable indicators of the presence of the particular, though unknown, arrangements of corpuscles that produce them (Locke 4.4.4 [1690] 1975: 563–64). More importantly, Hume himself continues to characterize objects as having colors despite his allowing that there is a "satisfactory" argument for the conclusion that no quality in bodies themselves resembles our ideas of colors; indeed, he appeals to the "reality" of colors to explain that of beauty:

If, in the sound state of the organ, there be an entire or a considerable uniformity of sentiment among men, we may thence derive an idea of the perfect beauty; in like manner as the appearance of objects in day-light, to the eye of a man in health, is denominated their true and real colour, even while colour is allowed to be merely a phantasm of the senses. (E-ST 234)

Second, the representation of causal pairs as having a "necessary connexion" as an intrinsic part – a representation that results from the "spreading" or projection of the impression – is not *essential* to the abstract idea of cause and effect itself. To overcome the illusion – as Hume implies can be done with care and attention (T 1.3.14.31, 1.4.3.9–10, 1.4.7.5–6, SBN 170, 222–24, 266–67) – is not to change the pairs of objects whose ideas constitute the revival set of the idea of cause and effect, but only to correct the way in which they are imaginatively represented. To include a lively idea of a pair of objects in that revival set when the pair does indeed "agree" with the abstract idea by resembling its other members in the manner picked out by the causal sense is, prima facie, to believe truly that the objects are related by cause and effect.

Projection and Determinacy

Even if causal judgments are sometimes properly considered *true*, however, it may still be objected that relations of cause and effect nevertheless cannot be *real* because the nature of the causal sense guarantees that whether two objects are related as cause and effect will sometimes be indeterminate, whereas every real relation is bivalent – that is, such that every pair of objects determinately does or determinately does not stand in it (even if it cannot always be known which is the case). Hume clearly allows that there is not always a determinate answer to every question of aesthetic or moral merit, especially when the questions concern comparative merit or the precise boundaries of aesthetic or moral qualities. This is because the precise delineation of moral and aesthetic qualities depends on there being a uniquely correct reconciliation among conflicting evaluative sentiments involving psychologically varying observers in a wide variety of circumstances.[8] Similarly, the objection may run, the causal sense cannot yield a determinate answer to every causal question because the precise delineation of causal relations depends on there being a single correct reconciliation of potentially divergent impressions of necessary connection and mental associations (which may be of varying strengths) among different observers (who may differ in psychological constitution) through exposure to constant conjunctions (which may be of varying constancy and numbers of instances) involving classes of objects whose members may be of varying degrees of resemblance. Thus, it may seem inevitable that some judgments of the form "A is the cause of B" will be of indeterminate truth-value, undecidable even by an ideally informed and ideally corrected causal sense.

Two replies are in order. First, it may be questioned whether the requirement of complete bivalence in the application of causal terms is too stringent, particularly in the context of Hume's philosophy. Although the revival sets of some Humean abstract ideas – such as those of single shades of color or of mathematical relations such as "being one greater than" – may admit of no vagueness or indeterminacy, the vast majority of

Humean abstract ideas will admit of at least some indeterminacy. The signification of an abstract idea depends on the revival set of resembling ideas that it does or would elicit, and, where precise degrees of resemblance are not easily measured or discerned, it will be common for some potential members of a revival set to be revivable only occasionally, variably, imperfectly, or hesitatingly, without any completely definite standard for correction. The general terms associated with such abstract ideas will, accordingly, be subject to what Hume calls irresolvable "verbal disputes."[9] It is not only abstract ideas derived from the moral, aesthetic, and causal senses that are potentially subject to such indeterminacy, but also ideas derived from the senses that pick out such qualities as colors, sounds, and smells. There are many different kinds of resemblance, both simple and complex, many of which are subject to variations of degree, some easily measurable and some not; and there are many different classes of resembling objects (and pairs of objects) corresponding to them. Hume can invoke his theory of abstract ideas to explain why many predicates fail to delineate sharply a single such class as opposed to other closely related ones; and given its pervasiveness, a modest amount of such semantic indeterminacy may well seem insufficient to reject the reality of the underlying relations themselves.

Second, however, and perhaps more importantly, although the class of pairs of objects picked out by the causal sense is *potentially subject* to vagueness and indeterminacy, it does not follow that it *is* vague or indeterminate. Hume believes, on the basis of inductive evidence derived from the past inductive successes of natural science, that the world is deterministic – that is, it is such that a finite set of generalizations is sufficient to determine without exception all of the qualities and relations of each state of the universe from those of the preceding state. Indeed, it is this evidence for determinism that provides the ultimate positive answer to the question of his first "neighbouring field" mentioned earlier, concerning the cause of our belief that "a cause is necessary for every beginning of existence." Hume expresses the Newtonian hope, and even the expectation, that the generalizations in question, though perhaps difficult of discovery, are both relatively simple and relatively few – providing what we might call a "unified theory of nature." In a relatively chaotic and indeterministic world, the set of pairs of objects picked out by an idealized human causal sense might be highly indeterminate – indeed, perhaps as indeterminate as the set of objects picked out by an idealized human aesthetic sense in the actual world. The set of objects picked out as "red" by an idealized human visual sense – a set whose membership is slightly vague and indeterminate in the actual world – might be much more indeterminate in such a conceivable world as well. But in a *deterministic* world entirely subject to a simple unified theory of nature, the idealized output of the causal sense may be entirely determinate – ultimately yielding precisely that theory. In such a world, causal relations may be very "real" – at least, as far as bivalence is concerned.

Projection and Mind-Independence

Even if many causal judgments are true and all are determinately true or false, however, it may still be maintained that causal relations are nevertheless too "mind-dependent" to qualify as real. For doesn't the very existence of causal relations *depend* on there being a human causal sense? And isn't the causal relation ultimately just *whatever* that human causal sense happens to pick out, so that *what causation is* depends equally on the operations of the mind?

Hume considers explicitly the objection that his theory of causation "reverse[s] the order of nature" by making causes depend on thought, rather than vice versa. In doing so, he imagines an opponent who exclaims,

What! the efficacy of causes lie in the determination of the mind! As if causes did not operate entirely independent of the mind, and wou'd not continue their operation, even tho' there was no mind existent to contemplate them, or reason concerning them. (T 1.3.14.26, SBN 167)

Hume's response is as follows:

As to what may be said, *that the operations of nature are independent of our thought and reasoning, I allow it*; and accordingly have observ'd, that objects bear to each other the relations of contiguity and succession; that like objects may be observ'd in several instances to have like relations; and that all this is independent of, and antecedent to the operations of the understanding. But if we go any farther, and ascribe a power or necessary connexion to these objects; that is what we can never observe in them, but must draw the idea of it from what we feel internally in contemplating them. (T 1.3.14.28, SBN 168–69; emphasis added)

The kinds of resemblance among pairs of objects that the actual human causal sense happens to pick out would continue to hold whether there were human beings or not, and events in nature would continue to exemplify the true generalizations of the unified theory of nature. Furthermore, although the "necessity" of causal relations would no longer be felt, the *basis* of that felt necessity in constant conjunction would continue to exist, in much the same way that, according to the "modern philosophy," the *basis* of sensory "redness" would continue to exist in the corpuscular structure of bodies even if the impression of red (which does not resemble its basis in the bodies) were never to occur. In much the same way, the necessity of mathematical relations would never be felt in the absence of minds, even though the *basis* of that felt necessity would continue to exist in the intrinsic natures of related things. Accordingly, Hume is willing to say that "the constant conjunction of objects constitutes the very essence of cause and effect" (T 1.4.5.33, SBN 250) and that "'tis from the constant union the necessity arises" (T 2.3.1.4, SBN 400). The causal relations that are in fact detected by a feeling of necessity – like the basis of that felt necessity in the constant conjunction of objects – are not dependent for their existence on the existence of the human mind or a causal sense that detects them.

Nor need we say that causal relations are *whatever* the causal sense happens to pick out, if this is taken to mean that a change in what produced the association, the inference, and the distinctive impression of necessary connection would also entail a change in what causation *is*. Consider an analogy. Suppose that the basis of redness consists in a particular complex (and perhaps highly disjunctive) structural surface reflectance quality. Suppose too that had the human sensory apparatus been different, a different quality of bodies would have produced the impression of red under standard circumstances. Then although it may be true that the quality of redness is what the visual sense of red actually discerns – and that this quality turns out to be a particular complex structural surface reflectance property – it will not follow that redness *would* have been a different property if the human sensory apparatus had been different. For the referent of "quality of red" may be fixed rigidly by the actual present human sensory apparatus – that is, in such a way that redness is that quality that produces the impression of red through the actual human sensory apparatus under standard circumstances in the actual world now, not whatever *would* produce the impression of red in another apparatus or under other circumstances. The quality of redness *itself* need not vary with the nature of the mind, even if a change in the nature of the human mind would lead to something other than *redness* playing the role (including producing the qualitatively distinctive "impression of red") that redness plays for us. Similarly, the referent of "causal relation" may be fixed rigidly by the causal sense – so that the causal relation is, in each possible world, that relation that actually produces the association, the inference, and the impression of necessary connection in normal human beings in the *actual* world, not whatever relation *would* produce it in that other possible world. So understood, the relation of causation itself need not vary with the nature of the mind, even if a change in the nature of the human mind would lead to a relation other than causation playing part of the role (including the production of the association, the inference, and an impression of necessary connection) that the relation of causation plays for humans in the actual world.

Alternatively, it may be proposed that causal relations must be mind-dependent, on Hume's account, because the causal pairs constituting the revival set of the abstract idea of causation will have no distinctive resemblance to one another *except* their tendency to produce the association, the inference, and the impression of necessary connection. However, the fifth of his "rules by which to judge of causes and effects" states that

> where several different objects produce the same effect, it must be by means of some quality, which we discover to be common amongst them. For as like effects imply like causes, we must always ascribe the causation to the circumstance, wherein we discover the resemblance. (T 1.3.15.7, SBN 174)

For Hume, at least, the ability of all causal pairs to produce the same effect on the mind indicates that there *is* some mind-independent respect – presumably, the causal relation itself – in which all such pairs do resemble one another.

Projection and Explanatory Role

Blackburn has recently proposed that projectivists can eschew what he calls "[t]heoretical or ontological ... [or] upper-case Realism" about a kind of entity by rejecting the claim that "we cannot understand what is going on [in discourse about the entity] except in terms of our responding to a world whose entities and properties and relations are the ones ostensibly referred to" in the discourse (2000: 110). However, it is at least debatable whether any full-fledged *explanation* of causal discourse could avoid making reference to causal relations as part of the explanation – by invoking, for example, our *responding* to exposure to constant conjunction and the role of such reactions in *producing* discourse. Without such references, it might be argued, one would have at most a narrative about, rather than an explanation of, causal discourse.

Thus, it may be granted that Hume's account of the operation of the causal sense involves the projection onto cause and effect pairs of an element of "necessity" that does not resemble anything in those pairs and which derives its origin instead from the constant conjunction of types of objects. It does not follow from this, however, that Hume cannot regard causal judgments as true and determinate, and causal relations themselves as mind-independent. He may even regard reference to causal relations as essential to any explanation of our discourse about them. He need not, therefore, regard ascriptions of causal relations as *mere* projections rather than true descriptions of reality.

4. CAUSAL REDUCTIONISM

Hume follows his account of the impression of necessary connection by declaring that he will "collect all the different parts of this reasoning, and by joining them together form an exact definition of the relation of cause and effect, which makes the subject of the present enquiry" (T 1.3.14.30, SBN 169). He proceeds, as we have seen, to define *cause* in terms of constant conjunction – that is, as "[a]n object precedent and contiguous to another, and where all the objects resembling the former are plac'd in like relations of precedency and contiguity to those objects, that resemble the latter" (T 1.3.14.31, SBN 170). He then cites this definition in seeking to justify a variety of further claims, including four "corollaries" concerning the causal relation (T 1.3.14.32–36, SBN 170–72) and his doctrine that human actions exhibit causal necessity (T 2.3.1). Thus, it seems that Hume offers a semantic analysis of the term *cause* in order to show that there is nothing more to causation than constant conjunction.

Reduction and Semantic Analysis

There are, however, several reasons to think that Hume's definition is *not* intended to provide a semantic analysis of the term *cause* – at least if this is understood to mean a synonymous term, one that can be substituted for it without change of meaning. First, as we have already seen, he offers not just one but two "definitions" of *cause*, the second of which defines the term quite differently, as "an object precedent and contiguous to another, and so united with it, that the idea of the one determines the mind to form the idea of the other, and the impression of the one to form a more lively idea of the other" (T 1.3.14.31, SBN 170). These two definitions are obviously not synonymous with each other, and hence at most one of them could be intended to be synonymous with *cause*. Yet he treats the two definitions entirely on a par, citing both together – for example, in his defense of his four "corollaries" and that of his doctrine of the necessity of human actions. It seems evident, then, that he must intend neither of them to be synonymous with *cause*.[10] Indeed, he rejects several other proposed definitions of "necessary connexion" precisely on the grounds that they *are* synonymous with their proposed definienda (T 1.3.2.10, SBN 77).

Second, Hume's account of the "rules by which to judge of causes and effects" is incompatible with regarding the first definition as a synonym for *cause*. His first three rules are:

1. The cause and effect must be contiguous in space and time.
2. The cause must be prior to the effect.
3. There must be a constant union betwixt the cause and effect.

(T 1.3.15.3–5, SBN 173)

As already noted, Hume characterizes all eight of the rules as "form'd on the nature of our understanding, and on our experience of its operations in the judgments we form concerning objects" (T 1.3.13.11, SBN 149). In addition, he gives an argument from the nature of time for the second rule (T 1.3.2.7, SBN 75–76), and he relaxes the first rule's requirement of spatial contiguity when dealing with unlocated entities (referring forward to T 1.4.5: T 1.3.2.6, SBN 75). Yet these first three "rules" constitute the primary elements in the first definition of *cause*. Accordingly, if that definition were intended to be synonymous with *cause*, these three rules would be trivial analytic truths for Hume and could not be discoveries grounded on experience – let alone properly subject to either further argumentation or later relaxation.

Third, the first definition is much too schematic to specify effectively the set of cause-and-effect pairs – at least for someone lacking the guidance of a causal sense. For a causal sense is required to discern what *kinds* of resemblance among objects are most significant – and what kinds of difference are insignificant – for determining that an object "of one kind" has been regularly followed by an object of "another kind." In fact, the *second* definition is *also* fundamentally unusable in the absence of a causal sense, for the question of whether an idea or an impression "determines" the mind to form another idea is itself a causal question, answerable ultimately only with a causal sense. Of course, in ordinary causal judgment, Hume surely thinks, one employs *neither* definition but simply utilizes (and corrects as appropriate) one's own causal sense.

If the two definitions are not intended to be synonymous with *cause*, then what is their purpose? Hume aims to explain the meaning of the term *cause* by indicating the set of ideas that constitute the revival set of the abstract idea of cause and effect. Both definitions serve this purpose – one by indicating the initial feature of cause-and-effect pairs that leads them to produce the impression of necessary connection and be discriminated by the causal sense, and the other by indicating the associative-plus-inferential effects on the mind of cause-and-effect pairs that lead to the same result. The term *cause* and its two definitions, taken together, indicate this revival set in three semantically distinct ways; hence, their coextensivity is an a posteriori truth, potentially requiring considerable investigation on Hume's part – or ours – to discover. This three-way coextensivity is not only an a posteriori truth but also presumably a *necessary* one (that is, a truth in every possible world) – just as the coextensivity of "red" with a particular description of a complex structural surface reflectance property (or, analogously, "virtue" with a particular description of features of character) might well be both a posteriori and necessary.

Reduction and the Nature of Causation

Because Hume's first definition is not intended as a synonym for *cause*, there is no reason to think that he regards causation as "nothing but" constant conjunction. On the contrary, because his two definitions already specify *two* different features that all cause-and-effect pairs have in common, he has no reason to deny that there may also be *other* features that all cause-and-effect pairs have in common as well. Such further additional commonalities, too, might have something to do with the way in which cause-and-effect pairs are picked out by the causal sense.

Thus, it may be granted that Hume's first definition of *cause* is intended to establish that constant conjunction, of the sort discriminated by the causal sense, is necessary and sufficient for causation; this conclusion is required for the applications he makes of the definition in his four "corollaries" and the argument for the causal necessity of human actions. His definition establishes this conclusion not through semantic analysis, however, but through an investigation of the basis of the discriminations made by the causal sense, analogous to an investigation of the underlying basis in bodies of the perception of redness. It constitutes a "reduction" of causation to constant conjunction only in the sense in which one might aim to "reduce" redness to a structural surface reflectance property of red bodies. It does not positively exclude the possibility that cause-and-effect pairs will have other important and relevant commonalities as well, and hence it does not entail that there is "nothing more" to causation that just constant conjunction.

5. CAUSAL REALISM

Does Hume hold that causal relations positively *do* consist of more than a particular kind of constant conjunction that gives rise to the association, the inference, and an internal impression of determination, an impression that is then mislocated in the objects themselves? His apparent references to "powers" by which objects "produce" one another, to "ultimate" and "operating principles," and to an impenetrable "reason of the conjunction" of causes and effects seem to imply that he does – even if he also thinks that the nature of the "something more" is unknown and incomprehensible.

Realism and "Power"

Hume can allow attributions of "powers" to objects without implying that causation is more than constant conjunction, for he takes the term power to signify "that very circumstance in the cause, by which it is enabled to produce the effect" (EHU 7.17, SBN 67–68; cf. T 1.3.14.13, SBN 161). He frequently writes of natural philosophy as discovering the powers of bodies, and of his own "science of man" as discovering powers of the mind. This usage is appropriate, on his view, because the discovery of the precise cause of some effect by means of the causal sense is, for him, ipso facto the discovery of the power that produced it. If, for example, the motion of one billiard ball is the cause of the motion of another, then the motion of the first is itself the "circumstance in the cause, by which it is enabled to produce the effect."[11] Similarly, the discovery of the effects that a given object or state produces is a discovery of the "powers" of that object or state to produce those effects. Many "powers" of things, in this sense, may be hidden from us in the unobserved microscopic or insensible structure of things in a way that does not require causation to be more than constant conjunction.[12]

However, because the mind tends to project the impression of necessary connection onto the objects themselves, it is natural to suppose that the idea of necessary connection represents a further feature intrinsic to the precise or particular cause itself that makes necessary its connection with its effect – that is, makes the separation of the effect from it unthinkable – and therefore constitutes the perception of an inner "power," "energy," or "efficacy" inherent in the particular cause itself.[13] Accordingly, Hume holds, the term power is often used with the intention of designating some intrinsic feature of the particular cause itself in which such a necessity of its being followed by its effect consists. Yet, because such a further feature is never observed at all, it cannot be observed to be constantly conjoined with causes and so cannot be inferred to exist by means of ordinary probable inference. Nor can we infer that such a feature must exist on the grounds that the regularity of nature would otherwise be improbable,[14] because for Hume the probability that nature will be regular is simply a direct function of the extent to which it has been regular in the past. Even more fundamentally, however, because "the necessity of causes" is in fact a psychological inseparability derived from constant conjunction via habitual association, it seems that no intrinsic causal necessity can be successfully conceived: the conditions that the necessity be both intrinsic and causal appear to be incompatible, so that they cannot be conceived to be jointly satisfied. Thus, he writes:

upon the whole we may infer, that when we talk of any being, whether of a superior or inferior nature, as endow'd with a power or force, proportion'd to any effect; when we speak of a necessary connexion betwixt objects, and suppose, that this connexion depends upon an efficacy or energy, with which any of these objects are endow'd; in all these expressions, so apply'd, we have really no distinct meaning, and make use only of common words, without any clear and determinate ideas. But as 'tis more probable, that these expressions do here lose their true meaning by being *wrong apply'd*, than that they never have any meaning; 'twill be proper to bestow another consideration on this subject, to see if possibly we can discover the nature and origin of those ideas, we annex to them. (T 1.3.14.14, SBN 162)

Particular allusions on Hume's part to secret or unknown powers may thus use the term *power* in either of these two ways – that is, as alluding simply to unobserved elements of constant conjunctions or as alluding to something that is both intrinsic to causes and yet causally necessitating – or may be intentionally ambiguous between the two. But even allusions to unknown "powers" and "principles" that were unambiguously intended in the second way would not entail that Hume acknowledges that something does or can meet both of the conditions. For just as Berkeley in the *Three Dialogues* first denies that we can *know* of qualities that both exist and are outside the mind and only later denies that any qualities *can* meet both of those conditions, so Hume may deny that we know of powers that are both intrinsic to causes and causally necessitating while also denying that anything can meet both of those conditions. Thus, in *An Enquiry concerning Human Understanding*, Hume alludes several times in his discussion of causal inference to our "ignorance" of the power located in causes themselves – an "ignorance" that is shown, he argues, by our inability to predict effects from causes prior to the experience of constant conjunction. But, as Winkler (2000b) emphasizes, these seeming references to "unknown powers" in the *Enquiry* occur prior to his explanation of the impression of necessary connection and its projective mislocation; and it is noteworthy that Hume remarks in a footnote to a typical such reference that "[t]he word, *power*, is here used in a loose and popular sense. The more accurate explication of it would give additional evidence to this argument. See Section 7 [i.e., "Of the Idea of Necessary Connexion"]" (EHU 4.16n7, SBN 33n). The "accurate explication" of "power," then, gives even greater force to the argument that we do not make causal inferences through knowledge of powers located in causes themselves by showing that such powers are not merely unknown but not fully conceivable.

Realism and "Ultimate Principles"

Like the term *power*, the term *ultimate principle* may be taken in more than one way for Hume. In the first, an "ultimate principle" is the topic of one of the final causal generalizations that can be reached in a true unified theory of nature – "ultimate" because it serves to explain more specific causal regularities by subsuming them as special cases though not itself being subsumable by any yet-more-inclusive generalization. Thus, he writes of "[e]lasticity, gravity, cohesion of parts, communication of motion by impulse" that "these are probably the ultimate causes and principles which we shall ever discover in nature" (EHU 4.12, SBN 30). Because of the projective mislocation of the impression of necessary connection, however, it is natural, he thinks, to suppose erroneously that we can discover "ultimate principles" involving a *necessity* of such generalizations' being true lying in the nature of the causes and effects themselves. Such "ultimate principles," one may then suppose, would help to explain regularities in nature by showing their intrinsic necessity. However, such supposed principles are just as inconceivable as powers located in objects:

> We wou'd not willingly stop before we are acquainted with that energy in the cause, by which it operates on its effect; that tie, which connects them together; and that efficacious quality on which the tie depends. This is our aim in all our studies and reflections: And how must we be disappointed, when we learn, that this connexion, tie, or energy lies merely in ourselves, and is nothing but that determination of the mind, which is acquir'd by custom, and causes us to make a transition from an object to its usual attendant, and from the impression of one to the lively idea of the other? Such a discovery not only cuts off all hope of ever attaining satisfaction, but even prevents our very wishes; since it appears, that when we say we desire to know the ultimate and operating principle, as something, which resides in the external object, we either contradict ourselves, or talk without a meaning. (T 1.4.7.5, SBN 266–67)

Hume's claims that we cannot "penetrate" to ultimate principles parallel his claims in *An Enquiry concerning Human Understanding* about our ignorance of powers in bodies; and for the same reason, they do not commit Hume to the view that there are such principles. His claim that we cannot know of things meeting the characterization at issue are compatible with his later and stronger claims that we cannot fully conceive of such things. Indeed, his practice with respect to "powers" and "ultimate principles" may be compared not only with Philonous's discussion of unperceived existence in the *Three Dialogues* but also with Cleanthes's discussion of "necessary existence" in Hume's own *Dialogues concerning Natural Religion*:

> It is pretended that the Deity is a necessarily existent Being; and this necessity of his existence is attempted to be explained by asserting, that, if we knew his whole essence or nature, we should perceive it to be as impossible for him not to exist as for twice two not to be four. But it is evident, that this can never happen, while our faculties remain the same as at present. It will still be possible for us, at any time, to conceive the non-existence of what we formerly conceived to exist; nor can the mind ever lie under a necessity of supposing any object to remain always in being; in the same manner as we lie under a necessity of always conceiving twice two to be four. The words, therefore, *necessary existence*, have no meaning; or, which is the same thing, none that is consistent.

But farther; why may not the material universe be the necessarily existent Being, according to this pretended explication of necessity? We dare not affirm that we know all the qualities of matter; and for aught we can determine, it may contain some qualities, which, were they known, would make its non-existence appear as great a contradiction as that twice two is five.... It must be some unknown, inconceivable qualities, which can make [God's] non-existence appear impossible, or his attributes unalterable: And no reason can be assigned, why these qualities may not belong to matter. As they are altogether unknown and inconceivable, they can never be proved incompatible with it. (DNR 9, 189–90)

Cleanthes's reference to our ignorance of any necessary existence on the part of the material universe in the second paragraph does not commit him to the claim that there actually is a quality of necessary existence, a claim that he has already rejected as either meaningless or inconsistent in the first paragraph.

Realism and Relative Ideas

Hume does not deny that objects may have unknown qualities that are unobserved and inconceivable by us, but he does question whether we have any basis for calling any of them "powers":

If we have really no idea of a power or efficacy in any object, or of any real connexion betwixt causes and effects, 'twill be to little purpose to prove, that an efficacy is necessary in all operations. We do not understand our own meaning in talking so, but ignorantly confound ideas, which are entirely distinct from each other. I am, indeed, ready to allow, that there may be several qualities both in material and immaterial objects, with which we are utterly unacquainted; and if we please to call these *power* or *efficacy*, 'twill be of little consequence to the world. But when, instead of meaning these unknown qualities, we make the terms of power and efficacy signify something, of which we have a clear idea, and which is incompatible with those objects, to which we apply it, obscurity and error begin then to take place, and we are led astray by a false philosophy. This is the case, when we transfer the determination of the thought to external objects, and suppose any real intelligible connexion betwixt them; that being a quality, which can only belong to the mind that considers them. (T 1.3.14.27, SBN 168)

Like Locke, Hume recognizes the existence of "relative ideas," which allow the mind to conceive of something simply as whatever it is that stands in a particular relation to something else. In order to have a relative idea of something, however – for Hume as for Locke – it is necessary to have an idea of one of the relata *and* an abstract idea of the relation. Thus, any attempt to regard an "unknown quality" as the intrinsic necessitating power of a cause faces a dilemma. If we merely conceive the unknown quality as *accompanying* the cause, we have not yet conceived it as an intrinsic necessitating power, but merely as another quality that is constantly conjoined with the cause and effect. If, on the other hand, we try to conceive of it as *causally necessitating* the effect, it appears that we can conceive of this necessitation only as an associative psychological connection grounded in constant conjunction – for that is what causal necessitation has proven to be – and hence not as a necessity *intrinsic* to the individual causes and effects themselves.

Yet this dilemma is not the end of the matter. To conceive of powers or ultimate principles in causes themselves would require the conception of a kind of necessity other than the causal necessity that lies in an associative psychological determination resulting from habit. It would also require the conception either of a kind of necessity entirely other than that which characterizes self-evident or demonstrable relations of ideas such as "twice two is four" or else of a very different kind of extension of it to an unknown kind of "idea." For although it might be proposed that *truly adequate* ideas of causes and effects would show the occurrence of each effect to be a self-evident or demonstrable matter of relations of ideas given only the occurrence of its cause, this proposal would require that our present ideas of things be erroneous even in representing causes and effects as *distinct* in Hume's sense of that term, which requires that distinct things be conceivable as existing without one another. That is, it would require that something like what Hume calls Spinoza's "hideous hypothesis" of "the simplicity [i.e., lack of distinct parts] of the universe" (T 1.4.5.18–19, SBN 240–41) – a doctrine to which Hume shows no evident attraction. The two kinds of necessity, causal and demonstrative, exhaust the relations of necessity that we can positively conceive; and we cannot therefore form a suitable relative idea of "power" simply by using an idea of the known relation of causal necessity or an idea of the relation of demonstrative necessity as applied to a known kind of idea. Nevertheless, we may seek to use the idea of a different relation – namely, the relation of resemblance – to form a *relative idea of the needed relation itself*. For it seems impossible to rule out positively the following hypothesis: that *if* we had experience of qualities of objects beyond those available to us now, we would *then* discern something characterizing cause-and-effect pairs themselves that we would find to *resemble* the two known kinds of necessity in some way that concerned (something resembling) the determination-of-thought or the inability-to-conceive-otherwise. Such a relation might even be assimilated to demonstrative necessity, if we form a relative idea of something resembling yet fundamentally different from our present human ideas to stand in such a relation. Indeed, Hume's qualifying phrase "while our faculties remain the same as at present" in the midst of Cleanthes's discussion of the meaninglessness of "necessary existence" may be understood as alluding to just such a hypothesis. By means of this hypothesis, then, one might form a *doubly-relative* idea – namely, the idea of a quality in or relation between objects such that, were we to acquire acquaintance with it through a radical alteration in our faculties, we would then find it somehow to *resemble* the kinds of necessity with which we are now familiar in such a way that we would see it as constituting a new and now-positively-unconceived kind of necessity, or a new and positively unconceived application of demonstrative necessity, between causes and effects.

Hume can allow that there may be *something* more to a causal relation than constant conjunction giving rise to association-plus-inference and a projected feeling of determination. Nor need he rule out the possibility of a quality or relation in causally related pairs that would resemble known kinds of necessity enough that, if we could discern it, we could regard it as some *third* kind of "necessity," one inherent in causes and effects themselves. Hume nowhere endorses a belief in such a species of necessity. Still, he might well allow that such a belief would be psychologically attractive to someone convinced by his argument about the projective mislocation of the impression of necessary connection and yet still attracted – by the residual force of that projection – to the doctrine that causes and effects have *some* kind of intrinsic necessity. Indeed, his many references (particularly in the first *Enquiry*) to our "ignorance" of secret powers and ultimate principles may well be intended, at least in part, to accommodate such a belief as compatible with his main arguments. He would certainly deny, however, that awareness or even postulation of such a species of necessity is required for the discovery of causal relations. Such discovery requires only a causal sense.

6. CONCLUSION

What then, according to Hume, is the causal relation? It is, as he promised at the outset of his explanation, the relation that is "discovered" by the process of causal inference whereby objects of types that are constantly conjoined produce association, inference, and an impression of determination or necessary connection. This process serves as the basis of a "causal sense." It is by means of this sense and the judgments based upon it that we discriminate cause-and-effect pairs from other pairs, in something like the way in which Hume's visual sense discriminates colors, his moral sense discriminates vice and virtue, and his aesthetic sense discriminates beauty and deformity.

In the course of explaining this causal sense and the causal judgments to which it gives rise, Hume asserts that it involves the projection onto cause-and-effect pairs of an element of felt necessity that does not resemble anything in those pairs, deriving its origin instead entirely from the experienced constant conjunction of types of objects. Yet at the same time, he regards many causal judgments as true and can regard all of them as determinately true or false; in addition, he can regard causal relations themselves as mind-independent and even as explanatorily basic. He grants that constant conjunction of the kind ideally detected by the causal sense is both necessary and sufficient for causation. Yet he denies that ascriptions of causation are synonymous with ascriptions of constant conjunction, and he does not assert that there is nothing more to causation than constant conjunction. He rejects the possibility of straightforwardly conceiving – and hence, too, of straightforwardly believing – that there are inherent necessitating powers or ultimate necessitating principles in causes and effects themselves. However, he does not positively rule out the possibility that some by-us-inconceivable analogues of such powers or principles may characterize causes and effects. His causal-sense theory allows him to do all of these things with complete consistency.

In light of these results, should we classify Hume's theory of causation as projectivism, reductionism, or realism? If my interpretation of Hume is right, then he concedes something to the motivations of each of these, and he could with some justice be classified as holding any of them – or all of them, or none of them – depending on the details of the more specific definitions that might be proposed for them. This result is, I think, all to the good: any plausible theory of causation *should* concede something to each of these approaches – as, perhaps, should any theory of the objects of at least some of the other Humean senses.

Hume's theory of causation is of historical interest not only because it has been an influential theory of causation but also because it sheds light on the many other aspects of Hume's philosophy to which it is related. Similarly, Hume's theory of causation is of philosophical interest not only because it is a deep and original theory of causation that offers to reconcile the insights of causal projectivism, causal reductionism, and causal realism, but also because it offers the prospect of illuminating the dialectic among projectivism, reductionism, and realism on other topics as well.

NOTES

This essay incorporates material from Garrett 2009 by permission of Oxford University Press.

1. Much of the recent debate about Hume's theory of causation has been provoked by striking readings of Hume as a causal realist – readings that exemplify what is now (following Winkler 2000b) commonly known as the "New Hume" interpretation. For a summary description of the debate and a collection of important contributions to it, see Read and Richman 2000.

2. Stroud (1977 and 1993) suggests an error theory version of projectivism. Blackburn (2000), Beebee (2006), and Coventry (2006) defend a sophisticated

projectivist interpretation. Examples of reductionist interpretations – setting out what is often called simply the "Humean view" of causation – include Robinson 1962; Ayer 1973; Woolhouse 1988; and Clatterbaugh 1999. See also Millican 2009. Recent realist interpretations include Broughton 1987; Wright 1983 and 2000; and Craig 1987 (but see Craig 2000), as well as Strawson 1989 and 2000. See also Costa 1989; Buckle 2001; and Kail 2001 and 2003.

3. For a fuller account of this argument, see Garrett 1997: ch. 4 and refinements in Garrett 1998 and 2001.

4. The term *relation*, Hume claims, may be understood in either of two senses. The first, "natural" sense is restricted to "that quality, by which two ideas are connected together in the imagination, and the one naturally introduces the other"; this sense includes the three associative relations of resemblance, contiguity, and causation. The second, "philosophical" sense encompasses more broadly any "particular circumstance, in which, even upon the arbitrary union of two ideas in the fancy, we may think proper to compare them"; and there are seven different species of such relations, including relations of resemblance, space and time, and causation, but also identity, contrariety, degrees in quality, and proportions in quantity or number (T 1.1.5.1–2, SBN 13–14).

5. These rules include the following such principles: "[t]he cause and effect must be contiguous in space and time"; "[t]he same cause always produces the same effect, and the same effect never arises but from the same cause"; and "where several different objects produce the same effect, it must be by means of some quality, which we discover to be common amongst them" (T 1.3.15.2–10, SBN 173–74).

6. As Hume explains in *Treatise* 1.4.2, the "vulgar" typically attribute a "continu'd and distinct existence" to impressions of sensations themselves, not distinguishing them from objects; in contrast, the more "philosophical" regard their impressions of sensation as caused by resembling qualities of objects.

7. Hume discusses the representation of large numbers in T 1.1.7.12 (SBN 23).

8. See, e.g., "A Dialogue," appended to EPM, and the essay "Of the Standard of Taste."

9. See, e.g., EPM App. 4, "Of Some Verbal Disputes."

10. Commentators have generally judged that the two definitions are not even coextensive. However, I have argued (Garrett 1997: ch. 5) that the two definitions of *cause* are each systematically ambiguous between a "subject-relative" reading and an "absolute" reading. On the subject-relative reading, the first definition concerns what has been observed to be constantly conjoined in a given subject's experience, whereas the second definition concerns the subjects of association and inference in that subject's mind. On the absolute reading, the first definition concerns what has been, is, and will be constantly conjoined through all time, whereas the second definition concerns the subject of association and inference in the mind of an idealized subject. So understood, the definitions are coextensive on their subject-relative readings and are again coextensive on their absolute readings; whereas the first reading specifies what a subject will include in his or her own revival set for the abstract idea of cause (and hence reflects what he or she takes to be causally related), the second

reading specifies what a fully corrected revival set would include (and hence what is in fact causally related).

11. Because his definitions of *cause* entail that a cause is always followed by its effect, one of the corollaries that he draws from them is that "[t]he distinction, which we often make betwixt *power* and the *exercise* of it, is ... without foundation" (T 1.3.14.34, SBN 171). Nonetheless, he later allows, in treating of the passions, a less "philosophical" conception of power, in which a part of a complete cause may also be considered a "power" when it seems possible or probable that the effect will occur – especially if volition is thought to be the needed completion of the cause (T 2.1.10.4–12, SBN 311–16).

12. This point is made in Winkler 2000b.

13. Presumably, when the same impression is spread onto the cause and effect together, rather than specifically onto the cause, it is taken to be an impression of a necessary connection or tie *between* the cause and effect, rather than a power *in* the cause alone.

14. This line of argument is suggested in Strawson 1989.

5   Scepticism with Regard to Reason

Until recently, philosophical scholarship has not been kind to Hume's arguments in "Of scepticism with regard to reason" (*A Treatise of Human Nature* 1.4.1).[1] Thomas Reid gives the negative arguments a pretty rough ride, though in the end he agrees with Hume's conclusion that reason cannot be defended by reason.[2] D. C. Stove's comment that the argument is "not merely defective, but one of the worst arguments ever to impose itself on a man of genius" (1973: 131–32), while extreme, is not atypical. Many important books on Hume (e.g., Stroud 1977) simply ignore it, though this may be because it is difficult to find any trace of the arguments in *An Enquiry concerning Human Understanding*.[3] Furthermore, when attention is paid to the arguments, it is devoted mainly to the second of the two negative arguments Hume puts forward, and that argument is held to contain an elementary mistake concerning beliefs about beliefs (MacNabb 1951).

Robert Fogelin's important work on Hume's scepticism shows the role that "Of scepticism with regard to reason" must play in any assessment of Hume's scepticism, but he is hardly friendly to the arguments of T 1.4.1 themselves.[4] A more sympathetic account of Hume's argument is presented in William Edward Morris's important 1989 article. Morris argues that the issue concerns the level of confidence we have in our beliefs and, furthermore, that the negative arguments are directed not at reason in general, but at a certain "formalist" conception of reason, a conception that Hume replaces with his own. Annette Baier (1991) follows Morris concerning this latter point. While agreeing with Morris's sympathetic rendering of the arguments, in Owen 1994 I argue that its target is not limited, but quite general. Fogelin (1993, following his 1985 and 1983) also argues that Hume's target is relatively general and concludes that Hume never entirely rejects the sceptical consequences of the negative arguments.

Although the sceptical arguments are generally held to show that beliefs based on reason are unjustified, Don Garrett (1997) and I (Owen 1999) argue that the negative arguments are not meant to show that such beliefs are in danger of being unjustified, but rather that they are in danger of ceasing to remain beliefs at all. One of our arguments hinges on treating Hume's use of "evidence" to mean not epistemological evidence, but "evidentness." This interpretation is challenged by Kevin Meeker (2000).

In section 1, I briefly outline the arguments of T 1.4.1, consider their origins, and investigate whether and to what extent they survive in Hume's later works. In section 2, I outline and assess some severe difficulties that Hume's arguments appear to face. In dealing with these difficulties, it emerges that Hume is more concerned with the retention of beliefs in the face of sceptical arguments than with their justification. In section 3, I argue that Hume attaches great importance to the arguments of T 1.4.1. I further argue that assessing Hume's negative arguments in this Section should be done in the context of his positive arguments. Because these arguments explain how we manage to retain beliefs in the face of sceptical arguments, it seems charitable to interpret his negative arguments as attempts to show that our beliefs based on reason threaten to cease to be beliefs at all. This position is discussed in the context of Hume's account of belief or assent as the more forceful and vivacious conception of an idea. In general, I argue that the negative sceptical arguments are to be interpreted not as showing that our beliefs lack justification, but instead as showing that the faculty of reason, considered as functioning alone, undermines itself. But I also argue that this is not a "merely psychological," nonsceptical thesis. It has significant epistemological import: reason cannot be defended just by reason. The workings of reason can be understood only by appeal to apparently trivial properties of the imagination.

I. THE ARGUMENTS

Outline of the Negative Arguments

Hume describes the result of the first negative argument in T 1.4.1 as "all knowledge degenerates into probability" (T 1.4.1.1, SBN 180) or "all knowledge resolves itself into probability" (T 1.4.1.4, SBN 181). The point is one about certainty and fallibility: although knowledge due to demonstration is certain, Hume's first argument purports to show that, as we are prone to error, we must make a probability judgment about whether we have performed any given demonstration correctly. Consider the very first sentence of this Section: "In all demonstrative sciences the rules are certain and infallible; but when we apply them, our fallible and uncertain faculties are very apt to depart from them, and fall into error" (T 1.4.1.1, SBN 180). Even if the rules of demonstration are "certain and infallible," we cannot be sure that the faculty of reason has functioned properly in any particular instance of demonstration. Reason is "a kind of cause, of which truth is the natural effect" (ibid.). But this effect is sometimes prevented from occurring "by the irruption of other causes, and by the inconstancy of our mental powers" (ibid.). Demonstration produces a claim to knowledge, something that we take to be true with full conviction. But consideration of our fallible natures produces "a new judgment, as a check or controul on our first judgment" (ibid.). This new judgment is only probable. Hume argues that it is this probable judgment that we rely on, not the original knowledge claim produced by the demonstration. The claim is a statement of fact, not a recommendation. Otherwise, he argues, why would a mathematician "[run] over his proofs" and seek "the approbation of his friends" (T 1.4.1.2, SBN 180)? Why else would a merchant not only seek an "accomptant" but also require the accomptant to keep records – that is, to create an "artificial structure of the accompts" (T 1.4.1.3, SBN 181)? The point is that our fallible faculties require a check to see that they are functioning properly. If they are not functioning properly, they will not produce truths. Such a check results in a belief that supplants the original knowledge claim, and hence the conviction is lowered from the certainty of demonstration to the lesser assent of high probability. It is rather like using an electronic calculator to perform a feat of long division: we believe the result because we believe that the engineers and production lines have designed and produced an accurate calculator. This is belief, not knowledge.

Hume goes on to argue that similar considerations concerning our fallibility apply to any probability judgment, including the probability judgment we may make about the result of a piece of demonstrative reasoning. "In every judgment, which we can form concerning probability, as well as concerning knowledge, we ought always to correct the first judgment, deriv'd from the nature of the object, by another judgment, deriv'd from the nature of the understanding" (T 1.4.1.5, SBN 181–82). The point is not just that every probability judgment is less than completely certain (doubt "deriv'd from the nature of the object"), but that further uncertainty concerning that probability judgment is increased by reflection on our fallibility (doubt "deriv'd from the nature of the understanding"). This new judgment is itself susceptible to reflection, and "we are oblig'd by our reason to add a new doubt deriv'd from the possibility of error in the estimation we make of the truth and fidelity of our faculties" (T 1.4.1.6, SBN 182). But this judgment, even if it

be favourable to our preceding judgment, being founded only on probability, must weaken still farther our first evidence, and must itself be weaken'd by a fourth doubt of the same kind, and so on in infinitum; till at last there remain nothing of the original probability, however great we may suppose it to have been, and however small the diminution by every new uncertainty.... Let our first belief be never so strong, it must infallibly perish by passing thro' so many new examinations, of which each diminishes somewhat of its force and vigour. (T 1.4.1.6, SBN 182–83)

Outline of the Positive Argument

The goal of both negative arguments is the reduction of the confidence or assurance we place in knowledge or belief claims.[5] If one accepted the results of these arguments, one would "be really one of those sceptics, who hold that all is uncertain, and that our judgment is not in *any* thing possest of *any* measures of truth and falshood" (T 1.4.1.7, SBN 183).[6] Hume's reaction to these arguments is neither to accept their results nor to find any fault in the arguments themselves. Both points are made in the following passage:

But as experience will sufficiently convince any one, who thinks it worth while to try, that tho' he can find no error in the foregoing arguments, yet he still continues to believe, and think, and reason as usual ... (T 1.4.1.8, SBN 184)

It is of course a question of some importance why and how we continue to reason, and believe on the basis of reason, in spite of these arguments. Hume gives an outline of his explanation in the remainder of the very same sentence:

he may safely conclude, that his reasoning and belief is some sensation or peculiar manner of conception, which 'tis impossible for mere ideas and reflections to destroy. (ibid.)

Hume is saying that some feature of his account of reasoning and belief explains how we manage to continue to put our faith in reason, despite these good, sceptical arguments. More strongly, Hume says that the whole point of his putting forward the sceptical arguments was to emphasize this feature of his account of reasoning and belief:

My intention then in displaying so carefully the arguments of that fantastic sect, is only to make the reader sensible of the truth of my hypothesis, *that all our reasonings concerning causes and effects are deriv'd from nothing but custom; and that belief is more properly an act of the sensitive, than of the cogitative part of our natures.* (T 1.4.1.8, SBN 183)

Hume's response to the negative arguments is not to find some flaw in the arguments, but rather to accept the arguments and nonetheless explain why we continue to reason and believe. Furthermore, he claims that his motivation for putting forward these arguments was to show that his own account of reason and belief was uniquely able to deal with them. These are complex matters, to which we will return in section 3.

Antecedents of the Negative Arguments

Whether and to what extent Hume's negative arguments have antecedents is a question of some interest, and not much discussed.[7] Hume's
reference to the sceptics is clearly a reference to the sceptical tradition of
ancient times, rediscovered in the sixteenth and seventeenth centuries
and transformed beyond all recognition by Descartes.[8] I know of no clear,
unequivocal antecedents to either of Hume's negative arguments, but
there are some suggestive similarities. In *Principles* I.5 ([1644] 1985
1:194), Descartes says, "Our doubt will also apply to other matters
which we previously regarded as most certain – even the demonstrations
of mathematics.... One reason for this is that we have sometimes seen
people make mistakes in such matters and accept as most certain ...
things which seemed false to us."[9] The argument is similar to Hume's
first negative argument: because we are fallible and make mistakes, we
cannot accept as certain even the results of demonstrations. An awareness of the unreliability of the faculty of reason causes us to treat the
conclusions of reason with less than full certainty.

It might seem that Hume's argument is different from Descartes's in
the following way. Descartes thought that error in others, and in our past
selves, gave us reason to wonder whether we might be making a mistake
in demonstrative reasoning, or whether a certain demonstrative
argument, or all of them, might be unsound. But it looks as if Hume is
arguing, concerning a demonstrative argument, not just that it might be
unsound, but that it actually turns into a probable argument. Fogelin
(1993) argues that this is a consequence of Hume's claim that "knowledge
degenerates into probability." Against Hume, Fogelin argues that "the
fact that there may be some chance that a demonstrative argument is
invalid does not change it into a different kind of argument" (1993: 103).[10]
But I think Hume need not disagree with this. His claim that "knowledge
degenerates into probability" must mean, as I argue below in section 2,
something like "knowledge claims become embedded in belief claims."
The result of the first part of the sceptical argument is to turn the claim "I
know that *p*" into the claim "I believe that I know that *p*." And like all
beliefs, such a belief is characterized by force and vivacity, which can
vary. The process of demonstration yields knowledge and certainty.
Hume's first argument purports to show that, as we are prone to error,
we must make a probability judgment about whether we have performed
the demonstration correctly; this doesn't change the demonstration,
though it does change the confidence with which we treat its result.

Indirect evidence for this analogy between Descartes's argument and
Hume's comes from the fact that at least two commentators suggest
that Hume's negative arguments in T 1.4.1 partially survive in Part 1,

Section 10 of the first *Enquiry*, which is explicitly about Descartes. Furthermore, reflection on the analogy with Descartes helps us counter a difficulty for Hume put forward by Thomas Reid. Philosophers, Reid plausibly reminds us, oppose probability to demonstration. But Hume, Reid accuses, must oppose probability to infallibility, because the only reason he gives for knowledge degenerating into probability is that we are not infallible (VII.4 [1785] 2002: 564). I think Reid's point rests on what I alleged to be a mistake in the previous paragraph. Hume doesn't turn demonstrations into probable arguments; he lowers the degree of certainty with which we treat the conclusion of demonstrations. But why should the mere fact of fallibility lead to that result? The answer is easy on the Cartesian picture: fallibility leads to doubt, hesitation, or lack of confidence. In Descartes's method, anything that could be doubted is to be treated as false. Because consideration of our fallibility leads to doubt about the truth of the conclusions of demonstrations, such conclusions must be treated as false and the demonstrations as unsound. Hume doesn't treat everything doubtful as false, but he does, like most philosophers of the early modern period, treat doubt and hesitation as a sign that we are dealing not with demonstrations, but with probabilities. The argument from fallibility to probability proceeds via the notion of doubt.[11]

Antecedents of Hume's second negative argument, which we will call the regress argument, are harder to find. Fogelin calls it an "ancient trope" but admits that Hume gives it a new twist by "suggesting that these successive evaluations must progressively drive the probability of the *original* judgment down to 'nothing' " (1983: 401).[12] Reid makes the intriguing suggestion that Hume's argument is based on Zeno's paradoxes of motion:

If we trace the journey of ACHILLES two thousand paces, we shall find the very point where the old man is overtaken: But this short journey, by dividing it into an infinite number of stages, with corresponding estimations, is made to appear infinite. In like manner, our author, subjecting every judgment to an infinite number of successive probable estimations, reduces the evidence to nothing. (Reid VII.4 [1785] 2002: 566)

So just as Zeno tries to show that a finite distance cannot be crossed with an infinite number of steps, so Hume's argument attempts to show that a finite amount of confidence or assurance cannot survive an infinite number of diminutions:

No finite object can subsist under a decrease repeated *in infinitum*; and even the vastest quantity, which can enter into human imagination, must in this manner be reduc'd to nothing. Let our first belief be never so strong, it must infallibly perish by passing thro' so many new examinations, of which each diminishes somewhat of its force and vigour. (T 1.4.1.6, SBN 182–83)

Fred Wilson (1985) reminds us that Hume himself explicitly links the regress argument to a consideration about chains of testimony:

the connexion betwixt each link of the chain in human testimony has been there suppos'd not to go beyond probability, and to be liable to a degree of doubt and uncertainty.... Every new probability diminishes the original conviction; and however great that conviction may be suppos'd, 'tis impossible it can subsist under such re-iterated diminutions. This is true in general; tho' we shall find afterwards [note referring to Part 4, Section 1 of Book 1], that there is one very memorable exception, which is of vast consequence in the present subject of the understanding. (T 1.3.13.5, SBN 145–46)

There is no doubt that comparison of the regress argument of T 1.4.1 to this point about testimony, which is itself just an instance of a general point about chains of reasoning, is crucial to understanding the regress argument. We will explore the comparison further in section 3.[13]

Successors of the Arguments in Hume

It is natural enough to think that "the argument of the *Treatise* which, as we saw, was intended to reduce all knowledge claims to probabilities and then drive all probabilities down to 'nothing' is nowhere to be found" in *An Enquiry concerning Human Understanding* (Fogelin 1983: 409). Instead, Fogelin claims, Hume's arguments in the *Treatise* concerning scepticism about reason are replaced in the *Enquiry* by the rather dull arguments about infinite divisibility found in Part 2 of Section 12.[14] But at least two commentators suggest that Hume's discussion of antecedent scepticism in the first four paragraphs of Part 1 of Section 12 of the *Enquiry* should be seen as reflecting the arguments found in "Of scepticism with regard to reason."[15] Antecedent scepticism, in its strong Cartesian form, starts from a doubt about our faculties of "whose veracity ... we must assure ourselves, by a chain of reasoning, deduced from some original principle, which cannot possibly be fallacious or deceitful" (EHU 12.3, SBN 149–50). Hume argues, as Reid argued against Hume's negative arguments of T 1.4.1 (Reid VII.4 [1785] 2002: 571–72), that there is no such principle and that, even if there were, we could not "advance a step beyond it, but by the use of those very faculties, of which we are supposed to be already diffident" (EHU 12.3, SBN 150).[16]

It might be thought that the very fact that Hume presents this as a Cartesian argument, which he rejects, is evidence that it is not to be treated as a successor to the negative arguments of T 1.4.1. But we must remember Hume's positive arguments in T 1.4.1 and the way he deals with the negative, sceptical arguments. He accepts them as good arguments but insists that we nonetheless retain beliefs. This is similar to the position developed in EHU 12.3 (SBN 150). He there claims that the Cartesian doubt can plainly never be attained (we still retain beliefs) and, furthermore, that this sort of scepticism, were it ever to be attained, is such that "no reasoning could ever bring us to a state of assurance and conviction upon any subject" (ibid.). Saying this in the *Enquiry* is similar to the position he takes in the *Treatise*: this sort of scepticism is not the sort one can argue one's way out of. It requires a different response. In addition, we should note that Hume's discussion (and rejection) of the extreme Cartesian scepticism is immediately followed by a description, and an acceptance, of a more moderate antecedent scepticism. This is the mature and reflective version of a little-noticed feature of the negative arguments of T 1.4.1: Hume never suggests that there are problems with the result of the first negative argument and appears to accept that all knowledge degenerates into probability. We will discuss this further in section 2.

Where else do Hume's arguments survive? Consider the following paragraph from the *Abstract*:

By all that has been said the reader will easily perceive, that the philosophy contained in this book is very sceptical, and tends to give us a notion of the imperfections and narrow limits of human understanding. Almost all reasoning is there reduced to experience; and the belief, which attends experience, is explained to be nothing but a peculiar sentiment, or lively conception produced by habit. Nor is this all. When we believe any thing of *external* existence, or suppose an object to exist a moment after it is no longer perceived, this belief is nothing but a sentiment of the same kind. Our author insists upon several other sceptical topics; and upon the whole concludes, that we assent to our faculties, and employ our reason only because we cannot help it. Philosophy would render us entirely *Pyrrhonian*, were not nature too strong for it. (Abs. 27, SBN 657)

Of the clause "Almost all reasoning is there reduced to experience," David Fate Norton and Mary J. Norton (2000: 568n27) say, "Hume argues that all demonstrative reasoning 'resolves itself' into probable reasoning – into reasoning based on experience." This seems plausible, because the whole paragraph can be interpreted as referring to Part 4 of Book 1 of the *Treatise*, "Of the sceptical and other systems of philosophy." Looked at in this way, the second sentence refers to T 1.4.1, the fourth sentence refers to T 1.4.2, the first part of the fifth sentence to the doubts raised in T 1.4.3 through T 1.4.6, while the rest of that sentence and the last sentence refer to T 1.4.7, "Conclusion of this book."[17]

The point is hardly crucial, but in fact I don't think the paragraph can bear this interpretation. Consider the second sentence again: "Almost all reasoning is there reduced to experience; and the belief, which attends experience, is explained to be nothing but a peculiar sentiment, or lively conception produced by habit." This would be a very strange way to sum up the point of T 1.4.1. First of all, "almost all reasoning" is unlikely to mean "demonstrative reasoning"; it is much more likely to mean "probable reasoning" because most reasoning *is* probable. Secondly, nowhere in T 1.4.1 does Hume explain belief. Rather he *uses* his explanation of belief, which occurs in Sections 7 through 10 in Part 3, to counter the conclusion of the negative arguments of T 1.4.1. So the above sentence is much more likely to refer to the main results of Part 3, "Of knowledge and probability." Those results were, firstly, showing that when making probable inferences we are not determined by reason, but rather by custom or habit ("Almost all reasoning is there reduced to experience") and, secondly, explaining belief, or the results of probable reasoning, not as a pale imitation of knowledge, but as something more like a feeling ("the belief, which attends experience, is explained to be nothing but a peculiar sentiment, or lively conception produced by habit").

Finally, as Fogelin (1983: 405–6) points out, Hume's claim that reason, considered in isolation, will self-destruct[18] and his explanation in T 1.4.1 of why nonetheless we do retain beliefs are echoed in the following passage from Part 1 of the *Dialogues*:

All sceptics pretend, that, if reason be considered in an abstract view, it furnishes invincible arguments against itself, and that we could never retain any conviction or assurance, on any subject, were not the sceptical reasonings so refined and subtile, that they are not able to counterpoise the more solid and more natural arguments, derived from the senses and experience. (DNR 1, 135)[19]

2. THE NEGATIVE ARGUMENTS

Knowledge and Probability

Although it is the second negative argument, the regress argument, that receives the most scholarly attention, the first, at the beginning of T 1.4.1 itself, raises some complex and interesting issues. One concerns the difference between demonstration and intuition. While intuition is the immediate apprehension of two ideas standing in a certain relation, demonstration is the indirect awareness of such a relation, mediated by a chain of ideas. Furthermore, Hume limits demonstration to relations of quantity and number, primarily algebra and arithmetic.[20] Now in these passages in T 1.4.1, Hume speaks only of demonstration, not of intuition, and it is perhaps important that all his examples are arithmetical. This fact supports the notion that his target here is the result of demonstration, not intuition. On the other hand, Hume sometimes uses "demonstrative" synecdochically for both intuition and demonstration.[21] Furthermore, his conclusion is that "all knowledge resolves itself into probability" (T 1.4.1.4, SBN 181), and there is no suggestion that he intends this to be limited to demonstrative knowledge. He says:

'tis easily possible, by gradually diminishing the numbers, to reduce the longest series of addition to the most simple question, which can be form'd, to an addition of two single numbers; and upon this supposition we shall find it impracticable to show the precise limits of knowledge and of probability. (T 1.4.1.3, SBN 181)

It is not just impractical to show that, while complex demonstrations are swallowed up by probability judgments, simpler demonstrations and intuitions remain knowledge. It may be incoherent: "if any single addition were certain, every one wou'd be so, and consequently the whole or total sum; unless the whole can be different from all its parts" (ibid.).

I think the situation is this. The more complex a process of demonstration is, by virtue of its complexity, the more prone it is to error and hence the more easily susceptible to this argument.[22] Naturally enough, Hume concentrates on examples of this kind. But once it is admitted that "none will maintain, that our assurance in a long numeration exceeds probability" (ibid.), the argument gets a foothold, and then Hume can extend it to simpler demonstrations and intuitions.[23]

Another issue that the first sceptical argument raises is this: Hume says that "knowledge and probability are of such contrary and disagreeing natures, that they cannot well run insensibly into each other, and that because they will not divide, but must be either entirely present, or entirely absent" (ibid.). Hume makes this claim in the course of arguing that if the argument applies to long numerations, it will apply to the addition of two single numbers as well. But this raises an interesting difficulty, perhaps even a profound issue. If knowledge and probability are of such differing natures, why need they conflict at all? Is not the knowledge that 2 plus 2 equals 4 one thing and the doubts about our performing calculations correctly another? Why does the certainty of the demonstration turn into the different sort of conviction or assent we give to belief?[24] There is no doubt that there is, at the very least, a prima facie problem here. Hume is quite clear about what characterizes the conviction or assent given to propositions that are known by intuition or demonstration:

In that case, the person, who assents, not only conceives the ideas according to the proposition, but is necessarily determin'd to conceive them in that particular manner, either immediately or by the interposition of other ideas. (T 1.3.7.3, SBN 95)

This passage occurs early on in Hume's discussion of belief and at first glance might seem to support the view that for Hume knowing and believing are much the same thing – namely, a manner of conceiving ideas. But a moment's reflection rules out that possibility. For one thing, it is supposed to be easy to see what the difference between assent and dissent is for knowledge, but very difficult for belief. There is no suggestion that knowledge requires the extra force and vivacity characteristic of belief. More importantly, Hume makes it quite clear what he means by "manner" in the above quotation about intuition and demonstration: it is conceiving propositions positively or negatively. In intuition and demonstration, we can conceive propositions only in one way (this is an "absolute necessity" [ibid.]), whereas in belief it is equally easy to conceive them positively or negatively.

So the certainty and assent characteristic of knowledge is due to the impossibility of conceiving an alternative, while the assent characteristic of belief is the force and vivacity of the ideas believed. But now it looks as if no probable belief could have any effect on a known proposition. If something known is such that its contrary is inconceivable, what effect could a belief have? Turn the inconceivable into the conceivable? If belief and knowledge were the same sort of thing for Hume – that is, if belief were on the same scale as knowledge only lower – this would not be a problem. But as the conviction or assent we give to belief is quite distinct from that we give to knowledge, according to Hume, the problem remains.[25] It is solvable, I suggest, not by converting the knowledge claim into a belief claim, but rather by embedding the knowledge claim inside a belief claim. "I know that p" becomes, under conditions of doubt or uncertainty about whether we have followed the rules of demonstration correctly, "I believe that I know that p." The conviction with which p is held will be no stronger than the assurance of the belief.

Treating Hume's conclusion of the first negative argument in this way has three advantages: it solves the problem of how probability can affect knowledge; it defends Hume against the charge, brought by Fogelin and Reid, that the possibility of error does not turn one sort of argument into another; and it does not have the consequence that demonstration and intuition effectively disappear from our cognitive repertoire. This last point is especially important because Hume allows the conclusion of the first negative argument to stand. But is it a plausible or even coherent interpretation? Antonia LoLordo (2002) suggests that it is not. Demonstration and intuition involve a robust sort of certainty, not reducible to force and vivacity. How could I have a probable belief that I am in the grip of such certainty? Wouldn't such a belief entail the absence of such certainty? This is an important point, and dealing with it adequately would require a thorough investigation of Hume's concept of demonstrative certainty.[26] One point to bear in mind is the similarity this issue has to the Cartesian question of how I can doubt what I clearly and distinctly perceive. Well, I can't, obviously, at least not as long as I am clearly and distinctly perceiving. But once I am distracted by thoughts of the errors that I, and others, have made in the past, it seems perfectly easy for doubt to creep in. One way of putting the point is this: when I know a proposition, I perceive that a certain relation holds between two ideas. I can't help but perceive that relation as long as the ideas remain the same. I have, as it were, a *de re* attitude toward those ideas and the relation in which they stand. It is quite literally inconceivable that they should fail to stand in that relation. But now suppose that I am no longer thinking directly about that proposition but am thinking a thought about that proposition. I might think, for example, that others had made errors about similar propositions in the past. I have something more like a *de dicto* attitude toward that thought. And now it seems perfectly possible to think that perhaps the ideas stand in the relation I took them to stand in and perhaps they do not. The sceptical consideration places me at one remove, as it were, from my own thoughts.

We should note that the eventual solution Hume presents later on in T 1.4.1 is a solution to the challenge posed by the second sceptical argument (i.e., that the assurance or conviction we have in any judgment threatens to disappear) and not this first argument (i.e., that all knowledge degenerates into probability). So it looks as if the conclusion of the first argument remains intact. This might well be considered unsatisfactory, but with a little adjusting, I think it can plausibly be seen as a stable position that may well be true. First of all, let us remember that according to the current interpretation we are treating in a nonstandard way Hume's claim that all knowledge degenerates into probability. It is usual to understand this claim as amounting to something like this: any claim that one has knowledge that p must be replaced by a claim that one has only probable belief that p. I have suggested that we treat it instead as saying that any claim that one has knowledge that p must be replaced by the claim that one has a probable belief that one has knowledge that p. It is not that the claim to knowledge drops out; it is just that it becomes embedded in a belief claim.

Suppose I claim to know that $3,467 = 2,895 + 572$, perhaps on the basis of using a calculator. In many contexts – for example, a discussion of the difference between demonstrative and probable arguments or an argument about scepticism – I can be persuaded that it is more precise to say that I believe with a high degree of probability that I know that $3,467 = 2,895 + 572$. In ordinary circumstances, it would rarely be appropriate to say that I believe that I know that $3,467 = 2,895 + 572$; we usually have only the simple attitude toward the arithmetical proposition. But philosophers can be interested in the more complex attitude. There are important differences between the arithmetic proposition, my cognitive state with respect to the arithmetical proposition, and my beliefs about that cognitive state. Nonetheless, if my belief turns out to be true, then so does the embedded knowledge claim.[27] On this view, the conclusion of Hume's argument is not that we can be certain that knowledge never obtains, but only that we cannot be certain just when it does. But we do have a highly probable belief, on various occasions, that it does. This seems to be a sustainable, indeed plausible, position for a cautious sceptic to take. Eschewing the excesses of negative dogmatism, Hume can be content with the moderate scepticism that entails a healthy sense of one's own fallibility.[28]

The Regress Argument

Hume goes on to argue that the very same considerations that lead us to doubt whether we have performed a demonstration correctly also apply to any probability judgment, including the probability judgment we make about the result of a piece of demonstrative reasoning. "In every judgment, which we can form concerning probability, as well as concerning knowledge, we ought always to correct the first judgment, deriv'd from the nature of the object, by another judgment, deriv'd from the nature of the understanding" (T 1.4.1.5, SBN 181–82). Our inherent fallibility is always a consideration, weakening the force with which the original belief is held. As this sort of judgment can reiterate, the result appears to be that the degree of assent will eventually reduce to nothing. We will, it appears, be left with a mere idea, with none of the force and vivacity that characterizes a belief: "Let our first belief be never so strong, it must infallibly perish by passing thro' so many new examinations, of which each diminishes somewhat of its force and vigour" (T 1.4.1.6, SBN 183). The point is not that a belief, with full force and vigor, is seen to be unjustified; rather, it is that because the force and vigor continually decrease, the idea seems in danger of ceasing to be a belief at all. As a matter of fact, our beliefs do not degrade in this matter, and Hume goes on to give an explanation of why they retain their force and vivacity. We will turn to that issue in section 3.

It is this regress argument toward which the vitriol, mentioned at the beginning of this paper, has been directed. There are, it seems to me, three basic objections to this argument. Objection 1, owing to MacNabb, is as follows:

Let us call a judgement which is not about judgements, but about other things, a first-order judgement, and a judgement about the reliability of a first-order judge- ment a second-order judgement. Now it seems evident to commonsense that the second-order judgement that I am very likely, though not certain, to be correct in some first-order judgement increases rather than diminishes the authority of that first-order judgement. (1951: 101)

The point is that when the result of a first-order judgment is itself the subject of a second-order judgment, our confidence in the first-order judgment does not necessarily decrease, as it would if that confidence was simply a probability considered as the product of the probability of the first-order judgment and the probability of the second-order judgment. MacNabb's point at least has the virtue of not assuming that Hume's argument is well represented as the apparent mathematical truism that a probability of less than one will continually decrease as it is successively multiplied by numbers less than one. But Hume's argument cannot be interpreted that way; the conclusion of the argument thus interpreted would be that, for any belief p, we end up believing p with zero probability – that is, we have a belief in not p with a probability of one. This clearly is not what Hume concluded. The point of Hume's argument is "a total extinction of belief and evidence" (T 1.4.1.6, SBN 183) or "a total suspence of judgment" (T 1.4.1.8, SBN 184). It is a sceptical argument, not the argument of a negative dogmatist.

MacNabb says that "it seems evident to commonsense that the second-order judgement that I am very likely, though not certain, to be correct in some first-order judgement increases rather than diminishes the authority of that first-order judgement." We have already seen that this claim is false in general: when the first-order judgment is a knowledge claim and the second-order judgment is a probability judgment, the authority of the knowledge claim is diminished. But does a judgment about a belief that p always reduce the certainty with which we hold p, given that we are not concerned with the simple product of probabilities? We will answer this question incorrectly unless we bear in mind, again, that Hume is not concerned with a scale of which the end point is a belief in p with a probability of zero. The bottom of Hume's scale is uncertainty, not the certainty of falsehood. One way of making the point is in terms of a Baconian rather than a Pascalian conception of probability. As Dorothy Coleman (2001: 198) says, "Pascalian scales take the lower extreme of probability to be disprovability or logical impossibility; the Baconian scale takes the lower extreme to be only non-provability or lack of proof."[29] Another way of making the point is to think of Hume's argument in the following way.[30] We must remember that each successive judgment is a judgment based on doubts about the reliability of our cognitive faculties – on our awareness of the mistakes that we and others have made in the past in making judgments or forming beliefs of just this sort. When we reflect on our fallibility, the appropriate response is to increase the margin of error concerning the belief that we are considering.

Suppose the first judgment results in a belief that p, which we hold at a very high level, say 0.9. The second judgment might lead us to think that this judgment involves a margin of error so that in fact we ought to revise our confidence level to somewhere – exactly where we are not sure – between, say, 0.81 and 0.95. A third judgment, again based on consideration of the fallibility of our faculties, might lead us to revise it yet again to somewhere – again, exactly where we are not sure – between 0.72 and 0.96. And so we continue, until the range in which our confidence level might fall is so great that it no longer makes sense to say that we have any confidence at all left in the belief. This is the extinction of belief and evidence that results in a total suspension of belief.

The second two objections are well presented in Fogelin 1985. They both share the assumption, already rejected, that Hume's argument is a matter of calculating formal probabilities. Objection 2 is that "we can imagine each diminution becoming progressively smaller such that the sum of the diminution approaches a finite limit" (1985: 17). But as Fogelin notes, this objection fails as long as "there is some finite degree of probability below which the chance of error never falls" (ibid.). The third objection is perhaps the most interesting.[31] If it is demonstratively certain that $2 + 2 = 4$, then, to the extent that it makes sense to assign a probability at all, the probability of that proposition is 1. Any subsequent doubts we might have about whether we have performed the demonstration correctly are irrelevant. The probability of a demonstrative proposition doesn't change; it is what it is – similarly with a proposition of probability of less than 1. "However certain or uncertain we are about our ability to calculate probabilities, if a proposition has a certain probability, that (tautologically) is the probability it has" (1985: 18). The probability, or certainty, of the original proposition does not change, whatever probability we assign to the proposition that our assignment of a probability to the original proposition was correct.

If my interpretations of Hume's negative arguments are correct, it is not difficult to see why these objections miss the mark. Suppose that it is demonstratively true that $2 + 2 = 4$. Of course, no doubts of mine will ever change that. Now suppose that the probability that the next roll of a fair die will show 4 is one in six. No doubts of mine will change that either, though weighing the die might. If I have got Hume right, he never questions any of this. Rather, his point is that because of our awareness of our fallibility, we can never rely on knowledge claims. We can at best rely on beliefs about our claim to knowledge. Similarly, because of our awareness of our fallibility, it looks as if we can't rely on any straightforward belief claim either. Whatever strength of belief we have in some proposition, it appears that we can at best rely only on some belief about that belief. And this results in an increase in the margin of error of each successive belief;

such an increase leads to a decline in confidence in the truth of the original proposition. One way to look at it is to think of each judgment after the first to be a matter of doubting. How could further doubt fail to decrease the confidence we have in any proposition?

Part of the point is that what Hume is concerned with in these negative arguments is not some formal assignment of probability, calculated according to the calculus. He is, instead, concerned with the confidence or degree of assent we have in any proposition.[32] For Hume, this confidence or degree of assent is simply a matter of the degree of force and vivacity the corresponding idea has. As the force and vivacity decreases, the danger is that it will cease to be a belief at all. The sceptical threat of the negative arguments of T 1.4.1 is not that the beliefs we have may turn out to be unjustified; it is that the beliefs, by losing their force and vivacity, may not survive as beliefs, but only as mere ideas. This is still a sceptical threat, but of a rather different sort from that which modern epistemologists are used to finding.[33] The negative arguments of T 1.4.1 do not show that there are no rational grounds for our beliefs; they show that our beliefs are in danger of ceasing to be beliefs at all. The problem is not that reason cannot justify our beliefs, or actually shows them to be unjustified; the problem is that our beliefs, as produced by causal or probable reasoning, threaten to disappear in the face of sceptical arguments. If sceptical arguments are arguments that produce doubt and uncertainty, then the negative arguments of T 1.4.1 are certainly sceptical in this sense. But it does not follow that they are sceptical in the sense with which most modern epistemologists are concerned.

When Hume worries about "a total extinction of belief and evidence" (T 1.4.1.6, SBN 183), the concern is not justification, but quite literally the extinction of belief.[34] This is a sceptical worry, in that it produces doubt and uncertainty. But does this characterization draw the teeth of scepticism? Doesn't Hume's argument have more epistemological bite than this? It helps to remember that Hume is concerned with scepticism with regard to reason, where reason is the faculty we use to reach truth, especially by inferential means – that is, by demonstrative and probable arguments. Hume's negative arguments show "that the understanding, when it acts alone, and according to its most general principles, entirely subverts itself, and leaves not the lowest degree of evidence in any proposition, either in philosophy or common life" (T 1.4.7.7, SBN 267–68). When a proposition is left only with "the lowest degree of evidence," it is conceived with very little force and vivacity and thus ceases to be believed. For Hume, the degree of assent, or amount of force and vivacity, simply is what we consider to be the likelihood of the belief's being true. "Our reason," Hume says in the opening paragraph of this Section (SBN 180), "must be consider'd as a kind of cause, of which truth is the natural effect."[35] If it turns out that the products of reason lose their force and vivacity, then they will cease to be beliefs. That is, they will cease to be ideas that we assent to as true. That would be a sceptical result, but not because it is a matter of showing beliefs to be unjustified. It is a matter of showing that they cease to be beliefs – that is, they cease to be things to which we assent as true.

Hume's negative arguments thus have real epistemological import: Unless the arguments can be dealt with, there is a serious problem with us assenting to anything as true. Furthermore, although the arguments do not directly concern justification, they certainly have a consequence for the way we think our beliefs are or are not justified. The faculty of reason is supposed to produce truths; that is its function. We are justified in believing propositions expressing these truths only insofar as the faculty of reason functions as it should. Hume's negative arguments cast serious doubt on this; the understanding, when it acts alone, entirely undermines itself. If reason functioned the way we thought it did and should, then the beliefs that reason gives rise to would be justified. But it doesn't, so they aren't, or at least not in the way we supposed them to be. Left to its own devices, reason cannot defend itself or the "truths" it purports to produce; the justification that we may have thought was available turns out to be lacking. The case for claiming that Hume's negative arguments have real sceptical bite, even when interpreted as I have interpreted them, is strengthened by consideration of the passage that opens and a passage that comes near the end of T 1.4.2 ("Of scepticism with regard to the senses"):

Thus the sceptic still continues to reason and believe, even tho' he asserts, that he cannot defend his reason by reason. (T 1.4.2.1, SBN 187)

This sceptical doubt, both with respect to reason and the senses, is a malady, which can never be radically cur'd, but must return upon us every moment, however we may chace it away, and sometimes may seem entirely free from it. 'Tis impossible upon any system to defend either our understanding or senses; and we but expose them farther when we endeavour to justify them in that manner. As the sceptical doubt arises naturally from a profound and intense reflection on those subjects, it always encreases, the farther we carry our reflections, whether in opposition or conformity to it. Carelessness and in-attention alone can afford us any remedy. (T 1.4.2.57, SBN 218)[36]

The apparent inability to retain beliefs in the face of sceptical arguments has profound sceptical consequences. It is not merely a psychological point; if reason cannot be defended by reason, then there is something self-defeating about being purely rational. This issue is best discussed in light of Hume's positive response to the negative arguments in T 1.4.1, to which I now turn.

3. HUME'S RESPONSE TO THE NEGATIVE ARGUMENTS

Outline of Hume's Response, and the Theory of Belief

Perhaps the best argument for my interpretation of Hume's negative arguments as being mainly concerned with the retention of beliefs in the face of sceptical arguments is his solution to the problem posed by those arguments. He claims that even though one "can find no error in the foregoing arguments" (T 1.4.1.8, SBN 184), we still continue to have beliefs. He does not proceed to show that these beliefs are in fact justified in spite of the arguments; rather, his concern is to show how it is possible that we can retain them at all. Consider these passages:

[A]fter the first and second decision; as the action of the mind becomes forc'd and unnatural, and the ideas faint and obscure; tho' the principles of judgment, and the ballancing of opposite causes be the same as at the very beginning; yet their influence on the imagination, and the vigour they add to, or diminish from the thought, is by no means equal. Where the mind reaches not its objects with easiness and facility, the same principles have not the same effect as in a more natural conception of the ideas; nor does the imagination feel a sensation, which holds any proportion with that which arises from its common judgments and opinions. (T 1.4.1.10, SBN 185)

No wonder, then, the conviction, which arises from a subtile reasoning, diminishes in proportion to the efforts, which the imagination makes to enter into the reasoning, and to conceive it in all its parts. Belief, being a lively conception, can never be entire, where it is not founded on something natural and easy. (T 1.4.1.11, SBN 186)

Hume explains how, given his theory of belief, the relevant ideas manage to retain enough force and vivacity, even in the face of sceptical arguments, to remain beliefs. It is difficult to understand Hume's response to these arguments without bearing in mind just what he thinks beliefs are, and how they are formed. Beliefs are distinguished by their feeling – that is, by their force and vivacity – and this feeling is analogous to that found in sense experience. Hume says, "[P]robable reasoning is nothing but a species of sensation" (T 1.3.8.12, SBN 103), a sentiment echoed in his response in T 1.4.1.10 (SBN 185), quoted above, where he claims that the subsequent judgments of diminishing probability are such that the imagination fails to feel the relevant sensation when considering them. As a result, the original "common judgments and opinions" retain the relevant force and vivacity, and remain beliefs. If Hume's problem were the justification of beliefs, this solution would completely miss the point. But, given the undeniable fact that we do retain beliefs, if the problem is how we manage to retain these beliefs in the face of sceptical arguments, Hume's solution, whatever one thinks of its merits, is at least on target.

In his resolution of the second negative argument of T 1.4.1, Hume does not try to show that the reasoning of that argument is faulty or even that our beliefs are after all justified. Rather, he immediately says that the point is really just to bolster his own account of belief:

My intention then in displaying so carefully the arguments of that fantastic sect, is only to make the reader sensible of the truth of my hypothesis, *that all our reasonings concerning causes and effects are deriv'd from nothing but custom; and that belief is more properly an act of the sensitive, than of the cogitative part of our natures.* (T 1.4.1.8, SBN 183)

He goes on to say, not that we should replace the principles of reasoning that lead to this impasse, but that we should recognize that it is the principles of reasoning we all use, *considered in isolation from the nature of the beliefs such reason produces*, that cause the trouble:

I have here prov'd, that the very same principles, which make us form a decision upon any subject, and correct that decision by the consideration of our genius and capacity, and of the situation of our mind, when we examin'd that subject; I say, I have prov'd, that these same principles, when carry'd farther, and apply'd to every new reflex judgment, must, by continually diminishing the original evidence, at last reduce it to nothing, and utterly subvert all belief and opinion. (T 1.4.1.8, SBN 183–84)

The problem is not so much with reason or reasoning, but with a failure to recognize the nature of belief:

If belief, therefore, were a simple act of the thought, without any peculiar manner of conception, or the addition of a force and vivacity, it must infallibly destroy itself, and in every case terminate in a total suspence of judgment. (T 1.4.1.8, SBN 184)

Because one "can find no error in the foregoing arguments" but one "still continues to believe," we may "safely conclude" that our "reasoning and belief is some sensation or peculiar manner of conception, which 'tis impossible for mere ideas and reflections to destroy" (T 1.4.1.8, SBN 184). Here again we get the comparison of probable reasoning and belief with sensation. When we reflect on how we reason and come to believe, we must keep this fact in mind. When we lose sight of it, we "lose ourselves in perpetual contradiction and absurdity" (T 1.3.13.20, SBN 155).[37]

What is needed is not a new theory of reasoning or a way of defending our reasoning by reason, but instead an answer to the question of *"how it happens, that even after all we retain a degree of belief, which is sufficient for our purpose, either in philosophy or common life"* (T 1.4.1.9, SBN 185). Hume's answer is disarmingly simple: we retain a degree of belief and conviction in spite of the regress argument because the reasoning is too complex and artificial to have any influence on us:

I answer, that after the first and second decision; as the action of the mind becomes forc'd and unnatural, and the ideas faint and obscure; tho' the principles of judgment, and the ballancing of opposite causes be the same as at the very beginning; yet their influence on the imagination, and the vigour they add to, or diminish from the thought, is by no means equal. (T 1.4.1.10, SBN 185)

There is nothing wrong with the reasoning; it is simply that it has, in these circumstances, no apparent lasting effect on our belief.

Considered in isolation, this is an odd response. It is odd not just because we might have expected an answer in terms of justification. Even once we realize that Hume's concern here is the retention, not the justification, of belief, we might still be surprised. Why should the complexity of the argument matter? Why should it be the case that after the first or second iteration, the subsequent judgments have no effect? We need to remember the general account of reason within which Hume is working. Hume is concerned, both positively and negatively, with an account of reasoning of the sort Descartes sketches in the *Regulae* (ca. 1628) – that is, an account in terms of "chains of ideas." Descartes, like Locke after him, thought that "reasoning" produced less certainty than intuition because the relation between the relevant ideas, while direct in the case of intuition, is mediated in the case of reasoning by intermediate ideas. As the number of intermediate ideas increases and the chain of reasoning becomes longer, the relationship between the ideas at each end of the chain of ideas becomes more indirect and the certainty of the conclusion is lessened. Intuitions are more certain than demonstrations, and longer and more complex demonstrations are less certain than shorter and simpler ones. It was a commonplace of seventeenth- and eighteenth-century theories of reasoning that complexity reduces certainty.[38]

Hume frequently comments on the difficulty of keeping one's attention on a long chain of reasoning and worries about its effect on the diminution of our beliefs. For instance, at the beginning of Book 3, he speaks of the trouble in retaining the convictions of reason, which seem to vanish "in the common affairs of life ... like the phantoms of the night on the appearance of the morning" (T 3.1.1.1, SBN 455). He goes on to say that

This is still more conspicuous in a long chain of reasoning, where we must preserve to the end the evidence of the first propositions, and where we often lose sight of all the most receiv'd maxims, either of philosophy or common life. (ibid.)

And in T 1.3.13 he is concerned about the fact that the impact of any piece of historical evidence is vitiated "by passing thro' many millions of causes and effects, and thro' a chain of arguments of almost an immeasurable length" (T 1.3.13.4, SBN 145). In fact, prima facie, any complex and lengthy chain of reasoning will have little influence on us. A special case must be made to explain the case in which, Hume wants to claim, a particular sort of complex and lengthy chain of reasoning does actually influence us. In the historical-evidence case, he argues that every step in the long chain of reasoning is the same: "There is no variation in the steps. After we know one, we know all of them; and after we have made one, we can have no scruple as to the rest.... By this means a long chain of argument, has ... little effect in diminishing the original vivacity" (T 1.3.13.6, SBN 146). And at the beginning of Book 3, he argues that his lengthy chain of reasoning should influence us, because of the importance of the subject matter:

Morality is a subject that interests us above all others: We fancy the peace of society to be at stake in every decision concerning it; and 'tis evident, that this concern must make our speculations appear more real and solid, than where the subject is, in a great measure, indifferent to us. (T 3.1.1.1, SBN 455)

But no such special circumstances attend the argument of T 1.4.1, and the reasoning there neither can nor does influence us. Hume's claim in general is that long and complex patterns of reasoning have less and less influence on us, in proportion to the length and the abstruseness of their subject matter. And as the number of steps increases – steps that are required to remove all the evidence or assent we attach to a proposition – so influence of the argument on our beliefs becomes vanishingly small.

Where reason is lively, and mixes itself with some propensity, it ought to be assented to. Where it does not, it never can have any title to operate upon us. (T 1.4.7.11, SBN 270)[39]

Reason's hold on us is limited, and that is a good thing. If its influence were unlimited, it would entirely destroy itself. It is only because its influence is limited by other aspects of our nature that it can have any influence. We can be rational only if we are only partly rational. If belief were "a simple act of thought" (T 1.4.1.8, SBN 184), governed entirely by the faculty of reasoning functioning in isolation, we could not retain our beliefs in the face of sceptical arguments. But we do retain beliefs, because *"belief is more properly an act of the sensitive, than of the cogitative part of our natures"* (T 1.4.1.8, SBN 183).

The Importance of Hume's Internal References to T 1.4.1: The Testimony Example

Hume took these sceptical arguments very seriously, at least in the *Treatise*. And it certainly looks as if he continued to accept the results of the first negative argument.[40] That Hume attached great importance to the second of these arguments is shown by the fact that he referred to it at least five times, twice before the argument occurs and three times afterward. Hume first refers to it in T 1.3.13, immediately after posing the historical-evidence conundrum, mentioned above and in the context of making a general point about human testimony.[41] He says:

[T]he connexion betwixt each link of the chain in human testimony has been there suppos'd not to go beyond probability, and to be liable to a degree of doubt and uncertainty.... Every new probability diminishes the original conviction; and however great that conviction may be suppos'd, 'tis impossible it can subsist under such re-iterated diminutions. This is true in general; tho' we shall find afterwards [footnote referring to T 1.4.1], that there is one very memorable exception, which is of vast consequence in the present subject of the understanding. (T 1.3.13.5, SBN 145–46)

At one point, Wilson interprets this passage as follows: "With a footnote, Hume explicitly identifies the structure of this regress with that of the regress that generates scepticism with regard to reason" (1985: 324). This is a natural way to interpret this forward-looking reference. Here is a defense of the natural reading: the general truth is that the longer a chain of a reasoning, the less certain we are of its conclusion. In the above passage in T 1.3.13.5 (SBN 145–46), Hume asserts a particular instance of that truth – that is, the longer the chain of testimony, the less credence we give to the content of that testimony. He then makes the forward reference to T 1.4.1. Wilson takes the reference to be explicitly to the second negative argument – that is, to the regress argument. Just as the testimony example shows that the credence we give to the content of testimony is lessened as the chain of testimony increases, so the regress argument shows that the credence we give to a belief is lessened, to the point of disappearing, as the regress continues. Furthermore, like the testimony case – at least as it occurs in the "very celebrated argument against the *Christian Religion*" – the regress argument turns out to be a "memorable exception" to the general truth. In fact, historical evidence does survive, in the right circumstances, and so too do our beliefs survive the regress argument. The survival of our beliefs "is of vast consequence in the present subject of the understanding" (ibid.).[42]

In spite of its initial plausibility, I do not think the natural reading can be correct. The general truth is that certainty decreases with complexity. Where does Hume deploy this truth in T 1.4.1? Not in the regress argument itself, but rather in his *response* to it. The regress argument fails to persuade us because it is too long and subtle. Although the first and second iteration may reduce the "original evidence" (T 1.4.1.9, SBN 184),

after the first and second decision; as the action of the mind becomes forc'd and unnatural, and the ideas faint and obscure; tho' the principles of judgment, and the ballancing of opposite causes be the same as at the very beginning; yet their influence on the imagination, and the vigour they add to, or diminish from the thought, is by no means equal. (T 1.4.1.10, SBN 185)

Testimony is supposed to *support* a belief, whereas the regress argument *undermines* a belief; so the apparent *failure* of long chains of testimony to support beliefs cannot be analogous to the apparent *success* of the regress argument in undermining beliefs. The general truth about length decreasing certainty shows that longer chains of testimony *reduce* the degree of belief. The same truth shows that the force of the regress argument begins to fade after the first few iterations, and that the original belief is *retained*. Under certain circumstances, outlined in T 1.3.13.6 (SBN 146), belief can be *retained* through a long chain of historical evidence; this is an exception to the general truth. It is an exception because as "most of these proofs are perfectly resembling, the mind runs easily along them, jumps from one part to another with facility.... By this means a long chain of argument, has as little effect in diminishing the original vivacity, as a much shorter wou'd have" (ibid.). If the same exception held in T 1.4.1, the regress would work, and we would be left with no beliefs. But it doesn't. There "the mind reaches not its objects with easiness and facility" (T 1.4.1.10, SBN 185). In sum, the increase of length and complexity tends to decrease belief; that is the general truth. The survival of historical evidence is an exception to the general rule, and we have historical beliefs. No such exception is available to the regress argument, and it fails because of the general truth. So we have beliefs.[43]

Here is my interpretation of the testimony passage in T 1.3.13.5, SBN 145–46. Hume says that it is true in general that lengthy chains of testimony reduce the original probability. We have a chain of judgments, one made by each person who passes on the original testimony that is the origin of an historical claim. What is true in general is that reiterated probability judgments, such as those found in these chains, tend to reduce the original conviction. Although true in general, Hume argues in the next paragraph that in the case of a historical chain of testimony, the original conviction survives this apparent diminution. And there is a sense in which, like the historical-evidence case, the argument in T 1.4.1 is a "memorable exception" to the general truth of probability diminution. It is an exception, like the historical-evidence case, because the conviction of the original judgment survives the long chain of reason. It is memorable because, unless it was an exception, we would retain no beliefs based on probable reasoning at all.[44]

This forward reference to T 1.4.1 is important. Not only does it show that Hume attaches great importance to the argument and to his response, but it also shows that Hume's response to the argument is yet another instance of a general truth of Hume's theory of reasoning. Long chains of reasoning have little effect on us, especially when the content is abstruse.

Other References to T 1.4.1

Hume next refers to T 1.4.1 at T 1.3.13.16–17 (SBN 152–53), just a few pages later. Here he is concerned with explaining why an "open and avow'd" violation of honor "the world never excuses, but which it is more apt to overlook, when the appearances are sav'd, and the transgression is secret and conceal'd" (T 1.3.13.16, SBN 152). The explanation is complex, but the reference to T 1.4.1 comes in the following passage:

> The labour of the thought disturbs the regular progress of the sentiments, as we shall observe presently [footnote referring to T 1.4.1]. The idea strikes not on us with such vivacity; and consequently has no such influence on the passions and imagination. (T 1.3.13.17, SBN 153)

This reference to T 1.4.1 is important because it indicates that the arguments of that Section, and Hume's response to it, are to be seen in the light of Hume's theory of belief and belief formation, a theory that treats belief and probable reasoning as more a matter of sensation than of calculation. The phenomenon referred to here is not the sceptical argument of T 1.4.1 but rather the feature of human nature that saves us from its consequences – that is, the quite general feature that abstruse arguments produce ideas that lack sufficient vivacity to have much influence on us.

Hume goes on, in the pages immediately following, to extol the virtues of his account of probable reasoning, largely because it is embedded in the larger context of belief formation. Unless a theory can account for the belief we have in the conclusion of an argument, it is going to run into just the problems that Hume outlines in T 1.4.1. Hume's theory of reasoning, like those of his predecessors, would face just those problems if it were not embedded in his overall account of belief as being formed by custom and the imagination. He says, having summarized his account of probable reasoning and having pointed out how it is sensitive to his account of belief as a more forceful and vivacious idea, that

> All these phænomena lead directly to the precedent system; nor will it ever be possible upon any other principles to give a satisfactory and consistent explication of them. Without considering these judgments as the effects of custom on the imagination, we shall lose ourselves in perpetual contradiction and absurdity. (T 1.3.13.20, SBN 154–55)

Hume seems to think that his account of belief and belief formation is uniquely able to deal with sceptical results; unless a theory treats belief as analogous to sensation, the result will be perpetual contradiction and absurdity.

The third and fourth references to the arguments of T 1.4.1 frame the discussion in T 1.4.2 and have already been discussed.[45]

The fifth reference to the argument in T 1.4.1 occurs in "Conclusion of this book" and is probably at least as important as the first reference:

For I have already shown [footnote referring to T 1.4.1], that the understanding, when it acts alone, and according to its most general principles, entirely subverts itself, and leaves not the lowest degree of evidence in any proposition, either in philosophy or common life. We save ourselves from this total scepticism only by means of that singular and seemingly trivial property of the fancy, by which we enter with difficulty into remote views of things, and are not able to accompany them with so sensible an impression, as we do those, which are more easy and natural. (T 1.4.7.7, SBN 267–68)

Although the dialectic of this Section is extremely difficult, it seems to me that we should read this passage in the following way: when the understanding, or reason, even on Hume's view of reason, acts alone, it is prey to the regress argument. On Hume's view, reason is not an independently functioning faculty that acts alone, following only its own rules. The beliefs we form as a result of a chain of reasoning are formed only when enough vivacity is communicated to the last idea in the chain. Beliefs cannot be formed in isolation from the sensitive side of our nature. That is the lesson of the negative arguments about probable reasoning, commonly called the problem of induction. And even if, counterfactually, beliefs could be formed by reason in isolation from the sensitive side of our natures, they would not survive sceptical arguments such as those of T 1.4.1. That is the lesson of "Of scepticism with regard to reason." It is the ability of ideas to be enlivened by their association with present impressions that explains the production of beliefs; it is the inability of that vivacity to survive complex and repeated patterns of reasoning that explains the retention of beliefs in the face of sceptical arguments.[46]

4. CONCLUSION

T 1.4.1, "Of scepticism with regard to reason," is important for many reasons. Although the second negative argument, the regress argument, has received the most attention, the first negative argument is itself interesting and important. If I am correct, the conclusion to that argument, suitably interpreted, stands: knowledge claims must be embedded in belief claims. Although this does not rule out the possibility of knowledge, it does drastically limit the range and frequency of knowledge claims. Even considered in isolation, this is an important sceptical result and survives as the moderate or mitigated scepticism of the first *Enquiry*.

The regress argument and the details it contains are difficult, and its interpretation, especially in light of the forward reference to it in the argument about historical evidence, controversial. But several points have emerged. To start with, the argument, or something closely related to the argument, has echoes in the first *Enquiry*'s antecedent scepticism. In each case, the argument cannot be rebutted; it is just not the sort of sceptical position out of which one can argue one's way. A different response is called for. Hume's response calls upon his theory of belief, and he thinks the fact that his theory of belief provides a way to avoid the conclusion of a sound argument is further evidence in support of that theory. A belief is distinguished from a mere idea by its extra force and vivacity. A piece of reasoning is a chain of ideas, and if an argument is to persuade us, the vivacity must be transferred along the chain of ideas and preserved in the conclusion. Such preservation is difficult in lengthy and complex arguments, especially those that concern abstruse subjects. The sceptical argument that would have us conclude that no beliefs can survive is itself of this sort: its conclusion has no apparent lasting effect on us, even though we can find no fault with the argument.

Hume says, "Nature, by an absolute and uncontroulable necessity has determin'd us to judge as well as to breathe and feel" (T 1.4.1.7, SBN 183). We are so constituted that we just cannot maintain acceptance of the sceptical conclusion, even though we can find no fault in the argument that supports it. This response raises several interesting issues concerning Hume's attitude toward scepticism. For one thing, we must bear in mind that, even though we cannot maintain the state of suspension of all belief, the reflective among us can and do achieve it for a short stretch of time when in the grip of philosophical reflection. And this is bound to affect us. That is why I said that the conclusion of the sceptical argument has no *apparent* lasting effect. As Fogelin remarks, the moderate scepticism that characterizes Hume's general attitude is a product of the collision of the unmitigated scepticism, which is supported by the regress argument, with our natural propensities to believe. Fogelin says that this "causal explanation of moderate skepticism as the natural terminus of philosophical reflection is, I believe, Hume's major contribution to the skeptical tradition" (1983: 399). Another consequence of Hume's solution to scepticism with regard to reason is shared by his response to scepticism with regard to the senses; in each case, one's beliefs survive only because nature "has not left this to his choice, and has doubtless esteem'd it an affair of too great importance to be trusted to our uncertain reasonings and speculations" (T 1.4.2.1, SBN 187). The sceptical considerations of the early Sections of Part 4 of Book 1 lead us to a very different view of the faculty of reason and the faculty of the senses from that with which we started. In the end, the workings of these faculties, and the way they produce beliefs, is to be explained in terms of principles of the imagination. Hume's scepticism supports his naturalism.

NOTES

A shorter version of this essay appeared as "Scepticism with Regard to Reason" in *Hume Readings*, ed. Lorenzo Greco and Alessio Vaccari (Edizioni di Storia e Letteratura, Rome: 2012), 59–89.

Parts 3 and 4 of this paper have a distant ancestor in chapter 8 of Owen 1999. Many thanks to Donald Ainslie, Lorne Falkenstein, Bob Fogelin, Don Garrett, Antonia LoLordo, Kevin Meeker, Ted Morris, Angela Coventry, and Wayne Waxman. I have learned much, not just from their published work, but also from many discussions concerning topics related to this paper over the past few years. Pressure from several of these friends has persuaded me that the negative arguments of T 1.4.1 have more epistemological import than I once thought. Various versions of this paper have been read at the Hume Society Conference in Helsinki, the Pacific APA, Departmental Colloquium at Uppsala University and the University of Quebec at Montreal, the Philosophy in Assos Conference, and the scepticism group lead by Plinio Junqueira Smith in São Paulo.

This paper was commissioned, in 2001, for *The Cambridge Companion to Hume's* Treatise, edited by Donald Ainslie. It was completed in June 2002, though minor revisions have been made since. It has been translated into Portuguese and published in a collection of essays on Hume, edited by Livia Guimarães. It is available in English at the author's section of the University of Arizona Philosophy Department's webpage (http://philosophy.arizona.edu/).

"Hume's Conclusions" (Garrett 2006) appeared long after this paper was written. His discussion of T 1.4.1, inter alia, is highly recommended, as is Garrett 2004. These papers, plus chapter 10 of Garrett 1997, constitute an important and significant account of Hume's scepticism. (April 2009)

1. Passmore's (1952: 134–37) discussion is a notable exception, though he does think that in the discussion of scepticism in the *Treatise* "Hume lapses into inconsistencies of the most startling character" (1952: 133). See also Fred Wilson's two articles, published in the mid-1980s. These are reworked in Wilson 1997.

2. Reid describes the claim that "the truth and fidelity of our faculties can never be proved by reasoning; and therefore our belief of it cannot be founded on reasoning" as "a manifest truth" (Reid VII.4 [1785] 2002: 572).

3. Compare Penelhum 1975: 198n7: "I omit discussion here of the unappetizing arguments of Section 1 of Part IV of Book I of the *Treatise*, 'of Scepticism with Regard to Reason'." Fogelin, having cited Penelhum here, continues, "He [Penelhum] then remarks, quite correctly, that this skeptical argument is not repeated in the *Enquiry*" (1985: 173n1). See section 1 of this paper for some evidence that the negative arguments of T 1.4.1 (at least the first negative argument) are represented in the *Enquiry*. It is likely that both Penelhum and Fogelin had in mind only Hume's second negative argument, and not the first.

4. See Fogelin 1983, 1985, 1993. See, especially, Fogelin 1985: 17–19.

5. "[E]ntire confidence in any truth," "his confidence increases," "universal assent and applauses of the learned world," "gradual encrease of assurance" (all from T 1.4.1.2, SBN 180), "our assurance in a long numeration" (T 1.4.1.3, SBN 181), "a greater assurance in his opinions" (T 1.4.1.5, SBN 182), "the original uncertainty," "a new uncertainty," "every new uncertainty" (all from T 1.4.1.6, SBN 182).

6. Note the problem the sceptic faces (or poses) is lack of certainty and hence uncertainty about truth, not lack of justification.

7. Among the few discussions I know of are Fogelin 1985: 173–74n2; Ainslie 2003; and Wilson 1985. Bennett (2001: 319) finds in Hume's first negative argument an echo of Descartes. Bennett also shares my view on the importance of this relatively neglected argument: "The heart of iv.1 is in its first paragraph – Hume's insight that *every* human faculty is a part or aspect of the natural world; its exercise involves the functioning of some mechanism; any mechanism can malfunction; so no human faculty is proof against error" (2001: 318; see note 25 below for further discussion of this point).

8. See Popkin 1979 and 1980; Hankinson 1995; Burnyeat and Frede 1998; and Fine 2000.

9. See also Part 4 of his *Discourse on the Method* (1985 1:127): "And since there are men who make mistakes in reasoning, committing logical fallacies concerning the simplest questions in geometry, and because I judged that I was as prone to error as anyone else, I rejected as unsound all the arguments I had previously taken as demonstrative proofs." And see also the first of the *Meditations on First Philosophy* (1985 2:14): "What is more, since I sometimes believe that others go astray in cases where they think they have the most perfect knowledge, may I not similarly go wrong every time I add two and three or count the sides of a square, or in some even simpler matter, if that is imaginable?"

10. Reid argues against Hume in a similar fashion: "one false step in a demonstration destroys the whole, but cannot turn it into another kind of proof" (Reid VII.4 [1785] 2002: 564).

11. Kemp Smith says that Hume does not "question the reliability of reason properly exercised" (1941: 358). It is "the irruption of other causes" (T 1.4.1.1, SBN 180) that prevents us from reaching truth, and truth is the "natural effect" of reason. This makes it look as if there is an important difference between Hume and Descartes here. Descartes wonders whether our faculty of reason might be inherently unreliable, whereas Hume, at least at the start of this Section, is happy to admit that in "all demonstrative sciences the rules are certain and infallible" (ibid.). But he immediately adds, "but when we apply them, our fallible and uncertain faculties are very apt to depart from them, and fall into error." So it looks as if Hume's position here is that if properly exercised, reason reaches the right results, but that the faculty of reason is such that it is liable not to be properly exercised. And surely this is to question the reliability of reason. Furthermore, Hume's conclusion is that, when left to its own devices, reason self-destructs. There is something dubious, if not exactly unreliable, about such a faculty.

Garrett (2006) suggests that Hume's characterization of reason as a cause of truth, where the production of truth is sometimes prevented by "the inconstancy of our mental powers" (T 1.4.1.1, SBN 180), invites us to think of Hume as appealing here to the probability of causes, "where there is a *contrariety* in our experience and observation" (T 1.3.12.3, SBN 131). Such a contrariety "may give us a kind of hesitating belief for the future" (T 1.3.12.6, SBN 132). So here is another route from fallibility to probability: reflection on our fallibility provides us with the mixed experience that leads to judgments of the probability of causes.

12. Fogelin makes it clear that the ancient trope he has in mind is the argument from the criterion of truth (1985: 173–74n2). Ainslie (2003) concurs with this as a point of similarity but argues, quite persuasively, that "it is hard to equate the ancient Pyrrhonists with Hume's 'total' sceptics" (2003: 256).

13. Hume's point about testimony in T 1.3.13.5 (SBN 145) is made in the context of his veiled reference to "a very celebrated argument against the *Christian Religion*." Norton and Norton mention both John Craig's argument in *Craig's Rules of Historical Evidence* and the anonymous argument of "A Calculation of the Credibility of Human Testimony" as possible candidates for the argument to which Hume is referring. See Norton and Norton 2000: 464n5. Wilson (1985: passim), although recognizing the importance of these sources, argues that Berkeley's *Alciphron* is a better candidate. The point about testimony weakening as the chain increases in length was, as Wilson documents, a commonplace in legal and philosophical discussion in the seventeenth and eighteenth centuries and was the basis for ruling out hearsay. See Locke 4.16.10 [1690] 1975: 663–64.

14. Beauchamp supports this in 1999: 54–56.

15. See Selby-Bigge 1975: xxxv. Cf. Passmore 1952: 134: "[T]here is *antecedent* scepticism, of the sort recommended by the Cartesians.... This antecedent scepticism is closely related to the 'scepticism with regard to reason' which Hume presents in the *Treatise*, although it is there commingled, as it is in Descartes, with what Hume calls 'consequent scepticism' – the scepticism which arises out of our discovery that our faculties not only might, but do in fact, lead us into error."

16. If Garrett (2006) is right about the first negative argument in T 1.4.1 being an instance of the probability of causes (see note 11 above), then that argument must be classified as a piece of consequent, not antecedent, scepticism, and the suggestion that the first negative argument of T 1.4.1 survives in some form in the first Part of the last Section of the *Enquiry* fails. In any event, the appeal to doubts about our faculties in each case is, at the very least, suggestive.

17. Norton and Norton (2000: 568n27) also point out, surely correctly, that the sentence "Philosophy would render us entirely *Pyrrhonian*, were not nature too strong for it" (Abs. 27, SBN 657) is a clear echo of T 1.4.1.7–8 (SBN 183–84).

18. "For I have already shown [here there is a reference to T 1.4.1], that the understanding, when it acts alone, and according to its most general principles, entirely subverts itself, and leaves not the lowest degree of evidence in any proposition, either in philosophy or common life" (T 1.4.7.7, SBN 267–68).

19. Assuming that this passage reflects what Hume actually believes, it lends support to the view argued for in the next section that the negative arguments, if not countered by Hume's positive account, would establish, not that our beliefs are unjustified, but that they would cease to be beliefs at all. Hume says, "[W]e could never retain any conviction or assurance, on any subject" (DNR 1, 135). Conviction or assurance *is* belief for Hume.

20. See Owen 1999: ch. 5 for a discussion of Hume on demonstration.

21. For example, Hume says, "If you assert, that vice and virtue consist in relations susceptible of certainty and demonstration, you must confine

yourself to those *four* relations, which alone admit of that degree of evidence" (T 3.1.1.19, SBN 463). By "demonstration," he must mean "intuition or demonstration," because he has already argued that only one of these four relations is capable of sustaining demonstrative reasoning. See T 1.3.1.3–5 (SBN 70–71).

22. Norton and Norton remind us, in the annotation to T 1.4.1.1, that for Locke the results of demonstration were less certain than those of intuition, in part because of comparative length and complexity of the former. This suggests that Hume in this paragraph can be taken to argue that demonstrations are even less certain than Locke thought. See Norton and Norton 2000: 470–71n1. For more detail, see Owen 1999: ch. 3.

23. See Garrett 1997: 223–24 for further argument that Hume intends his first negative argument to apply to both intuition and demonstration.

24. I was made aware of this interesting problem by Falkenstein 1997. Falkenstein thinks there is a good deal to be said for keeping the two cognitive modes separate and limiting the effect one can have upon the other.

25. For further discussion on Hume's distinction between knowledge and belief and its relation to Locke's, see Owen 2003. That paper begins to address a topic that deserves much further study. The results of both demonstrations and proofs ("proofs" in Hume's technical sense – i.e., "those arguments, which are deriv'd from the relation of cause and effect, and which are entirely free from doubt and uncertainty" [T 1.3.11.2, SBN 124]) are certain. But the certainty is of a different character and comes from a different source in each case. The certainty of a belief that results from a proof is just the manner of conceiving it – i.e., with a very high degree of force and vivacity. For Hume, the degree of certainty and the level of assent or degree of belief are the very same thing. And its source is the exceptionless uniformity of the proof of the belief. Now it is clear what the source of the certainty of an item of knowledge (the result of demonstration or intuition) is. It is the inconceivability of the alternatives. But what is the character of the certainty and of the assent we give to knowledge? It is not force and vivacity, surely. Could it be our literal inability to conceive of alternatives? The limits of our conceptual ability do not appear to be things we struggle with every time we claim to know something. Whatever the nature of demonstrative certainty, Hume appears committed to the view that it in part depends on our psychology or cognitive architecture. What we know depends on causal mechanisms, and those mechanisms (like all natural mechanisms) can go wrong. The first negative argument of T 1.4.1 forces us to confront these issues. Thanks to Donald Ainslie, Lorne Falkenstein, and Antonia LoLordo for pressing me on all this. Some of these points were made in Falkenstein 2002 and LoLordo 2002.

26. See preceding note.

27. The strategy of distinguishing between first-order knowledge and belief claims on the one hand and second-order belief claims about knowledge on the other was suggested to me by Nozick's well-known discussion of epistemology in Nozick 1981. He argues there for the now-familiar claim that it may be true that I know that p even though it is false that I know that I know that p. For instance, I may not know that I know that I am sitting in front of the fire, because for all I

know I may be asleep in bed dreaming. But if it turns out I am not dreaming but am awake in front of the fire, then I do know that I am sitting in front of the fire. Kevin Meeker tells me that most modern epistemologists would be unhappy with the rejection of the entailment of "knowing that one knows p" from "knows p." But this shouldn't affect our interpretation of Hume.

28. It is not completely clear whether Hume intended the conclusion of the first argument of T 1.4.1 to stand or not. In any case, the first argument is untouched by Hume's solution to the problem posed by the second argument. Furthermore, I think that the position of moderate scepticism I have just sketched is both a plausible conclusion to the first argument and consistent with the cautiously sceptical views Hume expresses elsewhere. For example, consider the concluding words of Book 1:

> On such an occasion we are apt not only to forget our scepticism, but even our modesty too; and make use of such terms as these, 'tis evident, 'tis certain, 'tis undeniable; which a due deference to the public ought, perhaps, to prevent. I may have fallen into this fault after the example of others; but I here enter a *caveat* against any objections, which may be offer'd on that head; and declare that such expressions were extorted from me by the present view of the object, and imply no dogmatical spirit, nor conceited idea of my own judgment, which are sentiments that I am sensible can become no body, and a sceptic still less than any other. (T 1.4.7.15, SBN 274)

See also Hume's description of moderate, antecedent scepticism (EHU 12.4, SBN 150).

29. The relevance of Coleman's point to my discussion was brought to my attention by Lewis Powell.

30. This interpretation of Hume's argument was first brought to my attention by Nicole Hassoun, in a paper she wrote for a seminar on Hume's *Treatise* at the University of Arizona, spring 2002. I have since discovered that is also put forward by Bennett (2001: 315).

31. Fogelin notes that it was made in essence by Reid and in detail by Hacking. See Fogelin 1985: 174n6; Hacking 1978.

32. This is the important lesson of Morris 1989. Of course, as Kevin Meeker reminds me, we can have a formal assignment of probabilities, where probability is interpreted subjectively. And Fogelin presents "a more sophisticated version of Hume's argument" (1985: 19), which he relates, via Hacking 1978, to Neyman's theory of confidence values (1985: 174n5). I am not sure that either Meeker or Fogelin would agree that thinking of Hume's argument in terms of a declining level of assent should lead one toward thinking of it less as a matter of declining rational grounds and more as a matter of declining evidence, where evidence is treated in the eighteenth-century sense of "evidentness." See the next note.

33. This interpretation is defended in Owen 1999: ch. 8, and a roughly similar one is defended in Garrett 1997: ch. 10. Both of these, as well as Morris 1989, are criticized in Meeker 2000. One of the main points of contention is Hume's use of the term *evidence*. Meeker treats it in the standard, epistemological way, whereas Owen and Garrett argue that Hume uses "evidence" more in the sense of "evidentness." The evidence of a belief, for Hume, is simply the degree of conviction or the assent we attach to it, that it is a matter of the force and vivacity of the relevant idea. When Hume

speaks of "a total extinction of belief and evidence" (T 1.4.1.6, SBN 183), he means the disappearance of the relevant force and vivacity that turns a mere idea into a belief. For details, see Owen 1999: 185–88. See also the glossary entry for "evidence" in Norton and Norton 2000: 575; and Bennett 2001: 315.

34. Consider also: "Let our first belief be never so strong, it must infallibly perish by passing thro' so many new examinations, of which each diminishes somewhat of its force and vigour" (T 1.4.1.6, SBN 183).

35. Hume makes a similar point about memory as a faculty in T 1.3.13.19 (SBN 153). Having characterized force and vivacity as the qualities that "constitute in the mind, what we call the BELIEF of the existence of any object," he says, "This force and this vivacity are most conspicuous in the memory; and therefore our confidence in the veracity of that faculty is the greatest imaginable, and equals in many respects the assurance of a demonstration." The faculty of memory produces the most forceful and vivacious ideas; that is why the ideas of memory are considered, with such a high degree of confidence, to be true.

36. Thanks to Donald Ainslie for pointing out to me that references to T 1.4.1 virtually frame the discussion of scepticism with regard to the senses in T 1.4.2. The symposium on Hume's scepticism, held at the Hume Society Conference in Helsinki, July 2002, was meant to encourage a look at the first two Sections of Part 4 of Book 1 of the *Treatise* as a continuous discussion. The other symposiasts were Donald Ainslie and Ken Winkler. See note 2 above for Reid's response to Hume's claim that we cannot defend reason by reason. Reid, and Beattie following him, thought that this was a "manifest truth," rather than a sceptical result.

37. The topic of this stage of T 1.3.13 is just the same as the topic of the stage of T 1.4.1 that we are now considering: the importance of Hume's "peculiar manner" account of belief.

38. In Hume's case, that length and complexity lessen the certainty with which the conclusion of an argument is held is partially due to his theory of the association of ideas:

> two objects are connected together in the imagination, not only when the one is immediately resembling, contiguous to, or the cause of the other, but also when there is interpos'd betwixt them a third object, which bears to both of them any of these relations. This may be carry'd on to a great length; tho' at the same time we may observe, that *each remove considerably weakens the relation.* (T 1.1.4.3, SBN 11; emphasis added)

This and other aspects of Hume's account of reasoning are discussed in Owen 1999. LoLordo (2000) also thinks that thinking of a piece of reasoning as a chain of ideas should affect the way we interpret the argument of T 1.4.1. Waxman (1998) interprets the argument in terms of the changing degree of our facility in moving from one idea to another. Lack of space prevents further discussion of these interesting accounts.

39. In Garrett 1997, this principle is called "The Title Principle" and is given an important role to play.

40. Consider the following, from the third Part of Section 12 of the *Enquiry*:

The greater part of mankind are naturally apt to be affirmative and dogmatical in their opinions.... But could such dogmatical reasoners become sensible of the strange infirmities of human understanding, even in its most perfect state, and when most accurate and cautious in its determinations; such a reflection would naturally inspire them with more modesty and reserve, and diminish their fond opinion of themselves, and their prejudice against antagonists. (EHU 12.24, SBN 161)

41. The full context of this passage is very complex. Hume is considering the third instance of unphilosophical probability. He starts out by once again pointing out that the length and complexity of arguments can diminish the certainty with which their conclusions are held: "tho' our reasonings from proofs and from probabilities be considerably different from each other, yet the former species of reasoning often degenerates insensibly into the latter, by nothing but the multitude of connected arguments" (T 1.3.13.3, SBN 144). The point is developed in the rest of the paragraph. He then raises the problem of historical evidence, already mentioned. The point about testimony follows, but it is made in the context of "a very celebrated argument against the *Christian Religion*" (T 1.3.13.5, SBN 145) (see note 13 above). If the argument were correct, then "there is no history or tradition, but what must in the end lose all its force and evidence." In other words, the argument against the Christian religion is just an instance of the general problem of historical evidence. Hume gives his solution to the problem on the next page. I outlined the solution in section 3 of this paper. Although Hume thought the historical-evidence problem could be solved, it still remains the case that the longer the chain of testimony, the less the certainty of the information testified to.

42. See also Ainslie 2003: "As David Owen has reminded us, it was a commonplace of early-modern logic to hold that the certainty of an argument was inversely proportional to its length and complexity. Hume's sceptical argument is meant to show that every argument should be infinitely complex, and thus we should have no faith in the verdicts of our reason" (2003: 255). Although Ainslie explicitly distances himself from Wilson's comparison of the testimony case to the regress argument, he nonetheless, like Wilson, considers the regress argument to be an instance of the general truth that complexity diminishes certainty. This is what I called "the natural reading." I argue, against the natural reading, that Hume's forward reference to T 1.4.1 is not to the regress argument, but rather to Hume's *response* to the regress argument.

43. Another point against the natural interpretation is that the point about conviction not surviving long chains of testimony is made in T 1.3.13 as a point of unphilosophical probability. But the second negative argument is supposed to rest on nothing but reason. It would be entirely out of keeping with Hume's purpose in T 1.4.1 for the negative argument to turn on a point of unphilosophical probability, but entirely in keeping with his purpose for his *response* to that argument to turn on such a point. Wilson argues that it follows from the natural reading that Hume regarded the second negative argument as unsound (Wilson 1984: 278–82). I agree with the inference but conclude by *modus tollens* that the natural reading is false. Further evidence for my interpretation comes from Hume's reference at T 1.4.7.7 (SBN 267–68), which is clearly to his response to the regress argument and not to the

argument itself: "We save ourselves from this total scepticism only by means of that singular and seemingly trivial property of the fancy, by which we enter with difficulty into remote views of things."

44. Strictly speaking, what Hume says here is misleading, and the T 1.4.1 case is not really an exception, though it is memorable. Hume's solution to the sceptical arguments of T 1.4.1 is to say that the effects of the negative arguments do not survive the lengthy chain of reason. This is what typically occurs with such a chain, so it is not an exception as is the historical-evidence case. It is true that there is a judgment that survives a lengthy chain of reason, but it is not the judgment that is the conclusion of the chain of reasoning; indeed, the latter judgment, which does not survive, is the negation of the first judgment, which does. This is not the only part of this passage that is misleading. Hume describes the apparent failure of long chains of testimony to support belief as follows: "Every new probability diminishes the original conviction; and however great that conviction may be suppos'd, 'tis impossible it can subsist under such re-iterated diminutions" (T 1.3.13.5, SBN 145). It is extremely difficult, especially with the footnote referring us to T 1.4.1, not to interpret this as an allusion to the second negative argument, as the natural interpretation does. But as I have argued, this is almost incoherent. It may be that Hume himself is confused here.

45. See section 2 of this paper.

46. In T 1.4.7, Hume treats the vivacity of ideas as the property of the imagination on which "the memory, senses, and understanding are, therefore, all of them founded" (T 1.4.7.3, SBN 265). This property is ("seemingly") "trivial" and "little founded on reason." Another, related property of the imagination (and surely a causal consequence of the first) is the "seemingly trivial property of the fancy, by which we enter with difficulty into remote views of things, and are not able to accompany them with so sensible an impression, as we do those, which are more easy and natural" (T 1.4.7.7, SBN 268). Now the understanding is constituted by "the general and more establish'd properties of the imagination," explicitly contrasted with "all the trivial suggestions of the fancy" (T 1.4.7.7, SBN 267). So it certainly looks here as if vivacity and the related inability of the mind to retain vivacity through complexity are trivial properties of the fancy or imagination, in contrast with those "general and more establish'd properties" that constitute the understanding. So the understanding, when it acts alone, cannot produce beliefs (when we reason probably, we are not "determin'd by reason" [T 1.3.7.7, SBN 97]); and even if it could, such beliefs would be unstable, as the understanding would self-destruct in the face of sceptical arguments.

6   Hume on Scepticism and the Senses

Asked to name the greatest blessing of his life, St. Thomas (according to G. K. Chesterton) answered, "I have understood every page I ever read" (Chesterton 1933: 16). I want to begin by acknowledging how far I am from this blessed condition, especially when it comes to *Treatise* 1.4.2, "Of scepticism with regard to the senses." What I have to contribute in the present essay is a reading of T 1.4.2 that is both tentative and partial. I concentrate on the theme of scepticism, and I ignore many interesting details in Hume's psychological account of our belief in body, so as to emphasize the bearing of that account on what I take to be the sceptical conclusion of the Section. I hope to support two main claims: that there is, in T 1.4.2, no indication that Hume – or the ordinary believer as portrayed by Hume, or even the "representative realist" philosopher as portrayed by Hume – believes in the existence of objects specifically different from perceptions; and, more controversially, I think, that T 1.4.2 presents a continuous sceptical argument opposing the "implicit faith" in the existence of bodies expressed by Hume as the Section begins. In developing the second claim, I will be portraying Hume's scepticism as a moral achievement. I conclude the essay by taking note, very briefly, of two further points: that the conclusion of Hume's sceptical argument is, despite its opposition to his earlier implicit faith, limited in certain ways; and that in *Treatise* 1.4.4, "Of the modern philosophy," the sceptical conclusion is strengthened or extended, though in a way consistent with the limitations Hume had imposed in T 1.4.2. I will not be discussing *Treatise* 1.4.7, the conclusion of Book 1, where Hume returns to the sceptical themes of T 1.4.2 (and other Sections in Part 4) and responds to them a second time. For all I say in the present essay, the sceptical argument of T 1.4.2 may be modified or even repudiated in T 1.4.7; my central claim is that the argument, as it is presented in T 1.4.2, is decidedly – and avowedly – sceptical.[1]

1. OBJECTS SPECIFICALLY DIFFERENT FROM PERCEPTIONS

My claim that there is, in *Treatise* 1.4.2, no sign that Hume (or any believer portrayed by Hume) believes in bodies specifically different from perceptions puts me at odds with what might be described as "strongly realist" readings of T 1.4.2, which hold that according to Hume, at least some of us – perhaps all of us – believe in the existence of objects specifically different from perceptions. Such readings have been defended, or suggested, by Donald W. Livingston and Galen Strawson, among others. Livingston (1984: 21), for example, writes that

Hume takes the doctrine of double existence presented in section ii [of *Treatise* 1.4] to be not simply a quirk of modern thought but a permanent tendency of the philosophical imagination whereby perceptions are treated as mere *appearances*, and objects, specifically different from perceptions, are treated as *realities*.

Strawson (1989: 52–53n32) writes:

The meaning of section 1. iv. 2. is endlessly disputed, and I wish to avoid the dispute as far as possible.... [But] it is worth adding that I will not take much notice of Hume's distinction between the "popular" and "philosophical" versions of the belief in truly external objects. This distinction would certainly be impor-tant in a full discussion of section 1. iv. 2.; but what matters here is simply that both versions of the belief in external objects are indeed that – beliefs in truly external objects.

These "truly external objects" are, as Strawson makes clear elsewhere (e.g., 1989: 136), specifically different from perceptions.[2]

My claim also puts me at odds with certain antirealist (or at least not strongly realist) interpreters of Hume. David Pears, for example, thinks that in T 1.4.2 Hume finds that the belief in body is "deficient ... in its content" (1990: 168) and that he accuses philosophers in particular of violating "canons of meaningfulness" (1990: 194). Unlike ordinary peo-ple, who assume that "our impressions continue to exist independently of our minds with the very same properties that they exhibit when they are present to our minds," the philosophers "borrow those properties and project them on to physical objects which are never present to our minds" (ibid.).[3] The nonpresence of these objects is, for Pears, a mark of their specific difference from perceptions.[4] Louis E. Loeb is another interpreter sceptical of strongly realist readings for whom the belief in body is, at least at times in T 1.4.2, a belief in objects specifically different from perceptions. In that form, Loeb suggests, Hume condemns the belief as meaningless.[5]

Now for the evidence on behalf of my claim.[6] Hume's account of our belief in body, which occupies fifty-seven paragraphs (T 1.4.2), is carefully framed by opening and closing references to objects supposed specifically different from perceptions. The opening reference, in the Section's second paragraph, dismisses such objects (or, more precisely, the supposition of such objects) from consideration. There Hume asks "whether it be the *senses*, *reason*, or the *imagination*, that produces the opinion of a *continu'd* or of a *distinct* existence" of body. He then writes:

These are the only questions, that are intelligible on the present subject. For as to the notion of external existence, when taken for something specifically different from our perceptions, we have already shown its absurdity. (T 1.4.2.2, SBN 188)

In case there should be any doubt that Hume is dismissing objects supposed specifically different, a footnote to the words "specifically different" refers us back to *Treatise* 1.2.6 ("Of the idea of existence, and of external existence"). There, immediately after a paragraph announcing that "'tis impossible for us so much as to conceive or form an idea of any thing specifically different from ideas and impressions" (T 1.2.6.8, SBN 67), Hume writes that

The farthest we can go towards a conception of external objects, when suppos'd *specifically* different from our perceptions, is to form a relative idea of them, without pretending to comprehend the related objects. Generally speaking we do not suppose them specifically different; but only attribute to them different relations, connexions and durations. But of this more fully hereafter. (T 1.2.6.9, SBN 68)

A footnote to the final sentence in this passage refers us forward to *Treatise* 1.4.2; the point, clearly, is that in T 1.4.2, where he attempts to explain what we do believe "generally speaking," Hume intends to ignore what we do not generally suppose.

Throughout the fifty-five paragraphs that follow T 1.4.2.2 (SBN 188), Hume consistently honors his dismissal of objects specifically different, concentrating, as T 1.2.6 anticipates, on the different relations, connections, and durations that we ascribe to perceptions. The notion of objects specifically different is entirely set aside. Hume does consider a "double existence" view of the philosophers, according to which our internal perceptions have external objects distinct from them, but the objects in the second set are themselves, as he repeatedly insists, perceptions. This is why, in the closing passage framing his official account of body, he speaks of philosophers as those who have "invent[ed] a new set of perceptions" (T 1.4.2.56, SBN 218). He adds:

I say, a new set of perceptions: For we may well suppose in general, but 'tis impossible for us distinctly to conceive, objects to be in their nature any thing but exactly the same with perceptions.

This is an indisputable indication that throughout T 1.4.2, where he gives his official account of belief in body, *Hume simply ignores the notion of objects as specifically different*. This notion is irrelevant to what Hume has to say in T 1.4.2, because his goal there is to *explain* our belief in continued and distinct existence. To explain it he needs to rely on the theory of ideas and his theory of belief (as he repeatedly indicates). The notion of objects as specifically different is irrelevant because we can have no idea of objects specifically different from perceptions, and therefore no belief in them.

It follows from all this that according to Hume, *our natural belief in body does not rest on an ability to suppose objects specifically different from our perceptions*. As Hume observes in T 1.2.6, "generally speaking," we do not suppose that there are such objects. The natural belief in body, in other words, does not depend essentially on the supposition that there are objects specifically different from perceptions. The "vulgar," for example, who do not so much as approach the supposition, believe wholeheartedly in body. Philosophers who accept the double existence view and do so clearheadedly – recognizing that the objects they invent are nothing but perceptions – are no less free of the supposition, but they too believe in body. What about philosophers who *do* suppose that there are objects specifically different? Perhaps they "take" (my word) the external objects they invent to be specifically different from perceptions, but Hume gives every indication that they must nonetheless *conceive* of these objects as perceptions and that they owe their belief in body to this conception rather than to their supposition. T 1.4.2 contains not a shred of evidence that the supposition of objects specifically different plays any role in anyone's belief in, or commitment to, body. Hume gives us no reason to think that the supposition has anything to do with the belief in the continued and distinct existence of body, and every reason to expect the opposite – every reason to expect, that is, that even in a philosopher who makes the supposition, the *belief* in the continued and distinct existence of body rests, as it does for others, on the mechanisms described in T 1.4.2. When it comes to explaining belief in body, in other words, the supposition is idle. It is not – at least not for most of us, most of the time – a working part of our cognitive economy. Hume seems to be suggesting that even philosophers who suppose that there are objects specifically different from perceptions owe their commitment to body to the new set of perceptions of which they, like the rest of us, conceive, despite (or alongside of) their supposition.

Hume's dismissal of objects specifically different from perceptions frames the sceptical argument of T 1.4.2. That argument, as I will now try to show, does not depend on the "unintelligibility" or "inconceivability" of our belief in body, but rather on its *falsehood* or *unjustification*. It is not until T 1.4.4, when Hume turns to the construal of body characteristic of "the modern philosophy," that the concern with intelligibility, first voiced in T 1.2.6, reemerges.

2. THE SCEPTICAL ARGUMENT OF TREATISE 1.4.2

Why does Hume give *Treatise* 1.4.2 the title "Of scepticism with regard to the senses"? It is a puzzling choice on at least two counts: first, the Section seems to have little to say about scepticism; and second, the scepticism it conveys does not seem on the whole to concern the senses.[7] The senses occupy Hume's attention only briefly (T 1.4.2.3–13, SBN 188–93), where they are commended for presenting sensations "as they really are" (T 1.4.2.5, SBN 189) and for their incapacity to deceive us regarding either the nature or the existence of their objects (T 1.4.2.7–11, SBN 190–92).

The title is intended, in part, as a companion to the title of *Treatise* 1.4.1, "Of scepticism with regard to reason." On one way of partitioning the powers of the mind, reason and the senses are the only ones that can justify belief; in that case, if Hume discusses scepticism with regard to them both, his coverage of scepticism will be complete. But I suspect that there is more to the title than this. In a telling sentence that appears very late in T 1.4.2, Hume writes that the argument of the Section inclines him "to repose no faith at all in my senses, or rather imagination" (T 1.4.2.56, SBN 217). He says "or rather imagination" because (as we will see) he believes that by this point, one page shy of the Section's end, he has shown that the imagination is responsible for our belief in body. This suggests that the initial object of concern in T 1.4.2 is not a particular power or faculty, but rather a particular belief – the belief in body – to which the power or faculty of sense is thought (perhaps mistakenly) to give rise. This suggestion is confirmed by Hume's observation that "[t]he subject . . . of our present enquiry" is the causes inducing us "to believe in the existence of body" (T 1.4.2.2, SBN 187–88) and by a summary remark that comes near the end of the Section: "Having thus given an account of all the systems both popular and philosophical, with regard to external existences, I cannot forbear giving vent to a certain sentiment" (T 1.4.2.56, SBN 217). Here Hume reports that he has surveyed what all systems, popular and philosophical, have to say about the external existence of body. His topic is scepticism with regard to the senses only insofar as the senses have usually been regarded as the source of that belief. So T 1.4.2 might have been entitled "Of scepticism with regard to the existence of body." If we understand the title Hume actually gave to the Section to be a way of expressing this one, the title seems much less puzzling, because the Section both begins and ends with remarks on scepticism concerning body.

The only problem remaining is that Hume seems not to be discussing scepticism in between the beginning and the end. This, I will argue, is merely an appearance. He is in fact concerned with scepticism throughout T 1.4.2. It is perhaps true that nonsceptical systems are the only ones Hume has talked *about*, but the sceptical system has been *enacted*. The nonsceptical systems are the objects of Hume's concern; scepticism is its *vehicle*. Hume permits himself a kind of identification with scepticism, an identification he denies himself when it comes to the others. The other systems are held at arm's length; Hume considers them objectively or scientifically. Scepticism, by contrast, is expressed and supported by justificatory argument. In effect, Hume repudiates "symmetry," as it came to be understood, two hundred years after his death, by the Edinburgh School: he gives an "account" of scepticism – the system he favors – that is radically different, in both method and manner of expression, from his accounts of the systems he opposes.[8]

Before I turn to the details of Hume's presentation, and to the clarification and defense of the conclusions just presented, I want to introduce three distinctions I employ throughout the rest of the essay.

The first is a distinction between justifying *what is believed* (a propositional content) and justifying – or defending, or vindicating – a particular person's belief or *doxastic commitment*.[9] I do think that Hume is interested in the justification of what is believed (or, perhaps, in the truth-or-justification of what is believed: he is not careful to distinguish matters of truth from matters of justification). But he is also interested in himself, insofar as he is productive of belief. He is interested in himself, that is, as a source or locus of doxastic commitment. As he says in T 1.4.7,

> I cannot forbear having a curiosity to be acquainted with the principles of moral good and evil, the nature and foundation of government, and the cause of those several passions and inclinations, which actuate and govern me. I am uneasy to think I approve of one object, and disapprove of another; call one thing beautiful, and another deform'd; decide concerning truth and falshood, reason and folly, without knowing upon what principles I proceed. (T 1.4.7.12, SBN 270–71)

Hume, it is clear, is not impartially curious about the principles on which he proceeds; he is hopeful that they will prove to be acceptable and that their discovery will vindicate him as a believer (and as an agent, though agency – a topic for Books 2 and 3 – is something I do not consider in this essay).

Reflexive self-acceptance or reflective endorsement, as described by Annette Baier (1991) and Christine Korsgaard (1996b: 51–66), is one example, or one possible upshot, of the task of self-assessment in which Hume is engaged. I believe that Hume sees it as a moral task. He asks, in a passage emphasized by Baier (T 3.3.6.6, SBN 620), whether the mind is able to "bear its own survey." Both Hume's words and the urgency of his concern echo Shaftesbury, who describes the virtuous mind as "such as can freely bear its own inspection and review" ([1711] 1999: 206). If, after philosophizing, "I am still the same mystery to myself as ever," Shaftesbury asks, "to what purpose is all this reasoning and acuteness? Wherefore do I admire my philosopher or study to become such a one myself?" ([1711] 1999: 134). Shaftesbury, who gave the name "soliloquy" to the enterprise of self-examination, was not the only one among Hume's predecessors in the science of man to pursue this scrutiny with a moral purpose (T Intro. 7, SBN xvii). In different ways, each of the five pioneers Hume identifies – Locke, Shaftesbury, Mandeville, Hutcheson, and Butler – was inspired with moral concern. Their method was new, but both their subject matter and the moral purpose of its study were traditional. M. A. Stewart (2005: 11) has recently called attention to a striking passage from Alexander Boswell's notes on the logic lectures Colin Drummond gave at Edinburgh in 1722–23, one year before Hume entered the university:

Such, in truth, are the faculties of human beings, and such the works of God, that when these have been duly reflected upon and properly attended to, more things about God and about the duty of humans towards God, self, and other humans come to be known without any positive and external revelation; and the knowledge acquired by these helps is called *philosophy*. (Translated by Stewart from the Latin)

"[W]e probably have here," Stewart surmises, "the first words of philosophy that Hume would have heard as a student at the College of Edinburgh" (2005: 11). In some ways they are not far from words Hume himself assembled many years later, again in defense of philosophy (though Hume dropped all of Drummond's references to God): "there are many positive advantages, which result from an accurate scrutiny into the powers and faculties of human nature" (EHU 1.13, SBN 13). In this particular passage from the *Enquiry*, the advantages Hume hopes for are not moral ones, but elsewhere, especially in the *Treatise*, he has moral advantages very much in mind.

Much more needs to be said about the import of the distinction between propositional content and doxastic commitment – more than I can say in this essay. But the distinction is relevant to a second one that runs through much of T 1.4.2. Hume speaks there at times of what a given faculty or principle *can* cause (what I will call the *competence* of the faculty) and at other times of what it *does in fact* cause (its *performance*). In the following passage, for example, he distinguishes between the competence and the performance of the senses:

But not to lose time in examining, whether 'tis possible for our senses to deceive us, and represent our perceptions as distinct from ourselves, that is as *external* to and *independent* of us; let us consider whether they really do so. (T 1.4.2.8, SBN 190)

In a second passage, he makes the same distinction with respect to reason:

So that upon the whole our reason neither does, nor is it possible it ever shou'd, upon any supposition, give us an assurance of the continu'd and distinct existence of body. (T 1.4.2.14, SBN 193)

Hume separates competence and performance – and, as the quoted passages indicate, recognizes that he does so – at least in part because he is sensitive to the distinction between an abstract propositional content and a concrete person's doxastic commitment. I may affirm a belief that is justified in the abstract (perhaps because some philosopher is in possession of an airtight argument in favor of it, a fact that places its justification within my competence, or at least within the competence of faculties I share with the philosopher), but I may not be justified in holding it (because the cause of my doxastic performance has nothing to do with the argument or with anything else able to confer justification on my commitment).

The third distinction I want to introduce is also related to the first. It is a distinction among three ways of explaining why I hold a given belief – three ways of explaining my doxastic commitments. A *justification-conferring* explanation accounts for a belief I hold by showing that I am justified in holding it. A *justification-undermining* explanation accounts for a belief I hold by showing (on the assumption that the account is complete) that I am not justified in holding it. A *justification-neutral* explanation is neither justification-conferring nor justification-undermining. In this essay I hope to show that Hume gives a justification-undermining explanation of our belief in body. Because the explanation is justification-undermining, the act of providing the explanation is a sceptical performance – a performance with doubt as its upshot – as I think Hume acknowledges in the concluding paragraphs of the Section. If the reader of those paragraphs is asked why Hume is sceptical, the answer – never given by Hume, but nonetheless communicated – is that he is sceptical about body because the correct explanation of his belief in body is justification-undermining. This is what I had in mind when I said that Hume repudiates symmetry: he explains why he and others believe in body in a way that is justification-undermining, but insofar as his doubt can be explained (and as I have tried to say, he does not officially undertake to explain it), it is explained in a way that is justification-conferring, because a justification-conferring explanation of a *doubt* (to extend my earlier definition to acts of doxastic suspension) can be derived from a justification-undermining explanation of the associated act of commitment.

Now to the details of Hume's presentation. My plan is to emphasize the kind of concern with justification that his presentation must exhibit if it is going to sustain the interpretive claims I have outlined.

The official subject of T 1.4.2, as I have already indicated, is the "*causes* which induce us to believe in the existence of body" (T 1.4.2.2, SBN 187–88). Here I want to add only that the investigation of the causes of that belief is offered to the reader as an escape from, or at least as an alternative to, scepticism. As Hume says at the end of the first paragraph of the Section, "We may well ask, *What causes induce us to believe in the existence of body?* but 'tis in vain to ask, *Whether there be body or not?* That is a point, which we must take for granted in all our reasonings" (T 1.4.2.1, SBN 187). As the Section proceeds, Hume will discover that this route of escape or avoidance in the end takes him back to scepticism, and when he returns to scepticism, the route cannot lure him a second time. "As the sceptical doubt arises naturally from a profound and intense reflection on those subjects, it always encreases, the farther we carry our reflections, whether in opposition or conformity to it" (T 1.4.2.57, SBN 218). The reasoning of T 1.4.2 commenced in opposition to scepticism but served only to return Hume to it. It remains true, perhaps, even at the end of T 1.4.2, that "all our reasonings" take for granted the existence of body. But this need not embarrass the sceptic. Even if his reasonings take for granted the existence of body, those reasonings can justify doubt in the existence of body if they explain that belief in a justification-undermining fashion.

Hume's first real step is to divide his question – Why do we believe in the existence of body? – into two parts. The first asks why we believe in the *continued* existence of objects "even when they are not present to the senses." The second asks why we believe in their *distinct* existence – distinct, that is, "from the mind and perception." He explains that under the heading of distinctness, he includes the "*external* position" of objects as well as "the *independence* of their existence and operation" (T 1.4.2.2, SBN 188). "External" and "independent" are to be understood in relation to the mind.[10] To say that an object has an external position is to say that it is outside the mind in space. To say that an object is independent in existence is to say that the object and the mind are, as Descartes might have put it, really distinct: either can exist apart from the other. And to say that an object is independent in its operations is to say that its operations do not depend on the operations (or even on the existence) of the mind. Continued existence and distinct existence are, in Hume's opinion, mutually implicatory: if an object has continued existence, then it has distinct existence (if its existence is not independent of the mind, it cannot exist unperceived); and if an object has distinct existence, then it will not fall out of existence merely because it is unperceived. Despite their close relationship, Hume thinks that distinguishing the two notions will enable us "more easily" to discover "the principles of human nature" responsible for our belief in body (T 1.4.2.2, SBN 188). It turns out that the belief in continued existence is, from an explanatory viewpoint, the more fundamental: it is through our belief in continued existence, according to Hume, that the imagination brings us to a belief in distinct existence.

The question of the Section, then, is whether it is the *senses, reason,* or *imagination* that produces the opinion of a continued or distinct existence. "These are the only questions, that are intelligible on the present subject. For as to the notion of external existence, when taken for something specifically different from our perceptions, we have" – as we noted above – "already shown its absurdity" (T 1.4.2.2, SBN 188).

The Senses

Hume's consideration of the senses as a potential source of the belief spans paragraphs 3 through 13 of the Section (SBN 188–93). He begins by observing that the senses can hardly produce a belief in the *continued* existence of body – that is, the existence of bodies when unsensed – because they could do so only on the assumption that they continue to operate after they have ceased operation. So the senses can support belief in body only insofar as they cause us to believe in their *distinct* existence.[11]

In order to do *that*, our senses must present "their impressions" either as images and representations, or as the distinct and external existences themselves (T 1.4.2.3, SBN 189). But they cannot present them as images, because the senses convey nothing but a single impression. "A single perception can never produce the idea of a double existence, but by some inference either of the reason or imagination" (T 1.4.2.4, SBN 189). This brings out a crucial assumption of this part of Hume's account: the senses are a *non-inferential* or *other-than-illative* faculty.

So our senses must convey the impressions *as* distinct existences, and they can do so, Hume concludes, only "by a kind of fallacy and illusion" (T 1.4.2.5, SBN 189). Here I want to pause to consider Hume's rapid step from *the senses present their impressions as distinct existences* to *the senses suffer from a kind of fallacy or illusion.*

My first observation is fairly straightforward: Hume's mention of fallacy and illusion shows that he has justification in view. His immediate concern is, I grant, an explanatory one, but at the same time he is keeping careful score; he wants the reader to know that if the senses present impressions as distinct existences, they are doing something *wrong*.

But this observation prompts a second and much more puzzling one: Hume's mention of fallacy and illusion is very surprising. It is as if he takes it to be obvious that the senses cannot present their objects as distinct existences, but the readiest explanation of his thinking *this* – that the objects of the senses cannot be distinct existences – is (or should be) unavailable here, since Hume will argue in just a few pages that the objects of the senses *can* be distinct existences. Here it is worth noting that at this point in Hume's discussion, we are considering whether it is *possible* for the senses to convey a belief in distinct existence. Whether they do so *in fact* is a question (one of performance rather than competence) that Hume postpones until the middle of T 1.4.2.8 (SBN 190). He will eventually argue that although the impressions of the senses *can* be distinct existences, they in fact are not.

Why, then, does Hume assume at T 1.4.2.5 (SBN 189) that the senses can convey the idea of distinct existence only by a kind of fallacy and illusion? The answer comes, I think, in the next few lines. "Upon this head," Hume writes,

we may observe, that all sensations are felt by the mind, such as they really are, and that when we doubt, whether they present themselves as distinct objects, or as mere impressions, the difficulty is not concerning their nature, but concerning their relations and situation. Now if the senses presented our impressions as external to, and independent of ourselves, both the objects and ourselves must be obvious to our senses, otherwise they cou'd not be compar'd by these faculties. The difficulty, then, is how far we are *ourselves* the objects of our senses. (T 1.4.2.5, SBN 189)

He then observes that "the nature of the uniting principle, which constitutes a person," is as abstruse as any in philosophy (T 1.4.2.6, SBN 189) and that it is therefore "absurd ... to imagine" that the senses could supply us with an answer to it (T 1.4.2.6, SBN 190). Furthermore, all the impressions of the mind, both internal and external, "are originally on the same footing," from which it follows that every impression must be felt by the senses in the same way (T 1.4.2.7, SBN 190). When Hume says that all impressions are "originally" on the same footing, I take it that what is "original" in our impressions is what they can be seen or felt to contain before we have had a chance to draw our experience together and reason on the basis of it.

Hume's primary point in all this is that the senses cannot present us with impressions of objects on one side ("external" impressions) and impressions of the self ("internal" impressions) on the other. If the senses were able to draw the boundary between the self and its external objects, "the uniting principle, which constitutes a person," would have to be within its grasp. Only by mastering that principle could the senses classify an impression as inward or outward. But that principle is far beyond the competence of the senses, and even if it fell within it, all the objects of the senses, "internal" as well as "external," present themselves ("originally") in just the same way, thereby rendering any "uniting principle" inapplicable. If the senses attempted to apply such a principle, they could succeed, as Hume says, only by a kind of "illusion": the illusion of a difference among impressions that would ground the application of the principle. To the question "how far we are *ourselves* the objects of our senses" (T 1.4.2.5, SBN 189), Hume's answer is: not far at all. We can, of course, *have* by sense the impressions that constitute the self, but we cannot by sense *view* them as impressions of the self.

Hume's distinction between the "nature" of impressions and their "relations and situation" is, incidentally, confirmation of the interpretive claims I defended in the first section of this essay. When we ask whether an object has an existence distinct from ourselves, we are asking not about its nature (as we would be doing if distinctness involved specific difference); we are asking only about its relations to other impressions and its situation relative to us.

Hume concludes his discussion of whether the senses *can* produce the idea of distinct existence with another indication of his interest in justification:

[S]ince all actions and sensations of the mind are known to us by consciousness, they must necessarily appear in every particular what they are, and be what they appear. Every thing that enters the mind, being in *reality* a perception, 'tis impossible any thing shou'd to *feeling* appear different. This were to suppose, that even where we are most intimately conscious, we might be mistaken. (T 1.4.2.7, SBN 190)

The implication here is that if the senses *could* present us with objects as distinct, those objects *would* be distinct – or at least that upon reflection we would have every reason to believe in their distinctness. The senses, as has been shown, are unable to present us with such objects. It is their primitiveness that disables them from doing so. Hume can, in one way, be a sceptic about the senses: they are primitive, or limited, and cannot be trusted to tell us everything. But he is, in another way, no sceptic about them: as a reflecting philosopher he has reason to trust them, with respect to the objects falling within their domain – the objects they actually, and "originally," present.[12]

When Hume moves to the question of whether the senses are *in fact* responsible for the idea of distinct existence (a question of performance), he considers, first, externality and, second, independence.

Turning to externality, and putting aside "the metaphysical question of the identity of a thinking substance," Hume declares that "our own body evidently belongs to us" (T 1.4.2.9, SBN 190). (Hume's language here confirms my earlier remarks on T 1.4.2.6, SBN 189–90.) The principle that unifies a person or thinking substance lies beyond the authority of sense, but the boundaries of the body may nonetheless be "evident" – available, even "originally," to the senses. He accordingly weighs the suggestion that "as several impressions appear exterior to the body, we suppose them also exterior to ourselves" (T 1.4.2.9, SBN 190). But, he cautions in response, for three reasons we should resist concluding that nothing but the senses is required to generate the belief in body (T 1.4.2.9, SBN 190–91). First, we do not perceive our body, properly speaking, but only certain impressions. This throws us back on the question of what induces us to ascribe a real and corporeal existence to impressions or their objects. Second, sounds, tastes, and smells do not appear to be external to the body, so the present approach cannot explain why we take *these* to have external existence. Third, our sight does not inform us of distance or outness immediately and without inference, "as is acknowleg'd by the most rational philosophers" (T 1.4.2.9, SBN 191), Berkeley presumably among them.

Hume turns next to independence, which is, he observes, on the whole a more important component of the belief in distinct existence than externality. "[W]hen we talk of real distinct existences," he writes, "we have commonly more in our eye their independency than external situation in place, and think an object has a sufficient reality, when its being is uninterrupted, and independent of the incessant revolutions, which we are conscious of in ourselves" (T 1.4.2.10, SBN 191). But independence, he insists, can hardly be an original object of the senses. A belief in independent objects can only be derived over time, from connected experience and observation.

After summarizing his argument (T 1.4.2.11, SBN 191–92), Hume offers, in the next two paragraphs, confirming evidence for its conclusion: colors, sounds, heat, and cold appear to the senses to exist just as motion and solidity do, hence the distinction we make between them as philosophers cannot take rise from perception alone (T 1.4.2.12–13, SBN 192). We can summarize Hume's progress up to this point as follows. After quickly discarding the possibility that the senses convey the idea of continued existence, he considers two ways in which they might convey the idea of distinct existence – two ways of explaining, by adverting to the senses, why we believe in objects distinct from ourselves. The first way, according to which the senses present impressions as images of distinct existences, would be justification-conferring, were the senses capable of such a dual presentation. But they are not. The second way, according to which the senses present impressions themselves as distinct, would (if it were the whole story) be justification-undermining, because the senses could present some impressions as external and others as internal only by suffering an illusion of difference. But the senses are incapable of any such illusion.[13] From this it follows that the senses cannot – and do not – explain the belief in body in the second way.

Despite Hume's distinction between competence and performance, it is clear that throughout his discussion of the senses, he has competence considerations uppermost in mind. The considerations are displayed in the following flow chart, where the words in small capitals are marks of logical structure.

Do the senses supply us with a belief in continued existence OR a belief in distinct existence?

NOT a belief in continued existence, because the senses cannot operate "after they have ceas'd all manner of operation" (T 1.4.2.3, SBN 188–89).

SO they can only impart a belief in distinct existence.

Would a perception then be conveyed as the image of a distinct existence OR as the distinct existence itself?

NOT as the image of a distinct existence, because the objects of the senses are single and the senses themselves are incapable of inference (T 1.4.2.4, SBN 189).

SO the perception must be conveyed as the distinct existence itself, meaning that it must be conveyed as something external to and independent of our selves (T 1.4.2.5, SBN 189).

BUT a perception could be so conveyed only by "a kind of fallacy and illusion" (T 1.4.2.5, SBN 189), and our senses cannot "convey a falshood" (T 1.4.2.11, SBN 192); they could convey perceptions as external and independent, moreover, only by fixing the boundaries of our selves and discovering that perceptions fall beyond them (T 1.4.2.6, 11, SBN 189–90, 192). It is "absurd" to suggest that they could manage this (T 1.4.2.6, SBN 190), and even if they somehow did, "they [would] not, nor is it possible they shou'd, deceive us" (T 1.4.2.11, SBN 192).

Every NOT or BUT in this display brings to bear some aspect of the competence whose limits Hume is investigating. That competence can be encapsulated under three headings: *influential only when stimulated; non-inferential, hence exhibiting their objects without intimating anything beyond them; exhibiting those objects as they truly are.* As the final heading indicates, and as Hume's choice of words ("fallacy," "illusion," "falshood," "they [would] not, nor is it possible they shou'd, deceive") confirms, that competence is, in part, normatively characterized. The normativity in Hume's characterization of the competence is clearest, perhaps, in the following passage from T 1.4.2.7 (SBN 190). Here again, Hume's assessment of sensory performance is led by considerations of competence.

[W]hatever other differences we may observe among [our impressions], they appear [to the senses], all of them, in their true colours, as impressions or perceptions. And indeed, if we consider the matter aright, 'tis scarce possible it shou'd be otherwise, nor is it conceivable that our senses shou'd be more capable of deceiving us in the situation and relations, than in the nature of our impressions. For since all actions and sensations of the mind are known to us by consciousness, they must necessarily appear in every particular what they are, and be what they appear. Every thing that enters the mind, being in *reality* a perception, 'tis impossible any thing shou'd to *feeling* appear different. This were to suppose, that even where we are most intimately conscious, we might be mistaken.

Reason

As the source of our belief in body, reason – that is, reason *uninflected by imagination* – is dismissed in a single paragraph (T 1.4.2.14, SBN 193). Hume begins by asking whether reason is *in fact* responsible for our belief in body. The arguments philosophers think they possess are, he says, "known but to very few"; it follows that it is not by their means "that children, peasants, and the greatest part of mankind are induc'd to attribute objects to some impressions, and deny them to others." And the conclusions of the vulgar on this topic are opposed to those of the philosophers, who assure us that everything appearing to the mind is "nothing but a perception, and is interrupted, and dependent on the mind." The vulgar attribute a distinct and continued existence "to the very things they feel or see." Since this conclusion is "entirely unreasonable," Hume concludes, it "must proceed from some other faculty than the understanding" (*understanding* serving here as another word for *reason*). Here again, Hume's treatment of performance is introduced by considerations of competence. Note that the unreasonableness of the vulgar belief functions as a premise, from which Hume (attentive, I am suggesting, to the normatively characterized limits of the competence of reason, when uninflected by imagination) infers that the belief is not produced by reason. Later in the Section, the inference is repeated: "'tis a false opinion [that objects are the same after interruption]; and consequently the opinion of their identity can never arise from reason" (T 1.4.2.43, SBN 209). The inference illustrates Hume's belief that reason operates by producing *good* arguments. Hence the competence of reason, like the competence of the senses, is normatively constituted. Were reason the cause of our belief in body, the explanation of our belief would be justification-conferring.[14]

Hume concludes by arguing that reason *could not possibly* produce the belief in body.

> To [this] we may add, that as long as we take our perceptions and objects to be the same, we can never infer the existence of the one from that of the other, nor form any argument from the relation of cause and effect; which is the only one that can assure us of matter of fact. Even after we distinguish our perceptions from our objects, 'twill appear presently, that we are still incapable of reasoning from the existence of one to that of the other. (T 1.4.2.14, SBN 193)

We cannot argue from impressions to objects if, like the vulgar, we identify them, and as we will see later on, we cannot hope for a better outcome if, like the philosophers, we distinguish them. "[U]pon the whole," Hume concludes, "our reason neither *does*, nor is it *possible it ever shou'd*, upon any supposition, give us an assurance of the continu'd and distinct existence of body" (emphasis added).

Imagination

If neither sense nor reason is its cause, the belief in body must be "entirely owing" to the imagination (T 1.4.2.14, SBN 193), which Hume addresses in the remainder of the Section. Reason, like sense, has the power to justify any belief whose presence it explains, but imagination, as we will see, carries no such privilege. Although scepticism is not an explicit theme in most of the rest of T 1.4.2 (it is officially reconsidered only at T 1.4.2.56 [SBN 217–18], after a brief mention at T 1.4.2.50 [SBN 214]), Hume calls attention throughout the Section to the justification-undermining character of the only kind of explanation of our belief in body that he can now provide.

That the source of Hume's scepticism lies in the justification-undermining character of the appeal to imagination is confirmed, I think, by a small but revealing fact. Only in the case of imagination is Hume's argument not divided into two parts, one concerning what the faculty in question *can* do, the other concerning what it does *in fact*. The reason, I suggest, is that an argument concerning the competence of the imagination (as opposed to its performance) is simply unavailable, because unlike sense and reason, imagination is not governed by norms internal to it, and it is constitutive norms that define the limits of competence as Hume understands it in T 1.4.2. To put it bluntly, the imagination is capable of almost *anything*.[15] The objects of sense, by contrast, always appear as they are, and the insights and deductions of reason, though not proof against all sceptical attack, satisfy standards constitutive of the faculty that delivers them.

Because impressions appear to be both "internal and perishing," the belief in their distinct and continued existence must, Hume proposes at T 1.4.2.15 (SBN 194), arise from a "concurrence" or interaction between their qualities and those of the imagination. And because we take only some of our impressions to possess (or represent) distinct and continued existence, careful comparison should reveal the qualities (on the side of the object or impression) that are at work.

The method of comparison shows that neither involuntariness nor vivacity is at issue. Pleasures and pains come to us whether we want them or not, and they often arrive with great force. Yet we do not deem them to have any existence beyond our perception. So we may dismiss those "vulgar opinions" that trace the belief in body to such causes. These opinions are not, despite the label, the views of ordinary men and women, but instead the "vulgar" – the usual or prevailing – opinions of philosophers. They can be found in – or at least extracted from – such works as Descartes's *Meditations* and Berkeley's *Principles* (Stroud 1977: 99). Hume does not represent himself as the first philosopher to try to explain our belief in body, or even as the first to try to explain it by appealing to the imagination.

Hume finds a more promising candidate in the "peculiar *constancy*" of the objects to which we ascribe a continued existence (T 1.4.2.18, SBN 194). These objects "present themselves in the same uniform manner, and change not upon account of any interruption in my seeing or perceiving them" (T 1.4.2.18, SBN 195). There are exceptions to this constancy. "Bodies often change their position and qualities," sometimes so much that they become "hardly knowable." But it is worth observing that even here, "they preserve a *coherence*, and have a regular dependence on each other; which is the foundation of a kind of reasoning from causation, and produces the opinion of their continu'd existence" (T 1.4.2.19, SBN 195). The fire in my chamber changes as it dies down, but I am familiar with such changes in other cases. So the opinion of continued existence, Hume suggests, depends on the coherence and constancy of certain impressions. The question now is "after what manner these qualities give rise to so extraordinary an opinion" (T 1.4.2.20, SBN 195).

Hume begins with coherence. The rough idea is that our perceptions change in regular ways. To say that one impression coheres with another is to say, for example, that an impression of the first kind is reliably succeeded by an impression of the second kind. As Hume explains at T 1.4.2.19 (SBN 195), "When I return to my chamber after an hour's absence," my fire is not as it was when I left it. But I am familiar, in other cases, with a pattern of change that makes the fire as it now appears just what we would expect to find given the fire as it was an hour ago. I therefore assume that the fire existed in my absence. In a sense – admittedly a very stretched sense – the fire's appearance upon my return contradicts my past experience of fires (T 1.4.2.20, SBN 196), in which the impression of a roaring fire is rarely (if ever) immediately succeeded by the impression of dying ashes. In order to "reconcile" the contradiction, I suppose that the fire existed for an hour during which it diminished gradually, as my past experience of fires suggests it should. The supposition of its continued existence "was at first entirely arbitrary and hypothetical," but it "acquires a force and evidence by its being the only one, upon which I can reconcile these contradictions" (T 1.4.2.20, SBN 197).

This reasoning is derived from custom and experience, but it bestows upon perceptions a greater regularity than they actually exhibit (T 1.4.2.21, SBN 197). The inference therefore "arises from the understanding, and from custom in an indirect and oblique manner." As he explains, "custom can only be the effect of repeated perceptions," from which it follows that "the extending of custom and reasoning beyond the perceptions can never be the direct and natural effect of the constant repetition and connexion, but must arise from the co-operation of some other principles" (T 1.4.2.21, SBN 198).

One of those other principles – the only one Hume specifies – is the tendency of the imagination, "like a galley put in motion by the oars," to continue any chain of thinking on which it has been set (T 1.4.2.22, SBN 198). "Objects have a certain coherence even as they appear to our senses; but this coherence is much greater and more uniform, if we suppose the objects to have a continu'd existence; and as the mind is once in the train of observing an uniformity among objects, it naturally continues, till it renders the uniformity as compleat as possible." This tendency has, of course, no justification.[16]

It is at this point that Hume shifts his focus from coherence to constancy.[17] It is a puzzling shift that deserves a close look. It will be best to begin a short distance back, with Hume's insistence that "the extending of custom and reasoning beyond ... perceptions" cannot be the effect of repetition alone. "[R]egularity in our perceptions," he had already written, "can never be a foundation for us to infer a greater degree of regularity in some objects, which are not perceiv'd; since this supposes a contradiction, viz. a habit acquir'd by what was never present to the mind" (T 1.4.2.21, SBN 197). Jonathan Bennett objects:[18]

This seems to imply that a Humean 'habit' can never lead to anything but the experiences that caused it in the first place – which is just to abandon the concept of habit and, with it, the entire theory of the association of ideas. That cannot be what Hume means. He must be aware of how it conflicts with his own theory according to which every causal prediction outruns its experiential basis. I am baffled by the 'degree of regularity' remarks. (2001: 296)

Bennett is of course right to say that habit must take us beyond its basis in experience. But consider the difference between the following two lines of reasoning:

> Half of all observed *A*s have been *B*s.
> I therefore expect half of all future *A*s to be *B*s.

> Half of all observed *A*s have been *B*s.
> I therefore expect three-quarters of all future *A*s to be *B*s.

In each case I form an expectation that runs beyond its experiential basis, but in the second case the expectation runs farther – far enough to make us wonder whether, if habit is responsible for the first expectation, something besides habit is helping to support the second. Hume was worried, I think, about audacious expectations of precisely the second sort: because my roaring fire perceptions have typically (but by no means universally) been followed by perceptions of gradual diminishment, I come to expect that in every such case, perceptions of a gradually diminishing blaze will be available. To insure their availability, I suppose that they continue to exist when unperceived. Here there is a move from *most* to *all* as daring as my imagined move from *one-half* to *three-quarters*. To explain it, Hume needs more than habit; he needs, as he says, a principle that urges us to render uniformity "as compleat as possible" – what Louis E. Loeb calls "the galley."[19]

After comparing the imagination to a galley, Hume observes that "[t]he simple supposition of ... continu'd existence ... gives us a notion of a much greater regularity among objects, than what they have when we look no farther than our senses" (T 1.4.2.22, SBN 198). His shift from coherence to constancy takes place in the very next sentence:

But whatever force we may ascribe to this principle, I am afraid 'tis too weak to support alone so vast an edifice, as is that of the continu'd existence of all external bodies; and that we must join the *constancy* of their appearance to the *coherence*, in order to give a satisfactory account of that opinion. (T 1.4.2.23, SBN 198–99)

What is the principle? Commentators generally take it to be the entire coherence-driven mechanism, what Loeb calls "custom-and-galley" (2002: 186): custom (or habit) joined to the inertia of an imagination that custom sets in motion. On this basis, Loeb argues that Hume shifts from coherence to constancy not because he is dissatisfied with the coherence account, but "simply because not all objects exhibit coherence" (2002: 191; indeed, Loeb adds, "most objects exhibit constancy rather than coherence"). I think there is some reason to believe that the principle in question is the galley principle alone.[20] But even if the principle in question is, as Loeb supposes, custom-and-galley, I think Hume in the end concludes that the galley cannot carry out the task he has assigned to it. It is too weak, even when joined to custom, to support so vast an edifice as the enduring external world, because if it were strong enough for that, it would be strong enough to make reckless inferences of my second sort standard rather than exceptional. The involvement of the galley accounts, I believe, for Hume's observation that although our "conclusion from the coherence of appearances may seem to be of the same nature with our reasonings concerning causes and effects; as being deriv'd from custom, and regulated by past experience; we shall find upon examination, that they are at the bottom considerably different from each other, and that this inference arises from the understanding, and from custom in an indirect and oblique manner" (T 1.4.2.21, SBN 197).[21] The obliquity of the mind's movement from custom to continued existence counts not only against the justification of that movement, but also against its strength or psychological force.

Whatever Hume's motive for shifting to constancy, he believes that it resembles coherence in first giving rise to a belief in continued existence, which gives rise in turn to a belief in distinct or independent existence. Our interrupted perceptions of the sun or ocean are different, Hume explains, but we "consider them ... individually the same, upon account of their resemblance" (T 1.4.2.24, SBN 199) – yet another conclusion with no color of justification. Because "this interruption ... is contrary to their perfect identity," we find ourselves "somewhat at a loss, and are involv'd in a kind of contradiction." To remove ourselves from the difficulty, we "disguise ... the interruption, or rather remove it entirely, by supposing that these interrupted perceptions are connected by a real existence, of which we are insensible." And this supposition – another unjustified invention – draws force and vivacity from "the memory of these broken impressions, and from that propensity, which they give us, to suppose them the same" (ibid.).

Having offered this summary, Hume then presents his account at greater length, in four parts. Rather than dwell on the details, I want to move directly to the great difficulty they present.[22] Imagination causes us to believe that our impressions have continued existence. And continued existence, as we earlier agreed, entails distinct existence. "But when we compare experiments, and reason a little upon them, we quickly perceive, that the doctrine of the independent existence of our sensible perceptions is contrary to the plainest experience" (T 1.4.2.44, SBN 210). The constancy account of our belief in continued existence is therefore justification-undermining.

Here are some of the experiments establishing that sensible perceptions do not exist independently.[23] We notice that when we press an eye with a finger, objects are doubled "and one half of them ... remov'd from their common and natural position" (T 1.4.2.45, SBN 210). We cannot attribute a continued existence to the objects in each pair, and "as they are both of the same nature, we clearly perceive, that all our perceptions are dependent on our organs, and the disposition of our nerves and animal spirits" (T 1.4.2.45, SBN 211). The opinion is confirmed by what is now called "perceptual relativity": apparent changes in size, figure, color, and other qualities that arise from changes in us. From all these we learn "that our sensible perceptions are not possest of any distinct or independent existence" (ibid.).

Now from this we should infer that objects do not have a continued existence.[24] But instead of reaching this conclusion, philosophers, at least, distinguish between perceptions and objects, the perceptions "interrupted, and perishing, and different at every return," and the latter uninterrupted and identical over time (T 1.4.2.46, SBN 211).

Hume makes two observations about this philosophical system. First, it "has no primary recommendation, either to reason or the imagination" (T 1.4.2.47, SBN 212). It has no primary recommendation to reason because there is no argument that can take us from the existence of perceptions to the existence of objects. Arguments from cause and effect are the only ones that could, but these arguments always rest on past experience. "But as no beings are ever present to the mind but perceptions; it follows that we may observe a conjunction or a relation of cause and effect between different perceptions, but can never observe it betwixt perceptions and objects" (ibid.). Note that there is no appeal here to specific difference. Hume is instead thinking, as T 1.2.6.9 (SBN 68) suggests he should be, of the attribution of "different relations, connexions and *durations*" (emphasis added). The only objects present to the mind are *interrupted* objects (i.e., "perceptions"). We cannot infer the existence of uninterrupted objects (i.e., "objects") because we never experience them.

Nor does the philosophical system have a primary recommendation to the imagination, which would never have arrived at the system were we not in the grip of a prior tendency toward the vulgar system. Given that our perceptions are "broken, and interrupted, and however like, [but] still different from each other," the "fancy" will not, "directly and immediately," proceed to a belief in another existence "*resembling these perceptions in their nature*, but yet continu'd, and uninterrupted, and identical" (T 1.4.2.48, SBN 213; emphasis added; note that the italicized words offer additional support to the reading I proposed in section 1).

Hume's second observation is that the philosophical system "*acquires all its influence on the imagination from the vulgar one*" (T 1.4.2.49, SBN 213). This is, he says, a "natural and unavoidable consequence" of the first observation (ibid.). Hume then gives another summary of his basic argument, as a way of displaying the relationship between the two systems:

The imagination naturally runs on in this train of thinking. Our perceptions are our only objects: Resembling perceptions are the same, however broken or interrupted in their appearance: This appearing interruption is contrary to the identity:

The interruption consequently extends not beyond the appearance, and the perception or object really continues to exist, even when absent from us: Our sensible perceptions have, therefore, a continu'd and uninterrupted existence. But as a little reflection destroys this conclusion, that our perceptions have a continu'd existence, by showing that they have a dependent one, 'twou'd naturally be expected, that we must altogether reject the opinion, that there is such a thing in nature as a continu'd existence, which is preserv'd even when it no longer appears to the senses. The case, however, is otherwise. Philosophers are so far from rejecting the opinion of a continu'd existence upon rejecting that of the independence and continuance of our sensible perceptions, that tho' all sects agree in the latter sentiment, the former, which is, in a manner, its necessary consequence, has been peculiar to a few extravagant sceptics; who after all maintain'd that opinion in words only, and were never able to bring themselves sincerely to believe it. (T 1.4.2.50, SBN 213–14)

Hume then takes note of the "great difference" between opinions formed after "a calm and profound reflection" and those embraced "by a kind of instinct or natural impulse" (T 1.4.2.51, SBN 214). The philosophical opinion may prevail in moments of intense reflective concentration, but when we "relax our thoughts," the instinctive opinions will reassert themselves (ibid.). After "leaving their closets," philosophers "mingle with the rest of mankind in those exploded opinions, that our perceptions are our only objects, and continue identically and uninterruptedly the same in all their interrupted appearances" (T 1.4.2.53, SBN 216). In two ways, even the philosophical opinion depends on the fancy. First, philosophers "suppose external objects to resemble internal perceptions" (T 1.4.2.54, SBN 216). They do not, in other words, suppose that external objects are specifically different from internal perceptions. "We never can conceive any thing but perceptions, and therefore must make every thing resemble them" (ibid.). Second, "we take it for granted, that every particular object resembles that perception, which it causes" (T 1.4.2.55, SBN 217).

Hume now reflects that despite the commonsense confidence with which T 1.4.2 began, he feels himself "*at present*" to be "of a quite contrary sentiment": more inclined to lose faith in sense or imagination altogether "than to place in it such an implicit confidence" (T 1.4.2.56, SBN 217). His actual words are worth quoting in full, because they put him at a considerable distance from sentiments he seemed previously to embrace with great sincerity:

I begun this subject with premising, that we ought to have an implicit faith in our senses, and that this wou'd be the conclusion, I shou'd draw from the whole of my reasoning. But to be ingenuous, I feel myself *at present* of a quite contrary sentiment, and am more inclin'd to repose no faith at all in my senses, or rather imagination, than to place in it such an implicit confidence. (T 1.4.2.56, SBN 217)

It may be worth recalling here the original meaning of "implicit faith" or *fides implicita*: blind persuasion in matters spiritual, resting not on one's own evidence, but rather on the authority of another person or institution.[25] Hume claims to have begun by premising that we *ought* to have an implicit faith in body, but this is not strictly accurate: he spoke not at all of what we ought to do, but only of what we "must" or cannot help but do. At the moment, of course, the word *ought* is exactly what he needs to express his disappointment. He sees, now, that the belief in body is not justified and that it would be wrong for him to place his trust in a process of imagination with which he cannot now identify. That imaginative process is, at the present moment, genuinely other. A faith in its deliverances would be "implicit" in something close to the original sense of that expression. It would be a faith in the authority of another, but in T 1.4.2, that authority has been exploded by the power of reason or reflection with which the "I" of Hume's text is now identified. That is why Hume's scepticism (at this moment, and when recollected at later moments) can fairly be described as a moral achievement: it alone is faithful to the I who has assumed the task of self-examination. Hume continues as follows:

I cannot conceive how such trivial qualities of the fancy, conducted by such false suppositions, can ever lead to any solid and rational system. They are the coherence and constancy of our perceptions, which produce the opinion of their continu'd existence; tho' these qualities of perceptions have no perceivable connexion with such an existence. The constancy of our perceptions has the most considerable effect, and yet is attended with the greatest difficulties. 'Tis a gross illusion to suppose, that our resembling perceptions are numerically the same; and 'tis this illusion, which leads us into the opinion, that these perceptions are uninterrupted, and are still existent, even when they are not present to the senses. This is the case with our popular system. And as to our philosophical one, 'tis liable to the same difficulties; and is over-and-above loaded with this absurdity, that it at once denies and establishes the vulgar supposition. Philosophers deny our resembling perceptions to be identically the same, and uninterrupted; and yet have so great a propensity to believe them such, that they arbitrarily invent a new set of perceptions, to which they attribute these qualities. I say, a new set of perceptions: For we may well suppose in general, but 'tis impossible for us distinctly to conceive, objects to be in their nature any thing but exactly the same with perceptions. What then can we look for from this confusion of groundless and extraordinary opinions but error and falshood? And how can we justify to ourselves any belief we repose in them? (T 1.4.2.56, SBN 217–18)

We cannot justify our belief in the continued and distinct existence of body. "This sceptical doubt," Hume continues, "is a malady, which can never be radically cur'd, but must return upon us every moment, however we may chace it away, and sometimes may seem entirely free from it" (T 1.4.2.57, SBN 218). He continues:

'Tis impossible upon any system to defend ... [our] senses; and we but expose them farther when we endeavour to justify them in that manner. As the sceptical doubt arises naturally from a profound and intense reflection on those subjects, it always encreases, the farther we carry our reflections, whether in opposition or conformity to it. (T 1.4.2.57, SBN 218)

Here Hume acknowledges that scepticism undermines the confidence with which the Section began. Hume's hope had been to put justification aside and to engage in a causal inquiry. That inquiry was conducted "in opposition" to sceptical doubt, or in spite of it, but the kind of scientific tunnel vision meant to keep doubt out of view brought us face-to-face with doubt at every turn. The only scientifically satisfying account of our belief in body proved to be not even justification-neutral but instead justification-undermining.[26]

There is, Hume concludes, but one remedy for this doubt, which can never be uprooted: "Carelessness and in-attention" (T 1.4.2.57, SBN 218). We will discuss its power to mitigate in just a moment. Because our capacity for carelessness insures that even the most sceptical philosopher will, upon relaxing his or her reflective intensity, be fully "perswaded" that there is "both an external and internal world," Hume announces his intention "to examine some general systems both antient and modern, which have been propos'd of both" (T 1.4.3 is on the ancient system of the external world, and T 1.4.4 is on its modern counterpart; T 1.4.5 is on the ancient system of the internal world, and T 1.4.6 is on its modern counterpart) before moving on, in Book 2, to "a more particular enquiry concerning our impressions" – that is, our passions (ibid.).

3. SCEPTICISM LIMITED, SCEPTICISM EXTENDED

I want to conclude by calling attention, briefly, to some of the ways in which the scepticism of *Treatise* 1.4.2 is limited or mitigated, and to an important way in which it is, in *Treatise* 1.4.4, "Of the modern philosophy," extended.

Near the end of T 1.4.2, Hume contrasts those "opinions as we form after a calm and profound reflection" with those "we embrace by a kind of instinct or natural impulse, on account of their suitableness and conformity to the mind" (T 1.4.2.51, SBN 214). The first or "philosophical" opinions are able to prevail so long as "our attention is bent upon the subject," but "the moment we relax our thoughts, nature will display herself, and draw us back to our former opinion." Sometimes, Hume testifies, nature "can stop our progress even in the midst of our most profound reflections, and keep us from running on with all the consequences of any philosophical opinion" (ibid.). The first way in which the scepticism of T 1.4.2 is mitigated, then, is that it is (at least in its active phase) *temporary*.[27]

It is, however, a *radical* scepticism in Fogelin's (1985: 5) sense: it condemns our belief in body as "wholly ungrounded"[28] – the vulgar belief because it is false, and the philosophical belief because it is unjustified (and unjustifiable). But this radical scepticism is *theoretical* rather than *prescriptive*. Radical theoretical scepticism (with regard to body) simply appraises our belief (1985: 6); it stops short of recommending that it be suspended.

The scepticism in *Treatise* 1.4.2 is, finally, *epistemological* rather than *conceptual*. "An epistemological skeptic accepts a system of beliefs as intelligible," Fogelin explains, "but challenges the supposed grounds for these beliefs. A conceptual skeptic challenges the very intelligibility of a system of beliefs" (ibid.). If the belief in body involved the idea of an object specifically different from perceptions (as Livingston, Strawson, and Pears all suppose), it would be open to a sceptical challenge of the second sort. But we have seen in section 1 that it does not and, in section 2, that Hume's case in T 1.4.2 against the belief rests entirely on its falsehood-or-unjustification .[29]

Despite these limitations or mitigations, the scepticism of T 1.4.2 is extended in T 1.4.4, "Of the modern philosophy." In the later Section, we encounter a conceptual scepticism – a scepticism of just the sort that Pears thinks he finds in T 1.4.2. There Hume argues that when, reasoning from cause and effect, we refine our conception of body, it vanishes:

When we reason from cause and effect, we conclude, that neither colour, sound, taste, nor smell have a continu'd and independent existence. When we exclude these sensible qualities there remains nothing in the universe, which has such an existence. (T 1.4.4.15, SBN 231)

As he later explains, it is not "possible for us to reason justly and regularly from causes and effects, and at the same time believe the continu'd existence of matter" (T 1.4.7.4, SBN 266).

Here, then, in a nutshell, is Hume's sceptical treatment of the belief in body: as T 1.4.2 begins, the meaning of the belief is carefully delineated, and a conception of bodies as specifically different from perceptions is swiftly (and, so far as T 1.4.2 is concerned, forever) set aside. In what remains of T 1.4.2, every form of belief in the continuous and distinct existence of perceptions (or in the continuous and distinct existence of objects specifically the same as perceptions) is shown to be false or unjustified. And in T 1.4.4, a prominent way of conceiving of bodies as specifically different from perceptions – the way characteristic of modern philosophy – is condemned as contentless.

In *An Enquiry concerning Human Understanding*, Hume's sceptical treatment of body is, in at least two ways, markedly different: he offers no real account of what the belief in body comes to, and he offers no explanation of its grip on us, attributing it simply to "natural instinct or prepossession" (EHU 12.7, SBN 151). But the broad structure of *Enquiry* 12, Part 1, is strikingly similar to that of T 1.4.2 and 1.4.4. Insofar as he explains what the belief in body comes to, he concentrates, as before, on continuity and independence: "we always suppose an external universe, which depends not on our perception, but would exist, though we and every sensible creature were absent or annihilated" (ibid.). He argues that the belief in body, in any form, is either "contrary to reason" or with "no rational evidence" (EHU 12.16, SBN 155, echoing T 1.4.2) and that the characteristically modern version of the belief "in a manner annihilate[s]" matter or body, leaving "only a certain unknown, inexplicable *something*, as the cause of our perceptions; a notion so imperfect, that no sceptic will think it worth while to contend against it" (ibid., echoing T 1.4.4). A more general notion of objects specifically different from perceptions is, as it was in the *Treatise*, simply set aside. Hume asks,

> By what argument can it be proved, that the perceptions of the mind must be caused by external objects, entirely different from them, though resembling them (if that be possible) and could not arise either from the energy of the mind itself, or from the suggestion of some invisible and unknown spirit, or from some other cause still more unknown to us? (EHU 12.11, SBN 152–53)

Notice the difference between this sentence, the first in Paragraph 11 of *Enquiry* 12, and the following one, the first in Paragraph 12:[30]

> It is a question of fact, whether the perceptions of the senses be produced by external objects, resembling them: How shall this question be determined?

The external objects of EHU 12.11 are "entirely different" from perceptions, but it is doubtful, as Hume's parenthetical comment indicates, that they are even possible. Because they are said to resemble perceptions, the objects cannot be "entirely" or "specifically" (in species or kind) different from them.[31] When, in EHU 12.12, the existence of external objects resembling our perceptions is, for the first time, firmly classified as a question of fact, Hume quietly drops all mention of "entire difference."

It is true that the sceptical conclusions of Part 1 of *Enquiry* 12 may be modified, perhaps even repudiated, in Parts 2 and 3. But this is one more respect in which this Part of the *Enquiry* resembles Sections 1.4.2 and 1.4.4 of the *Treatise*, whose conclusions may be modified, perhaps even repudiated, in T 1.4.7. My topic has been not T 1.4.7 but T 1.4.2, and the similarities I have enumerated help, in my view, to confirm the sceptical interpretation of T 1.4.2 developed in this essay.

NOTES

This essay was originally prepared for a symposium on "Skepticism in Hume's *Treatise*" at the 29th Hume Conference, Helsinki, Finland, August 2002. My fellow symposiasts were David Owen (the symposium's organizer) and Donald Ainslie; I thank them both for their detailed comments. An earlier version was presented at the conference "Humean Readings" at the University of Rome in June 2002; I am grateful to Tito Magri, Andrea Branchi, and their colleagues for the opportunity to participate and for their very stimulating comments. A later version was presented at Yale University in March 2004 and at the University of Notre Dame in April 2005; I thank audiences at both institutions for their questions and suggestions. I am also grateful to Donald Ainslie and Annemarie Butler for suggested changes, and to Butler for her careful work on the final version of the essay. Finally, I want to acknowledge the help of members of my graduate seminar on Hume at MIT in the fall of 2002: Mimi Cukier, Helena de Bres, Johanna Goth, Patrick Hawley, Sean Holland, Dilip Ninan, and Jessica Sin.

1. I discuss T 1.4.7, but in the context of inductive scepticism, in Winkler 1999.
2. Not every "realist" interpreter of Hume on our belief in body agrees with Livingston (1984) and Strawson (1989). John P. Wright (1983: 81n19) recognizes that "[t]hroughout 'Of scepticism with regard to the senses' Hume's conception of external objects is one which takes them to resemble perceptions totally; they are 'specifically' the same as those perceptions."
3. See also Pears 1990: 157, where even the plain man's belief in body is said to have "no coherent content."
4. Thus Pears (1990: 194) follows up the lines I have quoted with a discussion of T 1.2.6.9 (SBN 67–68), where Hume considers objects specifically different from perceptions.
5. See Loeb's very valuable study (2002: 164, 166, 169). See also Loeb 2001: esp. 156. Bennett 2001 may be another example, but his new book presents a confusing picture. He writes that in T 1.4.2 Hume "sets aside as dead the question of bodies which are ... 'specifically different from perceptions' " (2001: 286), but only three pages later he says that the philosophical version of the belief in body "is a belief in items that are categorially different from perceptions" (2001: 289).
6. I borrow here from Winkler 2000b: 74–84, 86–87; see in particular 78–79. Some of the same points are made by David Owen (2000: 325–26), though I do not share Owen's view that according to views expressed (I presume) elsewhere in the *Treatise*, "when we, as philosophers, think about trees, we take ourselves to be thinking of something specifically different from perceptions" (2000: 325). Here Owen seems to be moving toward Pears's reading.
7. For expressions of related perplexities, see Fogelin 1985: 64 and Baier 1991: 108.
8. On symmetry, see Bloor 1991: 7, 175–79.
9. My use of "propositional content" and "doxastic commitment" follows Robert Brandom's in (2000).
10. See, e.g., T 1.4.2.5 (SBN 189) ("external to, and independent of ourselves") and T 1.4.2.8 (SBN 190) ("distinct from ourselves").
11. Hume's argument here suggests that he is interpreting the belief in the continued existence of an object as the belief, held as it happens when the

object is unperceived, that the object exists, rather than as the belief that the object exists when unperceived. On the first interpretation, the continued existence of the object, falling outside the scope of the belief operator, is not really part of the *content* of the belief. That this is Hume's understanding is suggested not only at T 1.4.2.3 (SBN 188–89), but again at T 1.4.2.11 (SBN 191), where the earlier argument is summarized, and at T 1.4.2.38 (SBN 207), where he speaks of our saying of an object, "[w]hen we are absent from it," that "it still exists." These passages indicate the conceptual modesty of the belief in body as Hume interprets it. At one moment, we believe in the existence of a body because we are perceiving it. At the next moment, we continue to believe in its existence even though we are perceiving it no longer. There is no change in content from one moment to the next. The body may have vanished, but there has been no change in our concepts.

12. This is a theme developed at length by Wayne Waxman in (1994).

13. They cannot suffer such an illusion, as Hume contends at T 1.4.2.7 (SBN 190), and they do not in fact suffer such an illusion, as he argues in effect at T 1.4.2.9–11 (SBN 190–92).

14. Although I believe that Hume in T 1.4.2 views reason as a faculty that characteristically operates by producing good arguments, a very different view emerges elsewhere, for example in *An Enquiry concerning Human Understanding*, where he observes that nature would not entrust the life-sustaining operation of causal inference "to the fallacious deductions of our reason" (EHU 5.22, SBN 55). See also EHU 9.5 (SBN 106).

15. To be entirely accurate, there is at least one norm that governs even imagination, at least in T 1.4.2: the ideas and beliefs it engenders must be distinctly conceivable. Hume imposes this norm on every candidate faculty at T 1.4.2.2 (SBN 188), a passage I discuss at length in section 1. The imagination can also weary, or lose force over time.

16. In this respect, it may be worth comparing to the kind of illegitimate extension of causal or inductive reasoning condemned in Section 11 of the first *Enquiry*.

17. For an illuminating look at this shift and a survey of the literature it has provoked, see Loeb 2002: 188–93. My explanation of the shift is an instance of what Loeb calls "the dissatisfaction hypothesis" (2002: 191). Loeb argues that Hume is satisfied with his treatment of coherence and that he turns to constancy "simply because not all objects exhibit coherence; indeed, most objects exhibit constancy rather than coherence" (2002: 191).

18. For further discussion of some of the issues Bennett raises, see Gomberg 1976.

19. Or the "psychological galley": see Loeb 2002: 179ff. H. H. Price (1940: 55) calls it the "Inertia Principle."

20. The reason is narrowly textual: in T 1.4.2.21 (SBN 198), Hume says that the belief in continued existence cannot arise from custom alone, "but must arise from the co-operation of some other principles." In Paragraph 22 (SBN 198), he reminds us of the role of the galley principle in producing our standard of equality. "The same principle," he says, "makes us easily entertain this opinion of the continu'd existence of body." The next use of "principle" comes at the beginning of Paragraph 23 (SBN 198): "But whatever force we may ascribe to this principle, I am afraid 'tis too weak." So "this principle"

seems to be the same "principle" stated in Paragraph 23. Weighing against this is his comment that the principle is "too weak to support *alone* so vast an edifice" (emphasis added), but perhaps this means "too weak to support alone so vast an edifice, in response to the coherence of appearances."

21. If the inference arose from the understanding alone, it would, I assume, fall under "reason" as that term is understood in T 1.4.2, rather than under "the imagination."

22. For helpful discussion of some of the details, see Passmore 1952: 120–22; Stroud 1977: 100–5; Fogelin 1985: 70–75; and especially Bennett 2001: 297–304.

23. Hume nonetheless believes that it is *possible* for them to exist independently; his present complaint is that they do not in fact do so. Because the mind is nothing but a heap or collection of perceptions, united by certain relations, each of its perceptions is distinguishable – and therefore separable – from every other. Hume writes, "it evidently follows, that there is no absurdity in separating any particular perception from the mind; that is, in breaking off all its relations, with that connected mass of perceptions, which constitute a thinking being" (T 1.4.2.39, SBN 207). Hence there is "no contradiction" (T 1.4.2.40, SBN 208) in the supposition of continued existence. For an illuminating discussion of these claims, see Cook 1968.

24. Jonathan Bennett (2001: 305) objects that "[t]he facts that Hume adduces show at most that our organs affect what perceptions *we have in our minds*, and not what perceptions *there are*." Fair enough, but Bennett also says that Hume's empirical data "have no force" against the belief that some perceptions exist when nobody perceives them. These facts certainly count against the belief, and if, as Hume thinks, nothing counts in favor of it, the facts against would seem to be decisive.

25. "Implicit" is one of the characteristic descriptive categories of Hume's *History of England*, in which leading characters regularly place "implicit" trust or confidence in others, sometimes to their benefit and often to their detriment. There it stands, as it does here, for a resignation of judgment- or decision-making authority: its placement in the hands of someone (or something) else. Hume also speaks of "implicit faith" at EHU 4.3 (SBN 26). Its use there is strongly condemnatory: deeper inquiry into the topic of EHU 4 may, he says, destroy "that implicit faith and security, which is the bane of all reasoning and free enquiry." Here Hume seems to be thinking of a faith that would discourage philosophizing; perhaps the implicit faith of T 1.4.2 has (in Hume's view) the same lamentable potential. If so, Hume's assessment of implicit faith resembles that of Locke, who condemns it repeatedly in colorful terms. (See *Essay* 1.4.22, 2.33.17, 4.12.6, 4.17.4 in Locke [1690] 1975: 99, 400, 642, 671.)

26. Here I am especially indebted to Ira Singer (2000). See also Fogelin 1993: esp. 93, 107.

27. In its latent phase it is inexpungible, as Hume says at T 1.4.2.57 (SBN 218). Here I have been influenced by Terence Penelhum's striking comparison between sceptical doubt and positive religious commitment. Each may be "active" for only brief periods, but as Penelhum (2000: 192) argues, the fact that everyday circumstances weaken my religious attitudes "does not show that I did not really believe what I said to myself in the closet or in the

church." See too Singer 1995: esp. 617 on "background skepticism," which Singer describes as "a general willingness or tendency to doubt which allows for moments of conviction."

28. I have been helped not only by reading Fogelin's work, but also by Don Garrett (2004).

29. Fogelin (1985: 75–79) agrees.

30. These differences are neglected by Galen Strawson (2000: 39). Strawson writes, "It is, [Hume] says, a straightforward '*question of fact*, whether the perceptions of the senses be produced by *external objects ... entirely different from them*' (E153; my emphases). This is *very* clear." The words Strawson encloses in single quotation marks are stitched together from two separate sentences, in two separate paragraphs. The words he places before the elliptical dots come from the later paragraph, and the words he places after the dots come from the earlier one. When the paragraphs are separated, as above, and the context and order of Strawson's selections are restored, the point Hume is making seems to be the very opposite of the one Strawson takes him to be making.

31. For a view different from the one I take here, see Butler 2010b.

7 The Problem of Believing in Yourself: Hume's Doubts about Personal Identity

After considering the psychological propensities that produce the ordinary person's (the "vulgar") and the philosopher's beliefs in the existence of bodies, and after assessing a variety of philosophical distinctions about bodies, Hume turns to consider perceptions themselves. In *Treatise* 1.4.5, Hume rejects the existence of immaterial substances and the requirement that perceptions inhere in such substances (T 1.4.5.3–7, SBN 232–35). He argues that a perception may exist without location, and it is because of a psychological propensity to "compleat the union" that we attribute location to nonspatial perceptions (e.g., the taste of a fig) (T 1.4.5.8–28, SBN 235–46). Applying his account of causation, he discovers that motion of bodies may produce thought and that arguments that purport to prove otherwise rely on a mistaken account of causation (T 1.4.5.29–32, SBN 246–50).

In *Treatise* 1.4.6, Hume turns to the topic of personal identity, distinguishing between personal identity "as it regards our thought or imagination, and as it regards our passions or the concern we take in ourselves" (T 1.4.6.5, SBN 253). He focuses on the first in this Section. In *Treatise* 1.4.2, Hume explains that "identity" requires invariableness and uninterruptedness over time, and in *Treatise* 1.4.3, he holds that "simplicity" requires a lack of parts at a time. When certain philosophers believe in the perfect identity and simplicity of self, they claim that there is one thing (e.g., a soul or a self) distinct from perceptions that has no parts and continues to exist uninterruptedly and invariably over time. In *Treatise* 1.4.6, Hume argues that the true idea of a human mind is a collection of different and separable perceptions. It is neither perfectly identical nor simple, but he thinks that there are natural psychological propensities that lead us[1] to mistakenly attribute identity and simplicity to it.

In the Appendix to the *Treatise*, published along with Book 3 almost two years after Books 1 and 2, Hume confesses that he has discovered an inconsistency involving his account of personal identity. He rehearses the arguments that led him "to deny the strict and proper identity and simplicity of a self or thinking being" (T App. 10, SBN 633). But he admits to finding a "difficulty . . . too hard for my understanding" (T App. 21, SBN 636) in explaining "the principles, that unite our successive perceptions in our thought or consciousness" (T App. 20, SBN 635–36). Unfortunately, Hume's self-criticism is far from clear. He writes, "In short there are two principles, which I cannot render consistent; nor is it in my power to renounce either of them" (T App. 21, SBN 636). Most scholars acknowledge that the two principles are not by themselves inconsistent. So a wide range of interpretations has been offered to explain Hume's dissatisfaction.

This variety arises because Hume's account raises a host of interpretive issues. Some scholars take Hume to be addressing a metaphysical topic, concerning how perceptions are collected together into a single, identical mind; others take Hume to be addressing a psychological question, concerning the principles that lead us to the idea or belief in the simplicity and identity of the mind. I shall contend that Hume is best understood as offering a psychological account of how we come to *believe* in identity and simplicity.

Many scholars have wondered how a perception can represent a self.[2] Perceptions can represent objects, such as tables and chimneys, but not the perceiver herself. Jonathan Ellis (2006) has argued that this is the failure Hume discovers. I discuss two interpretations, both of which encounter textual and philosophical problems.

There has been a scholarly dispute about how to characterize higher-level perceptions and whether Hume's account of personal identity requires them. In the first Section of the *Treatise*, Hume distinguishes "primary" ideas from "secondary" ideas (T 1.1.1.11, SBN 6–7). Primary ideas are copies of impressions, and secondary ideas are copies of primary ideas. The precision of this distinction enables us to carefully interpret Hume's explanation of the mistaken belief in personal identity. As I show, Hume's self-criticism cannot be understood without it.

Finally, I argue, in substantial agreement with John Bricke (1977 and 1980), that Hume's crisis in the Appendix concerns problems with the explanations of personal identity (and simplicity[3]) involving resemblance and causation. Drawing on the distinction between the intentional object of belief and the perceptions that constitute the belief (the "vehicle" of the belief), and, further, paying special attention to the distinction between higher-level and lower-level perceptions, I argue that Hume's explanatory principles fail to connect present perceptions with temporally distant perceptions. For example, Hume cannot explain how I believe that I (now) am the same person as she who visited Hume's tomb years ago.

I. REJECTED ORIGINS OF THE IDEA OF PERSONAL IDENTITY

Prior to the Section on personal identity, Hume has already rejected the idea of a substantial self (T 1.4.5.3–4, SBN 232–33), failing to find an impression of it. Supposing for the sake of argument that substances are distinct from perceptions, Hume argues:

As every idea is deriv'd from a precedent impression, had we any idea of the substance of our minds, we must also have an impression of it; which is very difficult, if not impossible, to be conceiv'd. For how can an impression represent a substance, otherwise than by resembling it? And how can an impression resemble a substance, since, according to this philosophy, it is not a substance, and has none of the peculiar qualities or characteristics of a substance? (T 1.4.5.3, SBN 232–33)

The argument depends on the Copy Principle: any idea we have is ultimately derived from and resembles one or more impressions. Ex hypothesi, perceptions are unlike substances in qualities and characteristics. So perceptions cannot resemble substances. Therefore, there can be no impression of a substance. Nor can there be an idea of a substance. A fortiori, there can be no idea of a substantial mind.

A philosopher might try to evade this argument by definition: "a substance is *something which may exist by itself*" (T 1.4.5.5, SBN 233). Hume observes that this definition applies to perceptions too. He argues: "since all our perceptions are different from each other, and from every thing else in the universe, they are also distinct and separable, and may be consider'd as separately existent, and may exist separately, and have no need of any thing else to support their existence. They are, therefore, substances, as far as this definition explains a substance" (ibid.). The definition fails to distinguish substances from perceptions.

Having rejected the idea of substance, Hume concludes that the idea of inherence (or "inhesion") fails too. "Inhesion in something is suppos'd to be requisite to support the existence of our perceptions. Nothing appears requisite to support the existence of a perception. We have, therefore, no idea of inhesion" (T 1.4.5.6, SBN 234). Because we have no idea of the substance in which perceptions are supposed to inhere, the relation of inherence is not intelligible.

Hume begins *Treatise* 1.4.6 with the observation that some philosophers think that experience provides clear evidence of a continuously existing self that has perfect identity and simplicity.[4] In other words, these philosophers are committed to there being something simple, whose continued existence is somehow experienced. They resist offering any argument for such a self; because we are so "intimately conscious" of its existence, any discursive argument for its existence would carry less certainty. This implies that the philosophers consider the self a given datum of experience, not from discursive reasoning or the operations of the imagination.

Hume objects that such a view is not supported by experience: there is no simple, invariable, and uninterrupted impression from which an idea of self could derive.[5] The idea of an enduring simple self is not a straight-forward datum of the senses.

Satisfied that perceptions neither are supported by nor inhere in a self, Hume argues that there is no conceptual work for *self* to do that is not accomplished by perceptions. I do not use *self* to detect my existence; indeed, I never detect the continuous *self*, just particular perceptions. *Self* by itself (that is, without perceptions) would not enable me to continue to exist; if I have no perceptions, I do not exist:

> When my perceptions are remov'd for any time, as by sound sleep; so long am I insensible of *myself*, and may truly be said not to exist. And were all my perceptions remov'd by death, and cou'd I neither think, nor feel, nor see, nor love, nor hate after the dissolution of my body, I shou'd be entirely annihilated, nor do I conceive what is farther requisite to make me a perfect non-entity. (T 1.4.6.3, SBN 252)

Thus in order for self to exist, perceptions would have to exist. But since perceptions do not need to inhere in anything in order to exist, there is nothing necessary for the existence of perceptions. So self is constituted by perceptions alone (cf. T App. 17, SBN 634–35).

It is important to be clear that the view rejected by Hume is that there is any experience of *one simple and enduring* self. (See Green 1999: 115.) His uses of "self" in these opening paragraphs refer to variations of this rival view. As I see it, Hume is not thereby committed to denying that perceptions are experiential episodes; they are "sentient occurrences" (Garrett 1981: 344n4).[6] That is, on my reading, Hume does not disagree with Descartes's discovery that any kind of impression or idea ensures that I am thinking now; Hume's point is that what remains to be explained is the *belief* that the very same I who is thinking now is the same as the I who was thinking five minutes, weeks, or years ago. In other words, Hume denies that the momentary "I" exemplified by one perception can be known simply by sense or reason to be one and the same momentary "I" exemplified by another simultaneous or earlier perception. This is because the distinctness and separability of perceptions raise the problem of whether the "I" exemplified by each single perception is the same or different. Thus the explanandum in "Of personal identity" is how the (false) belief that I am one and the same "I" over time is produced from many distinct, successive perceptions.[7]

Yet it is difficult to make sense of how a single perception (or a group of perceptions) supplies an idea of "I."[8] Jonathan Ellis (2006) argues that

Hume's crisis is realizing that a perception of a tomato, for example, does not supply an idea of "I." Other scholars have offered different ways[9] of accomplishing this, but the explanations are found wanting. One holds that the momentary self is an impression distinct from, but always conjoined to, any perception (cf. Stevenson 1998). By Hume's separability principle, such an impression could exist separate from any perception. But Hume clearly denies that there is such an impression:

For my part, when I enter most intimately into what I call *myself*, I always stumble on some particular perception or other, of heat or cold, light or shade, love or hatred, pain or pleasure. I never can catch *myself* at any time without a perception, and never can observe any thing but the perception. (T 1.4.6.3, SBN 252)

So there is no distinct perception of self, either momentary or continuous, that accompanies other perceptions.

Another view maintains that the momentary self is an aspect of perceptions. Michael J. Green (1999) defends such a view, finding that Hume distinguishes two aspects of perceptions:

In thinking of our past thoughts we not only delineate out the objects, of which we were thinking, but also conceive the action of the mind in the meditation, that certain *je-ne-scai-quoi*, of which 'tis impossible to give any definition or description, but which every one sufficiently understands. (T 1.3.8.16, SBN 106)[10]

Green refers to this "je-ne-scai-quoi" as "consciousness" and identifies it with the momentary self (1999: 112; see also 110–11). This is the "little signatures" view that is appropriately ridiculed by John Haugeland (1998: 71n6).[11] Haugeland thinks that it is empirically implausible that I perceive a momentary self, but Green (1999: 114) argues that the view makes sense of Hume's claims to have an impression of the self, in Book 2 (inter alia, T 2.1.11.4, SBN 317). However, the claim that each momentary self resembles others would undermine Hume's explanatory emphasis on causation in *Treatise* 1.4.6, because on that view, resemblance alone could trigger the imaginative propensity to confound related perceptions.[12]

2. HUME ON PERSONAL IDENTITY

Hume takes himself to have shown that when we do not observe invariableness and uninterruptedness but nevertheless ascribe identity to plants, animals, churches, and rivers, there is a succession of objects connected by one or more relations (T 1.4.6.7–14, SBN 255–58). These relations make it so easy for the imagination to move from one perception to the next that the imagination fails to notice the difference. This leads the imagination to mistake the succession for one and the same perception over time. Hume notes that the imaginative transition from one object to the related one may be facilitated by one or more artifice. From this he concludes, "The identity, which we ascribe to the mind of man, is only a fictitious one, and of a like kind with that which we ascribe to vegetables and animal bodies. It cannot, therefore, have a different origin, but must proceed from a like operation of the imagination upon like objects" (T 1.4.6.15, SBN 259).

What does it mean to call the identity "fictitious"? As we have seen, neither the entire mind nor any of its parts remains uninterrupted and invariable over the course of a lifetime (T 1.4.6.2, SBN 251–52). Like plants and animals, the human mind may undergo a total change in a few years (T 1.4.6.12, SBN 257). Nevertheless, because of the easy transition of the imagination in following the relations among the perceptions that compose the mind, we ascribe identity to the whole collection and consider it to be one and the same over time. This ascription of identity is "improper," because the perceptions are not truly invariable and uninterrupted over time; and it is a "mistake" to suppose that the mind is uninterrupted and invariable, or that the perceptions are really connected by something "mysterious and inexplicable" (T 1.4.6.7, SBN 255).[13]

Hume offers another argument. All perceptions are different and distinguishable, and therefore may exist separately. When we attribute identity to the mind, we are "not able to run the several different perceptions into one, and make them lose their characters of distinction and difference, which are essential to them" (T 1.4.6.16, SBN 259). That is, the perceptions that compose the mind are sufficiently variable that one perception cannot be substituted for another without a sensible difference. Nevertheless, observes Hume, we do believe that the entire collection is simple and identical over time. So the explanation must lie either in some real connection that we observe between the perceptions or in a felt association among the ideas of the perceptions. Because Hume has argued at length against our ever perceiving real connections between things (and therefore we have no idea of such connections),[14] he concludes that it must be the association of ideas that leads us to pronounce the perceptions to be connected together (T 1.4.6.16, SBN 259–60).

This contrast is important, and it reappears in the Appendix (T App. 20–21, SBN 635–36). The rejected possibility is that there is a real bond between perceptions, and after observing every real bond, we pronounce the entire whole to be identical over time. The other alternative is that we do not perceive a real bond between perceptions, but instead come to associate the ideas of the perceptions together by resemblance or causation. Because "the very essence of these relations consists in their producing an easy transition of ideas" (T 1.4.6.16, SBN 260), the same relations by which we associate perceptions also cause us to ascribe identity to the whole collection. In effect, two beliefs occur together: the belief that the perceptions form a whole system and the belief that the whole collection is identical over time. Absent these, the perceptions are, so far as we judge, distinct existences.

Hume raises the question "by what relations this uninterrupted progress of our thought is produc'd, when we consider the successive existence of a mind or thinking person" (T 1.4.6.17, SBN 260). The three relations Hume considers are resemblance, contiguity in space and time, and causation. He notes that contiguity in space has no bearing on nonspatial perceptions, so he limits his discussion to resemblance and causation. He finds that the memory is crucially involved in each.

With respect to resemblance, Hume asks us to imagine being able to "see clearly into the breast of another, and observe that succession of perceptions, which constitutes his mind or thinking principle." He asks us also to "suppose that he always preserves the memory of a considerable part of past perceptions" (T 1.4.6.18, SBN 260). In such a case, I will come to have ideas of the other person's perceptions. I will find that many of my ideas resemble, because his perceptions resemble; memory replicates past perceptions (cf. T 1.1.3.2, SBN 9). The resemblance will enable me to pass easily from earlier to later ideas, and my imagination will cause me to mistake this smooth transition for the contemplation of a single, continuous perception. This causes me to believe that his perceptions (the perceptions from which my ideas are copied) are identical over time.[15] As in all cases of identity ascription, my imagination plays a fundamental role in confusing succession for identity. But in this case, the other person's memory also plays an important role in producing the belief in identity. Without the memory, there would be no (guarantee of) repeated resemblance among perceptions. The vast number of resembling perceptions so produced enables my imagination to mistake his succession of perceptions for a continuous, identical thing.

Hume turns to causation. Hume writes, "we may observe, that the true idea of the human mind, is to consider it as a system of different perceptions or different existences, which are link'd together by the relation of cause and effect, and mutually produce, destroy, influence, and modify each other" (T 1.4.6.19, SBN 261). Impressions cause ideas; in accordance with the principles of association, those ideas will call to mind other ideas; in accordance with Hume's theory of the passions, those ideas may arouse pride, love, desire, will, and other passions. Each of these successions is causal. Hume compares the entire system to a commonwealth, where the members succeed each other and reorganize according to new laws or constitutions. "[I]n like manner the same person may vary his character and disposition, as well as his impressions and ideas, without losing his identity. Whatever changes he endures, his several parts are still connected by the relation of causation" (ibid.). Again, memory plays a critical role in producing the idea of personal identity. Without memory, we would be unable to form the custom upon which causal inferences depend. Also, I have memories of many different particular causal chains of perceptions, all of which contribute to my belief in personal identity (T 1.4.6.20, SBN 261–62). As noted above, the very same action of mind by which I believe that many different perceptions are causally linked is the action by which I judge that the entire group is identical over time.

Hume notes that this cannot be the entire story. If memory were required for producing personal identity, then forgetting would remove past perceptions from the system. But, observes Hume, we can causally infer the existence of forgotten experiences. Although Hume may not remember his thoughts and actions from March 11, 1719, nevertheless his forgetting does not destroy his identity. Instead, because he remembers actions and thoughts from before or after that date, and he has developed relevant causal associations, he can infer that he existed at that time (and perhaps he can infer his actions or thoughts at that time too). In this respect, memory discovers and extends identity (T 1.4.6.20, SBN 262).

Hume concludes that "[i]dentity depends on the relations of ideas; and these relations produce identity, by means of that easy transition they occasion" (T 1.4.6.21, SBN 262). He adds that the same principles that explain our belief in identity also explain our belief in simplicity.[16]

3. "ALL MY HOPES VANISH"

In the Appendix to the *Treatise*, which accompanied the publication of Book 3 in 1740, Hume returns to the discussion of personal identity. He reports, "upon a more strict review of the section concerning *personal identity*, I find myself involv'd in such a labyrinth, that, I must confess, I neither know how to correct my former opinions, nor how to render them consistent" (T App. 10, SBN 633). Hume provides a summary of his arguments against "the strict and proper identity and simplicity of a self or thinking being" (ibid.). He rehearses arguments from *Treatise* 1.4.5 and 1.4.6, concluding that all perceptions are distinct and may exist separately. So a mind is simply a collection of related perceptions. Hume writes:

But having thus loosen'd all our particular perceptions, when I proceed to explain the principle of connexion,* which binds them together, and makes us attribute to them a real simplicity and identity; I am sensible, that my account is very defective, and that nothing but the seeming evidence of the precedent reasonings cou'd have induc'd me to receive it. (T App. 20, SBN 635)

Hume's footnote refers the reader back to the page that begins with the end of T 1.4.6.16 (SBN 260) and ends in the middle of T 1.4.6.18 (SBN 260).[17] On the positive side, he observes that his view is similar to other views about personal identity, which make identity depend on consciousness. Hume proclaims, "But all my hopes vanish, when I come to explain the principles, that unite our successive perceptions in our thought or consciousness. I cannot discover any theory, which gives me satisfaction on this head" (T App. 20, SBN 635–36). Hume articulates two principles that

... I cannot render consistent; nor is it in my power to renounce either of them, viz. that all our distinct perceptions are distinct existences, and that the mind never perceives any real connexion among distinct existences. Did our perceptions either inhere in something simple and individual, or did the mind perceive some real connexion among them, there wou'd be no difficulty in the case. (T App. 21, SBN 636)

Commentators note that the two principles do not contradict, so the inconsistency that Hume identifies must be with some other principle or principles. Moreover, the two resolutions of the purported inconsistency involve principles that Hume is strongly committed to rejecting (substances and perceived real connections).

What error is Hume confessing? One of the thornier fundamental interpretive issues about Hume's treatment of personal identity is whether he is primarily concerned with metaphysics or psychology.[18] If his focus is metaphysical, then he is interested in analyzing what it is for there to be one and the same person. Some metaphysical interpretations take the central problem to be the ownership of perceptions: Out of all the existing perceptions in the history of the universe, what relations distinguish my perceptions from others' perceptions?[19] On this interpretation, the error that Hume confesses concerns the principle of uniting or bundling perceptions into a single person. If Hume's focus on personal identity is psychological, then his primary aim is to explain the psychological operations that produce the belief in self: How do we compose the very idea of one and the same person,[20] and how does the belief in identity arise?[21] On either interpretation, scholars have criticized Hume for presupposing a unified self that perceives and manipulates perceptions[22] or for running into problems of self-reference.[23] On this interpretation, the Appendix problem concerns whether the psychological mechanisms are sufficient to produce the idea or belief in the identity and simplicity of myself.

In support of the metaphysical interpretation, scholars point to Hume's claim that human minds "are nothing but a bundle or collection of different perceptions, which succeed each other with an inconceivable rapidity, and are in a perpetual flux and movement" (T 1.4.6.4, SBN 252).[24] This view is opposed to the mistaken view of "philosophers" (T 1.4.6.1, SBN 251) and "metaphysicians" (T 1.4.6.4, SBN 252) who affirm that there is a self that is simple and identical over time. Later in the same paragraph, Hume compares the mind to a "theatre," where different perceptions enter, combine, and exit at different times. He cautions us not to be misled by the comparison: "They are the successive perceptions only, that *constitute* the mind; nor have we the most distant notion of the place, where these scenes are represented, or of the materials, of which it is compos'd" (T 1.4.6.4, SBN 253; emphasis added). The discussion of constitution looks to place Hume's thesis squarely in the camp of metaphysics. The Abstract (which is widely thought to be written by Hume) seems to support this interpretation. There, Hume's view about the mind is contrasted with that of Descartes. Hume's position is described as "our several particular perceptions ... compose the mind," and he calls our attention to the word *compose* (Abs. 28, SBN 657–58).

But in *Treatise* 1.4.6, immediately following this apparent analysis of the concept of mind, Hume asks, "What then gives us so great a propension to ascribe an identity to these successive perceptions, and to suppose ourselves possest of an invariable and uninterrupted existence thro' the whole course of our lives?" (T 1.4.6.5, SBN 253). His focus now seems to be on the psychological propension. He devotes an entire paragraph to reviewing the psychological propensities that produce beliefs in persisting objects.[25] Recall, in *Treatise* 1.4.2, that Hume introduces the problem as follows:

> We may well ask, *What causes induce us to believe in the existence of body?* but 'tis in vain to ask, *Whether there be body or not?* That is a point, which we must take for granted in all our reasonings. (T 1.4.2.1, SBN 187)

Hume proceeds to explain the psychological propensities that operate on perceptions and lead the vulgar and philosophers to believe in the external existence of bodies. In cases of constancy, the natural resemblance among the "interrupted" but invariable content of perceptions causes an association of their ideas. The imagination, when it considers the different contents, moves easily from the idea of the one to the idea of the next. This feels as if it is contemplation of a single object. These two relations (of ideas and acts of mind) trigger the "confounding principle" (as I call it): the imagination mistakes the different contents (of which it has perceptions) for an identical object. But the interruption of their appearance (from blinking, inattention, or sleep) is hard to ignore. So the imagination further supposes that the object continues to exist even when it is not perceived. This is a fiction, but it satisfies the imagination's propensity to confound as well as the undeniable interruption (T 1.4.2.43, SBN 209–10).

In *Treatise* 1.4.6, Hume rehearses this psychological account and claims that the "notion of a *soul*, and *self*, and *substance*" arises from the same psychological propensities (T 1.4.6.6, SBN 254). He proposes that any identity that we ascribe to objects whose invariableness or uninterruptedness is not observed will be a succession of related objects (T 1.4.6.7, SBN 255). In fact, Hume expands his explanation to describe circumstances in which we judge the identity of variable things (T 1.4.6.7–14, SBN 255–58).[26] He writes:

And here 'tis evident, the same method of reasoning must be continu'd, which has so successfully explain'd the identity of plants, and animals, and ships, and houses, and of all the compounded and changeable productions either of art or nature. The identity, which we ascribe to the mind of man, is only a fictitious one, and of a like kind with that which we ascribe to vegetables and animal bodies. It cannot, therefore, have a different origin, but must proceed from a like operation of the imagination upon like objects. (T 1.4.6.15, SBN 259)

Hume is addressing the *origin* of the fictional idea of the identity of the mind. The next paragraph (drawing on the separability principle) aims to make the same point ("lest this argument shou'd not convince the reader" [T 1.4.6.16, SBN 259]). After establishing the point that the idea of personal identity arises from associations of ideas, Hume remarks:

The only question, therefore, which remains, is, by what relations this uninter-rupted progress of our thought is produc'd, when we consider the successive existence of a mind or thinking person? (T 1.4.6.17, SBN 260)

His explanation describes how resemblance and causation between per-ceptions facilitate the transition along our ideas of them, thus triggering the confounding principle.[27]

Hume's retraction in the Appendix tends to be given greater interpre-tive weight. There, Hume opaquely criticizes his own account, identify-ing two principles that he cannot reconcile. Indeed, as Jonathan Ellis (2006: 204ff.) observes, Hume *himself* provides a footnote to the passage in *Treatise* 1.4.6 in which he characterizes his account as "very defec-tive" (T App. 20, SBN 635). In the first edition, the footnote points to where Hume explains "by what relations this uninterrupted progress of our thought is produc'd, when we consider the successive existence of a mind or thinking person" (T 1.4.6.17, SBN 260). Ellis concludes that Hume's self-criticism lies with his psychological account.[28]

Don Garrett (2011) concedes that there are psychological topics in addition to the metaphysical topic in "Of personal identity." But, he argues, a purely psychological interpretation cannot create the crisis that Hume experiences in the Appendix. Garrett contends that the psychological explanations presuppose that causal relations obtain between the bundled perceptions. If there were a failure in the bundling, then that would affect the success of the psychological explanations. But again, this requires Hume to say that the problem is in the bundling.

Hume offers two alternative views – that perceptions inhere in substances or that we perceive real connections between perceptions – either of which he thinks would solve his problem. Galen Strawson (2011) calls the psychological interpretation "The Problem of Detail" and argues that Hume's two solutions offered for the Appendix problem would not solve it.[29] But Hume's solutions aren't exclusively metaphysical ones.[30] The second "solution" requires that we *perceive* a real connection – Strawson (2011: 137–38) acknowledges this epistemological feature.[31] This It makes clear that this solution is not simply there being something (perhaps unknowable) that binds perceptions together; instead the solution requires some way for us to *discover* that perceptions are bound together. Observing such a bond would enable me to believe that the perceptions are connected together into a single system.

The first alternative seems even more clearly to be concerned with a metaphysical solution to Hume's difficulty.[32] I contend that it is a psychological solution too. To see how, recall the opening paragraphs of *Treatise* 1.4.6. There, Hume describes a view in which "we are every moment intimately conscious of what we call our SELF; that we feel its existence and its continuance in existence; and are certain, beyond the evidence of a demonstration, both of its perfect identity and simplicity" (T 1.4.6.1, SBN 251). The philosophers who endorse this view hold that every experience provides certain and immediate knowledge of the identity of self over time. Against this view, Hume reminds us of his argument that perceptions "have no need of any thing to support their existence" (T 1.4.6.3, SBN 252).[33] That is, the distinct existence of perceptions tells against this view. But if Hume were to give up the principle that "*all our distinct perceptions are distinct existences*" (T App. 21, SBN 636), he could adopt the philosophers' view that perceptions inhere in the self, and thereby acquire immediate and certain knowledge of the simple and continuous self.[34]

Notice that it is only the first of the alternatives that supplies a self that is (ex hypothesi) simple and identical over time. On the second solution, I perceive real connections between many different perceptions. The real connections guarantee the smooth transition along perceptions. But they do not provide one simple, invariable, and uninterrupted entity over time; there are multiple perceptions existing at different times, connected by real connections. Thus Hume's confounding principle would still be required for the belief that the different perceptions related by real connections are simple and perfectly identical. This indicates that Hume's self-criticism is not directed at the confounding principle. Instead, his concern lies somewhere with his account of the felt connection between distinct perceptions.

4. SECONDARY IDEAS

My interpretation of Hume's confession requires distinguishing levels of perceptions. Hume introduces the distinction between impressions and ideas in the first paragraph of the *Treatise*. He tells us that the distinction is the familiar one between feeling and thinking, respectively (T 1.1.1.1, SBN 1–2). In defending the Copy Principle (i.e., the principle that all ideas are ultimately copied from preceding impressions), he observes that it is possible to think about ideas too:

as our ideas are images of our impressions, so we can form secondary ideas, which are images of the primary; as appears from this very reasoning concerning them.... Ideas produce the images of themselves in new ideas; but as the first ideas are suppos'd to be deriv'd from impressions, it still remains true, that all our simple ideas proceed, either mediately or immediately, from their correspondent impressions. (T 1.1.1.11, SBN 6–7)

On this categorization, secondary ideas are ideas of ideas; primary ideas are ideas of impressions.[35] Secondary ideas (and higher-level ideas) are mediately derived from impressions. Our ability to think about ideas does not violate the Copy Principle.

But what content does a secondary idea copy? After explaining that belief is "nothing but a strong and lively idea deriv'd from a present impression related to it," Hume considers an objection (T 1.3.8.15, SBN 105–6). How do we come to believe that an idea was caused by a preceding impression when we have forgotten the impression? What enlivens the belief? Hume argues that in such a case, the present idea serves the role of an enlivening impression. Hume adds:

Upon the same principles we need not be surpriz'd to hear of the remembrance of an idea; that is, of the idea of an idea, and of its force and vivacity superior to the loose conceptions of the imagination. In thinking of our past thoughts we not only delineate out the objects, of which we were thinking, but also conceive the action of the mind in the meditation, that certain *je-ne-scai-quoi*, of which 'tis impossible to give any definition or description, but which every one sufficiently understands. When the memory offers an idea of this, and represents it as past, 'tis easily conceiv'd how that idea may have more vigour and firmness, than when we think of a past thought, of which we have no remembrance. (T 1.3.8.16, SBN 106)

I have already discussed this passage in the context of how perceptions represent an "I." Here I want to observe that the vehicle for thinking about the *je-ne-scai-quoi* is a higher-level idea: an idea of an idea. When I reflect on my own thought, the reflecting idea will be one level removed from the perception. The memory of an idea is an idea of an idea – that is, a secondary idea. The content of the secondary idea is the primary idea, and it also includes a conception of the action of the mind. This indicates that *remembering my thinking* requires the use of secondary ideas.

Why should we think that secondary ideas have a role in the belief in personal identity?[36] After rejecting that we perceive a real bond between distinct perceptions, Hume writes:

> For from thence it evidently follows, that identity is nothing really belonging to these different perceptions, and uniting them together; but is merely a quality, which we attribute to them, because of the union *of their ideas* in the imagination, when we reflect upon them. (T 1.4.6.16, SBN 260; emphasis added)

Hume's explanation of the belief in personal identity must then draw upon the resemblance or causation between *ideas of* the perceptions that are identified together. The beginning of Hume's explanation is where the Appendix footnote points.

Again in the Appendix, after rejecting observed "connexions among distinct existences," Hume concludes:

> It follows, therefore, that the thought alone finds personal identity, when reflecting on the train of past perceptions, that compose a mind, *the ideas of them* are felt to be connected together, and naturally introduce each other. (T App. 20, SBN 635; emphasis added)

Because both impressions and ideas belong to minds, in order to include past ideas, we need to feel a connection between current memories (i.e., higher-level ideas) of those ideas.

In the next two sections, I carefully distinguish the different perceptions that are involved in the belief in personal identity. I argue that Hume encounters problems with each of his explanations.

5. RESEMBLANCE

Let's return to Hume's illustration of the contribution of resemblance to the production of the belief in identity. He writes:

> suppose we cou'd see clearly into the breast of another, and observe that succession of perceptions, which constitutes his mind or thinking principle, and suppose that he always preserves the memory of a considerable part of past perceptions; 'tis evident, that nothing cou'd more contribute to the bestowing a relation on this succession amidst all its variations. For what is the memory but a faculty, by

which we raise up the images of past perceptions? And as an image necessarily resembles its object, must not the frequent placing of these resembling perceptions in the chain of thought, convey the imagination more easily from one link to another, and make the whole seem like the continuance of one object? (T 1.4.6.18, SBN 260–61)

First there are the perceptions of the other person; let's call him David. And there are my ideas of David's perceptions. My ideas are one level removed from David's perceptions. Because of the nature of memory, David's perceptions resemble. Thus my ideas resemble. I feel an easy transition from resembling idea to resembling idea. This easiness feels like a single act of mind. By the confounding principle, I mistake the easiness of the different perceptions for the easiness of the single perception. That is, I take the different resembling ideas to be one and the same perception.

This is the same account of belief in identity from T 1.4.2.31–42 (SBN 201–9), where the resemblance of distinct perceptions triggers the confounding principle and the fiction of continued existence arises from the undeniable "interruption" of resembling perceptions. I have argued elsewhere (Butler 2010) that the fictional idea of a body's identity over time should be understood as a complex idea. The present impression supplies the content of existence now. To get identity over time, we now add memories (i.e., primary ideas) to the present impression – both memories of having perceived the object and memories of perceiving things other than the object. These memories taken together supply the idea of the different times when the body is supposed (falsely) to have existed. All together, the fictional idea of a continuing body is a complex idea now of an impression and many memories of past impressions (i.e., primary ideas). Every single perception supplies content to the complex idea. The present impression supplies the content of the object as well as that of existing now. The memories resembling the present impression supply the content of observed existence at those different times. The nonresembling memories supply the content of times at which the object was not observed. Thus the entire idea is one of continued existence – existing when observed and when not observed.

There are two problems that arise for Hume's confounding resemblances account when applied to mental entities. First, Hume claims that "an image necessarily resembles its object" (T 1.4.6.18, SBN 260), so that would lead us to expect that resemblance can transcend the level of the perception: any level idea will resemble the impression from which it is derived. My seeing a tomato resembles my remembering having seen a tomato; and both resemble my remembering having thought about a tomato. This mediate derivation was advanced by Hume in T 1.1.1.11

(SBN 7). The problem arises from the *je-ne-scai-quoi* that is copied. Primary ideas of impressions will be ideas of feeling or doing: I remember seeing, smelling, or feeling. Secondary ideas will be ideas of thinking: I remember having remembered or thought about feeling. This distinction is significant. When I confound the resembling ideas, if my ideas are all primary ideas, I will believe that David was continuously sensing or feeling. If my ideas are all secondary ideas, I will believe that David was continuously remembering or thinking. If my ideas are an admixture of primary and secondary ideas, it is not clear what the content of my confused idea is.

There is an important caveat to this restriction, which is obscured in the example of peering into another's mind but is apparent from the case of body. A perception representing the object's occurrence *now* is one level lower than the others that now represent its past occurrences. In the case of body, I can have a present impression of the tomato. I confound that now with memories of resembling tomato impressions (i.e., primary ideas). In my own case, suppose that I am now *remembering having seen Hume's tomb*.[37] This memory is a primary idea and it occurs now. Memories that would resemble this would be memories of *remembering having seen Hume's tomb*. These memories of memories occurring now are secondary ideas; when the memories themselves occurred, they were primary ideas (i.e., memories). This caveat will become important when we examine Hume's account of how causation produces the belief in identity.[38]

The second problem from resemblance is that it looks to unavoidably produce belief in *continued existence* and *external existence*. In the case of body, there is an observed "interruption" in the succession of resembling perceptions. This "interruption" is simply that there are other nonresembling perceptions in the succession of perceptions. This may happen if I blink, become distracted, or fall asleep. The relation of resemblance transcends time; resembling items do not need to be temporally contiguous. So the confounding principle triggers a belief in identity of temporally distant perceptions. This identity conflicts with the interruption. To overcome this conflict, the imagination offers the supposition of continued existence (T 1.4.2.36, SBN 205). The perception is supposed to exist both when I perceive it and when I do not perceive it. But this means that I believe that when I am not perceiving it, the perception exists whole and entire *apart from my mind*. That is, I believe that it has distinct existence and external existence (T 1.4.2.2, SBN 188).

This is exactly the consequence Hume wants with respect to belief in bodies. But it seems most unwelcome with respect to perceptions in the service of belief in my own identity.[39] First, it commits me to believing that I am continuously thinking about or feeling the object of my belief.

Second, it is true that Hume thinks there is no contradiction in supposing a perception to exist apart from a mind (T 1.4.2.40, SBN 207). But on the supposition of continued existence, the perception exists unperceived by me. The confounding principle entails that I believe that the perception is mine. What is it for me to have a perception that I do not perceive?

6. CAUSATION

The problems I have pointed to for resemblance might be thought to be softened or eliminated by causal considerations. If I discover causal connections between the "interrupted" and "interrupting" perceptions, that would undercut the belief in continued existence. Causal relations can obtain between any two distinct things whatsoever, so it seems that there would be no restriction on the levels of causes or effects. If the explanation of the effects of causation in the belief in personal identity is unproblematic, then the explanation of the effects of resemblance in the belief in personal identity can be retained. Unfortunately, there is a problem with the former.

Hume is trying to explain how I (falsely) believe that I am the same person over time. Any such belief will involve some past perceptions, in order to supply the content of time.[40] Hume's psychological account requires my feeling a causal association among the successive perceptions. But in order for me to judge that these related perceptions are *mine*, there needs to be some felt connection to a present perception. Consider the succession where I run, trip, fall, scrape my knee, and now feel pain. I now remember the running, tripping, falling, and knee scraping. These are all primary ideas whose contents refer to past impressions. In addition, there is the present impression of pain. From customary associations, I judge these experiences to be causally related. That is, I feel an easy transition along the primary ideas and the current impression. The confounding principle is triggered; the current experience is (falsely) believed to be continuous with the past experiences. That is, I now judge that I am the same person as she who ran, tripped, fell, and scraped her knee.

But a problem arises. If the content of the perceptions is entirely of past objects, then I will judge now that those related past perceptions are continuous in the past, but there is nothing to link those objects to me now. The belief is consistent with those past experiences being had by someone or something else that I happen to have observed. It is helpful to return to Hume's example of peering into another's breast. As we have seen, the felt union among my ideas of past perceptions causes me to attribute a real union to the object of those perceptions. But the owner of the vehicle of the feeling is not regarded as the owner of the real connection; this would confuse me with David. Thus in order for me to believe that the past experiences were mine, I now must feel a connection between my present perception and the content of my past perceptions. In other words, some present perception needs to be included in the felt connection.

I might try to make the vehicle of thought the object of thought. Doing so introduces a higher-level perception at a later moment. And that pushes the problem back one further: What connects the owner of the current higher-level perception to the lower-level perceptions? In general, the problem is linking the vehicle of the belief with the content of the belief (cf. Bricke 1980: 88); this is how I understand Hume's inability "to explain the principles, that unite our successive perceptions in our thought or consciousness" (T App. 20, SBN 635). This problem arises only for mental unity and not bodily unity, because only in the former case do we make perceptions themselves the object of focus.[41]

We need some additional psychological principle. The alternative seems to be the "galley principle," which Hume employs in explaining belief in the continued existence of bodies from coherence (T 1.4.2.22, SBN 198). Setting aside the difficult issue of how exactly to understand the galley principle, it is clear that Hume's own assessment of it is that it cannot be the foundation of belief in continuity. The appeal to it here would make it responsible for all beliefs in personal continuity that are exclusively about past events, and that is a load Hume thinks it is "too weak" to bear (T 1.4.2.23, SBN 198).

My regress differs somewhat from Donald C. Ainslie's regress (2001 and 2008), which is a further labyrinthine problem. Ainslie observes that the philosopher who tries to connect *all* of her perceptions together will fail to do so, because the vehicle of her thought is not included in the object of her thought (Ainslie 2008, 153–54). Some of her perceptions, also, are not included in the content of her thought. This problem is especially acute for the belief in simplicity. Several scholars object that Hume's crisis in the Appendix is with anyone's belief in personal identity, not just that of certain philosophers.[42]

Jonathan Ellis (2006: 212–13) contends that Ainslie's problem can be handled so long as the philosopher successfully feels that some perceptions are connected together. Once she has some belief in identity, she can assimilate new perceptions to that belief. Garrett (2011: 26n12 and 13) and Ellis (2006: 212–13) contend that there is a general idea of myself; any particular belief in my existence will belong to its revival set.[43] Even if general ideas resolve Ainslie's problem, they will not work for the regress that I have identified. As I argued above, a succession of exclusively past perceptions would not have a perceived causal connection to any present perception. So to include the past perceptions in the revival set of "me" presupposes that they satisfy the belief. But that's precisely the issue at hand. Furthermore, the present moment continues to change. Past additions to the revival set will not settle whether those members of the revival set are connected to me now.

My regress bears some resemblance to casual regress interpretations, such as those advanced by Yumiko Inukai, Michael Jacovides, and Vijay Mascarenhas. Inukai (2007) thinks that Hume discovers that he presupposed that perceptions come bundled; without this assumption, associations of ideas cannot obtain. I argued that Hume is well aware that one has direct access to certain successive experiences; that is the psychological starting point of his explanation.[44] According to Mascarenhas (2001: 296), Hume cannot explain the unity of perception, which is presupposed in the association of ideas. In order to do so, there would need to be an impression of association. But that would be just another distinct impression standing in need of bundling. The problem is that this treats associations as perceptions distinct from the associated perceptions themselves.

7. OTHER PROBLEMS

Scholars have identified other problems with Hume's account, interpreted psychologically. A. E. Pitson raises a worry about discontinuities in perception. Specifically, Pitson (2002: 73) is concerned about the break caused by sound sleep (T 1.4.6.3, SBN 252).[45] Pitson thinks that noticing this discontinuity will interrupt the smooth transition of the mind. Baxter (2008: 80) replies that the vulgar are not likely to notice the discontinuities. But a philosopher might recognize the tension. And it is precisely the sort of problem that a substantial self or soul would be introduced to address. Bricke (1977: 172 and 1980: 92ff.) also notes discontinuities but adds to it that causation requires temporal contiguity. Since there are no perceptions during sound sleep, the perceptions that occur upon waking will not have perceptions as their causes.

Considerations of this sort have led scholars to think that Hume discovers that he needs to supplement his account. Wayne Waxman (1992) argues that the culprit is retentive memory. Annette Baier (2008: 164–69) thinks that Hume fails to realize that the conferring of vivacity from impression to idea is a perceived necessary connection. Several scholars suggest that Hume needs some nonperceptual causal relation, such as a psychophysical causal relation.[46]

Rather than complaining about the paucity of causal connections, Kenneth Winkler (2000) and Udo Thiel (2011: 399–400) think that there are too many causal relations; causation is insufficient to distinguish me from other things. I think Hume recognizes this point. In T 1.4.7.3, Hume reflects on the many different effects of the imagination:

Without this quality, by which the mind enlivens some ideas beyond others (which seemingly is so trivial, and so little founded on reason) we cou'd never assent to any argument, nor carry our view beyond those few objects, which are present to our senses. Nay, even to these objects we cou'd never attribute any existence, but what was dependent on the senses; and must comprehend them entirely in that succession of perceptions, which constitutes our self or person. (T 1.4.7.3, SBN 265)

That is, the imagination produces the belief in continued existence. Without it, we would think that every perception belongs to us. So Hume concedes Winkler and Thiel's point, but he thinks that the fiction of continued existence overrides the propensity to attribute sensory perceptions to ourselves. It requires further work to show that this project can be successfully completed; Abraham Sesshu Roth (2000) and Anik Waldow (2010) argue that it cannot be done.

NOTES

Thanks to Donald Ainslie and Travis Butler for generous and helpful feedback on earlier drafts of this paper.

1. On my interpretation, Hume sees himself as accounting for everyone's (false) belief in personal identity, not just that of philosophers. This will become clear in what follows.
2. Green 1999; Mascarenhas 2001: 288; and Ellis 2006: 218. MacNabb (1951: 151–52) raises the special problem of how a perception can be self-aware.
3. I focus on identity, though points can be brought to bear on simplicity.
4. There is scholarly disagreement about whose position Hume attacks or whether it is a straw man. See, inter alia, Bettcher 1999: 213n98; Penelhum 2000: 100–4; Winkler 2000; and Ainslie 2008: 143–44. It does not neatly match the views of Descartes, Locke, or Butler. David Raynor cites a 1727 letter (to William Mace) in which Francis Hutcheson rejects the bundle theory in favor of such a view. Raynor (1990: 237) does not suggest that Hume ever saw this letter; the point is that someone held the view Hume rejected.
5. This appeal to the Copy Principle is repeated in T App. 11 (SBN 633).
6. Strawson (2011: 37–38) calls them "conscious episodes"; cp. Stevenson 1999: 96–112; Waxman 1992; Ainslie 2001: 567–68 and n22; Bettcher 2009: 207ff.; and Thiel 2011: 403–8. The variety of interpretations provides reason to think that the expression "conscious" needs to be handled with care in interpreting Hume.
7. Bricke 1980: 83; Penelhum 2000: passim (e.g., 56–57).
8. There is a similarity between Hume's treatments of the idea of self and the idea of existence (T 1.2.6.4–6, SBN 66–67). Hume raises similar dilemmas in both cases: either we have a distinct idea of (self-) existence derived from a distinct impression, or the idea of (self-) existence is nothing other than the perception itself. (Compare T 1.2.6.2–4 [SBN 66–67] to T 1.4.6.2–3 [SBN 251–52] and T App. 12, 15–16 [SBN 634].) In the case of personal identity, the

duration is affected (cp. external existence at T 1.2.6.9 [SBN 68]). But the idea being accounted for in my present discussion is the momentary idea of "I" at a particular time, which is (falsely) believed to be continuous over time.

9. Don Garrett (1997: 168–69) offers an interpretation involving Hume's account of general ideas. As I argue below, populating the revival set presupposes success in identifying distinct perceptions as one and the same "I."

10. Ainslie (2001: 560n8) observes that impressions of reflection do not have objects.

11. See also Penelhum's last footnote in his contribution to this volume and Ellis 2006: 230n44.

12. Baxter (2008: 111n39) makes this point.

13. There are a number of scholars who follow Ashley and Stack (1974) in distinguishing between "perfect identity" and "imperfect identity." Ashley and Stack argue that Hume has shown that minds do not have "perfect identity" (invariableness and uninterruptedness over time), but that they do have "imperfect identity" ("uninterrupted progress of the thought" [T 1.4.6.9, SBN 256]). Ashley and Stack argue that "imperfect identity" is not a mistake or a fiction – there really is an uninterrupted progress of thought (1974: 245). It is true that the mistake that Hume identifies concerns attributing perfect identity to a succession of related objects. But even supposing that Hume countenances "imperfect identity," it is not clear that that is free of fictions. Relations among our ideas of objects may be facilitated by certain "artifice[s]" (T 1.4.6.11–12, SBN 257).

14. How to interpret Hume's denial is a subject of dispute. Certain "New Humeans" hold that Hume denies that we know anything about the *nature* of such connections but does not deny that we can intelligibly suppose that they exist. This requires that the idea of "real connections" not be meaningless. For arguments for and against such a view, see Read and Richman 2007. The possibility of such real but unknown entities forms the backbone of the interpretation advanced in Strawson 2011.

15. Hume adds, "The case is the same whether we consider ourselves or others" (T 1.4.6.18, SBN 261). This is doubtful, as I make clear below. See Bricke 1977: 168 and 1980: 87ff.; Biro 2004: 13; and Ainslie 2008: 153.

16. I have nothing more to say about simplicity in this essay. A number of scholars have raised appropriate worries. See Penelhum 2000: 118–19; Winkler 2000; Ainslie 2001.

17. Ellis (2006: 202) reports this from examining the original edition.

18. Stroud (1977: 133) offers a similar division. I say "primarily" because there are interpretations, such as that of Garrett (2011), that identify metaphysical and psychological theses. Nevertheless, Garrett maintains that Hume's confession concerns a metaphysical failure.

19. Stroud 1977; Garrett 1981; Pears 1990; Haugeland 1998.

20. Ellis 2006; Baxter 2008.

21. Bricke 1980: 83ff.; Roth 2000; Waldow 2010.

22. See, inter alia, Kemp Smith 1941: 73; Passmore 1952: 82–83; Stroud 1977: 140. McIntyre (1979: 87–88) raises the problem but argues that enduring memorial perceptions are the solution.

23. MacNabb 1951: 151–52; Passmore 1952: 82.

24. This point is foreshadowed in Hume's discussion of objects (T 1.4.2.39, SBN 207).

25. Many scholars have noted the parallel to *Treatise* 1.4.2. See Bricke 1980: 74; Roth 2000; Winkler 2000: 20ff.; Pitson 2002: 20, 72; Biro 2004: 17ff.; Baier 2008: 183 and passim.; Baxter 2008; Waldow 2010.

26. Pitson (2002: 73) thinks that a fundamental difference between Hume's account of body and his account of mind is that bodies exhibit either uninterruptedness or invariability, but minds exhibit neither. Against this, consider that the supplementary considerations in T 1.4.6.7–14 (SBN 255–58) are offered to handle bodily cases where neither condition obtains.

    Furthermore, many scholars misunderstand the two psychological operations that Hume describes in *Treatise* 1.4.2. They think that the "confounding principle" applies only to constant (or invariable) perceptions and the "galley principle" applies only to coherent, changing perceptions. So they accuse Hume of misapplying the confounding principle to variable perceptions. But Hume clearly indicates in T 1.4.2.34–35 (SBN 203–4) that he thinks *any relation* (not just resemblance) may trigger the confounding principle.

27. In a single paragraph, Hume addresses the question of the belief in simplicity of the self: "What I have said concerning the first origin and uncertainty of our notion of identity, as apply'd to the human mind, may be extended with little or no variation to that of *simplicity*" (T 1.4.6.22, SBN 263). Notice, again, that it is the *origin* and *uncertainty* of the idea.

28. Cf. Winkler 2000: 18–19.

29. See also Allison 2008: 307; Thiel 2011: 400n38; Winkler 2000: 18–20; Garrett 2011.

30. Cf. Thiel 2011: 399–400n38; Winkler 2000: 18–20.

31. This is confirmed by comparison with T 1.4.6.16 (SBN 259): "... a question naturally arises concerning this relation of identity; whether it be something that really binds our several perceptions together, or only associates their ideas in the imagination? *That is, in other words*, whether in pronouncing concerning the identity of a person, we *observe* some real bond among his perceptions, or only feel one among the ideas we form of them?" (emphasis added). In order for a real bond between perceptions to combine perceptions into an identical person, the bond must be perceived. In other words, for me to believe that these perceptions are the same person's, I would need to perceive the real bond between the perceptions.

32. See Strawson 2011: 137–38 and Stroud 1977: 133.

33. The Appendix uses "inhere," whereas T 1.4.3 (SBN 252) uses "support." The connection that other philosophers suppose between "inhesion" and "support" is identified by Hume in T 1.4.5.6 (SBN 234) and 1.4.3.7 (SBN 222).

34. Inukai misses this. She writes, "... if there were a substance to which all distinct perceptions belonged, then the togetherness of them would be explained by their inhering in one and the same substance, which in turn might allow them to be passively perceived as occurring together" (2007: 269). But co-occurrence of perceptions is not what I need; instead, I need to perceive some kind of connection between perceptions. But the substance "solution" would enable me to discover a thing that is simple and identical over time to which all of my perceptions belong. On such a solution, we could jettison Hume's psychological account of the fiction of identity and simplicity, because something really identical and simple exists and I know its existence.

35. See also Bricke 1977: 169ff. and 1980: 87ff.; Melchert 1975: 330.

There is a difference of scholarly opinion on how to characterize secondary ideas. Ainslie (2001: 563 and 2008: 146) thinks secondary ideas can be ideas of ideas or ideas of impressions. A memory of my idea *of a tomato* would be a secondary idea of an impression, whereas a memory of *my thinking* would be a secondary idea of an idea. On my taxonomy, there are no secondary ideas of impressions; the distinction between primary and secondary ideas tracks the number of copies.

Notice that Hume does not use the ambiguous expression "perception" in introducing the distinction in T 1.1.1.11 (SBN 6–7). Norton (2000: 119) thinks that secondary ideas are copies of "secondary impressions" (Hume's name for impressions of reflection in Book 2). Pitson (2002: 24) thinks that primary ideas are beliefs and secondary ideas are memories. On my interpretation, primary ideas can be memories of impressions and secondary ideas can be beliefs about primary ideas.

36. Bettcher (2009: 209–10n83) claims that "secondary ideas are not mentioned even once" in Hume's account of personal identity.

37. I have visited Hume's tomb only once. Examples of events that have been experienced multiple times introduce further complications.

38. It does raise a problem for resemblance: on Hume's account, I cannot believe that my memory now resembles the past impression from which it is copied. One and the same perception (i.e., the current memory) will have to represent both the present idea and the past impression. Bricke (1977: 170–71 and 1980: 88) notices this problem too.

There is a corresponding problem for causation. In the belief that my current higher-level perception was copied from the immediately preceding lower-level perception, the vehicle of my belief is one and the same higher-level perception. But ideas of causes are distinct from ideas of effects. This is a very limited problem; it is implausible that it gave rise to the despair of Hume's confession. See also Bricke 1977: 171.

39. Waldow (2010) comes to this problem by another route; cp. Roth 2000.

40. Hume writes, "the thought alone finds personal identity, *when reflecting on the train of past perceptions, that compose a mind*, the ideas of them are felt to be connected together, and naturally introduce each other" (T App. 20, SBN 635; emphasis added). This does not entail that no present impressions can be included; but it does require some past perceptions. This is because the idea of identity essentially involves time. Cf. Biro 1976: 28; Haugeland 1998: 65; Stevenson 1998.

41. Cf. Biro 1976: 30ff.

42. Pitson 2002: 79–80; Thiel 2011: 393n26; Baxter 2008: 79ff.

43. Michael J. Costa (1988–90: 102ff.) offers such a view with respect to Hume's account of belief in the external existence of bodies.

44. Traiger (1988) makes a point similar to mine in objecting to Grice and Haugeland's (1998) circularity objection.

45. In the Appendix, Hume repeats the claim that death is the "extinction of all particular perceptions," but there is no point made about sound sleep (T App. 17, SBN 634–35).

46. Bricke 1977: 172–73; Bricke 1980: 92ff.; Pears 1990; Wright 1996: 189–90; Thiel 2011: 425 and n63; Strawson 2011.

8 Sympathy, Self, and Others

Hume introduces the principle of sympathy in the Book 2 Section, "Of the love of fame," in order to show how other people's sympathetically communicated opinions and sentiments, when they concern ourselves, function as "secondary" causes of pride and humility (T 2.1.11.1, SBN 316). Our public identity – that is, "[o]ur reputation, our character, our name" – is of great importance to us yet depends to a significant extent on how others see us (ibid.). Before explaining further the importance of these seconding sentiments for our reputation and sense of self-worth, Hume notes that "'twill be necessary to take some compass, and first explain the nature of *sympathy*" (ibid.). He immediately alerts us to sympathy's importance: "[n]o quality of human nature is more remarkable, both in itself and in its consequences, than that propensity we have to sympathize with others, and to receive by communication their inclinations and sentiments" (T 2.1.11.2, SBN 316).

Indeed, we might fruitfully consider sympathy as the linchpin of Hume's narrative account of human nature in the *Treatise*. Book 1 anticipates sympathy's role in enhancing the operations of the understanding. Custom's enlivening of ideas produces a "system" (T 1.3.9.3, SBN 108) that is the object of judgment and "which peoples the world," moving us beyond both immediate sense perception and memory (T 1.3.9.4, SBN 108). Sympathy expands this system by making us enter into the passions and opinions of the persons in our belief-extended world. Through sympathy we come to care about the events and past lives presented in histories; to respond to persons who are culturally, socially, and physically distant from us; and even to be moved by the fictional characters of poets and dramatists. Book 2 details sympathy's crucial role in constituting the particular concerns we have for our "past or future pains or pleasures," which helps show how Hume's account of the passionate self "serves to corroborate" his metaphysical account of personal identity (T 1.4.6.19, SBN 261).[1]

Book 2's account of how others' sympathetic seconding of the indirect passions of pride or humility increases the durability of those passions, and of the part sympathy plays in producing a disinterested esteem or hatred of others, anticipates Book 3's discussion of the more extensive sympathy that produces our moral sentiments and allows us to reflect on our own moral identity. Sympathy serves as the source of our moral sentiments by making us sensible of the effects an agent's character has on those who associate with her. In addition, sympathizing with the sentiments that others entertain of us influences our sense of pride or humility with respect to our own character and thus helps to shape our moral identity.

Hume's appeal to the principle of sympathy rather than to reason, self-interest, or an innate moral sense renders unique and boldly original his project of giving a naturalistic account of ethical life. His account of sympathy also stands as a significant innovation in the theories of the mind and the moral psychology of the early modern period. In this essay, I begin by attending to Hume's initial account of how sympathy works and attempt to situate the theoretical implications of Humean sympathy in the broader historical context in which Hume is working. In the rest of the essay, I focus on a neglected aspect of Humean sympathy – namely, the importance of sympathy with belief – and I suggest that sympathy is a critical component of Hume's social epistemology.

I. HOW HUMEAN SYMPATHY WORKS

Hume's initial account of sympathy in *Treatise* 2.1.11 examines what happens when we sympathize with others and explains how we "receive by communication their inclinations and sentiments, however different from, or even contrary to our own" (T 2.1.11.2, SBN 316). Sympathy is not itself any particular emotion or passion, but is rather a means of communicating passions, sentiments, and opinions to one another, and Hume refers to it as a "principle" of "communication" (T 2.3.6.8, SBN 427). Like custom, sympathy is a principle of the imagination that works by conveying the "force" and "vivacity" from an impression to a related idea. Both custom and sympathy play an important role in how we experience the passions in our lives. Because we lack direct access to the minds of others, sympathizing with another's passion requires that we first form an idea of it. As Hume describes it, a person's countenance, demeanor, and conversation are the "effects" or "signs" that "convey an idea" of the passion she is experiencing (T 2.1.11.3, SBN 317).[2] Whereas custom produces in us a belief about the passion another person experiences, thereby convincing us of the real existence of the passion, sympathy in turn moves us beyond belief and makes our idea acquire "such a degree of force and vivacity, as to become the very passion itself, and produce an equal emotion, as any original affection" (ibid.).

To explain how an idea of a passion becomes "the very passion itself," Hume appeals both to the lively sense we have of ourselves and to the resemblance that others bear to us. Because the "impression of ourselves is always intimately present with us, and ... our consciousness gives us so lively a conception of our own person," whatever is related to us "must be conceiv'd with a like vivacity of conception" (T 2.1.11.4, SBN 317). Of the three natural relations that associate perceptions in the mind – causation, contiguity, and resemblance – the most important for sympathy is resemblance. There is first a "general resemblance" between ourselves and other persons in virtue of our passionate nature, construed broadly to include emotions, moods, attitudes, and convictions: "we never remark any passion or principle in others, of which, in some degree or other, we may not find a parallel in ourselves" (T 2.1.11.5, SBN 318). If in addition to this general resemblance, others also resemble us in more specific ways, by sharing, for example, "our manners, or character, or country, or language, it facilitates the sympathy" (ibid.). The relations of contiguity and causation also contribute to the easy production of sympathetic perceptions. Our perceptions of people or situations that are close to us strike the mind with more force, and the more forceful and vivid our conception of someone's situation, the easier it is to sympathize with her. Hume thinks of kinship relations as instances of causation, and acquaintances as influencing us in the same manner as "education and custom" – that is, through repeated contact (T 2.1.11.6, SBN 318). He suggests that we are more naturally sympathetic to our relatives and acquaintances, either because we care more for them than for others and so readily take up their concerns, or simply because they are more familiar to us.

Hume describes sympathy as working analogously to custom because both operate by transfusing the liveliness of an impression into an idea. So the account of sympathy provides "strong confirmation" to both his system of the understanding and his system of the passions (T 2.1.11.8, SBN 319). Although "sympathy is exactly correspondent to the operations of our understanding," its capacity to produce in us passions and sentiments by converting the ideas of others' affections "into the very impressions they represent" makes sympathy even "more surprizing and extraordinary" (T 2.1.11.8, SBN 319-20). It is important to bear in mind that, whereas a lively impression of the self is required to provide the force needed to convert an idea of another's passion into a passion, sympathy with another does not involve imagining oneself in place of the other.[3] When we sympathize with another person, "our own person is not the object of any passion, nor is there any thing, that fixes our attention on ourselves" (T 2.2.2.17, SBN 340). Sympathy interests us in the situations of others and "takes us so far out of ourselves, as to give us the same pleasure or uneasiness" that others experience (T 3.3.1.11, SBN

579). Our responsiveness to others depends on making the passions of others become "in some measure, our own," but this is so that "they operate upon us, by opposing and encreasing our passions, in the very same manner, as if they had been originally deriv'd from our own temper and disposition" (T 3.3.2.3, SBN 593). As M. Jamie Ferreira (1994) has rightly emphasized, in moving us beyond ourselves, sympathy may prompt us to imaginatively reconstruct the situation another person experiences.

Hume's attempt to explain sympathy and the passions systematically and as an extension of his explanation of belief and judgment makes his account of sympathy distinctive. Several of his early modern predecessors and contemporaries had noted an instinctive or mechanical communication of the passions, which they labeled "sympathy" or "contagion." For the dualist Nicolas Malebranche, who describes the human body as a machine, sympathy is a mechanical response that can occur without any interposing thought or belief. According to Malebranche (V.3 [1674–75] 1980: 348), an individual's passion has a certain corresponding facial expression or utterance that can mechanically excite the same passion in others.[4] This "communication of the soul's passions" may also elicit compassion or some other response that helps to preserve the social union (V.7 [1674–75] 1980: 377). Malebranche's explanation of sympathetic response is thus consistent with his view that the function of the passions is to protect and maintain the body-soul composite. Shaftesbury, too, notes that certain more "social and communicative" passions are conveyed by "aspect,... contact or sympathy"; and passions "raised in a multitude," or panics, are sympathetically conveyed by people's "very looks" ([1711] 1999: 10, cf. 374). Sympathy may be a source of ill, as with panics, or of pleasure, as when we communicate the good of others to one another. Joseph Butler also stresses the importance of sympathy for sociability. He argues that we have a prior disposition to associate, and a "bias of nature" (I.10 [1726] 2006: 50) makes us substitute the interest of others for our own so that we are "carried out, and affected towards the interests of others" (V.1 [1726] 2006: 72). People are so alike in terms of bodily and mental constitution "that in a peculiar manner they feel for each other, shame, sudden danger, resentment, honour, prosperity, distress" (I.10 [1726] 2006: 50). Although Malebranche, Shaftesbury, and Butler – each a philosopher respected by Hume – take note of the phenomenon of sympathy, they do not regard it, as Hume does, as a key principle that helps to explain the meaning and value of our passionate life.

Hume agrees that sympathy often operates with an immediacy akin to instinct, for we can "observe the force of sympathy thro' the whole animal creation, and the easy communication of sentiments from one thinking being to another" (T 2.2.5.15, SBN 363).[5] Certain passions and moods are contagious: "A chearful countenance infuses a sensible complacency and serenity into my mind; as an angry or sorrowful one throws a sudden damp upon me. Hatred, resentment, esteem, love, courage, mirth and melancholy; all these passions I feel more from communication than from my own natural temper and disposition" (T 2.1.11.2, SBN 317). Hume observes that people of the same temperament or disposition are naturally drawn toward one another: "men of gay tempers naturally love the gay; as the serious bear an affection to the serious," and this happens not only when we note the similarity between ourselves and others but also "by a certain sympathy, which always arises betwixt similar characters" (T 2.2.4.6, SBN 354). An "*immediate* sympathy" that precedes reflection makes us "enter with more warmth" into the sentiments of people with characters similar to our own (T 3.3.3.4, SBN 604).

But Humean sympathy goes beyond instinctive response. As we have seen, sympathy often requires that we notice the *effects* of someone's passion in order to form the idea of it that gets enlivened into our own passionate response. The judgments we form about the *causes* of various passions and how people experience them can also trigger our sympathy. Hume stresses this point in a vivid example of an upcoming surgery:

> Were I present at any of the more terrible operations of surgery, 'tis certain, that even before it begun, the preparation of the instruments, the laying of the bandages in order, the heating of the irons, with all the signs of anxiety and concern in the patient and assistants, wou'd have a great effect upon my mind, and excite the strongest sentiments of pity and terror. No passion of another discovers itself immediately to the mind. We are only sensible of its causes or effects. From *these* we infer the passion: And consequently *these* give rise to our sympathy. (T 3.3.1.7, SBN 576)

Further, the beliefs we form about the causes of the passions make it possible to sympathize with people even when they do not experience the emotion typically produced by their circumstances. For example, the magnanimous person who does not indulge in self-pity when misfortune befalls her often evokes a greater compassion in us, as does someone who is simply not conscious of his misfortune. And "[f]rom the same principles we blush for the conduct of those, who behave themselves foolishly" yet show no sense of shame (T 2.2.7.5, SBN 371). Hume describes these cases as involving a "partial" sympathy (ibid.) in which the sympathetically produced passion "acquires strength from the weakness of its original" (T 2.2.7.5, SBN 370). By a general rule, we form an idea of the passion usually produced by the situation in question, and this idea becomes livelier and the emotion more violent when we contrast it with the indifference or ignorance of the person with whom we sympathize.

Our sympathy can also extend beyond someone's present situation so that we concern ourselves with his "future possible or probable condition" (T 2.2.9.13, SBN 386). As in the case of partial sympathy, Hume focuses on explaining how the sympathetic perception is produced. Cases of "extensive" sympathy require that we have a sufficiently vivid conception of the person's current circumstances, because that vivacity provides the momentum to enliven our ideas of his future situation. Hume compares the mind's operations in such cases to hydrodynamics: just as a quantity of water is conveyed along pipes according to the pressure at the source, the more vivid our conception of someone's condition, the stronger our sympathy with both it and the related ideas we have of his future situation. It takes "a great effort of imagination" just to form lively ideas of someone's current passions, so a more extensive sympathy depends on our having a sufficiently vivid sense of his present condition that can enliven our ideas of his future probable or possible circumstances (T 2.2.9.14, SBN 386). Hume uses the term *extensive sympathy* in a similar way to refer to the sympathy that gives us an interest in the public good and serves as the source of our moral sentiments. In evaluating someone's moral character, we extend our sympathy to her "circle" of associates precisely to enliven the moral sentiments that will have her character as their object. Even in those cases in which we do not actually feel lively sentiments of praise or blame, we can still form notions of someone's praiseworthiness or blameworthiness by extending our sympathy to consider how her character affects the interests and sentiments of her associates.

Notice that in the discussion of the cases of partial and extensive sympathy, Hume appears to be working with a dual purpose. On the one hand, he is concerned to explain the circumstances that facilitate the production of a sympathetic passion *qua* perception. For this purpose, sympathy is conceived as a principle that transmits force from one perception to another, facilitating mental transitions (hence the usefulness of the hydrodynamics analogy). When sympathy is strong, partial or extensive, it is assisted by the vivacity of the idea or by general rules and so has more force. Sympathy is weak either when the principle of comparison keeps us focused on our own concerns or when the person with whom we sympathize is too remote for us to form a lively sense of him or his situation, so that sympathy fails to make us sufficiently interested in him.[6] This explanation of how our various perceptions arise in the mind fits with the aim of Hume's moral science – namely, to discover the fundamental principles of human nature.

Yet Hume's discussion of how these sympathetically produced perceptions inform our sense of ourselves, our understanding of others, and our ethical life goes beyond explaining how they are produced in the mind. In the case of partial sympathy, for example, Hume makes it clear that we reflect on someone's circumstances and make an evaluative judgment about why she might *deserve* greater compassion or contempt. And despite the mechanical analogy in the case of extensive sympathy, we must use our powers of inference and judgment about the person's future condition, even while sympathy works to *interest* us in the person's circumstances and to "take part with them" (T 2.2.9.14, SBN 386). As James Farr (1978: 295) has pointed out, Hume's causal-mechanistic and associative explanation "cannot quite contain sympathy." Association explains the movements of the mind and the transitions from one perception to another, but explanation at the level of association does not adequately capture the more normative versions of sympathy. The extension and correction of sympathy that occurs when we adopt the common point of view, as well as the delicate sympathy that is the hallmark of good aesthetic judgment, all suggest a cultivation of sympathy that involves reflective judgment. Hume remarks that sympathy is the "animating principle" of all our passions, and they would have no force "were we to abstract entirely from the thoughts and sentiments of others" (T 2.2.5.15, SBN 363). Sympathy does transmit force, but it also serves as the means through which the passions have for us the value and significance they do.

2. SYMPATHY AND THE SOCIAL CHARACTER OF BELIEF

I turn now to an important, although often neglected, aspect of Humean sympathy. In addition to sympathizing with one another's passions or the situations that typically produce the various passions, we also sympathize with *opinions*, *beliefs*, and *judgments*. Philip Mercer has noted that sympathizing with belief is consistent with Hume's account of how belief is produced:

In so far as Hume thinks that belief is merely a lively idea or impression, there can be no objections to saying that an idea that X is the case can, through being associated with an impression, be so enlivened as to become a belief that X is the case. It follows that beliefs, opinions, and attitudes are just as susceptible to communication from one person to another by means of the sympathetic mechanism as passions and emotions are. (1972: 34)[7]

As with the passions, sympathy with others' beliefs can be immediate and prior to reflection. Children, for example, "implicitly embrace every opinion propos'd to them" (T 2.1.11.2, SBN 316). And even when we know our own mind, sympathy makes us susceptible to others' eloquence or powers of persuasion and explains why we often find compelling the beliefs of those who have a sense of conviction. Thus even "men of the greatest judgment and understanding ... find it very difficult to follow their own reason or inclination, in opposition to that of their friends and daily companions" (ibid.; cf. T 2.3.6.8, SBN 427).

Any judgment or belief may be sympathetically communicated. Yet we are particularly disposed to sympathize with judgments either when they concern ourselves or when they are presented to us in a certain manner. In the first case, others' sentiments and judgments about us have "a peculiar influence," with the capacity "to disturb our understanding" because they either confirm or disconfirm the judgments we make about ourselves (T 2.1.11.9, SBN 321). In the second case, sympathy makes us susceptible to what Hume terms "artificial" causes of belief (T 1.3.9.19, SBN 117). Something repeated often enough or "painted out to us in all the colours of eloquence" has the same influence as truth or evidence in enlivening the imagination and making the mind acquiesce to the views presented (T 1.3.10.8, SBN 123). Both sympathy with judgments about ourselves and the sympathetic "absorption" of repeated judgment that occurs in education (or what Hume sometimes refers to as being "inculcated") play a significant role in how we understand and experience the indirect passions. I shall look at the significance of sympathizing with the judgments others make about us in the next section, after examining here the link between sympathy, belief, and education.

Many of the judgments or attitudes of others with which we sympathize embody elements of the collective social and moral beliefs of our community, which will include the "prejudices," both good and bad, borne of general rules. Both sympathy and custom serve as the means of transmitting these beliefs and hence help us acquire a competence in our community's beliefs and attitudes, ways, and values. Hume notes that although "education be disclaim'd by philosophy, as a fallacious ground of assent to any opinion" (T 1.3.10.1, SBN 118), examination would show that "more than one half of those opinions, that prevail among mankind" are owing to education "and that the principles, which are thus implicitly embrac'd, over-ballance those, which are owing either to abstract reasoning or experience" (T 1.3.9.19, SBN 117). Although Hume describes education as a process involving custom or repetition, he also observes that sympathy explains the "great uniformity we may observe in the humours and turn of thinking of those of the same nation" (T 2.1.11.2, SBN 316). And in the moral arena, we learn to have an esteem for justice and an abhorrence of injustice. Both civic education and moral education generally are promoted through custom and appeals to authority and honor that engage the sympathetic affections.

Although Hume observes that philosophers generally disclaim education, the question of how much of our knowledge results from education was an area of active debate in eighteenth-century Britain. Part of the debate concerned morality, and in Book 2 Hume alludes to the controversy about *"[w]hether these moral distinctions be founded on natural and original principles, or arise from interest and education"* (T 2.1.7.2, SBN 295). On one side of this particular controversy were those in the so-called selfish school, followers of Hobbes, such as Bernard de Mandeville, who argued that politicians cleverly exploited people's susceptibility to flattery in order to make honest and virtuous citizens of them. The other side was divided between those, such as Samuel Clarke, who held that reason allows us to discover the eternal and immutable moral distinctions, and others, such as Hutcheson, who argued for an innate moral sense that, uncorrupted by education and custom, approves of those natural affections that promote the public good. The debate also extended to accounts of the passions and judgment as well as of morality, and there were more moderate positions than that of Mandeville, such as those of John Gay and Hume, on the necessary role of education. If we look at the context in which Hume stakes out a role for the principles of association and sympathy in his account of how the mind works, we can see that he aims to construct an account of the passions and the moral sentiments that undercuts the prevalent teleological explanations that structured the work of moral sense theorists such as Shaftesbury and Hutcheson.

Locke introduced the term "association of ideas" in order to distinguish between those ideas that have a natural connection with one another and the accidental connections resulting from custom, education, or chance.[8] Hutcheson ([1728] 1969: 10) follows Locke in singling out the notion of the association of ideas as a troublesome "disposition in our nature," although both men acknowledge the need for the association of ideas since without it language would be impossible. In his *Inquiry* into the origin of virtue, which in its first edition was intended as a defense of Shaftesbury against the criticisms of Mandeville, Hutcheson ([1725] 1969: 268) argues for a natural moral sense that operates instinctively so that we perceive moral goodness independently of "custom, education, example, or study," for these latter "give us no new ideas."[9] In his essay on the passions, Hutcheson argues that education can corrupt both desires and values, and he expresses a particular worry about religious fanaticism. The problem as Hutcheson sees it is that desire and aversion arise in response to our apprehension of good and evil, yet that apprehension depends "much upon our opinions," which are often shaped by the influence of merely customary associations ([1728] 1969: 90). Custom and education make us form "wild associations of ideas" that, unless carefully regulated, distort the passions ([1728] 1969: 96). At their worst, such associations spread by "contagion" (ibid.) and prevent us from perceiving an object's "real good" by rendering the passions immune to reflection or argument ([1728] 1969: 95), and thus producing "endless labour, vexation, and misery of every kind" ([1728] 1969: 94).

Hume grants that customary mental associations may be a source of prejudice and error, just as he acknowledges that sympathetic contagion can produce or sustain factions. But he also holds that the only way we arrive at any of our beliefs in matters of fact is through habitual or customary associations, although we can and "ought to regulate our judgment" by some "rules," formed by the very same principle of custom but reflecting our experience of the operations of the understanding (T 1.3.13.11, SBN 149). In contrast to Locke and Hutcheson, Hume assigns the doctrine of the association of ideas a key explanatory role in his account of mental activity. A likely positive influence here is John Gay, an early critic of Hutcheson's moral sense doctrine. Gay argues that moral approbation and blame are indeed sentiments, as Hutcheson insists, but that we have no innate moral sense (or indeed any of the other internal senses) that operates independently of custom or instruction. With respect to the issue of the criterion of virtue, Gay finds that Hutcheson's account of the moral sense "relishes too much" of the doctrine of occult qualities, his explanation "rather cutting the knot than untying it" ([1731] 1964: 269). According to Gay, much of our moral knowledge results from customary associations of pleasure with things we perceive or imagine to be good or conducive to happiness. Many of these associations result not from our own experience, but are learned from others, particularly from those whom we esteem, and often by way of imitation.

Hume, perhaps for reasons of prudence, does not openly criticize Hutcheson as Gay does, yet he shares Gay's view that the diversity of human life, including morality, cannot be explained by the approvals and disapprovals of innate senses. Hume goes further than does Gay in explaining how association works and presenting a systematic account of how association and sympathy together help explain the origin of the indirect passions and moral sentiments that he repeatedly says are intimately linked with our moral responses to one another.[10]

It will be helpful to look in some detail at how sympathy and association work together to produce the indirect passions.[11] We can then see how sympathy is an important component, on Hume's view, of knowledge and belief as social in character. Hume emphasizes that the mind has a natural disposition to produce the indirect passions of pride, hatred, love, and humility (T 2.1.5.6, SBN 287). The indirect passions are counted as impressions in Hume's taxonomy of perceptions and have as "an original quality" a sensation "or the peculiar emotions they excite in the soul" (T 2.1.5.4, SBN 286). Regarded strictly as an impression, the sensation of an indirect passion – a pleasant one in the case of pride and love and a painful one in the case of humility and hatred – constitutes its "very being and essence" (ibid.). Yet our experience of an indirect passion such as pride encompasses more than sensation. Pride, like the other indirect passions, is "a passion plac'd betwixt two ideas, of which the one produces it, and the other is produc'd by it" (T 2.1.2.4, SBN 278). One of these ideas "represents the *cause*," while the other is of the object to which the passion is directed, which in the case of pride and its opposite, humility, is the self (ibid.). Pride thus depends on our having a belief about the value of some attribute of ours, the quality or possession that produces pride, and on our pride in turn producing an idea of ourselves as advantaged in virtue of the valuable quality (pride "always turns our view to ourselves, and makes us think of our own qualities and circumstances" [T 2.1.5.6, SBN 287]).

So although we should never be possessed of pride "were there not a disposition of mind proper for it" (ibid.), it is also the case "that pride requires the assistance of some foreign object" (T 2.1.5.7, SBN 287). The primary causes of pride and humility are "*natural*," Hume claims, in the sense that such things as wealth, power, beauty, and mental excellences, and the opposites of these, have regularly produced these affections across ages and cultures. So "we can know pretty nearly" what would influence the pride or humility "even of a stranger" (T 2.1.3.4, SBN 281). (As we'll see, this claim later gets qualified.)[12] Yet the causes are not *original* because there is no distinct mental principle to which each cause corresponds.[13] Not only do we find a "prodigious number" of causes of pride and humility, but many of the things that cause these passions are themselves produced or altered by art and tend to reflect particular technologies and varied material resources, local customs, fashion, or "caprice" (T 2.1.3.5, SBN 281). The task is to find some other circumstances common to all of them that explain their causal efficacy.

The investigation into these common circumstances and to see what determines each particular cause of pride "to be what it is" *qua* cause leads Hume to explain the origin of the indirect passions in terms of a double relation of ideas and impressions (T 2.1.3.1, SBN 280). The cause of pride is something related to the self, and the object of pride is the self; here is a relation of ideas. The thing that causes pride must be something that produces pleasure independently of pride, and the affective quality of pride is a pleasant feeling; so here we have two impressions related by their resembling feelings. As Hume explicitly notes in his later work on the passions, this double relation of ideas and impressions is "the real efficient cause of the passion" (DP 2.5).[14] Rather than attending to final causes and the question of what the passions are for, Hume's strategy is reductive. Any quality that produces pride, whether a beautiful *scritoire* or a shapely ankle or some other quality, is something pleasant related to the self. At the same time, however, this strategy accommodates the different historical and cultural contexts in which things are recognized as reasons for someone to feel pride or humility.

The point of claiming that the causes of pride are not original is to show that many of the particular causes of pride are shaped by everyday practice and social institutions, and so reflect a particular historical and cultural context. The causes of pride tend to fall into certain categories (this accounts for their designation as "natural"): qualities of mind or body, external advantages such as family lineage, and wealth – things that have, as Donald Ainslie (1999: 478) puts it, an *"existential connection"* to us in terms of making a difference to who we are.[15] Our beliefs about these causes include judgments about the value of the objects; it is *beautiful* houses, *virtuous* characters, and so on that are causes of pride. Yet how we respond to qualities of mind or bodily features, and the value we ascribe to material goods, will vary between and even within cultures, as well as over time, in relation to technological advance, for example. The limitations stipulating that we experience pride appropriately when what we take pride in has a close relation to us, when it is fairly rare as well as durable, and when it is recognized by others as a rare and durable source of pleasure will also reflect this variation (T 2.1.6).[16] Through sympathy we learn how to recognize and assess these existential connections. Different people will learn differently; think, for example, of how the delicate sympathy of the connoisseur reflects a specialized process of education, including a sympathetic appreciation for like-minded souls, that has helped her acquire superior powers of discernment and discrimination.

Sympathy is crucial to Hume's social epistemology, and this is made clear by his appeal to the influence of general rules or "general establish'd maxims" (T 2.1.6.9, SBN 294) as a final limitation on, but really an enlargement of, the system of indirect passions (T 2.1.6.8, SBN 293).[17] "[C]ustom and practice have brought to light ... the just value of every thing; [and] this must certainly contribute to the easy production of the passions, and guide us, by means of general establish'd maxims, in the proportions we ought to observe in preferring one object to another" (T 2.1.6.9, SBN 294). The general rules that lead us to think of particular qualities as having or lacking value often reflect the historical and cultural variations in how people recognize, describe, and classify the qualities that they take to be reasons for feeling pride or humility. We can now appreciate that regarding the causes of pride and humility as natural but not original suggests that we must *acquire* a competence in assessing the qualities in which different people will feel pride. Indeed, Hume now qualifies his earlier claim that we can pretty much know what will cause pride or humility in others, suggesting that we should not expect to have an automatic competence in such judgments when we encounter a culture other than our own. If a person from elsewhere "were on a sudden transported into our world, he wou'd be very much embarrass'd with every object, and wou'd not readily find what degree of love or hatred, pride or humility, or any other passion he ought to attribute to it" (T 2.1.6.9, SBN 293–94).[18]

With regard to the passions, general rules have normative weight.[19] Custom alone might explain how we come to have beliefs about such things as who should be proud of what. But our passionate education includes an often-insensible process of learning appropriate ways of expressing the passions, as well as being sensitive to who can do so and under which circumstances. Sympathetic imitation of others and inculcation of general rules helps us learn how to embody and enact our emotional life. General rules thus influence how we cultivate the character and conduct appropriate to, for example, our "sex," profession, or social class. They also govern our ascriptions of passions to others on the same bases. Hume identifies "rank," for example, as a key social category, because it reflects the importance that power, property, and wealth have for us (even though the existence of ranks depends on the "artifices" of government and are thus constructed rather than natural distinctions).[20] The rich are typically proud of their wealth, so we not only show the rich man greater deference but also attribute pride to him even if he does not in fact experience pride.[21] Hume notes that when we attribute a passion to someone that the person does not in fact experience, "[c]ustom readily carries us beyond the just bounds in our passions, as well as in our reasonings" (T 2.1.6.8, SBN 293).[22] Nevertheless, in order to navigate the social world it is convenient for us to identify people on the basis of their membership in a particular social group (or a plurality of such) and, through what we might think of as a variation of partial sympathy, attribute to them the passions, opinions, character traits, and so on that are typical of members of the group.

3. SYMPATHETIC COMMUNICATION AND THE NATURE OF THE PASSIONS

We might ask whether Hume gives a consistent account of how sympathy works. He sometimes appears to suggest that it is the natural commonality of our emotional lives that explains our capacity to sympathize with others' experiences, as is shown by the claim that "we never remark any passion or principle in others, of which, in some degree or other, we may not find a parallel in ourselves" (T 2.1.11.5, SBN 318). At other times, Hume indicates that sympathy explains that commonality. The mimetic and assimilative functions of sympathy that make it possible to share beliefs and values seem actually to construct a culturally organized set of emotional experiences, including the expression and recognition of emotions, as well as to produce similarities of manners and character. As Hume points out, thinking of sympathy in this way explains "the great uniformity we may observe in the humours and turn of thinking" among fellow citizens, a resemblance that "arises from sympathy" and preserves "the character of a nation" (T 2.1.11.2, SBN 316–17). Is commonality created through sympathy, or does our commonality make it possible for us to sympathize with one another?

Hume's assertion that the indirect passions are simple impressions creates some difficulty for him. Philip Mercer (1972: 34) argues that "on Hume's account we can only sympathize with feelings which we ourselves have already experienced." Because a passion is a simple impression, the idea we form of another's passion must be a copy corresponding to an impression that we have experienced ourselves. If we do form an idea of what is in fact the other's passion, then Mercer's point seems to hold. But Hume's explanation of what we do seems more qualified. When we sympathize with the beliefs, sentiments, or passions of others, Hume notes that we do so because others resemble us, and there is no "passion or principle ... of which, in some degree or other, we may not find a parallel in ourselves" (T 2.1.11.5, SBN 318; cf. T 3.3.1.7, SBN 575–76). A "parallel" passion resembling "in some degree" could be a passion similar but not identical to the one with which we sympathize. To suggest that sympathy sometimes produces a passion that is similar to but the not the same as what another actually experiences is in keeping with Hume's view that it is through the imagination that we interpret and reconstruct, rather than directly experience, the other's passionate experience.[23] Implicit in this view is that we may face limits in understanding one another.

Recall that the mind has a natural disposition to produce pride and the other indirect passions; so Hume clearly does think that some of the passions, or at least the tendency to experience them, are universal. Yet his account of the indirect passions limits the extent to which such innate dispositions determine how we actually experience such passions or our understanding of what the passions mean. Pride is a simple impression (essentially a pleasant feeling), but the claim that it is a passion "betwixt two ideas" should not mislead us into thinking that pride is simply a brute sensation – a primitive feeling – or that the ideas that produce pride and that which pride in turn produces are bare ideas (T 2.1.2.4, SBN 278). The indirect passions produce an idea of ourselves as attractive or unattractive, advantaged or disadvantaged in virtue of some publicly recognized quality or possession about which we typically form an evaluative opinion or judgment.

Annette Baier suggests that Hume's account of sympathy assumes both "a sort of intrinsic individualism of passions" (1997: 44) and "a common repertoire of emotions" (1997: 43) to which some seconding sentiments get added through sympathetic communication. Baier regards Humean passions as "primitive" elements of the mind (1997: 44), requiring no special skills and for which we need give no normative account of the standards for successful feeling, in contrast to the socially constructed standards we invoke to assess successful reasoning or moral evaluation.

The sympathetic communication of belief may be important in various contexts, but I have argued that it is especially so for Hume's account of the indirect passions, given their links to the moral sentiments. In any case, the role of sympathetically communicated belief suggests that the passions are socially constituted to a greater extent than Mercer and Baier allow. Baier notes that Hume allows for some cultural variation in our conception of the passions that influences how they might be cultivated, for example, with respect to what are deemed appropriate or acceptable expressions. My own view is that Hume comes closer to suggesting that the passions are fundamentally culturally structured (even if some of them are universal), hence the critical significance of sympathy as a principle of communication.

I have drawn attention to a distinct normative dimension of how we ascribe and experience at least some of the passions. The social categories that influence how we ascribe the passions to people will also contribute to structuring the cognitive and passionate realities of those who have membership in those categories. And they influence us in terms of how we treat one another in virtue of the social identities we recognize. Note that Hume identifies various forms of the key indirect passions of pride, humility, love, and hatred, and that these distinct forms of response are also guided by social norms. For example, the different causes of pride also engender different responses in us when we sympathize with the proud person such that we *esteem* the rich man but feel *moral admiration* for the virtuous one.

Although our experience of our emotional life is often personal and not shared, how we make sense of our emotional experience, and decide what to share and what to keep to ourselves, reflects the importance of sympathetic communication. We learn, for example, to disguise some of our real feelings in certain situations, just as we learn not to voice certain opinions. Hume's account of modesty and the rules of good breeding is a good illustration of emotional disguising – in this case with reference to pride. Pride is not only agreeable to the proud person, but also valuable, because it affords her a sense of her own merit and can make her "bold and enterprizing" (T 3.3.2.8–9, SBN 597). The proud person's good opinion of herself can, however, be disagreeable to others, by the principle of comparison. In order not to produce envy or hatred in others, and to carry on a conversation on equal terms with one another, good manners require that the proud person "shou'd avoid all signs and expressions" which betray her sense of pride (T 3.3.2.10, SBN 597). The rules of good breeding make up a set of norms that govern our expression of at least some of the passions.

I have also suggested that sympathy's role in communicating and impressing upon us meanings and values explains how we acquire a culturally and historically informed competence in those meanings and values. Sympathy is thus the means of *reproducing* forms of social life and schemes of value. The traits, attitudes, or manners we associate with particular nationalities, or those of a given rank or sex, are not natural or inherited features, but instead are patterns of feeling and behavior, transmitted by way of sympathy, to which people become accustomed. In this way, sympathy explains both the commonality and the variability of our emotional lives.

NOTES

1. A substantial body of important scholarly literature now exists on the relation between Hume's account of personal identity in Book 1 and the passionate self in Book 2. Among the most interesting discussions are Árdal 1966; Penelhum 1976; McIntyre 1979 and 1989; Baier 1991; and Ainslie 1999.

2. Ronald Butler (1975) and James Farr (1978) both raise the issue of whether Hume confuses the language of signs with causal language, as might be suggested by this passage. Butler resolves it by arguing that Hume is conscious of the distinction but that his analysis of causation denies the validity of it. Rather, both "the causal connexion and the relation between a sign and what it signifies" can be explained by reference to the "habitual determination of the mind to pass from one perception to another" (1975: 11).

   Farr is interested in a theory of signs as a feature of hermeneutics and argues that, although Hume's position is ambiguous, he clearly at times regards signs as things in need of decoding and interpretation – not only in histories, but as they are presented in human actions. Farr cites the first *Enquiry*, in which Hume writes that "we mount up to the knowledge of men's inclinations and motives, from their actions, expressions, and even gestures; and again, descend to the interpretation of their actions from our knowledge of their motives and inclinations" (EHU 8.9, SBN 84–85). I agree with Farr that we must often interpret the signs of actions and character and that Hume presents sympathy as the means of our acquiring skills in discerning and interpreting such signs. For another interesting hermeneutical approach to Hume's account of sympathy, see Weinsheimer 1993. Although he argues against Farr's particular interpretation of a hermeneutic Humean sympathy, Henrik Bohlin (2009) suggests that although there is some basis for placing Hume in the hermeneutic tradition of Schleiermacher and Dilthey, Hume does not develop his hermeneutics sufficiently.

3. Those who attribute to Hume an account of sympathy in which one imagines oneself in the place of the other include Mercer 1972; Capaldi 1976; and Hirschmann 2000.
4. See also Malebranche IV.13, V.3 [1674–75] 1980: 332 and 348–51, for further discussion of the *mechanical* nature of our sympathetic response to the emotions, pains, and pleasures of others. Malebranche devotes the first chapter of Book II, Part 3 of *The Search after Truth* to "the contagious communications of strong imaginations" ([1674–75] 1980: 161) and explains there how our disposition to imitate others spreads errors by communication.
5. Elsewhere, Hume writes, "'Tis evident, that *sympathy*, or the communication of passions, takes place among animals, no less than among men. Fear, anger, courage and other affections are frequently communicated from one animal to another, without their knowledge of that cause, which produc'd the original passion" (T 2.2.12.6, SBN 398).
6. Whereas sympathy with distant persons produces a weak passionate response, a sympathy that is weak because of comparison of oneself with another can result in strong other-directed emotions such as malice, respect, or contempt. See T 2.2.8–10 and 3.3.2.
7. The importance of sympathy with belief is also discussed by Árdal 1966: 46–48; Butler 1975: 15–19; Farr 1978; and O'Brien 2010.
8. Locke discusses the association of ideas in *Essay* 2.33. The concept of mental association is of course much older. Bacon's discussion of the "idols," in *Novum Organum*, is the first modern articulation, and his discussion of the negative effects of the associations produced by education, custom, accident, and philosophical sects had the most influence on his successors.

    For scholarly discussion of the development of the concept of the association of ideas, see Rapaport 1974 and Wright 1983: 203–10.
9. The full title of the first edition of this work is *An Inquiry Into the Original of Our Ideas of Beauty and Virtue; in Two Treatises. In which the Principles of the Late Earl of Shaftesbury are explain'd and defended, against the Author of the Fable of the Bees: And the Ideas of Moral Good and Evil are Establish'd, According to the Sentiments of the Ancient Moralists. With an Attempt to Introduce a Mathematical Calculation in the Subject of Morality* (1725). Beginning with the 1723 edition of *The Fable of the Bees*, Mandeville included a scathing critique of Shaftesbury's moral philosophy.
10. Hume connects the indirect passions and the moral sentiments in several places, including T 2.1.7, 3.1.2, and 3.3.1.
11. Hume makes it clear in the "Abstract" that the principles of association are important for giving an account of the passions and human sociality: they are of "vast consequence ... in the science of human nature,... [and] so far as regards the mind, these are the only links that bind the parts of the universe together, or connect us with any person or object exterior to ourselves. *For as it is by means of thought only that any thing operates upon our passions, and as these are the only ties of our thoughts, they are really to us the cement of the universe*, and all the operations of the mind must, in a great measure, depend on them" (Abs. 35, SBN 662; emphasis added).
12. "Can we imagine it possible, that while human nature remains the same, men will ever become entirely indifferent to their power, riches, beauty or

personal merit, and that their pride and vanity will not be affected by these advantages?" (T 2.1.3.4, SBN 281).

13. "The human mind ... may justly be thought incapable of containing such a monstrous heap of principles, as wou'd be necessary to excite the passions of pride and humility, were each distinct cause adapted to the passions by a distinct set of principles" (T 2.1.3.6, SBN 282).

14. As Hume emphasizes in Book 1, "all causes are of the same kind, and ... there is no foundation for that distinction" between efficient and other kinds of cause (T 1.3.14.32, SBN 171).

15. Ainslie (1999) gets the label "existential connection" from Hume's claim that the causes of pride and humility must be "connected with our being and existence" (T 2.1.8.8, SBN 302).

16. Hume writes that "these limitations are deriv'd from the very nature of the subject" (T 2.1.6.1, SBN 290). The last paragraph of T 2.1.6 suggests that the limitations state the conditions under which someone appropriately experiences pride, but that people may experience pride even when some limiting conditions are not met, and others may not experience it when all the limiting conditions are met.

17. In addition to Butler 1975 and Farr 1978, see also Baier 1994: ch. 5.

18. See Postema 2005 and Baier and Waldow 2008.

19. In Book 1, Hume noted that unphilosophical general rules or customary associations produce in us a lively anticipation that future encounters with situations that resemble past ones will be like those past ones in all respects. Our expectation is thus a kind of prejudice since we may encounter a future instance resembling only in some respects, and not in the causally efficacious ones, so that our expectation is contradicted by the evidence. We can correct the prejudicial belief through reflection, Hume notes, but "custom takes the start, and gives a biass to the imagination" (T 1.3.13.9, SBN 148). General rules have a different effect on the passions.

20. For a detailed discussion of sympathy and social relations, see Finlay 2007.

21. Here, "we form a notion of different ranks of men, suitable to the power or riches they are possest of; and this notion we change not upon account of any peculiarities of the health or temper of the persons, which may deprive them of all enjoyment in their possessions" (T 2.1.6.8, SBN 293).

22. John Gay ([1731] 1964: 284) notes that the power of association is so great as "to transport our passions and affections beyond their proper bounds, both as to intenseness and duration," and also "to transfer them to improper objects."

23. Of course, we do not here consciously aim to distort the experience of the person with whom we sympathize, but recall too that Hume notes the distorting effects of general rules when we ascribe passions that others do not in fact experience.

9   The Indirect Passions, Myself, and Others

In his anonymous attempt in the *Abstract* to draw attention to the neglected merits of the *Treatise*, Hume says of its second Book, "'Tis of more easy comprehension than the first; but contains opinions, that are altogether as new and extraordinary" (Abs. 30, SBN 659). In his concluding paragraph, he says that "if any thing can entitle the author to so glorious a name as that of an *inventor*, 'tis the use he makes of the principle of the association of ideas, which enters into most of his philosophy" (Abs. 35, SBN 661–62). These statements indicate that Hume thought highly of his treatment of the passions in Book 2 and thought his readers might follow him in this, at least with a little encouragement. On the whole, however, they have not. Commentators have tended to use Book 2, or at least its first two parts, merely as a source for teachings that are applied in Book 3 or to note that it corrects the unbalanced concentration on the understanding that has led Hume to sceptical grief at the end of Book 1. Admittedly, the greater clarity he boasts of in the *Abstract* is purchased at the price of some tedious detail, but the very quantity of this detail should make us recognize that these two Parts should be assessed primarily as what they purport to be: a sustained analysis of those fundamental human emotions that are their subject. I shall attempt such an assessment.

These Parts introduce us to the vital notion of sympathy, one that is central to Hume's understanding of human nature and to his ethical theory. They also contain some important statements about the self. I shall try to shed some light on these themes, concentrating throughout on what the two Parts tell us about them.

Hume's theory of the passions is a key component of his "science of man." He is famous (or notorious) for telling us that reason is, and ought only to be, the slave of the passions (T 2.3.3.4, SBN 415). Therefore, after we have finished reading Book 1 and have digested all the bad news it brings us about reason's limitations, it behooves us to take Hume seriously when he begins to anatomize the passions and to keep a sharp eye on such hints as he may give us about the tasks their slave is still able to perform. It is self-evident throughout that he wants to replace the rationalist tradition deriving from Plato, in which the passions are thought to be alien forces that assault our true self from without and in which true autonomy is to be found through the direction of reason. On that view, when we yield to the passions, we are in a state of *passivity*.[1] If reason's actual role is merely instrumental, and if there is no "true self" to be asserted in the face of passions, their actual operation and interrelationship has to be understood before human motivation can be seen for what it is.

Hume is not only an antirationalist thinker, however. He is also an antireligious one, or at least an anti-Christian one; and although this dimension of his purposes is less overt in the *Treatise* than in his later writings, it must be kept in mind when taking the measure of his account of human nature. Christian ethics emphasizes the centrality of love in human motivation and our need for humility. On Hume's analysis of the passions, neither is an immediate motive to action at all, and humility is a negative and debilitating state. Hume regards both the rationalist exaltation of reason and the Christian demand for humility as life-denying claims that can be exploded when we understand how our nature really functions and come to accept it as it is.

I. PASSION AND FEELING

In 1757 Hume published *Four Dissertations*, a work that included *A Dissertation on the Passions*, in which he gave his readers a brief recapitulation of the arguments of Book 2 of the *Treatise*. In its conclusion he says the following:

I pretend not to have here exhausted this subject. It is sufficient for my purpose, if I have made it appear, that, in the production and conduct of the passions, there is a certain regular mechanism, which is susceptible of as accurate a disquisition, as the laws of motion, optics, hydrostatics, or any part of natural philosophy. (DP 6.19)

This theoretical motive, perhaps almost spent by the time the *Dissertation* was published, is prominent in Book 2 of the *Treatise*. It has of course been prominent in Book 1 as well, but it appears there as the source of a mode of explanation that comes to our rescue when reason has been shown not to be the source of our key beliefs. In Book 2 we are dealing with experiences that the very rationalist tradition Hume is attacking has prepared us to view as phenomena that *happen* to us. Hume sees beliefs in this way too, but first has had to argue us out of our supposition that our intellect is in control of them. It is not surprising, then, that where the field is more open, Hume indulges himself at some length in demonstrating in detail that his mental science can anatomize our emotional life.

The analogy with natural philosophy, however, makes Hume prone to argue in another and less plausible way. It makes him construe the passions as mental *events* and to see his scientific task as that of discerning how they occur. Many of our emotions are like this, but many others seem equally clearly not to be. A surge of rage in response to an insult fits such a model well enough; but if instead of such a feeling one considers the contempt one person may feel for another, which has more obvious intellectual and dispositional features, the model seems Procrustean. In order to explain them all by a "regular mechanism," Hume treats them as though they are feelings. In the language of his system, introduced to us at the outset of Book 1, they must be classed as impressions. They are to be distinguished, however, from those impressions we have in sensory experience, by the fact that they are *secondary*. He also calls them *reflective*. These terms indicate their origins: they arise from causes that Hume's science shows to be mental ones – either prior impressions or prior ideas. The general model here is clear enough: our passions arise in us in response to our previous experience (actual or supposed) of outer or inner events.[2] There is a clear distinction implied between passions and their cognitive causes, the one being only contingently related to the other. Since the phenomena described by mental science can only have contingent relationships, no form of intrinsically necessary connections can be ascribed to them; each is complete in itself, as each phenomenon in the natural world is.[3] It is therefore only contingently true, for example, that love leads the person who feels it to seek the good rather than the harm of the beloved (T 2.2.6.3–5, SBN 367–68).

So the life of the passions is a sequence of feelings that can be understood when we know the mechanism that drives it. This mechanism is of course association, though Hume has to augment his earlier account of it to accommodate the emotional life.

He has three problems. First, he has to accommodate those emotions that do not look like feelings or events. Second, he has to accommodate the apparent intrinsic connections that we ascribe to the emotional life, as he has had to accommodate the necessity we ascribe to causal connections in the physical world. And third, he has to revise his theory of association to permit an association among impressions as well as ideas. The result is a theory that at least makes up in ingenuity what it may lack in plausibility.

He deals with his first problem by introducing a famous distinction between calm and violent passions. This is a distinction based on how intensely the passion is *felt*. Hume is aware that the term *passion* often connotes intense emotional disturbance and is most anxious to disabuse his readers of what he views as an implied bias, in our usage, against the recognition of the ultimate community of type among our feelings. We can come to recognize the primacy of the passions in human motivation, in his opinion, only if we acknowledge that many feelings of low intensity are passions nonetheless. So the calm passions are less intensely felt feelings. When he introduces this key distinction at T 2.1.1.3 (SBN 276), he gives as his example of calm passion "the sense of beauty and deformity in action, composition, and external objects." This is contrasted with love, hatred, grief, joy, pride, and humility, which he says are violent. He immediately concedes that in aesthetic rapture, what is usually a calm passion may be intensely felt and that those with which he has contrasted it may "decay" so much as to "become, in a manner, imperceptible." We make the clearest sense of his distinction if we assume that when he classifies a particular passion as calm or violent, he holds that it is one that is usually, though not invariably, gentle or intense in its tone. There does seem to be a serious systemic problem here when we recall that the initial distinction between impressions and ideas at T 1.1.1.1 (SBN 1) was one that defined the former in terms of their force and liveliness (even their force and *violence*). It is not easy to grasp how a mental item that has a sufficient force or vivacity to qualify for the title of "impression" can yet be in *any* manner imperceptible; but Hume's commentators have not made much of this. If we join them in ignoring this difficulty, we can recognize the value and power of this distinction for Hume's theory of human motives. A passion that is not violent may still be a strong one, in that it may well have a vitally important role in human choice and win out in a struggle with one that is violent (T 2.3.4.1, SBN 418–19). The most striking instance of this is perhaps "the general appetite to good, and aversion to evil, consider'd merely as such" (T 2.3.3.8, SBN 417) that can lead us to do things such as say no to insistent cravings in the interest of our health. Our lack of recognition of the fact that it is indeed a passion that wins out here leads many to ascribe the victory to reason, when (in Hume's view) reason can have nothing to do with it. We can reasonably equate violent passions with what Gilbert Ryle calls agitations; and we can easily see, now that Hume has pointed it out to us, that not all the phenomena he calls passions fall into this class. So far, so good; but it is not at all clear that this distinction, in spite of its value, can overcome all the difficulties attendant on the classification of passions as feelings. To stay with the same example, it is not at all clear that the general "appetite to good" is any sort of mental event, even if it is more accurate to class it as a passion than as a mode of reason. It seems to have irreducibly dispositional features and to be an ingrained tendency or orientation whose place in our natures demands a quite different sort of explanation.[4]

There is therefore good reason to think that the "regular mechanism" Hume thinks the emotions follow is one that can fit only the more obviously occurrent sorts of passion – that is, those that are feelings and can be discerned by introspection.[5] This leads to Hume's second problem. Impressions that arise according to such a mechanism are only contingently connected with the other phenomena that give rise to them or to which they lead. Yet we seem to believe in emotional necessities. We seem to think that there is an intrinsic or conceptual connection between loving someone and seeking that person's good or between being proud of something and its being connected with oneself. Hume firmly denies that the connections are of this sort and represents them as causal conjunctions. He distinguishes between love and hatred on the one hand, and benevolence and anger (desires for the happiness or misery of another) on the other hand, and tells us at T 2.2.6.3 (SBN 367) that each of the former pair is always followed by one of the latter pair. He finds these conjunctions remarkable and needing special explanation; but he insists that the benevolence is distinct from the love, and the "anger" from the hatred, these being joined together only "by the original constitution of the mind" (T 2.2.6.6, SBN 368). Hume may be guilty of denying conceptual connections where they really exist, but his procedure, especially in this Part of the *Treatise*, is quite deliberate and self-conscious and designed to replace our common ascription of such connections by something that he thinks his mental science shows to be wholly contingent and to be misrepresented by commonsense.[6]

This mental science, however, generates Hume's third problem. The mechanism that explains the coming and going of the passions is of course association. We are already familiar with association from Book 1. But when he introduces it (T 1.1.4.1, SBN 10), he tells us that the qualities from which association arises are resemblance, contiguity, and cause and effect. He writes there only of the association of ideas, and the passions are impressions. So we learn for the first time at T 2.1.4.3 (SBN 283) that there is an association of impressions also. It operates only by resemblance. (Hume considers it self-evident that impressions cannot be associated by contiguity or cause and effect; at least he offers no argument for this.) But the role of resemblance is at least superficially puzzling. For the passions are not only impressions but are said to be simple (T 2.1.2.1, SBN 277). Can simple impressions resemble one another, when (if they have no parts or separable aspects) they cannot resemble one another in this or that *respect*? Hume addresses this problem in relation to ideas in a note added to Book 1 in the Appendix; he says that simple ideas can resemble each other even though they are simple (T 1.1.7.7n5, SBN 637).[7] For example, blue and green are more alike than blue and scarlet. In T 2.1.4.3 (SBN 283) he does not acknowledge that the simplicity of impressions would make their resemblance problematic, but we do find the following:

All resembling impressions are connected together, and no sooner one arises than the rest immediately follow. Grief and disappointment give rise to anger, anger to envy, envy to malice, and malice to grief again, till the whole circle be compleated. In like manner our temper, when elevated with joy, naturally throws itself into love, generosity, pity, courage, pride, and the other resembling affections. (ibid.)

All passions in the first list are negative or unpleasant, and all those in the second, with the exception of pity, are positive or agreeable. It is therefore tempting to infer that it is just their pleasantness or unpleasantness in which their resemblance consists, provided that we do not suppose that pleasure or displeasure is a separately discernible feature of them. But it is not possible to be sure, and Hume has no accompanying theory of the nature of pleasure that would help us determine this.

It is certain, however, that pleasure and pain are the major causes of passions. Yet they are not the sole ones. This brings us to Hume's distinction between the direct and indirect passions.

2. DIRECT AND INDIRECT PASSIONS

Since Hume's mental science treats all connections between the passions as contingent, his classification of them reflects this. He divides them on the basis of what causes them. The *direct* passions, he tells us, are "such as arise immediately from good or evil, from pain or pleasure" (T 2.1.1.4, SBN 276). His immediate list of examples is "desire, aversion, grief, joy, hope, fear, despair and security" (T 2.1.1.4, SBN 277). The *indirect* passions "proceed from the same principles, but by the conjunction of other qualities"; the immediate list is "pride, humility, ambition, vanity, love, hatred, envy, pity, malice, generosity, with their dependants" (T 2.1.1.4, SBN 276–77). Even if we confine our attention to these lists and ignore other examples he mentions later, the heterogeneity is striking. In the case of the direct passions, which he has said are prompted by pleasure and pain, there is an obvious distinction to be drawn between those that relate to past pleasure and pain and those that relate to future pleasure and pain. Grief, though it can indeed be due to contemplation of the future (as one thinks, for example, of the future absence of the person one is mourning), is in an obvious way primarily centered on a past event. Desire, though it can be prompted by the presence of something (such as a television set in a store window), is for the most part directed toward future pleasures, as fear is directed toward future pains. It is the direct passions that Hume insists in Part 3 of Book 2 must be present before we can be motivated to action, and it is accordingly the direct passions of which reason is and ought only to be the slave (T 2.3.3.4, SBN 415). It is tempting to say that Hume has a wholly instrumental view of reason, but this is not quite accurate, for it is clear from the outset that one of the things reason does is *prompt* or *arouse* desires by making us aware of actual or possible situations we might want or fear, or prompt or arouse reactive passions such as joy or fear by enabling us to learn of events that please or displease us.[8]

The glib apposition of "from good or evil, from pain or pleasure" carries a strong and unfortunate suggestion of psychological hedonism. If Hume were inclined to this doctrine, it could well be pointed out that any plausibility it has derives in part from the ambiguity in the notion of pleasure between *being pleased* (i.e., evaluating some fact or situation positively) and experiencing enjoyment, and between being *dis*pleased and feeling pain. It may well be that everything we judge good is something that pleases us in prospect or retrospect, but it need not be something we get enjoyment from. (Think of losing weight or balancing a budget.) But it is plain from another passage of great importance that Hume is anxious to distance himself from psychological hedonism. He complicates his classification of the passions by saying that "the direct passions frequently arise from a natural impulse or instinct, which is perfectly unaccountable" and lists "the desire of punishment to our enemies, and of happiness to our friends; hunger, lust, and a few other bodily appetites" (T 2.3.9.8, SBN 439). He says that these passions "produce good and evil, and proceed not from them." His suggestion seems to be that although we may obtain pleasure when these desires are satisfied, it is not the prospect of such pleasure that prompts us to *have* these desires; we are, rather, unaccountably programmed to have them.[9] Earlier Hume offers examples of "certain calm desires and tendencies, which, tho' they be real passions, produce little emotion in the mind" (T 2.3.3.8, SBN 417). He says there are two kinds of these "calm desires": the first are "instincts originally implanted in our natures, such as benevolence and resentment, the love of life, and kindness to children," and the second consists of "the general appetite to good, and aversion to evil, consider'd merely as such" (ibid.). His purpose here is to show that it is calm passion and not reason that is at work when urgently felt desires are overridden; but his examples also require us to have motives that are not obviously activated by pleasure or pain.

Hume's classification of the passions is, accordingly, muddling, and this has led to some emendations by commentators. All desires are direct passions, though not all direct passions are desires. Desires may all yield pleasure when satisfied, but not all desires are desires *for* pleasure. The reactive direct passions, such as joy or despair, seem to be responses to pleasant or unpleasant impressions, or to the ideas of them. Norman Kemp Smith (1941: 164–69), and Páll Árdal (1966) following him, have called those desires that are not desires for pleasure (or for the avoidance of pain) "primary passions." Árdal (1966: ch. 1) develops this further and classifies all other passions, both direct and indirect, as "secondary." David Fate Norton (2000: 146–49) classifies similarly, dividing the passions into the "productive" and the "responsive," with all the former being desires that may yield, but are not prompted by, pleasures. I do not question the convenience of these amendments, but I will stay with Hume's own terminology: the direct passions are those that are prompted by pleasure or pain, or the idea of them, and those that yield pleasure when satisfied but do not require the idea of actual or envisaged pleasure or pain to activate them; and indirect passions are those that are prompted in part by pleasure or pain, or the ideas of these, but also require additional factors to arouse them. While Hume's most prominent theories of human motives center on the influence of the direct passions and their relation to reason, Parts 1 and 2 of Book 2 offer us an extensive analysis of the indirect passions, to which I now turn.

3. CAUSES AND OBJECTS

Part 1 of Book 2 describes the mechanisms that give rise to pride and humility, and Part 2 describes those mechanisms that give rise to love and hatred. Hume says that their indirectness consists in their being aroused by more than pleasure and pain, although these are necessary conditions for them. Since the direct passions include many that are prompted by reason, in the sense that they are generated by our aware-ness of those situations to which they are responses (in more modern parlance, since many of the direct passions have a cognitive core to them), the difference between direct and indirect passions cannot be merely that the indirect passions have ideas among their causes, for many direct passions also do. It has to be that the indirect passions are generated by a process in which ideas play a role in a special manner.

The role they play is a double one. They provide us with both the *cause* of the passion and its *object*. This distinction is the primary determinant of the mechanism to which Hume ascribes the generation of these four passions. We have to take special care in our day not to interpret Hume's distinction anachronistically. He introduces it at T 2.1.2.4 (SBN 278), where he tells us that we have to distinguish between "that idea, which excites them (i.e., the passions)" and "that to which they direct their view, when excited." This sentence does not make it unambiguously clear that both are *ideas*. But this is made certain for us later in this paragraph, where Hume says that each of pride and humility is "a passion plac'd betwixt two ideas, of which the one produces it, and the other is produc'd by it." He continues: "The first idea, therefore, represents the *cause*, the second the *object* of the passion." It is easy to suppose that Hume is making the same distinction between a passion's cause and its object that analytical philosophers have made in recent years;[10] but this supposition would be mistaken. For one thing, Hume stresses the distinction only in the case of the indirect passions, whereas the analytical contrast has far wider application. When we think of the cause of an emotion, we may well suppose it to be some phenomenon that the person having that emotion is aware of, but we may also suppose it to be something unknown to that person, such as a neurological disorder or a pill that an enemy has put into the person's drink. Hume does not think that we can be unaware of the cause of a passion; it is, after all, an idea, and I cannot have an idea without knowing it. When we think of the object of an emotion, on the other hand, we think of that which the emotion is *about*. We cannot be unaware of this if we have the emotion, although it may in fact be something that does not exist, as happens when I am angry about a supposed insult that has not been uttered. The objects of the indirect passions in Hume's sense cannot be purely imaginary in this way for the simple reason that they are *also* causes of the passions that they are the objects *of*. This is clear from the following:

> But tho' that connected succession of perceptions, which we call *self*, be always the object of these two passions (viz., pride and humility), 'tis impossible it can be their CAUSE, or be sufficient alone to excite them. (T 2.1.2.3, SBN 277–78)

The key word here is *alone*. Hume is arguing that although pride and humility have myself as their object, the idea of myself cannot be the only factor giving rise to them, since by itself it could not determine *which* of them would arise. But it is clear from his actual account of the associative mechanism that leads to pride and humility that it is a *necessary* condition of their arousal nevertheless and must therefore be listed among their causes. A look at this mechanism will clarify these matters.

Pride arises when some perceived quality of a thing or person (which is the cause of the passion) leads to a "pleasant sensation" (T 2.1.5.8, SBN 288), which in turn, through the association of impressions, arouses the similarly pleasant impression of pride; this ("not only by a natural but also by an original property" [T 2.1.3.2, SBN 280]) gives rise to the idea of the self, which is the object of the passion. We experience humility when the cause is unpleasant, but the sequence is otherwise the same. Love arises when the cause is a pleasant one, but the passion has another person for its object; if the cause is unpleasant, it is hatred rather than love that we experience.[11]

Hume modifies this story in one respect: he divides the cause of the passion into two – namely, the quality that excites the passion and the subject in which it inheres. To use his example, if I am proud of my beautiful house, the cause of my pride is the house's beauty, which inheres in the house as its subject. The object of my pride is myself as its owner. If the house is yours rather than mine, then its pleasing beauty leads to the passion of love toward you as its owner.

This story gives rise to many puzzles, some of great interest and others not. (1) Hume oscillates between identifying the cause of the passion as a thing or person, or rather a quality of that thing or person, and the idea or ideas of these; when most on guard, he holds to the latter, because only a perception can be a unit of association. (2) There is an unclarity about the pleasure or "pleasant sensation" to which the cause gives rise, and the nature of the resemblance this needs to have to the passion it leads to for the association of impressions to operate. Hume is emphatic that the cause of pride or humility generates a "separate pleasure" or "separate uneasiness" (T 2.1.5.1, SBN 285), but if this is indeed a separate item (an impression) from the idea that gives rise to it, and not a mere tonal quality of that idea, then it is not clear how its pleasantness, which would then be its whole content, resembles the impression of pride of which the pleasantness cannot similarly be the whole content – although its supposed simplicity might seem to require just this.

There is little chance of a puzzled reader finding enlightenment on these matters. (3) Much more significant, however, is the way the associative mechanism is supposed to lead the mind to the *object* of the passion. The object, which in the case of pride or humility is myself, comes last in the causal chain. This suggests that it is only *after* I feel pride that I become explicitly cognizant of the fact that the cause of it (viz., the beautiful house) has to do with *me*. It is true that if I feel pride in something that I own or have done, this in its turn may well generate self-absorbed reflections on my own merits. But it is also true that if it is indeed *pride* in the beautiful house that I feel rather than mere enjoyment, I must at least *already have noted* that the house is mine. Perhaps Hume could have accommodated this by putting the idea of the self earlier in the sequence and the pride later, but then the ultimate self-regard that he does explain would not make its appearance. There seems to be no way of amending his account while preserving the contingent separateness of the passion and its object that he regards as essential to that account.

(4) The "double relation of ideas and impressions" (T 2.1.5.5, SBN 286) that Hume uses to explain the emergence of pride or humility does not seem to come out quite right when we attempt to follow him and plot the course of our emotions. He gives two summaries, of which the first is this:

That cause, which excites the passion, is related to the object, which nature has attributed to the passion; the sensation, which the cause separately produces, is related to the sensation of the passion: From this double relation of ideas and impressions, the passion is deriv'd. (T 2.1.5.5, SBN 286)

This strongly suggests two concurrent processes of association. The first, that of ideas, yields the sequence: idea of beautiful-house, idea of myself. The second, that of impressions, yields the sequence: sensation of pleasure-at-the-beauty-of-the-house, pleasant impression of pride. Since Hume classes passions as *secondary* impressions, he has made room for the fact that the second sequence is triggered by the prior occurrence of the idea of the beautiful house that is the first item in the first sequence (just as the occurrence of the idea of a desirable object can trigger a desire in the realm of the direct passions). But if we read him strictly, his scheme does not allow for the key fact that the awareness that the house is mine is a key causal factor in my feeling pride in it – or indeed for the fact that my subsequent reflections on my own worth derive from that pride – because by his associative principles, the emergence of the idea of myself is the associative product of the prior idea of the house. Hume tries again with the following mind-bending passage (the bracketed interpolations are mine):

When an idea [of a beautiful house] produces an impression [of pleasure at its beauty], related to an impression [pride], which is connected with an idea [the self], related to the first idea [the house], these two impressions must be in a manner inseparable, nor will the one in any case be unattended with the other. 'Tis after this manner, that the particular causes of pride and humility are determin'd. The quality [the house's beauty], which operates on the passion [pride], produces separately an impression resembling it [pleasure at the house's beauty]; the subject, to which the quality adheres, is related to self, the object of the passion: No wonder the whole cause, consisting of a quality and of a subject, does so unavoidably give rise to the passion. (T 2.1.5.10, SBN 289)

Hume rightly emphasizes the inseparability of the cognitive and affective components in these emotional experiences; but the fact that his human science is so fundamentally committed to their contingent distinctness shows that in spite of the use of "No wonder . . .," he cannot easily make their interrelationship intelligible within that science.

A similar inadequacy appears with even greater clarity in Hume's treatment of love and hatred. The associative mechanism by which he explains their arousal parallels that which he claims to operate in the case of pride and humility. Here too there is a cause as well as an object, the double relation of impressions and ideas, and a conclusion in the idea of that object – the object in these two cases, however, being not oneself but another person. But there is one very obvious additional difference. Pride and humility are:

pure emotions in the soul, unattended with any desire, and not immediately exciting us to action. But love and hatred are not compleated within themselves, nor rest in that emotion, which they produce, but carry the mind to something farther. Love is always follow'd by a desire of the happiness of the person belov'd, and an aversion to his misery: As hatred produces a desire of the misery and an aversion to the happiness of the person hated. (T 2.2.6.3, SBN 367)

This naturally suggests that love and hatred have "an *end*, which they endeavour to attain" (T 2.2.6.4, SBN 367). But Hume firmly rejects this, insisting instead that the desire for the happiness or misery of the object (which he identifies with benevolence and anger, respectively) is merely conjoined with love or hatred "by the original constitution of the mind" and that there is no contradiction in supposing even the opposite sequences (T 2.2.6.6, SBN 368). Benevolence and anger are of course direct passions, each of which issues in a volition. But the result of Hume's insistence on the purely contingent character of the connections between the emotions is that none of the indirect passions is an immediate cause of choice.

4. PRIDE AND HUMILITY

Hume makes little or no attempt to distinguish pride from allied concepts such as vanity. More seriously, while describing the mechanism of the passions, he fails to distinguish the sort of pride that can plausibly be identified as a feeling from pride in the dispositional sense. The former, which we might call occurrent pride, is a "clockable" event that occurs, for example, when I feel it surge within me as my child crosses the stage to collect a prize. The latter does not *occur* at all, but manifests itself in such things as my tendency to expect deference or to disregard inferiors.[12]

The attempt to subsume dispositional features of emotions under a theory that takes occurrent feelings as the paradigm is even more obvious if we consider humility. Humility is manifestly not a feeling but a disposition or general moral attitude consisting in a low estimate of oneself. The corresponding occurrent feeling is of course shame. Just as someone who is dispositionally proud may be more likely to feel occurrent pride over actions and events that a more modest person would let pass without such a response, so a humble person is more likely than others are to feel ashamed, embarrassed, or diffident about actions or events that can be viewed as demeaning. But these connections are not universal. The person who feels proud when his or her children collect prizes can well feel this way without having a high self-estimate and indeed may well have his or her pride increased by the fact that the children have surpassed their parents. And I may well feel ashamed of some act or event because I feel it is beneath me to have done or experienced it – that is, as a manifestation of dispositional pride.

Even if we confine our attention to occurrent pride or shame, we must admit that Hume has mixed success in his interpretation. He is, in the first instance, right in holding that what he calls the cause of pride or shame, that which I am proud or ashamed *of*, must be something that I estimate independently to be admirable or bad. But he expresses this misleadingly. It is misleading to say that it must produce an "independent pleasure" or pain, for this suggests that in the case of pride it must be something *pleasant* and that in the case of shame it must be something *unpleasant*. But to be proud of something I have done, I do not have to have found it pleasant to do it. I can be proud of having paid my bills or fought a good fight or endured a disaster, none of which are *enjoyable*. And I can be ashamed of having done something I enjoyed doing, like wasting my paycheck in the casino. What pride or shame requires is that what Hume calls their cause be something that I can be *pleased* or *displeased* about, and these evaluative states are quite distinct from enjoyment. Roughly, the cause has to be something to which I give a positive or negative appraisal.

If we turn from occurrent pride and shame to dispositional pride and humility, each is something that can be fed or deepened by its occurrent counterpart but can control our conduct and our attitudes without its stimulus. My pride can make me feel disdainful of my less wealthy neighbors without my having first felt any glow of satisfaction at my own riches, and my humility can make me stand aside for a social inferior without having first blushed for shame at anything I have previously done to him or her. Dispositional pride and humility are character traits that indeed require heightened self-consciousness (in ways to be discussed) but do not require prideful or shameful feelings to activate them. Although occurrent pride and shame have to be because of something (i.e., they have to have a cause in Hume's sense), dispositional pride and humility do not.

Hume is fully aware that dispositional pride and humility are character traits, even if he is unaware that his psychical mechanics cannot do them justice. It is here that we find modest signs of the anti-Christian thrust of the arguments of the *Treatise*, albeit in a muted form. In *Treatise* 2.1.7, Hume opens his account of the various causes of pride and humility with virtue and vice. Awareness of my own virtuous behavior will please me as it pleases others, and awareness of my own viciousness will displease me and produce humility (shame). He adds, "'Tis evident the former impression is not always vicious, nor the latter virtuous" (T 2.1.7.8, SBN 297–98). These brief comments are augmented in *Treatise* 3.3.2, the Section entitled "Of greatness of mind." By this stage Hume has at his disposal the fourfold classification of the sources of virtue and vice and argues that "an over-weaning conceit of ourselves" is vicious because it is displeasing to others (T 3.3.2.1, SBN 592): it generates in them a reaction against the high valuation of himself or herself that the proud person projects. But this does not turn pride into a vice, because "nothing can be more laudable, than to have a value for ourselves, where we really have qualities that are valuable" (T 3.3.2.8, SBN 596). Pride, then, is a virtuous state, provided its expression is muted by good breeding. Modesty (or humility) comes off less well, because it "produces often uneasiness in the person endow'd with it" (T 3.3.2.9, SBN 597). He knowingly adds that "no one, who has any practice of the world, and can penetrate into the inward sentiments of men, will assert, that the humility, which good-breeding and decency require of us, goes beyond the outside, or that a thorough sincerity in this particular is esteem'd a real part of our duty" (T 3.3.2.11, SBN 598).

This rather gentle dismissal of humility is replaced in Section 9 of the second *Enquiry* by a famous diatribe against the "monkish virtues." Humility there is listed among those forms of life-denying mortification that render their practitioners less fit than they otherwise would be for the pleasures of society. Kant took exception to Hume's views on this matter, arguing that morality requires humility to ensure that we are aware of our shortcomings and are pleased with ourselves only for real merits ([1762–64] 1997: 16; Ak. 27: 39). I cannot explore how far Kant's opinion is from the less vitriolic Humean position of the *Treatise*. It is worth noting, however, that the most familiar Christian position known to us from Augustine – that pride is the deepest human sin – should be judged alongside some more recent Christian pronouncements about the importance of a proper pride in the face of systemic injustice. The former tradition, which is the one against which Hume is reacting, holds that pride, or self-assertion, is the primary source of sin and is ultimately a refusal to recognize that one is a creature brought into being by God out of nothing. In short, it is a denial of one's finitude. The latter tradition, found particularly in the works of feminist and African American theologians in our own time, argues in contrast that a high sense of self-worth is a precondition of righting the wrongs endured by the poor or oppressed, whose creaturely status and value are equal to those of the privileged.[13]

5. LOVE AND HATRED

Hume does not make any serious attempt to distinguish love from admiration or esteem, or hatred from allied attitudes such as contempt. (See T 2.2.5.1, 2.2.10, and esp. 3.3.4.2n88, SBN 357, 389–93, and esp. 608n.) Here also, his associationist psychology requires him to treat love and hatred as feelings and to overlook their important dispositional features. And we must bear in mind the fact that Hume insists that there is only a natural, and not a conceptual, connection between love and benevolence and hatred and anger – the desires respectively for the good or the misery of another person. Love and hatred, then, are not, as Hume interprets them, direct motives to action.

Donald Davidson says, correctly, that Hume accounts for "love for a reason" (1980: 278). If we compare what Hume says about love with what Plato says, then we find that both think that love has to have what Hume calls a cause in the form of some quality that we find admirable in the loved one. In contrast to Plato, however, Hume makes the object of love the individual person or self, not the perfection or beauty that he or she embodies. Yet both are far from the Christian view of love as *agape* or pure benevolence without any reason, which Hume thinks is rare or nonexistent and distinct from love even when it occurs (T 3.2.1.12, SBN 481).

Part 2 of Book 2 is lengthy, in spite of the simplicity of Hume's account of love and hatred. Its length (and occasional tedium) is due to the addition of two further theoretical components. The first is a series of "experiments" designed to confirm the system of analysis presented in this and the preceding Part. These experiments are all appeals to our observation or experience of the emotional life.[14] There are eight of them, and they are designed to show that the indirect passions will not be aroused unless the "double relation of impressions and ideas" is operative and that when it is operative, its effects are intensified when the other person with whom I am involved has a close relationship to me.

The second theoretical addition is a leisurely examination of what Hume calls the "compound affections, which arise from the mixture of love and hatred with other emotions" (T 2.2.3.1, SBN 347). Hume does not make it as clear as one would like what he means by calling these passions "compounds." His examples are benevolence and anger, compassion (or pity), malice, envy, respect, contempt, and sexual love. He explains the notion of compound passions almost casually at T 2.2.6.1 (SBN 366), where he tells us that although ideas can form compounds only by conjunction and not by mixture, "impressions and passions are susceptible of an entire union," like colors. Benevolence (the desire for another's happiness) and anger (the desire for another's misery) are, he insists, distinct from love and hatred, although they always accompany them. This, even if true, would hardly make them indiscernible compounds with love and hatred but would require their discernible distinctness from them! Here at most we have a compound *of* distinct passions. Compassion and malice[15] interest Hume because each yields a tendency to seek the good or the harm of another without the prior arousal of love or hatred, a fact Hume seems to think requires special explanation. It is a little hard to see why he should. Because he is so emphatic that seeking the good of the beloved or the harm of the hated is only a contingent consequence of love and hatred, it is hard to fathom why he discerns a puzzle in the fact that it might arise with different emotional antecedents. If one passion regularly follows another, it may be puzzling if the earlier one should sometimes appear to occur without the later one, but hardly if the later one arises independently. But if we grant the puzzle, it is still unclear why Hume thinks either of these passions are compounds that include love and hatred. We find ourselves considering something that more clearly resembles a compound or mixture in *Treatise* 2.2.9, where Hume addresses the challenge to his system presented by the fact that pity, once aroused, becomes mixed with love, and malice, once aroused, mixes with hatred. The puzzle here arises because his system has hitherto required that unpleasant passions should induce other unpleasant passions and pleasant passions should induce other pleasant ones. The core of his complicated answer is the assertion that the "character of any passion" is determined by the "general bent or tendency" that it has and that pity has the same tendency as love does to lead to goodwill toward its object (T 2.2.9.11, SBN 385). Even here there does not seem to be a clear example of love and pity being fused into one, rather than our feeling both together. We finally seem to achieve a real compounding of the feelings when, in *Treatise* 2.2.10, Hume considers respect and contempt. These do indeed seem to contain manifest admixtures of humility and pride respectively, the mixture in each case being, as Hume says, a result of the comparison of another's merits or demerits with one's own. Similarly, sexual love is plausibly represented as a compound of sexual desire, pleasure at beauty, and benevolence.

In these overelaborate Sections Hume shows a commendable awareness of the actual complexities of the emotional life, as well as a willingness to adjust his theories to the facts, rather than the opposite. But this good effect is lessened by his describing what he is doing as an explanation of how what are allegedly simple impressions can be compounded.

6. SYMPATHY AND THE SOCIAL SELF

It is in *Treatise* 2.1.11, late in the discussion of pride and humility, that Hume introduces the principle of sympathy, which all agree is fundamental to the ethical thought of the *Treatise*. Its importance there cannot be exaggerated. It is the key factor in the motivation Hume thinks we have for our allegiance to principles of justice, for example. Its role there is that of enabling us to appreciate the pleasures and pains caused by the character traits of others, an appreciation that is the essential preliminary to our approval or disapproval of them. This fundamental ethical role seems to be discharged in a less complicated manner in the second *Enquiry* by the sentiment of humanity. This apparent reincarnation in the later work has encouraged the conception of sympathy as almost exclusively a mechanism that enables us to come as near as our nature allows to the experiencing of others' pleasure and distress. But while this understanding of sympathy is not an incorrect one as far as it goes, we should also take careful note of what is taking place when Hume, in *Treatise* 2.1.11, first makes use of his principle. He offers it to us there as a mechanism that functions as a secondary source of *pride*. It is a mechanism that affects how I regard *myself*.

Hume introduces it by stressing how much each of us is imprinted with the "inclinations and sentiments" of those around us (T 2.1.11.2, SBN 316). (His first example of this imprinting is that of children, who "implicitly embrace every opinion propos'd to them." In Hume's world, beliefs are as catching as feelings are.) "Hatred, resentment, esteem, love, courage, mirth and melancholy; all these passions I feel more from communication than from my own natural temper and disposition" (T 2.1.11.2, SBN 317). Pride and humility are not on the list, but he soon makes up for this.

The mechanism of sympathy begins to operate when we become aware of the passion of another by observing its effects – that is, its external signs in the other's "countenance and conversation" (T 2.1.11.3, SBN 317). This far at least we have a standard-enough post-Cartesian view that we infer the feelings of others from their outward signs. The fruit of such an inference is, of course, the idea of that passion in the other. This idea, however, is converted, perhaps almost instantaneously, into an impression by being enlivened. What enlivens it is the "idea, or rather impression of ourselves" (T 2.1.11.4, SBN 317), aided by the fact that others resemble us and in many cases (the ones where the sympathy is strongest) are closely related to us in other ways also. Once enlivened, the original idea is converted into the very passion that the idea was an idea *of*.

The passions of pride and humility are strengthened, and even generated, by this mechanism when we are the recipients of the admiration or hostility of others. When another praises me, I will come, through sympathy, to feel the admiration of myself that he expresses, and similarly with his contempt. These effects are all the greater when the sentiments communicated by sympathy are those of persons whom we ourselves admire or are close to us in family or station.

So the phenomenon that Hume first uses sympathy to explain is the one that has come, much later, to be called that of internalization. It is a process whereby each of us comes to absorb the estimates of others into his or her own self-image. He uses a shrewd observation of our social natures to erect a general understanding of our social relationships. He expresses it in a passage whose importance Annette Baier (1991: ch. 7) has rightly stressed as a key to his theory of human nature:

In general we may remark, that the minds of men are mirrors to one another, not only because they reflect each other's emotions, but also because those rays of passions, sentiments and opinions may be often reverberated, and may decay away by insensible degrees. (T 2.2.5.21, SBN 365)

According to Hume, human beings are, by the structure of their emotional natures, conformists. It is no wonder that Hume is so negative in his judgments of those forms of life, such as that of religious contemplatives, that deliberately cut off their practitioners from the influence of society.

Hume's account of the indirect passions, and of sympathy, shows much insight into the ways our attitudes are affected by social interaction. I am prouder than before of some trait that a friend admires; if the same friend disparaged it, my own pride in it would be diminished. If some common motive is widely admired but I find it lacking in my own personality, I will "hate myself" (feel ashamed) for this and set about simulating its presence by doing what it would otherwise cause me to do naturally (T 3.2.1.8, SBN 479). Hume's system allows him to map many of the mechanisms whereby our personalities are developed and controlled by social pressures, and the operation of sympathy is a key component of this. (See, especially, T 3.3.2.2–3, SBN 592–93.) What does not emerge is any suggestion that one might judge, on one's own account, that one's whole society is wrong to prize something to which its members' emotions are attached. Hume's human beings are not, even potentially, revolutionaries. Hume's own rejection of religious values was a minority opinion in his time, yet the sort of change of which it is an example is less readily intelligible on his theory of the passions than is the conformity to which it is an exception.[16]

7. OUR SOCIAL IDENTITIES

Hume regards it as essential for his theory of moral judgments and moral motivation to be closely integrated with his theory of the passions, so it is easy to see why he spends so much time on the latter, even if we do not find it as interesting intrinsically as he does. Donald Ainslie (1999), in exploring their relationship, has developed an important insight into the role of Hume's lengthy treatment of the indirect passions. He maintains that the indirect passions, and most particularly pride as reinforced by the admiration (love) of others, serve to accustom us to regard certain qualities (those he regards as causes of the passions) as being existentially connected to us – that is, as helping define who we are. We think of ourselves *as* property owners, for example, because we are proud of our property and others admire us for having it. One is as vital as the other. In effect, we are confident of our identity insofar as we live in a world in which our values are shared – a world in which others admire us for whatever makes us regard ourselves highly. This is not a world in which we need be the same as our neighbors, for pride requires that its causes be distinctive and noteworthy and not shared by everyone. But it is a world in which others admire us for what we think is noteworthy, so our evaluations are likely to be the same even when our temperaments differ. Each of us has a social self, which is defined by his or her pride or shame and others' love or dislike. In such a world each of us has much the same understanding of what merits moral approval or blame, and we will tend to love those who merit the former and dislike those who merit the latter. In such a world, also, a dose of pride is a condition for social self-identity, and humility, in more than modest doses, is a recipe for social suicide. What this vision of our world does not make so readily intelligible is the personality that links its selfhood to resisting, rather than absorbing, social consensus.

8. THE SELF

The recognition of the way the indirect passions consolidate each individual's role in a social order leads naturally into one of the key interpretative puzzles of the *Treatise*.

The transition from Book 1 to Book 2 is more than a transition of mood. Readers of Book 2 have often been baffled by what Hume says in it about the self, which seems such a contrast to the sceptical arguments in Section 6 of Part 4 of Book 1. Their bafflement has good reasons, and their sense of an abruptness of transition is correct. But it is important to judge accurately whether this is a symptom of inconsistencies in his system or merely of incompleteness. I would argue that it is the latter.

In *Treatise* 1.4.6, Hume has done two things. He has, first of all, used his mental science to show that the mind is not possessed of "perfect identity and simplicity"; that is to say, it does not possess genuine identity through time (diachronic identity) or simplicity at any one time (synchronic identity). Hume maintains that introspective scrutiny of the mind reveals only a bundle of ever-changing perceptions, not a simple or identical mind whose perceptions they are. It is perceptions only that constitute the mind, and the "science of man" is the science of the relationships between those perceptions, which have no necessary relationship to any one mind rather than another or indeed to any mind at all. Hume then uses this same mental science to explain why we come to have our beliefs in diachronic and synchronic identity, an explanation that, roughly, tells us that we are led to overlook the heterogeneity and "changingness" of the mind's contents by the interrelationships between the perceptions that constitute it. This explanation shows us only how we come to have the beliefs in the mind's unity at a time and over time. It does not show us how we come to have the correlative beliefs in a plurality of minds or what enables us to individuate one mind from another.

In Book 2 the science of man is on extensive display. We must therefore assume that Hume is appealing to it when he tells us that the idea ("or rather impression") of the self is always present to us and serves as the source of the liveliness of the idea of another's feeling during the operation of the sympathetic mechanism, and also when he tells us that it is this idea to which the mind's attention is directed when we experience pride or humility. Many readers have found it puzzling that he makes these appeals so confidently, in view of the sceptical opening of *Treatise* 1.4.6, where he says that we do not even *have* the idea of the simple and identical self that he attacks there. It is a correct response to this puzzlement to point out that the idea of the self he uses in Book 2 cannot be, and is not, the idea he has argued in Book 1 that we do not even have. It must be the idea of "that connected succession of perceptions, which we call *self*" (T 2.1.2.3, SBN 277–78) – the idea of the series of perceptions whose interrelationships he appealed to in *Treatise* 1.4.6 – when explaining our belief in self-identity. But although this is true, it does not take us more than part of the way toward understanding the sort of self-consciousness Hume is appealing to in Book 2 and how this differs from the sort of self-consciousness he denies that we have in Book 1.

Let us consider first the role that the idea of the self plays in Book 2. It is the idea of the individual who is the unit of a social science: the owner of property, the bearer of virtue or vice, the possessor of talents and riches. The social science of which Hume gives us the elements in Books 2 and 3 is the study of the interrelationships between such an individual and others who are similar – so similar that they are mirrors to each other. Such individuals are above all participants in social relationships and could not be more different from the "strange uncouth monster" of T 1.4.7.2 (SBN 264) who is cut off from his physical environment and from other selves by the fact that he is unable to reason his way out of the confines of the impressions and ideas that he has, which could even exist, he thinks, without being *his* (T 1.4.2.39, SBN 207). The best Hume has been able to do in Book 1 is to show how those perceptions come to include the belief that they are all his and the belief that they represent an independent physical world. Nicholas Capaldi (1989) has expressed this well by saying that in moving from the world of Book 1 to that of Book 2 Hume takes us from an "I think" (Cartesian) perspective to a "We do" (social) perspective.

The trouble is that when we make this move by turning the pages, we find ourselves having leaped right into the social perspective. Once in it, we can learn how we come to be pleased with ourselves or ashamed, how we come to admire or despise others, and how we manage to empathize with our fellows and internalize their judgments of us. To learn all this is to learn how our social selves, our interpersonal identities, are created. The account Hume gives is every bit as original and perceptive as his sceptical analysis of our natural beliefs in Book 1, for all the tradition of scholarly obsession with the latter.

But for Hume's account of human nature to be even schematically complete, it should also provide us with some explanation of how we come to be *able* to construct the social self in the way we do. For we have seen that in order to feel pride, I must already realize that what I am proud of is some act or feature or possession that is *mine*. In order to love or hate someone for something they have or have done, I must already realize that it is *he* or *she* who has it or has done it. And in order to have the feelings of another communicated to me by sympathy, I must already be able to realize that although the feeling is his or hers, I might well feel the same way in his or her circumstances and have my imagination recreate their passion in parallel within myself. In other words, to create the social self in the way Hume describes, I must already have, *in my repertoire*, the ideas of myself and of a plurality of other individuals; I must be able to individuate in thought.

Manifestly, Hume assumes in Book 2 that I have these ideas and that I have this ability. He takes pains to make sure that we do not think, when we use these notions, that they entail the validity of the idea of the self that he attacks at the outset of *Treatise* 1.4.6. But beyond this, he does not offer us, from within the resources of his mental science, any theory of how we come to have these ideas in our repertoire, in the way he has shown us how we come to believe in our synchronic and diachronic identity or in the distinct and continued existence of physical objects.

There are suggestions in the literature that the stories of pride and sympathy are intended to provide this.[17] But when Hume tells us that pride or humility is a passion "betwixt two ideas, of which the one produces it, and the other is produc'd by it" (T 2.1.2.4, SBN 278), all he is able to show us is that, in his associative mechanism, the occurrence of the feeling of pride *calls up* the idea of self. He has not shown how it comes to be on call. The same is of course true for the correlative ideas of the other person or persons when the passion in play is love or hatred.

What seems to be missing, then, is any account of how we come to *have* the ideas of myself and others. Hume tells us that my idea of myself is the idea of a particular "connected succession of perceptions" (T 2.1.2.3, SBN 277). To this spare account of its content we have to add the fact that once launched on the social process of thinking and feeling, I ascribe to myself all those qualities that I take pride in or am ashamed of and ascribe to others all those qualities that cause me to love or hate them. As Annette Baier has pointed out, these include the physical qualities of my body and their bodies (1991: ch. 7). But by telling us this, Hume does not tell us how I come to be able to distinguish in my life-world between myself and other persons – how, that is, I come to believe that the connected series that makes up my history does make up *my* history and that there are others similarly constituted.[18]

In summary, two facts stand out. First, Hume's accounts of the genesis of pride and humility, love and hatred are accounts that require, and do not create or explain, the awareness that each of us is one among a plurality of selves or persons – even though the emotional life Hume describes is a life that fills in many crucial details in the social construction of our personalities. Second, the account in *Treatise* 1.4.6 of the ascription of diachronic identity to the self has provided us only one part of the story of how we come to have the awareness that Hume's theory of the passions requires – namely, the belief that each of us has that his or her biography possesses identity through time. The remaining elements in the required awareness that each of us is one of a number of individual selves are, quite simply, unaccounted for in Hume's system.

I have given no reason to suppose that Hume's system could not have provided an account of them, had he chosen to. Given his account in *Treatise* 1.4.2 of how I come to think that there are independent physical objects and his explanation in *Treatise* 1.4.6 of my conviction of the unity of my own self, he might have offered an equally plausible story of how I come to think that many of those independent objects are the bodies of selves like mine. But he has not done it or provided any hint of it.

NOTES

1. For an important discussion of this feature of our understanding of the emotions, see Peters and Mace 1961–62.

2. Hume modifies this in Part 3 by introducing a group of passions that he says are "unaccountable" in their origin (T 2.3.9.8, SBN 439). It does not seem possible, however, that he would deny that they need some impression or idea to call them into operation on particular occasions.

3. It is no part of my purposes in this essay to enter interpretative controversies about Hume's analysis of causal connections. I shall assume the following. First, Hume believes, as a central principle of his mental science and of his doctrine of the will, that there is no distinction between moral and physical necessity. (See T 1.3.14.33 [SBN 171].) Second, he also holds that the necessity that he believes to exist equally in the mental and the physical realms "lies in the determination of the mind to pass from the one (i.e., the cause) to the other (i.e., the effect)" (T 1.3.14.23, SBN 166; interpolations added). Hence

causes and effects are not intrinsically but contingently related, there being no absurdity in the suggestion that the one should not be followed by the other. Hume's mental science, which is on its most extensive display in his account of the passions, is a science that asserts what we would now call the logical independence of the impressions and ideas whose connections he describes. As it is no part of the essence of the motion of the first billiard ball that the second ball should move, so it is no part of the essence of one passion, such as love, that it should be followed by another, such as benevolence.

4. For the needed distinction between motives and agitations, see Ryle 1949: ch. 4.

5. I am indebted to Donald Ainslie here. My casual use of "emotions" rather than "passions" reflects a common reader's equation between them. In the *Treatise* and the *Dissertation*, Hume's use of the word *passion* is at least semitechnical. The passions, in his usage, are simple impressions that follow the associative mechanism he describes. Hume's use of the word *emotion* is not carefully circumscribed, but it would seem that we experience emotion whenever we are *moved*. He refers at T 2.2.8.4 (SBN 373) to "some emotion or movement of spirits," and at T 2.1.1.1 (SBN 275) he writes of "the passions, and other emotions resembling them." At T 2.3.5.2 (SBN 423) he refers to "the source of wonder, surprize, and of all the emotions, which arise from novelty." Emotions would seem to be the genus of which passions are species. The technical character of Hume's use of "passion" shows itself most clearly in the resistance he knows he must overcome to his concept of a calm passion.

6. Hume's argument here (T 2.2.6.4, SBN 367) seems to assume that an ascription of necessity would commit us to an unacceptable teleology. We must remember that for Hume "all causes are of the same kind" (T 1.3.14.32, SBN 171).

7. For a defense of Hume's position on this point, see Árdal 1966: 13ff.

8. Emphasizing this is one of the valuable features of the argument of Kydd 1946: esp. ch. 4.

9. Hume seems to have accepted Butler's ([1726] 2006: 110–18) arguments against psychological hedonism as found in his eleventh Rolls Sermon.

10. See, e.g., Kenny 1963; Wilson 1972.

11. Hume's argument at T 2.1.2.3 (SBN 277–78) seems to imply that the object of pride or humility is a partial, but not a total, cause of the passion. Yet when he describes the associative mechanism that produces pride or humility, the object (self) does not appear as the cause, which is instead my house or my virtue or my rank; and we reach the odd-looking claim that the pride I feel occurs *before* the idea of myself. That which he calls the passion's object seems both to be and not to be a cause of it. At this stage I can only note this fact, but will return to it.

12. As we shall see, Hume treats pride as a dispositional trait later, in Book 3. But this does not affect the fact that the ambiguity in our concept of pride is not reflected in Hume's mental science, which only permits accurate description of pride in its occurrent or episodic sense.

13. The best-known presentation of the Augustinian position in modern times is in Niebuhr (1941 and 1943). My other comments here are indebted to

Schweitzer 2000: 167–81. I do not wish to argue that these two theological positions cannot be reconciled.

14. See Norton and Norton (2000: 506) for a convenient summary.

15. For a useful discussion of the ambiguities in the notion of malice, see Árdal 1966: 62–65.

16. I am indebted here to Lionel Kenner.

17. See Henderson 1990.

18. There is a temptation, perhaps, to try to divine an answer in Hume's remark that "our consciousness gives us so lively a conception of our own person, that 'tis not possible to imagine, that any thing can in this particular go beyond it" (T 2.1.11.4, SBN 317) and to suppose him to think that the consciousness I have of my own perceptions includes an awareness that they are mine. He may reinforce this temptation by his remark that "as the immediate *object* of pride and humility is self or that identical person, of whose thoughts, actions, and sensations we are intimately conscious; so the *object* of love and hatred is some other person, of whose thoughts, actions, and sensations we are not conscious" (T 2.2.1.2, SBN 329). But to yield to this temptation would be to convict Hume of contradiction with the opening passages of *Treatise* 1.4.6.

Hume ascribes to consciousness a certainty that seems to assure us that our knowledge of our own perceptions is never deceptive. (See, especially, T 1.4.2.7 [SBN 190].) But this knowledge does not include a recognition that they are *ours*. This is the burden of the opening of *Treatise* 1.4.6. Consciousness does not deceive – Hume tells us this in Part 1 of Section 7 of the first *Enquiry*. (See also T 1.4.2.5 [SBN 189] and T 2.2.6.2 [SBN 366].) But it does not reveal, or (contrary to Locke) constitute, ownership. All that we are told in Book 2 is that consciousness is a concomitant of ownership, not that consciousness reveals it. To complicate our story, we must recall that at T 1.4.2.39 (SBN 207) Hume tells us that there is no absurdity in supposing that any particular perception might be wholly severed from the mind to which it happens to belong. He presents this as a clear consequence of his "bundle theory" of what the mind is. Whether or not this is a supposition that there might be unconscious unowned perceptions or that there might be conscious unowned perceptions (if either of these are intelligible) he does not tell us. But in Book 2 he tells us that each of us is made aware through outward signs, and then through sympathy, of the passions of other beings. This needs to come about because we are not conscious of the mental life of those beings, but the consciousness we have of our own perceptions yields for each of us a lively idea (even impression) of ourselves that gives vivacity to the ideas we have formed of the passions of others. It would seem, then, that he holds our consciousness to be a (the) cause of the idea of the self we have, but not to constitute the self's identity. Its identity is a fictitious construction based, or so *Treatise* 1.4.6 says, on a retrospective judgment on those perceptions of which each of us has been conscious and subsequently remembers. There is no parallel story of how such a fictitious identity is ascribed to other persons, because none of us has, and therefore none of us can remember, the perceptions of which each of *them* has been conscious.

10 "Hume's Lengthy Digression": Free Will in the *Treatise*

David Hume's views on the subject of free will are among the most influential contributions to this long-disputed topic. Throughout the twentieth century, and into this century, Hume has been widely regarded as having presented the classic defense of the compatibilist position, the view that freedom and responsibility are consistent with determinism. Most of Hume's core arguments on this issue are found in the Sections entitled "Of liberty and necessity," first presented in Book 2 of *A Treatise of Human Nature* (1739) and then in his *An Enquiry concerning Human Understanding* (1748). Although the general position in both these works is much the same, there are some significant points of difference relating to the way in which the core position is presented and also in the specific range of arguments covered. The focus of my concerns in this essay will not, however, lie with the relationship between the *Treatise* and the first *Enquiry* versions of "Of liberty and necessity." My discussion will center on the contrast between two alternative interpretations of Hume's views on this subject, with particular reference to the version presented in the *Treatise*. It will be my particular concern to explain and defend the naturalistic as against the classical compatibilist account and to explain the general significance of the naturalistic account for the contemporary debate.

I. SPONTANEITY, INDIFFERENCE AND THE LOGIC OF LIBERTY

The interpretation of Hume on free will that has been established for the past century or more is the classical compatibilist account, which places Hume at the heart of a tradition of empiricist-compatibilist thinking that stretches from Hobbes, through Hume, on to Mill, Russell, Schlick, and Ayer.[1] Classical compatibilists believe, with libertarians, that we need some adequate theory of what free action is, where this is understood as providing the relevant conditions of moral agency and responsibility. Compatibilists, however, reject the view that free action requires the falsity of determinism or that an action cannot be both free and causally necessitated by antecedent conditions. According to the classical compatibilist strategy, not only is freedom compatible with causal determinism, but the absence of causation and necessity would make free and responsible action impossible. A free action is an action caused by the agent, whereas an unfree action is caused by some other, external cause. Whether an action is free or not depends on the *type* of cause, not on whether it was caused or necessitated. An uncaused action would be entirely capricious and random and could not be attributed to any agent, much less interpreted as a free and responsible act. So construed, the classical compatibilist strategy involves an attempt to explain and describe the *logic* of our *concepts* relating to issues of freedom and determinism. It is primarily concerned with conceptual issues rather than with any empirical investigations into our human moral psychology. On the classical interpretation, this is how Hume's core arguments should be understood.

The very title "Of liberty and necessity" makes plain that the two key ideas in play are "liberty" (freedom) and "necessity" (causation and determinism). Although Hume emphasizes the point in his *Abstract* of the *Treatise* that his "reasoning puts the whole [free-will] controversy in a new light, by giving a new definition of necessity" (Abs. 34, SBN 661), the classical interpretation nevertheless places heavy weight on the significance of his views on the nature of *liberty* as the appropriate basis for explaining Hume's position on this subject. Hume, it is claimed, is generally following the same strategy that was pursued by Hobbes, and that strategy turns largely on a distinction between two kinds of liberty.[2] Hume's views on liberty, however, vary between the *Treatise* and the *Enquiry*.

In the *Treatise* Hume distinguishes between two kinds of liberty.

Few are capable of distinguishing betwixt the liberty of *spontaneity*, as it is call'd in the schools, and the liberty of *indifference*; betwixt that which is oppos'd to violence, and that which means a negation of necessity and causes. The first is even the most common sense of the word; and as 'tis only that species of liberty, which it concerns us to preserve, our thoughts have been principally turn'd towards it, and have almost universally confounded it with the other. (T 2.3.2.1, SBN 407–8)

Liberty of spontaneity involves an agent's being able to act according to her own willings and desires, unhindered by external obstacles that might constrain or restrict her conduct (e.g., the walls or bars of a prison [T 2.3.1.17, SBN 406]). A liberty of this kind does not imply an absence of causation and necessity, unless we incorrectly assume that what is caused is somehow compelled or forced to occur. In the *Enquiry* Hume drops the distinction between two kinds of liberty and instead provides an account of what he calls "hypothetical liberty" (EHU 8.23, SBN 95). A liberty of this kind involves *"a power of acting or not acting, according to the determinations of the will;* that is, if we choose to remain at rest, we may; if we choose to move, we also may." Hume goes on to claim that this sort of hypothetical liberty is "universally allowed to belong to every one, who is not a prisoner and in chains" (ibid.). Although Hume is committed to the existence of both liberty of spontaneity and hypothetical liberty, they are not the same. More specifically, a person may enjoy liberty of spontaneity and be able to act according to the determinations of her own will but nevertheless lack hypothetical liberty because, if she chose otherwise, her action might be obstructed (e.g., as with a person who chooses to remain in a room but could not leave if she chose to because the door is locked).

The variation between the *Treatise* and the first *Enquiry* accounts of liberty also reflect a variation in the way Hume presents his overall strategy and position in these two works. In the *Treatise* Hume tends to identify liberty with indifference rather than spontaneity and even suggests "that liberty and chance are synonimous" (T 2.3.2.8, SBN 412; cf. T 2.3.1.18, SBN 407; but see also EHU 8.25, SBN 96). For this reason he presents his arguments as aiming to show that liberty, so understood (*qua* indifference), is, if not contradictory, "directly contrary to experience" (T 2.3.1.18, SBN 407). In placing emphasis on this negative task of refuting "the doctrine of *liberty* or *chance*" (T 2.3.2.7, SBN 412), Hume is happy to present himself as coming down firmly on the side of "the doctrine of necessity" (T 2.3.2.3, SBN 409), which he is careful to define in a way that avoids any confusion between causation and compulsion or force (as is explained in more detail below). In the *Enquiry*, on the other hand, Hume strikes a more balanced note and presents his position as not so much a refutation of "the doctrine of liberty" or "free-will" (T 2.3.1.18, SBN 407; cf. T 2.1.10.5, SBN 312), but rather as a "reconciling project with regard to the question of liberty and necessity" (EHU 8.23, SBN 95; although even in the *Enquiry* his references to liberty are not uniformly to spontaneity). Having noted these differences, it is important not to exaggerate them. In the *Treatise* Hume makes clear that liberty of spontaneity is "the most common sense of the word" and the "only ... species of liberty, which it concerns us to preserve" (T 2.3.2.1, SBN 407-8). It is evident, therefore, that there is also a "reconciling project" implicit in the *Treatise* and that his arguments against "the doctrine of liberty" remain tightly focused on liberty of indifference.

For Hume, the original or interesting part of his contribution to free will is not the claim that liberty should be understood in terms of spontaneity as opposed to indifference. On the contrary, he is very clear, in both the *Treatise* and the *Enquiry*, that the primary obstacle to resolving this controversy is securing a proper definition or understanding of what we mean by *necessity* (T 2.3.1.18, 2.3.2.4, SBN 407, 409–10; see also EHU 8.1–3, 8.21–25, SBN 80–81, 92–96). According to Hume there are "two particulars, which we are to consider as essential to necessity, *viz.* the constant *union* and the *inference* of the mind; and wherever we discover these we must acknowledge a necessity" (T 2.3.1.4, SBN 400). To explain this, he begins with a description of causation and necessity as we observe it in "the operations of external bodies" (T 2.3.1.3, SBN 399) or in "the actions of matter" (Abs. 34, SBN 661). Here we find "not the least traces of indifference or liberty," and we can see that "[e]very object is determin'd by an absolute fate" (T 2.3.1.3, SBN 400). What this means, as Hume has explained at length in Book 1 of the *Treatise*, is that we discover that there exist constant conjunctions of objects whereby resembling objects of one kind are uniformly followed by resembling objects of another kind (e.g., Xs are uniformly followed by Ys). (See, in particular, T 1.3; Abs. 8–9, 24–26, SBN 649–50, 655–57; and also EHU 4 and 7.) When we experience regularities of this sort, we are able to draw relevant inferences, and we deem objects of the first kind causes and those of the second kind their effects.

What is crucial to Hume's account is that we can discover no further "*ultimate connexion*" (T 1.3.6.11, SBN 91) between cause and effect beyond our experience of their regular union. There is no perceived or known power or energy in a cause such that we could draw any inference to its effect or by which the cause compels or forces its effect to occur (T 1.3.12.20, 1.3.14.4–7, SBN 139, 157–59). Nevertheless, on the basis of our experience of regularities or constant conjunctions of objects, the mind, on the appearance of the first object, naturally draws an inference to that of the other (T 1.3.14.20–22, 31, SBN 164–66, 169–70; cp. EHU 7.28–29, SBN 75–77). In other words, our experience of regularities serves as the basis upon which we can draw inferences to the existence of an object on the appearance of another. According to Hume, then, all that we find of causation and necessity in bodies or matter is this conjunction of like objects along with the inference of the mind from one to the other. The relevant question, therefore, is do we find similar features in the operations of human action?

Our experience, Hume maintains, proves that "our actions have a constant union with our motives, tempers, and circumstances" and that we draw relevant inferences from one to the other on this basis (T 2.3.1.4, SBN 401). Although there are some apparent irregularities in both the natural and the moral realms, this is entirely due to the influence of contrary or concealed causes of which we are ignorant (T 2.3.1.11–12, SBN 403–4; cf. EHU 8.15, SBN 88).

[T]he *union* betwixt motives and actions has the same constancy, as that in any natural operations, so its influence on the understanding is also the same, in *determining* us to infer the existence of one from that of another. If this shall appear, there is no known circumstance, that enters into the connexion and production of the actions of matter, that is not to be found in all the operations of the mind; and consequently we cannot, without a manifest absurdity, attribute necessity to the one, and refuse it to the other. (T 2.3.1.14, SBN 404)

The relevant evidence that Hume cites for this claim comes, in the first place, from the regularities we observe in human society, where class, sex, occupation, age, and other such factors are seen to be reliably correlated with different motives and conduct (T 2.3.1.5–10, SBN 401–3). Regularities of this kind make it possible for us to draw the sorts of inferences that are needed for human social life, such as in all our reasoning concerning business, politics, war, and so on (T 2.3.1.15, SBN 405; EHU 8.17–18, SBN 89–90). In the absence of necessity, so understood, we could not survive or live together.

Hume goes on to argue that not only is this sort of necessity essential to human society, but it is also "essential to religion and morality" (T 2.3.2.5, SBN 410), because of its relevance to the foundations of responsibility and punishment. Human laws depend on the support of rewards and punishments for their enforcement. If these motives had no uniform and reliable influence on conduct, then law and society would be impossible (ibid.; cp. EHU 8.28, SBN 97–98; see also T 3.3.4.4, SBN 609). Moreover, whether we consider human or divine rewards and punishments, the justice of such practices depends on the fact that the agent has produced or brought about these actions through her own will. The "doctrine of liberty or chance," however, would remove this connection between agent and action and so no one could be properly held accountable for their conduct (T 2.3.2.6, SBN 411). It is, therefore, "only upon the principles of necessity, that a person acquires any merit or demerit from his actions, however the common opinion may incline to the contrary" (ibid.; EHU 8.31, SBN 99). On this (classical) reading, Hume is simply restating the familiar view about the need for necessity (determinism) to support a generally forward-looking, utilitarian theory of moral responsibility and punishment.[3]

Hume's observations on this subject make clear that although necessity is essential to all merit and demerit, the opposite is often asserted. The principal explanation for this resistance to "the doctrine of necessity" is found, according to Hume, in confusion about the nature of necessity as we discover it in *matter*.[4] Although in ordinary life we all rely upon and reason upon the principles of necessity, there may well be some reluctance to call this union and inference necessity.

But as long as the meaning is understood, I hope the word can do no harm.... I may be mistaken in asserting, that we have no idea of any other connexion in the actions of body.... But sure I am, I ascribe nothing to the actions of the mind, but what must readily be allow'd of.... I do not ascribe to the will that unintelligible necessity, which is suppos'd to lie in matter. But I ascribe to matter, that intelligible quality, call it necessity or not, which the most rigorous orthodoxy does or must allow to belong to the will. I change, therefore, nothing in the receiv'd systems, with regard to the will, but only with regard to material objects. (T 2.3.2.4, SBN 410; cp. EHU 8.22, SBN 93–94)

The illusion that we are aware of some further power or energy in matter, whereby causes somehow compel or force their effects to occur, is the fundamental source of confusion on this issue. It is this that encourages us to reject the suggestion that our actions are subject to necessity on the ground that this would imply some kind of violence or constraint – something that would be incompatible with liberty of spontaneity. When confusions of this sort are removed, all that remains is the verbal quibble about using the term *necessity* – which is not itself a substantial point of disagreement.[5]

Hume provides another explanation for our resistance to the doctrine of necessity, which has to do with "a *false sensation or experience* even of the liberty of indifference" (T 2.3.2.2, SBN 408, Hume's emphasis; cp. EHU 8.22n18, SBN 94n). He describes this "false sensation" in these terms:

The necessity of any action, whether of matter or of the mind, is not properly a quality in the agent, but in any thinking or intelligent being, who may consider the action, and consists in the determination of his thought to infer its existence from some preceding objects: As liberty or chance, on the other hand, is nothing but the want of that determination, and a certain looseness, which we feel in passing or not passing from the idea of one to that of the other. Now we may observe, that tho' in reflecting on human actions we seldom feel such a looseness or indifference, yet it very commonly happens, that in performing the actions themselves we are sensible of something like it.... We feel that our actions are subject to our will on most occasions, and imagine we feel that the will itself is subject to nothing. (T 2.3.2.2, SBN 408)

The difference between reflecting on and performing actions, in other words, corresponds to the difference in the stance of the spectator and the agent. From the agent's perspective we may experience an "indifference" that suggests the relevant uniformity and inference are absent, but spectators can, nevertheless, reliably infer our actions from our motives and character. For this reason, although we may in these circumstances find it hard to accept that "we were govern'd by necessity, and that 'twas utterly impossible for us to have acted otherwise" (T 2.3.2.1, SBN 407), the spectator's point of view reveals this to be an illusion or "false sensation." It is this deception in our experience of acting, along with our further confusions and mistaken suppositions concerning the nature of necessity (as it exists in matter), that largely account for "the prevalence of the doctrine of liberty [of indifference]" (ibid.).

One further explanation that Hume provides in this context is the influence of religion, which has been, he suggests, "very unnecessarily interested in this question" (T 2.3.2.3, SBN 409). In taking up this issue, Hume alludes to irreligious objectives that are fundamental to his core concerns throughout the *Treatise* – and, indeed, central to his whole philosophy. In this context, however, I will only briefly consider the irreligious aspect of Hume's aims and objectives.[6] First, although Hume suggests that the doctrine of necessity "is not only innocent, but even advantageous to religion and morality" (ibid.), he nevertheless goes on to point out that even if this doctrine had "dangerous consequences," this circumstance would not show that it was false.[7] Second, and more importantly, in the *Enquiry* Hume notes that while the doctrine of necessity is "absolutely essential" to morality (EHU 8.26, SBN 97), it *does* present intractable philosophical problems for religion (i.e., it is not as "innocent" as his remarks in the *Treatise* suggest). The most basic problem is that, given the doctrine of necessity, we can trace the origin of the whole causal series – including all evil action and conduct – back to God (EHU 8.32, SBN 99–100). Although he considers various ways in which the orthodox may try to evade these difficulties, he finds none of them convincing. The theist is left facing the following dilemma:

And we must therefore conclude, either that [human actions] are not criminal, or that the Deity, not man, is accountable for them. (EHU 8.32, SBN 100)

Hume rejects the first alternative on the ground that the distinction between virtue and vice depends on our natural sentiments and cannot be denied or rejected on the basis of "any philosophical theory or speculation whatsoever" (EHU 8.35, SBN 103). On the other hand, it seems impossible to deny that God is "the author of sin and moral turpitude" once we grant that we can trace the causal origins of all our actions back to him (EHU 8.36, 32, SBN 103, 99–100). Clearly, then, as Hume openly acknowledges in the *Enquiry*, the doctrine of necessity is far from "innocent" with respect to its implications for religion, contrary to what he suggests in the *Treatise*. Moreover, there is no reason to suppose that he was unaware of this when he wrote and published the *Treatise*.[8]

The account of Hume's views on free will provided so far suggests that it is Hume's primary concern in his discussion in "Of liberty and necessity" to defend an account of moral freedom understood in terms of liberty of spontaneity. Our tendency to confuse this form of liberty with indifference is rooted, he suggests, in confusion concerning the nature of causation and necessity. On this reading, Hume advances on Hobbes's distinction between two the kinds of liberty by supplementing it with his own insights relating to the nature of necessity and by showing that in the absence of necessity, understood in terms of uniformity and inference, no agent would be suitably connected with her actions whereby we could make sense of our attributions of merit or demerit.[9] All of this is generally consistent with the views subsequently advanced by other classical compatibilists following in Hume's footsteps (viz., Mill, Russell, Schlick, and Ayer, et al.). Suffice it to say that if this is a fair and full account of Hume's position, then it is liable to all the familiar criticisms leveled against classical compatibilism, most of which are very familiar and need not be reviewed and rehearsed in this context.[10] For our present purposes, what matters is to ask to what extent does the classical account adequately capture Hume's views and strategy on this subject?

2. THE NECESSITY OF MORAL SENTIMENT

When Hume came to present his views on liberty and necessity afresh in the first *Enquiry*, he positioned his discussion of this topic immediately after the Sections discussing necessity. This is not surprising because he had already indicated in the *Abstract* that "this reasoning puts the whole controversy in a new light, by giving a new definition of necessity." But this leaves us with a puzzle: Why did Hume originally present his discussion of liberty and necessity in "Of the Passions," Book 2 of the *Treatise*? In his highly influential study, *The Philosophy of David Hume*, Norman Kemp Smith describes the placement "Of liberty and necessity" as a "lengthy digression" in the context of Book 2 (1941: 161). Kemp Smith suggests that the "proper location of the two sections is not that of the *Treatise*, namely, as bearing on the treatment of the passions, but, as is recognised in the arrangement of the *Enquiry concerning Human Understanding*, in immediate sequence upon the section *Of the idea of necessary connexion*" (1941: 433). It is certainly true that on the classical interpretation Hume's discussion of free will at T 2.3.1–2 has little or nothing to do with the passions. On the naturalistic reading, however, there is an intimate and significant relationship between Hume's views on free will and his preceding discussion of the passions – in particular, his account of the mechanism of the indirect passions of pride and humility, and love and hate (T 2.1 and 2.2).

The key to the naturalistic interpretation, and the way in which it differs from the classical account, rests with Hume's claims that necessity is essential to morality and that liberty of indifference would make morality impossible (T 2.3.2.5–7, SBN 410–12). Hume's claim that necessity is essential to morality runs parallel to his claim that necessity is also essential to social life (T 2.3.1.8–15, SBN 401–5). For people to be able to live in society, they must be able to infer the actions of others from their motives and characters. In the opposite direction, we must also be able to infer character from action, because without this, Hume maintains, no one could be held responsible and morality would be impossible. To understand the thrust of Hume's argument here we need to get a clearer picture of what it is to be *held* responsible on Hume's account – a picture that is very different from anything suggested by the (forward-looking, utilitarian-oriented) classical interpretation. Holding a person responsible is, for Hume, a matter of regarding a person as an object of the moral sentiments of approval and disapproval. Approval and disapproval are "nothing but a fainter and more imperceptible love or hatred" (T 3.3.5.1, SBN 614). More specifically, approval and disapproval are calm forms of love and hatred, which are themselves indirect passions. To understand the relevance of necessity for the conditions of holding a person responsible, we must, therefore, also understand the workings of the "regular mechanism" of the indirect passions (DP 6.19).

In his discussion of love and hatred Hume writes:

One of these suppositions, *viz.* that the cause of love and hatred must be related to a person or thinking being, in order to produce these passions, is not only probable, but too evident to be contested. Virtue and vice, when consider'd in the abstract ... excite no degree of love or hatred, esteem or contempt towards those, who have no relation to them. (T 2.2.1.7, SBN 331)

Our virtues and vices are not the only causes of love and hatred, as our wealth and property, family and social relations, and bodily qualities and attributes may also generate love or hate (T 2.1.2.5, 2.1.7.1–5, SBN 279, 294–96; DP 2.14–33). It is, nevertheless, our virtues and vices, understood as pleasurable or painful qualities of mind, that are "the most obvious causes of these passions" (T 2.1.7.2, SBN 295; cp. T 3.1.2.5, SBN 473; and also T 3.3.1.3, SBN 574–75). In this way, virtue and vice, by means of the general mechanism of the indirect passions, give rise to that "faint and imperceptible" form of love and hatred that constitutes the moral sentiments, which are essential to all our ascriptions of moral responsibility.

Hume makes clear that it is not actions, as such, that give rise to our moral sentiments, but rather our more enduring or persisting character traits (T 2.2.3.4, SBN 348–49; and also T 3.3.1.4–5, SBN 575). The crucial passage in his discussion "Of liberty and necessity" is the following:

Actions are by their very nature temporary and perishing; and where they proceed not from some cause in the characters and disposition of the person, who per-form'd them, they infix not themselves upon him, and can neither redound to his honour, if good, nor infamy, if evil. The action itself may be blameable.... But the person is not responsible for it; and as it proceeded from nothing in him, that is durable or constant, and leaves nothing of that nature behind it, 'tis impossible he can, upon its account, become the object of punishment or vengeance. (T 2.3.2.6, SBN 411; cf. EHU 8.29, SBN 98; see also T 3.3.1.4, SBN 575)

Further on, in Book 3, Hume expands on these remarks:

'Tis evident, that when we praise any actions, we regard only the motives that produc'd them, and consider the actions as signs or indications of certain principles in the mind and temper. The external performance has no merit. We must look within to find the moral quality. This we cannot do directly; and therefore fix our attention on actions, as on external signs. But these actions are still consider'd as signs; and the ultimate object of our praise and approbation is the motive, that produc'd them. (T 3.2.1.2, SBN 477; cf. T 3.2.1.8, SBN 479; EHU 8.31, SBN 99)

In these two passages Hume is making two distinct but related points. First, he maintains that "action," considered as an "external performance" without any reference to the motive or intention that produced it, is not itself of moral concern. It is, rather, the "internal" cause of the action that arouses our moral sentiments. It is these aspects of action that inform us about the mind and moral character of the agent. Second, the moral qualities of an agent that arouse our moral sentiments must be "durable or constant" – they cannot be "temporary and perishing" in the way actions are. This second condition on the generation of moral sentiment is itself a particular instance of the more general observation that Hume has made earlier in Book 2: that the relationship between the quality or feature that gives rise to the indirect passions (i.e., its cause) and the person who is the object of the passion must not be "casual [or] inconstant" (T 2.1.6.7, SBN 293). It is, however, the first point that is especially important for our present purpose of understanding why necessity is essential to morality.

In order to know anyone's motives and character, we require inference from her actions to her motives and character (T 2.1.11.3, 3.3.1.7, SBN 317, 576). Without knowledge of her character no sentiment of approbation or blame would be aroused in us. Without inferences moving in this direction – from action to character (as opposed to from character to actions) – no one would be an object of praise or blame and, hence, no one would be regarded as morally responsible. In these circumstances, praising and blaming would be psychologically impossible. Along the same lines, external violence – like liberty of indifference – also makes it impossible to regard someone as an object of praise or blame. When an action is produced by causes external to the agent, we are led away from the agent's character. Clearly, then, actions that are either uncaused or caused by external factors cannot render an agent responsible, not because it would be unreasonable to hold the person responsible, but rather because it would be *psychologically impossible* to hold the person responsible, where this stance is understood in terms of the operation of the moral sentiments. It is in this way that Hume brings his observations concerning the operation of the indirect passions to bear on his claim that necessity is essential to morality and, in particular, to our attitudes and practices associated with responsibility and punishment.

It is evident, in light of this alternative account of Hume's arguments, that the nature of his compatibilist strategy is significantly misrepresented by the classical interpretation. Hume's arguments purporting to show that necessity is essential to morality are intimately connected with his discussion of the indirect passions and the specific mechanism that generates the moral sentiments. Whereas the classical interpretation construes his arguments as conceptual or logical in nature, the naturalistic interpretation presents Hume as concerned to *describe* the circumstances under which people are *felt* to be responsible. So interpreted, Hume's arguments constitute a contribution to descriptive moral psychology and should be considered an important part of his wider program to "introduce the experimental method of reasoning into moral subjects" (which is the subtitle of the *Treatise*).

In response to the naturalistic account of Hume's strategy as it concerns the free will problem, it may be said that the moral psychology involved, with its focus on the production of moral sentiment, is no longer of contemporary interest and that the classical interpretation is philosophically a more fertile way of reading Hume on this topic. However, the opposite is true. From a contemporary perspective, classical compatibilism seems too crude an account of both freedom and moral responsibility, and very few philosophers would still press the claim that incompatibilist prejudices can be explained simply in terms of confusion about necessity arising from a conflation between causation and compulsion. Hume's concern with the role and relevance of moral sentiment for our understanding of the free will problem, by contrast, anticipates several key features of P. F. Strawson's highly influential contribution to the contemporary debate. Strawson's "Freedom and Resentment" (hereafter, "FR") is arguably the most important and influential paper concerning the free will problem published in the second half of the twentieth century.[11] Perhaps the most striking affinity between the approaches taken by both Hume and Strawson is their shared appeal to the role of moral sentiments or reactive attitudes as a way of discrediting any supposed sceptical threat arising from the thesis of determinism.

According to Strawson, both classical compatibilists (who he refers to as "optimists") and libertarians (who he refers to as "pessimists," because they suppose that determinism threatens moral responsibility) make a similar mistake of "over-intellectualizing the facts" by seeking to provide some sort of "external 'rational' justification" for moral responsibility (FR 81). The classical compatibilist does this on the basis of a "one-eyed utilitarianism," whereas the libertarian, seeing that something vital is missing from the classical compatibilist account, tries to plug the gap with "contra causal freedom" – which Strawson describes as "a pitiful intellectualist trinket" (ibid.). By focusing attention on the importance of reactive attitudes or moral sentiments in this context, Strawson hopes to find some middle ground whereby he can "reconcile" the two opposing camps. Our reactive attitudes or moral sentiments, Strawson maintains, should be understood in terms of our natural human emotional responses to the attitudes and intentions that human beings manifest toward each other. We expect and demand some degree of good will and due regard, and we feel gratitude or resentment depending on whether or not this is shown to us (FR 66–67). Granted that these emotions are part of our essential human makeup and are naturally triggered or aroused in relevant circumstances, it is still important to recognize that they are in some measure under rational control and that we can "modify or mollify" them in light of relevant considerations (FR 68).

There are two kinds of considerations that Strawson distinguishes that may require us to amend or withdraw our reactive attitudes. First, there are considerations that we may describe as exemptions, where we judge that an individual is not an appropriate or suitable target of any reactive attitudes. These are cases in which a person may be viewed as "psychologically abnormal" or "morally underdeveloped" (FR 69; and also 71–72). On the other hand, even where exemptions of this sort do not apply, ordinary considerations about excuses may nevertheless require us to alter or change our particular reactive attitudes as directed toward some individual (FR 68). Considerations of this kind include cases in which an agent acts accidentally or in ignorance or was subject to physical force of some kind. Where these considerations apply we may come to recognize that the conduct in question, properly interpreted, does not lack the degree of good will or due regard that we may demand. Even if some injury has occurred, no malice or lack of regard has been shown to us. However, the crucial point for Strawson is that, although our reactive attitudes may well be modified or withdrawn in these circumstances, there is no question of us altogether abandoning or suspending our reactive attitudes (FR 71–73). In particular, there is nothing about the thesis of determinism that implies that either exemptions or excuses, as Strawson has described them, apply or hold universally (FR 70–71). Moreover, and more controversially, Strawson also maintains that even if determinism did provide some "theoretical" basis for drawing this sceptical conclusion, any such policy is "for us as we are, practically inconceivable" (FR 71). In other words, according to Strawson our natural commitment to the fabric of moral sentiment insulates us from any possible global sceptical threat to the whole fabric of moral responsibility based on theoretical worries about the implications of determinism.

Although both the interpretation of Strawson's naturalistic strategy and the various ways it relates to Hume's (similar) strategy are too complex to cover here in all their detail, the crucial point for our present purposes is to make clear where Hume stands with respect to the differences between classical compatibilism (Strawson's "optimism") and the alternative approach that Strawson has advanced. Whereas the classical interpretation would present Hume as an obvious and prominent *target* of Strawson's criticisms, the naturalistic interpretation presents Hume as broadly anticipating the key features of Strawson's approach – most importantly, his understanding of moral responsibility with reference to the role of moral sentiment. For both Hume and Strawson, moral responsibility, and the way in which it is related to issues of freedom and determinism, has to be explained and described with reference to the relevant psychological facts about our human emotions and the circumstances under which they are aroused or inhibited. This naturalistic approach, which is fundamental to Hume's entire program, constitutes its principal contemporary interest and significance.

3. BEYOND "THE MORALITY SYSTEM"

One of the most important philosophical differences between the classical and naturalistic interpretations, as they have been outlined above, concerns the relationship between freedom and moral responsibility. On the classical interpretation, this relation is simple: responsibility may be analyzed directly in terms of free action. That is, an agent is responsible for her action when it is performed freely, by way of her own willings and desires. (This simple view may be further refined by reference to the efficaciousness of rewards and punishments.) Where classical compatibilists differ from incompatibilists is that they reject the suggestion that free, responsible action requires indeterminism and some further form of "contra causal" or "metaphysical" freedom.[12] They are both agreed, nevertheless, that responsibility is essentially a matter of free action. On the naturalistic interpretation, however, Hume rejects this doctrine, which we may call "voluntarism."

As we have already noted, Hume thinks it is a matter of "the utmost importance" for moral philosophy that an action be indicative of durable qualities of mind if a person is to be held accountable for it (T 3.3.1.5, SBN 575). This claim is part of Hume's more general claim that our indirect passions (including our moral sentiments) are aroused and sustained only when the pleasurable or painful qualities concerned (e.g., the virtues and vices) stand in a durable or constant relation with the person who is their object. In the case of actions, which are "temporary and perishing," no such lasting relation is involved unless the action is suitably tied to character traits of some kind (T 2.3.2.6, SBN 411). We may, however, be able to infer a person's character through some medium other than her voluntary, intentional actions. A person may, for example, reveal her character through her "wishes and sentiments," gestures, mannerisms, carriage, and countenance, even though this is not done voluntarily and is not intentional (T 3.3.1.5, 2.1.11.3, SBN 575, 317; EHU 8.9, 15, SBN 85, 88). In these circumstances we may still find such mental qualities pleasant or painful, and they will, accordingly, generate moral sentiments in us. It is, therefore, a basic mistake, in light of the naturalistic interpretation, to read Hume as committed to the simple (voluntarist) understanding of the relationship between freedom and responsibility. While it is true that neither uncaused action nor action produced by causes external to the agent's willings and desires can arouse our moral sentiments, it is also true that our moral sentiments may be aroused through channels other than voluntary, intentional action.

This point should not be dismissed or set aside as an arcane point of scholarship or a mere curiosity of Hume's system. On the contrary, what these observations bring to light is the way in which Hume rejects central features of what Bernard Williams has described as "the morality system" (1985: ch. 10). Williams's (hostile) account of the morality system is layered and multifaceted and generally defies easy summary. There are, however, core features that he identifies and regards as especially problematic. In the first place, there is a special notion of moral obligation or duty, which is fundamental. Flowing from this concept of obligation are other key concepts, such as right and wrong, and blame and retributive punishment. Although the morality system takes various forms, and it is not simply a philosophical theory, it is still true that Kantian ethics represents the morality system in its "purest, deepest" form (1985: 174). For our purposes, what matters here is that Hume's views on free will, and on morality more generally, should not be forced into the restrictive, narrow framework of the morality system. Whereas the classical interpretation encourages such a view, the naturalistic interpretation suggests that it is mistaken.

When we attempt to understand moral responsibility in terms of obligations, as laid down by rules, principles, or laws (where violations constitute a wrong that is liable to punishment), the notions of choice, will, and voluntariness also become salient and essential to making sense of this aspect of moral life. The classical interpretation fits this model nicely and, indeed, does its best to accommodate it. Even within the naturalistic program, as recently revived by Strawson, there are efforts to reconstruct and amend this approach employing only the materials provided by the morality system.[13] Suffice it to say, however, that the apparatus that Hume provides takes us in a very different direction. Hume's account does not focus on choice and action, as such, but rather on virtues and vices understood as pleasurable and painful (and enduring) qualities of mind. While Hume allows that for the purposes of law and punishment the voluntary/involuntary distinction is of great importance, he explicitly denies that this should serve as the relevant basis for identifying the boundaries of praise and blame or moral responsibility.[14]

One reason the morality system places great weight on the importance of voluntariness in providing the relevant boundary for moral responsibility is that one of its central aims or ambitions is to establish that "morality" – and moral responsibility in particular – somehow "transcends luck" (Williams 1985: 195) and ensures that blame is allocated in a way that is "ultimately fair" (Williams 1985: 194). Despite the challenges this poses, compatibilists have generally tried to satisfy these demands of the morality system by way of offering a variety of arguments to show that compatibilist commitments do not render us vulnerable to the play of fate or luck in our moral lives.[15] Hume makes no effort to go along with these ambitions and aims. For example, Hume makes very clear, especially in the *Treatise*, that although our qualities of character may typically be *expressed* by means of our voluntary and intentional conduct, our character is not *acquired* through our own choices or decisions. This issue is addressed in the context of Hume's discussion of our natural abilities, where Hume says that it is "almost impossible for the mind to change its character in any considerable article, or cure itself of a passionate or splenetic temper, when they are natural to it" (T 3.3.4.3, SBN 608). Our will has no more influence over our moral virtues, including our natural abilities, than it does over our "bodily endowments" (T 3.3.4.1, SBN 606). In the final analysis, it is Hume's view that just as every body or material object "is determin'd by an absolute fate to a certain degree and direction of its motion, and can no more depart from that precise line, in which it moves, than it can convert itself into an angel, or spirit, or any superior substance" (T 2.3.1.3, SBN 400), so too our conduct and character is subject to an "absolute fate" as understood in terms of the inescapable "bonds of necessity" (T 2.3.2.2, SBN 408). For Hume, as for Williams, there is no reason to suppose that morality somehow "transcends luck" or that the allocation of praise and blame is in any way "ultimately fair." In this Hume perhaps shares more with the ancient Greeks than he does with moderns who embrace the aspirations of the morality system.[16]

There remains, however, a significant gap in Hume's scheme as we have so far described it. This is a gap that can also be found in Strawson's similar naturalistic account of the conditions of freedom and moral responsibility. Even if we eschew the aims of the morality system, any credible naturalistic theory of moral responsibility needs to be able to provide some account of the sorts of moral capacity involved in exempting conditions, whereby we deem some individuals and not others appropriate targets of moral sentiments or reactive attitudes. On the face of it, what Hume has to say on this issue is sorely inadequate. Hume treats it as an ultimate, inexplicable fact about our moral sentiments that they are always directed at people, either ourselves or others. It is simply a fact, to be observed and described, that the relevant feelings and attitudes are aroused by "mental qualities" – virtues and vices – and are targeted at the individuals these qualities belong or attach to. Clearly, however, this account leaves us unable to say why some people are *not* appropriate objects of moral sentiments (e.g., children, the insane, and so on). In general, then, Hume provides us with no adequate or clear account of the nature of the moral capacities required for a person to be deemed an appropriate object of moral sentiment. Strawson's effort to deal with this problem in "Freedom and Resentment" is not a great improvement on this. Although Strawson recognizes the need to be able to identify those who are "incapacitated" and those who are not, he simply categorizes the incapacitated as either "abnormal" or "immature," in contrast with ordinary, mature adults (FR 69–73, 75–76).[17] One reason this gap in the naturalistic program is especially problematic is that it leaves the field open to the incompatibilist to argue that the relevant moral capacities must include a capacity for categorical or "contra causal" freedom of some kind.[18] The situation is, however, not entirely dire for the naturalist approach because there are several proposals for dealing with this gap in the theory.

One proposal that is prominent in current compatibilist literature is to develop some general theory of reason-responsiveness or rational self-control. According to accounts of this kind, responsible agents need to have control over their actions, where this involves performing "those actions intentionally, while possessing the relevant sorts of normative competence: the general ability to grasp moral requirements and to govern one's conduct by the light of them" (Wallace 1994: 86).[19] Although theories of this kind face their own challenges and objections from incompatibilists, they do serve to plug a large gap in naturalistic approaches to the free will problem. However, in describing moral capacity directly in terms of rational self-control over action, theories of this kind provide an understanding of moral responsibility that is not entirely consistent with Hume's own account.

There are two considerations that suggest that Hume's theory should not be understood in terms of rational self-control models as generally presented. First, rational self-control may be explained in terms of specifically Kantian conceptions of practical reason and moral agency, as they are on Wallace's account.[20] Moreover, even if these specific commitments are avoided, as they may on other models, theories of this kind are still action-based interpretations of our ascriptions of moral responsibility, with a narrow focus on intentions and voluntariness ("quality of will") as the relevant basis of moral evaluation. This is, as we have noted, one way in which Hume plainly diverges from "the morality system" and the voluntarist doctrine associated with it. For Hume, our moral capacities do not relate only to our choices and intentions but must also engage wider patterns and dispositions of feeling, desire, and character. The scope of the ethical should not be reduced or narrowed to concern with (fleeting and momentary) acts of will modeled after legal paradigms but should comprehend a larger and more diverse set of propensities and abilities that make up our moral character.

Second, and perhaps more importantly, although Hume does not provide any substantial or robust theory of moral capacity, it is possible to find, within the resources of his philosophy, material that suggests a rather less "rationalistic" understanding of moral capacity. More specifically, it may be argued that there is an intimate relationship between virtue and moral sense, where this is understood in terms of our general capacity to feel and direct moral sentiments at both ourselves and others. Hume points out, for example, that children acquire the artificial virtues, involving the conventions of justice, not only by way of learning their advantages, but also by learning to feel the relevant moral sentiments when these conventions are violated (T 3.2.2.26, SBN 500–1). The mechanism of the moral sentiments both cultivates and maintains the artificial virtues. Hume has less to say about the role of moral sentiment in relation to the natural virtues, but similar observations would seem to apply. As children grow up and mature, they become increasingly aware that their qualities of character affect both others and themselves and that these will inevitably give rise to moral sentiments in the people they will deal with. This entire process of becoming aware of the moral sentiments of others and "surveying ourselves as we appear to others" (T 3.3.1.26, SBN 589; T 3.3.1.8, 3.3.1.30, 3.3.6.6, SBN 576–77, 591, 620; EPM 9.10, App. 4.3, SBN 276, 314) surely serves to develop the natural as well as the artificial virtues. Along these lines, Hume maintains that this disposition to "survey ourselves" and seek our own "peace and satisfaction" is the "surest guardian of every virtue" (EPM 9.10, SBN 276). Any person who entirely lacks this disposition will be shameless and will inevitably lack all the virtues that depend on moral reflection for their development and stability.

If this conjecture regarding the intimate or internal relationship between virtue and moral sense is correct, then it does much to explain and account for the range of exemptions that are required in this area. Hume's understanding of the operation of moral sentiment is not simply a matter of enjoying pleasant and painful feelings of a peculiar kind (T 3.1.2.4, SBN 472). On the contrary, the moral evaluation of character involves the activity of both reason and sentiment. The sort of intellectual activities required include not only learning from experience the specific pleasant and painful tendencies of certain kinds of character and conduct, as well as the ability to distinguish accurately among them, but also the ability to evaluate character and conduct from "some *steady* and *general* points of view" (T 3.3.1.15, SBN 581–82; EPM 5.41–42, SBN 227–28). Clearly, then, insofar as the cultivation and stability of virtue depends on moral sense, it also requires the intellectual qualities and capacities involved in the exercise of moral sense. Given this, an animal, an infant, or an insane person will lack the ability to perform the intellectual tasks involved in the production of moral sentiment. We cannot, therefore, expect virtues that are dependent on these abilities and intellectual activities to be manifest in individuals who lack them or when they are damaged or underdeveloped.

Interpreting Hume in these terms not only goes a long way to filling what looks to be a large gap in his naturalistic program, but it also avoids distorting his own wider ethical commitments by imposing a narrower, rationalistic conception of moral capacity on his naturalistic framework. Beyond this, interpreting moral capacity in these more sentimentalist terms is both philosophically and psychologically more satisfying and plausible. On an account of this kind, there exists a close and essential relationship between being responsible, where this is understood in terms of *being* an appropriate target of moral sentiments or reactive attitudes, and being able to *hold* oneself and others responsible, where this is understood as the ability to experience and entertain moral sentiments. It is a merit of Hume's system, so interpreted, that it avoids "over-intellectualizing" not only what is involved in holding a person responsible, but also what is involved in being a responsible agent.[21]

4. TWO PRESENTATIONS, TWO INTERPRETATIONS

In the introduction to this essay I indicated that my principal concern would be not to compare and contrast the *Treatise* and *Enquiry* versions of "Of liberty and necessity," but rather to compare and assess the opposing classical and naturalistic interpretations, with a view to defending the naturalistic interpretation and explaining its contemporary interest. Having given attention to these issues, it may, nevertheless, be appropriate to say something about the relationship between these two interpretations and the two versions of "Of liberty and necessity." It would not be correct to suggest that whereas the naturalistic interpretation can be derived from the *Treatise*, the classical interpretation sits more comfortably with the first *Enquiry*. This cannot be right, because the naturalistic interpretation suggests that *both* versions should be read in terms of the naturalistic interpretation. There is, however, something to be said for the claim that the first *Enquiry* version does *lend itself* to the classical interpretation.

As I have already mentioned, the *Treatise* and first *Enquiry* versions of "Of liberty and necessity" differ in where they are placed in their respective works. Whereas the discussion in the *Enquiry* is placed immediately after an extended analysis of our ideas of causation and necessity, the *Treatise* version is placed immediately following the discussion of the indirect passions, within Book 2 on the passions. There can be no doubt that the *Enquiry* format lends itself to the classical interpretation because the linkage with the wider theory of the passions and moral evaluation is entirely obscured, if not altogether severed. The difficulties here do not, however, rest exclusively with the first *Enquiry* version. It is not possible to appreciate Hume's arguments in *either version* of "Of liberty and necessity" if they are read as self-contained Sections or contributions needing no reference to other elements in Hume's system. Reading Hume on "free will" in this way inevitably distorts the arguments he is advancing in these Sections. The particular problem with the *Enquiry* version is that unless one turns back to the *Treatise* or refers (ahead) to the second *Enquiry* and *Dissertation on the Passions*, the relevance of what Hume has to say about liberty and necessity to the operation of the moral sentiments will be entirely lost. Although it may be true that Hume's discussion of moral responsibility in the *Enquiry* version of "Of liberty and necessity" (EHU 8) is "too brief and sketchy to give full satisfaction" (Botterill 2002: 299), this cannot be said of the *Treatise* discussion unless his discussion is severed from all its layered connections with other Sections and passages in the *Treatise* – which clearly it should not.[22]

One of the relative virtues of the *Enquiry* version is that it includes an extended discussion of the problems that "the doctrine of necessity" presents for religion, which makes it easier to identify the irreligious significance of Hume's views on free will. As already indicated, Hume's fundamental intentions throughout the *Treatise* – and, indeed, throughout his entire philosophy – are best understood as essentially irreligious in nature (and both his scepticism and naturalism are themselves guided by these more basic aims and objectives). This more general observation also applies to Hume's specific contributions on free will, which are, in both the *Treatise* and *Enquiry* versions, laden with irreligious significance. Appreciating this point should encourage us to avoid two methodological errors when approaching Hume's philosophy with a view to the relationship between the *Treatise* and the *Enquiries*. First, it is a mistake to overlook either the *Treatise* or the *Enquiries* as a proper basis for understanding Hume's philosophical intentions and the way they evolved. It is not possible to fully appreciate the *Treatise* or the *Enquiries* without some mutual reference. One obvious reason for this is that each of these works contains important passages and discussions missing in its counterpart, and each has its distinctive way of presenting shared themes and arguments. Second, and no less important, the *Treatise* remains Hume's fundamental work not only because it lays the foundations for his entire philosophical program, but also because, unlike the *Enquiries*, it presents Hume's philosophical system as more or less a whole, complete in itself. It is a mistake, therefore, not to give priority to the *Treatise* as his primary work that is most representative of his fundamental philosophical commitments and concerns. This is, as has been argued, especially important for appreciating and understanding what he has to say on a topic such as free will or "liberty and necessity."

I do not, however, want to close this discussion on the question of the relative merits of the *Treatise* and the *Enquiry* contributions (which is not an especially interesting or important debate unless one denies that both works deserve full and careful consideration). What is of central importance remains our assessment of the relative merits of the classical and naturalistic interpretations. It has been argued that the naturalistic interpretation properly captures Hume's core strategy, which involves essential reference to the role of moral sentiment in explaining why necessity is essential to morality – an issue that lies at the heart of Hume's position on the free will controversy. Beyond this, it has also been argued that, unlike the classical interpretation, the naturalistic interpretation brings to full and proper light where the contemporary interest and value of Hume's contribution lies. It rests, as we have seen, not only with its relevance to the efforts of P. F. Strawson and others to revive and defend the naturalistic strategy, but also, more radically, with Hume's anticipation of the critique of "the morality system" as it relates to the free will problem. An appreciation of these facets of Hume's thought on the problem of free will serves as a forceful example of the way in which issues of interpretation must be *fused* with any credible critical study of Hume's philosophy and its contemporary relevance.

NOTES

1. See, e.g., Hospers 1961: 140; Berlin 1969: xv; Glover 1970: 50n1; Davidson 1980: 63; Penelhum 1993: 129–32. See also Honderich 2002: 109–10, which provides a useful summary of some of the common points in the classical compatibilist position as generally understood.

2. Stroud 1977: 144–46, 153.

3. For more recent statements of this view see, e.g., Schlick 1966 (1939) and Smart 1970 (1961).

4. Although Hume considers our experience of matter as the most likely source of our idea of power or force, he also considers, and rejects, the "Cartesian" suggestion that the source of this idea comes from God's activity in the world (T 1.3.14.8–11, SBN 159–61; Abs. 26, SBN 656; cf. EHU 7.21–25, SBN 69–73). After publishing Books 1 and 2 (in 1739), Hume came to consider the mind or will as a third possible source of our idea of power and also rejected it (T 1.3.14.12, SBN 632; Abs. 26, SBN 656; EHU 7.9–20, SBN 64–69).

5. Although the verbal nature of the debate, understood in these terms, is noted in the *Treatise*, it is more strongly emphasized in the first *Enquiry* (EHU 8.1–3, SBN 80–81). It is a mistake, however, to conclude from this that Hume is somehow dismissive or cavalier about the difficulties involved. See, e.g., Flew 1961: 156–58.

6. A full account of Hume's fundamental irreligious intentions in the *Treatise* is provided in Russell 2008. On the particular relevance of Hume's irreligious aims and intentions for his discussion of free will, see Russell 1995: ch. 11 and Russell 2008: ch. 16.

7. Compare Hume's similar observation concerning the existence of God and a future state, as discussed in the first *Enquiry* (EHU 11.28–30, SBN 147–48).

8. It is entirely possible that the passages in the *Enquiry* directly concerning religion (EHU 8.32–36, SBN 99–103) were among those that were "castrated" from the *Treatise* prior to its publication (HL 1:25; HL 1:106, 111).

9. It may be argued that any effort to combine the (classical) empiricist-compatibilist strategy with the regularity theory of causation is problematic. More specifically, a regularity theory of causation, while it may avoid worries about compulsion or constraint involved in the causal relation, is neverthe-less an ontologically insufficient basis on which to ground the requirement that agents must be suitably connected or linked with action for them to be held responsible. On this criticism, see Russell 1988 and also Russell 1995: ch. 3.

10. See Russell 1995: ch. 1 for a brief review of these criticisms.

11. Strawson 2013 (1962). A number of important papers responding to Strawson's "Freedom and Resentment" can be found in McKenna and Russell 2008.

12. Some libertarians deny, of course, that they require any ("spooky") commit-ments of this kind. See, e.g., Kane 1996.

13. Wallace 1994: 39–40, 64–65.

14. Hume's specific argument to this effect is presented in a context in which he defends the claim that our natural abilities (e.g., wit, intelligence, imagina-tion, etc.) must also be deemed moral virtues or vices for which we are liable to praise and blame. We might well reject this specific claim concerning the

status of our natural abilities but still accept Hume's scepticism about the voluntary/involuntary distinction serving as the relevant boundary for moral responsibility. For a more detailed discussion of this, see Russell 1995: ch. 7 and also Russell 2013: 105–8.

15. See, e.g., Dennett 1984 for an assortment of arguments along these lines.
16. We might describe Hume's system, in this respect, as being a form of "Calvinism without God." (The same phrase was used by Eduard Bernstein to describe orthodox Marxism.)
17. In fairness to Strawson, it may be argued that he does provide some insight into the range of capacities involved. See, e.g., FR 75, where Strawson discusses the importance of "moral sense"; and also FR 77–78, where he describes aspects of moral development that are also relevant. Nevertheless, his remarks on this important issue are very slight.
18. On the significance of this vulnerability for Strawson's position, see Russell 1992.
19. Cp. Wallace 1994: 157–61, 181–85. See also Fischer and Ravizza 1998 for a similar theory.
20. Wallace 1994: 12–17.
21. See Russell 2004; and also Russell 2011 for further discussion of this issue in relation to the contemporary debate.
22. Botterill goes on to suggest that what Hume "was after was not a detailed account, but the basic necessary condition for responsibility," which is "that a person can only be responsible for what he does if his doing it is the result of an intentional state that can be attributed to him" (2002: 299). Botterill argues that this is "the essence of Hume's reconciling position on liberty and necessity" (ibid.). I have already argued that it is a mistake to read Hume as claiming that we are responsible only for our intentional, voluntary actions. I have also argued that if agents are to be held responsible for intentional actions, it is crucial on Hume's account that the actions be tied to (enduring) character traits, as otherwise no moral sentiments would be generated. To this we may add that Hume's most complete remarks about intention are found in the *Treatise*, in the context of his discussion of love and hate (T 2.2.3), and have no adequate counterpart in the *Enquiries*. On this see Russell 1995: 110–15.

11   Hume on Reason and Passion

Very few passages in Hume are better known or more often quoted than his declaration that "reason is, and ought only to be the slave of the passions, and can never pretend to any other office than to serve and obey them" (T 2.3.3.4, SBN 415).[1] This remark is often taken to epitomize his views not only on reason and motivation, but also (with just a bit more background) on reason and morality; indeed, Norman Kemp Smith (1941: 11) thought it provided the key to Hume's entire philosophy. It has been common to wonder about the role of the "ought only to be" in this manifesto,[2] but even if we dismiss that part of it as rhetorical flourish, I do not think this famous remark is well understood. Partly, I believe, this is because in some respects the claim really is opaque. It is very hard to find any doctrine that Hume affirms in the surrounding passage, or indeed anywhere in the *Treatise*, that it is plausible to take as a more literal rendering of the thesis that reason is slave to the passions (hereafter, RSP). In particular, one candidate often suggested – the so-called "Humean" view of motivation, the "belief-desire model" according to which motivation always depends ultimately on "passion," with beliefs functioning only to point the way to independently desired ends – suffers from the defect that Hume not only does not affirm it, but, as I shall argue, denies it. In the *Treatise*, I shall claim, it is not his view. So one of my conclusions in section 1 will be that there really is a problem about what Hume takes himself to mean by this famous slogan. Another will be that the most plausible explanation for Hume's rejecting this familiar account of motivation so often attributed to him is that he thinks that some desires, and therefore some actions, are motivated by reason rather than desire. Of course, this view conflicts with some other famous things he says, so it would be more plausible if we had a further argument for discounting those remarks.

The remainder of my discussion, in sections 2 and 3, will provide a further argument. Here I focus on a different reason why, in my view, Hume's remark is ill understood – namely, that there are some puzzles about it that *do* admit of resolution, and of a resolution that will advance our understanding of Hume but which are almost never noticed. Here is an example. Hume says that our reason is slave to our passions, but I have not been able to find anyone who calls explicit attention to the fact that, only a little over a page later, he declares just as emphatically that the reverse is true, that our passions are entirely subservient to our reason.[3] Here is the passage:

> Since a passion can never, in any sense, be call'd unreasonable, but when founded on a false supposition, or when it chooses means insufficient for the design'd end, 'tis impossible, that reason and passion can ever oppose each other, or dispute for the government of the will and actions. The moment we perceive the falshood of any supposition, or the insufficiency of any means[,] our passions yield to our reason without any opposition. (T 2.3.3.7, SBN 416)

Now, a natural first thought is that Hume must have switched to a different account of reason (or, as the quotation suggests, to a different sense of "reason") somewhere within the page between the earlier passage and this one. I believe this is correct. But this in itself is a noteworthy point, for Hume does not advertise any such shift, and commentators have generally not called attention to it. All that Hume advertises, in this Section on "the influencing motives of the will," is a contrast between *two* senses of "reason." There is a strict and philosophical sense insisted on at the beginning of the Section, in which reason does not conflict with the passions because it is slave to them (T 2.3.3.4, SBN 415). And there is an "improper sense," alluded to near the beginning of the Section and then explained in its final paragraphs, in which the calm passions count as reasonable, and conflict between reason and passion – that is, between the calm and the violent passions – is therefore possible (T 2.3.3.4, 8–10, SBN 415, 417–18).[4] But the notion of reason at work in the passage just quoted, midway through the Section, appears to be neither of these. For, as Hume presents it, it reverses the relation of subservience between reason and passion established by the former, making reason superior, but it does so without allowing for the conflict between them permitted by the latter. So Hume must be considering not just two but *three* different notions of reason in succession here, of which only the first is "strict and philosophi[cal]" (T 2.3.3.4, SBN 415). I have not found any commentators who emphasize this simple point about the structure of Hume's discussion. I intend to show that it is a point worth exploring.

For, when Hume's discussion is read with this structure in view, it quickly becomes apparent that, of the three accounts of practical rationality he considers, the philosophical interest resides entirely in the two he calls "improper"; and there are clear indications that, despite his dismissive language, he is aware of this. The only account he gives that seems devoid of philosophical interest is the one he labels "strict and philosophical," according to which reasonableness just consists in being a certain sort of true representation and unreasonableness in being a false one, with the consequence that only beliefs, and not passions, volitions, or actions, can be either reasonable or unreasonable. The other two accounts deserve rescuing. They need rescuing, however, because Hume's strategy is to denigrate them as nothing more than mistakes we might incautiously, if understandably, fall into. His official view of the judgments generated by either of these accounts is what J. L. Mackie has usefully called an "error theory" (1977: 35). Thus, he suggests, although only beliefs and not passions are strictly speaking reasonable, we might slide into calling a passion reasonable when it is *causally related to* or *accompanied by* a reasonable belief (one kind of mistake) or when it *resembles* a reasonable belief in being a calm rather than a violent "perception" in the mind (the other kind of mistake). But both the views presented in this way, viewed at all sympathetically, are far more interesting than these characterizations would indicate; and, I mean to show, Hume knows this.

For part of this last point I claim no originality. For Hume lists prominently among the calm passions "the general appetite to good, and aversion to evil, consider'd merely as such" (T 2.3.3.8, SBN 417), meaning by this a general desire for one's own pleasure together with an aversion to pain (T 2.1.1.4, 2.3.1.1, 2.3.9.8, SBN 276, 399, 439). And it has also not gone unnoticed – partly because Hume eventually calls attention to the point himself (T 3.1.2.1, 3.3.1.18, SBN 470, 583) – that the *moral* sentiment he says constitutes our admiration or blame for any character or action also falls among the calm passions. So Hume recognizes *one* account of reason on which a version of what Butler calls self-love – a desire for one's "greatest pleasure" – is intrinsically rational (XI.15, [1726] 2006: 115). And on that same account, despite all of Hume's explicit attacks on moral rationalism, morality turns out to be founded on reason as well. These implications embody what I shall call "motivational rationalism," the view that reason sets or constrains our ends; and they make that account of practical reason look like an interesting one, especially in Hume's naturalizing hands, as a number of commentators have noted.

But can we suppose that Hume himself thought this account at all plausible? There are two obvious and related obstacles to our doing so. One of course is that Hume denigrates this view as a mistake each of the first several times he mentions it (T 2.3.3.8–10, 2.3.8.13, 3.2.7.5, SBN 417–18, 437–38, 536). The other is that, as he initially presents it, it clearly *is* a mistake, for on no plausible view do desires become rational simply by being calm. No philosopher who found promise in the view Hume introduces under this banner would find it in his repeated official suggestion that the passions in question are to be identified just by their phenomenological calmness (T 2.1.1.3, 2.3.3.8–9, 2.3.8.13, SBN 276, 417–18, 437–38) or by their tendency to "produce little emotion in the mind" (T 2.3.3.8, SBN 417; cf. T 2.3.8.13, SBN 437). They would likely find it instead in passages in which Hume characterizes the calm passions as those "founded on some distant view or reflection" (T 3.3.1.18, SBN 583) – or, at any rate, as ones especially amenable to being "corroborated by reflection" (T 2.3.8.13, SBN 437) from such a perspective – and would understand him there to be spelling out a rational requirement of impartiality or objectivity on our motives. They would thus discount Hume's denigration of the position partly by reconstruing it so as to remove the grounds for the denigration. Of course, they could claim some textual support in Hume for this project. But since they would also have to ignore his official characterization of the position in question as well as some of his examples,[5] and would have to discount his official criticism of it, could they really still claim to be interpreting rather than merely criticizing Hume or spinning alternative theories under his inspiration?

I am not alone in thinking that, with proper cautions, the answer is yes, but I shall add two arguments to the others that might be given for this answer.[6] My arguments are largely indirect, for neither requires saying much more than I already have about the calm passions or about the way in which they either provide rational ends for us or set rational constraints on our ends. Both aim instead mainly to provide reasons for discounting Hume's repeated *dismissals* of the view that there is something rational about the calm passions. I shall argue in section 1 that the most plausible explanation for Hume's rejection of the belief-desire model of motivation is that he thinks of some desires and actions as motivated by reason. *That* motivation is not (or, at any rate, need not be) by the calm passions; but if this is Hume's view, then many of his antirationalist remarks, including ones that bear on the calm passions, have to be viewed with some suspicion. That is one argument. And my second argument, in sections 2 and 3, relies on what I have just said about the structure of Hume's discussion.

What I shall argue is this: that in interpreting Hume's *second* error theory (that passions are rational when calm) in the general manner I have described, we discount no more of his text than is standardly and very reasonably done in interpreting his *first* error theory (that passions are reasonable when accompanied by, or causally related to, a reasonable belief). For behind that first view too there lie at least one, and perhaps two, philosophically interesting accounts of practical reason. One of these is the "instrumentalist view" most commonly thought of as Hume's, that reasonableness is nothing but efficiency in the pursuit of one's ends. The other is a simple version of what Derek Parfit (1984: 118) has called the "deliberative" view, according to which passions are reasonable just to the extent that they are founded on reasonable beliefs.[7] (Call this the "foundation view.") I believe that writers who attribute one or the other of these views to Hume, on the basis of his presentation of what I am calling his first error theory (T 2.3.3.6–7, SBN 416–17), are not entirely mistaken to do so. But I also believe that they should notice, as they frequently do not, how much of Hume's presentation they are then required to discount. For they must ignore his calling the view he is presenting a mistake every time he describes it. *As* he describes it, moreover, it surely *is* a mistake and is not either of the more plausible views they want to find in him. That passions are reasonable whenever accompanied by or causally related to a reasonable belief is no more either the instrumental theory or the foundation theory than the view that passions are reasonable when tranquil is the theory that reason requires distance or impartiality. So they must determinedly set to one side many details of Hume's formulation as well. Having followed my argument this far, they might, of course, change their minds and conclude that Hume is not, after all, either an instrumentalist or a foundation theorist about practical reason.[8] The burden of my section 3, however, will be to argue, on the basis of details in Hume's discussion whose import is often overlooked, that there remains a reasonable case for interpreting him, cautiously, as committed to one of these views. But then, I shall conclude, this must be a reasonable strategy of interpretation on behalf of *both* the error theories he puts forward – the calm passion view as well as instrumentalism or the foundation theory.

About the "Humean theory of motivation," then – the belief-desire model – my conclusion will be that Hume does not hold it and that it is on that account an unpromising candidate to serve as RSP. About what is sometimes called the "Humean theory of practical reason" – the instrumental theory – my conclusion will be less iconoclastic. Despite the obstacles he places in the way of attributing it to him, there is a case for doing so; though, because of his rejection of the belief-desire model, one has to be careful about how to formulate it. But, as I shall argue, this case is balanced not only by one for attributing to him the not-quite-equivalent foundation theory, but also, and more importantly, for attributing to him a competing account, the "calm passions" account, on which our ends as well as our means are subject to rational assessment. And of course his *official* view still appears to be the "strict and philosophical" one, according to which neither our ends nor our means are subject to such assessment. His view is too complex for any of these positions to deserve to be called "the" Humean theory of practical rationality, but I shall argue that motivational rationalism has *at least* as strong a claim to that title as its competitors.

I

To begin with, then, what does Hume mean by RSP, the claim that reason is slave to the passions? It is not too difficult, I believe, to see what he must mean by the claim with which he introduces RSP – and which he appears to want to base on it – that "we speak not strictly and philosophically when we talk of the combat of passion and of reason" (T 2.3.3.4, SBN 415). The problem comes in seeing how RSP and this "No Combat" thesis are supposed to be connected. Passions are incapable of being either true or, more importantly, false copies "of any other existence or modification" (T 2.3.3.5, SBN 415). But since reasonableness in the strict and philosophical sense consists simply in being this sort of true representation and unreasonableness in being a false one,[9] this means that passions are neither reasonable nor unreasonable. A passion in combat with reason, however, would have to be an unreasonable passion; so there must be no such combat. This argument, though based on an account of reasonableness and unreasonableness that is wrong even for beliefs, is straightforward enough and gives us some idea what its conclusion, the No Combat thesis, is supposed at this juncture to mean: no motivational struggle, whatever its origins or outcome, *could* count as a conflict between passion and reason. But it leaves it entirely unclear how the No Combat thesis is supposed to depend on reason's being slave to the passions: What could this latter thesis be supposed to *mean* that would leave the two claims related as Hume suggests?

Now, the argument I just stated is not Hume's first for either of these two claims; it is one he adds to confirm them "by some other considerations" (T 2.3.3.4, SBN 415). And a reader may think (as I once did myself) that we would already have seen what these two claims are supposed to mean and how they are supposed to be related, if we had begun instead at the beginning with Hume's first argument for the No Combat thesis (T 2.3.3.3-4, SBN 414-15). For here he appears to rely only on a thesis about the limited role in motivation of beliefs arrived at by reasoning (call these "reasoned beliefs"),[10] which on the usual reading amounts to this: the only role of such beliefs, no matter how reasonable they may be, in the production of passions, volitions, or actions is to *extend* the effect of one's other passions (and in particular of one's other "propensit[ies]" and "aversion[s]"). In the familiar paradigm, if I desire a certain end and reason that an action open to me would secure that end, then my belief may give rise to a propensity toward that action, to a volition to perform it, and ultimately to the action itself. These effects might be prevented, on the other hand, if I thought that the action would have some other consequence, to which I had a strong enough aversion. But neither reasoned belief could either produce or prevent any of these things in the absence of the original aversion or propensity. That is why reason is "slave" to the passions: the beliefs it produces motivate only in their service. It does then follow, moreover, that reason and passion cannot conflict if that is understood to mean (now) that no reasoned belief could ever by *itself* block the motivational effect of a passion; though, of course, a reasoned belief in the service of some other passion might do so.

But this familiar account, which I shall continue to call the "belief-desire model" of motivation, faces several problems as a reading of Hume. One is that it appears not to depend on his strict and philosophical view of reason, though his statement of his conclusion (that it is only in an "improper sense" [T 2.3.3.4, SBN 415] that reason can be said to oppose passion) suggests that it is supposed to.[11] I shall pass this problem by, however, in order to focus on one of a different order, which is that in the *Treatise*, at any rate, Hume appears not to accept this account of motivation. In fact, as I shall now argue, on the most plausible reading, he repeatedly, and systematically, rejects it.[12]

This familiar account of motivation is supposed to be found, for example, in the third paragraph of the Section "Of the influencing motives of the will." But consider what Hume actually says.

'Tis obvious, that when we have the prospect of pain or pleasure from any object, we feel a consequent emotion of aversion or propensity, and are carry'd to avoid or embrace what will give us this uneasiness or satisfaction. (T 2.3.3.3, SBN 414)

The *prospect* of pleasure or pain, however, is surely a *belief* that pleasure or pain is somehow to be had, and any prediction of this sort will for Hume have to be arrived at by causal reasoning.[13] So it is a reasoned belief, not a passion, that begins the process Hume is describing, by giving rise to an aversion or propensity. If this is a slip, moreover, it is at least a persistent one; for four sentences later Hume says it again.

'Tis from the prospect of pain or pleasure that the aversion or propensity arises towards any object: And these emotions extend themselves to the causes and effects of that object, as they are pointed out to us by reason and experience. (T 2.3.3.3, SBN 414)

Much of the rest of the paragraph, on the other hand, at least appears to suggest the familiar belief-desire account (which would surely otherwise not have become so familiar).[14] And as will become clear, I am not denying that Hume thinks that account correct for many cases. So what should we think?

It may be tempting to dismiss these passages as just careless expression. After all, we *do* have to dismiss as misleading their suggestion that Hume's theory of motivation is entirely hedonistic, because it is not. But I believe we should take him at his word. My reasons are in the first instance textual. I shall show that Hume explicitly recognizes this sort of counterexample to the belief-desire account every time he summarizes his theory of motivation and, further, that the exceptions fall exactly where one would expect them to, in light of his repeated general characterization of the "direct passions," which include desire and aversion. One passage that might appear to threaten my view, moreover, can be shown on a close reading to support it. Of course, even faced with this evidence, we also want to know whether Hume's exceptions make any philosophical sense, and I shall show how they might.

(1) Each time Hume summarizes the ways in which passions may be founded on mistaken beliefs (T 2.3.3.6–7, 3.1.1.12, 3.1.1.16, SBN 416–17, 459–60, 462), he carefully distinguishes *two* cases: the first designed mainly to accommodate the sort of case we have just noted, in which it is a *belief* about pleasure or pain that initially gives rise to an aversion or propensity; and the second, by contrast, designed to cover cases that conform to the more familiar account. This contrast is clearest in a later Section of the *Treatise*. Reason influences our conduct, he says:

Either when it excites a passion by informing us of the existence of something which is a proper object of it; *or* when it discovers the connexion of causes and effects, so as to afford us means of exerting any passion. (T 3.1.1.12, SBN 459; emphasis added)

Here the second alternative fits the belief-desire account: a belief about causes and effects allows a desire for an end to be extended to what we take to be the means. But note the sort of example Hume gives of the contrasting case, in which the false belief involved is *not* said to be about the means to a desired end, but instead to be about the "proper object" of some passion:

A person may be affected with passion, by supposing a pain or pleasure to lie in an object, which has no tendency to produce either of these sensations, or which produces the contrary to what is imagin'd. (T 3.1.1.12, SBN 459)

And the same contrast, though explained far less clearly, receives a corresponding illustration in the earlier Section on the "influencing motives of the will." A passion may be "founded on the supposition of the existence of objects, which really do not exist"; this Hume contrasts with the case in which "we choose means insufficient for the design'd end, and deceive ourselves in our judgment of causes and effects" (T 2.3.3.6, SBN 416). This second case, again, clearly fits the familiar belief-desire account in which, as Hume repeats, we "will the performance of certain actions as means of obtaining any desir'd good" (T 2.3.3.7, SBN 417). But the description of the first case, with which the second is contrasted, is certainly opaque. Nor would Hume's illustration of the first case be of much help if we could not compare it with his other explanations of the same distinction. "I may," he says,

desire any fruit as of an excellent relish; but whenever you convince me of my mistake, my longing ceases. (T 2.3.3.7, SBN 416–17)

For how does this *contrast* with the second case? How is it not a mistake about the means to a "desir'd" good – for example, that biting into the fruit would be a way of obtaining that "excellent relish"? The answer, I suggest, depends on its being a belief, once again, about a "prospect of" pleasure. That is what is special about it and what keeps it from fitting the familiar account.[15] Hume does not take such beliefs to be about the means to a *desired* end because, remarkable as this may seem, he is not here thinking of the end as desired. That is why in his third brief summary he describes these beliefs as "prompting" passion rather than "directing" it (T 3.1.1.16, SBN 462): they produce a desire for something seen as a means, all right, but not because of any desire for the end. In all these passages, what Hume is very carefully avoiding ascribing to us is a desire for pleasure or an aversion to pain.[16]

(2) Exceptions on this pattern to the belief-desire model will appear less of an anomaly in Hume's theory if one notices that they can be seen simply as the application of a thesis he affirms several times in the *Treatise*, about the special relation of certain passions to pleasure and pain. The passions that may be called unreasonable, when "founded on the supposition of the existence of objects, which really do not exist," he says, are ones "such as hope or fear, grief or joy, despair or security" (T 2.3.3.6, SBN 416). These are not random examples, for these three pairs, along with desire and aversion (themselves obviously the main topic of this passage) make up Hume's usual list of the "direct passions" – passions distinguished precisely by the fact that they "arise immediately from good or evil, from pain or pleasure" (T 2.1.1.4, 2.3.1.1, 2.3.9.2, 3.3.1.2, SBN 276–77, 399, 438, 574).[17] In this formulation he clearly means, moreover, that these passions typically arise immediately, not from the experience of pain and pleasure but from their "prospect." He says, for example,[18] in one of his explanations of what is special about these passions, that

the mind by an *original* instinct tends to unite itself with the good, and to avoid the evil, *tho' they be conceiv'd merely in idea, and be consider'd as to exist in any future period of time.* (T 2.3.9.2, SBN 438; emphasis in final clause added)

So we have, in this repeated characterization of the direct passions, a powerful reason, quite independent of the evidence I cited above, for expecting that when Hume speaks of the "suppositions" on which *these* passions are founded, he means, always, suppositions about pleasure or pain.[19] And we also have less reason to be surprised when it turns out, as I have shown that it does, that perceived sources of pleasure and pain are the "proper objects" of these passions, in the sense that we need be attributed (for example) no desire for pleasure or aversion to pain to explain why the prospect of pleasure or pain should move us.[20]

(3) The textual evidence that Hume does not, in the *Treatise*, accept the belief-desire model of motivation usually ascribed to him is thus very strong; and the exceptions he allows fit nicely with a point he emphasizes about some of the direct passions. But do they make philosophical sense? There is one clear way in which they might and another that might explain at least part of his view on this issue.

(a) One possibility that comes to mind, of course, is that Hume thinks no desire for pleasure or aversion to pain is necessary for motivation by the prospect of pleasure or pain because it is *rational* to pursue one's own pleasure (which he regularly identifies, remember, with one's own good [T 2.1.1.4, 2.3.1.1, 2.3.9.8, SBN 276, 399, 439]) and to avoid pain (or evil) and that in such cases reason can set us on the pursuit of an end whether or not we desire it. This reading would further specify the sense in which an object that provides pleasure is a "proper object" of desire: not just that the prospect of pleasure can arouse desire for the pleasant object, without our needing a desire for pleasure, but also that it is rational for it to have this effect. It is a reading Hume invites, moreover, by so frequently appearing to assume, throughout his discussion of reason and passion, that these exhaust the possible sources of motivation.[21] For if that is so and if it is not passion that makes pleasure our end, then it must be reason that does so. And he invites it in a different way in the one passage in which he does acknowledge a third possibility. For he says about some of the direct passions – those not on his usual list – that they arise, not from reason and not from some (further) passion, but rather from "a natural impulse or instinct, which is perfectly unaccountable" (T 2.3.9.8, SBN 439). Part of the point of that very passage, however, is explicitly to *contrast* these unaccountable passions with those said to arise from "good and evil, or in other words, pain and pleasure." So these latter passions are *not* among the unaccountable ones, and we have seen that they are not due to any further passion, either; so, of the alternatives Hume mentions, that still leaves reason as the only alternative.[22]

Of course this is not what he says. And it appears to conflict with his claims, in passages immediately surrounding several I have just cited, that reason alone never motivates (T 2.3.3.1, SBN 413), that no pursuit is ever strictly speaking rational (T 2.3.3.4–5, 3.1.1.9–10, SBN 415, 458), and that there is no irrationality in knowingly choosing against one's own good (T 2.3.3.6, SBN 416). These considerations against this first suggestion are not decisive, for, as I have indicated, I shall show that there are strong independent reasons anyway for taking these claims about practical reason at less than face value. But since the full defense of this suggestion will depend on the argument of my next section, let me briefly turn to an alternate possibility – one that I think fails instructively as an explanation of the evidence considered so far, but which will nevertheless help illuminate an important feature of Hume's view.

(b) For at least part of Hume's view could be accounted for if he could be supposed to have learned a psychological lesson from his correspondent Francis Hutcheson. In Section I of *Illustrations on the Moral Sense*, Hutcheson qualifies a view of motivation many have thought very similar to Hume's, with a warning against

a mistake some fall into. They suppose, because they have formed some conception of an infinite good, or greatest possible aggregate, or sum of happiness, under which all particular pleasures may be included, that there is also some one great ultimate end with a view to which every particular pleasure is desired without farther view as an ultimate end in the selfish desires. It is true, the prospect of a greater inconsistent pleasure may surmount or stop this desire; so may the fear of a prepollent evil. But this does not prove 'that all men have formed ideas of infinite good, or greatest possible aggregate, or that they have an instinct or desire actually operating without an idea of its object.' ([1728] 1971: 124)

This passage suggests a reasonable argument, with which we may suppose Hume to have been acquainted, against supposing that people who choose pleasures over pains, and greater pleasures over lesser ones, are necessarily being motivated, when they so choose, by a desire for their maximum possible pleasure.[23] Of the points Hutcheson suggests, the most important for our purposes is this: that it requires some intellectual sophistication even to form the *idea* of such a "greatest possible aggregate,"[24] and we do not want to say that people are motivated by a desire for a goal of which they can form no conception. People without such a conception may have some tendency to forego pains for pleasures and lesser pleasures for greater ones, but this remains in them an underived disposition, not to be explained as the effect of a desire for the goal toward which it in fact propels them.

So we may take Hume to have been familiar with a good reason to deny that whenever anyone is motivated by a "prospect of pleasure," this is because she has a *general* desire for pleasure, a desire for as much pleasure as possible; and I shall point out below a way in which he acknowledges this point. Hutcheson, however, clearly takes the alternative to be that people are motivated by desires for *particular* pleasures, and Hume in the passages I have cited is careful not to appeal even to these. Why? Here I see no further help from this second suggestion.

The only serious alternative I can see to propose is the one I have mentioned under (a) above – a fact I take to lend that alternative significant support.

(4) One challenge is sure to be raised to my claim that Hume abandons the familiar belief-desire model for cases in which people are motivated by a "prospect of pleasure" and hence also to my search for an explanation of his doing so. For does Hume not at least once, in the very Section of the *Treatise* on which I have been focusing, *explicitly* ascribe to people a general desire for pleasure and aversion to pain of just the sort that would be needed to bring their pursuit of pleasure and avoidance of pain under the belief-desire account?

My answer is that he does, but that he does so with qualifications that support rather than undermine my reading of him. For he does not ascribe this desire to everyone. He is discussing, in a passage to which I have already referred, those "calm desires and tendencies, which, tho' they be real passions, produce little emotion in the mind" and which in consequence are often "confounded with reason by all those, who judge of things from the first view and appearance." And he offers the following list.

These desires are of two kinds; either certain instincts originally implanted in our natures, such as benevolence and resentment, the love of life, and kindness to children; or the general appetite to good, and aversion to evil, consider'd merely as such. (T 2.3.3.8, SBN 417)

"Good" and "evil," once again, are just pleasure and pain, so this last "calm passion" is, to be sure, a general desire for pleasure and aversion to pain. But notice that Hume says that these calm passions are of "two kinds." He does not say what is distinctive about the second kind, of which this general desire is his only example. But he says that the first kind are "instincts originally implanted in our natures"; and because there is supposed to be a contrast, I think we may take it that this general desire is *not* an instinct "originally implanted in our natures."[25] Presumably, then, it has to be acquired. And, plausibly, part of the reason for that, even if not for Hume's more general view about motivation by the prospect of pleasure or pain, is the one Hutcheson gives: that it requires some intellectual sophistication even to form the *ideas* of such abstract and general objects as pleasure and pain, "consider'd merely as such."[26] A similar but more distinctively Humean reason, moreover, concerns the role that we learn elsewhere in the *Treatise* this calm appetite for good and aversion to evil is supposed to play. For, by providing a psychological "distance" from anticipated pleasures and pains, it is supposed (for example) to counteract our natural tendency to prefer the near but lesser good to the remote but greater (T 3.2.7.2–5, SBN 534–36). This too is an accomplishment not to be attributed to everyone.[27]

Whatever the reason, however, what is clear is that we again find Hume carefully *not* ascribing to everyone a desire for pleasure or an aversion to pain; indeed, carefully contrasting these motives with those calm passions that he does attribute to persons generally as "instincts originally implanted" in their natures.[28] But, as we have seen, he includes no similar restriction in his attribution to people of a susceptibility to motivation merely by the prospect of pleasure and pain. So there is no reason to think that his ascription to (some) people of this calm passion is intended in any way to retract his view that the prospect of pleasure can motivate, whether or not we desire pleasure.[29]

So far, then, I have argued for two conclusions. One is that there is no doctrine about motivation that Hume advances in the *Treatise* that can plausibly be identified with RSP, the thesis that reason is slave to the passions. (Still less can I find any that depends, as Hume suggests this one should, on his "strict and philosophical" account of reason.) The most popular candidate, the familiar "belief-desire" account often referred to as the "Humean" theory of motivation, I have argued to be a view he repeatedly and systematically *rejects* for some cases.

Second, I have suggested that Hume's rationale in allowing exceptions to the belief-desire model is that he takes motivation by the prospect of pain or pleasure to be motivation by reason. He repeatedly identifies pleasure with the good and pain with evil, and, like many philosophers before and since, he takes our conscious tendency to pursue good and avoid evil to be a rational one. Unlike my first conclusion, this one flies in the face of some famous things Hume says, so my defense of it so far will be usefully supplemented when I display in my next section some additional reasons for taking those famous remarks at less than face value. At the same time, I have already offered serious reasons for my heterodox reading of Hume as a motivational rationalist, and they ought to have prepared the reader for the arguments to come. So these two portions of my argument should prove mutually supporting.

A careful reader might doubt in advance that this could be so, on the grounds that even if my two arguments are independently plausible, they will leave me with an embarrassment of riches. For I have already argued that Hume regards all motivation by the prospect of good and evil as rational, and I have promised to argue next that he regards motivation by such calm passions as "the general appetite to good, and aversion to evil, consider'd merely as such," as rational too. But I have *also* just argued that he refuses to identify these two sources of motivation, because he regards motivation by the prospect of pleasure and pain as ubiquitous but attributes motivation by the calm passions only to some people some of the time. And, the objection asks, if Hume were serious about attributing motivation to reason rather than passion, would he not have proposed a more unified account of rational motivation than the one I am pretending to uncover?

I think not. For, if one is able to bracket for a moment doubts about the portrayal of Hume as *any* sort of rationalist about motivation, then it is not hard to see how to unify the account. The view would be this. Any desire aroused by a prospect of good or aversion aroused by a prospect of evil counts as to that extent rational, just because of the nature of its object. But such desires may still be quite haphazard, in ways Hume catalogs: from comparison (T 2.2.8.2–3, 3.3.2.4, SBN 372, 593) or proximity (T 3.2.7.2–5, SBN 534–36) or other misadventures of the imagination, desires rational in this sense may nevertheless bear a relative strength all out of proportion to the value of their objects. "A trivial good may, from certain circumstances, produce a desire superior to what arises from the greatest and most valuable enjoyment" (T 2.3.3.6, SBN 416). The rational cure for *this* difficulty consists in achieving that "distant view or reflection" (T 3.3.1.18, SBN 583; cf. T 3.2.7.5, SBN 536) that is characteristic of the calm passions we are said to confuse with reason and that allows us to "give the preference to whatever is in itself preferable" (T 3.2.7.5, SBN 536). So there will be different levels and degrees of practical rationality, intelligibly related, and the accounts I am claiming Hume offers of them are in turn related just about as one would expect.

2

I now turn to my second argument, which is that the structure of Hume's discussion suggests that he puts greater store by the rationality of the calm passions than many of his official, and dismissive, remarks would suggest. Already I must modify one thing I have said about this structure. I argued above that when Hume says that our passions are subject to our reason, he must already be referring to reason in some sense other than his "strict and philosophical" one, on the ground that reason in the strict sense is supposed to be slave to the passions rather than a victor over them. We have just seen, however, that whatever Hume may mean by his thesis that reason is slave to the passions, it does *not* depend in any discernible way on his strict account of reason. Though my first argument must be rejected, however, I am sure the conclusion is correct, that Hume is no longer relying on his strict account of reason and reasonableness when he says that our passions always yield to our reason. I shall begin by establishing this point.

It is a point that Hume does his best to obscure. Immediately after having argued that actions, passions, and volitions can be neither reasonable nor unreasonable, in the strict sense, because they can be neither true nor false, he makes the following transition to the passage in which he says that our passions are subject to our reason.

What may at first occur on this head, is, that as nothing can be contrary to truth or reason, except what has a reference to it, and as the judgments of our understanding only have this reference, it must follow, that passions can be contrary to reason only so far as they are *accompany'd* with some judgment or opinion. (T 2.3.3.6, SBN 415–16)

But, of course, no such thing follows. All that *follows* is that, in the sense of "contrary to reason" that Hume has been employing to this point, passions cannot be contrary to reason at all. Nothing follows about any *other* sense in which they *can* be unreasonable. If there is such a sense, it must be one that Hume is here introducing and explaining for the first time.

And I believe it is obvious, both that this *is* what he is doing and that his explanation consists in tracing this new sense of the term to a confusion – actually, to any of several related confusions. Our reasoned beliefs really are, in the strict sense, reasonable and unreasonable: reasonable when true, unreasonable when false. Through carelessness we extend these epithets from the beliefs to which they strictly apply to those passions and actions to which they bear some salient relation. Hume initially says twice, as in the following summary of the paragraph just quoted, that what is required for the mistake to occur is just that the belief *accompany* the passion:

In short, a passion must be accompany'd with some false judgment, in order to its being unreasonable; and even then 'tis not the passion, properly speaking, which is unreasonable, but the judgment. (T 2.3.3.6, SBN 416)

He suggests in this same passage that one way for a judgment to "accompany" a passion is for the passion to be founded on it; but when he recurs to this topic in his later discussion of reason and morality, it appears that the judgment need not accompany the passion at all for the mistake to occur, so long as the two stand in some causal relation. He there considers the suggestion that, although no "will or action" may be "contradictory to reason" in the strict sense,

yet we may find such a contradiction in some of the attendants of the action, that is, in its causes or effects. The action may cause a judgment, or may be *obliquely* caus'd by one, when the judgment concurs with a passion; and by an abusive way of speaking, which philosophy will scarce allow of, the same contrariety may, upon that account, be ascrib'd to the action. (T 3.1.1.11, SBN 459)

To be sure, the "abusive way of speaking" Hume is contemplating here goes beyond any he describes elsewhere, by extending the epithet "unreasonable" not only to actions and passions *founded on* the agent's own unreasonable beliefs, but also to actions that *give rise* to unreasonable beliefs in others. That makes it a sillier view, based on a silly mistake that almost no one would make.[30] But it also makes clear that the former view, though based on a less silly mistake, derives nevertheless, according to Hume, from a mistake of the same general kind: that of extending the terms "reasonable" and "unreasonable" from items to which they strictly apply to other, related items to which they do not.[31]

So Hume has, as I alleged, two *different* "error theories" of practical reason, in addition to his "strict and philosophical" account, and in this Section on "the influencing motives of the will," he presents, and denigrates, them both. We call some passions reasonable, and others unreasonable, because they are *accompanied by* or are *causally related to* our reasonable or unreasonable beliefs. We also call the calm passions reasonable, whatever their accompaniments or causes, because they *resemble* our beliefs. And the former of these views, though less explicitly advertised, seems the more carefully worked out of the two, as an account of our mistake. For because the calm passions presumably resemble our calm, *un*reasonable beliefs as much as they do our calm, reasonable ones, the latter view does not really explain why we should slide into calling all these passions *reasonable*.

As I have indicated, this point alone is a sufficient basis for much of what I want to say in defense of my thesis that Hume takes motivational rationalism far more seriously than his official pronouncements suggest. For he certainly takes it seriously if he takes seriously the view that the calm passions are rational. He *appears* not to take the latter view seriously, because (1) he describes it as a mistake, and (2) as he describes it, it is a mistake. If resentment and kindness to children (to take two of his examples) are ever reasonable, this is not because they "produce little emotion in the mind" (T 2.3.3.8, SBN 417). But we have now seen that these same two points apply to a view many writers have *thought* Hume took very seriously indeed – the view that passions are unreasonable when and only when accompanied by or causally related to an unreasonable belief. He calls this a mistake, and as he describes it, it is: actions are not rendered unreasonable by causing unreasonable beliefs, nor (as we shall see) are they guaranteed reasonable when accompanied only by reasonable beliefs. Of course, many of Hume's *applications* of these views look quite plausible. A passion is unreasonable, he says, when it leads us to "choose means insufficient for the design'd end" or when it is founded on any unreasonable belief (T 2.3.3.6, SBN 416). These passages have led many to think Hume a proponent of an instrumental theory or else the foundation theory, views that are independently plausible.[32] But of course many of Hume's *applications* of the calm passions view look at least equally plausible. It is plausible, for example, that a preference for a lesser but near-future good, simply because it is nearer, is unreasonable (T 3.2.7.2–5, SBN 534–36) and also that moral appraisals are unreasonable unless made from a "steady and general" point of view (T 3.3.1.15–17, SBN 581–83). My conclusion, therefore, is that Hume takes these theses at least as seriously as he takes either the instrumental or the foundation view.

But how seriously is that? I may have discovered a problem for those who ignore Hume's denigration of the instrumental or the foundation view, only to take him at his word about the calm passions. But why not conclude that we should take him at his word about *both* error theories rather than (as I suggest) about neither?[33] Here my judgment is heavily influenced by a point I have alluded to: that when Hume *applies* these theories he represents as erroneous, in arguing for conclusions he cares about, he seems to be guided by plausible rather than obviously erroneous versions of them – even at a high cost in plausibility elsewhere in his views and even when either version might have secured his conclusion. To illustrate, I shall turn to an example I have had in view from the outset – namely, Hume's argument, based on his first error theory, that reason and passion never conflict because our passions always yield to our reason.

3

There can be no conflict between passion and reason, in Hume's *strict* sense of "reason," as we saw, because on that account no passion can be unreasonable and so in conflict with reason. Obviously, this argument is unavailable on his first error theory, because that *does* allow passions to be unreasonable when they are accompanied by or causally related to an unreasonable belief. So why does he take it to be an "evident" consequence of this view too that "'tis impossible, that reason and passion can ever oppose each other, or dispute for the government of the will and actions" (T 2.3.3.7, SBN 416)? I think the general idea is clear: it is that because there is, on this account, no unreasonableness in our passions *except* what is due to the unreasonableness of beliefs, and because reason is assumed to have the power to replace unreasonable beliefs with reasonable ones, reason must also have the power to produce reasonableness in our passions. But that still leaves crucial details to be filled in. It says nothing about why this effect on our passions, when we correct our beliefs, is always immediate, so fast as to count as "no dispute" between an unreasonable passion and a now-reasonable belief. And it does not say

which of the several possible versions of the first error theory is supposed to have this evident consequence. A look at the text, I shall now
suggest, shows that the version Hume is here relying on is a plausible
rather than an implausible one – even though an implausible, and so
more easily dismissed, version would have secured the same conclusion
about immediacy, and would have secured it (in a respect I shall explain)
at a lesser cost.

One version that I have mentioned, because Hume himself introduces
it elsewhere in deriding the theory as a mistake (T 3.1.1.12–16, SBN 459–62),
makes no appearance in this argument: my passions and actions are not
taken here to owe their unreasonableness to the unreasonableness of the
beliefs they cause in *others*.[34] What is more striking is that Hume also
avoids relying on a different version, which, unlike this one, certainly
would secure his No Combat conclusion and which does appear in this
passage. For suppose that all that made any passion unreasonable really
was just – as Hume says twice – its being *accompanied* by an unreasonable belief. Call this the "accompanying belief" account of reasonableness. It is a contrived view, easily represented as a mistake we might
fall into through carelessness; and it would certainly guarantee that the
replacement of an unreasonable accompanying belief by a reasonable one
would always, immediately, and without contest make the accompanied
passion a reasonable one as well. It would guarantee this because this
alteration in status would require *no change* in the passion.[35]

But that is not how Hume argues. He thinks that if combat between
reason and passion is to be avoided, when we correct unreasonable
beliefs, our passions are also required to change immediately. This is
clear from his examples.

The moment we perceive the falsehood of any supposition, or the insufficiency of
any means[,] our passions yield to our reason without any opposition. I may desire
any fruit as of an excellent relish; but whenever you convince me of my mistake,
my longing ceases. I may will the performance of certain actions as means of
obtaining any desir'd good; but as my willing of these actions is only secondary,
and founded on the supposition, that they are causes of the propos'd effect; as soon
as I discover the falsehood of that supposition, they must become indifferent to me.
(T 2.3.3.7, SBN 416–17)

Two points about this passage deserve comment. First, Hume is certainly
not relying on the accompanying belief account, which would rule out
combat between reason and passion in these cases, whether the passions
changed or not. The accompanying belief account seems in this respect
hardly a normative view, for although it provides us a way of labeling
passions as reasonable or unreasonable, it leaves reason no work to do
in making them reasonable, once our beliefs are in line. But Hume is

obviously relying on an account that is, by contrast, normative in at least this minimal sense, for it must be one that allows that *if* our desires did *not* change they *would* be unreasonable, despite our now-reasonable beliefs.[36] And it must also be one, therefore, that rules out combat between reason and passion only when conjoined with the strong psychological thesis that the requisite changes *always do* immediately take place.

That is one comment. And my second is that this strong psychological thesis, according to which the required changes always occur immediately, is implausibly optimistic about the rationality of our desires. Moreover, this is something that Hume says – or very nearly says – himself.

What account of reasonableness must Hume be relying on, then? I assume it must be either the foundation theory or the instrumental theory – one of the two that many have attributed to him, precisely on the basis of passages such as the one I just quoted. Now, one implication of the conclusion for which I argued in section 1, that Hume does not take all the beliefs in his examples to be about means to *desired* ends, is that there will be a complication in formulating a version of the instrumental view that could be ascribed to him: at the very least, it could not say that practical rationality consists in wanting or doing what is calculated to satisfy one's *desires*.[37] (For, recall, although the fruit is desired "as of an excellent relish," that is not because of a desire *for* the relish.) So, although I could illustrate my point using either the instrumental or the foundation theory, it is simpler to use the latter, and that is what I shall do here. According to that theory, any desire founded on an unreasonable belief is unreasonable. So if I were to desire that fruit for its relish and you were to "convince me of my mistake" but my longing were stubbornly to persist – because of the lingering influence of that unreasonable belief I have now abandoned – then my stubborn lingering desire would *be unreasonable* even though my current beliefs would not be. Reason and passion would thus be in conflict. That is the implication of the theory for such a case. Hume's response is to accept the implication of the theory but to deny that such a case ever occurs. Our desires never stubbornly linger, under the influence of thoughts we no longer credit.

But it is a commonplace that such cases occur, and Hume surely knows this. My objection could not be much better stated, in fact, than it is by Hume himself just a few pages later.[38]

Now, if we consider the human mind, we shall find, that with regard to the passions, 'tis not of the nature of a wind-instrument of music, which in running over all the notes immediately loses the sound after the breath ceases; but rather resembles a string-instrument, where after each stroke the vibrations still retain some sound, which gradually and insensibly decays. The imagination is extremely quick and agile; but the passions are slow and restive: For which reason, when any object is presented, that affords a variety of views to the one, and emotions to the other; tho' the fancy may change its views with great celerity; each stroke will not produce a clear and distinct note of passion, but the one passion will always be mixt and confounded with the other. (T 2.3.9.12, SBN 440–41)

Thus, as our views of an object change, our passions do *not* immediately follow suit, but sometimes linger even when the view on which the passion was based has disappeared.

I do not claim that Hume contradicts himself. In this passage he is explicitly confining his attention to cases of uncertainty in which optimistic and pessimistic views of a situation alternate, arousing hope and fear, each feeling lingering even as one's view shifts.[39] There is therefore room for him to claim, in response to the point I am now making, that confident belief differs from uncertainty precisely in eliminating this phenomenon.[40] But even if it is characteristic of beliefs to exercise *greater* control than do unconfident conjectures over feelings based on alternative (and so, in the case of belief, rejected) views, it is enormously implausible to claim that it eliminates them entirely. And I submit that if a writer as sensible and sensitive as Hume finds himself forced to say that it does, he must have been driven to do so by reasons he finds very compelling.

Part of his reason is clear. He hopes to show that he can derive the No Combat view from his first error theory of reason as well as from his "strict and philosophical" account. But *that* goal he could have achieved, without being forced to any dubious claims about the tractability of the passions, simply by relying on the accompanying belief version of that view: a version with the additional advantage, one would have thought, of making it obvious why his theory of judgments based on that account is an *error* theory, one that treats them as an expression of nothing more than a trick of the imagination in transferring epithets. Instead, he relies on a version that is independently plausible, interestingly normative, and far less obviously a mere mistake of the imagination; and it is that choice that then requires him to say, most implausibly, that the passions are like the notes of the woodwinds after all. No doubt some judgment is involved in deciding what Hume is claiming in any passage as complex as this one. But a reader could be forgiven for concluding, on this evidence, that Hume knows perfectly well which accounts of practical reason are independently plausible and that he argues as he does because he is *far more* concerned to show that he can derive his intended conclusion, the No Combat thesis, even from these plausible, normative accounts, than he is to argue that our entire habit of speaking of desires as reasonable and unreasonable is a mistake.

4

Obviously, my conclusion cannot be that Hume is, without qualification, a motivational rationalist. What I have just *argued*, after all, is that Hume takes much more seriously than his official pronouncements would indicate a view – either the foundation theory or the instrumental theory – that *denies* that our ends are subject to rational assessment. Indeed, I may need to remind the reader of how this helps my case. It does so because Hume officially and repeatedly denigrates these two views as mistakes, even silly mistakes, just as he does the view that the calm passions are rational; so if I can show that he recognizes them as plausible all the same, I strengthen my case that he also takes seriously some version of the calm passion view as well, in the passages where he appears to, and so finds it plausible that our ends are subject to rational assessment. Even if my argument is found convincing on these points, however, it still leaves the question of how these pieces fit together.

A rough comparison with Hume's discussion of inferences from experience in Book 1 of the *Treatise* may help. Many readers take Hume to be arguing on at least two different levels on that topic: on one, perhaps the deepest, he is a sceptic, but on another, he is interested in telling us how to make these inferences properly. When writers refer to "Hume's views" about such topics as causal inference, moreover, they are often talking about views he presents in this latter vein. It would suit many of my purposes in this paper if I had at least convinced a reader that the situation may be similar in his discussion of practical reason. Even if there is *a* level – that of his "strict and philosophical" account of reason – at which he denies that there is such a thing as practical reason at all, there is another at which he is deeply involved in laying out what practical rationality requires of us. And at that level it is at least as much "Hume's view" that reason requires distance and reflection as it is that it requires pursuing the means to one's chosen ends.

This comparison is imperfect in one way that challenges my case, but also in two others that may help it. (1) Hume seems to have a single account of how to reason from experience, but, when he is not being sceptical about practical reason, he appears to endorse conflicting accounts, only one of which allows for the rational assessment of ends. So more thought is needed about whether elements of these views can be fitted together into a consistent account plausibly attributed to him.[41] That is a problem. On the other hand, (2) I have provided strong evidence, quite apart from anything he says about the calm passions, that he regards motivation by the prospect of pleasure or pain as rational motivation, motivation by rational ends. This view seems built into his account of motivation, moreover, and is nowhere explained away as an error, as are his other accounts of practical reason, so it seems to be held on at least as deep a level as his "strict and philosophical" view. It may also provide help, therefore, in deciding which of his apparently conflicting remarks to take most seriously in addressing the difficulty I just mentioned. (3) Finally, it is difficult not to be struck by one contrast between his argument for scepticism about reasoning from experience and his argument that actions and passions are never either reasonable or unreasonable. The former argument is a philosophical masterpiece, fully meriting the attention philosophers continue to give it. His "strict and philosophical" account of reasonableness and unreasonableness, by contrast, is not worth taking seriously and properly receives almost no attention at all. As I have mentioned, its identification of reasonableness with truth and unreasonableness with falsity[42] is wrong even for beliefs. (The *challenge* Hume is typically credited with raising about practical reason is, instead, How can reason be more than instrumental? or How can we criticize actions and passions except by criticizing the beliefs on which they are based? But the "strict and philosophical" view denies, of course, that we can even get this far.[43]) It is a measure of my respect for Hume's intellect that I find it hard to believe that he took it very seriously either.[44]

NOTES

1. My interpretation is confined entirely to the *Treatise*; Hume's views on the topics I discuss appear to me to have changed a great deal in the second *Enquiry*.

2. Laird (1932: 203) apparently takes it to be about what we ought to *say* about reason (since to represent it otherwise is "mythical"). Mackie (1980: 45) follows Harrison (1976: 5) in taking it merely to deny that reason ought not to be slave to the passions. Baier (1980) speculates that Hume really means that (some) passions ought to control reason.

3. The most remarkable comment I have been able to find is in Harrison (1976: 8): "Hume supposed that, if only beliefs could be reasonable or unreasonable, it followed that reason was the slave of the passions, for the following reason." He then quotes the passage I here quote in the text – a passage, one should note, in which Hume (a) explicitly says that there *are* senses in which passions (as well as beliefs) can be unreasonable, and (b) concludes, *not* that our reason is slave to our passions, but rather that, in the circumstances he indicates, it always overcomes them.

Perhaps part of the reason for the general failure to remark on this shift is that Hume draws (verbally) the same conclusion in each passage: that *combat* between reason and passion is impossible. But it still does seem hard to miss that the reasons given in the two passages are, at least at the level of imagery, diametrically opposed. First, there is no contest because *reason* is impotent and passion always wins; a page later it is because *passion* immediately yields and reason always wins. Even if this is merely Hume being clever, cleverness on this order deserves notice.

4. At T 2.3.3.8–10, 2.3.4.1, and 2.3.8.13 (SBN 417–18, 419, 437–38), Hume says merely that there is a pervasive *mistake* of thinking the calm passions reasonable; but in his allusion at T 2.3.3.4 and 3.2.7.5 (SBN 415, 536), he indicates that this mistake creates an "improper sense" for the term "reason." (Of course, what makes any of Hume's "improper" senses improper has to be that the term is being applied, at bottom, in its *proper* sense but – by the standards of *that* sense – mistakenly.)

5. By this standard, for example, kindness to children (T 2.3.3.8, SBN 417) is *not* a calm passion; or, if it is calm (by a phenomenological standard), then Hume does not really think that we tend to confuse *all* the calm passions with reason. Except at T 2.3.3.8 (SBN 417), and also at T 2.3.8.13 (SBN 437) (where there are no examples), his examples of calm passions we call reasonable are all either of time-neutral prudence or some form of impartial approbation; and both are said to require achieving sufficient "distance" to overcome the distorting effects of perspective or context (T 2.2.8.2–3, 2.3.4.1, 3.1.2.2–4, 3.2.7.5, 3.3.1.15–18, 3.3.3.2, SBN 372, 419, 470–72, 536, 581–83, 603).

6. The most elaborate development of this view that I have seen is by Kydd (1946: ch. 5). I do not mean to endorse all of her speculations.

7. Parfit attributes a sophisticated version of this view to Brandt (1979).

8. Writers who have recently argued, with respect to at least one of these views, that Hume does not hold it, include Hampton 1995 and Millgram 1995. Both these authors rely, at least in part, on some of the considerations I shall mention in section 3.

9. Hume repeatedly equates "false," "unreasonable," and "contrary to reason," on the one hand, and "true," "reasonable," and "conformable to reason," on the other. For example: "In short, a passion must be accompany'd with some *false* judgment, in order to its being unreasonable; and even then 'tis not the passion, properly speaking, which is *unreasonable*, but the judgment" (T 2.3.3.6, SBN 416; emphasis added). But the qualification – that reasonableness is truth in the representation of "some other existence or modification" – is his own, and I have argued elsewhere (in Sturgeon 2001) that it matters for some purposes. It does not affect my argument in this paper, however.

10. The qualification is once again Hume's: he is talking about beliefs arrived at by reasoning either about relations of ideas (T 2.3.3.2, SBN 413–14) or about causes and effects (T 2.3.3.3, SBN 414). Even when they have noticed this qualification, commentators have tended to dismiss it, as Harrison does, on the grounds that "it is most implausible to suggest that how a belief is arrived at makes any difference to whether or not it moves us to action" (1976: 12) and thus to take Hume's claims to concern *all* beliefs. But I have argued (in Sturgeon 2001) that the qualification is important, for Hume means to allow that some beliefs *not* arrived at by reasoning *can* motivate by themselves. He means to allow this, in my view, about the noninferential belief that one *is having* a certain passion – for he takes such a belief to be identical

to the passion itself. (Though since the belief is entirely self-referential, its truth does not make the passion reasonable according to the qualification I have noted in the preceding note.) That is why beliefs about virtue and vice, if they are simply beliefs that one is having certain feelings (T 3.1.1.26, SBN 468–69), can motivate by themselves, even though reason cannot motivate by itself.

If I am right about this, it follows that Hume *already* allows what will on some formulations of it be exceptions to the belief-desire account. For he allows that beliefs can motivate by themselves – though not that they can motivate in the absence of passion, for the beliefs that can do this *are* passions. The exceptions to which I call attention in *this* paper, however, are very different, and my argument that Hume allows them in no way depends on the argument of that other paper. What I argue here is that Hume repeatedly allows that some *reasoned* beliefs can motivate, entirely in the absence of passion.

11. And a closely related difficulty is that this account makes it hard to see how Hume's second argument – the first I considered, which clearly *does* rely on that strict and philosophical view – is supposed to be an argument for the *same* conclusion, confirming it by "some other considerations." The No Combat thesis seems to have changed meaning between the two arguments: for the first argument implies nothing about whether passions can be reasonable, the second nothing about whether reasoned beliefs can, by themselves, motivate.

12. Some of the evidence I cite in my points (1) and (2), below, is also noticed by Kydd (1946: 103–10). She notes, correctly, that Hume thinks that "[t]he judgment that 'This apple is ripe' can affect my conduct independently of any prior desire to eat an apple of this kind" (1946: 103) and adds, also correctly, that "the fact that Hume allows that judgements can have this sort of influence is, prima facie, very surprising" (1946: 104). But she also thinks, for reasons I criticize below (note 17), that these claims can be reconciled with Hume's version of the belief-desire model.

13. Or at least – to use the term Hume himself prefers throughout his discussions of reason and passion at T 2.3.3.2–7 and 3.1.1.12–16 (SBN 413–17, 459–62) – it is a judgment, something capable of a truth-value. Almost nothing in my discussion depends on whether these all count as beliefs in Hume's somewhat special sense (T 1.3.7); but see note 40.

14. The very next sentence, for example, says:

It can never in the least concern us to know, that such objects are causes, and such others effects, if both the causes and effects be indifferent to us. (T 2.3.3.3, SBN 414)

And this of course sounds like the familiar view, *if* we assume (a) that "objects" here include pleasure and pain, not just the "objects" Hume speaks of as affording a prospect of these experiences, and (b) that what it takes for an object not to be "indifferent" to us is that we have an emotion of propensity or aversion toward it. (On the basis of my argument in this section, I would doubt at least that assumption (a) is correct, but I agree that it is a natural assumption if one has not focused on the difficulties I am calling attention to here.)

15. It also helps explain why Hume describes it as a mistake about the *existence* of something even though it is merely about what sensations the fruit has a "tendency to produce." (That it is not a mistake about the existence of the *fruit* is clear when Hume repeats the example [T 3.1.1.12, SBN 460].) As we have seen, Hume speaks of all beliefs about sources of pleasure as concerning the existence of "proper object[s]" for desire (T 3.1.1.12, SBN 459).

It has been suggested to me that any reasonable adherent of the belief-desire account of motivation will need to admit cases in which something is desired as an instance of a kind – for example, in which I want this bicycle because I want *a* sturdy bicycle and see that this is one – and that it is artificial to speak in such cases of desiring the item, or the getting of it, as a *means* to an end. So might not this be the class of cases Hume has in mind when he speaks of reason's informing us of the existence of a "proper object" for desire? Not if we go by his own examples: for his "proper objects" for desire and aversion are always objects identified precisely as means to the sensations of pleasure or pain that they have a "tendency to produce" (T 3.1.1.12, SBN 459).

16. Both Annette Baier and David Fate Norton have suggested to me, independently, that this point should be no surprise to anyone who has read Hume's discussion in *Treatise* 1.3.10, entitled "Of the influence of belief." (And see here Baier [1991: 157–59].) I agree with them in part. It is certainly instructive to notice, in that earlier passage, (a) that the beliefs whose extensive influence over our passions and actions Hume recounts are all of them about pleasure and pain and (b) that he nowhere says that this influence depends on our having a desire for pleasure or an aversion to pain; indeed, that he nowhere mentions such a desire or aversion. However, I do not think that one could be sure, just from his silence in this one passage, that he does not think that the motivating power of these beliefs depends on such a desire or aversion. One could easily suppose, after all, that he simply took this requirement to be too obvious to need stating there – especially if one also supposes, as I expect many readers have done, that he did state it later, in *Treatise* 2.3.3 or 3.1.1. It certainly advances the case, therefore, to note, as I have here, that on a plausible reading he states no such requirement in those later passages either; indeed, that he implicitly rejects it. And although my argument for that reading is also partly an argument from silence, it seems to me stronger than any argument just from *Treatise* 1.3.10 could be. For in the Book 2 and 3 passages, we need an explanation for Hume's repeatedly *contrasting* motivation by the prospect of pleasure or pain with other cases in which, as he says explicitly, the end *is* desired. Once this point is secured by appeal to the later passages, however, it certainly helps to see how unsurprising it can then look in light of the discussion at T 1.3.10.2–4 (SBN 118–20).

17. The complete list is at T 2.1.1.4 (SBN 277). These passages all make it sound as if immediate production by pleasure and pain were definitive of the direct passions, not just distinctive of this list of them. But at T 2.3.9.8 (SBN 439), Hume mentions other direct passions ("the desire of punishment to our enemies, and of happiness to our friends," plus some bodily appetites) that do not arise from pain or pleasure, but instead "from a natural impulse or instinct, which is perfectly unaccountable" and which "properly speaking,

produce good and evil, and proceed not from them." It is the postulation of *these* desires (as well as such calm passions as resentment and kindness to children [T 2.3.3.8, SBN 417]) that excuses Hume's motivational theory in the *Treatise* from being entirely hedonistic.

These other direct passions may appear to fit oddly into Hume's classification of the "perceptions of the mind," for if they arise from *no* other impression or idea, how can they count as secondary rather than primary impressions (T 2.1.1.1–2, SBN 275–76)? The answer, presumably, is that any desire, since it intrinsically "contains not any representative quality" (T 2.3.3.5, SBN 415), has an *object*, for Hume, only in virtue of being caused by an idea: so if I have a desire to punish my enemies simply from an unaccountable natural instinct, what this means is that I have, by an unaccountable instinct, a tendency to feel desire when I think of punishing my enemies.

Noticing this, Kydd suggests that there is no difference in principle between the two sorts of direct passions – it's just that some arise from ideas of pleasure and pain, others from ideas of punishing enemies – and that in consequence, "Hume's two views that judgements alone cannot cause passions, and that judgements can 'prompt' passions, are not, after all, incompatible" (1946: 107). But this seems wrong, for two reasons. First, Hume *says* that the difference is that some passions are caused by ideas of good and evil, some only by unaccountable instincts (T 2.3.9.8, SBN 439); so if ideas also come into the causation of the latter passions (as they must), one nevertheless expects their role to be importantly different from that assigned to ideas of pleasure and pain in the case of passions of the former sort. And, second, I have shown on textual grounds that it is. The idea of punishing enemies causes a desire, which is thus a desire *to punish enemies*. But Hume does not say that the idea of pleasure arouses a desire *for pleasure*. Rather, the judgment that eating a fruit would *cause* pleasure causes a desire *for the fruit*; no desire for the pleasure is invoked. So the problem of reconciling Hume's remarks remains.

18. The point is obvious too from Hume's statement that the "propense and averse motions of the mind," caused by pleasure and pain,

> are diversify'd into volition, into desire and aversion, grief and joy, hope and fear, according as the pleasure or pain changes its situation, and becomes probable or improbable, certain or uncertain, or is consider'd as out of our power for the present moment. (T 3.3.1.2, SBN 574)

The "situation" of the pleasure or pain is here clearly the situation it is *judged* to have (cf. T 2.3.9.1–7, SBN 438–39).

19. So they will *not* include beliefs about the existence of ghosts (Mackie 1980: 45), or about the existence of the Fountain of Youth (Stroud 1977: 160), or about the existence of burglars (Korsgaard 1996a: 318), except insofar as ghosts or the Fountain of Youth or burglars are seen as sources of pleasure or pain. And they will include beliefs about the *ripeness* of a fruit (in Kydd's paraphrase; 1946: 103–4) only on the assumption that ripeness guarantees an "excellent relish."

20. Perhaps one could not predict, merely from what Hume says about this list of direct passions, that he would make sources of pleasure and pain their

"proper objects" in this sense; one may have to turn to the passages I have cited under (1) to see that the belief-engendered desire is *for the object* or action – the fruit or biting into the fruit – seen as productive of pleasure. I think one *should* be able to tell, however, that his point cannot be merely that the idea of pleasure arouses a desire *for pleasure*. For, in that case, what significant contrast could he be drawing, at T 2.3.9.8 (SBN 439), between desires arising from pleasure and pain and those arising from unaccountable instincts, given that the latter desires are in his view engendered by ideas of their *objects*? See note 17.

21. He assumes this whenever he argues (as he of course appears to at T 2.3.3.4 [SBN 414–15]) that *because* reason does not govern the will, it must be passion that does so, for this conclusion follows only if there is no third possibility.

22. More explicitly: if there are unaccountable instincts, then it appears that Hume could in principle say about our disposition to desire objects seen as pleasurable that although (a) it is due to no further desire, such as a desire for pleasure, (b) it is not due to reason either. That would leave it unaccountable. But he does not say this; instead, he *contrasts* desires that arise in this way with the unaccountable ones. And that appears to suggest that, since they do *not* arise from any further desire, they must arise from reason.

If we probe a bit more deeply, I am not so sure that the option I have just described (and argued that Hume rejects) is an intelligible one anyway. I think that Hume can leave some basic desires just "unaccountable," but it is not clear what could be meant by saying this about a disposition to be motivated by a certain sort of *belief*. The reason is this. As Thomas Nagel has noted (1970: 29–30), there is obviously some sense in which anyone who is motivated to do or desire something by the belief that it will promote a certain goal has, and can appropriately be said to have, a desire for that goal. We might say that there is at least a *virtual* desire present in any such case. Hume will thus have to admit that in *this* sense all people have, and act on, a desire for pleasure (as at just one place [T 2.1.10.8, SBN 314] he does, in a passage in which the mechanism of motivation is irrelevant to his point and in a formula he nowhere repeats when he turns to his theory of motivation). The problem, then, for anyone who wishes to argue that in some cases the desire is *merely* virtual and that it is really just the belief that is doing the motivating, is to explain what distinguishes merely virtual desires from the more robust ones that, it is admitted, are operative in other cases. Nagel's answer (1970: 30–32) is that motivation can be ascribed to the belief, and the desire regarded as merely virtual, in precisely those cases in which the disposition to be so motivated is a necessary condition of rationality – that is, of the sort of ideal to which one must approximate if one is to count as having beliefs and desires at all. I find this plausible; and if it is correct, then it is not really an option for Hume to say that motivation by the prospect of pleasure is due *neither* to reason *nor* to our being moved by a desire for pleasure. For there is at least a virtual desire for pleasure in any such case. And if the motivation is not ascribed to reason, then there is no case for regarding that desire as merely virtual, so the desire for pleasure will have to be regarded as robust after all.

23. Or, more precisely, for their maximum possible balance of pleasure over pain.

24. In the first edition, Hutcheson attributes this mistake to those "who in their philosophical inquiries have learned to form very abstract ideas" ([1728] 1971: 124n3).

25. An alternative suggestion would be that the distinction here is the same (except for being confined to the calm passions) as the one Hume draws at T 2.3.9.8 (SBN 439) between passions that arise from "good and evil, or in other words, pain and pleasure," on the one hand, and others that "arise from a natural impulse or instinct, which is perfectly unaccountable," on the other. But, for reasons I have already suggested in notes 17 and 20, I think this cannot be right. For, crucially, the passions said at T 2.3.9.4–7 (SBN 439) to be engendered by good and evil are not desires *for* good or aversions *to* evil, but only desires for or aversions to the objects seen as providing a prospect of good or evil. The calm passion mentioned here, by contrast, is explicitly said to be an appetite to good and an aversion to evil.

26. For Hume, of course, such an idea is "nothing but a particular one consider'd in a certain view" (T 2.3.6.2, SBN 425; cf. T 1.1.7), but the adopting of such a view is still an intellectual accomplishment.

27. Hume seems to suggest at T 3.2.7.4 (SBN 535–36) that it is to be attributed to no one. He thus appears to fall there into what at T 2.3.3.10 (SBN 418) he calls the "common error of metaphysicians," of "ascribing the direction of the will entirely to one of these principles [i.e., the calm or the violent passions], and supposing the other to have no influence." He says that men "often counter-act a violent passion in prosecution of their interests and designs," but he appears at T 3.2.7.4 (SBN 535–36) to deny that this ever happens. He is perhaps not alone among political philosophers in coloring his account of human nature suddenly more pessimistic when the time comes to argue for the necessity of government.

28. This suggestion requires, of course, that Hume not take comparable points to hold for any of the calm passions on the *first* part of his list. This requirement would present a difficulty if "benevolence" here meant general benevolence, for Hutcheson offers about its role cautions exactly parallel to those he offers about the general concern for one's own good ([1728] 1971: 124–25). Since Hume doubts the existence of general benevolence (T 3.2.1.12, SBN 481), however, we may take him to be referring only to particular tendencies to kindness toward particular persons. Nor do any of the passions on this part of the list appear to require founding on a "distant view or reflection" (T 3.3.1.18, SBN 583); see note 5. There is also (just) one passage in which Hume says that "all men desire pleasure" (T 2.1.10.8, SBN 314); for my reasons for discounting it in this context, see note 22.

29. I thus take issue with Stroud, who suggests (1977: 163–67) that Hume introduces the calm passions in a largely question-begging attempt to *save* his view, that motivation always depends on passion, from counterexamples. For, first, I have argued that Hume's view is that motivation by the prospect of pleasure or pain does *not* depend on our having a passion (violent or otherwise) to obtain pleasure or avoid pain; so I deny that Hume ever advances, in the *Treatise*, the view Stroud thinks he wants to save. And, second, if Hume *did* intend his remarks about the calm passions to save that view, he

would need to attribute a calm desire for pleasure and a calm aversion to pain to everyone; but he does not.

30. Hume thinks William Wollaston made it, for this is his reconstruction of Wollaston's thesis that what makes actions at once immoral and contrary to reason is their making false assertions.

31. Indeed, Hume says as much, on the same page, in remarks confined to the less silly version of the accompanying belief account, according to which the relevant accompanying belief is the one on which the passion is founded.

> A person may be affected with passion, by supposing a pain or pleasure to lie in an object, which has no tendency to produce either of these sensations, or which produces the contrary to what is imagin'd. A person may also take false measures for the attaining his end, and may retard, by his foolish conduct, instead of forwarding the execution of any project. These false judgments may be thought to affect the passions and actions, which are connected with them, and *may be said to render them unreasonable, in a figurative and improper way of speaking.* (T 3.1.1.12, SBN 459; emphasis added)

32. Perhaps it is unnecessary to document in detail how often Hume has been read as advancing the instrumental or the foundation view. But a few references to recent discussions will provide a sense of the literature. Korsgaard (1996a: 312) takes Hume to be an instrumentalist. Gibbard (1983: 199–221 and 1990: 10) attributes the instrumental view to Hume, as does Harman (1977: 30–31, cf. 67). Harman also attributes the foundation theory to him (1977: 37), as Gibbard appears to in (1990: 39n). Parfit attributes to Hume both the instrumental and foundation theories (1984:117–18). He does not mention Hume's remarks about the calm passions, even though in complaining about the irrationality of a preference for near-future over distant-future goods (1984: 159), he cites a passage (T 3.2.7.5, SBN 536) in which Hume says that this preference represents a triumph of violent over calm passions and is thus (in an "improper sense") irrational.

33. See note 8.

34. If they did (as Hume notes at T 3.1.1.15n68 [SBN 461–62n]), then the beliefs reason would have to correct in order to render my actions reasonable would include *others'* as well as my own. So this version promises no support for the No Combat thesis, for it certainly allows that my passions and actions might be and remain unreasonable, even if all *my* beliefs are reasonable.

35. That is, it would require no *real* change; the passion's becoming reasonable would be what Geach (1969: 71–72) calls a merely Cambridge change, due entirely to a real change in the accompanying belief.

36. Nagel writes that "to hold, as Hume did, that the only proper rational criticism of action is a criticism of the beliefs associated with it, is to hold that practical reason does not exist" (1970: 64). But one should at least distinguish versions of this view. There is little interest in the claim that we *mistakenly* transfer epithets from beliefs to passions or actions, and not much more in the claim that it is correct to do so, but only in a way that guarantees our passions and actions to count as reasonable whenever our beliefs do. But practical reason acquires some normative bite on the sort of view Hume actually relies on, even though the reasonableness of passions and actions still derives in a complex way from that of beliefs.

Notice, incidentally, that Nagel is yet another writer who takes Hume to "hold" what is asserted by his first error view but not by his second.

37. We might finesse this difficulty as follows. Introduce the notion of a *goal* to include all ends desired for their own sake, but also to include such objects as pleasure and the absence of pain, when beliefs about pleasure and pain motivate as Hume thinks they do. (Goals will thus include the objects of what in note 22 I called virtual desires, as well as of robust desires.) Then the instrumental theory will be that actions (or desires) are reasonable just insofar as they are (or are for things) reasonably expected to promote one's goals. This view would support Hume's conclusions about his examples in the same way as would the foundation theory. (Incidentally, that the instrumental theory has to be formulated in this way, to be plausibly attributed to Hume, is a reason for doubting that *it* could be what he means by RSP. For even if it makes reason slave to our goals, it has to allow that not all of those goals are set by passion.)

In the background is of course the further problem, that the *same* evidence that shows that Hume does not think of pleasure and the absence of pain as ends set by passion is (I argued) evidence that he thinks they are ends set by reason. This view conflicts with the instrumental theory, which leaves no room for rational assessment of goals. But, on the assumption (which Hume appears here to endorse) that our goals are based on no beliefs, neither does the foundation theory. The argument of my section 1 provides reason for thinking that, if he takes these views seriously and also takes seriously the view that the calm passions are reasonable, he takes the latter somewhat *more* seriously.

38. I am grateful to Annette Baier for pointing out to me the relevance of this passage.

39. More precisely, he is discussing the alternation of grief and joy, and arguing (implausibly) that hope *just is* joy tinged by grief, fear grief tinged by joy. Hence the reference to the feelings mixing.

40. Here is the one place in my discussion in which it might matter that by "judgment" Hume appears to mean confident belief, rather than just any thought capable or truth or falsity, throughout his discussion of reason and passion. In the examples just cited, the judgments are ones we "perceive" to be true, or of which you "convince" me. See note 13.

41. There are useful suggestions in Falk 1986.

42. Strictly, with truth or falsity about "some other existence or modification"; see note 9.

43. See the quotation from Nagel 1970 in note 36; also Korsgaard 1996a: ch. 11. In attributing this challenge to Hume, writers sometimes *cite* his strict and philosophical view, but that appears always to be because they *have not seen* that it is distinct from his first error theory. They have not noticed that when Hume says that "it must follow" (T 2.3.3.6, SBN 416) that passions are unreasonable only when not instrumental, or when based on unreasonable beliefs, he is not drawing consequences from his strict and philosophical view but instead from a view he says is mistaken. But for this bit of misdirection by Hume, I doubt that his strict and philosophical view would have received any favorable comment at all.

44. A distant ancestor of this paper was read to the Society for the History of Ethics in 1981; David Fate Norton chaired, Annette Baier commented, and Stephen Darwall provided other remarks that forced me to rethink central portions of my argument. I am also grateful for discussions of more recent versions at the University of Vermont, at McGill University, and at the University of California, Irvine, as well as for helpful comments from Stephen Darwall (again), Paul Hoffman, Terence Irwin, Elizabeth Radcliffe, and John Robertson.

12   Hume and Moral Motivation

Hume devotes the two Sections of the first Part of Book 3 of the *Treatise* to an initial presentation of his sentimentalist moral theory. In Section 1, he argues against his rationalist opponents (such as John Locke, Samuel Clarke, and William Wollaston) who think that, in discerning moral properties, we use our reason to discover the truths of morality, usually construed as abstract eternal truths. Hume's primary objection to the rationalists is that their account of morality fails to account for the motivational force of morality. Reason, he has argued earlier, is inert, a mere "slave of the passions" (T 2.3.3.4, SBN 415), and thus, if morality were discerned by reason, it would leave us cold.[1] Or rather we would be moved by it only if there happened to be another motivational source on the scene, external to our moral faculties, that would engage our propensities to act. But Hume seems to suggest that we are fundamentally moved by morality. Moral rationalism, then, must be wrong.[2]

In the following Section of the *Treatise*, he argues that we recognize moral qualities by means of impressions, namely the moral sentiments. We *feel* the presence of virtue or vice in ourselves or others, rather than rationally *discovering* them by means of the relations of ideas that are the province of reason. The problem I explore in what follows is that Hume's invocation of sentiment as the key mental state in moral thought seems insufficient to create the kind of link between morality and our motivational propensities that he criticized the rationalists for having omitted. His own account of motivation by means of "direct" passions seems just as disconnected from his preferred account of moral discovery.

After detailing this problem in sections 1 and 2, I turn in section 3 to some possible responses that interpreters have offered on Hume's behalf. I argue that none succeeds, primarily because they have not sufficiently recognized that, in transitioning from his critique of the rationalists to his positive account, he has also moved to a different conception of morality. Thus I show in section 4 that, where the rationalists focus on deliberating moral *agents* as they decide what to do, Hume focuses on the moral *spectator* who tries to make ethical sense of the people around her (and sometimes also herself). So where the concern of the rationalists' agents is the choice of *actions*, the spectators trace behavior of all types – actions, reactions, thoughts, and passions – to the *character traits* that stand behind it as the focus for moral evaluation. And, as I show in section 5, it turns out that, for Hume, our moral responses to a trait, such as sentiments of approval or disapproval, are fully integrated into our affective responses to one another. We cannot help but take the recognition of virtue or vice to *matter*. In this sense, I suggest, Hume does offer an account of morality that explains its grip on us, even if it is not a grip on us as deliberating agents.

I. THE MOTIVATION ARGUMENT

Hume offers a number of arguments against the rationalist conception of morality. For example, his prior account of reason in Book 1 of the *Treatise* shows that it is deployed only for the discovery of relations and that these fall into seven classes: resemblances, qualitative relations, quantitative relations, contrarieties, identities, spatiotemporal relations, and causal relations (T 1.3.2.2, SBN 73; T 1.1.5). The first four are "relations of ideas" that admit of knowledge, while the last three concern "matter[s] of fact" that can be discovered only probabilistically (T 3.1.1.9, SBN 458; T 1.3.1). But Hume argues that the rationalists cannot easily fit immoral actions, such as incest (T 3.1.1.25, SBN 467), adultery (T 3.1.1.15, SBN 461), or ingratitude (T 3.1.1.24, SBN 466), into one of these categories. And if they did end up as immoral because they satisfied a relation, the same relation would apply just as much to inanimate objects. The moral rationalist, Hume says, cannot account for our blaming the son for killing his father when we do not blame the sapling for eventually overshadowing and killing its parent oak (T 3.1.1.24, SBN 467).

Hume's primary argument against the rationalists, however, holds that they cannot explain the link between moral judgment and our practical responses:

If morality had naturally no influence on human passions and actions, 'twere in vain to take such pains to inculcate it; and nothing wou'd be more fruitless than that multitude of rules and precepts, with which all moralists abound. Philosophy is commonly divided into *speculative* and *practical*; and as morality is always comprehended under the latter division, 'tis suppos'd to influence our passions and actions, and to go beyond the calm and indolent judgments of the understanding. And this is confirm'd by common experience, which informs us, that men are often govern'd by their duties, and are deter'd from some actions by the opinion of injustice, and impell'd to others by that of obligation. (T 3.1.1.5, SBN 457; see also T 3.1.1.6, 3.1.1.22–23, SBN 457, 465–66)

More specifically, he argues as follows (T 3.1.1.6, SBN 457):

(i) "[M]orals ... have an influence on the actions and affections."
"Morals excite passions, and produce or prevent actions."
(ii) "[R]eason alone ... can never have any such influence."
(iii) "The rules of morality, therefore, are not conclusions of our reason."[3]

The problem, then, is that the rationalists leave moral claims as mere facts – either natural facts true of the world or abstract rational facts that can be known independently of experience. But Hume takes himself to have shown in Book 2 that the discovery of facts does not directly motivate us to act (T 2.3.3). The ultimate source of action must be the passions (hence, ii). Thus the rationalists, by claiming that moral discoveries are ultimately the province of reason, fail to capture our *involvement* in it, our *caring* about what it has to say, in such a way that we are *moved* by it.

The traditional interpretation holds that, because Hume introduces his sentimentalist project by a criticism of rationalists for their failure to explain morality's motivating power, his positive view thereby treats the moral sentiments as themselves being motivating. They are pleasures and pains, after all, and these seem, on Hume's view, to be more bound up with our motivational propensities than do conclusions of reason. Not only is reason the "slave of the passions" (T 2.3.3.4, SBN 415), but pain and pleasure are the "chief spring[s] and moving principle" (T 1.3.10.2, SBN 118) of all actions. And thus interpreters such as Philippa Foot (1978: 79) conclude that, for Hume, "the moral sentiment, the special feeling which we call approbation, was a pleasurable sentiment, by which we were inclined towards those actions whose contemplation gave rise to it."[4]

2. MOTIVATION AND THE MORAL SENTIMENTS

The problem with the traditional interpretation is that when Hume discusses motivation by the moral sentiments, he does not seem to link them very tightly to action. Thus his criticism of the rationalists for their failing to account for morality's motivating power seems to apply equally to his own view. (See Brown 1988 and Sturgeon 2001: 20–21.)

As a preliminary, we must note that Hume thinks that the best kind of moral behavior is done spontaneously, without any thought of its moral praiseworthiness (T 3.2.1.1–7, SBN 477–79): a woman mowing her lawn might move on to do her neighbor's lawn at the same time simply because she feels like it. She never considers that it might be generous to help out and indeed might not engage in anything like deliberation over her choice to continue mowing. If this kind of nondeliberative helping behavior is typical for her, Hume would count her as generous and thus as meriting our approval. The contrast, where we are moved by thoughts with moral *content*, occurs when our natural tendencies do not incline us toward what we would approve of *and* where we are reflectively monitoring our behavior in such a way as to notice our omission.[5] For example, if a beggar is at the door asking me for money, I might have an initial inclination not to give. But if I recognize that not giving would indicate that I exemplified the morally disapproval-worthy trait of stinginess, I might be moved by this thought and donate a few dollars.

Hume gives the example in terms of someone who lacks gratitude to his benefactor:

When any virtuous motive or principle is common in human nature, a person, who feels his heart devoid of that principle, may hate himself upon that account, and may perform the action without the motive, from a certain sense of duty, in order to acquire by practice, that virtuous principle, or at least, to disguise to himself, as much as possible, his want of it. (T 3.2.1.8, SBN 479)

Two things should be noted about this passage: First, the man here is motivated to do what morality requires not, say, for duty's sake, but either to hide from himself his lack of virtue or to acquire the tendencies of mind that would allow him to express his gratitude spontaneously. Second, Hume suggests here that there is no guarantee that people will be moved by their self-disapprobation. Look at the qualifications in the passage: "a person ... *may* hate himself ... and *may* perform the action." And so in such cases not only will different people be motivated by different ends, but some people might not be moved at all. Hume certainly seems to leave open the possibility of people's having a kind of complacency about their moral deficits.

But this possibility means that Hume treats moral motivation as being independent from our moral evaluations. If only some people will be motivated by their moral sentiments, depending on their reactions to it, then moral motivation must depend on facts that are external to our moral evaluations. Charlotte Brown suggests that the relevant external facts have to do with how the person in question conceives of his happiness. She interprets Hume's reference in the quotation to the "sense of duty" as linked to the self-hatred that he also mentions there. And because his earlier analysis of hatred in the *Treatise* requires that it be directed at others (T 2.2.1.2, SBN 329), she takes his talk of *self*-hatred in the passage quoted above to be a sloppy invocation of the negative emotional response to the self that he classifies as the "indirect" passion of humility. Because, according to Hume, humility has no motivational efficacy (T 2.2.6.3, SBN 367), Brown suggests that the motivational force of the sense of duty ultimately depends on our desire for happiness. For Hume thinks that for us to be happy we must be able to survey ourselves approvingly (EPM 9.23, SBN 283). Moral disapprobation of one of our traits could thus motivate us to rid ourselves of the trait or to hide it from ourselves because the moral displeasure that the trait causes undermines our happiness.

But if this is Hume's view of moral motivation, then his argument against the rationalists fails. For they too could argue that our desire for happiness happens to fix on our character traits and that the *rational* recognition of a vicious negative trait links up with this desire so as to produce action. If Hume allows various desires and passions, different from the perceptions involved in a moral judgment, to play a role in his account of moral motivation, then the motivational argument no longer connects up with the moral epistemological conclusion that he wants to make. Brown's interpretation seems to force us to conclude that either Hume does not really subscribe to a conception of moral evaluations that makes it deeply connected with our motivations – in which case his antirationalist argument and subsequent adoption of sentimentalism are unsupported – or Hume does really subscribe to such a conception and his own positive sentimentalist position is a failure in not satisfying it.

3. POSSIBLE RESPONSES

There have been two kinds of responses to this dilemma. One is exemplified by Stephen Darwall, who argues that Hume's linkage of moral evaluation to motivation is meant only as an ad hominem argument against rationalists and that he is not committed to it himself. Another has been offered by Elizabeth Radcliffe, who suggests that the traditional interpretation of Hume as embracing this linkage can be saved if details of his moral psychology, different from those Brown examines, are taken into account. I will argue, however, that neither of these responses is adequate, although I will retain elements of each of them in my alternative response described in the following sections.

According to Darwall, Hume is not required to give an account of our moral evaluations as motivating, because he realizes that his appeal to the practical impact of morality in his antirationalist arguments has bite only because the rationalists themselves are committed to it. His aim, then, is only to show that they are inconsistent, not that they fail to live up to a criterion that applies to accounts of morality *in general*. For Darwall (1993: 445n49 and 1995: 305n30), Hume's real problem with the rationalists is that they are committed to an a priori connection between moral judgment and motivation; but on his view of causation, it is impossible to establish such necessary connections a priori (T 3.1.1.22, SBN 465–66). And this means that the kind of a posteriori connection between moral judgment and motivation that Hume offers within his own view does not conflict with his earlier criticisms of the rationalists.

Radcliffe (1996: 391) points out, however, that just because rationalists hold that we discover moral distinctions from a priori reasoning, they need not also be committed to the view that the motivating power of moral judgments must also be discovered a priori. (This is not to deny that some of Hume's actual historical opponents, notably Samuel Clarke, did make this argument a priori.) There is the possibility of using an a posteriori, empirical investigation of human nature to show that as a matter of fact moral judgments do motivate.

Radcliffe instead reinstitutes the traditional interpretation of the moral sentiments as fundamentally motivating. She argues that Hume means to identify them with a calm direct passion, the "general appetite to good, and aversion to evil, consider'd merely as such" (T 2.3.3.8, SBN 417). Thus she thinks that, for Hume, the impressions by means of which we approve of virtue or disapprove of vice are themselves motivations to be virtuous and to avoid vice. This is indeed an account of moral judgments that ties them tightly to our motivational propensities, but, for a number of reasons, I doubt that it is Hume's.

First, I think that it is hard to reconcile Radcliffe's suggestion with the detailed mechanism that Hume provides for how we come to have the moral sentiments. At the end of the *Treatise*, he summarizes his view by saying that "sympathy is the chief source of moral distinctions" (T 3.3.6.1, SBN 618), where sympathy is the mental principle that causes us to instinctively feel what others are feeling.[6] Our sympathetic tendencies explain how an impartial spectator can take disinterested pleasure or pain in behavior that might otherwise have nothing to do with him. Hume thinks that we approve of traits that are useful or agreeable to their possessors or to those who surround them because sympathy allows us to *share* in the pleasures that the traits bring to the relevant class of people. The problem for Radcliffe's interpretation is that it is hard to see that this sympathetically communicated pleasure or pain is motivating. Indeed in Book 2 of the *Treatise* Hume stresses that sympathetically felt pleasures and pains usually do not motivate us and that, when they do, the actions toward which we are motivated are not reliably of one kind or another (T 2.2.9).

It might seem that Hume's claim that the kind of sympathy involved in moral evaluation is what he calls *extensive* sympathy will help Radcliffe (T 3.3.1.23, SBN 586). This kind of sympathy involves our going beyond the momentary pain or pleasure of our sympathetic communicant and considering how it fits into his life as a whole. And this kind of sympathy *is* motivating; it leads us to care about the pain that we foresee someone will suffer, in such a way that we are moved to try to prevent it (T 2.2.9.11–16, SBN 384–87). But I do not think that Hume's invocation of extensive sympathy here gives Radcliffe what she needs. Consider my disapprobation of my stinginess when I encounter the beggar at my door. This feeling of uneasiness is brought about by my sympathizing with the disapprobation that an impartial member of my "narrow circle" (T 3.3.3.2, SBN 602) feels when she considers the effects of my trait. Sympathy here plays the role of "authority" (T 2.1.11.9, SBN 321), in that I must defer to the person who is properly situated to discern my traits. Extensive sympathy only enters in allowing the impartial spectator to reach her verdict; for she must consider not, say, the particular feeling of displeasure felt by the beggar at the door in the moment I refuse to offer him money, but the way this displeasure fits into his life overall and also the lives of others with whom I interact. She might then be moved to step in herself to help the beggar (or to chastise me), but I, in sympathizing with her, share only her negative feeling of disapprobation. If extensive sympathy is going to play any kind of motivating role in this story, it will affect an observer, not the person whose trait is being assessed.

A second concern with Radcliffe's interpretation is that it does not seem to fit with Hume's discussion of the motivating "direct" passions (T 2.3.9). There, he makes it sound as if the "general appetite to good, and aversion to evil" that Radcliffe relies on is triggered only *after* we have discovered what is good or evil. On this view, we could feel pained at how a particular future act might manifest our stinginess – this pain is our disapprobation of it. And *then* the "general appetite" comes in, causing us to be averse to performing the act that would make us stingy. Thus Hume says that "[u]pon the removal of pain and pleasure [i.e., the recognition of evil and good] there immediately follows a removal of . . . desire and aversion" (T 2.3.9.1, SBN 438). I think that this account of moral motivation is probably a more accurate description of his considered view than the one that Brown offered, which invoked humility and the desire for happiness,[7] but it still leaves Hume with a separation of moral evaluation from moral motivation. A "general appetite to good, and aversion to evil" does the motivating work, not the moral sentiments by means of which we identify good and evil in the first place. And this appetite could be called on by the rationalists to explain moral motivation in the very same manner that Radcliffe sees Hume as doing.

My third concern about Radcliffe's interpretation arises from some of the details of Hume's understanding of morality. For example, he allows that there are some virtues – those of the "great," such as "[c]ourage, intrepidity, ambition, love of glory, magnanimity" (T 3.3.2.13, SBN 599–600) – that most of us will approve of without thereby being moved to exemplify. (Indeed it would be quite an ugly world if we all wanted to be great leaders and none were willing to be "good" followers.) And what about such virtues as parental "indulgen[ce]" (T 3.3.3.9, SBN 606), which are only ever open to a restricted class of persons? This problem becomes especially severe when you recall that Hume includes involuntary aspects of our behavior, such as natural abilities, in his catalog of the virtues (T 3.3.4–5). But in approving of genius (T 3.3.4.2, SBN 608), are we thereby motivated to become so? Given that Hume makes it clear that we do not desire to achieve something that we know to be impossible (T Intro. 9, SBN xviii), I find it hard to see how the Humean moral sentiments *could* be motivating in all cases.

This does leave open the possibility that they are motivating in some cases but not others. Darwall (1995: ch. 10), for example, has argued that Hume ultimately takes judgments about justice to have motivational force, even if not all moral sentiments do. And Christine Korsgaard (1996a: ch. 2, esp. 69n11, 69n13, 70n21) has suggested that Hume means his claim in the motivation argument about the practical force of morality to apply only to the artificial virtues. For he says there that people are "deter'd from some actions by the opinion of *injustice*, and impell'd to others by that of *obligation*" (T 3.1.1.5, SBN 457; emphasis added), and he later suggests that the notion of obligation is coherent only in connection with justice (T 3.2.2.11, SBN 491; see also T 3.2.1.13, 3.2.2.15, SBN 482, 494). This does make it seem as if Hume restricts his concern about moral motivation only to justice.

Nonetheless, there are two problems with Korsgaard's and Darwall's suggestion. First, Hume does on occasion allow that there is after all a justice-independent notion of obligation, when, for example, omission of an action would indicate the presence of a vice in someone (T 3.2.5.4, SBN 517; also T 3.2.1.8, SBN 479). And second, Hume's antirationalist argument would no longer be valid if the claim about moral motivation is restricted to justice; for he would be entitled to conclude from his argument only that moral distinctions *relating to justice* are made by means of impressions and would have to leave open the possibility that moral distinctions relating to natural virtues could be made rationally.

The problem for Hume that we noted earlier – that his antirationalist argument requires that our moral evaluations motivate us, but his positive account of motivation does not seem to explain how such evaluations motivate – remains unresolved.

4. A DIFFERENT CONCEPTION OF MORALITY

Note that this problem presupposes that Hume's positive account of morality treats it in the same terms he uses to understand the rationalists, where morality is understood as primarily directing agents' choices when they deliberate over their actions. (We have seen that his examples focus on morally prohibited actions: patricide, murder, adultery, and so on.) I suggest, however, that in rejecting the rationalist account of moral evaluation, Hume also rejects their conception of morality. I hinted at this point when I noted his counting nonvoluntary and unchosen behavior – such as that resulting from a person's natural abilities – as morally salient. In fact, Hume's positive account radically downplays the significances of the moral *agent's* choices, instead focusing on the verdicts that a *spectator* feels when impartially observing someone's behavior, both chosen and unchosen. But if Hume's considered view of morality does not require moral evaluations to motivate our actions, how can he criticize the rationalists for their failure to explain this kind of motivation? Answering this question will require us to back up a bit and to come to grips with what is involved in a spectator theory. I return to the issue of moral motivation in the following section.

In this era of agent-centered moral theory, whether the approach be utilitarian or practical-reason based (and this latter in its Hobbesian, Kantian, or Aristotelian flavors), some have found it bizarre that anyone would privilege the spectator's evaluations. Korsgaard (1996a: 189), for example, says that it is an "obviously unattractive ... starting point in moral philosophy." But it would be uncharitable to think that Hume did not have reasons for taking this approach. The place to look for them must be in the early portions of Book 3 of the *Treatise*. For not only does he conclude from his antirationalist arguments that moral distinctions are a product of feeling, not reason, but he also seems to assume that his arguments allow him to move from an action-oriented agent perspective in his discussion of the rationalists to a character-trait-oriented spectator perspective in his presentation of his own view. I think that these three transitions – from reason to feeling, from agent to spectator, and from action to trait – need to be understood together if we are going to make sense of Hume's project, both negative and positive.

Let us start with Hume's emphasis on character traits as the primary objects of moral assessment, where actions are of interest only as "signs" of traits (T 3.2.1.2, SBN 477). Why would he think this? One problem with actions is that, at a fairly natural level of description, the same action can be morally admirable in some circumstances and despicable in others. Someone's shoveling a neighbor's walk after a winter storm might be generous, but if it is done in an attempt to make the neighbor feel indebted to the person in question, it is likely to be a less praiseworthy action. More dramatically, the doctor who lets a person in his care suffocate to death might be acting mercifully, neglectfully, or evilly, depending on the circumstances. Hume puts the point in these terms:

> Actions are by their very nature temporary and perishing; and where they proceed not from some cause in the characters and disposition of the person, who perform'd them, they infix not themselves upon him, and can neither redound to his honour, if good, nor infamy, if evil. The action itself may be blameable; it may be contrary to all the rules of morality and religion: But the person is not responsible for it; and as it proceeded from nothing in him, that is durable or constant, and leaves nothing of that nature behind it, 'tis impossible he can, upon its account, become the object of punishment or vengeance. (T 2.3.2.6, SBN 411)

Hume says here that if an action is not connected with the person who performed it in the right sort of way – if it is not "infixed" in him – it is a mere event. And this means that we cannot look at actions in isolation, but must instead connect them to the person's life as a whole. One way to do this is to consider the intention with which an action was performed, for "an intention shows certain qualities, which [remain] after the action is perform'd" (T 2.2.3.4, SBN 349). But what are these qualities? "Infixing" intentions is just as difficult as "infixing" actions, for people who perform the same action with the same intention might nonetheless merit different moral responses; it depends on how the intentional action fits into the person's life as a whole. And thus Hume concludes that we must look at the "mental qualities" or character traits from which our actions as well as our intentions spring. If the person's shoveling falls into a pattern of thought, feeling, and behavior that speaks to a general tendency to care for those around him, then it indicates his generosity. If the shoveling is accompanied by resentful feelings, and if he generally takes an accountant's outlook on all aspects of his life – entering debts and credits on an interior ledger indexed to the various people he encounters – this action speaks not to his generosity, but to his small-mindedness, his mercenary outlook.

It might seem as if Hume's emphasis on traits mixes up the causal and normative dimensions of our behavior. Kant ([1785] 1997: 7; Ak. 4: 393), for example, says of character traits that, although good traits might qualify as "gifts of nature," what matters morally is whether the person whose traits they are "use[s]" them with a good will. They are mere sources of inclination, over which the agent must deliberate to decide whether they qualify as the appropriate source of action. Hume sees things differently. For one thing, he denies that we primarily inhabit the deliberative posture. Not only are the trait-related feelings beyond our deliberative control, but most of the time we act spontaneously, without pausing to think about what we are doing (T 3.2.1.4–7, SBN 478–79). Moreover, on pain of a regress of deliberations, we cannot fully deliberate about whether to deliberate. Whether and when we enter into a normative consideration of how we should act is itself not up to us. (Kant attempts to escape this problem by making the relevant notion of agency nonempirical.) And, finally, even when we do deliberate, we are usually blind to how the action in question falls into place with our other behavior, chosen and unchosen, so as to speak to an enduring trait in us. It is all too familiar an occurrence for someone to think that she is free from moral blame for an action because, taken by itself, it is innocuous. A certain kind of racist, for example, can legitimately say that no single action of hers is wrong even though the actions fall into a pattern. For example, when a teacher unknowingly has a pattern of calling on and generally feeling more positively toward her white students, she is a racist nonetheless.

Once Hume concludes that traits are the ultimate objects of moral assessment, it is easy to see why he approaches moral theory from the point of view of the spectator. For having a trait involves more than deliberately choosing in such a way as to publicly manifest a certain pattern. It also involves thinking, feeling, and instinctively acting in a characteristic manner, and all of these elements of trait-related behavior are mostly independent of an agent's deliberative choices. That is why Hume is so willing to count nonvoluntary behavior as morally relevant (T 3.3.4). Indeed, two people could display in their *choices* identical behavior and yet bear different *traits*. If the choices of one of them are integrated into his life in such a way that they comport with a larger general outlook, affectively as well as actively, while the other only does the actions out of the thought that morality requires it of him, the former would have a genuine trait of, say, generosity or industriousness or parental solicitude, while the other would have instead the trait of dutifulness.

I have sketched why Hume might think that two of the three transitions that occur in Part 1 of Book 3 go together (from action to trait, and from agent to spectator) but what of the third transition, the one to which he gives the most direct attention – from reason to feeling? I think that one explanation for Hume's emphasizing our responding to traits with *feelings* of approval and disapproval has to do with epistemological issues connected with trait recognition. As we have seen, traits manifest themselves in a *pattern* of behavior – thoughts, feelings, actions, reactions, and so on. The epistemological question is how we are able to recognize the constituents of this pattern as hanging together, as having a kind of coherence that allows us to posit a common source – a trait – causally responsible for them.

One view would be that a trait is a natural entity that exists independently of our responses to it. Francis Hutcheson ([1725] 1969 and [1728] 1971), for instance, identifies virtue with benevolence. Though he thought that the positive response our moral sense has to benevolence is what identifies it as a virtue, his view leaves us in principle able to discover someone's benevolence independently of our sentimental response to her or him. This makes Hutcheson's view quite close to a kind of rationalism – not the a priori rationalism of a Clarke or Locke, but an a posteriori kind in which causal investigation of the sources of behavior in someone could discover her or his virtue. Hutcheson ([1728] 1971: 162–63) thus compares the moral sense to our sense of sight. But once we know which wavelength of light will be seen by us as red, it is possible for us to tell which things are red without having to see them – namely by designing an apparatus that identifies the wavelength of the light reflected off of various objects.

Hume, in contrast, is at pains to deny that virtue or vice can be discovered by causal reasoning (T 3.1.1.26, SBN 468). Instead, the pattern of behavior that indicates a trait counts as a pattern only because it elicits a feeling of approval or disapproval from us. The reaction is what indicates that there is a pattern present in the first place; it is not a response to something that exists independently of the reaction (even though the various items that go into the pattern do have an independent existence):

No one has ever been able to tell what *wit* [an exemplary character trait] is, and to show why such a system of thought must be receiv'd under that denomination, and such another rejected. 'Tis only by taste we can decide concerning it, nor are we possest of any other standard, upon which we can form a judgment of this kind. Now what is this *taste*, from which true and false wit in a manner receive their being, and without which no thought can have a title to either of these denominations? 'Tis plainly nothing but a sensation of pleasure from true wit, and of uneasiness from false, without our being able to tell the reasons of that pleasure or uneasiness. (T 2.1.7.7, SBN 297)

Similarly, then, a person who shovels a neighbor's walk, holds extra office hours for her students, and volunteers at the women's shelter is generous *because* impartial spectators bring these pieces of behavior (as well as others) together when they approve of them.

Hume's emphasis on feeling here often tempts interpreters to treat him as a subjectivist (or noncognitivist) so that there is no possibility of truth or falsity in our moral judgments. The quoted passage suggests otherwise. Character traits such as wit or generosity "in a manner receive their being" from our sentimental responses to them. Once they have that being, they are there to be discovered and evaluated by others who could then go wrong by failing to recognize the trait or by misjudging its moral features. Hume is thus what David Wiggins (1987: ch. 5) calls a "sensible subjectivist." Our subjectivities are relevant to our constituting such things as character traits; once so constituted they come to have an existence that is independent from the subjective responses of any given observer.

I have argued in this section that Hume's sentimentalism goes hand in hand with his moral theory's being trait-oriented and spectator-focused. To this extent, then, I agree with Annette Baier (1991: 185), who says, "Hume's disagreements with traditional moralists go deeper [than merely about how best to explain the link between moral evaluation and motivation]. He disagrees about the role morality plays, the content it has, and about the form it takes, as well as about its source." Radcliffe (1996: 391–92) suggests, however, that if Hume understands morality differently from his opponents, his objections to their view for failing to explain the link between moral judgment and motivation cannot count as a reason to abandon it. Hume should have concluded from his argument about moral motivation not that moral distinctions are discerned by feeling, but rather that the rationalists were wrong to think that moral judgments motivate. For it is hard to see that rationalists are *required* by their moral epistemological thesis to adopt the motivational thesis as well. Hume's antirationalist argument supports his sentimentalism only if he thinks that *any* account of our capacity for moral judgment must explain our being moved by morality. What does that requirement mean in a spectator theory?

5. THE SPECTATOR'S AFFECTIVE ENGAGEMENT

Hume criticizes the rationalists for opening up a gap between our recognizing a moral demand and our being moved by it. In the traditional interpretation, his own view supposedly bridges this gap by making the moral intrinsically attractive, so that to recognize it is to be moved by it. We saw in sections 2 and 3, above, that Hume's moral psychology does not link the moral sentiments to our motivational propensities in this way. But I suggested in section 4 that Hume rejects the conception of morality at work in the traditional interpretation, where he is viewed as accepting the rationalists' privileging of the deliberating agent. Nonetheless, even in an interpretation that emphasizes his preferred spectator-oriented analysis of morality, there could still be a gap between making a moral judgment and caring about it. Someone might suggest that the moral properties he discerns in people make no difference to how he conceives of them; he could say that such properties are not different from their nationality, their yearly income, their family background.

Nor, for that matter, are they different from such factors as their weight, the number of hairs on their heads, or what they ate for lunch on January 5, 1977. The gap here is not between the *deliberator's* recognition of a moral requirement and her being moved by it; it is a gap between the *spectator's* recognition of moral qualities in those she observes and her caring about them. Hume could close this gap that threatens his spectator theory if he could show that moral properties are different in kind from merely factual ones because they are fundamentally important in making people into who they are. Another way to put this challenge to Hume asks: Is it possible, in his analysis, for someone to treat the moral pleasure she takes in another's generosity to reveal just another fact about that person, with no special weight in how she understands him?

The important text to consider here is Hume's claim, shortly after he has introduced his sentimentalist treatment of moral assessment, that the "most considerable effect that virtue and vice have upon the human mind" (T 3.1.2.5, SBN 473) when they are recognized by a spectator is their eliciting one of the four "indirect passions" – pride, love, humility, or hatred. These passions involve a pleasant or painful feeling directed toward a person (oneself in the case of pride or humility, another in the case of love or hatred) on the basis of some of her agreeable or disagreeable qualities, in this case her virtue or vice. (See also T 3.3.1.2–6, SBN 574–75.)

This claim has not proved to be very easy to interpret, mostly because the point of Hume's treatment of the indirect passions, the subject of over two thirds of Book 2 of the *Treatise*, is obscure at best. Páll Árdal (1966) has offered one way to understand the importance of these passions; he suggests that Hume means to *equate* the moral sentiments with calm, impartial versions of them (see, especially, T 3.3.5.1, SBN 614).[8] I have argued against this interpretation elsewhere (Ainslie 1999), suggesting that it fits poorly with most of the text, in which Hume identifies the moral sentiments with an impartial pleasure or uneasiness in response to someone's *trait*, not the indirect passions they cause that will be directed at the *person* overall. That is, "we approve of his character [i.e., his character trait], and love his person" (T 3.3.3.2, SBN 602) when we recognize his virtue. Árdal's interpretation, in contrast, by assimilating the moral evaluation of the trait with the overall attitude toward the person, would collapse the distinction between recognizing virtue or vice and that recognition's "most considerable effect" (T 3.1.2.5, SBN 473), namely the indirect passions. I have suggested instead that Hume relies on these passions to escape a sceptical quandary about persons, one that "evidently" holds "a great analogy" (T 2.1.5.11, SBN 290) with his sceptical problems about causal connections.[9] The quandary is in understanding how, of the many facts that are true of someone – his virtue or vice, his nationality, his yearly income, his family background, his weight, the number of hairs on his head, what he ate for lunch on January 5, 1977 – only some of them play a role in making him into who he is, define him as a member of a certain kind, or, as Hume puts it at one place, are "connected with [his] being and existence" rather than being "in a manner separated from" him (T 2.1.8.8, SBN 302). But what is the nature of this "existential connection" between a person and his defining qualities?

Just as the necessary connection between cause and effect is not rationally discernible (T 1.3.6), neither is the existential connection between a person and her defining features. And just as, in light of this indiscernibility, Hume introduces an associative mechanism to account for our forming causal beliefs (T 1.3.8), so too he introduces an associative mechanism – the indirect passions – to account for our forming conceptions of persons in terms of their defining features. Hume does not however think that the associative origin of our causal beliefs means that they are immune from criticism. Rather he introduces "general rules" (T 1.3.13.7–12, SBN 146–50) to allow for the criticism of causal beliefs for failing to track the conjunction of events of the cause type and the effect type (T 1.3.15). So too in the case of our associatively engendered beliefs about persons that arise from the indirect passions: Hume introduces passion-related general rules that allow us to criticize the conceptions we form of one another. For he holds that when enough people start to take a particular kind of feature to be significant enough to define someone as being of a specific social type or "rank" (T 2.1.6.8–9, SBN 293–94), then that person comes to be of that rank independently of what people happen to feel about her. Our emotional responses to one another construct a social world of persons in which who a person is depends on how people generally respond to the various facts that are true of her.[10]

Hume specifies four general classes of objects that typically cause the indirect passions and thus typically structure our social worlds: virtue or vice (T 2.1.7); bodily qualities such as beauty or deformity (T 2.1.8); "external advantages [or] disadvantages" (T 2.1.9); and power and riches. Because of this, Hume thinks that a person's virtue or vice, nationality, yearly income (not the exact dollar figure, presumably, but the general range of his earnings), and his family background are not mere facts true of him, but are instead "connected with his being and existence," whereas his weight, the number of hairs on his head, and what he ate for lunch on January 5, 1977, are "in a manner separated from him" (although if his weight is abnormal in some way, excessive or extremely low, or if his number of hairs is steadily decreasing, these facts might relate to his beauty or deformity and would thus be bound up with the indirect passions).

In light of this interpretation of the indirect passions, let us go back to Hume's claim that the "most considerable effect" of a spectator's judgment of virtue or vice is the emergence of an indirect passion. We can now see that what this means is that recognizing virtue or vice by means of the moral sentiments and taking it to matter by means of the indirect passions go hand in hand. Approving of someone's generosity and taking that generosity to be a defining feature of him go together: "we approve of his character, and love his person" (T 3.3.3.2, SBN 602), thereby seeing him *as generous*. Note, however, that on this view not only moral qualities go into defining someone, because such things as approximate yearly income, looks, and nationality also play a role in making her into who she is. But a person's moral qualities pick out what is notable about her in relation to her *behavior*, in what she *does, feels, thinks, etc.*; the other kinds of qualities, though also person-defining, are not behavior-related. Hume stresses that moral traits are *mental* qualities because he thinks that our moral interest in one another has to do with the behavior – broadly construed – that we display to one another (and to ourselves).

I started this section by noting that Hume's concern about the rationalist account of morality was that it left a gap between our recognizing what morality required and our being moved by it. In his positive account of morality, he moves away from the rationalists' concern with the agent's deliberation, but he owes us an account in his preferred spectator model of the link between moral judgment and our caring about its verdicts. We can now see that, though as a spectator theorist he does not require us to *act* on our moral judgments, he does fully integrate the moral sentiments with the indirect passions, and thus the means of our making moral distinctions is internal to the means of our relating to one another as social persons. In support of my claim, look back at the passages where Hume first introduces the motivational thesis. In each case, he describes his view as relating to how moral judgment elicits actions *and passions*: "Morals excite passions" (T 3.1.1.6, SBN 457); "morality ... [has an] influence on human passions" (T 3.1.1.5, SBN 457) and "affections" (T 3.1.1.6, SBN 457). He hints at the fact that affective engagement for an agent-centered and a spectator-centered theory will be quite different, in the former case having to do with motivations to act, and in the latter having to do with the elicitation of passions, especially the indirect passions by means of which we form conceptions of one another.

Could a rationalist not make the same move? Why could a rational recognition of a moral trait (if that were possible) not also be integrated into the indirect passions? It could *if* the spectator happened to take pleasure or displeasure in what she discovered, for Hume thinks that these passions require a hedonic response to their causes as part of their structure, the "double relation of ideas and impressions" (T 2.1.5.5, SBN 286). But this would not allow the rationalist account to fully integrate morality and our affections. Recognizing a moral trait would be one thing; taking it to make a difference to the bearer would be another. The gap between moral recognition and moral engagement remains. Hume closes this gap by showing that traits "in a manner receive their being" (T 2.1.7.7, SBN 297) from our approval of them as they are taken up into the indirect passions. Morality is a precipitate derived from how we are affectively engaged with one another.

Perhaps, then, the rationalist could offer an account of existential connections – connections between persons and their defining features – different from Hume's passion-mediated story. But the problem is that if moral qualities are discovered by reason, then they are mere facts, and the difference between them and the other facts about persons disappears. Virtue is no longer different in kind from the number of hairs on a person's head. Even if reason is construed more broadly than Hume allows and is taken to include practical reason, it is hard to see how the rationalist can escape Hume's sceptical challenge. For reason's requiring someone to act in a particular way, on pain of irrationality, does not seem to play a role in defining him as who he is. His irrationality in this instance simply seems to be another fact about him. And so the rationalist can at best offer a theory of moral spectatorship that separates the recognition of moral features from our caring about them. Hume argues that they then falsify our moral phenomenology.

6. CONCLUSION

I have argued that taking seriously that Hume works with a different conception of morality from his opponents allows us to see how he can both reject rationalism for its failure to account for an agent's moral motivation and yet offer in his own theory an account that leaves motivation by a moral judgment dependent on contingent accompanying desires. For I have suggested that Hume does offer an account of moral spectatorship that shows how we are fully morally engaged: making a moral judgment about someone's traits and seeing those traits as a meaningful feature of her or him are, on his view, intimately linked.

NOTES

1. Hume's precise meaning in this claim is discussed in detail in Nicholas Sturgeon's contribution to this *Companion*.

2. This point is often made using Falk's (1947–48) terms, "internalism" and "externalism." An *internalist* in moral philosophy believes that morality is motivationally self-sufficient – that once we recognize a moral claim on us, there is no need for a motivational source distinct from this recognition in order for us to act on it. An internalist can still allow that people might not do what morality requires, even when they recognize the requirement, but she would have to explain this away as a case of vice, weakness of the will, or the like. The important point for an internalist is that there is no fundamental motivational gap between moral awareness and moral action. An *externalist*, on the other hand, thinks that recognizing moral properties is one thing; caring about them, and thus being moved by them, is another. An externalist thus thinks that a moral theory needs two components: an account of what moral requirements are and an explanation of what could move us to follow them (perhaps our self-interest or a special desire to be moral).

3. Cohon (2008: ch. 3, esp. 81ff.) argues convincingly that "reason" here must be understood to refer to the *process* of reasoning, not some independent and self-standing faculty of reason. In Book 1, Hume refuses to reify mental faculties (see, e.g., T 1.3.9.19n22, SBN 117–18n). Thus Hume's claim in the antirationalist argument is that the process of reasoning is different from the process of discovering moral features. The latter has an impact on our motivations, whereas the former does not.

4. See also Stroud 1977: 173 and Mackie 1980: 52–53.

5. Recall that in his discussion of personal identity at T 1.4.6.1–3 (SBN 251–52), Hume is at pains to deny that we are always engaged in this kind of self-monitoring. Instead, we must "enter most intimately" into ourselves before "observ[ing]" our perceptions.

6. That is, Hume uses "sympathy" in the sense of its Greek roots: feeling (*pathein*) with (*sun*) another. We might be tempted to use the word *empathy* where he uses *sympathy*.

7. Brown is not wrong, however, to see something like a concern for the negative impact of feelings of humility on our happiness at T 3.2.1.8, SBN 479.

8. Darwall (1995: 305) seems to accept Árdal's account of the indirect passions.

9. This is a different sceptical challenge from the one that asks whether and how we have a grasp on the mind's unity (T 1.4.6).

10. Hume is thus a "sensible subjectivist" about the features that define people.

13 Hume's Justice

Hume's phenomenology of justice goes as follows. In civilized societies, individuals generally observe rules concerning the ownership of goods, their transfer by consent, and the keeping of promises. (Hume calls these the "three main laws of nature.") These rules express the essential contents of justice and are closely related to rules of political obligation, international law, and chastity and modesty. The rules of justice are requisite for society to be possible at all. (Hume's theory of justice in the *Treatise* has no distributive concerns. It concentrates on justice understood as what makes social order possible.) While its contents come in the form of rules, justice figures in moral practice as a virtue and as a morally approved character trait. The authority of the rules of justice depends on the recognition of it as a virtue, where this recognition is owing to our moral sentiments.

Hume thinks that moral sentiments play this role with respect to all of the virtues. However, certain further facts about justice set it apart from the others. The first fact is that in the ordinary practice of justice, the only universal and real motive for performing just acts is a sense of duty or obligation. In the case of other virtues, particular motives for acting are drawn from the particular features of the actions. The second fact is that the rules of justice are perfectly general, inflexible, and determined. No gradual transition between right and wrong and no adjustment to particular circumstances are admissible (or admitted). The third fact is that conduct according to the moral rules of justice (unlike that expressing the other virtues) requires, in any large society, the backing of the sanctions of government. I think Hume is right in accepting these as facts about the present practice of justice. But, as he is well aware, this phenomenology of justice seems to be inconsistent with certain of his views about motivation and moral evaluation. Since no first-order scepticism about the practice of justice is viable, he must remove such inconsistency or face the threat of a *reductio* of his own account of morality. To remove the inconsistency, he proposes an account of justice as an artificial virtue – an account that is one of the most complex, original, and successful parts of the *Treatise*.

I. THE POSSIBILITY OF JUSTICE

The Paradox of Justice

The practice of justice, as described by Hume and in the context of his radical sentimentalism, is paradoxical because it seems to involve something *impossible*. This comes to light in the "absurdity" (T 3.2.5.4, SBN 517) of certain commonsense opinions concerning justice – for example, that it is the constant will of giving everyone his due or that the obligation of promises arises from an act of the mind (viz., the willing of that very obligation). Hume thinks that the "deceitful method of reasoning" we are prone to is evidence that "there are contain'd in the subject some obscurities and difficulties, which we are not able to surmount" (T 3.2.6.5, SBN 528). These "obscurities and difficulties" are in the very experience and practice of justice, not just in our ideas of it.[1] They spring from a gap that opens, in certain objective social circumstances, between our motivational endowment and the conditions of moral approval and moral regulation of conduct. This generates a problem of circularity: the motive and sentiments that support justice presuppose the idea and practice of it as a virtue. This circularity makes justice paradoxical and raises difficult explanatory problems; for Hume, it also motivates viewing this area of morals as an artifice. Hume's account of the paradox is in three steps: the first deals with the structure of moral evaluation; the second concerns the character of our motives for just conduct; and the third concerns certain facts about the contents of motivation.

The First Virtuous Motive and the Common Course of Passions

In Part 1 of Book 3 Hume has argued that "vice and virtue are not discoverable merely by reason, or the comparison of ideas," but rather "by means of some impression or sentiment they occasion," so that "morality, therefore, is more properly felt than judg'd of" (T 3.1.2.1, SBN 470). The relevant sentiment is a special sort of pleasure and pain: "virtue is distinguish'd by the pleasure, and vice by the pain, that any action, sentiment or character gives us by the mere view and contemplation" (T 3.1.2.11, SBN 475). Hume now adds a further a posteriori thesis about the objects of moral sentiments: "'Tis evident, that when we praise any actions, we regard only the motives that produc'd them, and consider the actions as signs or indications of certain principles in the mind and temper. The external performance has no merit. We must look within to find the moral quality" (T 3.2.1.2, SBN 477). Actions figure only because they are the "external signs" that give us access to the "motive, that produc'd them," which is the "ultimate object" of our praise. This is also true of moral prescription, despite its seeming to be inescapably linked to actions: "After the same manner, when we require any action, or blame a person for not performing it, we always suppose, that one in that situation shou'd be influenc'd by the proper motive of that action, and we esteem it vicious in him to be regardless of it." Therefore, "all virtuous actions derive their merit only from virtuous motives, and are consider'd merely as signs of those motives" (T 3.2.1.3–4, SBN 477–78). Motives are here understood as "durable principles of the mind, which extend over the whole conduct, and enter into the personal character" (T 3.3.1.4, SBN 575) and can only "influence" our moral sentiments: "We are never to consider any single action in our enquiries concerning the origin of morals; but only the quality or character from which the action proceeded. These alone are *durable* enough to affect our sentiments concerning the person" (T 3.3.1.5, SBN 575).[2]

This constraint on the *objects* of moral evaluation implies, according to Hume, a constraint on its *structure*: "From this principle I conclude, that the first virtuous motive, which bestows a merit on any action, can never be a regard to the virtue of that action, but must be some other natural motive or principle" (T 3.2.1.4, SBN 478). The principle is put forward not only as a "metaphysical subtility," but as a feature of "all our reasonings in common life" (T 3.2.1.5, SBN 478). If parental love were not a "natural affection," the care of children could not be a duty. We would not blame a parent for neglecting his or her child nor "have the duty in our eye" in this regard (ibid.). Hume thus establishes, as an "undoubted maxim" (which I dub "First Motive"), that *"no action can be virtuous, or morally good, unless there be in human nature some motive to produce it, distinct from the sense of its morality"* (T 3.2.1.7, SBN 479).

Hume's reasoning seems to be sound, on a priori grounds. It is reasonable that motivational principles, not actions, are the right level of moral evaluation. (Certain forms of utilitarianism deny this.) Thus the moral merit of actions cannot be recognized unless morally valuable motives are already given. But then, unless what confers moral value to motives is simply the *de dicto* content – "do the right thing" (certain forms of Kantianism accept this) – such motives cannot consist in regard for rightness of actions. In a radical sentimentalist setting, these a priori considerations mesh with a posteriori ones drawn from the natural objects of moral approval. Motives independent of the moral merit of actions make possible and are actually involved in moral evaluation. The alternative is impossible: "To suppose, that the mere regard to the virtue of the action, may be the first motive, which produc'd the action, and render'd it virtuous, is to reason in a circle" (T 3.2.1.4, SBN 478).[3]

First Motive explains, in turn, a constraint on the *determinants* and *contents* of moral evaluation. Hume remarks: "I shall add, as a corollary to this reasoning, that since no action can be laudable or blameable, without some motives or impelling passions, distinct from the sense of morals, these distinct passions must have a great influence on that sense. 'Tis according to their general force in human nature, that we blame or praise." He adds that we "always consider the *natural* and *usual* force of the passions, when we determine concerning vice and virtue; and if the passions depart very much from the common measures on either side, they are always disapprov'd as vicious." Hume then concludes: "Hence arise our common measures of duty, in preferring the one to the other. Our sense of duty always follows the common and natural course of our passions" (T 3.2.1.18, SBN 483–84).[4]

This principle (which I dub "Common Course") is explicitly linked by Hume to First Motive. I think that it is in effect an implication of it, given sentimentalism. But how does it follow? A possible answer again lies in the a posteriori fact that *sympathy* is the causal mechanism responsible for eliciting moral sentiments. Moral sentiments have their root in *vicarious* pleasures and pains, felt because of the lively ideas we can form of the impressions in the minds of others, by inference from their outward circumstances and signs. This inference relies on a background of beliefs concerning the similarity of the minds of all men or the general nature of the passions that give them motives for acting. Sympathetic feelings, like moral sentiments, thus cannot but be shaped by the general course of motivating passions. We blame, rather than praise, a father who neglects his children because of our acquaintance with the passions that commonly govern parental relations. Thus, Common Course is a necessary complement of First Motive. First Motive requires merit-independent motives for the occurrence of moral sentiments – that is, for moral evaluation. Common Course makes sense of the determinate character and contents with which moral sentiments occur, determining what is morally valuable and what is not. Together, these two principles determine, on the ground of basic facts about motivation, the possibility and nature of moral evaluation.

This is the first step of Hume's account of the paradox of justice. Assume that we can specify, for a class of moral sentiments individuated by their contents and directions, what motives would satisfy First Motive with regard to them. What would follow if there were a gap at this place in our motivational endowment? What if motives of that kind did not satisfy Common Course, in the circumstances that call for such moral sentiments and their authority? It would not simply follow that our moral sentiments and ideas were somehow mistaken or fallacious; there would be no such moral sentiments or ideas to harbor any mistake or fallacy. The conditions for these moral sentiments and ideas would simply be missing. If, on the other hand, the practice conforming to these sentiments and ideas is extant and in good order, we are plunged into paradox. The two principles, therefore, are the background against which to assess the "obscurities and difficulties" of justice.

Sense of Duty as the Motive for Justice

Hume accepts as a fact that our present practice of justice is motivated by a sense of duty. (This is the second step of his account.) If, as a civilized man, "train'd up according to a certain discipline and education," I ask myself what "*reason or motive*" I have for doing a certain act of justice, the "just and satisfactory" answer will be that "my regard to justice, and abhorrence of villainy and knavery, are sufficient reasons for me, if I have the least grain of honesty, or of sense of duty and obligation" (T 3.2.1.9, SBN 479). Within the practice of justice (in contrast with a "rude and more *natural* condition") we find a motive for justice simply by looking at the "*honesty and justice*" of prospective actions (ibid.). If we did not think that we were under a "moral obligation" with respect to them, "we never shou'd feel any inclination" to perform them (T 3.2.5.6, SBN 518).

This fact governs Hume's theory, since it must be explained consistently with the two principles about moral evaluation; and, as Hume remarks, "in this lies the great difficulty" (T 3.2.1.10, SBN 480).[5] Acting on duty is not *in general* problematic. First Motive and Common Course do not make it impossible; rather they set the conditions for it. Hume has a substantive account of acting on a sense of duty, in terms of motives springing from regret about lacking, on a certain occasion, a common virtuous trait. This account explicitly assumes that the motive the agent finds himself devoid of is one, independent of duty, that would produce actions of the same kind. In order to extend this explanation to justice, one must find a first motive for acts of justice and honesty. The difficulty is that, on a reasonable understanding of what it is for a motive to be "first" or "original," no such motive can be found in the case of justice. No common passion gives a merit-independent motive for justice that, by becoming an object of our moral sentiments, could give us the sense of the moral merit of just actions.

No First Motive for Justice

Hume argues for this conclusion by reviewing the different motives that could be candidates for this role. (This is the third step.) The first kind of motive that he considers is concern for private interest. Hume rejects it: "'tis certain, that self-love, when it acts at its liberty, instead of engaging us to honest actions, is the source of all injustice and violence; nor can a man ever correct those vices, without correcting and restraining the *natural* movements of that appetite" (T 3.2.1.10, SBN 480). The natural direction of the passion of self-interest is directly opposite to justice.

Hume's rejection of the second possible motive for justice, *"regard to public interest,* to which nothing is more contrary than examples of injustice and dishonesty," is better articulated (T 3.2.1.11, SBN 480). His first objection is that "public interest is not naturally attach'd to the observation of the rules of justice; but is only connected with it, after an artificial convention for the establishment of these rules, as shall be shown more at large hereafter" (ibid.). This is not a point about motivation, but a (very important) point about the act-consequence pattern that is distinctive of justice, to be discussed below. Hume's second objection is that, if an unjust act can be kept secret, so as not to give an example, "the public is no longer interested," while "there is no moralist, who will affirm, that the duty and obligation ceases" (T 3.2.1.11, SBN 481). His third objection concerns motivation. "Experience sufficiently proves" that regard for public interest is a "motive too remote and too sublime" to influence agents "in the ordinary conduct of life" (ibid.). More generally, "there is no such passion in human minds, as the love of mankind, merely as such, independent of personal qualities, of services, or of relation to ourself" (T 3.2.1.12, SBN 481). Therefore such a passion, even if it could occasionally motivate someone to perform a just act, would not satisfy Common Course.

The third kind of motivation Hume rejects is *"private benevolence, or a regard to the interests of the party concern'd"* (T 3.2.1.13, SBN 482). On this hypothesis, if what was prescribed by the rules of justice did not correspond to private benevolence, "the original motive to justice wou'd fail; and consequently the justice itself, and along with it all property, right, and obligation" (ibid.). Hume objects that private benevolence is influenced by personal characters, relations, and circumstances. It is too variable to motivate just acts in a general and reliable way.

The first and the third kinds of motives that Hume considered spring from the common course of passions. They do not depend on an antecedent sense of the moral merit of actions. They can well be objects of moral approval. But neither of them reliably motivates us to do just actions. There is a gap in our motivational endowment and no fit between First Motive and Common Course. Therefore, there are no structural grounds for our moral sentiments concerning justice; and there are no grounds for a sense of duty as the motivation to do just acts. Because this is the only general and reliable motivation for it, the practice of justice is tainted by paradox.[6]

Justice as Artifice

Hume thinks that the correct conclusion to draw from this paradoxical feature of the actual practice of justice is not that justice is impossible, but that it requires a special explanation, different from that of other areas of morals. Hume takes himself to have established that justice is an *artificial virtue*:

From all this follows, that we have naturally no real or universal motive for observing the laws of equity, but the very equity and merit of that observance; and as no action can be equitable or meritorious, where it cannot arise from some separate motive, there is here an evident sophistry and reasoning in a circle. Unless, therefore, we will allow, that nature has establish'd a sophistry, and render'd it necessary and unavoidable, we must allow, that the sense of justice and injustice is not deriv'd from nature, but arises artificially, tho' necessarily from education, and human conventions. (T 3.2.1.17, SBN 483)

Hume's argument is that justice would be impossible, as a practice and as a virtue, if we looked to human *nature* for satisfaction of its conditions. Human nature is the default explanans in the whole *Treatise*, so the structure of justice is problematic; but there is the alternative of its springing from artifice.

The above argument crucially turns on the notion of *natural motive*, because the conclusion that justice is naturally impossible (and is derived from artifice) depends on the assumption that the first motive for it should be found in our nature. Regrettably, Hume does not introduce this notion explicitly, so we are left to reconstruct it from the texts. There is a sense of "natural," as opposed to "rare and unusual" (T 3.1.2.8, SBN 474), in which any viable first motive for justice (which cannot but belong to the common course of passions) is natural. (Hume sometimes opposes "natural" to "moral," in reference to obligations. This raises complex interpretive issues, to be discussed below; but of course the first motive is by construction "natural" in this sense.) But Hume also sometimes means by "natural" "any thing that proceeds immediately from original principles, without the intervention of thought or reflection" (T 3.2.1.19, SBN 484). This is the relevant sense for Hume's argument about the artificiality of justice: in the common course of passions there are no first motives of this sort for justice.

It may be objected that motives that Hume recognizes as natural, such as self-interest or private benevolence, are not always unmediated by thought and reflection. But Hume does not mean that we always *act* on natural motives without thought or reflection; rather, the natural motives *themselves* are not grounded upon, or dependent on, thought and reflection. In general, motives are caused by the prevailing passions of the mind and the circumstances of action, as viewed by the agent.

Motives are natural if, in a given situation, they immediately spring from the corresponding qualities or principles of the mind, with minimal cognitive apparatus (essentially, what is required for recognizing their objects). In contrast, artificial motives depend on a quite complex cognitive appraisal and interpretation by the agents of their practical circumstances. It is only this appraisal and this interpretation that connect specific motives to a certain passion. (Notice that this makes possible a change in cognitive presuppositions yielding different motives with different practical implications from the same trait or passion. This point will prove important for the consistency of Hume's overall position about nature and artifice.)

This distinction between natural and artificial motives can be viewed from a slightly different but related perspective. Hume sometimes advances a particularistic view of motivation, insisting that "each action is a particular individual event" that "must proceed from particular principles, and from our immediate situation within ourselves, and with respect to the rest of the universe" (T 3.2.6.9, SBN 531). This conception of motivation could be used to identify "natural motives": motives are natural if they intelligibly connect particular actions and their particular consequences to the contents of certain passions or traits. In contrast, artificial motives are those that can refer to actions and their consequences (and connect with passions or traits) only under certain general descriptions. Such motives essentially depend on reflection and reasoning because they are general and descriptive in their contents and in the way they present actions and situations and direct us to act.

Natural and artificial motives are thus distinguished in terms of cognitive simplicity and complexity, and of particular and generalized content. On this understanding of natural motives, we can state Hume's conclusion as follows: from the viewpoint of First Motive and Common Course, if its first motive does not essentially depend on thought and reflection and if it is particular in its content, justice is impossible. Such motives cannot be first motives for just actions, they cannot provide an object for our moral approval of justice, and they cannot explain how a sense of duty can be a motive for justice at all. But justice is possible – as an artifice, grounded on artificial motives.

2. THE CIRCUMSTANCES OF JUSTICE

The problems, however, seem only to have been pushed back one step. For one thing, we still have to see what reflections and what descriptions are constitutive of the artificial motive for justice. For another, there are troubles with the very distinction of natural and artificial in this area. The motives, sentiments, and ideas required by Hume's justice are out of the reach of our nature. But then it is not clear how they can be put in place by artifice. Hume insists that "we can naturally no more change our own sentiments, than the motions of the heavens" (T 3.2.5.4, SBN 517); that "the will never creates new sentiments" (T 3.2.5.5, SBN 518); that the "natural and inherent principles and passions of human nature" are "inalterable" (T 3.2.5.9, SBN 521); and that "'tis impossible to change or correct any thing material in our nature" (T 3.2.7.6, SBN 537). But the invention of justice involves precisely this sort of change and correction. In general, Hume's radical empiricism and sentimentalism do not seem hospitable to the production of new, artificial mental contents by mental activity. There is thus a general problem concerning the very possibility of artificial motives – motives whose objects and directions are put in place by some mental activity or artifice.[7]

The same point can be made from a different perspective. Hume's solution to the paradox of justice is that first motives for justice spring from the passion or trait of self-interest. The rules of justice that make the advantages of society possible are in the interest of each and any of its members, so that a "concern for our own, and the public interest" makes us establish them (T 3.2.2.20, SBN 496). This claim may seem inconsistent with Hume's remark that self-interest, if pursued "without any precaution," causes us to act selfishly, not justly (T 3.2.2.21, SBN 497). Hume responds that the "interested affection" gives reasons for justice only "by an alteration of its direction" (T 3.2.2.13, SBN 492) or "in an oblique and artificial manner" (T 3.2.5.9, SBN 521); it cannot be produced by "*uncultivated nature*," nor by any "inartificial principle of the human mind" (T 3.2.2.8, SBN 488). But a difficulty remains. If the interest in restraining the pursuit of self-interest is (as Hume also says) "palpable and evident, even to the most rude and uncultivated of human race" (T 3.2.7.1, SBN 534) – if self-restraint or redirection "must necessarily take place upon the least reflection" (T 3.2.2.13, SBN 492) – it is not clear why the first motive for justice cannot be identified with a natural motive of interest. Why is this apparently straightforward causal and motivational connection not a natural motive? Naïveté and generality do not seem enough to distinguish nature from artifice in the mind.

Act-Consequence Structures

The two problems dovetail, one calling into question how something that is missing from mental nature can be put in place by mental activity; the other, how something that is present in the mind and close to its passions can fail to be natural. In Hume we find essentially the same answer to each question – one that explains how artifice can change something in mental nature and how self-induced redirection of interest can be artificial. But to see this we must go beyond the argument for the artificiality of justice as we have reconstructed it, looking at the different *act-consequence structures* of actions and at the relations between passions or traits, motives, and actions in different areas of morals.

Hume distinguishes two general kinds of act-consequence structures, which come into view precisely in the distinction between *natural virtues* and *justice*:

> The only difference betwixt the natural virtues and justice lies in this, that the good, which results from the former, arises from every single act, and is the object of some natural passion: Whereas a single act of justice, consider'd in itself, may often be contrary to the public good; and 'tis only the concurrence of mankind, in a general scheme or system of action, which is advantageous. (T 3.3.1.12, SBN 579)

The "good" is (in either case) the pleasant or useful consequences that follow from actions. But the causal production of this good is different in the two cases. In the case of natural virtues, any *single* act is followed (in the favorable cases) by the good consequences it is apt to produce. (The sum total of the good produced is an additive function of the single acts performed.) While it is obvious that such an act would not be morally meritorious if it did not express a natural virtue, the fact that it is such an instance does not affect its causal powers. In the case of justice, there is a gap between the actual consequences of single acts and the causal powers they have independently of the general practice of that virtue. The ultimate bearer of the causal powers of justice is, rather, the *general practice* itself, the scheme or system of the actions that conform to its rules. Particular actions have causal powers and can produce the good of justice only as instances of justice – that is, when they are included in its general practice or promote concurrence with it. The act-consequence structure of justice is in this sense *indirect* and practice-mediated.[8]

These different act-consequence structures underlie the contrast between natural and artificial motives and solve our two problems. Motives spring from passions or traits and from beliefs about the consequences of actions. (The trait of self-interest gives rise or fails to give rise to motives for acting on the basis of such beliefs.) Assuming that our beliefs are minimally accurate, the motives that arise from a certain passion or trait are determined in accordance with the act-consequence structure of the action. Now, the act-consequence structure of an action is an objective fact. This fact can act as an external factor on internal relations of mental causation: in particular, it can explain how motives can be in principle out of the reach of agents with otherwise suitable traits or passions – not because of unavoidable ignorance or rational flaws (which could not be repaired), but because of the practical structure of the relevant actions. If such structure can be changed, one can see how mental contents and states can be artificially put in place.

This also applies to the problem about artificial self-interest. Self-interest is, according to Hume, the natural trait or passion that supports justice. But, as with any other quality of the mind, it gives motives for actions only in reference to and within the constraints of act-consequence structures. This explains how it can have opposite motivational effects. It can fully motivate when the consequences of acting on it are caused by individual acts and can be "the object of some natural passion" (T 3.3.1.12, SBN 579); and it can fail to motivate if actions have a practice-mediated, indirect act-consequence structure. This is the case with just conduct, which cannot be motivated with reference to single acts: "tho' the rules of justice are establish'd merely by interest, their connexion with interest is somewhat singular, and is different from what may be observ'd on other occasions"; it cannot be determined with reference to single acts (T 3.2.2.22, SBN 497). This opposition grounds a distinction between natural and artificial motives. The interest in the restraint of self-interest according to rules of justice can well be palpable and evident and take place upon the least reflection. Still, it remains that such interest is necessarily practice-mediated, so as to reflect the structure of just conduct; and because practice-mediateness is something not given but produced, it is artificial in this specific and important sense. Again, it is the external factor of act-consequence structures that explains the gaps and continuities between the natural and artificial mental elements involved in the explanation of justice.[9]

Frequency Effects

Why is the act-consequence structure of justice indirect? It is crucial that the justice-constituting artifice is *social* – that justice proceeds from conventions or agreements, the choice, consent, or combination of mankind. This takes us to the deepest explanatory level of Hume's theory. He makes perfectly clear that justice is connected to specific social conditions. While society is in general necessary for mankind, not all social situations require and allow regulation by justice. Hume summarizes the circumstances that make sense of the need and possibility of justice in terms of the "concurrence of certain *qualities* of the human mind with the *situation* of external objects" (T 3.2.2.16, SBN 494). The qualities of the mind are our prevailing selfishness and our limited generosity (the second being almost as contrary to large societies as the first). The situation of the external objects is their "*easy change*," the fact that they can be taken from us to the advantage of others, and "their *scarcity* in comparison of the wants and desires of men" (ibid.). Thus, "'*tis only from*

*the selfishness and confin'd generosity of man, along with the scanty
provision nature has made for his wants, that justice derives its origin"*
(T 3.2.2.18, SBN 495).

But this is not all Hume has to say concerning the social grounds – the
true circumstances – of justice. A further, fundamental insight is that the
outcomes of actions, and thus the structure of different kinds of conduct,
are sometimes determined by the relative number of individual members
of a group that are disposed to act in certain ways and thus by the
frequency of acts of certain kinds. *Frequency effects* lie right below the
surface of the *Treatise* but come clearly to the fore in the second *Enquiry*,
which can thus be regarded as a helpful gloss to the earlier text. As in the
case of act-consequence structures, frequency effects are introduced in
terms of a distinction between justice and the other social virtues. But
what now becomes clear is that the different act-consequence structures
of actions and passions-motives relations depend on differences in frequency effects. *What others do* sometimes makes a difference in what
follows from *what each individual is doing*. In social virtues such as
humanity and benevolence, the good that results from single acts is
"compleat and entire," because it does not matter whether the other
members of society concur in the same acts. With justice, benefits arise
only if "the whole, or the greater part of the society," concur in observing
the rules of justice (EPM App. 3.3, SBN 304). The frequency of just acts
within society determines what follows from any particular act of an
individual; and this social fact – this social difference in respect of the
frequency effect – is the ultimate ground for the practical and motivational difference between act-consequence structures.[10]

The presence of frequency effects is a basic difference in social situations. Certain social situations have the structure of a "wall, built by
many hands; which still rises by each stone, that is heaped upon it." The
consequences of social action are (obviously) a function of the actions
performed by the individuals; but the consequences of each single act
are determined no matter what the others do. Other situations have
the structure of a "vault, where each individual stone would, of itself,
fall to the ground" (EPM App. 3.5, SBN 305). The individual agents and
their actions are *interdependent*: their actions' consequences display
frequency effects, being determined by what (many of) the others do.
Hume's fundamental idea is that justice is called upon to govern social
contexts where frequency effects are prevalent. This social fact is
the explanation of the different act-consequence structures. In the case
of justice, the demand for essentially practice-mediated motives is
grounded on the demand for essentially coordinated social action. And
this is required by the presence of frequency effects. To sum up, the
causal powers of single just acts are indirect (practice-mediated) because

they are determined by the relative number of agents performing just acts (by the coordinative social structure underlying justice).

These basic causal and social facts about justice constrain the motives for performing just acts and therefore, via First Motive and Common Course, the possibility of the sense of their moral merit. The facts explain how the gaps and the paradoxes of the ongoing, fairly successful moral practice of justice do not express a faulty understanding of it on the part of its practitioners; and the facts reveal the practice of justice's objective, motivational and social structure and conditions. They explain how such gaps and paradoxes do not mandate (at the motivational and evaluative level) anything that is not licensed by Hume's radical naturalism and sentimentalism; there is no need for principles of agency of a rational, intellectual, and spiritual kind.[11] They explain, by bringing causal and social external factors to bear on mental causation, how the *natural* mind and *inalterable* passions can be changed and redirected by artifice. Finally and most importantly, they tell us something vital about the justice-instituting artifice: it must have an effect on the contents of cognitive and motivational states, it must operate on act-consequence structures, and it must be a form of social action – an agreement or convention on a scheme of conduct – involving a distinctive pattern of frequency effects. "Whatever is advantageous to two or more persons, if all perform their part; but what loses all advantage, if only one perform, can arise from no other principle. There would otherwise be no motive for any one of them to enter into that scheme of conduct" (EPM App. 3.8, SBN 306–7).

3. THE ORIGIN OF JUSTICE

The idea that basic social rules can be fundamentally explained (starting from their very contents and the motives supporting them) by social action or agreement may seem to be in its turn paradoxical. Such an agreement is very naturally (and was traditionally) understood as a binding, voluntary engagement, on the model of a reciprocal promise or contract. But, on this understanding, it would fall short of the task assigned to it in Hume's theory. In the first place, a *binding* voluntary engagement requires recognized – and obligatory – rules, to determine what is to be undertaken and what sanctions follow their nonobservance. But rules of this kind are themselves rules of justice. In the second place, binding *voluntary* engagements presuppose that individuals have motives to undertake and observe them. But Hume introduces convention precisely because justice lacks the support of natural motives. How could it be that an agreement for justice expresses the will of the concerned agents? Hume advances a conception of agreement and social artifice that can answer this question.[12]

The Emergence of Justice

Hume insists that justice, though artificial, is neither accidental nor arbitrary: "where an invention is obvious and absolutely necessary, it may as properly be said to be natural as any thing that proceeds immediately from original principles, without the intervention of thought or reflection." He is even prepared to call the rules of justice "*laws of nature*" (T 3.2.1.19, SBN 484). These views can be reconciled with the artificial character of justice if its origin is gradual emergence through a process of social and psychological transformation.

If society were recommended only by the advantages of "conjunction of forces," "partition of employments," and "mutual succour" (T 3.2.2.3, SBN 485), we could not explain how it comes into being, because, "in their wild uncultivated state" and "by study and reflection alone," humans could not be "sensible of its advantages" (T 3.2.2.4, SBN 486). But this is a difficulty only for a mistaken, voluntaristic view of the origin of society. Sociability emerges from very different principles:

Most fortunately ... there is conjoin'd to those necessities, whose remedies are remote and obscure, another necessity, which having a present and more obvious remedy, may justly be regarded as the first and original principle of human society. This necessity is no other than that natural appetite betwixt the sexes, which unites them together, and preserves their union, till a new tye takes place in their concern for their common offspring. (T 3.2.2.4, SBN 486)

Parental care is also the principle of the "more numerous society" that comes to be established between parents and offspring. In the context of familial society, individuals not only come to understand the advantages of society, but gradually adapt to it: "In a little time, custom and habit operating on the tender minds of the children, makes them sensible of the advantages, which they may reap from society, as well as fashions them by degrees for it, by rubbing off those rough corners and untoward affections, which prevent their coalition" (ibid.).

This explanation extends to justice. In the context of early social relations, the "particulars in our *natural temper*" (selfishness and limited generosity), together with scarcity and interdependence, set a demand for (what we know as) justice (T 3.2.2.5, SBN 486). Of course, it would be reasoning in a circle to think that the origin of justice lies in the grasping and accepting of the idea by its prospective practitioners: "The idea of justice can never serve to this purpose, or be taken for a natural principle, capable of inspiring men with an equitable conduct towards each other. That virtue, as it is now understood, wou'd never have been dream'd of among rude and savage men" (T 3.2.2.8, SBN 488). The acquisition of the idea of justice is a crucial part of what is to be explained; but there is no need to involve such idea in the explanation of justice. Both the practice and the idea of it can be explained by gradual emergence. Humans cannot but recognize that the "principal disturbance in society" arises from the "looseness" and "easy transition from one person to another" of external goods. They are driven to "seek for a remedy" by rendering these goods "fix'd and constant" (T 3.2.2.9, SBN 489). (They are also driven to seek ways to ensure that such goods are where they are most usefully employed and ways to ensure commitment to exchange mutually beneficial services.)

Seeking such a remedy leads to the social artifice introducing justice – what Hume calls a "convention" – which is thus firmly and plausibly located within a gradually progressive view of social relations and individual cognition. In the fullness of time, property is instituted

by a convention enter'd into by all the members of the society to bestow stability on the possession of those external goods, and leave every one in the peaceable enjoyment of what he may acquire by his fortune and industry. By this means, every one knows what he may safely possess; and the passions are restrain'd in their partial and contradictory motions. (T 3.2.2.9, SBN 489)

The same holds for the rules for the voluntary transfer of property and (most importantly) the institution of promising (which is required for the exchange of services): "All of them, by concert, enter into a scheme of actions, calculated for common benefit, and agree to be true to their word; nor is there any thing requisite to form this concert or convention, but that every one have a sense of interest in the faithful fulfilling of engagements, and express that sense to other members of society" (T 3.2.5.11, SBN 522–23).

The gradual emergence of conventions and the rules and ideas of justice thus correct Hume's remark that "nature provides a remedy in the judgment and understanding, for what is irregular and incommodious in the affections" (T 3.2.2.9, SBN 489). Hume's historical (conjectural-historical, of course) gradualism removes the suspicion that judgment and understanding *presuppose* an understanding of justice. Conventions of justice are both the outcome and a part of a gradual process of cognitive, motivational, and social change driven by the common experience of social interaction (frequency effects and act-consequence structures included). This is an important insight – a radical revision of the natural law and social contract traditions. Still, this gradual progress has mainly the role of providing a context (and, to a certain extent, a model) for conventions, which have a distinct, irreducible explanatory weight. We must turn to it now.

Conventions

Convention is one of the most original and fruitful concepts in Hume's philosophy.[13] Conventions can explain, in a fundamental way, institutions such as justice, language, and money. We must now see how they do this. Hume characterizes convention by contrast with contracts: it is "not of the nature of a *promise*" (T 3.2.2.10, SBN 490). It does not consist in mutually binding engagements; it is rather the converging of individuals on certain patterns of conduct. What is crucial is that convention is itself a "scheme of action," a case of *social interaction* involving *frequency effects*. Participating in justice-instituting agreements is entering, "by concert" with others, into a specific pattern of social action (T 3.2.5.11, SBN 522). Because of its frequency effects on the consequences of actions, convention is a pattern of social action that can give self-interested motives for the conditional acceptance of rules of justice – motives that individuals otherwise would not have. The ultimate ground of the difficulty with justice is social in character; convention overcomes such difficulty precisely because of its social character and its frequency effects:

this may properly enough be call'd a convention or agreement betwixt us, tho' without the interposition of a promise; since the actions of each of us have a reference to those of the other, and are perform'd upon the supposition, that something is to be perform'd on the other part. Two men, who pull the oars of a boat, do it by an agreement or convention, tho' they have never given promises to each other. (T 3.2.2.10, SBN 490)

Frequency effects raise *coordination* problems – problems about whether and how individuals can converge on mutually beneficial patterns of actions. (These problems come into view, for individuals, in the act-consequence structure of their motivations.) Convention solves these problems by being a form of *coordinated* social action, instantiating such convergence on a certain pattern. In the case of justice, the pattern exhibits the right frequency effects for agents to converge in good numbers on conduct conforming to justice. Thus a justice-originating convention "immediately causes that interest to operate upon them; and interest is the *first* obligation to the performance of promises" (as well as to the other institutions of justice) (T 3.2.5.11, SBN 523). Frequency effects determine the indirect act-consequence structure of actions and the relation between passions, motives, and actions – of just conduct, in the present case. The lack of fit between those frequency effects that actually prevail and those that would be required for acting justly (for doing actions that, like actions of justice, have practice-mediated act-consequence structure) is the structural gap that makes impossible any natural motive for justice. Put in the most general terms, the role of conventions is to secure that frequency effects are the right ones for just actions – actions with indirect act-consequence structure – to be motivated on grounds of self-interest. They can do this precisely by being instances of social interaction of the right kind.

There is much else to be said about the structure of Humean conventions, of course, but their social, frequency-dependent character is centrally important. Notice that, on this understanding, conventions (in contrast with classical or contemporary social contracts) can play their theoretical role only if they count (if only hypothetically) as actual social processes – that is, as actual patterns of interaction. What makes justice possible is, ultimately, the causal influence of frequency effects on the likelihood that practice-mediated just actions will be performed out of motives of self-interest. But only actual social interactions can have such causal influence (or any causal influence). Hume's conventions, in this respect, differ radically from social contracts that can do their theoretical work as purely regulative notions, as in the theories of Hobbes, Rousseau, and Rawls. This is also perfectly coherent with the historical orientation of Hume's theory of justice: historical explanatory concepts (even *conjectural*-historical explanatory concepts) must be assumed to be actual – to be facts – if they are to do any theoretical work. Hume's historical gradualism (and its anticipation of evolutionary constructs) and the explanatory function of conventions thus dovetail perfectly. The social character of convention is confirmed by the *conditional* nature of the motives for justice that spring from it. Each and any of the individuals can observe and conclude that prospective just actions are in his interest only if the others (or enough of the others) perform actions of the same kind – that is, only taking into account the right sort of frequency effects. The conditional character of such motives does not express any sort of binding engagement, reciprocal promise, or contract. Rather, it is a consequence of frequency effects and individuals' awareness that their actions "have a reference" to those of others and to their reciprocal expectations.[14]

Of course, the individuals must have a capacity to judge what is in their self-interest and understand the causal and practical structure of the convention. This was our starting point. But this capacity to judge and understand is just what they acquire in the (historical and real) experience of convention. The crucial thing they learn is that convention-induced frequency effects make acting according to rules of justice (acting in a practice-mediated way) the best way to pursue self-interest. It is learning this that puts individuals in a position to be motivated to justice and accept it: "When therefore men have had experience enough to observe, that whatever may be the consequence of any single act of justice, perform'd by a single person, yet the whole system of actions, concurr'd in by the whole society, is infinitely advantageous to the whole, and to every part; it is not long before justice and property take place" (T 3.2.2.22, SBN 497–98). But, again, how do individuals engage in a convention before they learn to understand its structure and advantages? Hume's answer refers us back to historical gradualism. Engaging in a convention is not a particular decision made at a certain moment in time; conventions are an aspect of a historical and gradual progress. His "method of proceeding" in explaining the origin of justice is the following: "I here only suppose those reflections to be form'd at once, which in fact arise insensibly and by degrees" (T 3.2.3.3, SBN 503). Convention itself is a gradual process in time: "Nor is the rule concerning the stability of possession the less deriv'd from human conventions, that it arises gradually, and acquires force by a slow progression, and by our repeated experience of the inconveniences of transgressing it" (T 3.2.2.10, SBN 490). Hume's solution to the riddle of the origin of justice is, ultimately, that *there is no such origin*. Justice (like the artifice of language [ibid.]) emerges in the social practice and experience of it; it is not so much produced as instantiated by conventions.

Common Belief

This sketch of the nature and role of Humean conventions should be complemented by an appropriate interpretation of their structure. What must be shown, at least as to the essentials, is how, in what respects, and by what mechanisms convention successfully corrects frequency effects and makes motivational room for practice-mediated actions. In particular, what must be shown is how the necessary cognitive and motivational changes (the artificial creation of new mental contents and states) can be effected. It must also be shown how convention (which puts in place, as we have seen, essentially conditional motives) can result in or instantiate all-considered, effective motives for doing just actions. Hume is perfectly right in thinking that his account of justice requires such conditional motives. (After all, justice can emerge only within social coordinated activity actually engaged in by individuals.) It remains to be seen how the conditions of conditional motives for justice can be reliably satisfied.

Hume has the essential resources for explaining the working of convention and for solving this problem. Convention is a socially coordinated solution to a problem of social coordination. But the explanatory aims of Hume's convention (and what marks its difference from much contemporary work on this notion) are primarily cognitive and motivational (and implicitly even normative) rather than social-theoretical or decision-theoretical. In Hume's theory, the socially coordinated activity that achieves the status of a convention is framed in terms of cognitive and motivational change. Thus it contributes decisively to explain such a change and (via First Motive and Common Course) the idea and the sense of justice. *This* is Hume's ultimate target: considerations of social coordination are instrumental to clarifying the act-consequence structures underlying motivations and actions that are instrumental in explaining the cognitive and motivational changes resulting in justice.

The basic feature of convention, in this crucial regard, is that it consists in a system of *common belief*. Coordination in a pattern of conduct is achieved through the emergence of shared, mutually recognized beliefs with the appropriate content. (This feature is of course central for the contemporary theory of convention and social norms; I talk of common belief, rather than of common knowledge, in deference to Hume's highly technical use of these notions).[15] This is expressed repeatedly in the text:

This convention is not of the nature of a *promise:* For even promises themselves, as we shall see afterwards, arise from human conventions. It is only a general sense of common interest; which sense all the members of the society express to one another, and which induces them to regulate their conduct by certain rules. (T 3.2.2.10, SBN 490)

Every member of society is sensible of this interest: Every one expresses this sense to his fellows, along with the resolution he has taken of squaring his actions by it, on condition that others will do the same. No more is requisite to induce any one of them to perform an act of justice, who has the first opportunity. (T 3.2.2.22, SBN 498)

The common belief forms in the course of the social interaction of convention; it springs from the experience of such social activity and at the same time supports it as a rule-instituting convention. It is this that marks the difference between pre-convention and conventional social stages – between problematic and achieved coordination. To take part in the convention is to form the relevant common beliefs. The beliefs held in common are about or are a "sense" of "interest" – each individual's interest in safe possession and transfer of external goods, and in exchange of services. The beliefs are also about some obvious, easy, or salient way of solving the problems this raises – a way that all individuals can be expected to recognize ("it must immediately occur, as the most natural expedient, that every one continue to enjoy what he is at present master of" [T 3.2.3.4, SBN 503]). The beliefs, finally, are about the interest all the concerned individuals have in converging on these expedients and in others doing the same and about their awareness of such interest (a "*general* sense of *common* interest" [T 3.2.2.10, SBN 490; emphasis added]). (These beliefs must involve at least an implicit grasp of different act-consequence structures and the bearing of frequency effects on the results of actions.) Common beliefs about these objects, together with the corresponding interests, achieve coordination in the matters of concern for justice.

The crucial point is that such common belief marks an important *cognitive change*, not only in the sense that absent convention-constituting interaction there would be no matter of fact about which to have beliefs, but also in the more interesting sense that it is a kind of belief, as to its content and mental role, that can be held only as common – that is, shared and mutually recognized. Common belief is *shared* belief: many individuals have the same belief about the structure and the tendencies of patterns of action. Being a belief that can be held by all concerned individuals, it must have *general content* concerning actions, motives, and circumstances. By forming such shared belief, individuals thus come to think about these matters differently from how they did before. First, they come to entertain descriptions of actions and motives such that they can think of everyone performing (or failing to perform) the same action for the same motive. Second, this makes possible (and in fact mandatory) thinking of motives and actions as instantiating general schemes of conduct or general practices. (This is crucial for the cognitive control of act-consequence structures). Third, they come to have the idea of *rules of action*; they come to think about what to do in terms of patterns of conduct and related conditions (if such and such, do this and that) – rules that can be extensionally equivalent to the ordinary rules of justice. This cognitive change, springing from the appropriate common belief (which is in turn a central aspect of the social experience of convention), puts individuals in a position to think and be motivated to act in ways suitable to convergence on justice. Correspondingly, the general contents and importance of rules that are distinctive of artificial morals simply express their being grounded on convention and common belief.

But is this enough to achieve coordination on the contents of justice and to satisfy First Motive and Common Course? Common belief is not only shared but *mutually recognized*, and this makes for its different practical import.[16] Individuals not only have the same beliefs concerning what to do and think in terms of the same rules, but also they believe of each other that they all have the same beliefs and think in terms of these rules, and they believe that others believe the same and so on. (We can safely allow for iteration here: the flimsiness of imagination eventually takes hold and individuals stop worrying.) Mutual recognition strengthens beliefs concerning what one's interests are and that one should abide by the rules; it also strengthens the belief that the condition of the rule will be satisfied. The interested motive for doing just actions becomes effective in this way. Common belief redirects the natural motive of interest so that it takes as its content the relevant rules and effectively governs (ceteris paribus) the actions of individuals. This secures the success of coordination and satisfies First Motive and Common Course:

I observe, that it will be for my interest to leave another in the possession of his goods, *provided* he will act in the same manner with regard to me. He is sensible of a like interest in the regulation of his conduct. When this common sense of interest is mutually express'd, and is known to both, it produces a suitable resolution and behavior. (T 3.2.2.10, SBN 490)

The fact that common belief is progressively and gradually achieved through social experience only reinforces this result: "this experience assures us still more, that the sense of interest has become common to all our fellows, and gives us a confidence of the future regularity of their conduct: And 'tis only on the expectation of this, that our moderation and abstinence are founded" (T 3.2.2.10, SBN 490). Still, given Hume's beliefs-and-interests account of its structure, convention (the process and the rules it results in) can be rationally inspected and endorsed by its participants; historical gradualism does not leave individuals bereft of rational considerations in favor of justice.

To sum up, convention is actual, progressive, and coordinative *social interaction*. It involves and is supported by *common belief* concerning what is in everyone's interest. Common belief instantiates and makes available *general* and *rule-modeled* contents concerning what to do. The mutual ascription of such beliefs *redirects self-interest* in ways extensionally equivalent to (contemporary, moralized) justice. This redirected interest fits into the common course of passions and is the first motive to justice.[17]

4. THE VIRTUE OF JUSTICE

Hume is now in a position to account for several features of the phenomenology of justice: justice is strictly connected with *obligation*; it is ordinarily practiced as a *moral virtue*; our only real and universal motive for it is a *sense of duty*; and it needs the backing of the decisions and sanctions of *government*.

Natural Obligation

The contents of the body of common belief that constitutes justice-instituting conventions – and therefore the contents of the motive for and of the idea of justice itself – are necessarily general and consist of rule descriptions of actions. Such rule descriptions present actions as episodes of a general practice of justice and conditionalize our motivation to perform just actions on the expectation that there is convergence on them. The appropriate rule descriptions of actions are therefore essential to the motive for and the idea of justice – in contrast with any particularistic construal of them. The merit-independent motive for justice can respond only to prospective actions described in the right general kind of way. This fact helps explain why the laws of justice do not admit any "gradation" and are "rigid" or "perfectly inflexible" – what Hume regards as a mark of artificiality (T 3.2.6.8–10, SBN 531–33). Suitably to the constitutive position of rule descriptions in this area of morals, laws of justice are rigid and inflexible because they do not merely summarize just conduct, but are the principle and condition for it. Therefore they cannot be tested and corrected against any independent experience and practice of justice. Notice, also, that the rules of justice express the content of the convergent deliberations of prospective just agents. Because there is nothing else but the convergent deliberations and intentions of agents to support the practice of justice and because agents best (or even only) converge on fixed and well-determined patterns of action, it is necessary that the rules that express it are, in their turn, inflexible and invariant.[18]

The idea of essential or constitutive rule descriptions of actions has a strong, if generic, normative ring. Hume does not refrain from employing explicitly normative locutions in characterizing the motive for justice. Redirected (or rule-constituted) self-interest is identified with a *"natural obligation to justice"* (T 3.2.2.23, SBN 498) and the *"first obligation"* to perform acts of justice (T 3.2.5.11, SBN 523). Hume explicitly recognizes the *"natural obligations of interest"* (T 3.2.8.7, SBN 545) or the "natural obligation of interest" (T 3.2.9.3, SBN 551). However, he says precious little about this notion. Some suggestions can be derived from Hume's critique of the view that allegiance to government is based on the obligation of promises. Hume observes that political duties and the practice of promising derive from "nothing but self-interest" and that, because the ends and means of these interests are distinct, "we must also allow of a separate obligation" of two distinct "obligations of interest" (T 3.2.8.5–6, SBN 543–44). He then makes some remarks about the nature of the interest that imposes such obligations. There is a difference between the interest that is promoted by the practice of promising and other sorts of interests an agent can have – a difference that explains why he can bind himself by promises to do what would have been in his interest to do anyway. The difference is that

[t]he interest in the performance of promises, besides its moral obligation, is general, avow'd, and of the last consequence in life. Other interests may be more particular and doubtful; and we are apt to entertain a greater suspicion,

that men may indulge their humour, or passion, in acting contrary to them. (T 3.2.8.6, SBN 544)

The interest in government and civil duties is "as general and avow'd as the interest in the performance of a promise" (ibid.); this is why it does not need their support.

A suggestion can be drawn from this text. The interest that can impose an obligation is general, avowed, and important. General interests are more stable and more widely shared than particular ones: if they, and the means to them, are easily recognizable and of consequence, such interests cannot but have a greater potential weight on motivation. But practice-mediated, rule-constituted interest (the first motive for justice) is general by construction. Because it is necessarily the object of common belief, it is "obvious and avow'd" (T 3.2.8.6, SBN 545). Because the first motive for justice secures the possibility of social life, it is of the greatest importance. Therefore, the features that make self-interest the first motive to justice are the same as those that establish it as the natural obligation to do just actions. Natural obligation, in the first place, is a matter of the distinctive, reliable *force* with which redirected self-interest can override contrasting motives that spring from passions of a different nature and from particular, direct interest. (Force is not the same as agitation: naturally obligating self-interest looks more like what Hume calls a calm passion.) In the second place, even in cases where general, redirected self-interest and particular, direct self-interest motivate the same just actions, the former is *counterfactually distinct* from the latter. (We would be reliably motivated to do such actions even if our particular interests were different.) This principled distinctness and this motivational stability are elements that support Hume's view that the first motive to justice is a natural obligation to just actions. ("Natural" here is contrasted with "moral," of course, not with "artificial.") Justice is deeply and tightly connected to obligation in its structure and origin.[19]

Justice Morally Approved

The second question Hume asks about the origin of justice is *"Why we annex the idea of virtue to justice, and of vice to injustice?"* (T 3.2.2.23, SBN 498). There is a very tight connection between the inception of justice and our moral response to it: "After this convention, concerning abstinence from the possessions of others, is enter'd into, and every one has acquir'd a stability in his possessions, there immediately arise the ideas of justice and injustice; as also those of *property, right,* and *obligation*" (T 3.2.2.11, SBN 490–91). Hume insists that this is a natural development: "the sense of morality in the observance of these rules follows *naturally*, and of itself" (T 3.2.6.11, SBN 533).

This has to be handled with some care. Common Course implies that moral sentiments and ideas are historically and socially relative. In the "rude and savage" state that precedes justice, the common course of passions is very close to the "original frame of our mind," which is strongly partial to our favor and that of our relations and acquaintances. This partiality influences our ideas of vice and virtue, "so as to make us regard any remarkable transgression of such a degree of partiality" as "vicious and immoral" (T 3.2.2.8, SBN 488). Therefore, "our natural uncultivated ideas of morality, instead of providing a remedy for the partiality of our affections, do rather conform themselves to that partiality, and give it an additional force and influence" (T 3.2.2.8, SBN 489). Therefore, "a partial conduct must be suitable to the strictest morality" (T 3.2.6.9, SBN 532). Hume is perfectly aware that Common Course makes moral approval of justice problematic. So how can our approval of justice be immediate or natural?

Hume's account of the first motive for justice includes all the resources for answering this question. (In fact, this is one of his most interesting ideas in this area.) The interested affection, as modified by convention and common belief, gives motive to do just actions. This motive of interest is an ideal candidate for sentimental moral approval. It is a motive that is conducive to the utility of society and all its members. We feel vicarious, sympathetic pleasure in response to this motive because (in the context of the general practice of justice) the acts expressing it tend to favor the interests of the concerned individuals; and this makes us morally praise justice or blame injustice:

Nay when the injustice is so distant from us, as no way to affect our interest, it still displeases us; because we consider it as prejudicial to human society, and pernicious to every one that approaches the person guilty of it. We partake of their uneasiness by *sympathy*; and as every thing, which gives uneasiness in human actions, upon the general survey, is call'd *vice*, and whatever produces satisfaction, in the same manner, is denominated *virtue*; this is the reason why the sense of moral good and evil follows upon justice and injustice. (T 3.2.2.24, SBN 499)

As a natural obligation, it is a motive that is stable and permanent, that is recognizably distinct from the flux of particular, accidental passions: it is something like a character trait, which is what moral sentiments are most attuned to. Finally, by being structured by convention and common belief, it cannot but satisfy Common Course: it is widespread among prospective just agents and recognized to be such. But then moral sentiments cannot but fall in step with the motive for justice and approve of it. This is an immediate and natural development because it is made possible by the same process that makes possible the motive for justice. The progress and change of the motives we have for justice are also the progress and change of our moral evaluation of them.

The "moral obligation of duty" is in this way connected to the "natural obligation of interest" as to "its cause" (T 3.2.9.3, SBN 551). Hume emphasizes the connection of natural obligation to moral obligation and the priority of the first to the second: "there is first a *natural* union betwixt the idea of the person and that of the object, and afterwards a new and *moral* union produc'd by that right or property, which we ascribe to the person" (T 3.2.3.10n75, SBN 510n); "interest is the *first* obligation to the performance of promises" (T 3.2.5.11, SBN 523), then a sentiment of morals concurs with interest "and becomes a new obligation upon mankind" (T 3.2.5.12, SBN 523). The enormously interesting idea here is that the same cognitive and motivational changes serve as the origin of the rules and the practice of justice and make justice a virtue. (Virtue is a morally approved, permanent disposition to act that fits into the common course of passions.)[20]

Acting on Sense of Duty

The strongest and most general motives for performing just acts, within our present practice of justice, are moral. Moral obligation is a motive for justice *further* than and even *alternative* to natural obligation. We should make sense of this in terms of the overall theory of justice. In effect, there are two questions to be asked in this regard, the first being why our motive for justice *has to be moral*, and the second why it *has to be a sense of duty*.

The answer to the first question is that, in civilized societies and within an ongoing practice of justice, redirected self-interest is neither necessary nor sufficient for just conduct. Hume characteristically makes this point both in historical and structural terms. The interested obligation to justice is "sufficiently strong and forcible" only "on the first formation of society." "But when society has become numerous, and has encreas'd to a tribe or nation, this interest is more remote; nor do men so readily perceive, that disorder and confusion follow upon every breach of these rules, as in a more narrow and contracted society" (T 3.2.2.24, SBN 499). More extensive and complex social relations, however, would not make the benefits of justice so difficult to detect, were it not for the *motivational short-sightedness* of the individuals. The consequences of our actions are there, even when they are remote, but we are not equally aware of and motivated by them. So we will not be sufficiently motivated by natural obligation. By contrast, distance does not hinder, but rather helps, impartial praise or blame of characters and actions. Thus it can be expected that, with the progress and expansion of social relations, moral obligation will prevail over natural obligation as our motive for justice. So natural obligation will not be necessary for justice.

The structural counterpoint to this is the possibility, discussed in the second *Enquiry*, of a "sensible knave's" free riding on everyone else's just conduct. Hume's answer to the knave is not couched entirely in terms of interest. Although the knave is short-sighted in his perception of what is in his own interest, Hume does not rely on the correction of the effects of proximity. Rather, he makes essential recourse to moral sentiments and views, if not as resources that can be summoned by the knave, at least as the forces that can remedy, in part, the failure of redirected interest and that can prevent free riding from spreading in a large society (EPM 9.22–25, SBN 282–84).[21]

This does not amount to a recantation of the doctrine of the natural obligation to justice. For natural obligation plays a dual role in Hume's theory. *Historically*, it allows him to explain the origin of the rules of justice and the socially shared attitude of moral praise toward them. *Conceptually*, it allows him to overcome the vicious circle of moral motivation and moral evaluation that would otherwise make justice unintelligible. Neither theoretical role implies that, in the present conditions of its practice, compliance with justice is individually rational and justice is stable for merely self-interested agents. In the (conjectural) historical perspective, what is required is that natural obligation be a motive effective at some early stage of the progress of coordinated, justice-regulated sociability. In the conceptual perspective, what is required is that First Motive for justice be satisfied by self-interest redirected by convention and common belief (without further stipulations about particular contents or objects). To ensure that natural obligation is the *causal antecedent* of and *conceptual complement* to the moral sense of justice, Hume does not have to hold that natural obligation motivates presently to justice.

In general, Hume has no program to reduce the morality of justice to even redirected interest – causation and explanation are not reduction. He explicitly acknowledges that moral obligation can detach itself from natural obligation, and he hints at a cognitive explanation for this fact: "men are mightily addicted to *general rules*." Through such rules, the imagination often makes us carry our maxims beyond the reasons that first induced us to establish them. Thus "our moral obligation of duty will not cease, even tho' the natural obligation of interest, which is its cause, has ceas'd" (T 3.2.9.3, SBN 551). As a motive for justice, interest is "first in time, not in dignity or force" (T 3.2.8.5n79, SBN 544n1). Once the moral practice of justice is in place and intelligible, redirected self-interest has no further, necessary role.

But given that our universal and real motive for justice is moral, why does it have to be a sense of duty? This is not the only way in which we can be motivated morally. We can be motivated by moral sentiments, through the related indirect and direct passions: "These sentiments produce love or hatred; and love or hatred, by the original constitution of human passion, is attended with benevolence or anger; that is, with a desire of making happy the person we love, and miserable the person we hate" (T 3.3.1.31, SBN 591). This sort of motive has a normative character, because it presupposes that we have the appropriate moral attitude. It can also be regarded as a source of moral obligation: having moral desire for doing an action implies that the "neglect, or non-performance of it" would displease us *after a certain manner* – that is, as moral attitudes are felt – and Hume identifies this feeling with the recognition of an obligation (T 3.2.5.4, SBN 517). Moral motives, on this conception, are natural motives to do some determinate thing. But moral motivation can be of a different sort. An action may be performed "merely out of regard to its moral obligation" (T 3.2.1.8, SBN 479). Hume gives a substantive account of this possibility:

When any virtuous motive or principle is common in human nature, a person, who feels his heart devoid of that principle, may hate himself upon that account, and may perform the action without the motive, from a certain sense of duty, in order to acquire by practice, that virtuous principle, or at least, to disguise to himself, as much as possible, his want of it. (ibid.)

The motivational role of moral sentiments is, in this case, that they make us think of a certain trait as morally valuable and thus make us recognize and regret that we lack it. This regret may constitute a motive for acting out of "a certain sense of duty," but this will not be a natural moral motive. It does not respond to particular features of actions, but to the general feature of having moral merit (which is just what is required for regretting not being disposed to perform them) or being the right thing to do.

Why is a sense of duty (which, as Hume remarks, usually motivates only "on some occasions" [ibid.]) the *only* moral motive that in general supports justice? (In effect, Hume makes systematic recourse to the notion of moral obligation *only* in connection with artificial virtues.) The reason cannot be that redirected self-interest does not give sufficient support to the ongoing practice of justice. This can explain why only moral motives can in general support our just conduct, not why these motives must be a sense of duty or regard to moral obligation. We should answer, rather, by adapting to the case of justice the model of motivation by moral regret. The reason why there are no natural moral motives for justice is, at the root, the same reason that there are no natural motives of any kind for it. Natural motives, moral or nonmoral, are *particularistic*. They respond to the individual features of prospective actions. In the moral case, they respond to the particular features of actions that make them expressive of some morally approved trait. Moral regret can motivate us to act in cases in which we lack the feeling of approval of such a trait, where therefore no particular feature of any of our prospective actions can be attuned to such feeling and elicit a motive, and when we recognize that such action is the thing one ought to do. The case of justice is similar but also different. It is not that it just so happens that some agents lack the feeling of the moral merit of just actions: a sense of duty is the *only* general motive for justice. And it is not that we all lack the moral feeling for justice: this would make justice impossible as a virtue. The problem is not psychological; it is practical-structural. There are no natural, particular moral motives for justice, because there are no particular features of actions that are expressive of the moral trait of justice, and this is because it is of the nature of justice that its content comes only in the form of general rule descriptions of rules. What we approve of with regard to just actions is not that they have certain particular features, but simply that they are what is required by the rules of justice. The moral approval is *de dicto*; the moral motivation correspondingly is also *de dicto*. It might seem *as if* the feeling of moral approval for justice were lacking and we acted on regret; but it is rather that, if we look at the particular actions and at their particular circumstances and outcomes, we lose sight of their merit as just actions or as expressing the motive of justice. If moral desires respond to the features of actions that make them expressive of morally approved traits, then, in the case of justice, such desires cannot be particular or natural. They can be motives for doing actions only under a general moral description, as what it is just to do or what is our duty.

Justice and Government

The sense of morality in the observance of the rules of justice can be "augmented by a new *artifice*": the "public instructions of politicians" (together with the "private education of parents") (T 3.2.6.11, SBN 533–34). This artifice helps to associate a sense of honor and duty with just conduct. But government plays a more fundamental role in regard to justice. A fact about the present practice of justice is that it presupposes "the security and protection, which we enjoy in political society, and which we can never attain, when perfectly free and independent" (T 3.2.9.2, SBN 550–51). But our interest in the observance of justice is palpable and evident. How then can any disorder ever arise in society? Hume's answer refers (as in the case of the moral character of our present motives for justice) to the cognitive factors that influence evaluation and motivation and that give weight to proximity effects, because whatever is "contiguous to us, either in space or time," strikes with a strong and vivid idea and has a "proportional effect on the will and passions" (T 3.2.7.2, SBN 535). Even if we know that a more distant object is of greater value, this judgment cannot regulate our passions because of the countervailing effects of imagination and proximity. Proximity effects are "the reason why men so often act in contradiction to their known interest," why they prefer any trivial advantage "that is present" to the maintenance of order in society through the observance of justice (T 3.2.7.3, SBN 535).

Even the moral motivations that can be summoned for justice (the sense of duty, the sense of honor), though real and universal, may not be strong enough to stabilize the practice of justice. But, given that government is, for this reason, necessary, how is it possible, in light of proximity effects? Hume recognizes that sensitivity to proximity may appear "incapable of remedy," because any such remedy "can only come from the consent of men," and their being "incapable of themselves to prefer remote to contiguous" would work also against it (T 3.2.7.4, SBN 535–36). However, "this infirmity of human nature becomes a remedy to itself" (T 3.2.7.5, SBN 536). Following Hume's discussion of this point would take us too far afield. Suffice it to say that, though it would be hopeless to attempt to change or correct the natural disposition to prefer the contiguous over the remote, it is possible to change, with respect to a few persons, their circumstances and situation, so as to make the observance, execution, and decision of justice in their "immediate interest" (T 3.2.7.6, SBN 537). In particular, magistrates can be established with the relevant interest. Hume thus regards their institution, as well as our allegiance to government, as artifices that are well within our grasp – all the more so, considering that he regards the origin of government as a historical process and not (as in the social contract tradition) as an act that takes place at a given moment in time. This artifice is not of the nature of a convention: no coordination, no correction of frequency effects, and no common belief are involved. It is more directly and internally a process of cognitive and motivational change. Still, it is an artifice, having to do with motivation and evaluation, from which new kinds of moral sentiments and views can spring. This explains how it can be a part of the overall moral area of justice.

NOTES

1. Gauthier (1992: 403, 416) carefully articulates the sense and the limits in which Hume advances an error theory of justice but still regards Hume's justice as explainable only with recourse to systematic substantive error or self-deception. The same point is made, in a more sweeping way, by Haakonssen (1981: 34–35 and 1996: 108–9) (but why should Hume hold

that only the *purposeful* pursuit of social utility makes a motive for justice morally meritorious?) and by Baron (1982: 548–52), who insists on (functional) deception by politicians and educators concerning the need of universal compliance for the general practice of justice to subsist. See also Cohon (2008: 168), who identifies the problem with a defect in our application of moral concepts. Compare to Baier (2010: 27–28, 41ff., 68). Baier (rightly in my view) regards the paradox as a form of social reality (on Mandeville's model of private vices and public benefits).

2. Snare (1991: 171, 175, 181) finds fault with Hume's conflating, in this context, metaethical sentimentalism and substantive virtue ethics. I think, rather, that there are good, independent grounds in Hume's moral psychology for this position. See, for a reading closer to the one I propose, Darwall 1995: 301–2.

3. See, for a different interpretation, Bricke 1996: 179–80. Cohon (2008: 171, 179–80) denies that First Motive holds generally, but her grounds for this at most show that its satisfaction can be indirect.

4. This is consistent with virtuous and vicious actions (and even persons) being uncommon. We may judge the virtue or vice of particular actions and persons by comparison. But we compare them in terms of the degree in which, on particular occasions, they exemplify (or deviate from) the motivational traits that would be expected in those circumstances.

5. According to Bricke (1996: 192), Hume denies (or should deny) that a sense of duty is our only real and universal motive for justice. But I do not see how Hume could then argue for the artificiality of justice. I take up this issue in section 4. For Baier (2010: 49, 55, 63–64), self-interest remains a motive for justice throughout its historical development. This is consistent with its not being a universal and reliable motive.

6. Harrison (1981: 6, 10, 144) suggests an unnecessarily strong reading of Hume's argument, as proving that justice is not a virtue at all. A more equilibrate assessment is in Mackie 1980: 78–80. Snare (1991: 192–93) seems to suggest that the motivational circle cannot be overcome by Hume, but he subsequently (1991: 301n9) suggests a solution along the lines I propose. I also find confusing the suggestion that there is in Hume a problem of circularity issuing from sentimentalism, alongside that issuing from motivation (1991: 195–98). My account of these matters is very close to the beautiful discussion in Garrett 2007.

7. There is a similar problem with the change or production of ideas by imagination. I discuss the general problem of production of content in Magri 2012.

8. The idea of practice-mediated consequence is carefully articulated in Gauthier 1986; see also, for a Gauthier-related view, Part III of Thompson 2008.

9. The relevance of the indirect act-consequence pattern of justice is beautifully rendered by Mackie (1980: 81).

10. For this notion, see Maynard Smith (1982: 1, 55): "Frequency-dependent" population games are those whose payoffs "do depend on what other members of the population are doing."

11. I agree with Darwall (1995: 288) that justice involves a motivational state quite unlike any other Hume allows. But I do not think that this involves a form of practical reasoning substantially different from the other he

countenances (1995: 317). Rather, the explanation lies in the objective act-consequence structure of just conduct (that, of course, is reflected in sound deliberation).

12. Hume is often, and unsoundly, interpreted as a radical opponent of the natural law and social contract tradition. He, rather, offers a deep revision of that tradition – one that stands in close continuity with it. See Forbes 1975; Haakonssen 1981 and 1996; and Buckle 1991.

13. I follow Hume in taking conventions to be the processes instituting the rules of justice rather than the rules themselves. This explains Hume's (and my) concentration on the origins and practical and mental structure of such rules, rather than on their status *qua* rules. (Of course, the two considerations are strictly interconnected.)

14. Closer attention should be paid to the game-theoretical structure of Hume's convention. Some of the key points are these: what combination of pure coordination and conflict sets the stage for Hume's convention; what game-descriptions and solution-concepts best fit Hume's rules of justice; whether and how Hume makes room for the dimension of arbitrariness apparently involved in the notion of convention; what the relation is between Hume's view of repetition and learning and how these notions figure in contemporary research; how imagination and habituation individuate aspects of salience and prominence and contribute to equilibrium selection; how the flimsiness of Humean imagination assuages problems for cooperation arising from backwards induction in sequential games; and how evolutionary stability captures aspects of Hume's gradualist account of convention. See Lewis 1969 for the Hume-inspired, path-breaking study of convention; and, among others, see Gauthier 1979; Sugden 1986; Snare 1991; Magri 1994; and Vanderschraaf 1998 – a very careful review of Hume's game-theoretical insights. See also Rescorla 2011.

15. For the common knowledge assumptions underlying convention, see Lewis 1969: 58–59; Vanderschraaf 1998: 233–34; Vanderschraaf 2007; and Vanderschraaf and Sillari 2013.

16. On the epistemic and decisional difference between shared individual knowledge (mutual knowledge) and common knowledge, see Binmore 1992: 445–54, 472–81. A vivid presentation of these matters is in Nozick 2001: 197–201.

17. Interpreters differ widely in their opinions about the nature of the first motive for justice. Haakonssen (1996: 109) and Gauthier (1992: 422) deny that there is any such thing and opt for error theory. Snare (1991: 301–3) identifies the first motive with redirected self-interest but (surprisingly) denies that this is the motive that we approve. For Bricke (1996: 194), it is a combination of restrained self-interest and partial benevolence. Darwall (1995: 306, 313) identifies this motive with a state of acceptance of rules, regarded as authoritative, that is grounded on (but not reducible to) self-interest and strength of mind. Cohon (1997: 98–99) individuates it in a motivational consequence (pursuit or avoidance) of socially induced (and manipulated) moral attitudes to following the rules of justice.

18. This may be true even if such rules are the offspring of imagination and not of reason. Salience may impart uniqueness to the convergence point of deliberative processes. On the complementary roles of prominence and of imagination in fixing the contents of convention (for instance, the rules

concerning the assignment of property rights and their transferral), see Maynard Smith 1982: 96, 171, and Sugden 1986: 92–96.

19. Gauthier (1992: 409–10) understands natural obligation as the feeling of restraint left by redirection of interest. Darwall (1995: 298) makes a distinction between natural obligation, moral obligation, and what he calls "rule obligation." This latter is, however, much the same as natural obligation, on the reading of it that I have proposed. Baier (2010: 174) carefully examines the different meanings of "natural obligation" in the *Treatise*, pointing out irreparable equivocation.

20. See, for an analysis of the transition from (self-interested) conventions to (morally forceful) natural laws, Sugden 1986: 145–61; Lecaldano 2008: 265–66; and Taylor 1998: 19–20, 23–24. A Hume-related theoretical understanding of the relation between social evolution and moral emotion can be found in Gibbard 1990 and in Blackburn 1999.

21. I am far from having paid full justice to this important text (a faint anticipation of which can be found at T 2.2.11.4, SBN 395). See, for discussion, Postema (1988: 34–37), who argues that the knave's risk to lose his moral self (because of the necessity of permanent deception and limited communication with others) is Hume's best, if ultimately unsuccessful, answer to him; Gauthier (1992: 419–22) brilliantly argues that Hume must assume systematic self-deception about self-interest in the agents for just conduct to find moral support. (Gauthier underestimates the fact that, in Hume's framework, natural obligation can provide the origin of, and be a complement to, moral obligation without prescribing under all circumstances individual compliance to justice.) Baier (1992: 431–33) gives a very *nuancé* but persuasive defense of the moral grounds of Hume's answer.

14   What's So "Natural" about Hume's Natural Virtues?

Advocates and opponents of Humean ethics alike rely heavily on Hume's account of the natural virtues, an account to which we are introduced in the *Treatise*, but which is deployed throughout Hume's work.[1] Descriptions of Hume's ethics by his allies – whether as "a pioneer in the cause of a gentler morality" (Baier 1994: xi; see also ch. 13) or as providing a "more amiable, less duty-ridden conception of virtue" (Blackburn 1999: 32) – are often based largely on his catalog of natural virtues and vices (see Russell 1995: 116). Aristotelian critics of Hume have his natural virtues in mind when they complain that the Humean virtues are unreliable, unreflective, and isolable traits that prompt human conduct in a manner indistinguishable from the way in which a cat's behavior is prompted.[2] Likewise, Hume's account of the natural virtues plays a key role in grounding Kantian objections to Humean conceptions of moral value, moral motivation, and ethical normativity.[3]

Unfortunately, scholars typically begin their examination of the natural virtues by assuming that these laudable aspects of Humean character are "natural" in at least every sense in which the artificial virtues are "artificial" – i.e., conventional.[4] This is exegetically unwise and unwarranted. Both of these species of virtue may be, in many ways, the result of "the designs, and projects, and views of men" (T 3.1.2.9, SBN 474) without spoiling Hume's distinction between them.[5] All Hume needs in order to maintain his distinction between the artificial and natural virtues is for there to be *one* respect in which the former, but not the latter, are the products of human invention. The traditional tactic for understanding Hume's account of the natural virtues is backwards. Before we can say precisely what distinguishes the natural virtues from the artificial ones, we need to determine just what is so "natural" about the natural virtues.[6]

I argue that philosophers have grossly exaggerated the "naturalness" of Hume's natural virtues. According to the traditional interpretation, the natural virtues are: (1) dispositions whose objects, scope, force, and expression are dictated by the constitution of the human mind as such; (2) inalterable, or nearly so; (3) motivating dispositions in which the

agent's conception of value plays no essential role; (4) common; (5) culturally invariant; (6) traits neither wholly nor partly constituted by general
rules; (7) traits, our approval of which makes no necessary reference to
persons' general conformity in a particular "scheme or system of action";
and (8) dispositions, the content of which can be specified without reference to a particular "scheme or system of action." The first six of these
claims are mistaken; the seventh is true only with notable caveats.
Only the last can be said to mark a sharp edge between the artificial and
so-called natural virtues – and only if it is understood in a certain way.
Hume's natural virtues are far more complex than has been thought.

In the final section, I explore some of the important implications of
this new understanding of the natural virtues by focusing on two related
questions: (1) whether Hume is properly classified as a virtue ethicist, and
(2) whether it matters if we so categorize him. I argue that on the traditional interpretation of Hume's natural virtues, we are forced to conclude
that it is inappropriate to classify Humean ethics as a species of virtue
ethics and that Hume's failure to meet the qualifications for a "virtue
ethicist" is indicative of a deep inconsistency in his philosophical ethics.
On my interpretation of Hume's natural virtues, in contrast, there is no
such inconsistency in Hume's vision of ethical life, and the debate over
whether to categorize Humean ethics as "virtue ethics" is, as Hume
himself would say, a mere dispute of words.

I. NATURAL VIRTUES AS "INSTINCTS"

Accounts of Hume's natural virtues typically open with the assertion
that the natural virtues are "instincts" or "instinctual." At this level, the
traditional interpretation is not entirely lacking in textual evidence.
Hume does claim that the natural virtues "exert their influence immediately, by a direct tendency or instinct" (EPM App. 3.2, SBN 303). But the
mere invocation of the word *instinct* in this context tells us little.
Scholars have taken Hume to mean that the dispositions in question
are innate features of human psychology whose objects, scope, force,
and expression in action are also dictated by the constitution of the
human mind and which spontaneously (without reflection) give rise to
occurrent motives for acting.[7] We need not read Hume this way. After all,
Aristotelian virtues might also be said to "exert their influence immediately, by ... instinct," for the motive force of the Aristotelian virtues is
drawn from "instincts" that, when properly educated, become virtues. In
their instinctive form, these tendencies are little more than a certain
responsiveness to a broad scope of objects. Only once such instinctive
dispositions are educated (and thereby come to have definite objects, to
be expressed in particular contexts, etc.) do they begin to qualify as

candidates for Aristotelian virtues. Hume's natural virtues might be "instinctive" in this sense, rather than in the reductive sense captured by the traditional interpretation.

Why then do so many arrive at the traditional reductive interpretation of Hume's claim that the natural virtues "exert their influence . . . by . . . instinct"? Some ground this reading in an appeal to the "circle" concerning our motives to virtuous conduct found early in Book 3 of the *Treatise*.[8] Hume writes:

> To suppose, that the mere regard to the virtue of the action, may be the first motive, which produc'd the action, and render'd it virtuous, is to reason in a circle. Before we can have such a regard, the action must be really virtuous; and this virtue must be deriv'd from some virtuous motive: And consequently the virtuous motive must be different from the regard to the virtue of the action. (T 3.2.1.4, SBN 478)

At most, however, what this "circle" establishes is that for every virtue, there must be a wholly nonmoral motive that characteristically motivates acts expressive of that virtue.[9] To jump from this conclusion to the further claim that those motives are instincts in the reductive sense, one must suppose that there is nothing else for the motive in question *to be* if it is wholly nonmoral. That is simply not the case. Consider, for instance, parental affection. It is not contrary to Hume's circle to hold that the fact that parental affection typically takes children as its object, and not also, say, one's spouse, is the result of our upbringing and social structure rather than some innate feature of human psychology. The same can be said for the ways in which adult members of a human society express parental affection, the typical motive force of that affection among adults, and so on.

Other passages commonly adduced as evidence for a reductive reading of Hume's claim that the natural virtues motivate through instinct admit easily of alternative interpretations. Charlotte Brown draws our attention to Hume's reflection that:

> we always consider the *natural* and *usual* force of the passions, when we determine concerning vice and virtue; and if the passions depart very much from the common measures on either side, they are always disapprov'd as vicious. A man naturally loves his children better than his nephews, his nephews better than his cousins, his cousins better than strangers, where every thing else is equal. Hence arise our common measures of duty, in preferring the one to the other. Our sense of duty always follows the common and natural course of our passions. (T 3.2.1.18, SBN 483–84)

In part on the basis of this passage, Brown concludes that the "content of our natural duties coincides with the untutored play of our common affections as they would operate in the state of nature" (1988: 81).

One might, instead, interpret Hume as claiming only that our *"measures of duty"* follow the "common and natural course of our passions." Because "we perceive, that the generosity of men is very limited, and that it seldom extends beyond their friends and family, or, at most, beyond their native country," "we expect not any impossibilities" of them (T 3.3.3.2, SBN 602). That is, as broad as the responsiveness of each of our instinctive passions may be, in terms of their possible objects, this responsiveness is not infinitely broad. If we were to extend the measures of our duties too far, "our affections and actions would be dissipated and lost, for want of a proper limited object" (EPM 5.43n25, SBN 229n).[10] Accordingly, our instinctive passions do establish very broad parameters for the content of our duties. We do not, for instance, expect people to love society as a whole as they love their spouse, and this is reflected in, for instance, the fact that people have more extensive duties to their spouses than to the society as a whole. But none of this entails, *pace* Brown (1988: 81), that we approve of our affections "as they would operate in the state of nature."[11] Within the broad range of what is possible for most human beings, a range that establishes the measure of duty, we might well expect a great deal of the "naturally" virtuous.[12]

By far, the strongest support for the reductive interpretation lies in three passages that invoke parental affection as a prime example of a natural virtue.[13] In one of these passages, Hume writes:

> We blame a father for neglecting his child. Why? because it shows a want of natural affection, which is the duty of every parent. Were not natural affection a duty, the care of children cou'd not be a duty; and 'twere impossible we cou'd have the duty in our eye in the attention we give to our offspring. In this case, therefore, all men suppose a motive to the action distinct from a sense of duty. (T 3.2.1.5, SBN 478)

At first glance, the suggestion seems to be that all defects of (natural) virtue are indicative of a "want" of some (innate) nonmoral affection. Were that so, there might be the beginnings of a case for the traditional interpretation. But Hume chooses his words carefully here. This passage appears immediately after Hume's argument that "the first virtuous motive, which bestows a merit on any action, can never be a regard to the virtue of that action, but must be some other natural motive" (T 3.2.1.4, SBN 478). To illustrate *that* claim, Hume needs an example of someone who is blameworthy *merely because* he lacks a given nonmoral affection. So he imagines a parent whose vice is that of "neglect." The very word suggests the *absence* of concern.

It does not follow that Hume believes that possession of whatever form parental affection human beings would have in the state of nature would be tantamount to possession of a *virtue*. He could hold that anyone who has some measure of parental affection thereby escapes the charge of being vicious, without also holding that all forms of parental affection qualify as virtuous.[14] Alternatively, he might hold that the presence of some form of parental affection is not sufficient to qualify the agent as having the virtue of parental concern *and* that the presence of parental affection is no guarantor that one will not act viciously as a parent. The latter, in fact, is Hume's view. In "A Dialogue," for instance, while in the same breath condemning the Athenians for infanticide, he acknowledges that had one "asked a parent at ATHENS, why he bereaved his child of that life, which he had so lately given it. It is because I love it, he would reply; and regard the poverty which it must inherit from me, as a greater evil than death" (D 30, SBN 334).[15] The Athenian has the "instinct" of parental concern and yet acts viciously. Hume endorses both sides of the proposed view: something more than an instinct of parental concern is required for the virtue of parental affection, because the Athenian has that instinct and yet performs a blameworthy act; and some vicious acts are motivated by a form of parental concern. To be *virtuous*, one's parental concern must, at least, not prompt one to leave one's child outside to die of exposure.

The second passage involving parental concern cited as support for the reductive reading of the role of "instinct" in the natural virtues appears in Hume's discussion of promising. In the course of asking the reader to recall his earlier argument concerning our first motives to virtuous conduct, Hume notes that the father who "knows it to be his duty to take care of his children . . . has also a natural inclination to it. And if no human creature had that inclination, no one cou'd lie under any such obligation" (T 3.2.5.6, SBN 518–19). This need not mean we approve of parental concern in its instinctual form. The following might be the case. Many human beings are "hardwired" to have some concern for their children. If no human being ever had such concern, there could be no *virtue* of parental concern. But it is only when a parent's concern for his or her children motivates certain kinds of actions, is felt under specified circumstances, etc., that it becomes a *virtue*. These aspects of parental concern, one might plausibly suppose, are not determined solely by the makeup of the human mind.

Even a third, rather strongly worded, passage concerning parental affection, found in "Of the Original Contract," admits of the proposed interpretation:

All *moral* duties may be divided into two kinds. The *first* are those, to which men are impelled by a natural instinct or immediate propensity, which operates on them, independent of all ideas of obligation, and of all views, either to public or private utility. Of this nature are, love of children, gratitude to benefactors, pity to the unfortunate. When we reflect on the advantage, which results to society from such humane instincts, we pay them the just tribute of moral approbation and esteem: But the person, actuated by them, feels their power and influence, antecedent to any such reflection.

The *second* kind of moral duties are such as are not supported by any original instinct of nature, but are performed entirely from a sense of obligation, when we consider the necessities of human society, and the impossibility of supporting it, if these duties were neglected. (E-OC 479–80)

Parents who are virtuous or who avoid acting viciously toward their children, we might say, are "impelled by a natural instinct," only in the sense that the *motivating force* of parental affection is not *derivative* of their conception of value. This is very different from claiming that we do, or ought to, approve of *whatever* parents might do if impelled to act by such parental affection in the same manner as they would have in the state of nature.

There is, in short, insufficient evidence for the reductive reading of Hume's claim that natural virtues motivate through instinct. There is also a good deal of evidence that Hume rejected this reductive account of the natural virtues. In the second *Enquiry*, for instance, he distinguishes between the affective state of a man living outside society and the affective state of "we, accustomed to society." His comparison does not speak well for "instincts":

It seems certain, both from reason and experience, that a rude, untaught savage regulates chiefly his love and hatred by the ideas of private utility and injury, and has but faint conceptions of a general rule or system of behaviour. The man who stands opposite to him in battle, he hates heartily, not only for the present moment, which is almost unavoidable, but for ever after; nor is he satisfied without the most extreme punishment and vengeance. But we, accustomed to society, and to more enlarged reflections, consider, that this man is serving his own country and community; that any man, in the same situation, would do the same; that we ourselves, in like circumstances, observe a like conduct; that, in general, human society is best supported on such maxims: And by these suppositions and views, we correct, in some measure, our ruder and narrower passions. (EPM 9.8n57, SBN 274–75n)

Elsewhere, Hume makes the same basic point in a different way – that is, by offering us illustrations of ways in which the structure of one and the same affective disposition may make it either a vice or a virtue. Hume tells us that "liberality," for instance, though it can be a natural virtue, is a vice when it leads a prince to convert the "homely bread of the honest and industrious" into "delicious cates for the idle and the prodigal" (EPM 2.20, SBN 181). The ambition of a king whose powers are limited may lead to tyranny and thereby the "perilous situation" of justly provoked revolt (E-PO 492). Hope, "warm imagination," and pride, when both forceful and combined, lead to the extremes of enthusiasm (E-SE 74). Love sometimes "renders a man a total slave to the object of his passion" (E-Sc 180), and when cheerfulness is "without a proper cause or subject" it becomes the vice of folly (EPM 7.22n49, SBN 258n). According to Hume, liberality, ambition, hope, pride, love, and cheer are all, at least in some form, natural virtues. But since he also holds that all of these affections can qualify as vices, the relevant natural virtues must consist in more than the mere possession of an affective disposition; there is more, for instance, to the virtue of being loving than being disposed to feel love. The affections must, at the very least, take appropriate objects, not be expressed in "perilous" ways, and not be so forceful or have so significant a place in the structure of a person's motivational psychology as would make a man a slave or an enthusiast.

Were all these dimensions of our passions also inborn aspects of human psychology, we would be forced to conclude that the above-mentioned vices arise from the corruption (via culture and upbringing) of minds that would otherwise be hardwired for virtue. We would also have to conclude that the vast majority of us have thus been corrupted by our upbringing and society, for Hume frequently comments that although morality requires an "impartial conduct,... 'tis seldom we can bring ourselves to it," and "our passions do not readily follow the determination of our judgment" (T 3.3.1.18, SBN 583).[16] Since the passions that are the objects of our moral evaluations are not often brought in line with those assessments, a fortiori, our passions (here, dispositionally understood) are not often entirely virtuous. Hence, the supposition that (natural) vice results from the corruption of human psychology should lead us to conclude that the rude, untaught savage is in a far better position, morally speaking, than are most of us who are "accustomed to society." But we already know from the second *Enquiry* comparison between the "rude, untaught savage" and "we, accustomed to society" that this is not Hume's view. It is thus far more tenable to hold that, on Hume's account, our innate affective dispositions require education in order to *acquire* the appropriate range of objects, strength, responsiveness, etc., before they are candidates for natural *virtues*.

2. THE RECALCITRANCE OF NATURAL VICE

Even supposing that our affections require education to become virtues – or perhaps precisely because they do – the traits we have as adults may be relatively immune to improvement, particularly by the agent herself. Paul Russell, for instance, claims that Humean persons "are essentially *passive* with respect to their own moral character" (1995: 128).[17] The presumed connection between the "naturalness" of natural virtues and their being inalterable is indirect, proceeding sometimes via the assumption that these traits are instincts in the reductive sense discussed above and sometimes through Hume's general commentary on the extent to which it is possible to reform one's own character.

It is true enough that when we speak, colloquially, of "instincts," we often mean to convey the thought that a disposition is unchangeable. One might, for example, remark that in spite of a lifetime indoors a domesticated cat still exhibits an "instinct" for burying her food. Hume recognizes that we speak this way:

But though animals learn many parts of their knowledge from observation, there are also many parts of it, which they derive from the original hand of nature; which much exceed the share of capacity they possess on ordinary occasions; and in which they improve, little or nothing, by the longest practice and experience. These we denominate *instincts*, and are so apt to admire, as something very extraordinary, and inexplicable by all the disquisitions of human understanding. But our wonder will, perhaps, cease or diminish; when we consider, that the experimental reasoning itself, which we possess in common with beasts, and on which the whole conduct of life depends, is nothing but a species of instinct or mechanical power, that acts in us unknown to ourselves; and in its chief operations, is not directed by any such relations or comparisons of ideas, as are the proper objects of our intellectual faculties. (EHU 9.6, SBN 108)

We tend to reserve the word *instinct* for dispositions that do not alter with "the longest practice and experience," assuming that any disposition that is derived (partly) "from the original hand of nature" and can operate in us without conscious awareness is also inalterable. Hume thinks that this is a significant mistake. Some dispositions that are "instincts" in other senses, such as (notably) the disposition that provides us with a foundation for experimental reasoning, do substantially improve with practice.[18]

So does Hume think our laudable and despicable affective dispositions are more like experimental reasoning in this respect or more like a cat's tendency to "bury" her food? In favor of the latter option, Annette Baier (1991: 186–87) and Paul Russell (1995: 126–29) point readers to the following *Treatise* and second *Enquiry* remarks:

many of those qualities, which all moralists, especially the antients, comprehend under the title of moral virtues, are equally involuntary and necessary, with the qualities of the judgment and imagination. (T 3.3.4.3, SBN 608)

'tis certain we can naturally no more change our own sentiments, than the motions of the heavens ... (T 3.2.5.4, SBN 517) this, in the mean time, must be allowed, that *sentiments* are every day experienced of blame and praise, which have objects beyond the dominion of the will or choice, and of which it behoves us, if not as moralists, as speculative philosophers at least, to give some satisfactory theory and explication. (EPM App. 4.21, SBN 322)

it being almost impossible for the mind to change its character in any considerable article, or cure itself of a passionate or splenetic temper, when they are natural to it. (T 3.3.4.3, SBN 608)

This natural infirmity [a preference for the contiguous to the remote] I may very much regret, and I may endeavour, by all possible means, to free myself from it. I may have recourse to study and reflection within myself; to the advice of friends; to frequent meditation, and repeated resolution: And having experienc'd how ineffectual all these are, I may embrace with pleasure any other expedient, by which I may impose a restraint upon myself, and guard against this weakness. (T 3.2.7.5, SBN 536–37)

The first of these passages is drawn from "Of Natural Abilities," where Hume argues that a trait *need not* be voluntary in order for attributions of responsibility to be appropriate. The truth of that claim does not entail the further proposition that the traits for which we are held responsible are *involuntary*. Moreover, what Hume says in that passage is only that *some* virtues are just as ("equally") involuntary as some natural abilities. And Hume does not think that "natural abilities" are immune to self-directed improvement. At one point, for instance, he lauds a middle-class existence as "the most favourable to the improving our natural Abilities," because in leading such a life we frequently find reason to exercise our natural abilities and thereby improve them (E-MSL 548). In addition, on the page of the *Treatise* following the first passage cited above, Hume tells us that one difference between natural abilities and moral virtues is that "the former are almost invariable by any art or industry; while the latter, or at least, the actions, that proceed from them, may be chang'd by the motives of reward and punishment, praise and blame" (T 3.3.4.4, SBN 609).[19] The second and third passages above both refer to Hume's view that the "will never creates new sentiments" (T 3.2.5.5, SBN 518); this is the sense in which Hume thinks we cannot "change our own sentiments" and the sense in which some of the objects of our praise and blame lie "beyond the dominion of the will." In the last two passages, Hume's claim is that a person can purge from her psychology neither a passionate or splenetic temper nor the inherently human tendency to prefer lesser, more immediate goods. (See T 3.2.7.6, SBN 537.) He makes the same claim about "a certain degree of selfishness in men" (T 3.3.1.17, SBN 583) and anger (T 3.3.3.7, SBN 605). But neither the claim that one cannot create a susceptibility to an affective disposition by an act of will nor the claim that there are affective dispositions ineliminable from "our frame and constitution" (T 3.3.1.17, SBN 583) entail the further claim that we cannot substantially alter the content and force of the passionate dispositions to which we find ourselves subject.

In addition to the passages quoted above, Baier (1991: 186) and Russell (1995: 128–29) also refer readers to Hume's essay "The Sceptic" for evidence that Humean character traits are inalterable. The irony is that in so doing, they attribute to Hume a view about the possibility of character reform that is *more* sceptical than the view Hume attributes to the sceptic.[20] The passages from this essay cited by Russell and Baier actually make two weaker claims. First, Hume claims that we cannot "Proteus-like" alter the whole "fabric and constitution of our mind" (E-Sc 168). Second, he claims that the influence of philosophy – that *"medicine of the mind"* – over our character is limited. This latter claim is restricted in two ways. For one, Hume's claim is not that philosophical reflection has no influence, only that its influence is *limited*. In Hume's words, such reflection will not make it "always in a man's power ... to correct his temper" (E-Sc 169). For another, Hume's claim concerns not the general question of the extent to which we can reform our own character, but the more specific question of what influence *philosophical reflection* can have in such endeavors (E-Sc 169–71). Shaftesbury is clearly one of Hume's targets here. In "Soliloquy," Shaftesbury argues that character reform is possible through what he calls "self-converse" ([1711] 1999: 75; see also 75–86), a method of reflection that is nothing other than "philosophy which by nature has the pre-eminence above all other science or knowledge" ([1711] 1999: 133). Hume's "sceptic" retorts that Shaftesbury has grossly exaggerated the practical significance of philosophical reflection.[21] Yet "the Sceptic" argues that if we look beyond philosophical reflection, we *will* find sufficient means to reform our own character:

The prodigious effects of education may convince us, that the mind is not altogether stubborn and inflexible, but will admit of many alterations from its original make and structure. Let a man propose to himself the model of a character, which he approves: Let him be well acquainted with those particulars, in which his own character deviates from this model: Let him keep a constant watch over himself, and bend his mind, by a continual effort, from the vices, towards the virtues; and I doubt not but, in time, he will find, in his temper, an alteration for the better. (E-Sc 170)

Elsewhere, Hume is equally optimistic. In "Of the Delicacy of Taste and Passion," he argues that developing a "cultivated taste for the polite arts" can improve one's "tender and agreeable passions" (E-DT 6). Similarly, in "Of the Middle Station of Life," Hume argues that the opportunities for the exercise of virtue afforded by a middle-class life are such that "a Man may ... be much more certain of his Progress in Virtue, than where his good Qualities lye dormant" (E-MSL 547).[22] In the *Treatise* no less than these later works, Hume also reveals his belief that meaningful character reform is possible. In the midst of arguing with advocates of "the doctrine of liberty," for instance, he complains that they cannot explain why "repentance wipes off every crime, especially if attended with an evident reformation of life and manners." Hume's explanation is that "actions render a person criminal, merely as they are proofs of criminal passions or principles in the mind; and when by any alteration of these principles they cease to be just proofs, they likewise cease to be criminal" (T 2.3.2.7, SBN 412; cf. T 2.3.6).[23]

In short, there are only two limitations Hume places on the possibility of self-improvement, neither of which excludes the possibility of substantial character reform: we cannot create the susceptibility to a particular affect by an act of will, and there are some affective dispositions that we cannot entirely purge from our psychology.

3. MORALITY AND THE NATURAL VIRTUES

The traditional interpretation of Hume's natural virtues would be unrecognizable as such without the contention that an agent's sentiments of moral approbation and moral disapprobation play no role in the dispositions constitutive of her natural virtues.[24] The primary source of this assertion is "Hume's circle":

> To suppose, that the mere regard to the virtue of the action, may be the first motive, which produc'd the action, and render'd it virtuous, is to reason in a circle. Before we can have such a regard, the action must be really virtuous; and this virtue must be deriv'd from some virtuous motive: And consequently the virtuous motive must be different from the regard to the virtue of the action. (T 3.2.1.4, SBN 478)

Hume's claim is that if our motives for virtuous conduct were our "sense of duty" – that is, our sense of what is worthy of moral approval or disapproval – then our moral approval would lack a proper object. Of what do you approve? Motives. What motives? Moral approval and disapproval. Of what? Motives. We have no noncircular way to say what our moral approval is moral approval *of*.[25] Hence, scholars routinely conclude, the dispositions constitutive of the Humean virtues (or at least the natural ones) must be motivating dispositions that do not implicate the agent's conception of value.

This radical conclusion is unwarranted. The upshot of Hume's circle is not that an agent's conception of value plays no role in the dispositions constitutive of her virtues, but that those dispositions cannot consist *solely* in an agent's conception of value. One can hold that possession of a (natural) virtue involves both a nonmoral affection and good moral sense without running afoul of Hume's circle.[26] To see this, we can begin where sections 1 and 2 (above) leave off. We already know that any natural Humean virtue involves, among other things: a nonmoral affective disposition, which takes an appropriately specified range of objects, under appropriate circumstances, which is expressed only as appropriate and when appropriate, and which does not lead to some other vice (such as when love makes a man slavish). It is not contrary to Hume's circle to hold that what ensures that the virtuous agent's nonmoral affections are laudable in each of these respects is his conception of value. It is, let's say, the fact that David regards parental affection as morally appropriate when expressed in saving for his child's college education (rather than buying the child expensive toys) that leads him to take the former course of action. His moral approval thereby plays an essential role in the conduct expressive of his parental affection. Of what do we then approve when we approve of David's parental affection as virtuous? A morally regulated nonmoral affection. Of what does David approve, as an agent, when he brings his moral sense to bear on his conduct as a parent? The *nonmoral* affection of parental concern, as expressed in certain ways, under certain circumstances, and so on. There is no circle involved in specifying either the object of the agent's approval or the object of our approval of the agent's conduct. The agent, *qua* agent, approves of a nonmoral affection under a description that includes a specified set of objects, etc. The object of his approval is, thereby, and in that context, wholly nonmoral. But when either we or David himself then approve of David's conduct as indicative of his possession of a virtue, the object of our approval is a *morally regulated* nonmoral affection.[27]

The limitations on our conception of the virtues imposed by "Hume's circle" are, thus, far more narrow than scholars have supposed. The first restriction is this: we must allow for the *conceptual* possibility of agents who are in no way motivated by their moral commitments, but who are nevertheless virtuous. An agent (were there one) motivated to save for his child's college education would be virtuous, even if his moral commitments played no role in so motivating him. In some sense, it is such an agent that David (in our example) has in mind when he judges that parental affection expressed through saving money for his child's education is virtuous. The reason we must allow for the conceptual possibility of such an agent is that we will otherwise be unable to specify of what David approves in making judgments (in the course of deciding how to act) about which expressions of parental love are virtuous. Second, the dispositions constitutive of natural virtues cannot consist solely in an agent's conception of value. An agent who found herself lacking in parental affection, and hence moved to save for her child's education only in order to avoid the pain of disapproving of her own conduct would be performing an action merely imitative of the *virtue* of parental love (T 3.2.1.8, SBN 479).

But David, in our example, is motivated neither by a nonmoral affection of parental concern alone nor by his moral commitments alone. Rather, his moral commitments govern his nonmoral affection of parental concern; they play the role of second-order motives in prompting virtuous conduct. That is, David's conception of value moves him to express his parental affection in certain ways, to direct it toward his children (rather than his spouse or colleagues), to govern the strength of his parental concern, and so on. It is the possibility of agents motivated in this way that scholars have consistently failed to consider in their interpretations of "Hume's circle." Brown, for instance, tells us that together, Hume's distinction between the artificial and natural virtues and the distinction between "whether or not an action is performed with a regard for its moral worth" yield "four cases of being moved to do the virtuous or right thing":

An agent may be moved to do the naturally virtuous or right thing from a nonmoral motive (1a) or from a moral motive (1b). Or an agent may be moved to do what is artificially right from a non-moral motive (2a) or from a moral motive (2b). (Brown 1988: 79)

"Moral motive" in this context refers to the agent who is motivated solely by a sentiment of moral approbation or disapprobation. The possibility that Brown and other Hume scholars fail to consider is, we might say, (1c): an agent may be moved to do the naturally virtuous thing by a combination of moral and nonmoral motives – that is, by a nonmoral sentiment that is informed and influenced in its direction and significance within the larger picture of the agent's motivational psychology by that agent's conception of value. There is nothing in Hume's circle that either excludes this possibility or demands that we treat agents thus motivated as merely imitating genuine virtue in the way that Hume suggests we ought to regard those motivated solely by their moral sentiments.

It remains to be seen whether Hume himself ever considered this third possibility. If he did, the issue would then become whether Hume thought that naturally virtuous conduct was typically, always, or sometimes motivated in the manner of (1a) or else motivated always, sometimes, etc., in the manner of (1c).

Hume does at least hint that he had this possibility (1c) in mind in constructing the argument concerning our first motives for virtuous conduct. In the next paragraph, he writes of parental affection: "Were not natural affection a duty, the care of children cou'd not be a duty; and *'twere impossible we cou'd have the duty in our eye in the attention we give to our offspring*" (T 3.2.1.5, SBN 478; emphasis added). This phrasing suggests that we *do* have our duties toward our children "in our eye" in the attention we afford them, guiding our nonmoral concern for our children in light of our conception of the value of that concern. One might think that all Hume means is that we can have our duties to our children "in our eye" in that we can perform those actions "from a certain sense of duty" (T 3.2.1.8, SBN 479) when we lack parental concern. But first, if all Hume intended to say here is that "were not natural affection a duty, the care of children could not be a duty, and it would be impossible for a parent to perform those duties merely out of regard for his obligations," he could have said precisely that, just as he does in T 3.2.1.8 (SBN 479). Second, if I am right, then T 3.2.1.5–8 (SBN 478–79) covers all of the basic possibilities for what might prompt an agent to a certain course of conduct: she might be prompted by a nonmoral affection alone, by her sense of duty alone, or by nonmoral affection guided by her sense of her duties. If the imagined interlocutor is right, Hume failed to even consider the second possibility.

The remarks with which Hume concludes the "circle" argument may seem more difficult to square with the interpretation I have been urging. There, Hume writes of those who, in an attempt to imitate true virtue, act solely out of their sense of duty:

still this supposes in human nature some distinct principles, which are capable of producing the action, and whose moral beauty renders the action meritorious. (T 3.2.1.8, SBN 479)

On one reading, Hume concludes the "circle" argument with the claim that what "renders" an action "meritorious" is nothing more than an affection that is "distinct" from the agent's sense of duty – that is, (natural) virtues are constituted by wholly nonmoral affections.[28] But that would be a puzzling conclusion for Hume to reach, because, as we have seen, it is not entailed by the argument of T 3.2.1.5 (SBN 478) that precedes it.

Perhaps Hume is merely jumping the gun, telling us that (natural) virtues are nothing more than nonmoral affections before his arguments demand that conclusion. But there is another, better possibility. At this point in the text, a distinction between aspects of our conception of the virtues that can be specified in the absence of an account of morality's authority, and those that can be specified only after we have our account of morality's authority in hand, is becoming increasingly important to Hume. According to Hume, we can make two claims about the virtuous without understanding the source of morality's normativity (the justification for the kinds of claims ethical life makes on us). First, a disposition must be one of which we approve from the moral point of view in order to count as virtuous, for by definition only then is it a virtue. Second, the virtuous disposition must consist in something more than an agent's sense of duty, or we will be unable to specify of what we are approving when we approve of her conduct as virtuous. All actions are then "rendered meritorious" by some nonmoral affection in the sense that, but for that nonmoral affection, the action could not be virtuous. And since neither of these restrictions on what qualifies as a virtue requires an agent's sense of morals to play a role in the dispositions constitutive of her virtues, it is *conceivable* that an action may be "rendered meritorious" solely by a nonmoral disposition.

At the same time, however, Hume also holds that once we understand morality's authority – why we make distinctions between virtue and vice, the normative force of those distinctions, and the justification for morality's normativity – we will see that no human being does, or could, possess a virtue comprised solely of a nonmoral affection. We human beings depend on the authoritative force of our sense of moral worth, just as David in our example depends on his sense of morals to regulate his parental concern. The reason for this, on Hume's account, is that the same features of our psychology that give rise to the need for a shared normative standard of character are also inevitable sources of temptation once that standard is adopted.

Imagine life without moral value, without distinctions between virtue and vice, and without the normative standard of character that those distinctions bring with them, Hume argues, and one begins to see why adoption of that standard is justified:

When we form our judgments of persons, merely from the tendency of their characters to our own benefit, or to that of our friends, we find so many contradictions to our sentiments in society and conversation, and such an uncertainty from the incessant changes of our situation, that we seek some other standard of merit and demerit, which may not admit of so great variation. (T 3.3.1.18, SBN 583)

Similar passages are found throughout the *Treatise* and the second *Enquiry*.[29] Nowhere does Hume elaborate on the content of these "contradictions," nor does he explain *why* the threat of such "contradictions" justifies the adoption of the Humean moral point of view as a normative standard of character. The result has been substantial scholarly controversy.[30] Fortunately, it is clear – at least in outline – what Hume thinks are the *sources* of these "contradictions": our tendency to prefer more immediate, though lesser, goods; our tendency to evaluate persons and traits from the perspective of self-interest; and our tendency to evaluate traits and persons from the perspective of our concern for our loved ones. These three basic human propensities combine to give us four perspectives from which we tend to evaluate persons and traits: short-term self-interest, long-term self-interest, concern for the short-term interests of loved ones, and concern for the long-term interests of loved ones. Eliminate entirely these four evaluative propensities from the human mind and one eliminates the source of the "many contradictions ... in society and conversation" that Hume tells us give us a need for a normative standard of character. Eliminate these evaluative propensities, in other words, and Humean morality is superfluous for humankind. Purge these evaluative tendencies from an individual human mind, and Humean morality becomes superfluous for that agent.[31]

At the same time, for the person who has adopted the Humean standard of character, self-interest, concern for her loved ones, and the all-too-human tendency to prefer lesser, more immediate goods will inevitably give rise to temptations to stray from virtue. Even the most caring parent, for instance, will sometimes face conflicts between the long-term interests of his child that he knows ought to guide his concern for the child and the child's present desires and will sometimes find himself in situations in which his known duties toward his child conflict with his own interests. Hume is hardly shy, as we have already seen, about reminding us that we are chronically tempted in these ways. Although morality "requires an impartial conduct," "'tis seldom we can bring ourselves to it" (T 3.3.1.18, SBN 583).[32] In short, there are three features of human psychology – self-interest, concern for loved ones, and our preference for lesser, more immediate goods – that are primarily responsible on Hume's account for both the necessity of a normative standard of character and a substantial portion of our temptations to vice. Hence, as long as we have a need to make moral distinctions among characters and persons – vicious and virtuous, praiseworthy and blameworthy – we will inevitably be tempted.

Unless we are all hopelessly vicious, something must move us to resist those temptations. What does so, according to Hume, is our moral sentiments. This is not mere exegetical speculation or "filling in." Hume's laudatory remarks about morality's great practical force – commentary that makes little sense if morality has no practical influence over the natural virtues, as the traditional reading claims – begin on the first page of Book 3 of the *Treatise*. Famously, he writes:

If morality had naturally no influence on human passions and actions, 'twere in vain to take such pains to inculcate it; and nothing wou'd be more fruitless than that multitude of rules and precepts, with which all moralists abound. Philosophy is commonly divided into *speculative* and *practical*; and as morality is always comprehended under the latter division, 'tis suppos'd to influence our passions and actions, and to go beyond the calm and indolent judgments of the understanding. And this is confirm'd by common experience, which informs us, that men are often govern'd by their duties, and are deter'd from some actions by the opinion of injustice, and impell'd to others by that of obligation. (T 3.1.1.5, SBN 457)

Later, in the second *Enquiry*, Hume is even more explicit about morality's practical role as guardian against temptation:

What wonder then, that moral sentiments are found of such influence in life. ... They form, in a manner, the *party* of human kind against vice or disorder, its common enemy. ... Other passions, though perhaps originally stronger, yet being selfish and private, are often overpowered by its force, and yield the dominion of our breast to those social and public principles. (EPM 9.9, SBN 275–76)

These passages, and many others besides, must be read out of Hume's moral theory by advocates of the traditional reading. They tell us that Hume's praise for morality's practical force in the *Treatise* is a *reductio* of peculiarly rationalist views, or that all such remarks are mere rhetorical flourishes, or that Hume intended such remarks to apply only to the artificial virtues. These are far from the obvious ways to read these passages.[33] The burden of argument is on those who would thus read Hume to show why we must so interpret these passages. That burden, perhaps, seemed possible to meet as long as "Hume's circle" was thought to entail the claim that our motives to virtuous conduct must be wholly nonmoral affections. But "Hume's circle" does not have this implication.

On my reading, the dispositions of which we approve under the title "natural virtues" are comprised of nonmoral affections whose strength, vivacity, objects, subjects, and expression in action or "on the countenance" are all governed (against the force of temptations to the contrary) by the agent's sense of moral worth. Moral sentiments, on this account, function as second-order motives, but their motive force is not so limited as of a "limiting" motive – a motive that prevents an agent from acting on a desire that would otherwise prompt action. Humean moral sentiments also govern the *way* an agent acts on his desires (as in the example of David, who saves for his child's education rather than buying him toys), the objects of his nonmoral affections, the subjects of those affections, the expression on his face, and the relative weight that those affections are afforded in the agent's psychology as compared to other affections.[34]

It is human psychology, rather than the concept of a "virtue" as such, that requires an agent's sense of morals to govern her natural affections in this way, but that does not make Humean morality a mere "back-up system" to nonmoral dispositions. To say that Humean morality is, in practical terms, a "back-up system" *for this reason* is to imagine that in the absence of the facts of psychology that make us tempted to vice our character would be, by Hume's lights, virtuous. That is false. On Hume's account, were human psychology such as it would have to be in order for morality to play no practical role in the natural virtues, we would have no need to construct a moral point of view, in which case we would not denominate any disposition either virtuous or vicious.[35]

4. NATURAL VIRTUES AS COMMONPLACE

Yet another sense in which Hume's natural virtues are traditionally thought "natural" is in being "common" as opposed to "rare and unusual."[36] Baier, for instance, writes: "Hume requires of a natural virtue that it be the norm, not the exception, in a human population" (1994: 75). Elsewhere she tells us that "there is a realism constraint built into [Hume's] theory, which amounts to the requirement that vice be the exception, virtue the rule" (1991: 187). We are referred, in this context, to Hume's *Treatise* discussion of "common" as one meaning of *natural*:

if ever there was any thing, which cou'd be call'd natural in this sense, the sentiments of morality certainly may; since there never was any nation of the world, nor any single person in any nation, who was utterly depriv'd of them, and who never, in any instance, show'd the least approbation or dislike of manners. (T 3.1.2.8, SBN 474)

Hume's claim here is that nothing could be more common than sentiments of moral approval and disapproval. This leaves wide open the question of whether the *dispositions* of which we approve are also themselves common. A second passage frequently cited as evidence that Hume's natural virtues are commonplace is the *Treatise* passage in which Hume tells us that our "measures of duty" follow "the common and natural course of our passions" (T 3.2.1.18, SBN 484).[37] I have argued that this passage ought to be read as claiming only that we cannot expect what would be impossible for most people, such as we would if our "measures of duty" required agents to love society as we do our spouses or have the same extensive duties to society as we do to our spouses. The natural virtues may be rare, even if we restrict our "measures of duty" in this way. Suppose that most people are capable, at some basic psychological level, of cultivating the virtue of "parental concern" when it comes to their own children, but incapable of cultivating such concern for all the world's children. Parents may nevertheless fail to cultivate "parental concern" for their own children or fail to develop that virtue to its full perfection.

In fact, Hume makes it clear in various ways that he does not believe that any virtues are commonplace. For instance, he pokes fun at those who deplore humanity on the grounds that there are few truly wise or virtuous among us, writing:

the honourable appellations of wise and virtuous, are not annexed to any particular degree of those qualities of *wisdom* and *virtue*; but arise altogether from the comparison we make between one man and another. When we find a man, who arrives at such a pitch of wisdom as is very uncommon, we pronounce him a wise man: So that to say, there are few wise men in the world, is really to say nothing; since it is only by their scarcity, that they merit that appellation. (E-DM 83; cf. E-ST 238)

We should also remember that all Humean virtues give rise to pride (if our own virtues) or love (if someone else's virtues) (T 3.3.1.3, 26, 31, SBN 574-75, 589, 591). To be proud, Hume argues, we must believe that the subject of our pride is "peculiar to ourselves, or at least common to us with a few persons" (T 2.1.6.4, SBN 291). Because all of our own virtues give rise to pride, they must also all be, to some degree, seen by us as rare. And unless we are guilty of a global mistake in this respect, they also must actually be, to some degree, rare. Hume seems to think this is even true of "good nature," a trait rare enough to give rise to pride but common enough that it only gives rise to the smallest tincture of pride.[38] The many passages in which Hume reminds us of how often our passions are slow to "follow the determinations" of our moral evaluations also imply that the natural virtues are rare (T 3.3.1.18, SBN 583).[39] Were they, as Baier claims, "the norm in a human population," then at least with respect to the affective dispositions constitutive of those virtues, Hume would have to say that our passions *do* readily follow the determination of our moral evaluations. Moreover, Hume cautions us that some natural virtues, including ambition and courage, are apt in men of "ordinary talents and capacity" to "degenerate into a turbulent ferocity" (EPM 2.3, SBN 177). These natural virtues must be particularly rare – as rare as men and women of extraordinary talent and capacity.[40]

5. CONVENTIONAL NATURAL VIRTUES?[41]

There are two additional respects in which both our approbation of and the content of the natural virtues *is* straightforwardly conventional.[42] Although there is less scholarly unanimity in these two respects, some have claimed that "one of the marks of ... the artificial virtues," in contrast with the natural virtues, is the fact that only the former admit of "cultural variation" (Baier 1991: 230; cf. Whelan 1985: 221n47). Perhaps the thought is that whether a disposition is praised as "virtuous" will culturally vary in the case of the artificial but not the natural virtues. Alternatively, the thought might be that the particular contours of the descriptive content of the artificial but not the natural virtues is culturally variable. But neither thought fits the text. Hume's works are replete with examples of natural virtues that he claims properly receive culturally varying degrees of approbation and/or whose descriptive content varies among societies, including magnanimity, inflexible rigor, integrity, courage, clemency, tranquility, wit, ingenuity, and "good-nature."[43] In this sense, then, both the content and our approbation of the dispositions praised as "natural virtues" is conventional on Hume's account.

Second, some scholars have thought that Hume's natural virtues are nonconventional in that, as Tito Magri puts it, they need "general rules only as rules of thumb," whereas "general rules are constitutive of justice" (1996: 233). Magri himself qualifies this claim because of some peculiar features of the Humean moral point of view – that is, "extensive sympathy" (1996: 233, 238–39).[44] The affective aspects of extensive sympathy make us sensitive to, and aware of *as relevant*, features of traits and situations to which "general rules" could not sensitize us.[45] Yet our sympathetic deliberations must be structured by the general rules involved in "extensive sympathy," for only then do the resulting affective responses count as *moral* approval and disapproval. Hence, Magri (1996: 238–39) and others have argued, Humean sentiments of moral approval and disapproval are conventional.[46] In that case, our approval of the natural virtues is conventional. But we also know from the reflections of section 3 that a virtuous Humean agent's sentiments of moral approval and disapproval play a necessary role in motivating her virtuous conduct. If we put that conclusion together with Magri's important point about the role of general rules as partly constitutive of moral approbation, we are led to the further conclusion that insofar as sentiments of moral approval and disapproval play a role in the dispositions constitutive of the natural virtues, the natural virtues themselves are also, and in that sense, partly conventional.[47]

6. A SUMMARY OF THE "NEW" (OR, RATHER, "ORIGINAL") NATURAL VIRTUES

Hume's natural virtues, it turns out, are not so natural. They are not "instincts" in any robust sense; nor are they inalterable, wholly nonmoral, culturally invariable, or dispositions in which general rules function only as rules of thumb. Instead, Hume's natural virtues are dispositions in which nonmoral affections are regulated by the agent's moral sentiments; dispositions that can and must be cultivated and improved upon by the agent; dispositions that vary across cultures and in which general rules play a circumscribed but constitutive role.

There are nevertheless two ways in which Hume's natural virtues are clearly nonconventional. The goods that result from acts of justice, and that make justice a *virtue*, result only when there is general conformity to certain cooperative schemes of action.[48] A promise-respecting act, for instance, may have all sorts of beneficial effects in a particular instance, but the effects that entitle us to treat such acts as expressive of *virtues* can occur only where there is general conformity to the "schemes or systems of action" constitutive of the practice of promising.[49] In contrast, the typical effects of traits that lead us to approve of them as natural virtues when we adopt the moral point of view could occur even if only one person, in one instance, were motivated by that trait.[50] Thus, our approval of the artificial virtues – "our sense of [those] virtues" (T 3.1.2.9, SBN 475) – necessarily makes reference to persons' general conformity to certain schemes of action. This is not true of our approval of the natural virtues. Similarly, many scholars have thought that the dispositions constitutive of the artificial virtues must make necessary reference in their content to the schemes of action in which context those dispositions are expressed; such is not the case for the dispositions constitutive of the natural virtues.[51]

7. VIRTUE ETHICS AND HUME'S NATURAL VIRTUES

I would like to conclude by taking a step back and placing the two interpretations of Hume's natural virtues that have been at issue throughout this piece – the traditional interpretation and my own – in the context of the broader issue of Hume's status as a "virtue ethicist." My hope is to begin to show that there are significant issues involving Hume's place in contemporary ethics that turn on our understanding of the natural virtues.

"Virtue ethics," its advocates often tell us, is a distinct approach to theorizing about ethics, a full-blooded alternative to Kantian, contractarian, and utilitarian moral theories. A central aspect of this approach, as it has developed in recent years, is the virtue ethicist's theory about the relationship between moral judgment and character. At the heart of that theory are two claims:

(1)   Good moral sense – the ability and willingness to make accurate judgments of moral value – is essential for possession of any virtue.[52]

(2)   One cannot have the good moral sense essential for possession of any particular virtue without actually possessing that virtue.[53]

Hume has widely been seen as offering one version of virtue ethics, at least since the publication of Baier's *Postures of the Mind*. It has escaped notice that the traditional interpretation of Hume's natural virtues throws serious doubt on this view of Humean ethics. On the traditional reading, natural virtues are nothing but innate dispositions to have, and act on, certain nonmoral affections.[54] The virtue ethicist's first thesis would not then apply to the natural virtues; the ability to make accurate judgments of moral value is not, by definition, essential to the possession of those virtues. For the same reason, the virtue ethicist's second claim would then have no content as a claim about good Humean moral sense. Suppose, by analogy, I say that you cannot have the sense of perfect pitch necessary for being physically strong unless you are in fact physically strong. This claim tells us nothing about what is required to have perfect pitch, because perfect pitch is not essential to the possession of physical strength. Similarly, the virtue ethicist's second claim tells us nothing about what is required for good Humean moral sense, because (on the traditional reading) good moral sense is not essential to the possession of a natural virtue.

It might seem that a measure of the second thesis can be preserved by appealing to the fact that some of the affective dispositions involved in Humean moral assessment also qualify as natural virtues.[55] For instance, one cannot engage in Humean moral evaluation if one is incapable of feeling pride and love, and due pride and love can be natural virtues.[56] So one cannot have good moral sense about any virtue without possessing at least some capacity for some virtues. But this feature of Humean moral evaluation differs from the virtue ethicist's second claim in at least two important respects. First, it concerns our judgments *about* virtues, not judgments of value essential *for* possession of a virtue. Second, even a more stringent requirement that one possess some laudable qualities (e.g., sympathy) in order to have good moral sense about the virtues in general is not equivalent to the virtue ethicist's claim that one must possess a particular virtue in order to have good moral sense when it comes to *that* trait.

Hume's apparent rejection of the two claims concerning the relationship between moral judgment and character central to contemporary virtue ethics makes it difficult to see what could justify calling him a "virtue ethicist." Still, the category of virtue ethics is a recent invention, and other aspects of Hume's ethics are difficult to square with prevailing categories in contemporary ethics. So why should we be worried if we cannot classify Hume as a "virtue ethicist"?

What is potentially troubling here is that there seem to be good *Humean* principles underlying the virtue ethicist's two claims about the relationship between moral judgment and character. The assumptions that underwrite those two claims include the views that (1) a trait must be reliable and reliably good in order to qualify as a "virtue";[57] (2) virtues are not entirely discrete, isolable traits;[58] and (3) there are distinct benefits in being virtuous that are unavailable to the vicious, (some of) which cannot be seen *as* benefits by the vicious and which accrue to the virtuous just insofar as they are virtuous.[59]

Hume endorses all three of these claims about the virtues. He repeatedly tells us that an affection "must depend upon durable principles of the mind, which extend over the whole conduct" (T 3.3.1.4, SBN 575) in order to qualify as a virtue and frequently warns that we must attend only to the tendencies of affections – their typical effects – in evaluating traits in order to ensure that the traits of which we approve are reliably good (T 3.3.1.19, SBN 584; EPM 5.41n24, SBN 228n).[60] And while no advocate of a strong version of the unity of the virtues, Hume is equally averse to the claim that the virtues are entirely discrete, isolable traits. He tells us, for instance, that whether as a society or as an individual, we cannot cultivate all virtues alike but must sacrifice some of the "*useful*, if we be very anxious to obtain all the *agreeable* qualities; and cannot pretend to reach alike every kind of advantage" (D 47, SBN 339). Were virtues entirely isolable – traits with no intrinsic relationship to one another – there would be nothing in principle excluding the possibility that we *could* cultivate all the virtues. This is certainly not the relationship among the virtues at which neo-Aristotelians drive via something like the unity thesis, but it is a rejection of the claim that the virtues are entirely isolable (D 47, SBN 339). Finally, Hume recognizes at least two "benefits" of virtue that accrue to the virtuous because they are virtuous: (a) the pleasures involved in knowing that one is virtuous and (b) the "benefit" of virtue that simply consists in conducting oneself in a manner in which one sees as justified. It is the latter at stake, for instance, in Hume's remark that the sensible knave misses out on that "consciousness of integrity" that "every honest man" understands as "requisite to happiness" (EPM 9.23, SBN 283).[61]

The virtue ethicist tells us that one cannot adopt these three views and yet simultaneously reject the virtue ethicist's theory about the *relationship* between moral judgment and character. The traditional interpretation of Hume's natural virtues, however, forces us to reject the latter. Much more worrisome, if the traditional interpretation of Hume's natural virtues were correct, then Hume would not be entitled to make the sensible claims – to which he does seem committed, as we have seen – that the virtues are reliable, are not entirely isolable, and accrue special benefits to the virtuous. In other words, on the traditional interpretation, Hume avows what he is not entitled to avow, and what he is not entitled to avow are perfectly sensible views (a)–(c).

If, for instance, the natural virtues were "instinctive" in the reductive sense at issue in the traditional interpretation, they must also be isolable traits. Otherwise, we could not identify them *as* "instincts" in this reductive sense. If an agent's conception of value plays no role in her natural virtues, those traits could not plausibly be supposed to be reliably good for exactly the reasons that Hume in fact thinks that an agent's conception of value must play an essential role in her natural virtues. Similarly, Hume holds that both the pleasures resulting from one's awareness that one conducts oneself in praiseworthy ways and the "benefit" of simply being able to rightly judge that one conducts oneself in praiseworthy ways depend on an agent's ability to correctly assess her traits. But on the traditional reading, an agent's possession of the natural virtues does not depend on her having good moral sense. This makes possible the "naturally sound person" whom Brown describes – one who has all the natural virtues but lacks a moral sense, and so lacks "any awareness of doing something with moral worth" (1988: 81). On the traditional interpretation, then, the two "benefits" at issue accrue to an agent only insofar as she is both virtuous *and* aware that she is praiseworthy. They are not, in other words, benefits of virtue per se. For the same reason, there is no assurance that the naturally virtuous will see the benefits in question *as* benefits. Brown's "naturally sound person" cannot see the justified regulation of his conduct as tantamount to doing well by himself and can have no notion of the special pleasures that accrue to those who are aware that they conduct themselves well. An understanding of these benefits, on the traditional interpretation, is also the result of more than virtue alone.

All this changes if we adopt my interpretation of Hume's natural virtues. True, Hume does not quite hold the virtue ethicist's view about the relationship between character and moral evaluation. A Humean agent's conception of value plays a necessary role in the dispositions constitutive of her natural virtues on my account, but the "necessity" at issue here is psychological and part of the justificatory structure of Humean ethics rather than strictly conceptual or definitional, as today's virtue ethicists claim.[62] So too, a naturally virtuous Humean's ability to make the judgments of value relevant to the exercise of her virtues is entirely derivative of the fact that her conception of value plays this psychologically necessary role in her natural virtues. In contrast to the virtue ethicist's view, Hume's view leaves open the possibility that an agent might have good sense about all that is involved in the exercise of a natural virtue without actually possessing that virtue.[63]

Even so, Hume can consistently avow the three key views that underwrite the virtue ethicist's claims about the relationship between character and judgment. First, Hume holds that our moral sentiments must govern the natural virtues, precisely because virtues are, by definition, reliably good. Our moral sentiments enable us to resist temptation and so enable us to maintain reliably laudable traits. Second, that virtues are not isolable traits on Hume's account is reflected in the fact that he does not view those traits as "instincts" in the reductive sense. Recall that his examples of corrupted innate dispositions include the combination of hope, warm imagination, and pride that gives rise to enthusiasm and the form of love that in itself makes "a man a total slave" (E-Sc 180). Hume's description of these vices is a description of two ways in which virtues are not isolable: whether a trait is a virtue depends on its relationship to the agent's other dispositions, and a trait is not entirely virtuous if its presence makes the agent, in another sense, vicious.[64] Moreover, the temptation to allow our laudable dispositions to "go bad" in ways that implicate the relationship among the virtues is among the temptations that our moral sentiments enable us to resist. Hume's account of the role of moral sentiments in the natural virtues also thereby reflects his acknowledgment that the virtues are not isolable.

Third, consider the virtue ethicist's claim that there are distinct benefits in being virtuous that are unavailable to the vicious – benefits that accrue to the virtuous just insofar as they are virtuous and some of which cannot be seen as benefits by the vicious. Hume's account of morality's practical role in the natural virtues makes room for his commitment to this thesis.[65] On the one hand, a naturally virtuous Humean is the recipient of two sorts of specifically moral "benefits." First, in treating her moral sentiments as authoritative governors of her other affections, she treats the moral regulation of her (nonmoral) affections as tantamount to doing well by herself, just in the sense that she conducts herself in ways that she rightly sees as justified. One who lacks natural virtue(s), in contrast, cannot rightly judge that she conducts herself in ways she sees as justified. Second, to have an appropriate moral sentiment is to understand, in situ, what is praiseworthy and blameworthy. Since the moral sentiments play a necessary practical role in the natural virtues, the particular pleasures produced by the knowledge that one conducts oneself in praiseworthy ways necessarily accrue to the naturally virtuous Humean. On the other hand, those who are lacking in natural virtue will not be able to see some of the benefits that accrue to the virtuous *as* benefits. If, for instance, one's lack of virtue is the result of a mistaken notion of the laudable or the failure to judge one's traits as either praiseworthy or blameworthy, it will be definitionally true that one cannot see the justified moral regulation of one's affections as tantamount to doing well by oneself. And since those who lack natural virtue(s) cannot be aware that they conduct themselves in praiseworthy ways – they do not – the pleasures produced by such awareness are unavailable to them.

Insofar as they do not have experience of those pleasures, they cannot fully understand the content of those pleasures and so cannot fully understand the content of this "benefit" that accrues to the virtuous.[66]

The mistake contemporary virtue ethicists have made is in holding that their three fundamental theses about the reliability of, relationships among, and benefits of the virtues can be maintained only by adopting the two views about the relationship between character and moral judgment mentioned at the beginning of this section. Hume manages to preserve the former three theses without adopting the two views. If rejection of those two views disqualifies him for the title "virtue ethicist," so be it. What was troubling was the possibility that Hume could not maintain the three theses on the nature of the virtues that contemporary virtue ethicists treat as *underwriting* their claims concerning the relationship between moral judgment and character, both because the former three theses are explicitly avowed by Hume and because they are plausibly thought necessary to any adequate treatment of the virtues. But the purported link between these two sets of views has been broken. With the source of the concern eliminated, the question of whether Hume qualifies as a virtue ethicist is then nothing more than a "verbal dispute."[67]

NOTES

1. Hume did not use of the terms "artificial" and "natural" virtues in his later work, but he continued to mark the distinction between them as two central categories of virtue. He does so, for instance, in the third appendix to EPM, as well as in his essay "Of the Original Contract." Speculations abound as to why Hume dropped the nomenclature of "artificial" and "natural" virtues in his later work. My own view is that this has largely to do with the fact that many of Hume's eighteenth-century interlocutors, such as Hutcheson, Wishart, and "that silly fellow" Beattie, used the term *artificial* as one of disapprobation. Hume never used "artificial" in this evaluatively laden manner when speaking in his own philosophical voice and would have been right in seeing a number of misreadings of his account of the artificial virtues as arising partly from the mistaken assumption that he intended disapprobation when using the term.
2. See, e.g., Broadie 1991: 215–16, 359–60; and Hursthouse 1999a: 103–6, 154.
3. See, e.g., Darwall 1995: 321; and Korsgaard 1996a: 47–51.
4. A prime example of this assumption at work can be found in Mackie 1980. Having argued that our approval of natural virtues is, in one sense, conventional, Mackie concludes that "[this] is rather devastating for Hume's theory. For it means that the natural virtues are, after all, a further set of artificial virtues" (1980: 123). Annette Baier (1991: 178–79) and Jean Hampton (1997: 88–89) reach similar conclusions on the basis of the same (mistaken) assumption.

   The reason I say, above, that Hume's natural virtues are commonly presumed "natural" in *at least* every sense in which the artificial virtues are "artificial" is that some traditional claims about the naturalness of the natural virtues have nothing to do with whether they are "artificial." For instance, it is often claimed that the natural virtues are common. But a trait may be common (or not) irrespective of whether it is also conventional (or not).

5. See also T 3.2.1. In introducing the distinction between artificial and natural virtues in T 3.1.2, Hume does not claim that the content of the former is conventional in a way (or ways) in which the content of the latter is not. Rather, the distinction there drawn is between our *approbation* of two species of virtues. He writes, "Perhaps it will appear afterwards, that our sense of some virtues is artificial, and that of others natural" (T 3.1.2.9, SBN 475). Only later, in T 3.2.1, does it become clear that Hume holds that the content of the dispositions constitutive of these two species of virtue also differs in terms of the degree, or manner, in which they are conventional.

6. We ought not to be deterred by the fact that Hume's account of the artificial virtues precedes his account of the natural virtues in the *Treatise*. There are many reasons Hume might have chosen this order of exposition. Just as with the question "What is so natural about Hume's natural virtues?" the question of whether this order of exposition was meant to suggest to the reader that the natural virtues are nonconventional in every sense that the artificial virtues are conventional can be answered only once we have a full understanding of the "naturalness" of the natural virtues in hand.

7. See, e.g., Stewart 1963: 102; Árdal 1966: 168; Whelen 1985: 220–21; Brown 1988: 69–82, esp. 78–81; Norton 1993a:164–65; Penelhum 1993: 135–36; and Korsgaard 1996a: 49–50. However, Baron (1988) disputes the common claim that the dispositions constitutive of the natural virtues *spontaneously* give rise to occurrent motives for acting, and J. L. Mackie (1980: 120) claims that the expression of these dispositions in action is sufficiently constrained by artifice (convention) to spoil Hume's distinction between the artificial and natural virtues. (See also the discussion of Baron and Mackie's views in sections 3 and 5.)

8. Brown 1988; Norton 1993a: 164–66; and Korsgaard 1996a: 49–51.

9. My description of the conclusion of Hume's argument in T 3.2.1.4 (SBN 478) is a close paraphrase of that provided by Rachel Cohon (1997: 92). The difference is only that I have inserted into her version of that conclusion the word "wholly," for reasons that will become obvious in section 3.

10. In the revised version of this passage that appears in the EPM, Hume also cautions us that "a small benefit done to ourselves, or our near friends, excites more lively sentiments of love and approbation. ... But still we know here, as in all the senses, to *correct* these inequalities by reflection, and retain a general standard of vice and virtue" (emphasis added).

11. In the passage quoted above, Brown tells us that the "content of our natural duties coincides with the untutored play of our ... affections as they would operate in the state of nature" (1988: 81). Donald Ainslie has suggested to me that this phrasing opens the door to a distinction between (1) traits that enable us to "perform our duty" and avoid vice and (2) traits that merit approval and the title of "naturally virtuous." This distinction would make it possible to claim that the affections we would have in the state of nature would *neither* be regarded as "vicious" *nor* "virtuous" by a judicious Humean

spectator. That is, we do not approve of affections "as they would operate in the state of nature," but neither do we disapprove of them.

I am not convinced that Hume couples the performance of "duties" with the avoidance of vice in the manner Ainslie suggests. But the distinction to which Ainslie points between that which is required in order to avoid meriting disapproval (to avoid vice) and that which is required in order to merit approval (virtue) does, I believe, have a place in Hume's moral theory. (See note 14 below and corresponding text.)

On the other hand, Brown does not draw any such distinction. In the passage in question, she is using the phrase "the content of our natural duties" to refer to the content of our "natural virtues." This is made clear, for instance, by the fact that shortly before the passage about the "content of our natural duties" quoted above, Brown writes, "The natural virtues are those tendencies and patterns of behavior which human beings would possess and exhibit even in the state of nature prior to societal influences" (1988: 78; see also 79). What concerns me above is the claim that we would *approve* of the traits "human beings would possess and exhibit even in the state of nature," for this is a claim about the content of Hume's natural *virtues.* Many scholars in addition to Brown have read Hume in this way as well. (See citations in note 7 above). It is this reading of the natural virtues as "instincts" in the reductive sense that I wish to argue against in section 1 above.

12. Much of my alternative reading of T 3.2.1.16 (SBN 483) is compatible with that which Tito Magri (1996) offers. In particular, the proposed reading is one way in which we might understand Magri's claim that "Hume seems sometimes to suggest that the general features of our motives are regulative for sympathetic appraisal" (1996: 237). I am less certain that Magri and I agree in two other respects about this passage. First, in introducing this *Treatise* passage, Magri writes that it "seems to be put forward by Hume as a complete theory of moral ... evaluation" (1996: 236). A short while later, Magri argues that we need not read the *Treatise* passage in this way but as one of two principles that play "different but complementary roles in the process of moral evaluation" (1996: 237). I am not yet convinced that this *Treatise* passage even *seems* to be put forward as a complete theory of moral evaluation. Second, Magri offers as an explanation for why our measures of duty are constrained by the general features of our natural motives that our "[s]ympathy [in its role in moral appraisal] would be blind if it were not directed towards a specific class of persons and if the set of consequences of actions that are relevant for moral appraisal were not in this way fixed" (1996: 237). As a claim about the ways in which our sympathy must be restricted or directed if moral appraisal is to work (in particular, if our moral sentiments are to have intersubjective validity), I quite agree with Magri here. But as I argue above, I think the explanation for Hume restricting our "measures of duty" to the "common and usual course of our passions" lies elsewhere.

13. See, e.g., Baron 1988: 43–45; and Whelan 1985: 220–21.

14. I owe this point to Donald Ainslie, who mentioned this possibility to me in helpful comments on an early version of this piece. I find Ainslie's suggestion intriguing, particularly insofar as what he is pointing to is the possibility of a category of affections that Hume could regard as, strictly speaking, neither

virtuous nor vicious. Still, for reasons mentioned above, I do not believe that "parental affection as it would exist in the state of nature" falls into this category for Hume. It's also worth noting that, in general, it is difficult to find room in Hume's account of moral evaluation for the proposed category of traits that are neither virtuous nor vicious. Whether we can find that room depends in large part on our understanding of Hume's criterion of virtue. (See Abramson 2008 for an argument that the traditional reading of this criterion is seriously misguided.)

15. Hume is sometimes read as advocating relativism in "A Dialogue," and accordingly read as explaining, without condemning, Athenian practices of infanticide. I argue against such interpretations in Abramson 1999b.

16. Some scholars read this passage as claiming only that, while we cannot often bring ourselves to *feel* moral approbation or disapprobation, we know what our sentiments would be were we to adopt the Humean moral point of view, and so correct our *language* (Baron 1988 and Magri 1996). In a telling emendation to the *Treatise*, however, Hume writes that of the "principle of sympathy" – "extensive sympathy" – that is the source of our moral sentiments, "This latter principle of sympathy is too weak to controul our passions; but has sufficient force to influence our taste, and give us the sentiments of approbation or blame" (T 3.2.2.24, SBN 670). Here Hume says explicitly that extensive sympathy *does* give us "sentiments of approbation or blame." The passions that extensive sympathy is too weak to control are, accordingly, those that are the *objects* of our moral sentiments. (The reading of this and similar such passages that I favor can also be found in Darwall 1995 and Radcliffe 1996.)

17. Thanks to Ken Winkler for raising the question of whether the naturalness of natural virtues consists partly in their being inalterable and for pointing me to EHU 9.6 (SBN 108).

18. On EHU 9.5n20 (SBN 107n), Hume makes it eminently clear that he thinks experimental reasoning improves with practice. For instance, he claims that practice using analogies and greater experience with "books and conversation" both improve one's skill in experimental reasoning.

19. Russell (1995: 133n4) reads T 3.3.4.4 (SBN 609) as claiming that although we cannot change our passions, we can learn to suppress them (not act on them). For reasons explored above, I do not believe this was Hume's considered view.

20. Neither Baier nor Russell seriously entertains the possibility that the voice of "The Sceptic" is not Hume's own. For purposes of my argument above, I similarly assume that "the sceptic" speaks for Hume, for even on that assumption, the essay does not provide evidence that Humean character traits are inalterable.

21. A similar line of thought, I believe, is also what underlies Hume's claim in the *Treatise* that it is "almost impossible for *the mind to change its character* in any considerable article" (T 3.3.4.3, SBN 608; emphasis added).

22. In the same vein, Hume draws a picture in "The Stoic" of a "true sage" in whom "the most turbulent passions [are] tuned to just harmony and concord." Having sketched this magnificent figure, Hume asks, "What must be the effects of [such] moral beauty? And what influence must it have, when it ... *is the result of our own reflection and industry?*" (E-St 153; emphasis

added). As with "The Sceptic," it is not obvious to what extent we can identify the voice of "The Stoic" with Hume's own. My own view is that the voice of "the Stoic" is much closer to Hume's than is commonly thought. Unfortunately, making out that argument would take us far afield from our present concerns. Doing so would require, among other things, a detailed analysis of the nature of Hume's appropriations of Stoicism (which proceed largely through Cicero's own appropriation of Stoicism in *De Officiis*) and a more general examination of the methods and goals that guided the genre of early modern essay writing to which such essays as "The Stoic" belong.

23. See also EPM 1.7, 9.8n57, 9.9–11 (SBN 172, 274–75n, 275–76). Russell takes the "sceptic's" claims about how we can improve our character to "substantially qualify" the claim that Humean traits are unchangeable (1995: 129). But since neither Hume nor "The Sceptic" ever says that our traits are unchangeable, the sceptic's claims about how we can improve our character cannot be read as qualifications on that general claim.

24. Stewart 1963: 102; Árdal 1966: 168; Whelan 1985: 220–21; Baier 1988: 757–78 and 774; Brown 1988: 78–83; Baier 1991: 183–85; Darwall 1993: 416–17; Haakonssen 1993: 186–87 and 191; Norton 1993a: 164–65; Penelhum 1993: 135–36; Korsgaard 1996a: 48–51; Korsgaard 1996b: 57–58; Radcliffe 1996: 406; Cohon 1997: 92–95; and Blackburn 1999: 416–17. In what follows, I argue that this traditional assumption about the natural virtues is mistaken. In Abramson 2002, I argue that an agent's conception of value plays a (conceptually) necessary role in two very exceptional natural virtues, goodness and greatness of mind, which (in part because of the ways in which they are exceptional natural virtues) I do not consider here. I will, however, mark in the notes some of the most significant differences between goodness and greatness of mind and the rest of the natural virtues with which I am here concerned.

25. Cf. Cohon 1997: 95; and Korsgaard 1996a: 48.

26. Here, and in what follows, *nonmoral* means simply this: not structured by nor in any other way necessarily implicating the agent's conception of (ethical) value.

27. See also T 3.2.5.6 (SBN 518); EPM App. 3.2–3 (SBN 303–4). I argued in section 1 that a similar passage in "Of the Original Contract" (E-OC 479–80) can be read as claiming that parents are "impelled by a natural instinct" *only* in the sense that the *motivating force* of parental affection is not *derivative* of their conception of value. We do not, however, approve of *whatever* parents do when they act out of their (instinctive) parental concern. This reading is compatible with the reading proposed above of T 3.2.1.4 (SBN 478). Moreover, in "Of the Original Contract," Hume distinguishes between the artificial and natural virtues by claiming that artificial virtues are "not *supported* by any original instinct" (emphasis added). Once again, this suggests that something more than an "original instinct" is involved in the motives that prompt action indicative of the natural virtues.

28. Thanks to Tito Magri for pointing me to this passage.

29. See also: T 3.2.2.6, 3.2.2.9, 3.2.2.14, 3.2.2.16, 3.3.1.15, 3.3.3.2 (SBN 487, 489, 493, 494, 581–82, 602–3); and. EPM 5.42 (SBN 229).

30. See, e.g., Baier 1991: 181–85; Bricke 1996: 138–39; and Korsgaard 1999: 10–17.

31. Hume clearly did not think morality superfluous. Our moral practices, he holds, *are* justified – as a whole and for every individual (see note 28 and T 3.3.6.3 [SBN 619]). The fact that self-interest, our concern for loved ones ("limited generosity"), and our preference for the contiguous to the remote *are* the primary sources of the "contradictions" at issue is clear on a close reading of any of these passages. For instance, in T 3.3.1.18 (SBN 583), Hume writes that in the absence of morality, such contradictions arise "when we form our judgments of persons, merely from the tendency of their characters to our own benefit" (self-interest) or "to that of our friends" (limited generosity) and because of the "uncertainty from the incessant changes of our situation" (preference for contiguous to remote; its link to the "incessant changes of our situation" is explained on T 3.2.7.2–6 [SBN 535–37] in Hume's account of the origins and justification for government).

32. See also T 3.3.1.23, 3.2.2.24 (SBN 586, 670 [emendation to SBN 499]). The fact that Humean persons are chronically tempted also plays an important role in my argument for the claim that moral sentiments play a necessary role in "goodness," as offered in Abramson 2002. One important difference between goodness and greatness of mind and other natural virtues is that in the former, the necessity of morality's practical role is conceptual. That is, the very concepts of "goodness" and "greatness of mind" involve the thought that an agent's conception of value is essential to the dispositions constitutive of those virtues.

33. See also T 3.1.1.1, 3.3.6.6 (SBN 455–56, 621); E-DT 7–8; EPM 1.7–8, App. 4.7 (SBN 172, 317). For attempts to read out such remarks, see, e.g., Baier 1991: 183–85; Korsgaard 1996a: 70n21; and Radcliffe 1996. Brown (1988) claims instead that Hume just contradicts himself – founding his case against rationalism on premises about morality's practical import that he cannot accommodate in his own moral theory.

34. Baron (1988) argues that Humean moral sentiments do function as "limiting motives," hence the allusion to limiting motives above. This way of understanding Hume, she contends, affords two advantages. First, Hume can countenance the possibility that it may be appropriate for me to feel *x* but not appropriate for me to act out of *x* (1988: 40–42). Second, Hume can then countenance the possibility that some laudable nonmoral affections arise (in the occurrent sense) only upon reflection (1988: 44–45). In these latter cases, it seems to me that moral sentiments function not as motives but – borrowing Brown's (1988) language – as "triggers," raising a motive from antecedently given motivating disposition. There is, however, room for both of these possibilities on my interpretation of the role of moral sentiments as well.

Barbara Herman (1996) has attributed to Kant a view about moral motivation that is strikingly similar to that which I here attribute to Hume – i.e., a view on which moral evaluations function as second-order motives. There are, nevertheless, significant differences between the view I attribute to Hume and that which Herman attributes to Kant – differences at which I can only gesture here. Among other things, on Herman's account, the virtuous agent's conception of value influences the structure of her desires, including the objects of those desires and the agent's conception of the value of the objects of those desires, both of which Herman takes to be internal to the desires themselves. When the virtuous agent acts, her conception of value is thus embedded in the structure of her desires, and to the extent that it is not, she is lacking in virtue. In contrast, I take it that on Hume's account, an agent's moral sentiments may function as second-order motives that are, psychologically, *external* to her nonmoral affections without this being a mark of a defect in her character. If, for instance, an agent is tempted to express her anger inappropriately, her moral sentiments may move her to express that anger in an alternative course of action, even as she continues to desire to perform the viciously angry action from which she refrains. See also Abramson 2002: esp. 334n38, where I briefly discuss these issues insofar as they concern Hume's portrait of perfect virtue.

35. Baron (1988: 27) describes the "back-up" model of morality's practical force this way: "According to this picture there is a perfect correspondence between the goodness, appropriateness or (in some instances of the view) 'naturalness' of the agent's unmediated desires and affections, and the moral rectitude of her conduct. If the affections are what they should be, the ensuing actions will be morally right."

The motives of the naturally virtuous nevertheless aim at goods that are not, themselves, irreducibly moral. This is true even insofar as the agent's conception of value plays a necessary role in the dispositions constitutive of her natural virtues. What the agent, *qua* agent, takes to be valuable traits are traits that are seen, from the general point of view, to be typically productive of nonmoral goods. (In Abramson 2002, I argue that there is one exception to this claim about the natural virtues: "greatness of mind.") On some interpretations, the dispositions constitutive of the artificial virtues, in contrast, aim at irreducibly moral goods.

36. Mackie 1980: 3, 76–77; Whelan 1985: 220–21; Baron 1988: 44–45; Brown 1988: 80–82; and Baier 1991: 187 and 1994: 75.

37. See, e.g., Brown 1988: 81; and Baier 1994: 75.

38. "Suppose, therefore, an object to be presented, which is peculiarly fitted to produce love, but imperfectly to excite pride; this object, belonging to another, gives rise directly to a great degree of love, but to a small one of humility by comparison; and consequently that latter passion is scarce felt in the compound, nor is able to convert the love into respect. This is the case with good nature, good humour, facility, generosity, beauty, and many other qualities. These have a peculiar aptitude to produce love in others; but not so great a tendency to excite pride in ourselves" (T 2.2.10.8, SBN 392). Good nature cannot then be commonplace. If it were, it could not give rise to a "small degree" of pride. Baier glosses over this when she reads Hume as claiming "we can love a person for his common good nature, while not taking any pride in our own good nature" (1991: 147).

Baier also claims that Hume abandons the second restriction on pride in Book 3, citing T 3.3.2.7 (SBN 596): "those, who have an ill-grounded conceit of themselves, are for ever making those comparisons, nor have they any other method of supporting their vanity. A man of sense and merit is pleas'd with himself, independent of all foreign considerations: But a fool must always find some person, that is more foolish, in order to keep himself in good humour with his own parts and understanding." The virtuous need not make judgments about the rarity of their traits, Baier claims, to recognize that they are virtuous and to be proud (1991: 207). That is not Hume's claim. Hume's claim is that the virtuous need not compare themselves to *fools*. Their pride is "independent of all foreign considerations" in that they can compare themselves with anyone and remain proud, because their traits are truly rare. The conceited, in contrast, must find fools with whom to compare themselves, because only then will their traits *seem* rare enough to warrant pride.

39. See also T 3.3.1.23, 3.2.2.24 (SBN 586, 670 [emendation to SBN 499]).

40. The difficult question on this count, as Donald Ainslie pointed out to me, concerns the artificial virtues, for it seems that the artificial virtues must be, at least to some extent, common if the "schemes of action" to which those virtues make necessary reference are to be maintained.

41. The understanding of "convention" embedded in Hume's account of the artificial virtues is notoriously complicated. Fortunately, as our topic is Hume's natural virtues, we only need to sketch the basic outlines of Hume's account of "convention" here.

42. Some scholars allege that the natural virtues are nonconventional because and insofar as they are "instincts" in the reductive sense. See Brown 1988: 78–79; Haakonssen 1993: 191; Norton 1993a: 165–66; and Penelhum 1993: 135–36. We rejected this claim in section 2.

43. See, e.g., D 38–43 (SBN 336–38); EPM 7.15, 7.18, 8.4 (SBN 255, 256–57, 262); E-ST 227; E-RA 280.

44. For other accounts of the role of general rules in extensive sympathy, see, e.g., Stroud 1977: 202; Baier 1988; Darwall 1994; Sayre-McCord 1994; and Abramson 1999a.

45. T 3.3.1.15–23 (SBN 581–87); EPM 1.9 (SBN 173); E-DT; E-ST; E-SR.

46. See also Mackie 1980: 123; Baier 1991: 178–79; and Hampton 1997: 88–89.

47. Mackie (1980: 122–23) and Magri (1996: 240–41) gesture toward this possibility but do not pursue it. Because nonmoral affections (e.g., parental concern) play a role in the natural virtues, those virtues are – to that extent – not constituted wholly by general rules. The same cannot be said, on most readings, of artificial virtues. On many interpretations, the motives of which we approve in the artificial virtues are nothing but moral approval and disapproval. (See Árdal 1966; Mackie 1980; Korsgaard 1996a; and Cohon 1997.) On Darwall's (1995) reading, the motive of which we approve in the case of the artificial virtue is a motivational state of "rule-regulation."

48. T 3.2.2.10–22 (SBN 490–98); EPM App. 3.1–8 (SBN 303–6); Árdal 1966: 117; Baron 1982: 541–42; Baier 1991: 231; Haakonssen 1993:186; Darwall 1995: 292–93; Bricke 1996: 199ff.; and Magri 1996: 233–34.

49. The qualification that promising may have all sorts of beneficial effects that are not relevant to its being virtuous is important. Haakonssen, attentive to this point, reminds us: "My giving money to another person does not constitute 'paying rent' merely because we have, respectively, intentions of giving and receiving. The transaction is given its particular meaning because it involves a social practice or institution, in this case a special form of contract" (1993: 187). The act of giving money to Jane may make her happy, whatever may be the operative social practices, but it has

consequences that make property-respecting acts expressive of a virtue only because it is an act of "paying rent."

50. My reference to the "typical" effects of traits we call natural virtues and my claim that the consequences at issue "could" (rather than "will") result under the scenario described are deliberate. In describing the differences between the artificial and natural virtues, scholars sometimes claim that acts expressive of the artificial virtues "*need* do no good to any specified individual" (Baier 1985: 300; see also Árdal 1966: 117; and Norton 1993a: 16). This is also true, however, of the natural virtues. We judge traits (both "natural" and "artificial") according to their *usual* effects, approving of typically beneficial traits even where they fail to have their usual effects (T 3.3.1.19, SBN 584).

51. See, e.g., Árdal 1966; Mackie 1980; Darwall 1995; Magri 1996; Cohon 1997; and EPM App. 3.1–2 (SBN 303).

52. See McDowell 1979; Broadie 1991: 201; Swanton 1995: 55ff.; Williams 1995; Slote 1997: ch. 3.6–11 and 270ff.; Hursthouse 1999a: 12–13, 154; and Kamtekar 2004. It may well be argued that there is no such thing as "virtue ethics" if that is to be understood as a single, distinctive approach to philosophical ethics. Those who hold this view may regard the argument that follows as one that concerns what are now the recognizably dominant forms of virtue ethics. I note in passing as well that these forms of virtue ethics came to prominence on the scene of contemporary ethics long after the publication of Anscombe 1958, now treated as foundational to the field, and some time after the publication of Baron 1985 – which is largely, though not wholly, concerned with forms of dispositional reductionism that reject both of the theses about the relationship between moral judgment and virtue mentioned above.

53. McDowell 1979: 332ff.; Broadie 1991: ch. 1; Swanton 1995: 50; Williams 1995; Slote 1997: ch. 3.6–11 and 270ff.; Hursthouse 1999a: 80–81, 129–30; and Kamtekar 2004. This is almost always viewed as a matter of degree; one who lacks a virtue will not be *as* morally perceptive as one who possesses that virtue.

54. See, e.g., Stewart 1963: 102; Árdal 1966: 168; Whelan 1985: 220–21; Baier 1988: 774; Brown 1988: 81; Darwall 1993: 416–17; Haakonssen 1993: 186–87, 191; Norton 1993a: 164–65; Penelhum 1993: 135–36; Korsgaard 1996b: 51; Radcliffe 1996: 406; and Cohon 1997: 92–95.

55. These reflections were spurred by a related passage in Baier 1991. "Clearly," Baier writes, Hume's judicious spectator "needs the capacity for sympathy, and surely also equity, delicacy of discrimination, delicacy of taste in pleasures, and lack of stupidity. The hard-hearted, stupefied, unimaginative, and sour-tempered will be effectively disqualified as moral judges, as 'judicious spectators.' They will be incapable of sympathizing with all those affected by the particular character trait that is up for judgment, of putting themselves imaginatively into the shoes of representative persons who have 'commerce' with a person with such a character trait" (1991: 217). Baier's list of "mental qualities" in this passage is a bit odd. Some of them, such as "delicacy of discrimination," are difficult to distinguish from the ability to make moral assessments itself. The ability to make accurate moral evaluations may be a virtue, but it cannot be a "natural" virtue if natural virtues are nothing but

innate dispositions to have and act on some set of nonmoral affections. Other "mental qualities" on Baier's list, such as "equity," might refer either to one of the artificial virtues or one of the natural virtues. In the case of equity, for instance, Baier might have in mind some aspect of the just man's character or that "disinterestedness" that Hume names as a natural virtue (T 3.3.3.3, SBN 603).

56. My claim that the capacity for love is essential to Humean moral evaluation does not rest on the assumption that Humean moral sentiments are a species of the indirect passions (pride, humility, love, and hatred). On my reading, love plays an important role for Humean moral evaluation, because moral approbation of traits gives rise to a special kind of love (or esteem) for the agent who possesses that trait. This love constitutes our praise for the agent as virtuous. Those who follow Árdal, Brown, Korsgaard, and others in claiming that Humean sentiments of moral approbation are themselves a species of love and pride have different, though equally powerful, reasons to view the capacity for love as a requisite part of the capacity for making Humean moral evaluations.

57. See, e.g., McDowell 1979: 331–32; Broadie 1991: 54; Swanton 1995: 47; Hursthouse 1999a: 13, 101–2, 154–55; and Kamtekar 2004.

58. See, e.g., McDowell 1979: 343–45; Hursthouse 1999a: 154; and Kamtekar 2004.

59. See, e.g., McDowell 1980; Slote 1997: 209–33, 270ff.; and Hursthouse 1999b: 70. There are, of course, many other assumptions underlying the virtue ethicist's theory about the relationship between moral judgment and character.

60. See also T 2.3.2.6, 3.2.1.2–3, 3.3.1.4, 3.3.1.13–23 (SBN 411, 477–78, 575, 580–87); EPM 5.42–47 (SBN 228–30).

61. See, e.g., T 3.3.6.3–6 (SBN 619–21); and E-DM 85–86.

62. See, e.g., McDowell 1979: 331–32; Broadie 1991: 201, 257–58; and Hursthouse 1999a: 13, 103–6, 154.

63. Cf. Hursthouse 1999a: 130.

64. That Hume does not treat the virtues as isolable traits becomes even clearer in his account of goodness and greatness of mind. In Abramson 2002, I argue that both of these virtues implicate an agent's character as a whole. Goodness is the virtue of being a reliable friend and thus consists in all the virtues that make one a reliable friend. Greatness of mind is strength of mind in the pursuit of virtue. Hence, one will lack in greatness to the extent that one lacks any Humean virtue.

65. The naturally virtuous are not *motivated by* contemplation of the "benefits" of virtue described above – at least, not under *that* description.

66. There is a suppressed premise here drawn from Hume's epistemology – the priority of impressions to ideas. This will, however, be a matter of degree. If I lack only one natural virtue, I may be able to do a fair job of estimating the pleasures to which people who have that virtue have access, but if I am completely lacking in natural virtues, I will be able to form no notion of those pleasures.

67. My tremendous gratitude to all of the following: to Donald Ainslie for the invitation to write this piece for the collection and his generous comments on an earlier version; to those who responded to an earlier version of this

piece presented at the University of Rome, in particular to Tito Magri and Ken Winkler for prodding me where I needed it; to Steve Darwall and Don Garrett for comments on earlier drafts; to the ever-Kantian (but in a good way) David Sussman for harassing me one more time about "Hume's circle"; and to Rachana Kamtekar for helpful and encouraging comments on earlier drafts.

Bibliography

Abramson, Kate. 1999a. "Correcting Our Sentiments about Hume's Moral Point of View." *Southern Journal of Philosophy* 37(3): 333–61.

——. 1999b. "Hume on Cultural Conflicts of Values." *Philosophical Studies* 94(1–2): 173–87.

——. 2002. "Two Portraits of the Humean Moral Agent." *Pacific Philosophical Quarterly* 83(4): 301–34.

——. 2008. "Sympathy and Hume's Spectator-Centered Theory of Virtue." In *A Companion to Hume*, edited by Elizabeth Radcliffe, 240–56. Oxford: Blackwell.

Ainslie, Donald C. 1999. "Scepticism about Persons in Book II of Hume's *Treatise*." *Journal of the History of Philosophy* 37(3): 469–92.

——. 2001. "Hume's Reflections on the Identity and Simplicity of Mind." *Philosophy and Phenomenological Research* 60(3): 557–78.

——. 2003. "Hume's Scepticism and Ancient Scepticisms." In *Hellenistic and Early Modern Philosophy*, edited by Jon Miller and Brad Inwood, 251–73. Cambridge: Cambridge University Press.

——. 2008. "Hume on Personal Identity." In *A Companion to Hume*, edited by Elizabeth S. Radcliffe, 140–56. Oxford: Blackwell.

Allison, Henry E. 2008. *Custom and Reason in Hume: A Kantian Reading of the First Book of the* Treatise. Oxford: Clarendon.

Annand, M. R. 1930. "An Examination of Hume's Theory of Relations." *The Monist* 40(4): 581–97.

Anscombe, G. E. M. 1958. "Modern Moral Philosophy." *Philosophy* 33(124): 1–19.

Árdal, Páll S. 1966. *Passion and Value in Hume's* Treatise. Edinburgh: Edinburgh University Press.

Ashley, Lawrence and Michael Stack. 1974. "Hume's Theory of the Self and Its Identity." *Dialogue* 13(2): 239–54.

Ayer, A. J. 1973. *The Central Problems of Philosophy*. Harmondsworth, UK: Penguin.

Baier, Annette C. 1980. "Master Passions." In *Explaining Emotions*, edited by Amélie Oksenberg Rorty, 403–23. Berkeley: University of California Press.

——. 1985. *Postures of the Mind: Essays on Mind and Morals*. Minneapolis: University of Minnesota Press.

——. 1988. "Hume's Account of Social Artifice–Its Origins and Originality." *Ethics* 98(4): 757–78.

——. 1991. *A Progress of Sentiments*. Cambridge, MA: Harvard University Press.

——. 1992. "Artificial Virtues and the Equally Sensible Non-Knaves: A Response to Gauthier." *Hume Studies* 18(2): 429–39.

——. 1994. *Moral Prejudices: Essays on Ethics*. Cambridge, MA: Harvard University Press.

——. 1997. *The Commons of the Mind*. Chicago and La Salle, IL: Open Court Press.

——. 2008. *Death and Character: Further Reflections on Hume*. Cambridge, MA: Harvard University Press.

——. 2010. *The Cautious Jealous Virtue: Hume on Justice*. Cambridge, MA: Harvard University Press.

——. 2011. *The Pursuits of Philosophy: An Introduction to the Life and Thought of David Hume*. Cambridge, MA: Harvard University Press.

Baier, Annette C. and Anik Waldow. 2008. "A Conversation between Annette Baier and Anik Waldow about Hume's Account of Sympathy." *Hume Studies* 34(1): 61–87.

Barfoot, Michael. 1990. "Hume and the Culture of Science in the Early Eighteenth Century." In *Studies in the Philosophy of the Scottish Enlightenment*, edited by M. A. Stewart, 151–90. Oxford: Clarendon.

Baron, Marcia. 1982. "Hume's Noble Lie: An Account of His Artificial Virtues." *Canadian Journal of Philosophy* 12(3): 539–55.

——. 1985. "Variety of Ethics of Virtue." *American Philosophical Quarterly* 22(1): 47–53.

——. 1988. "Morality as a Back-Up System: Hume's View?" *Hume Studies* 14(1): 25–52.

Baxter, Donald L. M. 2001a. "Hume on Steadfast Objects and Time." *Hume Studies* 27(1): 129–48.

——. 2001b. "Hume on the Simplicity of Moments." Paper presented at the 28th Annual Hume Conference at University of Victoria in Victoria, British Columbia, Canada, July 2001.

——. 2008. *Hume's Difficulty: Time and Identity in the* Treatise. London: Routledge.

Beauchamp, Tom L. 1999. Editor's Introduction to *An Enquiry concerning Human Understanding*, by David Hume, 7–62. Edited by Tom L. Beauchamp. Oxford: Oxford University Press.

——. 2000. "Editorial Appendix: Emendations and Substantive Variants." In *David Hume: An Enquiry concerning Human Understanding, A Critical Edition*, edited by Tom L. Beauchamp, 206–71. Oxford: Clarendon.

Beebee, Helen. 2006. *Hume on Causation*. London: Routledge.

Bennett, Jonathan. 2001. *Learning from Six Philosophers*, vol. 2. Oxford: Oxford University Press.

Berlin, Isaiah. 1969. *Four Essays on Liberty*. Oxford: Oxford University Press.

Bettcher, Talia Mae. 2009. "Berkeley and Hume on Self and Self-Consciousness." In *Topics in Early Modern Philosophy of Mind*, edited by Jon Miller, 193–222. Studies in the History of Philosophy of Mind, vol. 9. Dordrecht, NL: Springer.

Binmore, Ken. 1992. *Fun and Games. A Text on Game Theory*. Lexington, MA: D. C. Heath and Co.

Biro, John I. 1976. "Hume on Self-Identity and Memory." *Review of Metaphysics* 30(1): 19–38.

——. 2004. "Cognitive Science and David Hume's Science of the Mind." In *Truth, Rationality, Cognition, and Music: Proceedings of the Seventh International Colloquium on Cognitive Science*, edited by Kepa Korta and Jesús M. Larrazabal, 1–20, vol. 102. Dordrecht, NL: Kluwer Academic Publishers.

Blackburn, Simon. 1999. *Ruling Passions*. Cambridge: Cambridge University Press.

——. 2000. "Hume and Thick Connexions." In *The New Hume Debate*, edited by Rupert Read and Kenneth A. Richman, 100–12. London: Routledge.

Bloor, David. 1991. *Knowledge and Social Imagery*, 2nd edition. Chicago: University of Chicago Press.

Bohlin, Henrik. 2009. "Sympathy, Understanding, and Hermeneutics in Hume's *Treatise*." *Hume Studies* 35(1–2): 135–70.

Botterill, George. 2002. "Hume on Liberty and Necessity." In *Reading Hume on Human Understanding: Essays on the First* Enquiry, edited by Peter Millican, 277–300. Oxford: Clarendon.

Brandom, Robert. 2000. *Articulating Reasons: An Introduction to Inferentialism*. Cambridge, MA: Harvard University Press.

Brandt, Reinhard. 1977. "The Beginnings of Hume's Philosophy." In *David Hume: Bicentenary Papers*, edited by G. P. Morice, 117–27. Edinburgh: University of Edinburgh Press.

——. 1979. *A Theory of the Good and the Right*. Oxford: Oxford University Press.

Bricke, John. 1977. "Hume on Self-Identity, Memory and Causality." In *David Hume: Bicentenary Papers*, edited by G. P. Morice, 167–74. Edinburgh: Edinburgh University Press.

——. 1980. *Hume's Philosophy of Mind*. Princeton: Princeton University Press.

——. 1996. *Mind and Morality: An Examination of Hume's Moral Psychology*. Oxford: Oxford University Press.

Broad, C. D. 1961. "Hume's Doctrine of Space." *Proceedings of the British Academy* 47: 161–76.

Broadie, Sarah. 1991. *Ethics with Aristotle*. Oxford: Oxford University Press.

Broughton, Janet. 1987. "Hume's Ideas about Necessary Connection." *Hume Studies* 13(2): 217–44.

Brown, Charlotte. 1988. "Is Hume an Internalist?" *Journal of the History of Philosophy* 26(1): 69–87.

Buckle, Stephen. 1991. *Natural Law and the Theory of Property: Grotius to Hume*. Oxford: Oxford University Press.

——. 1999. "Hume's Biography and Hume's Philosophy." *Australasian Journal of Philosophy* 77(1): 1–25.

——. 2001. *Hume's Enlightenment Tract: The Unity and Purpose of An* Enquiry concerning Human Understanding. Oxford: Clarendon.

Burnyeat, Myles and Michael Frede, eds. 1998. *The Original Sceptics: A Controversy*. Indianapolis, IN: Hackett Publishing Co.

Butler, Annemarie. 2010a. "Hume on Believing the Vulgar Fiction of Continued Existence." *History of Philosophy Quarterly* 27(3): 237–54.

——. 2010b. "On Hume's Supposed Rejection of Resemblance between Objects and Impressions." *British Journal for the History of Philosophy* 18(2): 257–70.

Butler, Joseph. (1726) 2006. "Fifteen Sermons Preached at the Rolls Chapel." In *The Works of Bishop Butler*, edited by David E. White, 33–146. Rochester, NY: University of Rochester Press.

Butler, Ronald J. 1975. "T and Sympathy." Supplement, *Proceedings of the Aristotelian Society* 49: 1–20.

Capaldi, Nicholas. 1976. "Hume's Theory of the Passions." In *Hume: A Re-Evaluation*, edited by Donald W. Livingston and James T. King, 172–90. New York: Fordham University Press.

——. 1989. *Hume's Place in Moral Philosophy*. New York: Peter Lang.

Chesterton, G. K. 1933. *St. Thomas Aquinas*. London: Hodder and Stoughton.

Clatterbaugh, Kenneth. 1999. *The Causation Debate in Modern Philosophy: 1637–1739*. London: Routledge.

Cohon, Rachel. 1997. "Hume's Difficulty with the Virtue of Honesty." *Hume Studies* 23(1): 91–112.

———. 2008. *Hume's Morality: Feeling and Fabrication*. Oxford: Oxford University Press.

Coleman, Dorothy. 2001. "Baconian Probability and Hume's Theory of Testimony." *Hume Studies* 27(2): 195–226.

Connon, R. W. 1977. "The Textual and Philosophical Significance of Hume's MS Alternations to *Treatise* III." In *David Hume: Bicentenary Papers*, edited by G. P. Morice, 186–204. Edinburgh: University of Edinburgh Press.

Cook, John W. 1968. "Hume's Scepticism with Regard to the Senses." *American Philosophical Quarterly* 5(1): 1–17.

Costa, Michael J. 1988–90. "Hume and Belief in the Existence of an External World." *Philosophical Studies* 32: 99–112.

———. 1989. "Hume and Causal Realism." *Australasian Journal of Philosophy* 67(2): 172–90.

Coventry, Angela. 2006. *Hume's Theory of Causation: A Quasi-Realist Interpretation*. London: Continuum.

Craig, Edward. 1987. *The Mind of God and the Works of Man*. Oxford: Clarendon.

———. 2000. "Hume on Causality: Projectivist and Realist?" In *The New Hume Debate*, edited by Rupert Read and Kenneth A. Richman, 113–21. London: Routledge.

Cummins, Phillip D. 1973. "Hume's Disavowal of the *Treatise*." *Philosophical Review* 82(3): 371–79.

Darwall, Stephen. 1993. "Motive and Obligation in Hume's Ethics." *Noûs*, 27(4): 415–48.

———. 1994. "Hume and the Invention of Utilitarianism." In *Hume and Hume's Connexions*, edited by M. A. Stewart and John P. Wright, 58–82. University Park: Pennsylvania State University Press.

———. 1995. *The British Moralists and the Internal 'Ought': 1640–1740*. Cambridge: Cambridge University Press.

Davidson, Donald. 1980. *Essays on Actions and Events*. Oxford: Clarendon.

Dennett, Daniel C. 1984. *Elbow Room: The Varieties of Free Will Worth Wanting*. Oxford: Clarendon.

Descartes, René. 1985. *The Philosophical Writings of Descartes*. Translated by John Cottingham, Robert Stoothoff, and Dugald Murdoch. 2 vols. Cambridge: Cambridge University Press.

Echelbarger, Charles. 1997. "Hume and the Logicians." In *Logic and the Workings of the Mind: The Logic of Ideas and Faculty Psychology in Early Modern Philosophy*, edited by Patricia A. Easton, 137–51. Atascadero, CA: Ridgeview Publishing Co.

Ellis, Jonathan. 2006. "The Contents of Hume's Appendix and the Source of His Despair." *Hume Studies* 32(2): 195–232.

Elmen, Paul. 1951. "Richard Allestree and *The Whole Duty of Man*." *The Library*, s5–VI(1): 19–27.

Emerson, Roger L. 2009. *Essays on David Hume, Medical Men and the Scottish Enlightenment: Industry, Knowledge and Humanity*. Surrey, UK: Ashgate.

Falk, W. D. 1947–48. "'Ought' and Motivation." *Proceedings of the Aristotelian Society* n. s. 48: 111–38.

——. 1986. *Oughts, Reasons and Morality: The Collected Papers of W. D. Falk*. Edited by W. D. Falk and Kurt Baier. Ithaca, NY: Cornell University Press.

Falkenstein, Lorne. 1997. "What Happens When Beliefs Conflict?" Paper presented at the 24th Annual Hume Conference in Monterey, California. August 1997.

——. 2002. Paper presented at an "Author Meets Critics" panel on David Owen, *Hume's Reason*. The American Philosophical Association, Pacific Division meeting in Seattle, Washington. March 2002.

Farr, James. 1978. "Hume, Hermeneutics, and History: A 'Sympathetic' Account." *History and Theory* 17(3): 285–310.

Ferreira, M. Jamie. 1994. "Hume and Imagination: Sympathy and 'the Other.'" *International Philosophical Quarterly* 34(1.133): 39–57.

Fine, Gail. 2000. "Descartes and Ancient Skepticism: Reheated Cabbage?" *Philosophical Review* 109(2): 195–234.

Finlay, Christopher J. 2007. *Hume's Social Philosophy: Human Nature and Commercial Sociability in* A Treatise of Human Nature. London: Continuum.

Fischer, John Martin and Mark Ravizza. 1998. *Responsibility and Control: A Theory of Moral Responsibility*. Cambridge: Cambridge University Press.

Flew, Antony. 1961. *Hume's Philosophy of Belief: A Study of his First Inquiry*. London: Routledge and Kegan Paul.

——. 1976. "Infinite Divisibility in Hume's *Treatise*." In *Hume: A Re-Evaluation*, edited by Donald W. Livingston and James T. King, 257–69. New York: Fordham University Press.

Fogelin, Robert J. 1983. "The Tendency of Hume's Skepticism." In *The Skeptical Tradition*, edited by Myles Burnyeat, 397–412. Berkeley: University of California Press.

——. 1985. *Hume's Skepticism in the* Treatise of Human Nature. London: Routledge and Kegan Paul.

——. 1993. "Hume's Scepticism." In *The Cambridge Companion to Hume*, edited by David Fate Norton, 90–116. Cambridge: Cambridge University Press.

Foot, Philippa. 1978. *Virtues and Vices and Other Essays in Moral Philosophy*. Berkeley: University of California Press.

Forbes, Duncan. 1975. *Hume's Philosophical Politics*. Cambridge: Cambridge University Press.

Franklin, James. 1994. "Achievements and Fallacies in Hume's Account of Infinite Divisibility." *Hume Studies* 20(1): 85–101.

Frasca-Spada, Marina. 1998. *Space and the Self in Hume's Treatise*. Cambridge: Cambridge University Press.

Garrett, Don. 1981. "Hume's Self-Doubts about Personal Identity." *Philosophical Review* 90(3): 337–58.

——. 1997. *Cognition and Commitment in Hume's Philosophy*. Oxford: Oxford University Press.

——. 1998. "Ideas, Reason, and Skepticism: Replies to My Critics." *Hume Studies* 24(1): 171–94.

——. 2001. "Replies." *Philosophy and Phenomenological Research* 62(1): 205–15.

——. 2004. "'A Small Tincture of Pyrrhonism': Skepticism and Naturalism in Hume's Science of Man." In *Pyrrhonian Skepticism*, edited by Walter Sinnott-Armstrong, 68–98. Oxford: Oxford University Press.

——. 2006. "Hume's Conclusions in 'Conclusion of this Book.'" In *The Blackwell Guide to Hume's Treatise*, edited by Saul Traiger, 151–75. Oxford: Blackwell.

———. 2007. "The First Motive to Justice: Hume's Circle Argument Squared." *Hume Studies* 33(2): 257–88.

———. 2009. "Hume." In *The Oxford Handbook of Causation*, edited by Helen Beebee, Christopher Hitchcock, and Peter Menzies, 73–91. Oxford: Oxford University Press.

———. 2011. "Rethinking Hume's Second Thoughts about Personal Identity." In *The Possibility of Philosophical Understanding: Reflections on the Thought of Barry Stroud*, edited by Jason Bridges, Niko Kolodny, and Waihung Wong, 15–40. Oxford: Oxford University Press.

Gauthier, David. 1979. "David Hume, Contractarian." *Philosophical Review* 88(1): 3–38.

———. 1986. *Morals by Agreement*. Oxford: Clarendon.

———. 1992. "Artificial Virtues and the Sensible Knave." *Hume Studies* 18(2): 401–27.

Gay, John. (1731) 1964. "*Concerning the Fundamental Principle of Virtue or Morality,*" 5th edition published in 1781. First printed as a Preliminary Dissertation to Edmund Law's translation of Archbishop King's *Essay on the Origin of Evil*. In *British Moralists*, edited by L. A. Selby-Bigge, vol. 2: 267–85. Indianapolis, IN: Bobbs-Merrill.

Geach, Peter. 1969. *God and the Soul*. New York: Schocken Books.

Gibbard, Allan. 1983. "A Noncognitivistic Analysis of Rationality in Action." *Social Theory and Practice* 9(2–3): 199–221.

———. 1990. *Wise Choices, Apt Feelings: A Theory of Normative Judgment*. Cambridge, MA: Harvard University Press.

Glover, Jonathan. 1970. *Responsibility*. London: Routledge and Kegan Paul.

Gomberg, Paul. 1976. "Coherence and Causal Inference in Hume's *Treatise*." *Canadian Journal of Philosophy* 6(4): 693–704.

Graham, Roderick. 2004. *The Great Infidel: A Life of David Hume*. East Lothian, UK: Tuckwell Press.

Green, Michael J. 1999. "The Idea of a Momentary Self and Hume's Theory of Personal Identity." *British Journal for the History of Philosophy* 7(1): 103–22.

Greig, J. Y. T. 1931. *David Hume*. Oxford: Oxford University Press.

Haakonssen, Knud. 1981: *The Science of a Legislator: The Natural Jurisprudence of David Hume and Adam Smith*. Cambridge: Cambridge University Press.

———. 1993. "The Structure of Hume's Political Theory." In *The Cambridge Companion to Hume*, edited by David Fate Norton, 182–221. Cambridge: Cambridge University Press.

———. 1996. *Natural Law and Moral Philosophy: From Grotius to the Scottish Enlightenment*. Cambridge: Cambridge University Press.

Hacking, Ian. 1978. "Hume's Species of Probability." *Philosophical Studies* 33(1): 21–37.

Hampton, Jean. 1995. "Does Hume Have an Instrumental Conception of Practical Reason?" *Hume Studies* 21(1): 57–74.

———. 1997. "The Hobbesian Side of Hume." In *Reclaiming the History of Ethics: Essays for John Rawls*, edited by Andrews Reath, Barbara Herman, and Christine M. Korsgaard, 66–101. Cambridge: Cambridge University Press.

Hankinson, R. J. 1995. *The Sceptics*. London: Routledge.

Harman, Gilbert. 1977. *The Nature of Morality: An Introduction to Ethics*. Oxford: Oxford University Press.

Harrison, Jonathan. 1976. *Hume's Moral Epistemology*. Oxford: Clarendon.

———. 1981. *Hume's Theory of Justice*. Oxford: Oxford University Press.

Haugeland, John. 1998. *Having Thought: Essays in the Metaphysics of Mind*. Cambridge, MA: Harvard University Press.

Hendel, Charles W. 1963. *Studies in the Philosophy of David Hume*. Indianapolis, IN: Bobbs-Merrill.

Henderson, Robert S. 1990. "David Hume on Personal Identity and the Indirect Passions." *Hume Studies* 16(1): 33–44.

Herman, Barbara. 1996. "Making Room for Character." In *Aristotle, Kant and the Stoics*, edited by Stephen Engstrom and Jennifer Whiting, 36–60. Cambridge: Cambridge University Press.

Hirschmann, Nancy J. 2000. "Sympathy, Empathy, and Obligation: A Feminist Rereading." In *Feminist Interpretations of David Hume*, edited by Anne Jaap Jacobson, 174–93. University Park: Pennsylvania State University Press.

Holden, Thomas. 2001. "Hume, Infinite Divisibility and Actual Parts Metaphysics." Paper presented at the 28th Annual Hume Conference at University of Victoria in Victoria, British Columbia, Canada, July 2001.

Honderich, Ted. 2002. *How Free Are You? The Determinism Problem*, 2nd edition. Oxford: Oxford University Press.

Hospers, John. 1961. "What Means This Freedom?" In *Determinism and Freedom in the Age of Modern Science*, edited by Sidney Hook, 126–42. New York: Collier.

Huntington, Edward V. 1917. *The Continuum and Other Types of Serial Order*, 2nd edition. Cambridge, MA: Harvard University Press.

Hursthouse, Rosalind. 1999a. *On Virtue Ethics*. Oxford: Oxford University Press.

——. 1999b. "Virtue Ethics and Human Nature." *Hume Studies* 25(1–2): 67–82.

Hutcheson, Francis. (1725) 1969. "An Inquiry into the Original of Our Ideas of Virtue or Moral Good," 4th edition published in 1738. In *British Moralists 1650–1800*, edited by D. D. Raphael, vol. 1: 261–99. Oxford: Oxford University Press.

——. (1728) 1969. *An Essay on the Nature and Conduct of the Passions and Affections*, 3rd edition published in 1742. Gainesville, FL: Scholars' Facsimiles and Reprints.

——. (1728) 1971. *Illustrations on the Moral Sense*, 5th edition published in 1769. Edited by Bernard Peach. Cambridge, MA: Belknap Press.

Inukai, Yumiko. 2007. "Hume's Labyrinth: The Bundling Problem." *History of Philosophy Quarterly* 24(3): 255–74.

Jacovides, Michael. 2010. "Hume's Vicious Regress." *Oxford Studies in Early Modern Philosophy* 5: 247–97.

Jacquette, Dale. 2001. *David Hume's Critique of Infinity*. Leiden, NL: Brill.

Kail, P. J. E. 2001. "Projection and Necessity in Hume." *European Journal of Philosophy* 9(1): 24–54.

——. 2003. "Is Hume a Causal Realist?" *British Journal for the History of Philosophy* 11(3): 509–20.

Kamtekar, Rachana. 2004. "Situationism and Virtue Ethics on the Content of Our Character." *Ethics* 114(3): 458–91.

Kane, Robert. 1996. *The Significance of Free Will*. Oxford: Oxford University Press.

Kant, Immanuel. (1762–64) 1997. *Lectures on Ethics*. Edited by Peter Heath and J. B. Schneewind and translated by Peter Heath. Cambridge: Cambridge University Press.

——. (1785) 1997. *Groundwork of the Metaphysics of Morals*. Edited and translated by Mary Gregor with an introduction by Christine M. Korsgaard. Cambridge: Cambridge University Press.

Kemp Smith, Norman. 1941. *The Philosophy of David Hume: A Critical Study of Its Origins and Central Doctrines*. London: Macmillan.

Kenny, Anthony. 1963. *Action, Emotion and Will*. London: Routledge.

Korsgaard, Christine M. 1996a. *Creating the Kingdom of Ends*. Cambridge: Cambridge University Press.

———. 1996b. *The Sources of Normativity*. With G. A. Cohen, Raymond Geuss, Thomas Nagel, and Bernard Williams. Edited by Onora O'Neill. Cambridge: Cambridge University Press.

———. 1999. "The General Point of View: Love and Moral Approval in Hume's Ethics." *Hume Studies* 25(1–2): 3–41.

Kydd, Rachael M. 1946. *Reason and Conduct in Hume's Treatise*. Oxford: Oxford University Press.

Laird, John. 1932. *Hume's Philosophy of Human Nature*. London: Methuen.

Lecaldano, Eugenio. 2008. "Hume's Theory of Justice, or Artificial Virtue." In *A Companion to Hume*, edited by Elizabeth S. Radcliffe, 257–72. Oxford: Blackwell.

Leibniz, Gottfried Wilhelm. (1684) 1956. "Meditations on Knowledge, Truth, and Ideas." In *G. W. Leibniz: Philosophical Papers and Letters*, edited by Leroy E. Loemker, vol. 1: 448–54. Chicago: University of Chicago Press.

Lewis, David. 1969. *Conventions*. Cambridge, MA: Harvard University Press.

Livingston, Donald W. 1984. *Hume's Philosophy of Common Life*. Chicago: University of Chicago Press.

Locke, John. (1690) 1975. *An Essay concerning Human Understanding*, 4th edition published in 1700. Edited by Peter H. Nidditch. Oxford: Oxford University Press.

Loeb, Louis E. 2001. "Hume's Explanations of Meaningless Beliefs." *Philosophical Quarterly* 51(203): 145–64.

———. 2002. *Stability and Justification in Hume's Treatise*. Oxford: Oxford University Press.

LoLordo, Antonia. 2000. "Probability and Skepticism about Reason in Hume's Treatise." *British Journal for the History of Philosophy* 8(3): 419–46.

———. 2002. Paper presented at an "Author Meets Critics" panel on David Owen, *Hume's Reason*. The American Philosophical Association, Pacific Division meeting in Seattle, Washington. March 2002.

Mackie, J. L. 1977. *Ethics: Inventing Right and Wrong*. Harmondsworth, UK: Penguin.

———. 1980. *Hume's Moral Theory*. London: Routledge.

MacNabb, D. G. C. 1951. *David Hume: His Theory of Knowledge and Morality*. London: Hutchinson's University Library.

Magri, Tito. 1994. *Contratto e Convenzione: Razionalità, Obbligo e Imparzialità in Hobbes e Hume*. Milan: Feltrinelli.

———. 1996. "Natural Obligation and Normative Motivation in Hume's *Treatise*." *Hume Studies* 22(2): 231–53.

———. 2012. "Imagination and Convention." In *Hume Readings*, edited by Lorenzo Greco and Alessio Vaccari, 263–89. Rome: Storia e Letteratura.

Malebranche, Nicolas. (1674–75) 1980. *The Search after Truth*, 7th edition published in 1712. Translated by Thomas M. Lennon and Paul J. Olscamp. Columbus: Ohio State University Press.

Mascarenhas, Vijay. 2001. "Hume's Recantation Revisited." *Hume Studies* 27(2): 279–300.

Maynard Smith, John. 1982. *Evolution and the Theory of Games*. Cambridge: Cambridge University Press.

McDowell, John. 1979. "Virtue and Reason." *The Monist* 62(3): 331–50.

———. 1980. "The Role of *Eudaimonia* in Aristotle's Ethics." In *Essays on Aristotle's Ethics*, edited by Amélie Oksenberg Rorty, 359–76. Berkeley: University of California Press.

McIntyre, Jane L. 1979. "Is Hume's Self Consistent?" In *McGill Hume Studies*, edited by David Fate Norton, Nicholas Capaldi, and Wade L. Robison, 79–88. San Diego: Austin Hill Press.

——. 1989. "Personal Identity and the Passions." *Journal of the History of Philosophy* 27(4): 545–57.

McKenna, Michael and Paul Russell, eds. 2008. *Free Will and Reactive Attitudes: Perspectives on P. F. Strawson's "Freedom and Resentment."* Farnham, UK: Ashgate.

Meeker, Kevin. 2000. "Hume's Iterative Probability Argument: A Pernicious *Reductio.*" *Journal of the History of Philosophy* 38(2): 221–38.

Melchert, Norman. 1975. "Hume's Appendix on Personal Identity." *Philosophy Research Archives* 1: 323–35.

Mercer, Philip. 1972. *Sympathy and Ethics: A Study of the Relationship between Sympathy and Morality with Special Reference to Hume's* Treatise. Oxford: Clarendon.

Millgram, Elijah. 1995. "Was Hume a Humean?" *Hume Studies* 21(1): 75–93.

Millican, Peter. 2009. "Hume, Causal Realism, and Causal Science." *Mind* 118(471): 647–712.

Morris, William Edward. 1989. "Hume's Scepticism About Reason." *Hume Studies* 15(1): 39–60.

Mossner, E. C. 1980. *The Life of David Hume*, 2nd edition. Oxford: Oxford University Press.

Nagel, Thomas. 1970. *The Possibility of Altruism.* Oxford: Clarendon.

Nelson, John O. 1976. "Has the Authorship of *An Abstract of a Treatise of Human Nature* Really Been Decided?" *Philosophical Quarterly* 26(102): 82–91.

——. 1991. "The Authorship of the *Abstract* Revisited." *Hume Studies* 17(1): 83–86.

Niebuhr, Reinhold. 1941 and 1943. *The Nature and Destiny of Man.* New York: Scribners.

Norton, David Fate. 1993a. "Hume, Human Nature, and the Foundations of Morality." In *The Cambridge Companion to Hume*, edited by David Fate Norton, 148–81. Cambridge: Cambridge University Press.

——. 1993b. "More Evidence that Hume Wrote the *Abstract.*" *Hume Studies* 19(1): 217–22.

——. 2000. Editor's Introduction to *A Treatise of Human Nature*, by David Hume, I9–I99. Edited by David Fate Norton and Mary J. Norton. Oxford: Oxford University Press.

——. 2007. "Historical Account of *A Treatise of Human Nature* from Its Beginnings to the Time of Hume's Death." In *David Hume: A Treatise of Human Nature, A Critical Edition*, vol. 2, edited by David Fate Norton and Mary J. Norton, 433–588. Oxford: Clarendon.

Norton, David Fate and Mary J. Norton. 2000. Supplementary Material to *A Treatise of Human Nature*, by David Hume, 421–622. Edited by David Fate Norton and Mary J. Norton. Oxford: Oxford University Press.

Nozick, Robert. 1981. *Philosophical Explanations.* Cambridge, MA: Harvard University Press.

——. 2001. *Invariances: The Structure of the Objective World.* Cambridge, MA: Belknap.

O'Brien, Dan. 2010. "A Feminist Interpretation of Hume on Testimony." *Hypatia* 25(3): 632–52.

Owen, David. 1994. "Reason, Reflection, and *Reductios.*" *Hume Studies* 20(2): 195–210.

——. 1999. *Hume's Reason.* Oxford: Oxford University Press.

——. 2000. "Reply to My Critics." *Hume Studies* 26(2): 323–337.

——. 2003. "Locke and Hume on Belief, Judgment and Assent." *Topoi* 22: 15–28.

Parfit, Derek. 1984. *Reasons and Persons.* Oxford: Clarendon.

Passmore, John. 1952. *Hume's Intentions.* Cambridge: Cambridge University Press.

Pears, David. 1990. *Hume's System: An Examination of the First Book of His* Treatise. Oxford: Oxford University Press.

Penelhum, Terence. 1975. *Hume.* London: Macmillan.

——. 1976. "Self-Identity and Self-Regard." In *The Identities of Persons*, edited by Amélie Oksenberg Rorty, 253–80. Berkeley: University of California Press.

——. 1993. "Hume's Moral Psychology." In *The Cambridge Companion to Hume*, edited by David Fate Norton, 117–47. Cambridge: Cambridge University Press.

——. 2000. *Themes in Hume: The Self, the Will, Religion.* Oxford: Clarendon.

Peters, R. S. and C. A. Mace. 1961–62. "Emotions and the Category of Passivity." *Proceedings of the Aristotelian Society* n. s. 62: 117–42.

Pitson, A. E. 2002. *Hume's Philosophy of Self.* London: Routledge.

Popkin, Richard H. 1979. *The History of Scepticism from Erasmus to Spinoza.* Berkeley: University of California Press.

——. 1980. *The High Road to Pyrrhonism*, edited by Richard A. Watson and James E. Force. San Diego: Austin Hill Press.

Postema, Gerald J. 1988. "Hume's Reply to the Sensible Knave." *History of Philosophy Quarterly* 5(1): 23–40.

——. 2005. " 'Cemented with Diseased Qualities': Sympathy and Comparison in Hume's Moral Psychology." *Hume Studies* 31(2): 249–98.

Price, H. H. 1940. *Hume's Theory of the External World.* Oxford: Clarendon.

Radcliffe, Elizabeth S. 1996. "How Does the Humean Sense of Duty Motivate?" *Journal of the History of Philosophy* 34(3): 383–407.

Rapaport, David. 1974. *The History of the Concept of Association of Ideas.* New York: International Universities Press.

Raynor, David R. 1990. "Hume and Berkeley's *Three Dialogues.*" In *Studies in the Philosophy of the Scottish Enlightenment*, edited by M. A. Stewart, 231–50. Oxford: Clarendon.

——. 1993. "The Author of the *Abstract* Revisited." *Hume Studies* 19(1): 213–15.

Read, Rupert and Kenneth A. Richman, eds. 2007. *The New Hume Debate*, revised edition. London: Routledge.

Reid, Thomas. (1785) 2002. *Essays on the Intellectual Powers of Man: A Critical Edition.* Edited by Derek R. Brookes. University Park: Pennsylvania State University Press.

Rescorla, Michael. 2011. "Convention." In *The Stanford Encyclopedia of Philosophy.* Edited by Edward N. Zalta. http://plato.stanford.edu/archives/spr2011/entries/convention/.

Robinson, J. A. 1962. "Hume's Two Definitions of 'Cause.' " *Philosophical Quarterly* 12(47): 162–71.

Rorty, Amélie Oksenberg. 1990. " 'Pride Produces the Idea of Self': Hume on Moral Agency." *Australasian Journal of Philosophy* 68(3): 255–69.

——. 1993. "From Passions to Sentiments: The Structure of Hume's *Treatise.*" *History of Philosophy Quarterly* 10(2): 165–79.

Rosenberg, Alexander. 1993. "Hume and the Philosophy of Science." In *The Cambridge Companion to Hume*, edited by David Fate Norton, 64–89. Cambridge: Cambridge University Press.

Roth, Abraham Sesshu. 1990. "What Was Hume's Problem with Personal Identity?" *Philosophy and Phenomenological Research* 61(1): 91–114.

Russell, Paul. 1988. "Causation, Compulsion, and Compatibilism." *American Philosophical Quarterly* 25(4): 313–21.

——. 1992. "Strawson's Way of Naturalizing Responsibility." *Ethics* 102(2): 287–302.

——. 1995. *Freedom and Moral Sentiment: Hume's Way of Naturalizing Responsibility.* Oxford: Oxford University Press.

——. 1997. "Wishart, Baxter and Hume's *Letter from a Gentleman*." *Hume Studies* 23(2): 245–76.

——. 2004. "Responsibility and the Condition of Moral Sense." *Philosophical Topics* 32(1–2): 287–305.

——. 2008. *The Riddle of Hume's* Treatise*: Skepticism, Naturalism and Irreligion.* Oxford: Oxford University Press.

——. 2011. "Moral Sense and the Foundations of Responsibility." In *The Oxford Handbook of Free Will*, 2nd edition, edited by Robert Kane, 199–220. Oxford: Oxford University Press.

——. 2013. "Hume's Anatomy of Virtue." In *The Cambridge Companion to Virtue Ethics*, edited by Daniel C. Russell, 92–123. Cambridge: Cambridge University Press.

Ryle, Gilbert. 1949. *The Concept of Mind.* London: Hutchinson's University Library.

Sayre-McCord, Geoffrey. 1994. "On Why Hume's 'General Point of View' Isn't Ideal – and Shouldn't Be." *Social Philosophy and Policy* 11(1): 202–28.

Schlick, Moritz. (1939) 1966. "When Is a Man Responsible?" Reprinted in *Free Will and Determinism*, edited by Bernard Berofsky, 54–63. New York: Harper and Row.

Schweitzer, Don. 2000. "Pride as Sin and Virtue." *Studies in Religion/Sciences Religieuses* 29(2): 167–81.

Selby-Bigge, L. A. 1975. "Comparative Tables of Contents of the *Treatise* and of the *Enquiries and Dissertation on the Passions*." In *Enquiries concerning Human Understanding and concerning the Principles of Morals*, xxxiii–xl. Edited by L. A. Selby-Bigge with notes by P. H. Nidditch. Oxford: Clarendon.

Shaftesbury, Anthony Ashley Cooper, third Earl of. (1711) 1999. *Characteristics of Men, Manners, Opinions, Times*, 2nd edition published in 1714. Edited by Lawrence E. Klein. Cambridge: Cambridge University Press.

Sher, Richard B. 1990. "Professors of Virtue: The Social History of the Edinburgh Moral Philosophy Chair in the Eighteenth Century." In *Studies in the Philosophy of the Scottish Enlightenment*, edited by M. A. Stewart, 87–126. Oxford: Clarendon.

Singer, Ira. 1995. "Hume's Extreme Skepticism in Treatise I IV 7." *Canadian Journal of Philosophy* 25(4): 595–622.

——. 2000. "Nature Breaks Down: Hume's Problematic Naturalism in *Treatise* I iv." *Hume Studies* 26(2): 225–43.

Slote, Michael. 1997. "Virtue Ethics" and "Reply to Baron and Pettit." In *Three Methods of Ethics*, edited by Marcia W. Baron, Philip Pettit, and Michael Slote. Oxford: Blackwell.

Smart, J. J. C. (1961) 1970. "Free Will, Praise and Blame." Reprinted in *Determinism, S Free Will and Moral Responsibility*, edited by Gerald Dworkin, 196–213. Englewood Cliffs, NJ: Prentice Hall.

Snare, Francis. 1991: *Morals, Motivation and Convention: Hume's Influential Doctrines*. Cambridge: Cambridge University Press.

Spencer, Mark G. 2003. "Another 'Curious Legend' about Hume's *An Abstract of a Treatise of Human Nature.*" *Hume Studies* 29(1): 89–98.

Stevenson, Gordon Park. 1998. "Humean Self-Consciousness Explained." *Hume Studies* 24(1): 95–129.

Stewart, John B. 1963. *The Moral and Political Philosophy of David Hume*. New York: Columbia University Press.

Stewart, M. A.. 1990. "Introduction." In *Studies in the Philosophy of the Scottish Enlightenment*, edited by M. A. Stewart, 1–9. Oxford: Clarendon.

——. 1995. "An Early Fragment on Evil." In *Hume and Hume's Connexions*, edited by M. A. Stewart and John P. Wright, 160–70. University Park: Pennsylvania State University Press.

——. 2005. "Hume's Intellectual Development, 1711–1752." In *Impressions of Hume*, edited by Marina Frasca-Spada and P. J. E. Kail, 11–58. Oxford: Clarendon.

Stove, David C. 1973. *Probability and Hume's Inductive Scepticism*. Oxford: Clarendon.

Strawson, Galen. 1989. *The Secret Connexion: Causation, Realism, and David Hume*. Oxford: Clarendon.

——. 2000. "David Hume: Objects and Power." In *The New Hume Debate*, edited by Rupert Read and Kenneth A. Richman, 31–51. London: Routledge.

——. 2011. *The Evident Connexion: Hume on Personal Identity*. Oxford: Oxford University Press.

Strawson, Peter. (1962) 2013. "Freedom and Resentment." In *The Philosophy of Free Will: Essential Readings from the Contemporary Debates*, edited by Paul Russell and Oisin Deery, 63–83. Oxford: Oxford University Press.

Stroud, Barry. 1977. *Hume*. London: Routledge, Kegan and Paul.

——. 1993. "'Gilding or Staining' the World with 'Sentiments' and 'Phantasms.'" *Hume Studies* 19(2): 253–72.

Stuchbury, Oliver. 1989. "Two Puzzles in Mossner's *Life of David Hume.*" *Hume Studies* 15(1): 247–53.

Sturgeon, Nicholas L. 2001. "Moral Skepticism and Moral Naturalism in Hume's *Treatise.*" *Hume Studies* 27(1): 3–83.

Sugden, Robert. 1986. *The Economics of Rights, Co-operation and Welfare*. Oxford: Blackwell.

Swanton, Christine. 1995. "Profiles of the Virtues." *Pacific Philosophical Quarterly* 76(1): 47–72.

Taylor, Jacqueline. 1998. "Justice and the Foundations of Social Morality in Hume's *Treatise.*" *Hume Studies* 24(1): 5–30.

Thiel, Udo. 2011. *The Early Modern Subject: Self-Consciousness and Personal Identity from Descartes to Hume*. Oxford: Oxford University Press.

Thompson, Michael. 2008. *Life and Action: Elementary Structure of Practice and Practical Thought*. Cambridge, MA: Harvard University Press.

Traiger, Saul. 1988. "The Ownership of Perceptions: A Study of Hume's Metaphysics." *History of Philosophy Quarterly* 5(1): 41–51.

Vanderschraaf, Peter. 1998. "The Informal Game Theory in Hume's Account of Convention." *Economics and Philosophy* 14(2): 215–47.

——. 2007. "Covenants and Reputation." *Synthese* 157(2): 167–95.

Vanderschraaf, Peter and Giacomo Sillari. 2013. "Common Knowledge." In *The Stanford Encyclopedia of Philosophy*. Edited by Edward N. Zalta. http://plato.stanford.edu/archives/fall2013/entries/common-knowledge/.

Waldow, Anik. 2010. "Identity of Persons and Objects: Why Hume Considered Both as Two Sides of the Same Coin." *The Journal of Scottish Philosophy* 8(2): 147–67.

Wallace, R. Jay. 1994. *Responsibility and the Moral Sentiments*. Cambridge, MA: Harvard University Press.

Waxman, Wayne. 1992. "Hume's Quandary concerning Personal Identity." *Hume Studies* 18(2): 233–54.

——. 1994. *Hume's Theory of Consciousness*. Cambridge: Cambridge University Press.

——. 1998. "The Point of Hume's Skepticism with Regard to Reason: The Primacy of Facility Affect in the Theory of Human Understanding." *Hume Studies* 24(2): 235–73.

Weinberg, Julius R. 1965. *Abstraction, Relation, and Induction: Three Essays in the History of Thought*. Madison: University of Wisconsin Press.

Weinsheimer, Joel C. 1993. *Eighteenth-Century Hermeneutics: Philosophy of Interpretation in England from Locke to Burke*. New Haven, CT: Yale University Press.

Whelen, Frederick G. 1985. *Order and Artifice in Hume's Political Philosophy*. Princeton, NJ: Princeton University Press.

Wiggins, David. 1987. "A Sensible Subjectivism?" In *Needs, Values, Truth: Essays in the Philosophy of Value*, 185–214. Oxford: Blackwell.

Williams, Bernard. 1985. *Ethics and the Limits of Philosophy*. Cambridge, MA: Harvard University Press.

——. 1995. "Acting as the Virtuous Person Acts." In *Aristotle and Moral Realism*, edited by Robert Heinaman, 13–23. London: UCL Press.

Wilson, Fred. 1984. "Is Hume a Sceptic with Regard to Reason?" *Philosophy Research Archives* 10: 275–319.

——. 1985. "The Origins of Hume's Sceptical Argument against Reason." *History of Philosophy Quarterly* 2(3): 323–35.

——. 1997. *Hume's Defence of Causal Inference*. Toronto: University of Toronto Press.

Wilson, J. R. S. 1972. *Emotion and Object*. Cambridge: Cambridge University Press.

Winkler, Kenneth P. 1999. "Hume's Inductive Skepticism." In *The Empiricists: Critical Essays on Locke, Berkeley, and Hume*, edited by Margaret Atherton, 183–212. Lanham, MD: Rowman and Littlefield.

——. 2000a. "'All is Revolution in Us': Personal Identity in Shaftesbury and Hume." *Hume Studies* 26(1): 3–40.

——. 2000b. "The New Hume." In *The New Hume Debate*, edited by Rupert Read and Kenneth A. Richman, 52–87. London: Routledge.

Wolterstorff, Nicholas. 2001. *Thomas Reid and the Story of Epistemology*. Cambridge: Cambridge University Press.

Woolhouse, Roger S. 1988. *The Empiricists*. Oxford: Oxford University Press.

Wright, John P. 1983. *The Sceptical Realism of David Hume*. Manchester, UK: University of Manchester Press.

——. 1996. "Hume, Descartes and the Materiality of the Soul." In *The Philosophical Canon in the 17th and 18th Centuries: Essays in Honor of John W. Yolton*, edited by G. A. J. Rogers and Sylvana Tomaselli, 175–90. Rochester, NY: University of Rochester Press.

——. 2000. "Hume's Causal Realism: Recovering a Traditional Interpretation." In *The New Hume Debate*, edited by Rupert Read and Kenneth A. Richman, 88–99. London: Routledge.

——. 2003. "Dr. George Cheyne, Chevalier Ramsay, and Hume's Letter to a Physician." *Hume Studies* 29(1): 125–41.

——. 2006. "*The Treatise*: Composition, Reception, and Response." In *The Blackwell Guide to Hume's* Treatise, edited by Saul Traiger, 5–25. Oxford: Blackwell.

——. 2012. "Hume on the Origin of 'Modern Honour.'" In *Philosophy and Religion in Enlightenment Britain: New Case Studies*, edited by Ruth Savage, 187–209. Oxford: Oxford University Press.

Yolton, John W. 1980. "Hume's Ideas." *Hume Studies* 6(1): 1–25.

——. 1984. *Perceptual Acquaintance from Descartes to Reid*. Minneapolis: University of Minnesota Press.

Index of Passages Cited

383

Index of Names and Subjects